TENNESSEE 〰 A SHORT HISTORY

SECOND EDITION

DISCARDED

9/11

TENNESSEE

 A SHORT HISTORY

SECOND EDITION

Updated through 1989

by *Robert E. Corlew*

*Incorporating revisions developed by
the late Stanley J. Folmsbee
and the late Enoch Mitchell*

THE UNIVERSITY
OF TENNESSEE PRESS
KNOXVILLE

The paper in this book meets the minimum requirements of the American
National Standard for Permanence of Paper for Printed Library Materials.
♾ The binding materials have been chosen for strength and durability.

Library of Congress Cataloging in Publication Data

Corlew, Robert Ewing.
    Tennessee, a short history.
    Edition for 1969 by S. J. Folmsbee, R. E. Corlew, and E. L. Mitchell.
    Includes index.
    Summary: A general survey of Tennessee history from the earliest
settlements to the present.
    1. Tennessee—History. [1. Tennessee—History]
I. Folmsbee, Stanley John, 1899–   Tennessee.
II. Mitchell, Enoch L., 1903–   III. Title.
F436.C78   1981   976.8   80-13553
ISBN 0-87049-646-8 (cloth: alk. paper)
ISBN 0-87049-647-6 (pbk.: alk. paper)

For my daughter MARY CATHERINE
   *whose grandfather—six generations removed—was Tennessee's
   first governor*

Contents

Illustrations

PHOTOGRAPHS

Preface

A social and political revolution has taken place in both Tennessee and the nation since the late 1950s, when first I was privileged to collaborate with Professors Stanley J. Folmsbee and Enoch Mitchell on a history of the state. The past quarter-century has brought about changing attitudes toward women and minorities. Schools have been racially integrated, the population has tended to cluster more in and near urban areas, and tremendous progress has been made in transportation, education, industry, and commerce. Since 1969, when the first edition of our *Tennessee, A Short History* was published, a majority of voters, while remaining Democrats, have nevertheless elected two Republican governors and two Republican United States senators. For a time, a majority of the state's congressmen also were Republicans.

In this edition, I have not only attempted to recount events since the last writing but have also rewritten the first edition completely in order to incorporate new scholarly research and new interpretations that add to a knowledge of Tennessee's history. To devote more space to the twentieth century, I have condensed sections about the eighteenth century and such nineteenth-century topics as public lands, the disappearance of the Indians, and transportation.

This second edition would not have been possible without the first, and I continue to be indebted to all those who contributed to make the earlier volume possible. In particular, this revision reflects the scholarship of my two collaborators on the earlier work and on the four volumes of *A History of Tennessee* (New York, 1960). Professor Folmsbee died before the present revision began; Professor Mitchell died in 1965.

I thank the Center for Business and Economic Research of the University of Tennessee for use of maps 10-15 and the figure "Percentage Change in Population, Tennessee and the United States, 1820-1890," from *Tennessee Statistical Abstract, 1977* (Knoxville, 1977), as well as for the figure "Manufacturing Income," from Ormond C. Corry and Patricia A. Price, *Population and Personal Income Estimates for Tennessee Counties, 1950-1964* (Knoxville, 1964); the University of Tennessee Press for maps 8 and 9, from Joseph H. Cartwright, *The Triumph of Jim Crow: Tennessee Race Relations in the 1880s* (Knoxville, 1976), and for the photograph of eight of the Grand Ole Opry's best-known performers, from the collection of Charles K. Wolfe; and the Tennessee State Library and Archives for two cartoons illustrative of the women's suffrage movement.

A number of individuals and institutions have generously furnished photographs for this and the earlier edition of *Tennessee, A Short History*. Pictures of Governors William Blount, John Sevier, James K. Polk, DeWitt Clinton Senter, Gordon W. Browning, Prentice Cooper, Buford Ellington, Winfield Dunn, and Ray Blanton, and illustrations showing David Crockett, Mrs. James Robertson, Andrew Jackson, John H. Eaton, Nathan Bedford Forrest, Gustavus A. Henry, Philip Lindsley, Kenneth D. McKellar, Cordell Hull, Edward H. Crump, the Indian burial grounds, Rocky Mount, the block house at Benton, the Dean Cornwell murals, the homes of James K. Polk and Sam Davis, Fort Donelson, the governor's mansion, the tobacco and cotton scenes, the Country Music Hall of Fame, and the state buildings at Nashville are reproduced courtesy of the Tennessee Department of Conservation. I thank S. N. McMinn of Lascassas for the print of Governor Joseph McMinn; the Greene County Chamber of Commerce for Andrew Johnson's tailor shop; the University of Tennessee Library at Knoxville for the photograph of Governor John Buchanan; the Walden S. Fabry Studios of Nashville for the photograph of Governor Frank G. Clement; the Nashville Chamber of Commerce for pictures of Fort Nashborough and the Hermitage; the Knoxville Chamber of Commerce for Blount Mansion; Tracy Photography for the aerial view of Knoxville; the Memphis Chamber of Commerce for the photographs of the city and the W. R. Grace Company; Chattanooga Area Convention and Visitors Bureau for the aerial of Chattanooga; the Tennessee Valley Authority for pictures of Norris Dam, dairying, river transportation, and recreation; the Minnesota Historical Society and the University of Tennessee Press for the reproduction of the oil painting of the Battle of Nashville by Howard Pyle, reprinted from Stanley F. Horn, *The Decisive Battle of Nashville* (Knoxville, 1968); the Wiles-Hood Studio of Nashville for the William Jennings Bryan group; Thompson's of Knoxville for the Great Smoky Mountains scene; the public relations departments of Tennessee's seven state universities and of Vanderbilt University for pictures of their institutions; the United States Atomic Energy Commission for photographs of a graphite reactor and an Oak Ridge plant; the offices of Governor Lamar Alexander and Senators Jim Sasser and Howard F. Baker, Jr., for their pictures; Jack Ross for the pictures of Governor McWherter and Otis Floyd; Gunter's Studio for the photograph of Dorothy Brown; the Trustees of the British Museum for the engraving of Little Carpenter and six other Cherokees; the Mississippi Valley Collection for the picture of marchers in Memphis, Tennessee, in 1968; and the Thomas Gilcrease Institute of American History and Art for its permission to reproduce Francis Parsons' portrait of Standing Turkey. Photographs of Benjamin Hooks and Hollis Price appear courtesy of Hooks Brothers, Photographers, C. S. Hooks, Memphis, Tennessee. The rendering of Dragging Canoe (from Pat Alderman, *The Overmountain Men*) is reproduced courtesy of The Overmountain Press, Johnson City, Tennessee. I am especially indebted to Marcia Brubeck for careful editing, and to my wife, Mary Scott Corlew, who devoted considerable time to reading proof.

Robert E. Corlew
Murfreesboro
January 1990

Abbreviations

AHM	*American Historical Magazine*
AHR	*American Historical Review*
ETHSP	*East Tennessee Historical Society's Publications*
GHQ	*Georgia Historical Quarterly*
JAH	*Journal of American History*
JNH	*Journal of Negro History*
JOP	*Journal of Politics*
JSH	*Journal of Southern History*
MVHR	*Mississippi Valley Historical Review*
NCHR	*North Carolina Historical Review*
PSQ	*Political Science Quarterly*
THM	*Tennessee Historical Magazine*
THQ	*Tennessee Historical Quarterly*
WTHSP	*West Tennessee Historical Society Papers*

TENNESSEE ❧ A SHORT HISTORY

SECOND EDITION

1.

HISTORIANS of the Volunteer State have traditionally written of "three states of Tennessee." Constitution-makers wrote in the fundamental law of the three "grand divisions"—East Tennessee, Middle Tennessee, and West Tennessee, shown in map 1—and legislators have defined these divisions in the statutes and delineated the counties in each.

For Tennesseans, as for people everywhere, geography has determined the economic, social, and political life. Those who settled in the fertile Mississippi Valley, for example, found a daily existence different from that of their parents who lived in the Cumberland Basin and their grandparents who established homes in the mountains of East Tennessee and western North Carolina.

Boundaries ॐ Since 1818, when the Chickasaw title to West Tennessee was cleared, the state of Tennessee has extended from the Unaka Mountains in the east to the Mississippi River in the west. Long, narrow, and rhomboidal in shape, the state covers some 430 miles from east to west and 110 miles north to south. Its 42,244 square miles make it 34th in size, or about one-sixth as large as Texas. Nearly 450 square miles are lakes, both natural and man-made.

The eastern boundary follows the crest of the Unakas, and the western traces the Mississippi River. Tennessee was an extension of North Carolina, and the northern boundary of that colony was placed at 36° 30' in a charter issued to eight friends of King Charles II in 1665. (Two years earlier, another charter had placed the line at 36°.) The southern border was established at 35° following negotia-

3

4

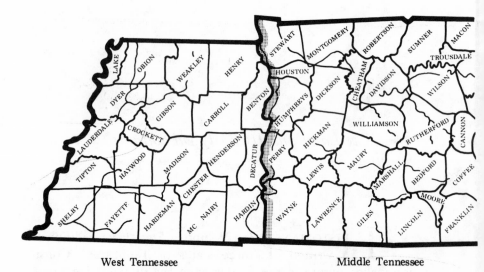

West Tennessee   Middle Tennessee

Map 1. The Three Grand Divisions and Counties in Tennessee

tions between Georgia and Carolina officials. Both lines have been
the occasion for disputes between Tennessee and the neighboring
states. Governors Carroll (1831) and Jones (1845) gave attention to
the problem, and Georgia officials sought a new and more accurate
survey of the southern line as late as the 1940s.

In 1749, Peter Jefferson, father of the president, surveyed the
northern line for a short distance to Steep Rock Creek (now Laurel
Creek), a tributary of the Holston River in present Johnson County.
No further surveys were made until 1779, one year after Virginia
and North Carolina had appointed commissioners—Thomas Walker
and Daniel Smith of Virginia and Richard Henderson and others
from North Carolina—to extend the line westward. By the time of
this appointment, Walker had served in the North Carolina Assembly, and as Indian commissioner for Virginia he had become close
friends with the Cherokee diplomat Little Carpenter. Smith, then a
young man of thirty-one, later became secretary of the Southwest
Territory and was active on the Tennessee frontier. Henderson, a
prominent and wealthy North Carolinian, had been inspired by
Daniel Boone's descriptions of the west to organize a land company
and attempt a colony.

Walker and his party were unable to find the exact point where
Jefferson had ceased his survey thirty years earlier, and the commis-

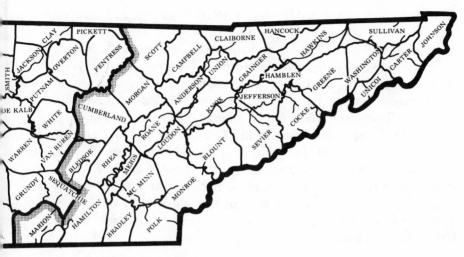

East Tennessee

sioners agreed upon a starting place on Steep Rock Creek and moved westward about forty-five miles to Carter's Valley, west of the Holston River. There they had a disagreement, and after the Henderson party insisted that the boundary should be two miles north of the Walker line, it was decided to run two separate surveys. The Carolina commissioners abandoned the attempt when they reached Cumberland Mountains, but the Virginia group—enduring considerable physical hardships during the winter—continued all the way to the Tennessee River, except for a gap between Deep Fort and the first crossing of the Cumberland River. By that time, owing to some error, they were actually at about 36° 40′, more than twelve miles (on a direct line) north of 36° 30′.

North Carolina approved the Walker line in 1790, and the Virginia legislature did so in 1791, three years before Walker's death. After Tennessee was admitted to statehood in 1796, a dispute arose over the part of the line separating Tennessee from Virginia, and in 1802 those states appointed a commission (consisting of Governor John Sevier and others) to study the matter. Neither side prevailed; ultimately they agreed upon an east-west boundary between and equidistant from the Henderson and Walker lines. When Virginia attempted in 1893 to have the line established at 36° 30′, the United States Supreme Court ruled that the agreement of 1802, coupled with long usage, precluded change. In 1818, when the land between the Tennessee and Mississippi rivers (now West Tennessee) was purchased from the Chickasaw Indians, an accurate survey was made of the Tennessee-Kentucky line along the 36° 30' parallel. Two years later, the two states agreed upon that boundary for the area west of the Tennessee River, but they allowed the old Walker survey between the Tennessee River and Cumberland Gap to stand in order not to disturb the citizenship of many Tennesseans who lived on the intervening land. The east line—between North Carolina and Tennessee—was surveyed partly in 1799 and partly in 1821. When members of the joint commission of 1821 reached the Hiwassee River, they realized that they had come to the end of the Unicoi Mountains, and from that point they surveyed due south to the Georgia boundary.

Physiographic Regions Geographers have divided Tennessee into six major and two minor natural regions that are sections of larger geographic districts extending far beyond the borders of the state (see map 2). The most eastern is the Unaka Mountains. It is the western front of the "Blue Ridge" province of the major geographic division called the Appalachian Highlands, which extends from New Brunswick southward to Alabama and Georgia. The area includes mountainous sections with local names such as Bald, Great Smoky, Stone, and Unicoi. To the west lies the Great Valley of East Tennessee, a succession of parallel ridges and valleys, followed by the Cumberland Plateau or "Cumberland Table Land." Next is the Highland Rim, which encircles another main region, the Central Basin. At the western edge of the Rim is one of the minor sections—a narrow, irregular, and swampy area—called the Western Valley of the Tennessee River. The sixth major region is the Gulf Coastal Plain of West Tennessee, followed by the second minor district—an area fertile but spotted with lakes and marshes—called the "Mississippi Bottoms" or Flood Plains of the Mississippi River.

The *Unaka Mountains,* with their rugged surface and tall peaks, cover a total area of about 2,600 square miles. A dozen or more peaks, including Clingmans Dome, Mount Guyot, and Mount Le Conte, rise to heights of 6,000 feet or more; the highest is Clingmans Dome, at 6,643 feet. The region is drained by the branches of the Tennessee River, which occupy steep-sided valleys and afford many excellent power sites. The jagged mountains and rivers, which have cut deep gorges through the area, constituted an almost impenetrable barrier between the Tennessee Country and the Atlantic coast. For many years they isolated the mountain people of the region and even shaped their political thought and patterns to some extent.

Most of the ridges and mountains are too steep for row crop farming. There is an ample supply of timber, however, and lumbering for many years has been a principal occupation of the inhabitants. Iron, copper, zinc, and manganese are mined here. With the coming of the automobile, the tourist business became important, bringing income rivaling that of the lumbermen and the "moonshiners." Several thousand acres have been set aside by the federal government in the Great Smoky Mountains National Park, where rhododendron and many other botanical specimens attract many visitors.

The *Great Valley of East Tennessee*, sometimes referred to as the *Ridge and Valley Country*, lies just west of the Unaka region and extends from southwest Virginia into northern Georgia. It is a segment of the Ridge and Valley province of the Appalachian Mountains, which runs in a northeastern-southwestern direction from New York to central Alabama, varying in width from thirty-five to fifty-five miles and covering about 9,200 square miles. It consists largely of long, narrow ridges separated by broad and fertile valleys. Some of the ridges, including Clinch Mountain in the northwestern part, rise a thousand feet or more above the floor.

The underlying rocks are almost wholly sedimentary and in large measure of a limestone character but also include some shale and sandstone. The erosion of the soluble limestone gave rise to the long, fertile valleys, while the more resistant sandstone and chert beds remained as ridges. The area is drained to the southwest by the Tennessee River, which with its tributaries has played a very significant role in the transportation system of the state.

The region as a whole has been productive agriculturally. Inadequate transportation facilities have hindered people in sending their crops to market, but there has been considerable specialization

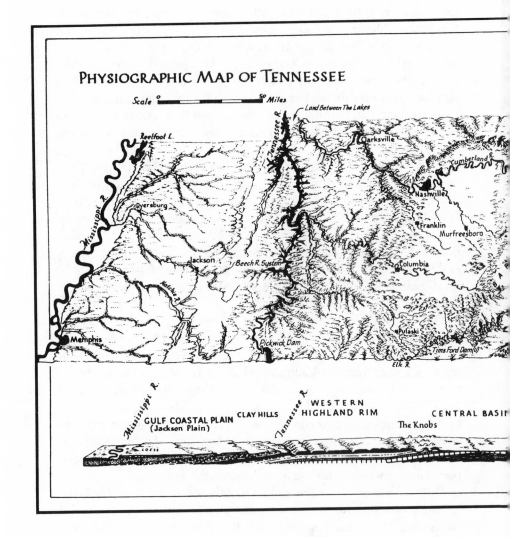

PHYSIOGRAPHIC MAP OF TENNESSEE

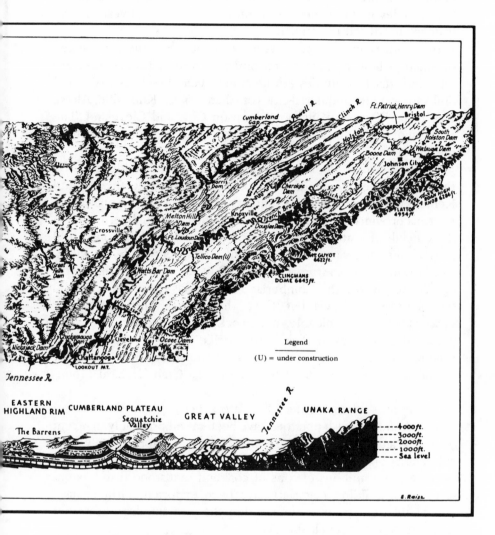

Map 2. Physiographic Map of Tennessee. Physiographic map from *The Geography of Tennessee,* by H. C. Amick and L. H. Rollins, copyright 1937 by Ginn and Company.

in tobacco in the northern half of the valley, and most of the farmland
has been devoted to general agriculture. Grain crops, livestock, and
fruit are produced in abundance.

In comparatively recent years this has become the state's
outstanding industrial area. It encompasses four of Tennessee's leading industrial counties—Anderson, Hamilton, Knox, and
Sullivan—and the industrial cities of Chattanooga, Knoxville, Alcoa,
Oak Ridge, Bristol, Kingsport, Johnson City, and Cleveland. The
creation of the Tennessee Valley Authority has been of great help to
the region.

The *Cumberland Plateau*, sometimes called the "Wilderness" by
the early settlers, extends from central Alabama northward into
Kentucky. It constitutes the southern segment of the Appalachian
Plateaus province of the Appalachian Highlands, which terminate in
the Catskill Mountains in New York. It has an area of about 5,400
square miles and varies from about fifty to seventy miles in width.
The elevation ranges from 1,800 to 2,000 feet except in the northeast corner, where the Cumberland Mountains rise to about 3,500
feet. To the east is Walden Ridge, the edge of which one writer
described as a "formidable, gray, rocky, cliff-lined rampart." The
region also includes the fertile Sequatchie Valley, a great cove extending almost halfway across the state (north to south) from the
Tennessee River at the Alabama line to the Crab Orchard Mountains.

The early settlers avoided the plateau because the soil was not
fertile. Although Irish potatoes have been raised profitably in recent
years, agricultural activity for generations has afforded only bare
subsistence. Later settlers found the region to be rich in minerals,
however, and millions of tons of coal and sandstone (used extensively as a building material) have been exported. Drillers have
sought oil from time to time within the past hundred years but
generally without much success.

The *Highland Rim*, a region that almost completely encircles the
Central Basin, lies west of the Cumberland Plateau. Both belong to
the Interior Low Plateaus province of the Interior Plains, major
physiographic division which extends from northern Alabama to
beyond the Ohio River. The Rim encompasses an area of about
10,650 square miles and is the largest of the state's six natural
regions. It ranges in width from about twenty-five miles in the east to
about seventy-five miles in the northwest. The eastern section is a

gently rolling plain about 1,000 feet lower than the Cumberland Plateau and about four hundred feet higher than the Central Basin. The rocks of the Rim are sedimentary in origin and are chiefly limestone and shale but include some sandstone. The acidity of the underground water has worn away some of the limestone in places, causing the formation of sinkholes, some 15 to 20 feet deep. The limestone and chert soils are well suited for the production of grain, cotton, tobacco, and other crops. Tobacco is the principal crop in the northern counties—primarily in Robertson and Montgomery—and cotton is grown profitably in the southern counties. The Rim also has an abundance of timber and minerals, including iron. Although much of the timber has been cut during the past quarter-century, the steeper slopes and hills still have thousands of acres of oak, ash, hickory, and cedar.

The *Central Basin* (sometimes called the *Nashville Basin*) ranges from 50 to 60 miles in width and covers an area of about 5,500 square miles. This highly fertile soil, closely resembling the Blue Grass region of Kentucky, was a paradise for the early settlers. Writing more than a century ago, Joseph B. Killebrew saw the fertile land as "the bottom of an oval dish, of which the highlands form the broad, flat brim."[1] For four decades before the Civil War the region rivaled the counties of West Tennessee in the production of cotton, but in more recent years the chief crops have been grains, hay, vegetables, tobacco, and livestock. The recent quarter-century has been a time of considerable industrial expansion, and many factories have located in Nashville and other nearby towns and cities.

At the western edge of the rim is the long and narrow *Western Valley of the Tennessee River*, the first of the two minor divisions. Although its surface is broken and irregular, its soil is productive. This area covers about 1,200 square miles, with an average width of about 12 miles.

The *Gulf Coastal Plain of West Tennessee* lies within the physiographic division called the Coastal Plain, which extends along the Atlantic Coast and the Gulf of Mexico. The broad plain covers about 9,000 square miles and slopes gently to the west. It is divided into two parts: the Plateau, or Slope, of West Tennessee and the Flood Plain of the Mississippi River (frequently called the "Mississippi

---

[1] Joseph B. Killebrew, *Introduction to the Resources of Tennessee* (Nashville, 1874), 3.

Bottoms"), which is the second of the minor natural regions of the state. In the extreme northwest corner of the flood plain is Reelfoot Lake, the only large natural lake in the state, which was formed by the earthquakes of 1811–1812. Cotton and grain have been the principal crops; by the time of the Civil War, cotton had built Memphis into a major city larger than Nashville.

River System ৯ With the exception of one small area in the southeast, the entire state is drained by the Mississippi River system, most of it by two branches of the Ohio—the Tennessee and the Cumberland—and their tributaries. In the western part, the rivers flow directly into the Mississippi.

The Tennessee is formed by the junction of the Holston and French Broad rivers a few miles above Knoxville. The Holston, which rises in Virginia, has two main forks that converge at Kingsport after the South Fork has received the historic Watauga, which originates in North Carolina. The French Broad and its main tributaries, Nolichucky and Pigeon, also rise in North Carolina, as does the Hiwassee, a tributary of the Tennessee. From the west, the upper Tennessee receives the Clinch and its branch the Powell, which rise in southwest Virginia, as well as the Emory, which starts in the Cumberland Plateau.

The Tennessee flows in a relatively placid manner out of the upper valley, but near Chattanooga it abruptly changes course several times as it cuts through Walden Ridge into the valley of the Sequatchie. Before the Tennessee was tamed by TVA, perils such as the "Suck," the "Boiling Pot," and the "Narrows" confronted navigators. Emerging from the Sequatchie Valley, the river resumes a southwest course to Guntersville, where it turns northwest across Alabama, creating "Muscle Shoals," another hazard well known to early navigators. There it receives the Elk River, which rises in Franklin County. Below Florence, the Tennessee turns northward and flows for nearly 200 miles, crossing Tennessee a second time and thence into Kentucky, where it empties into the Ohio at Paducah. As it travels north, the stream receives the major tributaries of the Duck, which enters from the east, and the Big Sandy, which flows from the west. As a result of dam building by TVA, much of the course of this river system consists of artificial reservoirs such as the Kentucky, Chickamauga, and Fort Loudoun lakes in the main stream, and the Norris,

Melton Hill, Cherokee, Douglas, Holston, and Watauga lakes in various tributaries.

The Cumberland River, the second major stream that flows through the state, begins in southeastern Kentucky, runs across northern Middle Tennessee, and then parallels the Tennessee River on its way across Kentucky to a junction with the Ohio. Its southern tributaries—the Obey, the Caney Fork, the Stone, the Harpeth, and the Yellow—drain most of northern Middle Tennessee. The Red, a northern branch, starts in Tennessee, passes through Kentucky for a few miles, and enters the main stream near Clarksville. Like the Tennessee, the Cumberland system is being converted into a series of artificial reservoirs.

The largest of the rivers flowing across West Tennessee into the Mississippi is the Forked Deer, formed by the union of the North Fork and the South Fork about fifteen miles from the Mississippi. Its largest branch, the Obion, has two major forks as well as a small branch coming from Reelfoot Lake. Farther south the Mississippi River receives the Hatchie (once called the Big Hatchie) and the Wolf, both rising in Mississippi, and between them the small Loosahatchie, which rises in Hardeman County.

Natural Resources ∻ The soils of Tennessee constitute the state's most important natural resource, and farmers have produced corn, tobacco, cotton, and a variety of other crops since the early days. The state leads all others of the South in dairying and is a leader in swine production. All of the major cities are important for meat packing, and Memphis is one of the leading cottonseed processing centers in the world. Forests have been one of the state's most important natural resources. The most productive areas are in the Unaka Mountains, the Highland Rim, and the lowlands of West Tennessee. Tennessee is the South's leading producer of hardwood lumber, which accounts for about two-thirds of the state's current lumber production. Oak provides about 40 percent of the hardwood, and cedar, pine, and hemlock are the leading softwoods. The state has about 60 percent of the commercial red cedar land of the nation. Because of wasteful exploitation and delay in instituting adequate reforestation programs, Tennessee's forest resources had been seriously depleted by 1930, but since that time effective conservation measures have revitalized the lumbering industry.

Climate and weather have contributed to the state's agricultural success. Tennessee has a mild climate with an average annual temperature of 60° F. The length of the growing season varies from about 150 days in the Unaka Mountains to about 220 days in West Tennessee. The prevailing winds are westerly or southwesterly. Those coming from the Gulf of Mexico are usually moisture-laden and provide the state with an adequate rainfall, averaging about fifty inches per year.

Tennessee is one of the leading states of the South in the variety and value of its mineral production. Its fifty or more minerals include zinc, stone, coal, Portland cement, phosphate, and copper. For years the state has ranked first in the production of ball clay, pyrite, and zinc, and third in phosphate rock and dimension marble. Until 1958 bituminous coal ranked first in tonnage and in value. Its availability on the Cumberland Plateau has been important for the industrial development of Tennessee. The rise of stone to first place has been due mainly to the great increase in the demand for crushed stone for highway construction but has also reflected a decline in the production of coal and an increase in the value of marble. Marble is found primarily in the Great Valley, and Knoxville is the center of the marble industry in the state. Tennessee marble has been widely accepted throughout the nation, particularly for constructing public buildings. The copper deposits in the Ducktown area were opened in 1847 and have been worked almost continuously since that time. Sulphur fumes resulting from the smelting process destroyed practically all the vegetation in the surrounding area until it was discovered that the fumes could be utilized in the production of sulfuric acid, a by-product even more valuable than the copper.

The First Americans ᣬᣠ Insofar as we can tell, there was no human life in North America before the last glacial period, which probably began 20,000 to 30,000 years ago. But the Ice Age hunters of Asia, finding North America and Asia connected by a broad rolling plain at the present Bering Sea, traversed the land connecting Siberia and Alaska and spread throughout Canada before turning southward. These people became Tennessee's first inhabitants, known to archaeologists chiefly from the fluted spearpoints and stone tools found throughout the state. Just when they came cannot be determined because of the absence of organic materials suitable for radiocarbon dating, but judging from artifacts and remains found in Alabama, there is a good reason to believe that they were in Tennessee well before the Ice Age ended.

Recent excavations have uncovered many artifacts, leading archaeologists to believe that the lower Tennessee Valley was as heavily populated with Ice Age hunters as any part of the United States. Fluted points, cutting and scraping tools, and other remains have been found near Chattanooga, where the hunters apparently established a campsite. The Highland Rim and Central Basin were probably their favorite hunting areas. Many spearpoints have been found in Bedford, Sumner, Robertson, Davidson, and other rim and basin counties. The area probably was a rich pasture for mastodons and other wild animals, making it a natural habitat for the nomadic hunter. Descendants of these early inhabitants continued to live in the area and mixed with other groups arriving later. These Paleo-Indians with their Old Stone Age culture were the first Americans.

The Archaic Indians succeeded the Paleolithic group. Radiocarbon dating has placed their life in Tennessee from about 8,000 years ago to shortly after the birth of Christ. They settled in villages, built houses, cooked over open fires, and shaped and polished their stone spearpoints and other weapons and tools. They also domesticated the dog and devised improved instruments for procuring fish and game, such as bone fishhooks, traps, and nets. Their dress became more elaborate, and they developed ornaments fashioned from bone, shell, and copper. The earliest sites of the Archaic Indians include one in Benton County, near the town of Eva and the junction of Cypress Creek with the Tennessee River; a second has been found in Henry County on the Big Sandy River.

The next inhabitants have been named Woodland Indians because they lived in eastern woodlands from Canada to the Gulf of Mexico. They probably came into Tennessee between 1000 B.C. and 500 B.C. and gradually developed a life based upon agriculture. It was they who first cultivated corn in the state. They used bows and arrows as well as spears in hunting game and fighting the enemy, and they made pottery, including large vessels for cooking. Their homes were circular huts or wigwams, made by pushing small poles into the ground and bending them to form a dome-shaped framework.

Later generations of the Woodland Indians were responsible for many of the Indian mounds so widely scattered over Tennessee, most of which served as a burial ground for the dead. The growth of a belief in a life hereafter led to ceremonial burials with accompanying objects for use in the world to come. As bodies were added to the mounds, they reached heights of fifteen or more feet. The Woodland Indians probably also built "Old Stone Fort" in Coffee County, between A.D. 100 and 500.

Another group constructed even larger "temple" mounds, which were substructures for religious and community buildings. These builders were the Early Mississippian Indians, who concentrated in the Mississippi Valley. They came into Tennessee about 1000 or a little thereafter. The mounds found on Hiwassee Island in East Tennessee and on the Forked Deer River in West Tennessee were formed in the course of many years. As a group of two or three built together deteriorated, the structures were apparently destroyed, and several feet of soil were added to the remains. Another group of temples would then be constructed on the summit. This process was repeated several times, with the top one or two layers seemingly added by Indians who either succeeded the Early Mississippian tribe or amalgamated with it. Some of the temple mounds grew to great size; the Pinson mound in Madison County, more than seventy feet high, is the second tallest in the United States.

The Early Mississippians constructed rectangular dwellings by setting long saplings upright in trenches to form the walls and weaving the bent tops together to make a base for a thatched roof. Their pottery was quite distinctive. Their crops included beans, potatoes, squash, and pumpkins as well as corn.

Historic Tennessee Indians ⟩⟩ Because prehistoric Indians lived before the time of written records, our information concerning them depends largely upon the results of archaeological investigations. The historic Indians came into contact with European explorers, who left written descriptions of these encounters. Hernando de Soto led expeditions into Tennessee in 1540, and Juan Pardo came twenty-five years later, but they left little information of benefit, and more than a hundred years elapsed before accounts of Indian-white relations reported much about the red culture. The Tennessee Indians of that period had a late Mississippian culture and were called by tribal names that have survived into modern times. The Creeks and the Chickasaw, like the neighboring Choctaw of south central

Mississippi, were of the Muskhogean[2] language group, but the Shawnee, Yuchi, and Cherokee were not. The Chickasaw, who seceded from the Choctaw, lived in northern Mississippi but claimed all of West Tennessee and part of Middle Tennessee as their hunting grounds. They did not have any towns in present-day Tennessee until about the time the state was admitted into the Union and a trading post was established at the site of Memphis.

Nevertheless, excavations in East Tennessee have unearthed evidence indicating, when it is related to other data, that much of this area was occupied by the Creek Indians from before 1300 to about 1700 or 1715. The name "Creek" came to be applied to this great confederacy of tribes as a shortened form of "Ochesse Creek," now the Ocmulgee River in Georgia, near which some of them lived. The confederacy included tribes residing in Alabama, Florida, Georgia, and, for the period mentioned above, Tennessee as well.

The Creeks had two types of towns—"red" ones devoted to making war and "white" ones to preserving peace. Inhabitants agreed that war should occur between them, so they substituted "brother of war" ball games, the ancestor of modern lacrosse. Each town had a "chunkey" court, where young men equipped with 10-foot poles played a game with a symmetrical disc six inches in diameter. The towns were never large, because war and disease took their toll. An examination of skeletal remains indicates that few Creeks lived beyond forty and that infant mortality was high. The dead were buried in or near the towns, with food and weapons interred for use on the way to the happy hunting grounds. Life in Creek towns concentrated in the public square, an outdoor council ground flanked on all sides by buildings and with a sacred fire, symbol of the heavenly sun, at the center. Each building was open on the side facing the square and was supplied with two tiers of mat-covered benches. In the squares were held the daily council meetings and periodic impressive assemblies of the whole confederacy. One such festival, held in mid-summer, was the "Boskita." shortened by European traders to "Busk."

Another tribe, of uncertain origin, was the Yuchi or Euchee ("Children of the Sun"), which temporarily occupied East Tennessee

---

[2] The Indian languages of the United States have been classified into the Muskhogean, Caddoan, Iroquoian, Siouan, and Algonquin groups.

during the early proto-historic period. They may have come from the "Chisca" province mentioned in accounts of the de Soto expedition. Juan Pardo, the Spaniard who invaded their land in 1566, described the people as living in houses built partly underground in a fortified village; later excavation of Yuchi sites in East Tennessee confirmed his descriptions.

It was the powerful Cherokee Nation that forced both the Creek and Yuchi Indians to migrate from East Tennessee in the early 1700s. In 1714 the warriors of the Yuchi town of Chestowee on the Hiwassee River, fearing capture and enslavement by the Cherokee, massacred their fellow townsmen and then committed suicide. Soon thereafter the remaining Yuchi moved to the Chattahoochee Valley in Georgia and joined the Creek Confederacy.

Another non-Muskhogean tribe, the Shawnee Indians, occupied the Cumberland Valley in Middle Tennessee during and shortly after the proto-historic period. The French had a trading post at the site of Nashville from 1710 to 1714. On early French maps the Cumberland River is called the Chaouanon, the French name for Shawnee. About 1714 the Cherokee and Chickasaw combined forces to drive the Shawnee out of the Cumberland Valley. Most of the Shawnee settled north of the Ohio River.

The Cherokee Indians ⟨⟩ After expulsion of the Creek, Yuchi, and Shawnee Indians during the early years of the eighteenth century, the Cherokee were the only Indians who occupied land in Tennessee. Their towns were located in the Southern Appalachians—in East Tennessee and in the neighboring regions of North Carolina, South Carolina, and Georgia. Cherokee claims to hunting grounds extended to the Ohio River on the north, to the Kanawha and its branch the New River on the east, and to the northward-flowing Tennessee (in conflict with the Chickasaw) on the west. In view of the absence of Indian towns after about 1715 in all of Tennessee except the southeastern corner and in most of Kentucky and western Virginia, this immense area was an Indian no-man's-land, traversed by many tribes with war and hunting expeditions but permanently settled by none.

The Cherokee were the largest single tribe of the South and one of the largest north of Mexico; with some justification they called themselves "Principal People." Because they belonged to the

The first "Tennesseans" were the Indians. Pictured above are Indian burial grounds at Chucalissa in Shelby County.

Iroquois language group, their Muskhogean neighbors called them "Tciloki," or "people of a different speech." The Spanish rendered the word "Achelaque," and the Cherokee adopted it in the form "Tsalagi." From these words the name Cherokee was derived.

The Cherokee probably first came into the Southeast and into Tennessee more than a thousand years ago. At the beginning of the historic period their estimated population was 22,000 and they lived in about eighty towns varying in size from a dozen to 200 families.

Cherokee towns were concentrated in four large groups. The lower settlements were along the Keowee and Tugaloo rivers in South Carolina and Georgia; the middle settlements, the heart of their nation, were located near the headwaters of the Tuckaseegee and Little Tennessee rivers in North Carolina; and the valley towns, also in North Carolina, were along the Valley, Notteley, and upper Hiwassee rivers. The fourth group, the only one in Tennessee, consisted of upper or overhill towns located on the other side of the mountains from the Carolina settlements. These towns were placed chiefly along the Little Tennessee River, but a few were situated on the Tellico and the Hiwassee. On the west side of the public square in the center of each town was the council house or temple. Grouped around the temple and square were the dwelling houses, which like those of other Late Mississippian Indians were built of upright logs. In the center of the dirt floor was a scooped-out fireplace, flanked by a hearthstone for use in baking corn bread. At one end were the beds, made of saplings and woven splints. In cold weather the families slept in the adjacent "hot house," a small, dirt-covered, cone-shaped structure supplied with beds and a fireplace in which a fire was kept burning all day and was banked at night. Similar hot houses were used by the medicine men for giving sweat baths as a means of treating certain diseases and as a purification ritual.

The council house was used mainly as a temple for religious rites but also as a public hall for civil and military councils. Usually large enough to seat 500 persons, it was seven-sided to correspond to the seven clans of the Cherokee Nation, with each clan assigned seats in a particular section. Seven large pillars lined the outer walls, and within were two concentric series of seven posts and a large central pillar. Three tiers of benches lined the walls, and one area near the sacred seventh pillar of the outer wall was reserved for the main officials. Near the central pillar and in front of the officials' seats was the altar, at which a fire was kept burning perpetually except for periodic and ceremonial extinguishing and rekindling. Lieutenant Henry Timberlake, who visited the Cherokee in 1761–1762, described the town house at Chote as having been built in the form of a "sugar loaf" large enough to hold 500 people and having "the appearance of a small mountain." He found the interior "extremely dark."[3]

Within the national government the Cherokee had one chief for the nation, who was aided by seven counselors in conducting the civil and religious affairs. There were also many minor officials, including medicine men, whose duties combined magic with practical surgery. Women had an important role in time of war, particularly the "Honored Woman," who had a vote in deciding for or against war and exercised the power of life and death over captives. The last and best known of the "War Women" was Nancy Ward, who was credited with warning settlers of the danger of attacks and with saving at least one white captive from being burned at the stake.

The Cherokee had a concept of creation as well as life after death. They spoke of a supreme being called "Yowa," they fasted, and they offered sacrifices. Their religious organization was closely tied to the civil government. Those who were ultimately to become the priests and medicine men were selected in early childhood and received special training.

Before the beginning of historic times the Cherokee were farmers, although they depended on hunting and fishing for their meat supply. Their chief crop was corn, but beans, squash, gourds, pumpkins, and sunflowers were also grown. Farming was carried on mainly by the women and old men, because warfare and hunting absorbed the time of the able-bodied males. Between wars, however, men tilled the soil.

The craft specialties of the Cherokee were stamped pottery and stone pipes skillfully carved in the shape of birds, animals or, occasionally, human beings. The Cherokee also were adept at wood carving and wove baskets and mats out of colored strips of cane. Clothing was made of turkey feathers as well as of animal skins, and feathers of more brilliantly colored birds were used as trimmings and headdresses.

The women wore skirts and shoulder mantles, and the men breech clouts and sleeveless shirts. Both wore moccasins. The men's garb

[3] Samuel C. Williams (ed.), *Lieutenant Henry Timberlake's Memoirs, 1756–1765* (Johnson City, Tenn., 1927), 59.

was brighter than that of the women and included earrings, neck-
pieces, and bracelets to supplement the painting or tattooing of the
body. When several young Cherokee chiefs visited London in 1730
and were presented to the royal family, a newspaper described their
attire as follows:

> The Indian king had on a scarlet jacket, but all the rest were naked
> except an apron about their middle and a horse's tail hung down
> behind. Their faces, shoulders, etc., were spotted with red, blue, and
> green. They had bows in their hands and painted feathers in their
> heads.[4]

The Cherokee were somewhat taller and more robust than other
Southern Indians. They had coarse, black hair and a rather light
complexion. Timberlake described them as having an "olive colour"
and noted that the men usually shaved their heads or had all their hair
plucked out by the roots "except a patch on the hinder part of the
head, about twice the bigness of a crown-piece, which is ornamented
with beads, feathers, wampum, stained deer hair, and such like
baubles." He also said that they slit their ears and stretched them to
an enormous size in order to adorn them with pendants and rings,
but he explained that this custom was borrowed from the Shawnee
Indians. The women wore their hair long, "sometimes to the ground,
club'd and ornamented with ribbons of various colours."[5]

Marriage customs seem to have been influenced by the near-
equality of the sexes, which resulted from the matrilineal system of
the Cherokee. Elaborate negotiations were carried on by the kinfolk
of the couple. Once marriage was agreed upon, the groom sent the
bride a piece of venison as a pledge that he would provide an ample
food supply, and the bride sent the groom an ear of corn as a token
that the crops would be tended and the food prepared. It seems that
the life of Cherokee women was confined to drudgery and un-
requited toil. Marriages were of short duration, and adultery was so
prevalent as to provoke comment from early European visitors.

Effects of Indian—White Contacts ᜮ Before the coming of
the white man, the life of the Cherokee and other Indians was
leisurely and pleasant. The forests teemed with game and the streams

---

[4] Williams (ed.), *Early Travels in the Tennessee Country* (Johnson City, Tenn.,
1928), 129n.
[5] Williams, *Timberlake,* 75ff.

were well stocked with fish. Without much cultivation the fertile soil produced corn and other vegetables. There was plenty of time for fun and entertainment. The Cherokee as well as the Creeks indulged in "ball play," the ancestor of lacrosse, played chunkey, and gambled on the results of the games.

Large-scale wars were not prevalent before the whites came and incited one tribe to war against another. Neighboring tribes engaged in commerce, transporting goods along Indian trails and on the rivers in dugout canoes. But with the development of trade relations with the whites, wars became more prevalent, and hunting became a business instead of a sport. As their primitive weapons for war and hunting were replaced or supplemented by firearms, the Indians became dependent on the whites for a regular supply of ammunition. Other European goods gradually became necessities. From the whites the Indians obtained horses and other domesticated animals and learned better methods of agriculture. They were also taught the doctrines of Christianity, but while adopting the white man's religion and customs, they acquired many of his vices to add to their own.

In a similar way white civilization was influenced by contacts with the Indians, with both beneficial and injurious results. The white man's diet was greatly enriched by food products contributed by the American Indians, and the billion-dollar tobacco industry had its origin in a weed first cultivated by those aborigines. The natives also taught the white pioneers how to survive in a wilderness environment. The opportunity to occupy great stretches of Indian country stimulated the white man's greed, and the natives were frequently dispossessed by dishonorable means. Although the Indians suffered perhaps inevitable casualties from the march of civilization, they left indelible marks on the character of modern American society.

SUGGESTED READINGS

Books
John P. Brown, *Old Frontiers: The Story of the Cherokee Indians from the Earliest Times to the Date of their Removal to the West, 1838* (Kingsport, 1938); Robert S. Cotterill, *The Southern Indians* (Norman, 1954); Donald Davidson, *The Tennessee: The Old River, from Frontier to Secession* (1946; rpt. Knoxville, 1979); Charles H. Faulkner, *The Old Stone Fort: Exploring an Archaeological Mystery* (Knoxville, 1968); Ralph O. Fullerton and John B. Ray (eds.), *Tennessee: Geographical Patterns and Regions* (Dubuque, 1977);

Harry Law, *Tennessee Geography* (Oklahoma City, 1961); Thomas M. N. Lewis and Madeline Kneberg, *Hiwassee Island: An Archaeological Account of Four Tennessee Indian Peoples* (Knoxville, 1946); Lewis and Kneberg, *The Prehistory of the Chickamauga Basin in Tennessee, A Preview* (Knoxville, 1941); Lewis and Kneberg, *Tribes That Slumber: Indians of the Tennessee Region* (Knoxville, 1958); James H. Malone, *The Chickasaw Nation* (Louisville, 1922); Laura Thornborough, *The Great Smoky Mountains,* rev. ed. (Knoxville, 1962); Samuel C. Williams (ed.), *Lieutenant Henry Timberlake's Memoirs, 1756–1765* (1927; rpt. Marietta, Ga., 1948).

Articles
E. Morton Coulter, "The Georgia-Tennessee Boundary," *GHQ,* 35 (Dec. 1951), 269–306; Cecil C. Humphreys, "The Formation of Reelfoot Lake and Consequent Land and Social Problems," *WTHSP* 14 (1960), 32–73; Robert A. McGaw and Richard W. Weesner, "Tennessee Antiquities Re-Exhumed: The New Exhibit of the Thruston Collection at Vanderbilt," *THQ* 24 (Summer 1965), 121–42; James R. Montgomery, "The Nomenclature of the Upper Tennessee River," *ETHSP* 28 (1956), 46–57; Charles H. Nash, "The Human Continuum of Shelby County, Tennessee," *WTHSP* 14 (1960), 5–31; Ann Harwell Wells, "Early Maps of Tennessee, 1794–1799," *THQ* 35 (Summer 1976), 123–44.

2.

ᢒᢌ Europeans Struggle for Control

THE discovery of America by Columbus in 1492 gave Spain a strong impetus to explore and colonize the new world. Not long after the discovery, Spain occupied the West Indies, Central America, and Mexico, acquiring convenient bases from which to begin exploration of the southeastern part of the United States. Initial attempts at occupation by England and France were not successful, but within the first decade of the seventeenth century both nations had footholds on the continent.

Spain did not become a strong contender for Tennessee, but France and England fought for three-quarters of a century for the territory east of the Mississippi River before France was finally expelled after the French and Indian War.

Tennesseans still repeat a legend of a Welsh prince called Madoc, who reportedly came in the twelfth century and built the Old Stone Fort at Manchester. As noted in the preceding chapter, however, it is now known that the fort was built by Woodland Indians some 1,500 to 2,000 years ago, and the Madoc story remains only a legend.

Early Explorations ᢒᢌ Hernando de Soto, a Spanish nobleman, was probably the first European in Tennessee. He landed at Tampa with 625 men in 1539, after procuring from his king permission to explore and settle Florida. Having heard from Indians of "gold-bearing mountains" to the north, he soon made his way through the tangled underbrush and swamps of Florida, Georgia, and South Carolina. By 1540 he had come to the headwaters of the Little Tennessee River in North Carolina, and thence across an

Indian trail to a site on the Tennessee River just north of Chattanooga. He camped for a time at the Creek town of Chiaha on an island a few miles below Chattanooga and sent out scouts to find an Indian town called "Chisca," which Indians said was rich in gold and copper. Vainly searching for the yellow metal, he then moved southwest and fought his way through Chickasaw territory across Alabama and Mississippi. In May 1541, he arrived at an Indian town called Quizquiz (pronounced "keys-keys")—or perhaps it was Chucalissa—in southwestern Tennessee or northwestern Mississippi. He died in the following spring (1542), and his men buried him in the waters of the great stream he had discovered.

A quarter-century later (1566–1567), Juan Pardo led expeditions into Tennessee, seeking alliances with the natives as well as gold. He built a fort at the Creek town of Chiaha but soon abandoned it and returned to South Carolina. Although the Spaniards were the first Europeans in Tennessee, they left no trace of their civilization, except perhaps ill will among the Indians, who told succeeding generations of their cruelties.

Of much greater significance was the coming of the English and, at about the same time, the French. John Cabot had been only a few years behind Columbus, and in 1497 he claimed North America for England. But Cabot's voyage was considered a failure because he found no precious metals, and the English were too busy with problems at home to give much attention to colonization. England's navy was inconsequential and church disputes rivaled economic interests in the minds of the leaders. During the reign of Queen Elizabeth I (1558–1603), however, matters changed. Catholics and Protestants had fought for two generations, but the specter of religious persecution vanished as the new monarch turned her attention toward building England into a nation that could rival Spain and its European neighbors. She unified the people, built a navy, improved the economy through the "enclosure" of farmland for sheep raising, and encouraged "Elizabethan sea dogs" to prey upon Spanish commerce. Finally, in 1588, her splendid navy—aided by a severe storm—defeated the "Invincible Armada" of Spain in its attempted invasion of English coasts.

Even before that victory, England had attempted colonization in the new world. Businessmen, making money from the manufacture of woolen goods, were willing to risk capital in attempting colonization; farm workers, displaced by the enclosure movement, were ready to seek new opportunities elsewhere. Consequently, Sir Humphrey Gilbert secured from Queen Elizabeth authorization "to discover and inhabit strange places," and in 1583, he landed with 250 men at Newfoundland. The colony was soon abandoned, however, and Gilbert lost his life at sea on his return voyage. In the following year, Gilbert's half-brother, Sir Walter Raleigh, received a charter from the queen to "discover, search, find out, and view such remote, heathen and barbarous lands, countries, and territories, not actually possessed of any Christian prince, nor inhabited by Christian people." Those who went with Raleigh were accorded the same rights and privileges as if they were "personally resident within our said Realme of England, any law, custome, or usage to the contrary notwithstanding." After a voyage of three months Raleigh reached the coasts of North Carolina, claimed all the land from Florida to Canada for England, and named it "Virginia" after Queen Elizabeth, the virgin queen. This first colony of Roanoke lasted for less than a year, but the settlers did discover three plants that were to become extremely important to later settlers and indeed to the entire world: corn, tobacco, and the "Irish" potato. A second colony of more than 100 people, including women and children, was established in 1587 under Governor John White, but this one—"the Lost Colony of Roanoke"—also failed.

Two decades elapsed before England attempted another colony, but this one was successful. A group of businessmen known as the "London Company" received a charter in 1606 to plant a colony on the Virginia coasts—a "sea-to-sea" grant between the 34th and 41st parallels, which of course included Tennessee. In the following year they sailed into the Chesapeake Bay and up a river they called "James" to a point where they established a settlement. This they named "Jamestown" in honor of King James I, who had succeeded to the English throne upon the death of Elizabeth I.

Within a few years some Virginians began to follow rivers and trails into the back country, where they traded with the natives. James Needham and Gabriel Arthur were the first Englishmen recorded as having come into present-day Tennessee. Arriving in 1673, they were told by Indians that Cherokee efforts to trade with the Spanish in Florida had resulted in death and captivity for some of their tribesmen and that the Indians preferred to develop trade with the English. Needham was subsequently killed, but Arthur lived to help the Virginians develop good trade relations with the red men.

In 1663 King Charles II had given the land between the 31st and 36th parallels to eight Englishmen who had helped restore the monarch to the English throne; this gift was modified two years later to include land to 36° 30'. Inasmuch as this was also a "sea-to-sea" grant, Tennessee was included within the new colony of Carolina. Trade developed rapidly as Carolina grew, and well before the turn of the century a lucrative fur trade had been developed with the Overhill Cherokee Indians.

While the English were settling Virginia and North Carolina and moving up navigable streams into the mountains, the French built settlements along the St. Lawrence River and explored the Great Valley of the Mississippi southward to the Gulf of Mexico. Under the aggressive policy of Count Frontenac, who came in 1672 as governor of the French dominions, explorers went forth into the west in large numbers, determined to claim the vast area for France. They included a Jesuit missionary, Father Jacques Marquette, and a fur trader, Louis Joliet. In 1673 they descended the Wisconsin River to the Mississippi and proceeded thence as far south as the Arkansas River, supposedly stopping for a short time at the Chickasaw bluffs. Nine years later Robert Cavelier de la Salle led an expedition to the Gulf. Near the mouth of the Hatchie River he temporarily lost one of his men, Pierre Prud'homme, and built a fort named in his honor. In 1692 Martin Chartier married a Shawnee and lived on the Cumberland River near Nashville. Shortly after the turn of the century Jean de Charleville conducted a lucrative fur trade with the Shawnee at the site of Nashville, which became known as "French Lick." This post was continued until 1714, when the Shawnees were forced out.

Indian Trade Increases Anglo-French Rivalry ⁀ᴥ The British and French traders played an important role in the conflict between their countries to gain control of the Mississippi Valley. The Indians became increasingly dependent upon goods of European manufacture, especially gunpowder, and they tended to favor the European country most generous and consistent in supplying their needs. Within most Indian nations one faction favored the British and another supported the French. Generally, however, the French were able to control the Creeks and Choctaw, while the British usually held sway over the Cherokee and Chickasaw. But each country and its traders continued to try to break in on the other's trade. The result was lack of harmony within each tribe and frequent wars between the tribes, with one contestant supported and armed by the British and the other by the French.

The English had left no stone unturned in their efforts to win Cherokee friendship, and as elusive as it was, they found that it had to be maintained with gifts and supplies. Expeditions were sent from time to time for parleys and to bear gifts. In the late 1720s Sir Alexander Cuming appeared in South Carolina, and he soon did more than anyone else to cement relations between the English and the Overhill Cherokee. With a display of force he overawed and mesmerized the warriors, compelled them to acknowledge King George II as their sovereign, and in the summer of 1730 carried six young braves, including the Little Carpenter, to England to visit the king. The visit became a powerful force in maintaining friendship among the Cherokees—the Little Carpenter, who returned to become the chief diplomat among the Cherokee, always remained friendly to the whites and often expressed a desire to return to visit "the great white chief' in London. Before they departed, the six young men as deputies of their nation signed a treaty of friendship with the English.

The Chickasaws, who lived in northern Mississippi but who claimed western Tennessee as a hunting ground, were also friendly to the British. They disrupted French communications between the trading posts near the Gulf of Mexico and those in the Illinois country and Canada. Unable to lure them from their adherence to the English, the French adopted a policy of destruction, first by inciting the Choctaw against England and then by direct force of French arms. The warlike Chickasaw succeeded in 1736 in defeating two French expeditions before finally being forced to surrender at Memphis to an army of 3,500 Frenchmen. Weakened after this, the Chickasaw still continued to act as a thorn in the flesh of the French by harassing convoys on the Mississippi River.

A profitable Indian trade developed before mid-century. Charles Town became the chief market for Indians goods, but other posts grew in North Carolina and Virginia. The journey from Charleston into the back country, where the Overhill trade was lucrative, required three to four weeks. Several traders traveled together for protection, and some caravans had a hundred or more horses to carry goods. The principal commodity supplied by the Indians was deerskins. In 1748, for example, 160,000 skins worth £250,000 were

Attakullakulla ("Little Carpenter"), far right, with six other Cherokees who visited London in 1730. Engraving by Isaac Basire.

exported from Charleston alone. Large quantities of beaverskins and other pelts were also involved in the market. Some slaves—men captured from other tribes—were sold to the whites, but the Indian did not take well to slavery, and that practice was soon abandoned as unprofitable. In exchange for the skins, the English trader supplied a variety of goods. Clothing and all sorts of adornments—shirts, laced hats, petticoats, colored stockings, striped calico, ribbons, buttons, beads, bracelets, ear bobs, and looking glasses—were among them. The men were interested in guns, gunpowder and bullets, knives, hatchets, and whiskey; women, in kettles, hoes, axes, and scissors.

The British and French Fight for America ঌ The contest between the English and French for control of the eastern part of the Mississippi Valley erupted into a series of four wars from 1689 to 1763 between those nations and their allies in Europe as well as between their colonists. The first conflict, known in Europe as the War of the Palatinate and in America as King William's War, was fought entirely in New England, the Great Lakes country, and the Hudson Bay region. It had resulted in no significant land gains for either side when peace was declared in 1697. This peace was uneasy, however, and in 1702 war broke out again. In Europe it was called the War of Spanish Succession, and in America it was Queen Anne's War. By then French traders had swarmed over the back country, and an important segment of the conflict was fought on the borderlands between the Carolinas, Florida, and Louisiana. When Spain joined with France, the English attacked Spanish posts along the coast of Georgia. By the time the treaty of peace was signed in 1715, England had taken from France Newfoundland, Acadia, and the Hudson Bay area, leaving unresolved the question of control over the transmontane area, where French and British traders continued to struggle for dominance. King George's War (called the War of Austrian Succession in Europe) was fought in the 1740s and resulted in no significant land gain. It was the fourth and final of these conflicts that held great significance for the American colonies because the outcome determined whether France or England would control North America. Known in Europe as the Seven Years' War and lasting on that continent from 1756 to 1763, the war actually began in America in 1754 and for all practical purposes had ended in America by 1760, when Montreal was surrendered to the English; General James

Wolfe had taken Quebec in heroic action one year earlier. Known in America as the French and Indian War, the contest in the Tennessee country was primarily a war between the English and French traders and their supporting Indian allies, with such English regulars as could be spared from the war in the north. When the treaty of peace was ultimately signed in 1763, the French had been driven from the continent, and the transmontane country was now free—at least from French obstruction—for English settlement.

Of considerable importance in the French and Indian War in the back country was Fort Loudoun, the first structure built in Tennessee by Anglo-Americans and one that protected the Carolinas from French troops who might invade from the south and west. The idea of a British fort in the Overhill Cherokee country had been suggested as early as 1746, when Chote and the other Little Tennessee River towns were under French influence. The plan seemed essential to both South Carolina and the Cherokee, especially if the English were to preserve their trade relations with the Indians. The French had established posts at New Orleans, Mobile, Fort Massoc near the mouth of the Tennessee River, and Fort Toulouse on the Alabama River, and they referred to the Cherokee country as the "key to Carolina" because of the ease with which the colony could be invaded through the Cherokee domain. In 1753 the English had built Fort Prince George near the Lower Cherokee town of Keowee some 250 miles away, and this caused the Overhill group around Chote to renew its claim for a fort. In the following year, the French threatened to invade the Overhill area because the Cherokee around Chote were friends of the English. In the summer of 1755, 500 Cherokee met with the governor of South Carolina, and he promised to build a strong fort at once in the Overhill Country. Several months later, when the Little Carpenter and 150 warriors visited Charleston, the South Carolina legislature appropriated money to begin the fort. Yet it was fall 1756 before work began, with additional funds coming from the colony of Virginia and Prince George himself (later George III) just as the Cherokee became more restive. William De Brahm—a German engineer who had earlier supervised the fortification of Charleston, 500 miles away—was engaged to build the fort with troops commanded by Captain Raymond Demere. The site selected was on the south bank of the Little Tennessee near the mouth of the Tellico (in present-day Monroe County, about thirty miles southwest of Knoxville) and partly on a ridge above the river, which was considered essential in the fort's defense. The fort was built of heavy logs, a well was dug within the enclosure, and the ridge was cleared of heavy timber within the range of rifle fire. The enclosure was roughly diamond-shaped, with a projecting bastion for the mounting of three cannon from each corner. Around the fort a ditch was dug, and locust trees were planted in it—the sharp thorns, De Brahm declared, would render the fort "impregnable at least against Indians who always engage [in battle] naked." The embankment along the ditch was provided with a palisade fifteen feet high. Adequate supplies, including twelve small cannon, were brought in on the backs of horses. As construction of the fort proceeded, the Cherokee became less restive.

On June 26, 1757, Captain Demere informed his superiors that the fort had been completed according to specifications. Named in honor of the Earl of Loudoun, commander in chief of all British troops in America, the fort occupied nearly two acres. A few weeks after its completion, Demere departed and was replaced by his brother, Captain Paul Demere, as commander of the garrison. With the arrival of traders and settlers, a thriving settlement soon grew up around the fort. At first they were welcomed by the Indians, who increased their hunting and trapping activity to meet the new demands for skins and pelts.

For the English, Fort Loudoun more than anything else secured the southern frontier during the early years of the French and Indian War. The French had powerful allies in the Shawnees of the Ohio Valley and the Creeks of Alabama. Had the Cherokees joined the French in 1756 or 1757, as they probably would have done if Fort Loudoun had not been built, the outcome of the war for the British could have been tragic.

The Cherokee War ⧉ Despite the construction of Fort Loudoun, relations between the English and the Cherokee soon became strained and flared into actual warfare before the end of 1759. A combination of causes brought on the conflict. The Cherokee, who had readily marched northward to participate in the war against the French in Virginia, believed that they had not been treated with proper respect or rewarded adequately. The Little Carpenter, second in power among the Cherokee, had been arrested and put in chains when he abandoned a march against Fort Duquesne.

While he readily forgave the whites after a conference with Governor Francis Fauquier of Virginia, his people did not so quickly forget the insult. Deteriorating trade relations, failure of the English to furnish the red men with adequate supplies (particularly war paint but also necessary guns and ammunition), and other misunderstandings, some of which seemed of somewhat small consequence to the English engaged in fighting the French, inevitably brought warfare on the frontier between the whites and their erstwhile allies, the Cherokee. The catalyst was the slaughter by the English of 21 hostages after the Cherokee leader Oconostota, also known as Great Warrior, had sanctioned the killing in ambush of Lieutenant Richard Coytmore, commander of Fort Prince George. The hostages, all leading chieftains of the Cherokee, were visiting Governor William Henry Lyttelton to discuss negotiations when they were arrested. The arrest outraged Oconostota, and in retaliation he lured Coytmore outside the fort, ostensibly for a conference, and then watched impassively as the Englishman was killed by Indians firing from ambush. The English soldiers then attempted to place the hostages in irons and massacred them when they resisted. This incident brought the whole Cherokee nation into war against the English, with the exception of the Little Carpenter, who had tried to preserve peace. Standing (or Stalking) Turkey, the emperor newly elected to replace Old Hop (who recently had died), concentrated hostilities upon the isolated Fort Loudoun.

As mentioned earlier, Loudoun was placed under the command of Captain Paul Demere soon after its completion. An able career soldier, he had brought about fifty regulars to occupy the fort in August 1757. Demere set out immediately upon a number of projects designed to improve the fort, including the building of guardhouses, storage bins, and chimneys for fires. In addition, small reinforcements were sent in. But Demere was unhappy; he soon chafed under the isolation of the frontier and complained about a lack of cooperation and aid from Governor Lyttleton and the British high command in general.

The Indians soon tried to take the fort. Unable to do so by direct assault, they determined to starve the post into submission, and for a year it was a beleaguered garrison plagued by desertion, illness, and demoralization. Demere received little assistance, although English forces under Lieutenant Colonel Archibald Montgomery wrought havoc among Cherokee Middle Towns in western North Carolina

Standing (or Stalking) Turkey, a portrait by Francis Parsons, reproduced courtesy of the Thomas Gilcrease Institute of American History and Art, Tulsa, Oklahoma.

that had cooperated with the French. Colonel William Byrd III was
sent with troops to reinforce Loudoun but was turned back at the
Holston River in southwestern Virginia.

Finally, in August 1760, Demere surrendered to Oconostota. The
arrangement provided that able-bodied soldiers could march out
with arms and baggage to Fort Prince George or to Virginia; soldiers
too ill to march could be cared for by Indians until they were able to
leave. The fort, with all remaining supplies, would be left to the
Indians. After marching fifteen miles, however, the hapless soldiers
were ambushed by 700 warriors who proceeded to massacre many of
them. Demere was shot, scalped, and tortured until he died. Captain
John Stuart, an aid to Demere, escaped, and most of the whites taken
prisoner later were ransomed by the English.

When the news of the Fort Loudoun massacre reached British
authorities, the governors of several colonies raised troops to re-
taliate. Soon the Cherokee sued for peace, and after troops from Fort
Prince George devastated Middle and Valley towns and destroyed
growing crops, a treaty was consummated in December 1761. The
Cherokee had lost 2,500 of their 5,000 warriors in their unfortunate
war on the back-country English.

Even as the Cherokee besieged and took Loudoun, British soldiers were winning Canada and driving France from the continent.
When the Treaty of Paris was written in 1763, England controlled
North America east of the Mississippi (except New Orleans), while
Spain was given the area west of that river. This of course opened up
for settlement the vast transmontane area into which hunters had
been going for several decades in their trade with the Indians.
Concerned with the restlessness of the frontier Indians now that
their French and Spanish allies had been defeated, the English did
announce the establishment of a definite boundary line beyond
which colonists could not go; still, it was not permanent. The line
passed along the crest of the mountains established by the Proclamation of 1763, and was generally ignored by the restless Virginians and
North Carolinians in their hunger for western lands.

SUGGESTED READINGS

Books
John Richard Alden, *John Stuart and the Southern Colonial Frontier* (Ann

Arbor, 1944); Charles W. Alvord and Lee Bidgood, *The First Exploration of the Trans-Allegheny Region by the Virginians* (Cleveland, 1912); John A. Caruso, *The Appalachian Frontier* (Indianapolis, 1959); David H. Corkran, *The Cherokee Frontier, 1740–1763* (Norman, 1962); Vernon W. Crane, *The Southern Frontier* (Durham, 1928); Gilbert E. Govan and James W. Livingood, *The Chattanooga Country*, 3d ed. (Knoxville, 1976); Chapman J. Milling, *Red Carolinians* (Chapel Hill, 1940); Constance L. Skinner, *Pioneers of the Old Southwest* (New Haven, 1919); Samuel Cole Williams, *The Dawn of the Tennessee Valley and Tennessee History* (Johnson City, Tenn., 1937); Williams, *Beginnings of West Tennessee in the Land of the Chickasaws* (Johnson City, Tenn., 1930).

Articles
Vernon W. Crane, "The Tennessee River as a Road to Carolina," *MVHR* 3 (March 1916), 3–18; Stanley J. Folmsbee and Madeline Kneberg Lewis (eds.) and Gerald W. Wade (trans.), "Journals of Juan Pardo Expeditions, 1566–1567," *ETHSP* 37 (1965), 106–21; W. Neil Franklin, "Virginia and the Cherokee Indian Trade," *ETHSP* 4 (1932), 3–21, 5 (1933), 22–38; Paul Kelley, "Fort Loudoun: The After Years, 1760–1960," *THQ* 20 (Dec. 1961), 303–22; Charles H. Nash, "Human Continuum of Shelby County," *WTHSP* 4 (1960), 5–31; Nash and Rodney Gates, Jr., "Chucalissa Indian Town," *THQ* 21 (June 1962), 103–21; Mary U. Rothrock, "Carolina Traders in the Overhill Country," *ETHSP* 1 (1929), 3–18, reprinted in Robert H. White et al. (eds.), *Tennessee: Old and New*, vol. 1 (Nashville, 1946), 69–83; Craig Symonds, "The Failure of America's Indian Policy on the Southwestern Frontier, 1785–1793," *THQ* 35 (Spring 1976), 29–45.

3.

Seedtime: Permanent Settlements Are Established

F OR several years before the beginning of the French and Indian War, traders and hunters visited the western country on a regular basis. At mid-century Samuel Stalnaker, a Cherokee trader and friend of Dr. Thomas Walker, and perhaps others had settled just north of the present Tennessee-Virginia line near Abingdon. A year or two earlier Dr. Walker and others had claimed land in the vicinity of Bristol and Kingsport, and in 1749 they had organized the Loyal Land Company, which secured the title to 800,000 acres for the purpose of establishing families "upon the western waters."

The French and Indian War accentuated the dreams of settlement on rich and fertile land across the mountains. Scarcely were arms stacked before the restless spirit of frontiersman was aroused again. As one scholar has written,

> Every ragged colonist in Virginia and Carolina (and some as far away as Maryland and eastern Pennsylvania) increasingly saw the west as a veritable pot of gold. Land in the distant west became a magnet, and the older hills and uplands of the eastern piedmont lost their attractiveness compared to the fertile valleys beyond the mountains.[1]

The Proclamation Line of 1763, announced by the British in that year to pacify Indians, forbade Europeans from settling beyond the crest of the Appalachian Mountains. This stricture was of course denounced by settlers, who believed that they had played a major role in driving the French from North America and in winning the vast West and consequently felt entitled to an opportunity to gain

---

[1] Max Dixon, *The Wataugans* (Nashville, 1976), 3.

western lands after the war. Fortunately, the line was not to be permanent. Two superintendents of Indian Affairs, in cooperation with the colonial governors, were authorized to negotiate with the Indians for cessions of land. The two superintendents in 1763 were Sir William Johnson (for the region north of the Ohio River) and John Stuart, a survivor of the Fort Loudoun massacre (for the South). By 1768, Stuart had obtained Cherokee consent in the Treaty of Hard Labour to a line running from Reedy River in South Carolina past Tryon Mountain to Chiswell's Mine (at the site of Wytheville, Virginia) and thence in a direct line to the mouth of the Kanawha River. In the same year, Johnson at the Treaty of Fort Stanwix asked the Iroquois to relinquish all claims to the region south of the Ohio River as far west as the mouth of the Tennessee, even though they had only a shadowy claim to that territory; superior titles to that no-man's-land were held by the Cherokee and Chickasaw, who had driven the Shawnee out of the Cumberland Valley early in the eighteenth century.

Land-hungry speculators and settlers naturally assumed that the Treaty of Fort Stanwix had opened to legal settlement all of southwest Virginia, West Virginia, and much of Kentucky and Tennessee, but at the Treaty of Lochaber in 1770, John Stuart—with the reluctant acquiescence of the governor of Virginia—confirmed the Cherokee title to much of that country. He nevertheless acquired from those Indians a new cession of land north and east of a line running along the 36° 30' parallel to the Holston River near Long Island (the site of Kingsport) and thence northward to the mouth of Kanawha. When that line was surveyed in 1771 by John Donelson and Alexander Cameron, the Cherokee accepted two important modifications. As the Little Carpenter explained it, the Indians "pitied" some settlers they found north of the South Fork of the Holston but south of the 36° 30' parallel and allowed the South Fork to be considered the boundary line to the vicinity of Long Island. Since the 36° 30' parallel was supposed to be the Virginia–North Carolina boundary, the Donelson line of 1771 following the South Fork of the Holston was accepted temporarily as the line dividing those colonies, and the portion of Tennessee lying "north of the Holston" (South Fork) was governed by Virginia until the boundary was surveyed in 1779. The other modification of the Lochaber line accepted in 1771 made the new boundary run northwest from the vicinity of Long Island to the Kentucky River and along that stream

The Dean Cornwell murals, depicting the history of Tennessee, are on the walls of the State Office Building at Nashville. The mural panel above shows some of the explorers and pioneers who figured prominently in the early history of the state; the panel below shows later figures who contributed to the development of the state.

to the Ohio, rather than north to the mouth of the Kanawha (see map 3).

The several years after the conclusion of the Cherokee War has been called "the decade of the long hunters." A "long hunter" was a person who went into the wilderness to hunt, trap, and trade for

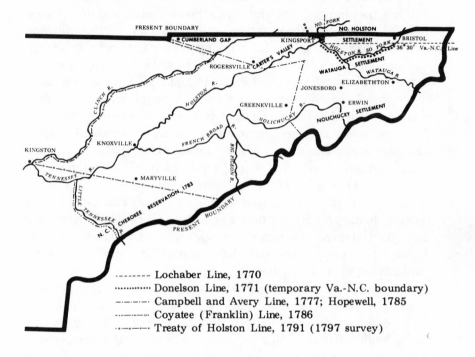

Lochaber Line, 1770
Donelson Line, 1771 (temporary Va.-N.C. boundary)
Campbell and Avery Line, 1777; Hopewell, 1785
Coyatee (Franklin) Line, 1786
Treaty of Holston Line, 1791 (1797 survey)

Map 3. Early East Tennessee Settlements and Treaties

several months—or perhaps in a few cases for several years. He seldom established a home and had no intention of making permanent settlement; he only sought pelts and skins from the wilderness and planned to return to the seaboard to market them. But he did pave the way for permanent settlements. Some long hunters prepared rough maps, made friends with the Indians, and even made small clearings; all returned to the East with such tales of the richness of the West that hundreds wanted to follow them into the wilderness. Many of them left their names on a river, creek, mountain, or ridge.

Long hunters often traveled in groups. In 1761 Elisha Walden (for whom Walden Ridge was named) led a group of eighteen or twenty hunters into the Tennessee country from Virginia. After hunting for a while near present-day Johnson, Sullivan, and Hawkins counties, he turned northward through Cumberland Gap and into Kentucky. Eight years later, Kasper Mansker came with a group about the same size. Mansker and his associates, who included Abraham Bledsoe, Uriah Stone and others, entered the country from Abingdon. Like Walden, they hunted for a while in the eastern sector and then turned north into Kentucky through the Cumberland Gap. By the following year they had been successful in taking hundreds of pelts, and some of them, including Mansker, turned southward in hastily constructed canoes and boats. At French Lick they stopped long enough to kill a few buffalo and add more hides to their cargo, and thence they moved down the Cumberland, Ohio, and Mississippi rivers to Natchez, where they sold their wares. Mansker continued to hunt and trap sporadically for another decade. Ultimately he became associated with James Robertson, and in early 1780 he signed the Cumberland Compact. Hundreds of others came into the Tennessee wilderness; they included Andrew Greer, James Harrod, Michael Stoner, Julius Dugger, Gilbert and Robert Christian, William and George Anderson, Thomas Sharp Spencer and, of course, Daniel Boone. Some were not only long hunters but also, surveyors, explorers, and land speculators.

Among the best known of the long hunters were Spencer and Boone, perhaps because the aura of romance was associated with their venture into the wilderness. Boone, reared by Quaker parents in the Yadkin Valley of North Carolina, was by 1760 in present-day Washington County, where he carved on a beech tree a terse statement of his exploits with a "bar" which he had "cilled" nearby. A few years later he became a land agent for Judge Richard Henderson, a North Carolina jurist and land speculator, and played a prominent role in the establishment of settlements in Kentucky. Spencer had hunted and explored parts of Kentucky earlier, but his first foray into Tennessee was in 1776, when he traveled by way of Kentucky into present-day Sumner County near Bledsoe's Lick. It was at that time, according to an oft-repeated story, that he acquired the sobriquet of "Big Foot." In pursuit of a wounded buffalo, he had dashed by a cabin built by Timothy Demonbreun and occupied at that moment by a hunter from the Illinois country. The hunter, on seeing the enormous prints of Spencer's oversized bare feet, fled for his life and informed the first traders he met that the area was inhabited by giants. Spencer is also alleged to have spent at least one winter in a hollow sycamore tree, to which Sumner natives could point as late as 1839.[2] He claimed cleared land, planted a crop of corn, became associated with Robertson's settlement at French Lick, and is sometimes referred to as the "first white settler" in Middle Tennessee. Like some others, he thus developed from a long hunter into a permanent settler. He was granted several thousand acres of land and lived in the Cumberland region until 1794, when he was shot to death in an ambush near the present location of Crab Orchard.

Some of the hunters developed frontier business enterprises. Most left the meat to spoil when they slaughtered an animal for his hide, but in the late 1760s Joseph Hollingshed developed a meat-packing operation on the Cumberland and Tennessee rivers. There he cured and casked buffalo beef and venison and rendered tallow from buffalo fat as well as gathering deerskins, all of which he sent to the New Orleans market and the Fort Chartres market in the Illinois country. His operations were naturally confined to the winter months. Timothy Demonbreun, a French Canadian, established a store or trading post at French Lick about 1796 and was one of the first settlers on the Cumberland frontier.

Settlements in East Tennessee 8~ At about the time that Demonbreun and Spencer were settling on the Cumberland, William Bean and a group of relatives and friends from Pittsylvania County, Virginia cleared land and built cabins along the Watauga River. Often called the "first permanent settler," Bean may have been preceded by others whose names are not known to us. In the same year (1769) Gilbert Christian and others, having ventured across the valley in December 1768 and found "nothing . . . but a howling wilderness," were astonished upon their return trip to find small cabins "on every spot where the range was good."[3] In spring of the following year James Robertson came from Orange County,

---

[2] Contemporaries told of his tremendous physical strength. One remarked, "He was the stoutest man I ever saw. Indeed, he was a Hercules—stronger than two common men." Still another told how he lifted an antagonist by the seat of the trousers and threw him over an eight-foot rail fence. The man, somewhat humbled but nonplussed, simply arose from the dust and, while Big Foot glared, exclaimed, "Mr. Spencer, if you will be kind enough to pitch my horse over, I will be riding."

[3] James G. M. Ramsey, *The Annals of Tennessee to the End of the Eighteenth Century* (Charleston, 1853), 93–94.

Charlotte Reeves Robertson came with her husband from Virginia in 1770 to settle at Watauga. A few years later they settled at Nashborough.

North Carolina, destined to play a role not only in the development of Watauga but in the settlement of Nashborough on the Cumberland River as well. Born and reared in Brunswick County, Virginia and of Scotch-Irish ancestry, he had lived in Orange only four years when he determined to move westward. With him came his wife, Charlotte Reeves, their child, born in 1769, his brother-in-law William Reeves, his brothers Charles and Mark, and perhaps other relatives and friends.

Hundreds of people moved into the area during the next twelve to fifteen months. Various developments pushed people from Virginia and North Carolina into the transmontane area; dissatisfaction with the North Carolina government stands foremost. The county was the unit of representation, and since the eastern counties outnumbered the western, settlers in the Piedmont were generally outvoted in the assembly. In the early 1770s, for example, seven western counties had seventeen representatives, or one for every 7,300 people, while the eastern counties had sixty-one representatives—one for every 1,700 people.

Not only was the west under represented, but the undemocratic character of local government was even more irritating to the western folk. The county court, made up of justices of the peace who held their positions for life, appointed (or nominated for gubernatorial appointment) practically all county officeholders. Some of the appointed officials even came from outside the county of their supposed residence. "Big government" resulted in discriminatory tax policies that did much to unify the people of the west—particularly in Orange, Anson, Halifax, and Granville counties—into protest movements. Calling themselves "Regulators," the dissident groups held meetings and circulated leaflets as early as 1765, but the year 1768 brought formal organization to the activity. Governor William Tryon had complained to English authorities in the preceding year that the western people paid less than one-third the amount of taxes levied, and he had told of plans for a stricter policy of enforcement. When the assembly a short time later announced a new tax to raise funds for a governor's mansion—called "Tryon's palace" by the westerners—the frontiersmen exploded. They held meetings, refused to pay taxes, disrupted court proceedings when lands and chattels were being foreclosed upon, threatened death to certain judges and lawyers, and otherwise engaged in mob action. At length Tyron called out 1,500 militiamen and marched on the Regulators.

At Alamance Courthouse on May 16, 1771, he encountered 2,000 armed Regulators and fired upon them when they refused to obey an order to surrender. Less than a dozen men were killed on each side; a number of the Regulators were captured and some were convicted of treason, but the majority fled and were later pardoned by the governor. Many came across the mountain to take up lands in their flight from oppression.

Other reasons for heavy immigration into East Tennessee involved many fundamental differences between the eastern and western North Carolinians. Geography, ethnic origin, religion, social background, and economy conspired to separate them into two peoples. The east, composed largely of English and Scot Highlanders, owned plantations and slaves; the westerners, Scotch-Irish and Germans, had small farms and depended upon their own labor for subsistence. The eastern people were Anglicans; the westerners were affiliated with the more fundamentalist groups. Commercially, the east had ties with England, the other coastal colonies, and the West Indies; westerners were highly restricted in their markets. Social structure, based upon wealth, naturally favored the east.

As people were being pushed from the east, they were being beckoned by the overmountain country with promises of a better life. Long hunters brought reports of better relations with the Cherokee, who now appeared eager to exchange rights to land for commodities of all sorts. In October 1770, for example, the treaty of Lochaber ceded land west of the Hard Labor Line in the Holston Valley. An important consideration for the Cherokee, of course, was their war with the Chickasaw, which occurred just as hundreds of whites were moving across the mountain and accentuated the Indians' need for arms and other supplies. Curiosity and the sheer love of adventure also pulled the people westward. After visiting John Honeycutt in his hut "high on the flank of a mountain," Robertson returned to Orange County to tell of the beauty of the terrain, the relative ease with which the mountains could be traversed, and the economic opportunities the area offered. Certainly to Robertson and others the prospect of relief from discriminatory taxation and the sheer hope of "beginning again" must have been important attractions of new homes in the west.

Within a very short time four pockets of settlement developed (see map 4). The Watauga settlement centered at Sycamore Shoals (present-day Elizabethton) but soon spread along the Watauga River and its tributaries. To the north of Watauga on the Holston River was Sapling Grove, an early name for Bristol, where Evan Shelby in 1770 built a store and stockade. To the Wataugans, Shelby's Station was

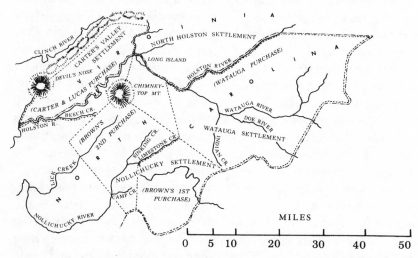

Map 4. Early Settlements, Adapted from Map in Garrett and Goodpasture, *History of Tennessee.* "Map showing the supposed line between Virginia and the Western Territory of North Carolina, from 1772 to 1779, and the two Tennessee settlements on either side of said line in 1772; and also the limits of the several private purchases from the Indians, by the Watauga settlers, Jacob Brown, and Carter and Lucas, in 1775."

the "North of Holston" settlement, and it soon became an important trading post and rendezvous for expeditions northward. One early settler was Valentine Sevier, father of John Sevier, who also lived in the North Holston area before removing to Watauga. North Holston was governed as a part of Virginia, but as a western settlement it was closely tied to Watauga. Carter's Valley, west of North Holston and Watauga, formed a third region. It lay between present-day Kingsport and Rogersville and was established by John Carter, a Virginia merchant who opened a store in the area. Problems with the Cherokee forced these people to remove to Watauga in 1772, however. The fourth settlement lay to the south of Watauga, near the site of Erwin on the Nolichucky River. In 1771 Jacob Brown, a small merchant from South Carolina, bought rights from John Ryan, who had had a preemption claim as early as 1768, and came, bringing with him settlers said to be Regulators. A gunsmith and blacksmith as well as a storekeeper, Brown found his services much in demand by Indians as well as whites.

The western people apparently thought they were within the jurisdiction of Virginia and east of the Proclamation Line. A survey conducted in 1771 by John Donelson assisted by the Little Carpenter and John Stuart's chief deputy, Alexander Cameron, however, clearly indicated that all the settlers at Watauga and Nolichucky were on lands reserved for the Indians. North Holston, governed by Virginia, was within the Lochaber cession, but the other areas were not. Cameron therefore proclaimed the Wataugans to be squatters and ordered them to move. Jacob Brown and his people immediately departed the Nolichucky settlement and joined the Wataugans. The Wataugans, however, determined not to leave.

It was again Little Carpenter who came to the rescue of the whites. With the authorization of the Watauga leaders, James Robertson and John Bean visited the Cherokee chiefs at Chota, sacred city of the Overhill Cherokee, and urged them to lease the land on which they had settled for ten years in exchange for "merchandise and trade goods, plus some muskets and household articles." The Cherokee agreed. As the Little Carpenter said, "It is but a little spot of ground you ask, and I am willing that your people should live upon it. I pity the white people. . . ."[4] Learning of the success of Robertson and Bean, Jacob Brown made a similar lease with the Indians for land on both sides of the Nolichucky. He then returned to his settlement and reopened his store. The westerners now had reason to rejoice. As one scholar has written,

> They had achieved a real backwoods coup. Their red adversaries were now their landlords, a clear improvement, and a decade of peace with them seemed ahead. Moreover, tenancy, which gave them a legal toehold on the land, might lead to possession. The lease in any event was a key to their survival.[5]

The settlers of Watauga and Nolichucky were outside the bounds of any organized government. Like the signers of the Mayflower Compact of 1620, they therefore developed a homespun government; they called it the "Watauga Association." As leaders explained

[4] John P. Brown, *Old Frontiers* (Kingsport, 1938), 130–31.
[5] Dixon, *The Wataugans,* 15.

to North Carolina authorities, they were on the frontiers of civilization, and

> being apprehensive that, for the want of a proper legislature, we might become a shelter for such as endeavored to defraud their creditors; considering also the necessity of recording Deeds, Wills, and doing other public business; we by consent of the people, formed a court . . . taking (by desire of our constituents) the Virginia laws for our guide. . . . This was intended for ourselves, and was done by the consent of every individual. . . .[6]

They then agreed upon a document that they called "Written Articles of Association," by which they established a court of five members having powers to exercise both legislative and judicial functions, along with a sheriff, clerk, and other officials. Although the records of the proceedings have been destroyed, the judges probably were John Carter, James Robertson, Charles Robertson (James Robertson's cousin), Zachariah Isbell, and Jacob Brown.

Writers for 200 years have debated the intent of the Wataugans. The Earl of Dunmore, royal governor of Virginia, viewed Watauga as a "Separate State," a condition constituting a "dangerous example"; other ambitious frontiersmen, he said, might try the same thing elsewhere. Nineteenth-century historian George Bancroft wrote of the "Republic of Watauga," and Theodore Roosevelt, writing near the end of the same century, saw the Wataugans as having "exercised the rights of full statehood." Two able twentieth-century historians, however, have not viewed the movement in that light. Philip Hamer, writing in 1932, saw the government as "simply designed . . . to meet a particular emergency;" the people "had no intention of exercising . . . all the purposes of a sovereign and independent state." Stanley J. Folmsbee, writing three decades later, agreed; "independence," he wrote, "was not the design."[7] Still, the Watauga movement may safely be considered a precursor of later movements of a similar nature, such as the Cumberland government of 1780 and Franklin of 1784.

For several years Wataugans lived in peace with their neighbors and landlords. In 1774, Lord Dunmore's War developed between Virginia and the Indians of the Ohio River region, but fortunately the Cherokee remained quiet. During the war, King's Mill Fort and

[6] Ramsey, *Annals,* 134–38.

[7] Philip M. Hamer (ed.), *Tennessee, 1673–1932,* vol. 1 (New York, 1933); Folmsbee *et al., Tennessee, A Short History,* 1st ed., 57.

Eaton's Station were built near the site of Kingsport for the protection of settlers who were moving into that area, and Shelby's Fort, named for Captain Evan Shelby, was constructed at Sapling Grove.

The successful conclusion of Lord Dunmore's War stimulated the activities of speculators, who organized land companies. One of the most important of such companies was the Transylvania Company, formed by Judge Richard Henderson of North Carolina, who planned to establish a colony west of the mountains on land he would purchase from the Cherokee. Early in 1775, he arranged a treaty conference with the Indians at Sycamore Shoals. For goods costing £10,000, Henderson purchased an enormous tract bounded on the north and east by the Ohio and Kentucky rivers and on the south by the ridge dividing the waters of the Tennessee and Cumberland rivers. Although Dragging Canoe, a son of the Little Carpenter, warned his fellow Cherokee during the negotiations that they were paving the way for the ultimate extinction of their race, he was overruled by the older chiefs. He then stalked out of the council chamber, where negotiations were being conducted, staying only long enough to warn whites that they were purchasing a "dark and bloody ground."

The Wataugans were interested spectators at the treaty negotiations in the midst of their settlement. On March 19, two days after the Transylvania Treaty was signed, Wataugans bought from the Cherokee all the land that they had leased and more. This purchase included all the land on the Watauga River, land below the South Holston and the Virginia line, and the headwaters of the New River, consisting of much of the present-day Virginia counties of Allegheny, Ashe, and Watauga. Thus the Watauga country of the early 1770s, now free of Indian title, consisted of some 2,000 square miles. Jacob Brown, hearing that the Cherokee were in a trading mood, on March 25 purchased his settlement on the Nolichucky River. His land, two separate but adjoining counties, bordered Watauga on both sides of the Nolichucky River and was almost equal in size to the Watauga purchase.

Before the treaties had been concluded, Henderson dispatched Daniel Boone and a party of axe-wielders to mark a trail (later called the Wilderness Road) through Cumberland Gap into Kentucky, and he followed a little later with a group of settlers. Although he was at first primarily interested in Kentucky, Henderson turned his attention to the Tennessee portion of his purchase when Virginia refused to recognize the company's title, and in 1779–1780 he sponsored the settlement of the Cumberland Valley.

The Cumberland Settlements ᏋᎧ After Virginia nullified the Transylvania Company's claim to land in Kentucky in 1778, Judge Henderson turned his attention to that part of his purchase which lay below the Virginia–North Carolina line. To determine positively that the French Lick was not in Virginia, Henderson employed James Robertson and a party of eight of Robertson's companions to go into the Cumberland Valley "with instruments" to make an accurate survey. If the Lick proved to be in North Carolina, Henderson counseled, Robertson should plant corn and otherwise prepare for settlers.

Inasmuch as the survey showed the Lick to be clearly south of 36°30' Robertson returned, according to his daughter Lavinia Robertson Craighead, with "a glowing description of the country . . . [and] made up a large party to go and settle . . . where Nashville now stands." John Donelson, who had settled in Pittsylvania County, Virginia, had joined Robertson in conferences with Henderson on several occasions, perhaps as early as the time of Henderson's Transylvania purchase. The current plan for settlement provided that Robertson would take most of the men overland and Donelson would lead a flotilla of women and children and the remaining men by river.

Robertson therefore left his home on the Holston and with a party of some two hundred men, including his brothers Mark and Joe and his ten-year-old son Jonathan, set out in October 1779 for French Lick. Driving before them pack horses, mares and colts, cattle, hogs, sheep, and other stock, the party moved northward from Fort Patrick Henry at the present site of Kingsport and then turned abruptly westward at the Block House, a Virginia station built in 1777 on the North Fork of the Holston. From that point they proceeded west, traveling through Cumberland Gap, over the Cumberland Road, and on through much of Kentucky. In the vicinity of the Powell River they met John Rains (or Raines) and others bound for Harrodsburg, but Robertson persuaded them to join his group headed for the Cumberland. They entered Tennessee just north of present-day Clarksville; from there they journeyed south, probably stopping at Kilgore's and Mansker's stations before continuing to the French

Lick. They arrived during Christmas week and, finding the Cumberland River frozen solid, completed the 400-mile journey by driving their stock and wagons across the ice on Christmas Day.

In the meantime, Donelson had constructed a large flatboat (such vessels were customarily about 100 feet long and 20 feet wide) called the *Adventure* to serve as his flagship. Other smaller craft, probably a dozen or more boats capable of transporting several families, made up the flotilla. Because Donelson told of his fascinating experiences in a well-kept journal, the story of the journey has become a favorite saga among Tennesseans.

Donelson and his party departed Fort Patrick Henry on December 22, 1779, determined to float down the Tennessee to the Ohio and up that river to the Cumberland; from the mouth of the Cumberland they would proceed to French Lick. Cold weather and other problems caused them to stop after only a few miles, and the journey was not resumed until about the middle of February. On February 20 they reached Cloud Creek, where they were joined by other vessels. A little later they arrived at the Clinch River, where still more flatboats joined them. On March 2, they reached the mouth of the French Broad, and two days later, the mouth of the Little Tennessee.

Many problems attended the journey. On March 7, Ephraim Peyton's wife was delivered of a child who died several days later, when its mother was forced to help fight off an Indian attack. A smallpox epidemic broke out on one boat, one or more boats ran aground, Indian attacks were frequent, and the food supply was almost exhausted. Navigating the "Suck" at Chattanooga and "Muscle Shoals" in northern Alabama was difficult. Some families quit the voyage at the shoals and settled in that vicinity, others decided to go to Natchez; and still others joined Moses Renfroe at Clarksville to settle in the valley of the Red River. On April 23 those who remained reached Eaton's Station, a small settlement recently established by Amos Eaton, who had also established a station between Ready Creek and the Holston River before moving westward. On the following day the group arrived at French Lick. The eloquent Donelson closed his journal on that day with the statement:

> This day we arrived at our journey's end at the Big Lick where we have the pleasure of finding Captain Robertson and his company. It is a source of satisfaction to us to be enabled to restore to him and others their families and friends, who were entrusted to our care, and who sometime since, perhaps despaired of ever meeting again.

Interestingly, Judge Henderson arrived at the same time, having left the commission appointed to establish a boundary between the western claims of Virginia and North Carolina. His real interests lay at French Lick, and he took the lead in formulating a frontier government there. It was Henderson who insisted upon the name of Nashborough for the new settlement. General Francis Nash, of Hillsborough, North Carolina, who before the Revolution had been clerk of the court over which Judge Henderson presided, had been killed three years earlier in the Battle of Germantown.

As mentioned earlier, several people had settled in the Cumberland country before Robertson and Henderson arrived. Timothy Demonbreun was at the Lick by the time the Revolution began and two years later told of seeing seven whites on the Cumberland River in present-day Montgomery County. In 1773 about thirty Tory families, apparently driven from North Carolina because of their support of the British, sought to form a colony on the Cumberland. At the same time Thomas Kilgore, at the age of 62, established himself in the Clarksville vicinity and in 1779 built a small stockaded fort called Kilgore's Station near present Palmyra. Others had established themselves, and still more arrived daily even as Henderson, Robertson, and Donelson contemplated a form of government.

The Cumberland settlement was within the bounds of Washington County, created from the transmontane settlements at the beginning of the Revolution but separated from Watauga by more than 200 miles of wilderness. The leaders organized a temporary government somewhat similar to that established under the Watauga Compact. The Cumberland Compact provided for a tribunal of twelve judges apportioned among the eight stations in the vicinity as follows: Nashborough, three; Mansker's (in Sumner County), two; Eaton's (on the east side of the Cumberland two or three miles below Nashville), two; Bledsoe's (near Castalian Springs), one; Asher's (on Station Camp Creek near Gallatin), one; Stone's River (west of the Hermitage at Clover Bottom), one; Fort Union (about six miles up the Cumberland from Nashville), one; and Freeland's one-half mile northwest of Nashville), one. The judges (variously called "Triers," "Notables," and "General Arbitrators"), who were to be elected by all free men twenty-one years of age or older, had certain defined judicial and legislative powers. Their decisions were to be enforced by a militia composed of all men above the age of sixteen. Although their rulings could not be appealed, the judges were subject to recall if they failed to act within the best interests of all concerned. In the event that a major crime was committed, the felon was to be "safely bound" and returned to a place where a fair trial could be given him. Until "the full and proper exercise of the laws of our country can be in use," each signatory agreed to "most solemnly and sacredly declare and promise to each other" that they would "faithfully and punctually adhere to perform, and abide by this our association, and at all times, if need be, compel by our united force a due obedience to these our rules and regulations." Two hundred and fifty-six names were signed to the document.

During the first few years the operations of the government were suspended because the settlements were almost destroyed by the Indians. It would become necessary for the people to abandon some of the weaker forts and flee to Nashborough in the event of a full-fledged attack. Joseph Renfroe's station on the Red River was the first to feel the resentment of the Chickasaws. About twenty of the settlers, including Renfroe, were killed as they attempted to flee to the safety of Nashborough. In the fall of 1780, several of the settlements were assaulted by the Chickamaugans. Mansker's Station sustained such losses that many of the survivors, including John Donelson, decided to move to Kentucky. James Randolph Robertson, the eldest son of Captain Robertson, was killed. As supplies ran low, Robertson went into Kentucky to seek food and weapons. Upon his return in January, 1781, he stopped at Freeland's Station, where he helped the people at that fort fight off an attack by the Chickasaws. In April 1781, Nashborough was invaded by the Chickamaugans under Dragging Canoe. Robertson and a party of twenty mounted men were ambushed and cut off from retreat to the fort. Fortunately, the attention of the Indians was distracted by the fleeing horses of the ambushed men and by a pack of dogs that Mrs. Robertson released from the fort, and most of the men were able to return safely. It was late in 1783 when Robertson negotiated a treaty with the Chickasaw and even later—when he led troops against the Chickamaugans in the Nickajack Expedition—before the Cumberland settlers got some relief from the Indian assaults.

Because of relief from Indian depredations, the Cumberland government was able to resume operations in 1783. The judges elected Robertson as their chairman, Andrew Ewing (whose qualifications included being able to write legibly and spell correctly, apparently a part of his Quaker heritage) as clerk, and John Montgomery as sheriff. They took their work seriously. They sought to regulate the Indian trade, build roads leading out of Nashborough, regulate the price of whiskey, and try suits concerned with such matters as breach of contract, theft, slander, and trespass. They also petitioned North Carolina for official recognition, and the legislature of that state responded by forming Davidson County. Named for General William Davidson, the new county included all of the Cumberland country.

Recognition by North Carolina also meant the end of the government under the Cumberland Compact. As was the custom in North Carolina, members of the county court were appointed by the legislature and were not elected by the people. Consequently, North Carolina appointed a new court, five members of which, including Robertson, had been judges under the Cumberland Compact. One of the first acts of the new court when it assembled in October was to provide for the building of a log courthouse eighteen feet square and a log jail fourteen feet square, both "of hewed logs of a foot square." The court also elected Robertson as the first representative from Davidson County to the North Carolina General Assembly. In the following year the name of the county seat was changed to Nashville. Thus by the mid–1780s the Cumberland settlements, having withstood the worst of the Indian assaults (but by no means the end of them) and the insecurity incident to frontier life, and having gained recognition of the North Carolina legislature, apparently had acquired prospects for permanence, although a wilderness of 200 miles lay between them and Watauga and 600 miles separated Nashville and Raleigh, the capital of North Carolina.

Growth and the Spanish Intrigue 🙠 At the end of the Revolutionary War in 1783 Spain held Florida and the Louisiana Territory west of the Mississippi River. She had urged Great Britain in the Treaty of Paris, which ended the war, to limit the boundary of the United States to that area east of the Appalachian Mountains, but the British of course refused. Spain now viewed the aggressive frontiersmen of Tennessee and Kentucky as a serious threat to her colonies in Florida and elsewhere.

Within the two or three years following the Revolution considerable dissatisfaction developed among the American people with the new government under the Articles of Confederation. Among the

many complaints was one voiced by George Washington and certainly shared by the Cumberland people. There was an inadequate
"peace establishment" (standing army), wrote Washington, and
Robertson and others also expressed that sentiment to the North
Carolina legislature. The Cumberland population was growing
rapidly—two new counties, Tennessee and Sumner, were carved
from Davidson in 1788—but isolated as they were, they remained at
the mercy of the Indians.

The Cumberland people had two main complaints. Soon after the
American Revolution, the weakened Chickamaugans joined with
the warlike Creeks under the leadership of Alexander McGillivray,
and together they began a savage war against the widely spread
settlements. Robertson believed that they were being instigated by
the Spaniards in Florida and Louisiana, and he promptly protested to
North Carolina authorities, who largely ignored his grievance. The
second complaint was that although the population on the frontier
increased daily, the economy had become stagnant because the
settlers were unable to transport their crops to market economically.
To float them down the Cumberland, Ohio, and Mississippi rivers to
New Orleans would be simple and highly profitable, but Spain
owned New Orleans and both sides of the Mississippi for a hundred
miles north of New Orleans. Although Spain had previously permitted limited commerce, in 1784 she threatened to close it. When it
became known that John Jay, the United States envoy designated to
develop a commercial treaty beneficial to the seaboard states, was
willing to trade free navigation on the Mississippi for economic
benefits for the New England states, the Tennessee and Kentucky
frontiersmen were irate. Mass meetings of protest were held. Colonel Daniel Smith was named chairman of the group at Nashville,
which had as one of its tasks the development of committees of
correspondence similar to those formed in the pre-Revolutionary
years.

It was under these circumstances that Robertson, the spokesman
for the Cumberland people, opened negotiations with the Louisiana
governor, Don Estevan Miró. In 1788 he persuaded the North
Carolina legislature to honor the Spanish governor by naming a
newly created judicial district in the Cumberland region the "Mero
District." Robertson and Daniel Smith wrote Miró early in 1789 to
appeal for peace with the Indians and improved commercial relations. Both couched their letters in very careful language, but the

courier who carried the Smith letter, a Spanish military officer and St. Louis trader named Don Antonio Fagot, reported to Miró that he had been assured of the Cumberland people's intention to petition the North Carolina General Assembly for permission to separate from the state in the autumn of 1789. Once that was accomplished, they would look with favor upon sending representatives to Miró to discuss allegiance to Spain. Robertson, who was not as circumspect as Daniel Smith, had hinted at this possibility in his communications to Miró, although he (like other Davidson leaders) much preferred a cession of the western lands to the United States. Smith learned the nature of Fagot's report to Miró through a mutual friend, and in September 1789, Smith informed Miró that Fagot was mistaken. "The people here," he wrote, "wish to be in the closest friendship tho' not subject to his Catholic Majesty." By that time the partial opening of the river and the influence of Miró in the lessening of the Indian raids had greatly improved the situation, for which the Cumberland leaders profusely thanked the Spanish governor.

The Cumberland leaders obviously negotiated with the Spaniards mainly to obtain concessions, especially cessation of Indian raids and the right to navigate the Mississippi, and some material benefits were indeed secured. The Cumberland group had no desire, as Smith admitted, to become subjects of the Spanish ruler, except perhaps as a last resort. Another purpose of the intrigue was probably to nudge North Carolina into ratifying the Constitution and ceding the western lands to the United States. If this were accomplished then they could soon attain statehood, they believed, which would bring at least some measure of relief to their problems. While the leaders were dealing with Miró, they also were informing the governor of North Carolina of the separatist feeling and its encouragement by the Spaniards, warning that the population of the western districts might be reduced by Spain's new immigration policy. One of Smith's letters to the governor hinted very strongly that ratification of the Constitution and the cession of the western lands by the Old North State would bring the intrigue to an end. Thus, the ultimate passage of those measures late in 1789 may be considered a fullfillment of the hopes of the western people, as it accomplished the goal that they had had in mind when they first began to confer with Spanish leaders. After the Tennessee country became the Territory of the United States South of the River Ohio and later a new state, its inhabitants no longer saw any need to consider intrigue with Spain.

SUGGESTED READINGS

Books

Thomas P. Abernethy, *From Frontier to Plantation in Tennessee* (1932; rpt. University, Ala., 1967); Pat Alderman and Lee B. Andrews, *The Overmountain Men* (Johnson City, Tenn., 1970); Clarence W. Alvord, *The Mississippi Valley in British Politics,* 2 vols. (Cleveland, 1916–17); John Bakeless, *Master of the Wilderness: Daniel Boone* (New York, 1939); John A. Caruso, *The Appalachian Frontier: America's First Surge Westward* (Indianapolis, 1959); Carl Driver, *John Sevier: Pioneer of the Old Southwest* (Chapel Hill, 1932); Walter T. Durham, *The Great Leap Westward: A History of Sumner County, Tennessee, from its Beginning to 1805* (Gallatin, Tenn., 1969); Archibald Henderson, *Conquest of the Old Southwest* (New York 1920); William S. Lester, *The Transylvania Colony* (Spencer, Ind., 1935); Constance Skinner, *Pioneers of the Old Southwest (New Haven, 1919);* Samuel C. Williams, *Dawn of the Tennessee Valley and Tennessee History* (Johnson City, Tenn., 1937); Williams, *William Tatham: Watauga* (Johnson City, Tenn., 1947).

Articles

Katherine R. Barnes, "James Robertson's Journey to Nashville: Tracing the Route of Fall, 1779," *THQ* 35 (Summer 1976), 145–61; Louis De Vorsey, Jr., "The Virginia-Cherokee Boundary of 1771," *ETHSP* 33 (1961), 17–31; Paul M. Fink, "Jacob Brown of Nolichucky," *THQ* 21 (Sept. 1962), 235–50; Anita S. Goodstein, "Leadership on the Nashville Frontier, 1780–1800," *THQ* 35 (Summer 1976), 175–98; Archibald Henderson, "The Spanish Conspiracy in Tennessee," *THM* 3 (Dec. 1917), 22–43; J. W. L. Matlock, "John Cotten: Reluctant Pioneer," *THQ* 27 (Fall 1968), 277–86; Frederick J. Turner, "Western State Making in the Revolutionary Era," *AHR* 1 (Oct. 1896), 70–87; Harry W. Wellford, "Dr. Thomas Walker, His Uncelebrated Impact on Early Tennessee," *THQ* 34 (Summer 1975), 130–44; Arthur P. Whitaker, "Spanish Intrigue in the Old Southwest: An Episode, 1788–1789," *MVHR* 12 (Sept. 1925), 155–76; Samuel C. Williams, "Shelby's Fort," *ETHSP* 7 (1935), 28–37.

4.

The Revolution in the Tennessee Country

GRENVILLE and Townshend Plans, Boston Tea Parties, writs of assistance, and Cape codfish had no real fascination for the frontiersmen of the Tennessee country. But just as New England patriots fumed over the Stamp Act and other laws enacted by the British Parliament, so it was that Regulators and others in the southern mountain country resented oppressive taxes levied by the royal colony of North Carolina. Soon after the Revolution began, westerners raised troops to fight both Indians and Englishmen in a struggle for freedom to live and hold land on the frontier. The victory at King's Mountain, won in 1780 by Over Mountain people led by John Sevier and Isaac Shelby, became a turning point for victory in the war in the South.

The fall and winter of 1774–1775 was a difficult time in British-colonial relations and led to the Revolutionary War. Colonial defiance of British authority ultimately caused King George III to instruct General Thomas Gage, commander in chief of the royal forces in America, to crush colonial resistance before it became unmanageable. He was too late. In May and June 1774, Virginia and Massachusetts had taken the lead in calling for an assemblage of delegates at Philadelphia in September to discuss common problems. When North Carolina's royal governor, Josiah Martin, sought to forbid the selection of delegates, patriots met anyway; they met in August at New Bern in defiance of the governor's wishes. The First Continental Congress duly assembled, and its delegates denounced tax laws enacted by Parliament; that assembly, they said, had no authority over colonials who had established their own lawmaking bodies. Spring brought armed conflict in Massachusetts when at

Concord's "rude bridge" patriots and British soldiers exchanged shots "heard round the world."

It was not long before people in Virginia and North Carolina seized the reins of government of those states. Patrick Henry, Richard Henry Lee, and Thomas Jefferson took the lead in Virginia and moved more swiftly than did patriots in North Carolina. Even George Washington, by no means as extreme as Henry, Lee, and Jefferson, expressed sentiments that "the crisis is arrived when we must assert our rights, or submit to every imposition that can be heaped upon us. . . . " But under the influence of Henry's charismatic oratory, the Virginia patriots quickly raised troops. Within a few months they had driven Governor Dunmore from the colony and prepared to propose a declaration of independence in the Philadelphia convention. The North Carolinians moved more slowly, so that for a while Governor Martin believed he could hold the colony for the Crown. Martin was a sensible soldier as well as governor, however, and after seeing people rallying to the committees of safety, organizing troops, and procuring military supplies, he quietly left the colony on May 31, 1775. On the same day, a gathering at Charlotte resolved that all parliamentary laws affecting the colonies were "annulled and vacated" and urged the people to establish an army and government "independent of Great Britain."

At the time of the British and American confrontation at Lexington and Concord in April 1775, the North Holston settlers at Sapling Grove were under the wing of the Virginia government and were recognized as citizens of Fincastle County. There were also many settlers west of the Holston near Long Island (present Kingsport) who felt greater affinity for Virginia than for North Carolina. Together they organized a governmental district of their own, called "Pendleton" in honor of the Virginia patriot and statesman, Edmund Pendleton, and formed a revolutionary committee of safety. Early in the next year they petitioned Virginia for a definite extension of governmental jurisdiction over them. With a revolutionary war in prospect, they wished to "contribute their Mite to Support the glorious Cause," they wrote, and to make "a Cheerful Contribution of their Quota of the general exigencies."[1] Settlers south of the Holston on the Watauga and Nolichucky rivers were definitely

---

[1] Samuel C. Williams, *Tennessee During the Revolutionary War* (1944; rpt. Knoxville, 1974), 15–17.

within the boundaries of North Carolina, and they also formed a revolutionary committee of safety. Meeting in the fall of 1775, they organized the "Washington District"—perhaps the first use of the illustrious leader's name for a governmental subdivision—and raised a company of soldiers under the command of James Robertson. A district Committee of Thirteen, with John Carter as chairman, was appointed to direct affairs. Other committee members included James and Charles Robertson, John Sevier, William Bean, Jacob Womack, and Jacob Brown. At least four of them were from the Sycamore Shoals area, four were from Bean's Pittsylvania area, and at least one came from Nolichucky and South of Holston.

Impressed with the spirit of independence developing in both North Carolina and Virginia, the Wataugans petitioned both states for annexation. No reply was immediately forthcoming from Virginia, but the committee of safety of North Carolina responded by recommending that the people hold a "free and impartial election" and choose delegates scheduled to meet in Halifax in November 1776 to frame a constitution for the "independent state of North Carolina." Leaders of the new district promptly complied and chose five delegates, including John Sevier; four of them attended and became signers of North Carolina's first constitution.

The framers of the new fundamental law asserted the state's title to the Tennessee country but wrote nothing in the body of the document about a government for the area. Still, perhaps as an afterthought, they did append an "ordinance" to the constitution naming twenty-one justices of the peace for the new "District of Washington." A little later, when voters in statewide elections chose members of the first general assembly of the new state, an election was also held in the new district. Voters chose John Carter as senator and John Sevier and Jacob Womack as members of the lower house (called the house of commons). In 1777 the North Carolina legislature changed the district to "Washington County," thus eliminating confusion about the definition of a "district." Included within the new county was practically all of present Tennessee. The exceptions were the North Holston settlement and the Pendleton District sections of Washington County, Virginia. Later, in 1779, this territory was restored to North Carolina when the North Carolina–Virginia boundary was surveyed, and the area became Sullivan County, named for General John Sullivan, a Revolutionary leader from New Hampshire.

Why were the Wataugans aroused—they who drank no tea, used little or no refined sugar, and felt none of the effects of the Intolerable Acts? For one thing, they had experienced enough Indian warfare (their role in Lord Dunmore's War had just concluded) to keep them, as one frontiersman said, in a "fighting mood." It was easy to imagine that someone—probably an unscrupulous British official—was inciting the Indians to assault the frontier settlers. Too, the Regulator spirit had been brought across the mountains, and a latent hatred of taxation (either with or without representation) was in the minds of most people. None had forgotten the Proclamation Line of 1763 which, despite a lease and purchase of the land they occupied, still made the Wataugans mere squatters on the land. British officials continued to consider the settlers' transaction illegal, and the British Indian agents John Stuart and Alexander Cameron naturally tried to enforce British policy. Finally, frontier pride, always worn on one's sleeve, was easily hurt as the mountaineers contemplated both real and imagined privileges reserved for island Englishmen and specifically denied colonials. At any rate, the committee of safety formed in the Washington District resolved "to adhere strictly to the rules and orders of the Continental Congress" and to volunteer to bear their "full proportion of the Continental expense." In preparation for war they organized a unit under Colonel John Carter and a company "of fine riflemen" under Colonel James Robertson to "act in the common cause on the sea shore." Although a group under Lieutenant Felix Walker did help defend Charleston against a British assault in June 1776, the majority of the fighting men were retained at home to defend the settlements against the Cherokees.

The Cherokee War, 1776 ॐ Unable fully to comprehend many of the ways of the white man and never fully understanding his inclination to make war, the Cherokee were astounded to learn that white brothers of the same language now were engaged in serious disagreement. Still, the preparations for war and the formation of provisional governments made deep impressions upon them, and despite their affection and animosity for both groups, the Cherokee leaders eventually decided to support the Crown.

Although Indian Agent John Stuart at first advised chieftains to remain neutral in the conflict, the Cherokee soon indicated where their sympathies lay, especially after Stuart (whom they believed to be their close friend) was forced to flee from Charleston to Savannah and then to British Florida. Too, they blamed the frontiersmen when Indian trade with the British at Charleston was interrupted and, with good reason, when the flow of British arms and ammunition was curtailed. Leaders refused to talk with American commissioners from the Continental Congress in a conference arranged for Fort Charlotte near Salisbury in the winter of 1776, but instead trudged to St. Augustine to assure Stuart of their loyalty to the Crown. By the time of their arrival in St. Augustine, Stuart had received instructions from General Thomas Gage to persuade the Indians to "take up arms against his Majesty's Enemies." Stuart was therefore forced to change his policy advice from neutrality to aggression, and he advised the Cherokee to become involved in joint operations with Loyalists or British troops. To put the recommendation into effect, Stuart dispatched his brother, Henry Stuart, as a special agent to the Indians with 30 horseloads of ammunition.

Henry Stuart determined to carry out his assignment with haste. At Mobile he met Dragging Canoe, who voiced his hatred of the encroaching whites and revealed the plans of the younger Cherokee to recover land even if they had to resort to an indiscriminate slaughter of the settlers. By the time Stuart reached the Overhill towns, he knew that the Indians were serious. In a meeting of some 700 Cherokees at Chota, Stuart told his listeners of the intention of the British government to support their territorial claims and explained that they could be accomplished only if the Cherokee helped the Crown in the Revolution. As the aroused Indians joined in a cry for immediate war on the western people, Stuart asked for time so that the whites could remove peacefully and voluntarily.

Then followed an interesting exchange of correspondence that bought sufficient time for the Wataugans to prepare better to defend themselves. On May 17, Stuart and Alexander Cameron dispatched a letter to the people at Watauga and Nolichucky, ordering them to vacate their homes in twenty days. The patience of the Indians had long been sorely tried, the message continued; the agents had "little hope of being able to restrain them" any more. But any Wataugans willing to become "good and peaceable subjects" abiding by the Proclamation of 1763 would be given land in British West Florida. The message caused some degree of consternation among the settlers, and a few removed immediately, but the majority determined to remain. They then developed a ruse to gain more time in

Dragging Canoe, a son of Attakullakulla (the "Little Carpenter"), shown here in a drawing by Bernie Andrews.

which to prepare for their defense and seek aid. In a reply drafted by Chairman John Carter to Stuart and Cameron, the Wataugans expressed surprise that the Indians should not respect the legality of the land purchase and amazement that their "brothers" (the Cherokee) should wish to destroy the settlers' homes and farms. Still, they would move; "Subjects must Obey Their Sovereign," they wrote, "which we as subjects sincerely determine to do." The Indians thereupon granted them twenty additional days in which to move and the ruse thus succeeded.

Meanwhile, the Wataugans attempted to secure aid from Virginia, but to their disappointment they were rebuffed by authorities at both Fincastle and Williamsburg. Fincastle wanted no part of an Indian war; leaders there advised the Wataugans to evacuate Indian property and retreat to safety behind the Donelson Line of 1771. The Williamsburg people had more important matters to attend to.

At this point the Wataugans, realizing that they must fight within the bounds of their own resources or surrender, prepared to defend their homes. First they increased their defenses by building Fort Watauga (later called Fort Caswell) near Sycamore Shoals and a second fort on the Nolichucky frontier on Big Limestone Creek. Second, they increased their efforts to procure help from anyone in Virginia or North Carolina who was of revolutionary persuasion. They circulated a letter, purportedly signed by Henry Stuart but later proved to have been forged by a Wataugan, that told of a combined British-Indian plan to destroy the west. The Crown, the message indicated, with Creek, Chickasaw, and Cherokee Indians, had raised a large army that would march from West Florida to the Virginia and North Carolina frontier and would destroy the settlements on the western frontier in its wake. When the letter reached Fincastle, the committee of safety of that county reversed its position. Not only were the Revolutionary Wataugans worthy of recognition, leaders concluded, but they needed help. Accordingly, Fincastle supplied the Wataugans with ammunition and even hinted that payment for it might not be required. A Fincastle company of troops commanded by Captain John Shelby joined a company under James Robertson and visited some seventy known Loyalists in the vicinity, forcing them to take an oath of allegiance to the Revolutionary cause. Finally, the Fincastle leaders warned the Cherokee against "evil and designing men" who would involve them in a war with their white brothers that could ultimately only result in the "destruction and perhaps the utter extirpation of the Cherokee nation."

The Cherokee, who had waited the agreed-upon forty days to find the Wataugans not only still in the area but feverishly building forts and seeking aid, then realized that they had been duped. In mid-June 1776, fourteen chiefs from Northern tribes arrived in the Overhill towns to offer an alliance with the Cherokee. Dragging Canoe and the other young chiefs responded enthusiastically as they contemplated an alliance of the Delaware, Mingo, Mohawk, and Shawnee that might drive the white men from the land. With the whites now fighting each other, the time was opportune to strike.

Accordingly, in mid-July, 700 warriors set out to destroy not only the settlements at Watauga and Nolichucky but those at Long Island and Carter's Valley as well. In a three-pronged assault, Dragging Canoe struck Long Island, Old Abram invaded Watauga and Nolichucky, and the Raven assaulted Carter's Valley. Although whites had been alerted to the impending attacks, for two or three weeks they sustained heavy losses. Lieutenant John Sevier had to abandon Fort Lee, and the people of that settlement were forced to flee into the mountains or to Watauga. The Raven scoured Carter's Valley and moved northward to Virginia, burning cabins, destroying growing crops, and driving away horses and cattle before him. On July 20, the red men were defeated near Eaton's Station at the Battle of Island Flats and Dragging Canoe was wounded, but on the following day Old Abram moved against Fort Watauga. There he found some 200 people crowded into the small one-acre enclosure with troops commanded by Captain James Robertson and Lieutenant Sevier. Unable to take the fort by direct assault, Old Abram lingered in the area for several weeks to harass the people and to forage in the countryside. During this time one effort of the Indians to set fire to the fort was foiled when James Robertson's sister, Anne, poured scalding water down from the palisades upon the torchbearers. It was also during this time, according to tradition, that Sevier laid the groundwork for a second marriage. Several young women were outside the fort milking cows when a dozen or more Indians ambushed them. All reached the gate except a young woman named Catherine Sherrill, who was rescued dramatically by John Sevier. With one hand the Old Indian fighter pulled her over the palisades, and with the other he fired into an Indian who pursued her closely. Four years later, after the death of his first wife, Sarah Hawkins,

Sevier married Catherine Sherrill. She assumed the care of his ten children and in due time bore him eight more.

Substantial aid arrived soon after the Tennessee country folk had withstood the July assault. Virginia sent troops under Colonel William Christian, and North Carolina forces were led by Joseph Williams (whose son, John, later represented Tennessee in the United States Senate); their 1,800 men met at Fort Patrick Henry in September 1776 and made plans to destroy the Cherokee towns. Georgia sent 200 men under Major Samuel Jack, and South Carolina marched nearly 1,200 men in under Colonel Andrew Williamson. In September, General Griffith Rutherford of North Carolina led 2,400 men down the valley of the French Broad River and cooperated with Williamson in the destruction of the Middle and Valley towns.

The combined assaults were too much for the Cherokee, who soon sued for peace. Although Dragging Canoe refused to join in this effort and lurked in the Chattanooga vicinity with an unruly Cherokee element that became the core of the "Chickamauga" Indians, the other chiefs met with representatives of Virginia and North Carolina at Long Island in June and July 1777.The Virginia commissioners were headed by Colonel Christian, and those of North Carolina by Waightstill Avery. To Virginia the Cherokee ceded the land north of a line beginning at the lower corner of the Donelson line, following the river to the mouth of Cloud's Creek (a few miles from Rogersville), and then running in a straight line to a point between three and five miles west of the Cumberland Gap. Included was a considerable stretch of country south of the 36° 30' parallel that technically belonged to North Carolina but over which Virginia for some years had exercised jurisdiction. To North Carolina the Indians ceded the country north and east of a line running from the mouth of Cloud's Creek northeast to the highest point on a mountain called Chimney Top, thence south to the Nolichucky River at the mouth of Camp Creek (a few miles southeast of the site of Greeneville), and from there southwest to the mountains dividing the hunting grounds of the Overhill and Middle Cherokee.

The defeat of the Indians in the Cherokee War and the subsequent negotiation of a peace treaty with them had considerable significance in the outcome of the Revolutionary War. The continued occupation of the East Tennessee country kept the road open to Kentucky, without which the settlements in that area could not have been maintained. And if those settlements had not been held, there would probably have been no conquest of the Illinois country by George Rogers Clark and the frontier would not have been pushed westward to the Cumberland while the war was in progress. It is also unlikely that there would have been a battle at King's Mountain.

King's Mountain Campaign ᖷ While colonial troops fighting Indians on the frontier were meeting with success at home, American forces contesting Philadelphia and other points in the East with the British were not so fortunate. Still, they did win a significant victory in October 1777 at Saratoga, New York, and this was sufficient to turn the British attention away from the area for a while. Instead of continuing in the northeast, the British leader, Major General Lord Cornwallis, turned to Georgia, the soft underbelly of the colonies, where he expected to find considerable Loyalist support and little or no opposition from the revolutionaries. Cornwallis, who had arrived in America with 4,500 troops in the second year of the war, was not to be disappointed. He landed at Savannah on December 29, 1778 and immediately took that town without difficulty. A few months later he seized Charleston and soon was free to run at large in Georgia and South Carolina, although he did meet troublesome resistance from guerrilla bands skillfully and ably led by Francis Marion and Thomas Sumter. Next, he turned his attention to the western settlements, and there, at King's Mountain, the British troops met their match.

Before they were able to participate effectively in campaigns east of the mountains, however, westerners first had to turn their attention to the troublesome Indians led by Dragging Canoe, who continued to harass the settlers. The Cherokee remnant was joined by Creek warriors and relocated on Chickamauga Creek just east of Lookout Mountain. There 1,000 "Chickamaugans" threatened the revolutionaries until Colonel Evan Shelby and Major Charles Robertson laid waste their towns and drove their troops southward.

Meanwhile, the western country received a new tide of immigrants from the east. The fleeing Tory refugees proved especially embarrassing, and the newly organized court of Washington County had to devote much of its time to considering cases of persons charged with being disloyal or with harboring Loyalists. Those convicted were imprisoned or, in some cases, subjected to exile and confiscation of property.

Having at least temporarily pacified the Indians, western troops now were able to help more effectively in the fight against British armies. Lord Cornwallis felt secure after his victory at Charleston; he established seaboard bases at Savannah, Beaufort, Charleston, and Georgetown, and in the interior he extended his line along the Savannah River, westward to Ninety-six, and thence northward to Camden and Rocky Mount. The area was too large to protect, and he assigned Major Patrick Ferguson to protect his left flank, which was exposed to the west. In the summer and early fall Ferguson scoured the Piedmont, destroyed the cabins of American sympathizers in his path, and won Tories to his cause. In an effort to curtail some of this destruction, Colonel Charles McDowell, Colonel Isaac Shelby, and Major Charles Robertson led troops against Ferguson and his Tory detachment. They picked at Cornwallis's flank by taking a small fort at Thicketty Creek and then defeated a detail of men at Musgrove's Mill but were forced to retreat before a superior British force at Cedar Springs. Finally, in August, Camden, South Carolina fell to Cornwallis's army, and this loss forced western troops to retreat to the back-country hills.

Greatly encouraged, Ferguson spread the word that the war was over for the colonials, and thus had little trouble in gaining recruits among Loyalists. But when Shelby and the backwoodsmen refused to obey his blanket order to lay down their arms and return allegiance to the Crown, Ferguson threatened to "march his own men over the mountains, hang their leaders, and lay their country waste with fire and sword."[2] Shelby and Sevier, their troops eager and ready to fight, now decided to regroup their Sullivan and Washington forces, gather in Colonel McDowell and Colonel William Campbell (of southwestern Virginia), and meet Ferguson before his command had been expanded by additional Tories.

The frontier troops assembled at Sycamore Shoals on September 25, 1780, armed with rifles and dressed in hunting attire. After receiving the blessings of Samuel Doak, a frontier Presbyterian preacher, they marched southwest to meet Ferguson. They soon found him at King's Mountain, a narrow ridge located in the north-

[2] Lyman Draper, *King's Mountain and Its Heroes* (1881; rpt. Baltimore, 1971), 562.

western corner of South Carolina due north from Ninety-Six. There
Ferguson and his forces of perhaps 1,000 men had ensconced themselves and boasted that even "the Almighty" could not drive them
away.

American troops arrived in the vicinity in early October and on the
seventh day of that month assaulted the mountain position; they
fastened themselves around the enemy and slowly ascended the
ridge. Ferguson had ordered his men to use the bayonet where
possible, but the American troops were so well camouflaged behind
trees, logs, and rocks that they were able to decimate the enemy
before he was close enough to use the dreaded weapon effectively.
The westerners were forced to fall back three times, but each time
they rallied from all sides of the mountain. After about sixty minutes
of fighting, the British surrendered. Ferguson lay dead, and Abraham de Peyster, who assumed command, saw no chance for retreat.
Few if any of his men escaped—as one Loyalist survivor remarked,
"the cursed rebels . . . killed and took us every soul." Reports of the
casualties are conflicting, but according to Shelby's personal account,
28 Patriots were killed and 62 wounded, while 157 British were
killed, 153 wounded, and 706 captured.

The victory was of great significance, and the battle has justifiably
been called the turning point of the Revolutionary War in the South.
It greatly encouraged the Southern Patriots and correspondingly
discouraged the Loyalists. It caused Cornwallis to curtail his operations in North Carolina until he could receive reinforcements. Ex-
planations of the remarkable success of the frontier troops have been
many. Some people have attributed it to the "hunting rifle," and
others to Indian tactics of camouflage. Still others have pointed to the
able leadership on the part of the westerners and to overconfidence
and other flaws in the leadership of Ferguson. At any rate, these "tall,
rawboned, sinewy" men from the west had won the respect of the
infant nation, and Sevier was on the threshold of a successful political
career.

Western troops continued to fight both the British and the Indians
until the war ended. More than one hundred men joined General
Nathaniel Greene, who had recently replaced Horatio Gates in the
South, in checking Cornwallis at Guilford Courthouse in March
1781. Another group of 600 under Sevier and Shelby aided Francis
Marion in South Carolina. And in late 1781, more than one hundred

Wataugans under Elijah Clark of Georgia fought to repel an attack on Augusta.

The war did not end officially until the Treaty of Paris was signed in 1783, but it had ended for all practical purposes in late 1781 when fighting ceased. Although independence meant that conflict with the British was over, it did not mean that violence on the frontier had ended. Unfriendly Indians continued to attack, and problems of government were not easily solved.

SUGGESTED READINGS

Books
Thomas P. Abernethy, *From Frontier to Plantation in Tennessee: A Study in Frontier Democracy* (1932; rpt. University, Ala., 1967); John A. Caruso, *The Appalachian Frontier* (New York, 1959); Carl Driver, *John Sevier: Pioneer of the Old Southwest* (Chapel Hill, 1932); William H. Masterson, *William Blount* (Baton Rouge, 1954); Helen T. Miller, *The Sound of Chariots: A Novel of John Sevier and the State of Franklin* (Indianapolis, 1947); Samuel C. Williams, *History of the Lost State of Franklin* (Johnson City, Tenn. 1924).

Articles
G. H. Alden, "The State of Franklin," *AHR* 8 (Jan. 1903), 271–89; John Allison, "The Mero District," *AHM* 1 (April 1896), 115–27, reprinted in White, *Tennessee: Old and New,* Vol. 1, 145–54; Walter F. Cannon, "Four Interpretations of the History of the State of Franklin," *ETHSP* 22 (1950), 3–18; Paul M. Fink, "Some Phases of the History of the State of Franklin," *THQ* 16 (Sept. 1957), 195–213; Thomas B. Jones, "The Public Lands of Tennessee," *THQ* 27 (Spring 1968), 13–36; Eric R. Lacy, "The Persistent State of Franklin," *THQ* 23 (Dec. 1964), 321–32; J. T. McGill, "Franklin and Frankland: Names and Boundaries," *THM* 8 (Jan. 1925), 248–57; Arthur P. Whitaker, "The Muscle Shoals Speculation, 1783–1789," *MVHR* 13 (Dec. 1926), 365–86.

5.

T HE national government, in dire need of funds after the Revolutionary War, urged states claiming western lands to cede them to the United States. The territory would be surveyed and sold, and the funds received would be used toward necessary operating expenses. Most of the claims were not well founded anyway, and the states, including North Carolina, promptly complied with the request. North Carolina, however, after ceding her claims (present-day Tennessee) in April 1784, repealed the act of cession a few months later. In the meantime, the people of Washington, Greene, and Sullivan counties formed a separate state that they named Franklin, in honor of Benjamin Franklin. It was a short-lived and unsuccessful venture, but it has been the subject of both factual and fictional writings and has sometimes been called the "lost state" of Franklin.

Beginnings ੴ Even before the Revolutionary War ended, Congress anticipated victory and independence, by declaring that new states would ultimately be formed from western territory ceded to the national government by the already existing states. The understanding was that such newly formed states would be admitted into the Union without undue delay and on terms of equality with the original states.

Many transmontane people received this information with considerable interest, including Arthur Campbell of southwestern Virginia, who was already giving thought to establishing a new state consisting of the counties of southwestern North Carolina and Virginia. Like many others in the west, Campbell visualized the unfolding of great economic opportunities for land development there and dreamed of the power and prestige that the government of new states would bring. He also shared the belief prevalent among westerners that people of the older settled regions east of the mountains viewed their ambitions with distrust and were oblivious to their needs and demands. Thus he and many others became leaders in the development of a strong competitive spirit of independence among the people of the west. As early as 1782 Campbell had proposed a convention of delegates from southwest Virginia and North Carolina to meet in Abingdon to discuss statehood for that area.

Two years later, in 1784, Thomas Jefferson presented to Congress an elaborate plan for western statehood. Displaying a giant map, the Virginian proposed the formation of eighteen or more states in the west, including one constituted from southwestern Virginia and North Carolina. News of his plan, along with that of the act of cession and the ambitions of Arthur Campbell, aroused latent interests of frontiersmen who already viewed with alarm the haste with which North Carolina speculators were buying western land.

Along with Virginia and other states, the legislature of North Carolina (on June 2, 1784) ceded her western lands to the central government. Congress was given one year to accept. Some of those favoring the passage of the act noted that North Carolina would be relieved of the need to defend the westerners from Indian assaults, and others referred to the transmontane folk as "fugitives from justice" and "offscourings of the earth"—words that among westerners aroused bitterness and accentuated their desire for separation. Five months later, however, a new legislature elected in the summer repealed the act of June 2 and thus denied Congress the opportunity of accepting the cession.

Several months before the repeal of the act, western leaders from the Holston-Watauga area enthusiastically met in Jonesboro on August 24, 1784 to organize a new state. They chose John Sevier as chairman of their convention, asserted their right "to petition Congress to accept the cession made by North Carolina," and expressed a willingness to include "any contiguous part of Virginia" in their "separate government" to be organized "agreeable to a resolve of Congress." After determining to meet again within a few weeks, they adjourned.

Following a second brief meeting in November, delegates assembled on December 14 in Jonesboro and resolved to form "a separate and distinct State, independent of the State of North Carolina." It was no more than " a decent respect to the opinions of mankind," they wrote, which made "it proper that we should manifest to the world the reason which induced as to a declaration." The reasons were carefully outlined: (1) North Carolina's constitution and cession act implied consent to separation, (2) North Carolina had provoked Indians to hostile acts, (3) congressional resolutions regarding new states gave them "ample encouragement," (4) union with North Carolina appeared incompatible with the region's interests because the two were separated "by high and almost impassable mountains," and "5th and lastly," the lives, liberty, and property of the western people would be better protected by separation.

Before Congress could act on the matter, the newly elected legislature in North Carolina repealed the act of cession on November 20. This action, legislators said, was taken because the cession act had failed to give North Carolina credit for the expenses of an Indian expedition carried out on behalf of the central government, but westerners knew that it also reflected the influence of land speculators who stood to profit as long as the land remained under state control. But at the same time, North Carolina leaders sought to placate westerners by organizing the Tennessee country into a new district named Washington. David Campbell was appointed superior court judge; this meant that litigants—who had complained about the inconvenience of crossing the mountains to obtain formal justice—could now try their cases at home. Most significantly, a militia brigade was authorized for the district, and John Sevier was appointed brigadier general. Commissioners were appointed to negotiate and settle disputes with the Cherokee Indians.

Sevier, a western leader commanding great respect after his victories at King's Mountain and elsewhere, vacillated in his eagerness for statehood and thus delayed plans for formal organization. He at first expressed a belief that the concessions granted by North Carolina would satisfy the western people. His own appointment as brigadier general he had considered "an honour," and he believed that North Carolina's attempt to control the Indian raids should please everyone. Too, he feared that separation from North Carolina would interfere with the land speculation in which he, William Blount, Richard Caswell, and others were engaged at Muscle Shoals. But William Cocke, also a Revolutionary hero and a leader influential in the separate statehood movement, was able to persuade Sevier that his best interests and the interests of the western people lay in separation. As Sevier later explained, he was "dragged into the Franklin measures by a large number of the people. . . ." Indeed, Carl Driver, Sevier's biographer, has observed that Sevier "opposed the movement until he saw that it would proceed without him and then [he] grasped the reins of power."[1]

With Sevier now safely within the fold, the first legislature of the new state met at Jonesboro in March 1785 and chose officials in accordance with a constitution drafted earlier at Jonesboro. The Hero of King's Mountain was chosen as governor. Landon Carter, a son of John Carter, a Revolutionary officer who had served under Sevier, and was a prime mover in the statehood venture, was named secretary of state. Stockley Donelson, a noted surveyor and one of the most successful of land speculators, became surveyor general. William Cocke was named brigadier general, as was David Kennedy, another soldier who had fought under Sevier at King's Mountain.

Legislators enacted a variety of measures before adjourning. They levied taxes, but, because of the scarcity of money, gave tax collectors authority to accept tax payments of flax, linen, woolen and cotton linsey, woolen cloth, bacon, tallow, beeswax, sugar, rye whiskey, peach and apply brandy, "good country made sugar," tobacco, and skins from beaver, deer, fox, otter, and raccoon. They also formed a judicial system, reincorporated Doak's academy, and created four new counties, naming them for Sevier and other frontier leaders.

In the meantime, news of the venture had reached North Carolina authorities, and Governor Alexander Martin promptly addressed to Sevier a letter of inquiry. "With some concern," he wrote, "I have heard that the counties of Washington, Sullivan, and Greene, have lately declared themselves independent of the State of North Carolina and have chosen you as governor." Expressing surprise at the development after North Carolina had attempted to redress "every grievance" of the frontiersmen, he commanded Sevier to furnish him with a full "account of the late proceedings." Sevier transmitted the message to the legislature, and on March 27 (three weeks after receiving Martin's letter) that body addressed a formal reply to the North Carolina governor. The document was a description of the circumstances under which Franklin had been formed and

---

[1] Driver, *Sevier*, 87.

a justification of its existence. While legislators thanked North Carolina for its expression of "every sentiment of regard," they could not dismiss lightly the neglect and lack of protection from the Indian raids. They rhetorically questioned whether they had "deserted North Carolina or [whether] North Carolina, [had] deserted" them. Expressing the "sanguine hopes" that North Carolina authorities would help instead of hinder their reception into the Federal Union, the legislators concluded by expressing a determination "never to desert that independence which we are bound by every sacred tie to honor and religion to support."

Governor Martin, however, responded on April 25 with a "manifesto" commanding an end to Franklin and a return of the people to allegiance to North Carolina. He urged the people not to "tarnish the laurels you have so gloriously won at King's Mountain" or to be "led away with the pageantry of a mock government" or to "be hurried on by blind ambition to pursue your present unjustifiable measures." Persistence in defending the state of Franklin would "open afresh the wounds of this late bleeding country and plunge it again into all the miseries of a civil war." Sevier stood firm, however, and responded with a proclamation enjoining the people to be loyal to the new state; to do otherwise, he wrote, would "destroy that peace and tranquility that so greatly abounds among the peaceful citizens of the new happy country." Further action in the dispute was postponed until the North Carolina legislature convened in the autumn of 1785, by which time Richard Caswell, a friend of Sevier, had replaced Martin as governor. Franklin officials in the meantime carried their appeal for statehood to the Congress of the United States. William Cocke was dispatched to New York (where Congress was then meeting) with a memorial officially adopted by the Franklin legislature and signed by Governor Sevier.

Relations with Congress and North Carolina ⮞ At first it appeared that Congress would act favorably upon the westerners' appeal for statehood. The congressional committee to which the memorial was submitted took the position that Congress could accept North Carolina's cession at any time within the time limit of one year included in the original cession law. It therefore recommended that Congress accept the western territory, an action that would have paved the way for Franklin's statehood. Seven states voted in favor of the recommendation and only two against it, but the measure was defeated because passage under the Articles of Confederation required favorable votes from nine states. Those who opposed or failed to vote apparently wished to support North Carolina's right to rescind her act of cession. Congress by a majority vote then asked that the North Carolina legislature rescind its repeal law, but North Carolina lawmakers ignored the request. Franklin's hopes of federal approval at this point were blasted.

Later, Cocke sought advice from Benjamin Franklin, in whose honor the state had been named. Franklin, however, urged Cocke to submit the dispute to Congress. Still later, in 1787, members of the Constitutional Convention included in the new Constitution a clause providing that no state could be divided without its consent, and Franklin advised Sevier that the proper procedure was to apply to North Carolina for a satisfactory compromise.

Franklin leaders had already sought to settle matters amicably with North Carolina. Thomas Stuart in April 1785 had been appointed head of a commission to seek North Carolina's consent to peaceful separation. Unfortunately, however, the North Carolina assembly was controlled by a conservative group opposed to the statehood movement. Not only did they ignore the Stuart Commission's appeal, but they offered pardons to those Franklinites willing to renew their allegiance to the mother state.

Although the Franklin movement encountered some local opposition from the beginning, most of the people apparently supported it for at least two years. In August 1786, however, a strong anti-Franklin group emerged in Washington County and attempted to elect delegates to the North Carolina legislature. John Tipton, a Revolutionary War veteran and able leader who had opposed the Franklin efforts from the beginning, was seated in the North Carolina legislature as a senator from Washington County. He had assured Governor Martin of his loyalty at the time of the governor's manifesto, and now he loudly proclaimed his adherence to the mother state. Under his leadership, the North Carolina legislature attempted to pull the grass-roots support from under Sevier by again offering pardons to residents of Franklin who returned to North Carolina allegiance, remitting taxes for the past two years, creating a new county of Hawkins, and appointing Evan Shelby to replace Sevier as brigadier general of Washington District. These acts caused many people to conclude that separation could be attained only after submission, and they therefore returned their allegiance to North Carolina.

A substantial group of people (especially those living south of the French Broad) remained loyal to Sevier, however, and they became infuriated by the actions of North Carolina and particularly those of Tipton. Outright hostilities between the Franklin militia and forces supporting Tipton were prevented only for a short time through efforts of Evan Shelby and Sevier. Franklin leaders faced not only internal dissension but also hostilities from the Cherokees in the area south of the French Broad, which North Carolina recognized as Indian country.

Indian Relations ࢟➤ The first assembly of Franklin authorized the governor to negotiate with the Cherokee Indians, and in June 1785 several prominent chiefs signed the Treaty of Dumplin Creek, which permitted settlement south of the French Broad River as far as the ridge dividing the Little River from the Little Tennessee. Although this region was within the Cherokee reservation set aside by North Carolina in 1783, Franklinites moved in so rapidly that by 1786 Blount County had been created.

This southwestern migration was not confined to the region opened by the Dumplin Creek Treaty. Lands outside the reservation, north of the French Broad River and also west of the Tennessee and Holston, were occupied. James White, speaker of the Franklin senate, Francis Ramsey, and others settled in 1785 in the forks of the French Broad and Holston rivers, and the next year White established a settlement called White's Fort at the site of Knoxville, west of the Holston (now Tennessee) River. But after that, the Indians stiffened their resistance and refused to permit other attempts at settlement, particularly in the Muscle Shoals region.

Warfare soon developed. When whites continued to occupy territory identified as Indian land by the Treaty of Hopewell (November 1785), the Cherokee went on the warpath. Franklin leaders retaliated, defeated the red men, and forced them in August 1786 to sign the Treaty of Coyatee, which permitted white settlement as far south as the Little Tennessee River. As soon as possible, the Indians repudiated the treaty and massacred whites along the river; whites in turn destroyed towns along the Hiwassee River and murdered the Cherokee leader Old Tassel and other chiefs who came in to negotiate under a flag of truce. Sevier and others soon talked of joining with Georgia in an effort to drive the Creeks from the Muscle Shoals area, but Georgia leaders abandoned war plans after initially offering encouragement to the Franklinites.

Intrigue with Spain Even before warfare with the Indians became acute, Franklin leaders consulted with the neighboring Spanish officials. Spain at the time occupied territory along the Gulf of Mexico and west of the Mississippi River. To protect her claims against western aggression, Spain closed the Mississippi to navigation so as to discourage settlements dependent upon the river as an outlet to market. In addition, Spain made friends with neighboring Indians and encouraged secession movements in the American West. The Franklinites were among those western people who by 1786 were becoming disillusioned with the national government. They were especially unhappy with the conciliatory policy of Congress regarding the Southern Indians, whom they wanted removed or at least pacified, and with Secretary of Foreign Affairs John Jay's proposal in 1786 that the United States forego for twenty-five to thirty years the right to navigate the Mississippi River in exchange for commercial concessions that would please merchants in the northeast. At this point serious negotiations with Spain began—so serious, in fact, that Sevier was quoted to Spanish officials as stating that citizens of Franklin "wished to place themselves under the protection of the King [of Spain.]"[2]

Other western leaders, distressed over the prospects of losing their economic lifeline, the Mississippi River, also talked of a union with Spain and found Spanish leaders receptive. Congressman James White of North Carolina,[3] who had extensive land holdings on the Cumberland, told Don Diego de Gardoqui, the Spanish diplomatic representative, that western leaders would surely separate from the United States and ally themselves with either England or Spain. If Spain opened the Mississippi immediately to western navigation, her

[2] Arthur P. Whitaker, "The Muscle Shoals Speculation," *MVHR* 13 (1926), 379; D. C. Corbitt and Roberta Corbitt (trs. and eds.), "Papers from the Spanish Archives Relating to Tennessee and the Old Southwest, 1783–1800," *ETHSP* 18 (1946), 144.

[3] Not the same James White who was speaker of the Franklin senate and founder of White's Fort.

action would win western allegiance forever, White said. White became friends with the Spanish representative and in 1788 carried a message from him to Sevier, denying that Spain had ever incited Indian assaults on western people and expressing the belief that Spain was "much disposed" to give the residents of Franklin "all the protection" from the Indians they needed. It was Sevier, however, who, greatly encouraged as he expressed opinions of Franklinites in general, now entered directly into negotiations with the Spanish. In September 1788 he addressed several letters to Gardoqui. The "principal men" of Franklin, he wrote, were "as well disposed and willing" as he was, and were "very ardent" regarding the "future probability of an alliance and a concession of commerce." The people of Franklin, he said, "have come to realize truly upon what part of the world and upon which nation depend their future happiness and security." The new state's needs were several, Sevier said, including navigation of the Mississippi, Spanish protection while Franklin speculators expanded Franklin borders down the Tennessee River past Muscle Shoals to the headwaters of the Alabama and the Yazoo rivers, and a loan of a few thousand pounds that would be repaid by the export of produce to the Spanish ports. In return, Franklin would pledge allegiance to Spain, providing that the state could retain control of its domestic affairs. Other western settlers, Sevier believed, would follow Franklin's example.

True to Sevier's predication, leaders on the Cumberland soon began negotiations with Spain. By 1788, these settlers had sustained so many Indian assaults that they were willing to turn almost anywhere for protection. Negotiations continued for about a year, during which it was believed that the Cumberland people would declare their independence from the United States and then, in concert with the people of Franklin, join with Spain.

Spanish officials were interested in the western people but were also suspicious of them. One wrote of his firm belief that the westerners were interested in the establishment of their own "independence rather than a *rapprochement* with Spain."[4] Finally, Governor Miró addressed a "Memorandum of Concessions of Westerners" dated April 20, 1789, in which he expressed the Spanish position. Because Spain and the United States were at peace, Miró wrote, he could not encourage annexation at that time. But if the westerners

[4] Whitaker, "Muscle Shoals Speculation," 384.

obtained their independence on their own, Spain would grant them favors "compatible with the interests of the Crown." As an immediate alternative, Miró encouraged the westerners to immigrate into Spanish Louisiana, where they would be given land and religious freedom, although they would be required to take an oath of allegiance to Spain. Those who migrated and became Spanish citizens would of course be permitted to navigate the Mississippi River without the payment of any duties.

Despite the apparent seriousness of their negotiations, western leaders considered becoming subjects of Spain only as a last resort. They also apparently hoped that their negotiations with Spain would encourage the national government to repudiate Jay's position with regard to navigation of the Mississippi River and would bring some relief from Indian raids. At the same time they hoped that their actions would encourage North Carolina to ratify the Constitution and cede her western lands to the national government. In April 1789, George Washington became president of the United States under the new Constitution, and late in that year North Carolina ratified the Constitution and again ceded Tennessee to the United States. To the western people, these measures represented a fulfillment of desires expressed in the Spanish intrigue, and the settlers abandoned further negotiations with Spain.

Franklin Comes to an End ঌ Franklin was slowly coming to an end, probably after 1786, and Franklin leaders knew it. This realization partly explains their negotiations with Spain. In a desperate effort to bring about reconciliation with North Carolina, Franklin voters elected General Evan Shelby as governor in August 1787, although few if any had lost confidence in Sevier. Shelby declined, however, and also resigned his position as brigadier general of Washington District. He wrote a strong recommendation to North Carolina officials that Sevier be chosen in his place, but the officials, apparently disillusioned with Sevier, appointed Joseph Martin instead.

Sevier retained leadership of the Franklin people, and soon his disagreements with John Tipton flared into a bitter feud and civil war. Tipton was colonel of the militia in his county and used his power and influence to obstruct the Franklin movement. He had also urged his partisans to carry out raids designed to seize Franklin court records, and this had resulted in hard feelings. Finally, early in 1788, bloodshed resulted. Washington County Sheriff Jonathan Pugh, acting on Tipton's advice, seized some of Sevier's slaves to satisfy a judgment issued by a North Carolina court. At Tipton's suggestion, Pugh took the slaves to Tipton's home, on the outskirts of present-day Johnson City, for safekeeping. Sevier, infuriated upon hearing of these developments, determined to organize a force of fifty or more men to march on Tipton's home and recover the slaves. In anticipation of the assault, however, Tipton also amassed a small group of his own partisans. In the resulting skirmish, one of his men was killed and Sheriff Pugh received an injury from which he died a week later. Several others were wounded and captured. Tipton captured two of Sevier's sons and threatened to hang them but, acting on the advice of his friends, wisely released them.

By spring 1788, Sevier was ready to make peace with North Carolina but was apparently reluctant to desert his ardent supporters, especially those south of the French Broad who had sustained so many assaults from the Cherokee. His term as governor officially expired on March 1, 1788, however, and no one took his place. Shortly thereafter a new governor of North Carolina, Samuel Johnston, instructed Judge David Campbell to issue an order for Sevier's arrest on charges of high treason. Campbell refused, but another North Carolina judge sitting at Jonesboro complied with the governor's request. The order was given to Tipton for execution, and on October 10, 1788, Sevier peacefully surrendered to his old enemy of long standing. The Franklin leader was taken to Morganton for trial, where General Charles McDowell, a fellow commander at King's Mountain, signed his bail bond and obtained his release. Later, as preparations were made for a trial, Sevier's sons and others came to "rescue" him and were apparently allowed to escort him home without interference. Thus a trial was never held.

By this time the state of Franklin was dead except in the region of the Cherokee reservation south of the French Broad, where a "lesser Franklin" existed for a few months. In contrast to the many Franklinites, who had settled outside the reservation where land titles could be obtained under North Carolina's laws, the settlers south of the French Broad had title to their lands only from the state of Franklin, because North Carolina had prohibited settlement in that area. The settlers' status under the federal Indian policy was even worse, for the line established by the Treaty of Hopewell ran far to the northeast, on the other side of Greeneville.

The people south of the French Broad, like the Wataugans in 1772, attempted to solve their problem by drafting in Janury 1789 "articles of association" similar to the Watauga Compact. Instead of adopting the laws of Virginia, however, they adopted those of North Carolina and agreed to ask the next general assembly of that state "to receive us into their protection." Although they recognized John Sevier as their commander and Indian commissioner, the extent to which he was connected with the "association" is unknown. At the February term of the Greene County court, Sevier took an oath of allegiance to North Carolina and in August was elected to the state senate. Not only was he allowed to take his seat, but he was declared by the assembly to be the brigadier general of Washington District under his original appointment of 1784.

Thus the conciliatory policy of North Carolina, so successful in destroying the state of Franklin, was finally extended to its leader, who was permitted to assume a position of power in the same government he had tried to disrupt. After North Carolina ratified the Constitution later in 1789, Sevier was elected as a representative in Congress from the state's most western district. Although the state of Franklin failed because of its inability to gain recognition and because of dissension within its own ranks, the idea of a separate state for the area now known as East Tennessee did not die.[5]

SUGGESTED READINGS

Books

Thomas P. Abernethy, *Western Lands and the American Revolution* (New York, 1959); John R. Alden, *The South in the Revolution, 1763–1789* (Baton Rouge, 1962); Pat Alderman, *One Heroic Hour at King's Mountain, October 7, 1780* (Erwin, Tenn., 1968); John P. Caruso, *Appalachian Frontier* (Indianapolis, 1959); Carl Driver, *John Sevier: Pioneer of the Old Southwest* (Chapel Hill, 1932); Gilbert E. Govan and James W. Livingood, *The*

[5] As late as 1959 a bill was introduced in the legislature whereby "the historic state of Franklin" would be re-created from the eastern third of Tennessee. For a perceptive article about the Franklin idea, see Eric R. Lacy, "The Persistent State of Franklin," *THQ* 23 (Dec. 1964), 321–33.

Chattanooga Country (1952; rpt. Knoxville, 1976); Thomas E. Matthews, *General James Robertson* (Nashville, 1934); William H. McRaven, *Life and Times of Edward Swanson* (Nashville, 1937); Constance L. Skinner, *Pioneers of the Old Southwest* (New Haven, 1919); Samuel C. Williams, *Tennessee During the Revolutionary War* (1944, rpt. Knoxville, 1974).

Articles
Randolph G. Adams, "Two Documents on the Battle of King's Mountain," *NCHR* 8 (1931), 348– 52; Randolph C. Downes, "Cherokee-American Relations in the Upper Tennessee Valley, 1776– 1791," *ETHSP* 8 (1936), 35– 53; Stephen Foster, "The Battle of King's Mountain," *AHM* 1(1896), 22– 45; Robert L. Ganyard, "Threat from the West: North Carolina and the Cherokee," *NCHR* 45 (Jan. 1968), 47– 66; Philip M. Hamer, "John Stuart's Indian Policy During the Early Months of the American Revolution," *MVHR* 17 (Dec. 1930), 351– 66; Hamer, "The Wataugans and the Cherokee Indians in 1776," *ETHSP* 3(1931), 108– 26; Archibald Henderson, "The Treaty of the Long Island of the Holston, 1777," *NCHR* 8 (Jan. 1931), 51– 116; Ben H. McClary, "Nancy Ward," *THQ* (Dec. 1962), 352– 64; Mary H. McCown (ed.), "A King's Mountain Diary," *ETHSP* 14 (1942), 102– 5; James H. O'Donnell, "The Virginia Expedition against the Overhill Cherokee, 1776," *ETHSP* 39 (1967), 13– 25; Carol F. Young, "A Study of Some Developing Interpretations of the History of Revolutionary Tennessee," *ETHSP* 25 (1953), 24– 36.

6.

The Southwest Territory Becomes the Sixteenth State

T HE half-decade following the American Revolution was a traumatic period for the new nation. Problems along the eastern seaboard as well as on the frontier were varied and many. Finally, in 1787, delegates from the states met in convention in Philadelphia and wrote the new fundamental law—the Constitution of the United States—which was designed to give stability to the American government and economy and correct some of the problems that the country could not solve under the Articles of Confederation. William Blount was one of the delegates from North Carolina who affixed his signature to the historic document.

Most of the states readily ratified the Constitution, but North Carolina at first refused. A group called the "Radicals" dominated the state convention assembled specifically to vote on the matter, and members of that party expressed a deep-seated fear of the strong government that would develop under the Constitution. They believed particularly that such a government would levy high taxes and jeopardize liberty. Only if a bill of rights were added with specific guarantees, they said, would they reconsider the matter.

George Washington became president in April 1789, and only North Carolina and Rhode Island remained outside the Union at that time. In order to win the laggard states, Congress agreed that they could trade with the other eleven without any tariff duties, but only until January 15, 1790. In the meantime, Franklin leaders of the west no longer considered themselves separate from North Carolina and now began to participate again in the affairs of the mother state. Consequently, when delegates were chosen for a new ratifying convention to be held late in 1789, Sevier and others from the west, anxious to see North Carolina become part of the Union, helped overthrow the Radicals. In November 1789, delegates ratified the Constitution in a second convention by a vote of 195 to 77 and North Carolina became the twelfth state of the Union. Three weeks later, on December 12, legislators enacted a second cession law, again transferring western land to the national government. Congress readily accepted the territory this time, and on May 26, 1790 created the Territory of the United States South of the River Ohio, which eventually became the state of Tennessee.

The provisions of the new cession law were very similar to those of the act of 1784, which had been repealed. All land claims under North Carolina laws were to remain valid. The Military Reservation Act passed in 1782 had set aside millions of acres of Cumberland lands for Revolutionary soldiers, and the cession law provided that if there was not enough "good" land in the reservation to satisfy the veterans' claims, the remaining warrants could be located elsewhere in the region ceded. Finally, the cession law provided that one or more states should ultimately be formed, and until that time the territory would be governed under the provisions of the Northwest Ordinance of 1787, except that slavery would be permitted.

Under the Northwest Ordinance, originally written to apply only to territory north of the Ohio River, residents were guaranteed many rights, including freedom of religion, trial by jury and, ultimately, statehood. As long as the population consisted of fewer than 5,000 free adult males, a federally appointed governor, a secretary, and a body of judges should make, execute, and apply all laws for the district. After acquiring a population of 5,000 adult males, the territory could form a house of representatives which, with the governor and a legislative council of five members, would constitute a lawmaking body known as the General Assembly. When the free population reached 60,000, then the territory could be admitted as a state "on an equal footing with the original States in all respects whatsoever." Such admission was possible before the territory acquired the requisite 60,000 people, the ordinance provided, if it could be shown that this was "consistent with the general interest" of the central government.

William Blount was appointed territorial governor, an appointment that carried with it the position of superintendent of Indian affairs south of the Ohio. The 41-year-old speculator and businessman had campaigned actively, and the appointment did not come

William Blount was appointed governor of the Southwest Territory by President Washington, and served throughout the territorial period, 1790–1796.

about without negotiation. Others had also been interested in the position. Patrick Henry, a former governor of Virginia, suggested George Mason and General Joseph Martin. General Anthony Wayne, a Revolutionary War hero, also sought the appointment, and John Sevier received the warm support of probably a majority of the transmontane people. Blount had the support of the North Carolina delegation, however, and on June 8, 1790 was appointed governor.

Blount had served in the army during the Revolution and, more significantly, had known George Washington as a member of the Constitutional Convention of 1787. As a representative of North Carolina, he had been among the fifty-five delegates who had drawn up the new federal compact, and he was among the thirty-nine members who finally signed the Constitution. With Congressman John Steele's help he gained the support of all of North Carolina's senators and representatives and in 1790 was probably at the pinnacle of his political career.

The son of well-to-do North Carolina parents, Blount and others of his family had played active roles for years in the civil and military affairs of their colony and state. With his brother, John Gray Blount, William Blount had engaged in a variety of commercial enterprises, but the one most intriguing to him was always speculation in western lands. He claimed more than a million acres, and as he stated after his appointment as territorial executive, the governorship would not only give him an opportunity to serve his country but would also enable him to keep a close and careful eye on his land holdings and enhance their value.

President Washington named other territorial officials at the same time. General Daniel Smith of Sumner County became secretary. As events developed, this proved to be a significant appointment, because in Blount's frequent absences Smith served as acting governor, a post that employed his seasoned judgment to good advantage. The three judges were David Campbell, John McNairy, and Joseph Anderson. In accordance with the Ordinance of 1787, they, along with Blount, constituted the governing body until a legislature was formed in 1794.

As early as March 1790, Blount had been confident of his eventual appointment as governor, and he wasted no time in taking up his duties. By early October he had settled his affairs at home, taken the oath of office, and called upon the president at Mount Vernon. In the same month he established headquarters on the fork of the Holston

Above: Fort Nashborough, existing now in partial replica, was the site of the "Battle of the Bluffs." *Below:* Rocky Mount, near Johnson City, was the first capitol of the Southwest Territory.

and Watauga rivers at "Rocky Mount," the home of William Cobb, a
well-to-do pioneer who numbered among his friends the high and
powerful of North Carolina.

The Southwest Territory (as the new land came to be called)
contained nearly 43,000 square miles, but the population consisted
of two pockets of settlements separated by more than 100 miles of
wilderness. The eastern valley, now divided into the counties of
Washington, Greene, Sullivan, and Hawkins, had a population of
28,000. The Cumberland settlements, consisting of Davidson,
Sumner, and Tennessee counties, had about one-fourth that number.

On October 23, Blount arrived in Washington County to take up
residence at "Rocky Mount." He hastily called together a group of
influential citizens and informed them of his appointment as territorial governor. He read to his listeners the Ordinance of 1787 and
North Carolina's act of cession of 1789, told of the territory's acceptance by Congress, declared all appointments under North Carolina
law henceforth null and void, and read the names of newly appointed
officials. Within the next ten days he visited Sullivan, Greene, and
Hawkins counties and repeated the procedure. On December 15, he
arrived at Nashborough and was the house guest of James Robertson
for nearly two weeks. There he performed the same ceremonies for
the three Cumberland counties that he had in the eastern district. He
returned home at the end of the month, where he took up his
multifarious duties with vigor, not least among which were attention
to the troublesome Indian question, consideration of a permanent
location for a territorial capital, and plans for a census.

The most serious problem faced by Blount as superintendent of
Indian affairs was Cherokee resentment of the government's failure
to enforce the Treaty of Hopewell. Thousands of whites had moved
into the area south of the French Broad under the treaties made by
the defunct state of Franklin, many others had built homes just west
of the Holston and Tennessee rivers, and still others continued to
settle in the Cumberland areas. The Chickamaugans had returned to
the Cherokee fold and demanded, with the Creeks, the release of at
least some of the land, particularly that in the Cumberland Valley,
which they considered a common tribal hunting ground.

The federal government at first offered help. Secretary of War
Henry Knox instructed Blount to negotiate with the Cherokee and
offer them an annuity of $1,000 if they would permit whites to
remain in the disputed territory. Accordingly, Cherokee leaders met

Blount at White's Fort (soon to become Knoxville) late in June 1791 and signed the Treaty of the Holston. In this agreement, the Cherokee confirmed the Transylvania Purchase of the Cumberland area and granted land bounded on the west by the Clinch River and on the south by a line running from near the mouth of the Clinch to the North Carolina border. The United States would guarantee protection of the Cherokee trade, "gratuitously" supply the Indians with "useful implements of husbandry" and instructions in their use, and pay an annuity of $1,000.

The expected peaceful relations failed to materialize. In the following year (January 1792) a delegation of Cherokee visited the national capital and attempted to persuade Secretary Knox that the Cumberland Valley, the "joint lands" of several tribes, should be evacuated by the whites. Knox satisfied them for the moment by increasing their annuity to $1,500 and showering them with presents. But other developments soon made the Indians restive and encouraged them to believe that they might be successful in expelling the whites. In November 1791 the northern Indians resoundingly defeated the army of Arthur St. Clair, governor of the Northwest Territory—a development that encouraged the southern tribes to hope for similar success in their area. In addition, Secretary Knox, hoping yet to promote peace between the Indians and whites, gave firm orders that people in the southwest should launch no offensive assaults against the Indians. As soon as the red men heard of this, they renewed their attacks with less fear of white retaliation. Still another important cause of accelerated Indian warfare was the aggressive Spanish policy inaugurated by Baron de Carondelet, who succeeded Don Estevan Miró on December 30, 1791, as governor of New Orleans and immediately revitalized the coalition under Spanish protection of the Creek, Choctaw, Chickasaw, and Cherokee. Carondelet wrote his superior that he planned "underhandedly [to] Supply the Cherokees and Creeks with sufficient arms and munitions to maintain themselves. . . ."[1]

Under these circumstances, Governor Blount's task of maintaining peace was extremely difficult. The Cherokee chief Hanging Maw kept the Upper Cherokee relatively quiet, but the raids of the Lower Cherokee and Creeks became so serious in the spring and

[1] D. C. and Roberta Corbitt, "Papers from the Spanish Archives," *ETHSP* 28 (1856), 139–41.

summer of 1793 that the settlers throughout the Southwest Territory were forced to crowd within the walls of the various station forts. For Blount it became increasingly difficult to enforce the federal order against offensive operations, and the fury of the settlers was expressed in a variety of ways as they struck back indiscriminately at their foe. The most serious raid occurred in June, while Blount was in Philadelphia. Captain Hugh Beard launched an offensive war against the Upper Cherokee and in the process captured and slaughtered the family of Hanging Maw. When the formerly peaceful chieftain received the news, he was beside himself with grief and promptly rallied support to launch a general war against the whites.

It was fall 1793 before the westerners, in disregard of federal policy, developed concentrated offensive operations and began to get the better of the enemy. After Cherokee and Creek warriors brutally massacred whites at Cavet's Station, about eight miles east of Knoxville, John Sevier pursued the Indians with a force of several hundred militiamen, soundly defeated them at the Battle of Etowah (near present-day Rome, Georgia), and destroyed several Cherokee and Creek towns in the area. This crushing defeat quieted the enemy long enough for Blount again to seek help from Philadelphia. The Washington administration responded by authorizing a few garrisoned posts along the Little Tennessee and Clinch rivers and increasing the Cherokee annuity to $5,000. Then, in the summer of the following year, James Robertson authorized Major James Ore to march from Nashville with 550 men to a point below the mouth of the Sequatchie River and attack the Indian town of Nickajack. The small army did this with great success and returned to Nashville. Finally, the defeat of the northern Indians at Fallen Timbers by General Anthony Wayne in the summer of 1794 exerted a calming effect upon the southern tribes, and the Spanish policy also became less aggressive. In the Treaty of San Lorenzo (Pinckney's Treaty) of the following year, the Spanish not only granted to the Americans navigation rights on the Mississippi River but also agreed to evacuate the territory north of the 31st parallel. This meant that the southern Indians, now within the jurisdiction of the United States, could no longer look for help from Spain. Thus the end of the territorial period was approaching before an era of peace came to the Indians and whites.

A second problem—and perhaps the least troublesome of all those facing Governor Blount—was the selection of a permanent location for a territorial capital. James White had explored, purchased, and erected a fort on land a few miles below the juncture of the Holston and French Broad rivers. Blount, himself owning land nearby, decided upon that general vicinity for the capital. He had already used White's Fort as a place to meet Cherokee leaders and develop a treaty with them, and he soon began to build a cabin on a hill very near the Tennessee River that would serve as both the territorial capital and a residence for his family. White immediately began to mark off and sell lots near the governor's mansion, and a town developed in short order. Blount named it Knoxville, in honor of the secretary of war.

By 1792, several buildings had been erected, and in June, Knox County was carved from Hawkins; Knoxville, of course, now became not only the capital of the new territory but also a county seat. At the same time the politically astute governor formed Jefferson County and, grouping Knox and Jefferson into a military and judicial district, honored the third member of Washington's cabinet by naming the district "Hamilton."

The census takers reported a population of 35,691, but Blount made no immediate effort to call together a legislature, as the Ordinance of 1787 gave him the right to do. Ambitious residents, however, frequently reminded him of his right and obligation. Accordingly, on October 19, 1793, the governor called for an election to be held in late December. A house of representatives consisting of thirteen members was to be chosen by all freemen having a freehold of at least fifty acres.

The election was duly held, despite riots and disturbances at some of the voting places. The successful candidates, including John Tipton, whose political power in Washington County had increased after the Franklin fiasco and who continued to manifest little regard for either Sevier or Blount, assembled in Knoxville on February 24. According to the law, they were to select a group of ten men from whom President Washington would select five to serve as a "council" or upper house. The five council members eventually selected by the President included Sevier, Griffith Rutherford, James Winchester, Stockley Donelson, and Parmenas Taylor.

It was not until August 1794 that the whole assembly convened. They enacted laws incorporating the town of Knoxville, establishing a tax rate, creating Sevier County south of the French Broad River,

Above: Blount Mansion, home of the territorial governor, was one of the first frame houses west of the Blue Ridge. *Below:* This block house at Benton guarded the supply lines to Andrew Jackson at the Battle of New Orleans.

and chartering Greeneville and Blount colleges. They chose Dr. James White[2] as delegate to Congress.

Participation in the first legislative session whetted the lawmakers' desire for statehood. Blount was by no means averse to the idea; indeed, for some time he had foreseen himself as a United States senator from the new state. But the procedure by which a territory became a state had not been clearly defined. The thirteen colonies had declared their independence and had then fought the Revolutionary War to secure it. Kentucky and Vermont had been admitted after the war, but they did not go through a territorial stage. Blount turned to Dr. White for advice on procedure, and White urged him to take the initiative. "Nothing will be done by Congress," he assured the governor, until you "come forward with a petition for the purpose." Some authorities had suggested, White wrote, that proper procedure would include a referendum to determine the will of the people, to be followed by a constitutional convention that would prepare a basic document for the prospective state. Blount agreed, and accordingly called the legislature into special session on June 29, 1795 to consider statehood. He told the assembled lawmakers that he believed it to be "the wish of the majority of the people that the territory should become a State."[3]

Upon Blount's recommendation, the legislature provided for a census and a poll on the question of statehood. Each free adult male was asked, "Is it your wish if, on taking the enumeration there should prove to be less than sixty thousand inhabitants, that the territory shall be admitted as a State. . . ?" Although some opposition to statehood was expressed by a few legislators, particularly Thomas Hardeman of Davidson County, the Blount forces were confident of the outcome. They were not to be disappointed. The final count showed a population of 77,262 and the vote on the question of statehood favored it 6,504 to 2,562 (see table 1). The eastern counties voted for admission, but the western counties were overwhelmingly against it. Perhaps Representative Hardeman had expressed the sentiment of the Cumberland people when he argued that statehood meant increased taxes. Probably even more important was the fear on the part of these western people that they would be domi-

---

[2] Dr. James White, earlier a North Carolina congressman with extensive holdings on the Cumberland, was not the same as James White who established "White's Fort" where Knoxville was built.

[3] Masterson, *Blount,* 284.

Table 1.

CENSUS OF 1795 OF TERRITORY OF THE UNITED STATES SOUTH OF THE RIVER OHIO

County	Free white males		Free white females	All others free	Slaves	Total	Yeas*	Nays*
	16 and over	under 16						
Jefferson	1,706	2,225	3,021	112	776	7,840	714	316
Hawkins	2,666	3,279	4,767	147	2,472	13,331	1,651	534
Greene	1,567	2,203	3,350	52	466	7,638	560	495
Knox	2,721	2,723	3,664	100	2,365	11,573	1,100	128
Washington	2,013	2,578	4,311	225	978	10,105	873	14
Sullivan	1,803	2,340	3,499	38	777	8,457	715	125
Sevier	628	1,045	1,503	273	129	3,578	261	55
Blount	585	817	1,231	00	183	2,816	476	16
Sumner	1,382	1,595	2,316	1	1,076	6,370	00	00
Tennessee	380	444	700	19	398	1,941	58	231
Davidson	728	695	1,192	6	992	3,613	96	517

*Each free adult was asked, "Is it your wish if, on taking the enumeration there should prove to be less than sixty thousand inhabitants, that the territory shall be admitted as a State in the Federal Union with such a number or not."

nated by the eastern part of the state; they looked forward to the day when they might become a state in their own right.

When Blount learned of the results of the referendum, he made plans immediately for a convention at which delegates would draft a constitution and otherwise make plans for statehood. He proclaimed December 18–19 as the dates for an election of five representatives from each county. When the delegates had been elected and duly certified, they would assemble in Knoxville on January 17, 1796, to begin their work.

Some of the territory's ablest men were chosen. Blount was selected chairman. The delegates included Territorial Judges Joseph Anderson and John McNairy, Secretary Daniel Smith, and the congressional delegate and large landholder, James White. James Robertson, Andrew Jackson, and Thomas Hardeman were among those from the Cumberland area. James Houston, father of Sam Houston, represented Blount County. John Tipton and Landon Carter, former speaker of the Franklin legislature, represented Washington County. Men destined to serve later as governor of Tennessee or to represent the state in Congress included William Cocke, Joseph McMinn, John Rhea, and Archibald Roane, in addition to Andrew Jackson. Sixteen members listed their place of birth as Virginia, eight mentioned Pennsylvania, seven North Carolina, four South Carolina, and three Maryland.

Debates were spirited. The Blount group consisted of such stalwarts as Daniel Smith, Judge McNairy, James Robertson, and Andrew Jackson, and it generally prevailed, but Judge Anderson and his father-in-law, Alexander Outlaw, were joined by Joseph McMinn and Joseph Hardeman in opposing some of Blount's recommendations. The latter group took the initiative, for example, in preparing a bill of rights—a matter upon which the Blount faction wanted to proceed with caution—and worked to curtail the powers of the upper house after failing in an attempt to establish a unicameral legislature. Fundamentalistic in religion, they vainly sought to include a requirement that officeholders believe in the "divine authority of the old and new testament." With an independent spirit reminiscent of Franklin days, they urged delegates to agree to function as an independent state under the new constitution if the central government refused to admit them to the Union with rights and privileges equal to those of the other states.

The constitution, later described by Thomas Jefferson as "the least imperfect and most republican," began with a preamble in which "the people" were proclaimed as ordaining and establishing the law. Legislative authority was vested in a bicameral legislature. Membership in the house or senate was open only to free males twenty-one years of age or older who owned at least 200 acres and had resided for three or more years in the state. The legislature had broad lawmaking powers not fettered by a gubernatorial veto.

The executive power was vested in a governor who served a term of two years and was limited to three consecutive terms. (It was not unt'l the limited constitutional convention of 1953 that the executive's term was expanded to four years.) To serve as governor, one had to be at least twenty-five years of age and own a freehold of at least 500 acres. The chief executive was given various powers, the most important of which was to "take care that the laws shall be faithfully executed."

The judicial branch consisted of "such superior and inferior courts of law and equity as the legislature should create." Judges served for life on good behavior.

All freemen who were at least twenty-one years of age and had been residents of a county for at least six months could vote. A declaration of rights guaranteed freedom of speech, press, religion, peaceable assembly, trial by jury, and security against unjustifiable search and seizure. Although some of the passages were original, much of the constitution was copied from those of other states, particularly Pennsylvania and North Carolina.

The draft was finished in three short weeks, and on February 9 convention members sent a copy to Philadelphia by Joseph McMinn. They instructed McMinn to remain at the nation's capital long enough to determine how the statehood request would fare and to urge the territorial delegate, Dr. James White, to apply immediately for statehood.

Although proclaiming the sovereignty of "the people," the delegates did not refer the constitution to a popular referendum for ratification. Haste was necessary, they believed, to carry the matter of admission to Congress before that body adjourned. Some complained, however, including Arthur Campbell, who had earlier sought to play a major role in the making of western states. Campbell voiced his objections to President Washington and opposed immediate statehood and the manner in which the constitution was shaped. The convention had been called in too great a haste, he said, and had acted precipitately without adequate deliberation and judgment. He urged that Congress take sufficient time to deliberate on so important a subject as statehood, and thought that although "a delay of one or two years" might disappoint some of the ambitious politicians of the west, it would "be found to accord with the interest and safety of the people."[4] The Blount-Sevier forces were not to be deterred by protests from Campbell, though, and there is no evidence that Washington gave the slightest attention to Campbell's concern.

Before the convention adjourned, members authorized Governor Blount to conduct an election for a governor and a General Assembly so that the state might be prepared to function even before it was officially admitted to the Union. Accordingly, on February 6, Blount issued writs of election to county sheriffs instructing them to hold the required election. Sevier appeared from the beginning as the likely choice for governor, and in the eastern counties even the friends of John Tipton did not oppose him. In the Cumberland region Thomas Hardeman, Colonel James Winchester, and Colonel Robert Hayes tried vainly to develop support for Judge Anderson. But James Robertson, John McNairy, and others countered successfully with strong support for Sevier, and Anderson withdrew shortly before the election so that Sevier was chosen without opposition.

Governor Blount had proclaimed March 28 as the day on which the General Assembly should convene. This would be the last day of the territorial government. The two houses met on the specified day and elected James Winchester of Sumner County as speaker of the senate and James Stewart of Washington County as speaker of the house.

The next two days were busy ones for the legislature. On March 29 the legislators began the day by opening and publishing the returns from the several counties in the gubernatorial election. "Citizen John Sevier," the members proclaimed, was "duly and constitutionally elected. . . ." Committees were formed to assist in the inauguration. On the following day Sevier was inaugurated and two United States senators were elected. In a brief inaugural address, Sevier expressed gratitude for the confidence reposed in him and promised "to labor to discharge with fidelity" the office of governor of Tennessee. Blount, William Cocke, Dr. James White, and Judge Anderson were

[4] Masterson, *Blount,* 291.

nominated for the two Senate seats. The election of Blount was assured from the first, but Cocke was not selected until after Anderson and White had withdrawn. Immediately following their selection, Blount and Cocke delivered brief acceptance speeches and a few weeks later departed for the nation's capital.

Believing Tennessee would be allowed two representatives and thus four presidential electors, the lawmakers divided the state into two congressional districts and chose Joseph Greer, Daniel Smith, Hugh Nielson, and Judge Anderson as presidential electors. Daniel Smith had urged during the convention that the territory bear the name of Tennessee. Members, concerned that the state and one of the counties now had the same name, moved to divide Tennessee County into Robertson and Montgomery. The former was named for James Robertson, and the latter for Colonel John Montgomery, who had migrated to the west from Virginia. Grainger County, named for Blount's wife, Mary Grainger, was created at the same time.

In the meantime, McMinn had arrived in the nation's capital with the constitution and an official communication from Blount explaining in detail what had taken place in the Territory South of the River Ohio. On April 8 President Washington forwarded both documents to Congress, along with a presidential message. Among the "privileges, benefits, and advantages" that Congress had conferred upon the territory when it accepted the cession from North Carolina, the president said, was "the right of forming a permanent constitution and State Government, and of admission as a State. . . on an equal footing with the original States, in all respects whatever, when it should have therein 60,000 free inhabitants. . . ."[5] The matter was then referred to appropriate committees.

Had Tennesseans applied for admission a year or two earlier, chances are they would have encountered little or no opposition in Congress. As it was, however, considerable debate and several weeks of delay ensued before Tennessee became the sixteenth state. By 1796, the political climate had changed markedly from what it had been two years earlier. Washington's two main cabinet members, Secretary of State Thomas Jefferson and Secretary of the Treasury Alexander Hamilton, had disagreed over a philosophy of govern-

[5] James D. Richardson, *A Compilation of the Messages and Papers of the Presidents, 1796–1897*, vol. 1 (Washington, D.C., 1896), 197.

ment and had particularly disputed the issue of a national bank. When Washington supported Hamilton, Jefferson had resigned in disgust and frustration. Jefferson returned to Monticello where, upon receiving messages of support, he made plans for a presidential campaign. His followers, disillusioned with the direction of Federalist leadership, spoke of themselves as Republicans and hoped to elect Jefferson and Aaron Burr to the top posts in the federal government.

Federalists, realizing that Washington would retire at the end of his term, groomed John Adams and Thomas Pinckney for president and vice president. They knew of the Republican proclivities of the western people and, realizing that the election probably would be close, reasoned that three or four electoral votes might determine the winner. In order to be safe, they determined to delay Tennessee's admission until after the election.

By the time Tennesseans applied for admission, the Republican party had experienced such growth that its leaders controlled the House of Representatives. Consequently, a House committee to which the matter had been referred responded with a recommendation of immediate admission; the territory, the committee said, should be "declared to be one of the sixteen United States of America." This report became the signal for protracted debate.[6]

Although the House committee reported on April 12, debate on John Jay's treaty with Great Britain delayed the discussion of statehood for more than three weeks. By that time Federalists, although in the minority, had planned their strategy to delay admission in that legislative session until after the presidential election. They could distract attention from the sectional nature of their action by having the argument against immediate admission opened by one of the South's ablest Federalists, William Loughton Smith of South Carolina.

In a succinct, legalistic argument, Smith established the guidelines for other Federalists who were to follow. What rights did the territory people have, he asked rhetorically, as conferred upon them by Congress in the Ordinance of 1787 and the act of 1790 accepting North Carolina's deed of cession? A territory had no rights of its own to form itself into a state, because Congress alone could do that. The

[6] The debates are found in *Annals of Congress,* 1 sess., *passim.*

Tennessee convention had therefore acted illegally and improperly in drafting a constitution, electing officers, and considering itself to be a state. Furthermore, the territory had no authority to take a census. While the territorial legislature could enact laws "for the good government of the district," it was incompetent to legislate on matters of "great and external" concern. The figures proclaimed were inaccurate anyway, because Congress in prescribing a requisite number for statehood had used the term "inhabitants," while the Tennesseans had enumerated "persons." There was a distinct difference, he said, because the exodus of people through the state enroute to Kentucky and the Northwest Territory filled Tennessee with people passing through who had no intention of becoming permanent residents. The census was "unfair" because it was taken at a time of the greatest migration. Moreover, the fact that sheriffs were allowed one dollar for each 200 persons enumerated encouraged fraud.

The new constitution was subjected to Congressman Smith's careful scrutiny. It carried, he said, "the same marks of haste and inaccuracy as the rest of the proceedings." Several provisions contravened the federal Constitution, including the provision that made all lands equally liable to taxation, the provision that no citizen should be fined more than $50 except in jury trials, the exemption from taxation of articles manufactured from the produce of the state, and the section respecting navigation of the Mississippi River. Two other provisions were objectionable if not illegal, namely, the right of the legislature to instruct congressmen and the omission of military officers from the requirement that officials must believe in God and a future state with rewards and punishments. Too much power, he thought, was placed in the legislative branch.

The South Carolina congressman would not oppose admission of Tennessee if it were accomplished "correctly and constitutionally." But it was a matter of great concern, he thought, to the entire union because it would establish a precedent for other territories. The correct threefold course of legal and constitutional action for admission, he said, required Congress to declare the territory a state and define its boundaries; order an enumeration of the territory's free inhabitants; and, upon finding the state to contain the requisite 60,000 free inhabitants, admit it into the union. Other Federalists supported Smith's position.

Federalists were answered effectively by a dozen Republicans, including James Madison, Thomas Blount,[7] and Albert Gallatin. Madison, who would become president in 1809, was already recognized as one of the ablest men in the young nation and had played a dominant role in the Constitutional Convention of 1787. He chided Federalists for trying to delay admission by "spinning a finer thread" of legalism than was necessary. The western people were having to obey laws made by a body in which they had no representation, he said, as he urged a vote for immediate statehood.

Thomas Blount, a younger brother of William Blount, had been elected to the House from North Carolina in 1795. Although a freshman member of Congress, he spoke strongly in favor of immediate statehood. Albert Gallatin, soon to become President Jefferson's able secretary of the treasury, joined Blount and argued that a territory automatically became a state "the moment they amounted to 60,000 free inhabitants."

After two days of debate the House voted on May 6 to admit Tennessee to statehood, but the Senate, dominated by Federalists, at first refused. Three weeks of serious debate on the Tennessee matter then ensued in the upper house. In the meantime, on May 23, William Blount and William Cocke arrived in Philadelphia and presented letters to the Senate stating that they "had been duly and legally elected . . . to represent the State of Tennessee in the Senate." The Senate, however, refused to accept them but did vote to receive them as "spectators" until "the final decision of the Senate shall be given on the bill proposing to admit the Southwestern Territory into the Union."

Republicans opened up the matter in earnest on May 25. They proposed a compromise whereby Tennessee would have one representative in Congress instead of two, as they originally had hoped. This would mean that the new state, if admitted, would have three electoral votes instead of four, which, Republicans believed, would satisfy Federalist opposition. A few days later senators voted to form a joint conference committee consisting of members of both the House and Senate to work out details upon which the Congress could agree. Tennesseans were fortunate in that Aaron Burr, a Republican senator from New York, was one of two senators appointed and became chairman of the committee. The Republican nominee for vice president in 1796, Burr counted many of the

---

[7] A brother to William Blount, then serving in Congress from North Carolina.

western people, including Blount and Cocke, among his close friends. After only brief deliberation, the committee reported in favor of immediate statehood with the understanding that "the said State of Tennessee shall be entitled to one representative in the House of representatives. . . ." Both houses accepted the report, and President Washington signed the statehood bill on June 1, 1796, thereupon making Tennessee the 16th state.

Still, Federalist senators would not accept Blount and Cocke until they had been elected by the voters of the State of Tennessee and not the voters of the Southwest Territory. Governor Sevier accordingly called the legislature into special session on July 30 for the purpose of electing two senators, providing for the election of a congressman, and selecting three presidential electors. Blount and Cocke were elected again without difficulty, although Judge David Campbell and Dr. James White were also nominated. The legislature rescinded an act that had divided the state into the Holston and the Cumberland congressional districts and provided instead for one district to embrace the entire state, in accordance with the understanding reached at the time of admission. A congressional election was held early in October, and Andrew Jackson was chosen over negligible opposition. In revising legislation for choosing presidential electors, the General Assembly divided the state into three electoral districts— Washington, Hamilton, and Mero—and named three people from each county to choose an elector from each of the three districts.

When Congress assembled in January, 1797, the Tennessee senators and congressman proudly took their seats, signaling the end of the brief but eventful struggle of Tennesseans for equal status in the young nation. The electors had met in December 1796 and, fulfilling the fears expressed earlier by the Federalists, cast their votes for Thomas Jefferson and Aaron Burr.

SUGGESTED READINGS

Books

Thomas P. Abernethy, *From Frontier to Plantation in Tennessee* (1932; rpt. University, Ala., 1967); *The South in the New Nation, 1789–1819* (Baton Rouge, 1961); John A. Caruso, *Appalachian Frontier* (Indianapolis, 1959); Robert E. Corlew, *Statehood for Tennessee* (Nashville, 1976); Carl Driver, *John Sevier: Pioneer of the Old Southwest* (Chapel Hill, 1932); Walter

Durham, *Daniel Smith, Frontier Statesman* (Gallatin, Tenn., 1976); William H. Masterson, *William Blount* (Baton Rouge, 1954); Thomas E. Matthews, *General James Robertson* (Nashville, 1934); Samuel C. Williams, *Phases of Southwest Territory History* (Johnson City, Tenn., 1940); Williams, *Beginnings of West Tennessee in the Land of the Chickasaws, 1541– 1841,* (Johnson City, Tenn., 1930).

Articles
John D. Barnhart, "The Tennessee Constitution of 1796: A Product of the Old West," *JSH* 9 (Nov. 1943), 532– 48; James W. Hagy and Stanley J. Folmsbee, "Arthur Campbell and the Separate State Movements in Virginia and North Carolina," *ETHSP* 42 (1970), 20– 46; David E. Harrell, "James Winchester, Patriot," *THQ* 18 (Dec. 1958), 301– 17; William H. Masterson, "William Blount and the Establishment of the Southwest Territory, 1790– 1791," *ETHSP* 23 (1951), 3– 31; Isabel Thompson, "The Blount Conspiracy," *ETHSP* 2 (1930), 3– 21; Charlotte Williams, "Congressional Action on the Admission of Tennessee into the Union," *THQ* 2 (Dec. 1943), 291– 315, reprinted in White, *Tennessee: Old and New,* Vol. 1, 27– 50; Samuel C. Williams, "The Admission of Tennessee," *THQ* 4 (Dec. 1945), 291– 319; Williams, "French and Other Intrigues in the Southwest Territory, 1790– 1796," *ETHSP* 13 (1941), 21– 35.

7.

?~ *Social and Economic Life*
on the Frontier

THE Tennessee territory was transformed from a wilderness into a state within a quarter-century after the first settlers crossed the Appalachians. The population grew from a few families along the Holston Valley in the late 1760s to 105,602 people in 1800. Settlers in the east, scattered among eight counties, lived as far west as the Clinch River. Those west of the Cumberland Plateau lived in four counties chiefly along the Cumberland River between the present-day towns of Carthage and Clarksville and centered at Nashville. The area between the two groups was Indian country, as indeed was all of the land between the Mississippi and Tennessee rivers that later became West Tennessee. While the majority of the people were of English descent, approximately 25 percent were Scotch-Irish. About half that number were Negro slaves, and there were scatterings of German, Irish, French, and perhaps other nationalities.

Pioneer Life ?~ The long hunters—nomadic individuals who came into the Tennessee country ahead of the permanent settlers—had not been particularly concerned with a place to stay. Most of them, like the wild animals whose furs and skins they sought, simply slept in the woods when night came or wandered until they found a cave or other natural shelter where they might remain for a few days. Some, like Thomas "Big Foot" Spencer, mentioned earlier, found a hollow tree big enough to sleep in and called it home while they hunted and trapped in the surrounding area. For a meal they roasted game over a campfire or ate provisions that they brought with them from the east.

The permanent settlers were not far behind the long hunters. They hastily constructed temporary shelters consisting of forked stakes driven into the ground with poles laid over the top and sloping to the ground in the rear. On the poles they placed thick brush, which provided shelter from the weather. They then felled trees in the immediate area, stripped branches from the logs to build a cabin, and planted a crop of corn between the stumps. If two or more families came together—which usually was the case—they could work together and build cabins within a few days.

Most of the people came in small groups and established "stations" in both the eastern and Cumberland areas. As protection from hostile Indians, they built a stockade, or fort, which was nothing more than a high fence of logs placed in the ground side by side. As one contemporary described it,

> a ditch was dug three feet deep. . . . Logs twelve or fifteen inches in diameter and fifteen feet long, were cut, and split open. The top ends were sharpened, the butts set in the ditch with the flat sides all in, . . . The dirt was then thrown into the ditch and well rammed down.[1]

At each of the four corners of the stockade a blockhouse was built—a two-story log cabin. It served as a lookout for the approach of hostile foe and was also frequently used as a place for storing supplies in the event of an Indian raid.

Most people lived in log cabins reasonably near the fort. The typical cabin seldom measured more than fifteen or twenty feet square, depending not so much on the size and quality of logs as upon the availability of manpower among neighbors and friends to handle the heavy unseasoned timbers. The first cabins were of round logs from which the bark had been removed; they were notched on the ends. If a builder had sufficient labor available, he would hew two sides flat or, if he had even more time and help, he would square the logs to insure a snug fit. Air space between would be "chinked" with mud or clay. Holes for doors and windows were cut after the logs were in place. Interior walls were left unfinished, except for a few pegs or deer's antlers for hanging clothes. Floors were of earth or of puncheons—logs split in two and laid with the flat side up. A fire-

---

[1] James A. Crutchfield, "Pioneer Architecture in Tennessee," 165.

place in one end, with a chimney of sticks and mud, provided heat for warmth and cooking. Roofs consisted of clapboards laid on poles running the length of the cabin and held in place by wooden pegs.

By the time of statehood and as the frontier grew in size, people were building larger and more expensive homes. The double-unit or "dog-trot" cabin (such as Rocky Mount, where Blount established territorial headquarters in 1790) was in widespread use by the time of statehood. It consisted of two distinct cabins, with a single roof over them, and a porch—the dog-trot—between. The porch often served as an additional room, especially for sleeping on hot nights. Later, as family needs increased, the dog-trot was enclosed.

Homes of a few prosperous families were more elaborate. Some were two-story frame houses with shingled roofs, plank floors, and glass windows, while others were of brick or stone. By 1792 William Blount had moved the territorial capital to Knoxville, where he built his "Mansion," one of the first frame houses west of the mountains. Francis A. Ramsey constructed "Swan Pond" near Knoxville, and General James Winchester settled near Gallatin in "Cragfont" a few years later. Both built elaborate homes of stone.

Furnishings, food, and clothing were simple on the frontier. Tables, benches, and stools were made of split logs sometimes supported by wooden pegs. Mattresses were bed ticks filled with straw and covered with animal skins. Wild and domestic animals supplied meat, and corn ground into meal was made into cornbread. Hominy was another of the products made from corn, and by no means the least was corn whiskey. Spring and summer brought a variety of fruits and vegetables, some of which were dried and preserved for winter. Food was eaten from pewter or wooden plates and bowls, often with wooden spoons. Clothing was made in the homes and was similar to that worn by the Indians. Hunting shirts, generally of deerskin, fitted loosely and reached halfway down the thighs and were fringed at the bottom. Trousers of similar materials, leggings of deerskin wound around the ankles to protect against poisonous snakes and briars, and moccasins of buckskin or buffalo hide were what the well-dressed frontiersmen of the 1790s wore. Women wore dresses of linsey, cotton, or wool, often dyed in different colors.

Frontier Towns ⧉ As observed earlier, James White had established "White's Fort" in 1786 in the vicinity of present-day

Knoxville, and it was there that William Blount established the territorial capital after a brief stay at Rocky Mount. The town was laid out in 1791 by Charles McClung, a Philadelphia surveyor, and Blount took considerable interest in its development. He watched with pride as homes and places of business were begun, and before the year was out he had brought in George Roulstone as territorial printer and publisher of the town's first newspaper, the *Knoxville Gazette*. Blount College, ultimately the University of Tennessee at Knoxville, was established in 1795.

Many visitors came from the East and even from abroad to see the transmontane capital. Blount entertained Louis Philippe of France shortly before the territory became a state, and another Frenchman, André Michaux, visited shortly after the turn of the century. Michaux wrote that Knoxville had about 200 homes, fifteen to twenty stores, and a thriving trade with New Orleans.

Nashville, even older than Knoxville, was not as large as the state's capital at the turn of the century but was the fastest growing town in Tennessee. It consisted of about 100 homes at the time of statehood, but the number increased daily because of the large number of people moving in from the east and from Kentucky. One traveler, visiting in 1796, referred to a "deluge of immigration" and predicted that the population of the Cumberland country would double in less than a year. Nashville's public square, where a long courthouse and jail had been built and where fifteen or twenty stores were operating, was the center of activity. Two newspapers, the *Intelligencer*, established by John McLaughlin in 1799, and the *Tennessee Gazette*, begun a year later by Benjamin J. Bradford, were published. Thomas B. Craighead had opened an academy and for some years had preached to Presbyterian congregations of the area. Farmland near Nashville was quoted in 1795 at one dollar or less per acre, but within a year brought twice that amount.

Other towns, smaller in size, were developing in both east and west. Jonesborough, (now Jonesboro) the state's oldest, had a hundred or more homes, Greeneville thirty, and Kingston about half that number. Rogersville, the county seat of Hawkins, was probably as large as Kingston, and boasted several places of business dealing in a variety of goods. Clarksville, the seat of Tennessee County until 1796 and after that of Montgomery, was second in size to Nashville among towns in the western section at the turn of the century.

Some manufacturing was carried on in the frontier towns. Knoxville had tanneries and also sent flour, cotton, and lime to the New Orleans markets. John Hague smuggled out of England designs for cotton manufacturing machinery and in 1791 established in Davidson County the first cotton factory in the South. Although Hague abandoned his enterprise two years later, other cotton factories were established in Nashville by the turn of the century or shortly thereafter.

The frontier merchant apparently did a thriving business with neighborhood farmers as well as eastern wholesalers. Merchants advertised their wares in the newspapers and took in a variety of farm produce in exchange for goods. A merchant in tiny Rogersville announced in Roulstone's *Gazette* on January 14, 1792, that he had for sale clothes, velvets, buff denim, poplins, calicoes, muslins, men's and women's stockings of both cotton and silk, Irish linen, blankets, bed ticks, hats, powder, pewter, playing cards, coffee, chocolate, tea, Bibles, knives "and [other] articles too numerous to mention." He purchased or took in exchange for goods skins and furs of bear, deer, otter, wildcat, muskrat, mink, fox, and raccoon as well as all other "kinds of fur whatever." A Knoxville merchant announced at about the same time that he not only sold the usual staples, hardware, and dry goods but also had "a few young and likely Virginia born negroes" for sale. Most merchants sold Bibles, hymnals, dictionaries, and a few other books that might be demanded by the reading public.

While some roads were being developed at the time of statehood, much of the commerce and travel was by water. The *Knoxville Gazette* in the summer of 1795 reported the frequent arrival and departure of flatboats; one bound for New Orleans for example, was laden with bar iron, whiskey, bacon, lime, flour, and cotton. After navigation rights on the Mississippi River were gained from Spain in 1795, both Nashville and Knoxville developed a brisk market with New Orleans. Materials from Knoxville were sent down the Tennessee River to the Ohio, and thence down the Mississippi; those from Nashville floated on barges, flatboats, or keelboats down the Cumberland to the Ohio and thence down the Mississippi to New Orleans. John Coffee was among the boat owners who operated a lucrative "carrying trade" and transported for Middle Tennessee vendors such items as hams, salt, bacon, brandy, whiskey, butter, hemp, tobacco, cotton, flour, lime, animal skins, and bar and cast iron. Boatmen often sold both boat and cargo at the port and then returned 550 miles through the wilderness over Natchez Trace (a path or trail made into a road by

1802), or took passage on sailing vessels to Philadelphia, Baltimore, or Charleston.

Rough wagon roads were also traveled, leading from Knoxville to Baltimore, Richmond, and Philadelphia, the last-named city being 650 miles away. Some wagons traversed the mountains and valleys to Nashville, but most of the imports into the Cumberland country came from Philadelphia to Pittsburgh, then on water to the mouth of the Cumberland, and thence upstream or overland into Nashville. Inns dotted the wagon roads along the way. I. A. Parker, of Nashville, for example, announced in 1804 that he, in tendering "his services as an innkeeper to the public in general," would "most studiously attend to the accomodation of all Genteel Guests (and no others are welcome) who may please to call upon him."

Travel was precarious even at its best. By water, Muscle Shoals was difficult to navigate, and hills and valleys posed major problems for wagons and pack animals crossing the land. Travelers always had to be on the lookout not only for hostile Indians but for thieves and robbers as well. As tough and notorious as any were Micajah and Wiley Harpe ("Big Harpe" and "Little Harpe"), brothers who robbed and sometimes murdered people along the secluded roads and trails. Finally apprehended, Big Harpe was shot and killed shortly after the turn of the century, when he resisted capture, and his brother was hanged in Mississippi in 1804. Others, perhaps less notorious but every bit as vicious, continued to harass travelers and merchants.

Frontier Feuds, Fights, and Frolics The Tennessee frontiersmen of course had few of the means of entertainment enjoyed by the present generation, but they probably had as much fun. "House-raisings" and "barn-raisings" always brought folk together. After the house or barn had been built, or perhaps new ground cleared, brush and branches would be gathered into a common heap and burned. The fire supplied sufficient light to attract people from miles around for an all-night dance and frolic. The blaze, ever shooting skyward as more fuel was piled on, served as an invitation to all.

Corn huskings and quilting parties were held in the autumn at harvest time. Modern farmboys could probably see little amusement in "shucking" corn. The frontier youths, however, chose sides and husked the corn with fervor, always mindful of prizes and refreshments after the task was done. Anticipating a cold winter and the chilling wind that whistled through windows, doors, and cracks between logs, the ladies made quilts—and talked.

Hunting was a sport enjoyed by all; indeed, proper use of guns often meant the difference between life and death on the frontier—or at least between good fare and a vegetarian diet. The meat of wild turkeys, squirrels, venison, and bear graced the tables of frontiersmen. When the men were not on a hunt they often practiced using targets—or perhaps boasted of their skill with a flintlock. When Captain John Rains killed thirty-two bears with his gun, affectionately called "Betsy," he swore that "she" was "a gun that never missed."

Whiskey drinking and tobacco chewing were almost universal vices on the frontier. Most farmers had a "still" with varying capacities for production. Bishop Francis Asbury of Virginia was astounded at the bibulous habits of frontiersmen and lamented that many tavern keepers sold their wares in defiance of scriptural injunctions. Tough old Methodist circuit rider Peter Cartwright, however, knew that it was not uncommon for preachers and laymen alike to take "snorts of redeye" to keep off the winter chills, to ease the pains of rheumatism, or simply for "old times' sake."

Whiskey drinking may have been responsible for some of the fights and brawls on the frontier, but apparently hundreds fought for the sheer love of combat. Although antagonists chiefly used fists, they often resorted to kicking, biting, and clawing. The nose and ears of an opponent were especially vulnerable to biting and clawing, and many a youth was scarred for life after such an encounter. Not infrequently spectators would become so aroused over a fight that they would join in on one side or the other or else start a new one among themselves. At Elkton (in Giles County) in 1816 the champion of the Price family fought the best man of the McKinneys. Before the principals had struck a half-dozen blows, half the crowd had stripped to fight. For hours the community echoed with the sounds of the free-for-all.

Wrestling and boxing—or a combination of both—could be expected at almost any kind of gathering. Political speakings, court meetings, weddings, or even religious revivals were places where one man would pit his strength against that of another. David Crockett once told of attending a wedding party at which even the bride and groom staged a wrestling match just before vows were said. To the amusement of the crowd, Crockett related, the buxom female threw her nervous and fidgety husband-to-be three times in a row.

Horseracing and cockfighting were enjoyed by many. Andrew Jackson's racehorse, Truxton, was known by all people in Middle Tennessee and was a source of great pride to the rising young attorney. William B. Stokes owned Ariel, which competed occasionally with Truxton, and John Coffee, William Dickinson, and others had horses of similar high quality.

People in all walks of life engaged in duels and tavern brawls, but none were more spectacular than those involving Andrew Jackson. As mentioned earlier, Jackson had come into Nashville soon after the frontier town was established, participated in the development of the state constitution, and became Tennessee's first representative to Congress. Born of Scotch-Irish parentage in the Waxhaw area near the boundary of North Carolina and South Carolina, Jackson had participated as a teenager in the Revolution and had settled to practice law in Salisbury, North Carolina, where one contemporary described him as "the most roaring, rollicking, game-cocking, card-playing, mischievous fellow that ever lived in Salisbury." He had little or no formal education but had learned law by reading and observing in the office of a North Carolina attorney. He lingered for a while in Salisbury and then in Jonesboro before coming to Nashville. There he became financially successful, acquired land, married, built a home, and became prominent politically.

When Jackson first came to Nashville he lived at the boarding-house of Mrs. John Donelson, whose husband had commanded the *Adventure*, which had brought settlers to Nashborough. Donelson then died, supposedly at the hands of the Indians, and Mrs. Donelson had to rent rooms. Jackson soon fell in love with her daughter, Rachel, who was married to Lewis Robards. The Robards had been unhappy together and had applied for a divorce in the District of Kentucky, where Robards was a legal resident, and Rachel had come home to her mother. Apparently thinking that the divorce had been granted, Jackson and Rachel went to Natchez and were married. Later, learning that the divorce had not been consummated until sometime after their marriage, they applied for another license and were wed a second time. Consequently, much gossip developed, and Jackson was always very sensitive about the matter.

Jackson seldom fought with ordinary people, but he had a special knack for involving himself with prominent people. He and John

Sevier had quarreled as early as 1796, when the state's brigadier generals, under Sevier's influence, elected George Conway instead of Jackson as major general of the state militia, the highest military position in the state. Jackson could do little about Sevier's preference for Conway, but he became extremely angry when he learned that the governor had referred to him as a "poor, pitiful, pettyfogging lawyer." In the gubernatorial campaign of 1803, in which Sevier defeated Jackson's friend, Archibald Roane, Jackson accused the governor of obtaining thousands of acres of public lands by fraud and bribery. Sevier denied the charge and was furious when Jackson made it public. When the two encountered each other on the public square of Knoxville in October 1803, neither was in a peace-making mood. Both engaged in name-calling and personal abuse, and both boasted of their public services. In response to Jackson's claims, Sevier in disgust and anger spoke words that cut Jackson to the quick. "Services?" shouted the governor. "I know of no great service you have rendered. . . , except taking a trip to Natchez with another man's wife." "Great God," Jackson exclaimed, "do you mention her sacred name?" Both men quickly drew weapons, but bystanders separated them before blood was shed.

The reference to Rachel was too much for Jackson, and on the next day he challenged Sevier to a duel. Sevier suggested that they meet outside the state because dueling was unlawful in Tennessee, but Jackson insisted upon meeting either "in the neighborhood of Knoxville" or near "the Indian boundary line." Although Jackson publicly called Sevier a "coward," tempers cooled sufficiently to avoid a duel. Shortly thereafter, the two met apparently by chance outside Kingston, and after another exchange of harsh words, both went their respective ways without bloodshed. Although Sevier lived for another decade, the two never became friends.

Jackson's most famous duel was fought in 1806 with a young Nashville lawyer named Charles Dickinson after disagreements over horseracing and, according to some reports, more uncomplimentary remarks about Rachel. At any rate, Jackson challenged Dickinson to a duel, and they agreed to meet in Kentucky to avoid violating Tennessee law. Dickinson was probably the best marksman in the state, and Jackson's friends urged the General to call off the fight. Jackson refused. Instead, he planned his strategy well. He knew that if he fired hastily he would miss his target; therefore, he determined to hold his fire until after his opponent had shot. Then, if he were still on his feet, he would take deliberate aim. According to tradition, he carefully selected a coat that was too large for him in order to give a false impression of his size. At the signal given by John Overton, Jackson's second, Dickinson fired hastily. Although Jackson received the bullet in the chest, he did not fall. Showing great pain and bleeding profusely, Jackson raised his gun, took careful aim, and pulled the trigger, but the gun did not fire. Then once again he carefully cocked his pistol, deliberately aimed and fired, and this time mortally wounded the young lawyer. Jackson recovered, but his popularity declined after the duel, and some people considered him little more than a murderer.

Of the frontier brawls and saloon fights, none was better known than a tavern brawl involving Jackson and Thomas Hart Benton in September 1813. Benton and his brother, Jesse, both of Franklin, had been close friends of Jackson; so had William Carroll of Nashville, who later became governor. In June 1813, Jesse, the younger of the brothers, had fought Carroll in a duel in which neither was seriously injured. Jackson had served as Carroll's second. The elder Benton had been in Washington at the time, but when he returned and learned of the duel and Jackson's role in it, he became highly incensed. He believed that the General, being older and more mature than the two contestants, should have prevented the duel; at least he should not have acted as Carroll's second. Talebearers and gossips magnified the quarrel.

In early September, Jackson and his friend John Coffee encountered the Bentons at a Nashville tavern. Soon more than a dozen men were engaged in a brawl featuring gunplay, stabbing, wrestling, fistfighting, and shoving. In the fracas both Jackson and Coffee fired at Thomas Hart Benton but succeeded only in ripping holes in the sleeve of his shirt. One of the Bentons (Jackson never knew which but always thought it was Thomas) shot Jackson in the left shoulder; an artery was severed and the General fell to the floor, bleeding profusely. At this point the brawl ended, and Jackson's friends carried the wounded warrior to the Nashville Inn. There several doctors gathered to attempt to stop the bleeding and succeeded only after the General's blood had soaked through two mattresses. While doctors insisted that Jackson's left arm should be amputated at the shoulder, the Bentons departed defiantly. Jackson recovered, of course, and he and Thomas Benton later became reconciled. The Dickinson-Jackson duel and the Benton-Jackson tavern brawl were by no means unique on the Tennessee frontier, but they gained more publicity than most of the others because of the people involved.

Participants in the frontier feuds and fights often found themselves in court. Long and dramatic trials punctuated by courtroom oratory offered observers relief from the monotony of life on the farm and at home. Whenever court was in session and able lawyers performed, farmers left their crops and headed for the county seat. Not everyone sat in the courtoom, of course. Many swapped horses or bought and sold farm produce on the public square while proceedings were going on inside.

Typical of the many cases tried in the state was one in Franklin in 1811, known as the Magness case, which drew hundreds to the Williamson County courthouse. In October 1810, on the public square at Shelbyville, a close friend of Andrew Jackson named Patton Anderson became involved in a heated argument with three brothers, Jonathan, Perry Green, and David Magness. For years the Magnesses and Andersons had been enemies, and their family feud was known throughout Bedford County. Soon words led to violence, and Anderson drew a dirk. Bystanders separated the antagonists before blood was shed, but Patton Anderson continued to lurk about the court square, exchanging curses with the Magnesses. Finally David Magness pulled a pistol, took a few steps in Anderson's direction, fired, and mortally wounded his enemy of long standing. The three Magnesses were arrested and, when they alleged that they could not get a fair trial in Bedford County and asked for a change of venue, were arraigned in Franklin.

The case attracted an array of legal talent and a courtroom filled with spectators. Appearing for the prosecution were John Haywood, a well-known writer, lawyer, and judge; Jenkins Whiteside, recently elected to the United States Senate; and Thomas Hart Benton and Andrew Jackson. The Magnesses secured Felix Grundy of Nashville, who probably was the best criminal lawyer in the state. After a long trial in which forty-two witnesses were called, David Magness was sentenced to be branded with the letter M (for murderer) and to serve an eleven-month prison term. The other Magnesses were set free.

The amount of violence in early Tennessee probably differed little from that in any other frontier community. The people struggled daily with nature, the elements, and hostile Indians; their hardships had made them fiercely independent and quick to take offense. The severity of the violence was partly offset, perhaps, by fun and frolics, neighborly conduct, and the religious enthusiasm found in most communities.

Frontier Agriculture and Industry ？᳒ The early settlers raised a variety of crops and livestock. Corn was the chief crop because it could be raised so easily and produced so bountifully, requiring a very short growing season; indeed, the soil was so fertile that it required no fertilizer and bottom lands produced sixty bushels an acre. Many other crops were also raised, including wheat and other grain, flax, tobacco, and a variety of vegetables. Cotton became an important product for export especially after Eli Whitney's cotton gin came into use around the turn of the century. Tobacco also became a crop for export. In 1799 the state legislature established inspection stations in Greene County and at four locations in the Cumberland area to determine that tobacco for sale was packed in the prescribed manner and that no foreign matter was included.

Cattle and hogs were so numerous that it is difficult to determine whether a farmer's major interest was livestock or row crops. John Rains, who came to Nashborough with James Robertson, was said to have brought the first "neat cattle" into Tennessee. He had nineteen cows, two steers, a bull, and seventeen horses. Everybody's cattle ran at large, so it was necessary to brand the animals in order to identify them.

Agricultural implements were primitive and were similar to those used in the days of Moses. Plows were made of wood except for an iron point, which was bolted on. Moldboards and iron shares came into use about 1800. Hoes, rakes, and similar implements were widely used. Grain was cut with a sickle or cradle and was separated from straw by the use of a flail or the feet of horses.

An adequate labor supply was no major problem for frontier Tennesseans. "Working parties" filled the need for social activity and also assured farmers of additional hands when house-raisings and barn-raisings required several men. Frontier people married young and soon had a half-dozen or more children who at a very early age performed many necessary chores around the house. As they reached their teens, they took their place with the older children and parents in the fields of corn and cotton. Records indicate that there were a few indentured servants on the early frontier, but by the time

Tennessee became a state the day of the indentured servant had ended. Those who had come to the seaboard states earlier were probably among those who crossed the mountains into Tennessee and Kentucky to assume independence and take up lands of their own.

Negro slaves, never numerous on the Tennessee frontier, nevertheless played a role in the development of the economy. Among the early Wataugans, John Sevier, James Robertson, John Carter, and a few others owned slaves, but the vast majority on the frontier came carrying all of their worldly possessions on a packhorse or two and were too poor to own slaves. The territorial census of 1791 indicated a black population of 3,417. Slaves lived in all the counties; in Hawkins the population was 11.6 percent of the total, and in Davidson County it was nearly 20 percent. By 1800—the date of the first official census after statehood—the slave population of 13,584 made up 12.8 percent of the total. The number of free blacks had declined by that date from 361 to 309. The vast expansion of slavery in the state was to await the development of West Tennessee and the widespread use of the cotton gin, although slaves did play an important role in the development of the iron industry at the forges and furnaces of Montgomery Bell and other entrepreneurs.

Because of the isolation of the Tennessee settlements, the people made much of their clothing and other supplies and thus contributed to the development of manufacturing. Women made cloth at the spinning wheels and hand looms and rendered lard and soap at the kettles. The men in the early days made their own farm implements and household furniture. The first manufacturing establishments outside the homes were blacksmith shops, tanneries, and gristmills for the grinding of wheat and corn.

The development of iron was the largest single industry on the frontier. David Ross, a Virginian of vision, enterprise, and wealth, had already established iron works on the North Fork of the Holston (Hawkins County) by the time William Blount arrived as territorial governor. Moses Cavitt, John Sevier, and others soon became interested in exploiting the rich ore of the eastern mountains, and by the time the territorial legislature met in 1794, lawmakers deemed many of the artisans working at the forges and furnaces to be of such significance that they could be exempted from militia duties. In Middle Tennessee James Robertson established works around

Cumberland Furnace in the 1790s but sold the establishment to Montgomery Bell just after the turn of the century.

Several dozen furnaces and bloomeries were probably in use by 1800. Bloomeries were small forges at which rough wrought iron could be produced, but cast iron came from the larger furnaces. By the turn of the century there were several refinery forges, where the pigs of cast iron were hammered into a finer grade of wrought iron, and a few crude rolling mills, which produced the long flat strips required for making cut nails. Water power was necessary to turn the heavy machinery, so the furnaces were generally built on rivers. Charcoal was the fuel required to separate the ore from the impurities, but it was abundant because of the availability of wood from the nearby virgin forests.

Schools and Churches ⧉ There were no public schools on the frontier and the few private schools afforded only a very small part of the population an opportunity to learn the fundamentals. It seems safe to say that only a small minority of people could "read and write" in the modern sense of the term, although the early records do reveal "signatures" instead of "marks" in the various legal and governmental documents of the time. Private schools were few and many were short-lived. Terms were short. Literate parents no doubt taught their children in the homes when they had time from household chores, while others who could afford a tutor hired one who traveled from farm to farm.

Ministers of the gospel, often among the few who were educated and had the inclination and time during the week, were the teachers and educational leaders. Presbyterian ministers especially were active in establishing frontier schools with terms of short duration and curricula centered upon the classics and Scriptures. The first ministers included Samuel Doak, Thomas Craighead, Hezekiah Balch, and Samuel Carrick.

Doak, a Virginian of Scottish parentage, had come into the Watauga area as early as 1777 as a frontier preacher, and three years later he opened a school at his church near Jonesboro. In 1783 the North Carolina legislature chartered the school as Martin Academy (in honor of Governor Alexander Martin); twelve years later the territorial government issued a new charter and called it Washington

College. Today the school is known as Washington College High School and is a part of the secondary system of Washington County. Craighead, a Princeton classmate of Doak, established Davidson Academy in 1785 in Nashville. Among the first members of the board of trustees was William Polk, grandfather of James Knox Polk. He was replaced as a trustee in 1791 by Andrew Jackson. Davidson became Cumberland College in 1806 and was reincorporated as the University of Nashville in 1826. Balch's school, although chartered in 1794, opened in 1802 as Greeneville College. Carrick opened a "seminary" at his home near Knoxville in the early 1790s, and in the following year the school was chartered as Blount College, after William Blount. Carrick announced publicly that he offered instruction not only in Latin and Greek but also in geography, logic, natural and moral philosophy, astronomy, and rhetoric. Carrick admitted women as well as men, and at least five women attended, including Barbara Blount, a daughter of the territorial governor and first United States senator from Tennessee. The institution grew rapidly after a slow beginning and in 1807 became East Tennessee College and received a land grant under the terms of the Compact of 1806. In 1840 it became East Tennessee University and in 1879 The University of Tennessee.

The anniversary of the first decade after statehood was a significant year for the chartering of academies in Tennessee. According to the Compact of 1806, an agreement among the United States, Tennessee, and North Carolina, chartered academies were to be given grants of land that could be sold to provide operating capital. Unfortunately not all received land, and those that did failed to realize much financial return. Nevertheless, in the legislative session of 1806, petitions for charters were brought from each of the twenty-seven counties of the state. Some of the chartered academies did not open until several decades later, and some never opened. The only other schools known to have existed before 1806 were Union Academy (a predecessor of Maryville College), begun in Knox County in 1806 by the Reverend Isaac Anderson, and Valladolid Academy, started near Nashville in 1805.

The self-confident people who developed the virgin resources of the Tennessee frontier probably would have ignored spiritual matters completely had it not been for a handful of Presbyterian and Baptist ministers who came along with them or soon after the first settlements were made. These frontier preachers helped to counteract the materialistic influences of the frontier environment, baptized converts, performed marriages, conducted funeral services, and otherwise ministered to the needs of the people.

The first Presbyterian preachers to serve Tennessee congregations actually lived in southwestern Virginia. The Reverend Charles Cummings, who had established a church at the site of Abingdon by 1772, considered the people of the North Holston region his spiritual responsibility. Possibly for his convenience, a "meeting house" was built near the site of Blountville. Both Cummings and the Reverend Joseph Rhea, another Presbyterian preacher, accompanied the Christian expedition of 1776 as chaplains. The Reverend Samuel Doak moved from the North Holston settlement to the vicinity of Jonesboro in 1780 and organized the Salem congregation. Not long thereafter came other Presbyterian ministers, including Balch, Carrick, Samuel Henderson, and Gideon Blackburn.

The vast number of Scotch-Irish Presbyterians on the frontier brought about the formation of the Abingdon Presbytery in 1785. In the following year it was divided; the new presbytery, Transylvania, assumed jurisdiction over the churches of the Cumberland Valley as well as the Kentucky region. The first Presbyterian minister of record in the Cumberland settlements was the Reverend Thomas Craighead, who established a church and school at Haysboro in Davidson County (near the present Spring Hill Cemetery). William Hume, encouraged by the settlement of Scotch seceders on the Cumberland, came not long thereafter.

Almost simultaneously with the Presbyterians, ministers of the Baptist faith became active in the Tennessee country. The first two known to have settled there were Matthew Talbot and Jonathan Mulkey, who came into Watauga and Carter's Valley, respectively, as early as 1775. Some Baptist historians contend that Talbot organized in the mid–1770s the first Baptist church in the Tennessee country; others point to Tidence Lane's Buffalo Ridge Church of Washington County, organized in the late 1770s, as being the first.

Seven Baptist churches in the East Tennessee region were organized into the Holston Association in 1786, the same year that the first Baptist church in the Middle Tennessee country was established by the Reverend John Grammer. Ten years later five churches in Middle Tennessee were organized as the Mero Association. By 1803 East Tennessee had about forty-six churches divided between two associations, Holston and Tennessee, in addition to an unknown number of churches not represented in any association—a result of the Baptist policy of emphasizing the independence of individual congregations. Another reason for the rapid growth of the Baptists on the frontier was their willingness to ordain ministers who had little formal education. A special "call" to preach, together with the inspiration of the Spirit, was considered an adequate qualification. Actually, the unlettered frontiersmen felt more at home with the uneducated preachers than with the learned Presbyterian divines.

Another type of preacher who could talk easily with the illiterate pioneers was the sturdy Methodist circuit rider. The first of these in Tennessee was Jeremiah Lambert, who was assigned by the Annual Conference of 1783 to the newly formed Holston Circuit in what is now southwestern Virginia and northeastern Tennessee. The Holston Circuit had about sixty members, and Lambert preached to them—and seventeen more by the end of the year—in their scattered homes. In 1786, the first Methodist church in Tennessee, Acuff's Chapel, was built near Blountville. The next year Holston became a district composed of two circuits, and in 1788 it held the first conference west of the mountains, at Keywood in Virginia. For that occasion the famous Methodist leader, Bishop Francis Asbury, made the first of his sixty-two trips across the Appalachians. While traveling over the district he commented in his *Journal* on the disorders in the state of Franklin. In 1787 a new circuit, a part of Kentucky District, was created for the Cumberland settlements, with Benjamin Ogden as its preacher. Methodism expanded rapidly in that area as well as in East Tennessee. Although the Methodist circuit system was well suited to the frontier, many circuit riders died of consumption or other lingering diseases from the hardships involved in regularly covering circuits that were 400–500 miles in length.

The churches attempted to regulate the conduct of their members, admonished parishioners, and sometimes excommunicated them for such offenses as drunkenness, fighting, dishonesty, and marital unfaithfulness. At Tidence Lane's Bent Creek Baptist Church, for example, both blacks and whites came before the church council when they were accused of sinful acts. Men predominated in the churches. At the Turnbull Baptist Church, for example, a Sister Barfoot was excluded from the fellowship after a church trial "for taking up with a married man" (no reference was made to any punishment for the "married man"), and another woman was admonished for "not being obedient to her husband as directed by Saint Peter."

Apparently the church courts were not very successful in regulating conduct, because the county records abound with criminal and tort suits. Bishop Asbury on one occasion complained of disorders in the state of Franklin and despaired lest frontiersmen should "lose their souls." The Presbyterian General Assembly observed in 1798 "with pain and fearful apprehension" a "general dereliction of religious principles and practices among" the people. "Profaneness, pride, luxury, injustice, intemperance, lewdness, and every species of debauchery and loose indulgence," they said, "greatly abound."[2] Students at one school formally debated the question of whether Christianity had been injurious or beneficial to mankind.

Perhaps the time was ripe for a spiritual awakening and the "Great Revival," which started in the West in 1799. Beginning under the leadership of the able Presbyterian preacher James McGready, in Logan County, Kentucky (commonly called at the time "Rogue's Harbor" and the "Devil's Camp Ground"), the revival had spread into Tennessee by 1800 and had aroused the interest of Baptists, Methodists, and Presbyterians alike. By the fall of 1800 dozens of "protracted meetings" were being held on the Tennessee frontier, with thousands of people in attendance. An amazing lack of decorum characterized the services. Frequent shouts and emotional outbursts were heard in all services and such manifestations as "falling, running, barking, and jerking" transpired. One contemporary in 1808 described the jerking exercise as follows:

> The exercise commonly began in the head which would fly backward and forward, and from side to side with a quick jolt, which the person would naturally labor to suppress, but in vain; and the more one laboured to stay himself and be sober, the more he staggered, and the more rapidly his twitches increased. . . . Head dresses were of little account among the female jerkers. Even handkerchiefs bound tight round the head would be flirted off almost with the first twitch, and the hair put into utmost confusion.[3]

Presbyterians viewed the physicial extravagances with surprise and perhaps disdain, but Methodist and Baptist leaders considered them as a normal response to the demands of a heartfelt religion. Consequently, Presbyterians generally withdrew from the revival

[2] William W. Sweet, *The Story of Religions in America*, 324.
[3] Richard McNemar, *The Kentucky Revival* (Cincinnati, 1808), 61–62.

movement and left the field largely to the other groups. Only a spin-off Presbyterian group organized in Tennessee and called "Cumberland Presbyterians" participated vigorously in revival activities.

The Great Revival had a tremendous effect upon frontier Tennessee and stimulated religious life of the new state. Although the extremes of emotionalism subsided, the camp meeting and summer revival remained a basic feature of the Cumberland Presbyterians, Methodists, and Baptists for many years.

SUGGESTED READINGS

Books

Thomas P. Abernethy, *From Frontier to Plantation in Tennessee* (1932; rpt. University, Ala., 1967); Harriette Arnow, *Seedtime on the Cumberland* (New York, 1960); Arnow, *Flowering of the Cumberland* (New York, 1963); Howard E. Carr, *Washington College* (Knoxville, 1935); Catharine C. Cleveland, *The Great Revival in the West, 1797–1805* (Chicago, 1916); Robert E. Corlew, *A History of Dickson County, Tennessee* (Dickson, 1956); Albert C. Holt, *The Economic and Social Beginnings of Tennessse* (Nashville, 1924), rpt. from *THM* 7 (1921–22), 194–230, 252–94, 8 (1924), 24–86; William H. McRaven, *Life and Times of Edward Swanson* (Nashville, 1937); Walter B. Posey, *The Baptist Church in the Lower Mississippi Valley* (Lexington, Ky., 1957); Posey, *The Development of Methodism in the Old Southwest, 1783–1824* (Tuscaloosa, 1933); Posey, *The Presbyterian Church in the Old Southwest* (Richmond, 1952); O. W. Taylor, *Early Tennessee Baptists* (Nashville, 1957); Ernest T. Thompson, *Presbyterians in the South, 1607–1861* (Richmond, 1963).

Articles

Theron Alexander, Jr., "The Covenanters Come to Tennessee," *ETHSP* 13 (1941), 36–46; Ward Allen, "Cragfont: Grandeur on the Tennessee Frontier," *THQ* 23 (June 1964), 103–20; Elizabeth Skaggs Bowman and Stanley J. Folmsbee, "The Ramsey House: Home of Francis Alexander Ramsey," *THQ* 24 (Fall 1965) 203–18; James A. Crutchfield, "Pioneer Architecture in Tennessee," *THQ* 35 (Summer 1976), 162–74; Pauline Massengill DeFriece and Frank B. Williams, Jr., "Rocky Mount: The Cobb-Massengill Home: First Capitol of the Territory of the United States South of the River Ohio," *THQ* 25 (Summer 1966), 119–34; Margaret Burr DesChamps, "Early Days in the Cumberland Country," *THQ* 6 (Sept. 1947), 195–204; Walter T. Durham, "Kasper Mansker:

Cumberland Frontiersman," *THQ* 30 (Summer 1971) 154–77; Durham, "Thomas Sharp Spencer, Man or Legend," *THQ* 31 (Fall 1972), 240–55; Stanley J. Folmsbee, "Blount College and East Tennessee College, 1794–1840: The First Predecessors of the University of Tennessee," *ETHSP* 17 (1945), 22–50, reprinted in the University of Tennessee *Record,* 49: 1 (Knoxville, 1945), 11–23; Folmsbee and Susan Hill Dillon, "The Blount Mansion: Tennessee's Territorial Capitol," *THQ* 22 (June 1963), 103–22; Anita S. Goodstein, "Leadership on the Nashville Frontier, 1780–1800," *THQ* 35 (Summer 1976), 175–98; Neal O'Steen, "Pioneer Education in the Tennessee Country," *THQ* (Summer 1976), 199–219; Walter B. Posey (ed.), "Bishop Asbury Visits Tennessee, 1788–1815: Extracts from His Journal," *THQ* 15 (Sept. 1956), 253–68; William Flinn Rogers, "Life in East Tennessee Near the End of the Eighteenth Century," *ETHSP* 1 (1929), 27–42; Samuel C. Williams, "Early Iron Works in the Tennessee Country," *THQ* 6 (March 1947) 39–46; Williams, "The South's First Cotton Factory," *THQ* 5 (Sept. 1946), 212–21.

8.

🦢 The Young State, 1796–1821

THE first two and one-half decades after statehood were years of considerable growth and activity. Governor Sevier, the old hero of King's Mountain and many Indian battles, proved his political charisma and was elected six times to the governor's chair. Also serving as governor during the twenty-five years after statehood were Archibald Roane, Willie Blount, and Joseph McMinn, but none had the personal charm and appeal of Nolichucky Jack. Rivaling political events for first place in the attention of the people was a two-year war with Great Britain in which Tennessee earned the sobriquet of "Volunteer State," experienced prosperity and economic development, and finally suffered financial depression culminating in the Panic of 1819.

John Sevier was the logical choice to head the young state and was elected governor in 1796 without opposition. Again in 1797 and 1799 he was chosen without difficulty, and he was prevented from running again in 1801 by a constitutional provision that limited governors to three consecutive terms. His interest in politics was far from satisfied, however, and he was chosen for three additional terms beginning in 1803. Defeated for the United States Senate in 1809 by Joseph Anderson, he was elected to the state legislature in the same year and to Congress in 1811, 1813, and 1815.

During his twelve years in the gubernatorial chair, considerable growth came to Tennessee; the population expanded from about 85,000 in 1796 to nearly 250,000 in 1809 when his final gubernatorial term expired. West Tennessee remained in the hands of the Chickasaws, but most of Middle Tennessee (then called the "Western District") and the counties of the east had been cleared of Indian claims. More than 60 percent of the people lived in Middle Tennessee in 1809 as compared with about 30 percent when Sevier became governor. Most Tennesseans supported the Jeffersonian Republicans instead of the Hamiltonian Federalists. Sevier and Blount were the dominant political figures and both had little or no difficulty in voting for Thomas Jefferson for president. Sevier was a son of the frontier; although Blount had been an eastern Federalist in his early political career, he became identified with the West through his land speculations and his six years as territorial governor. The strong personal animosity that developed between him and Federalist leaders during the territorial period, the criticism of his administration during the debates over admission, and the refusal of the Federalist-dominated Senate to seat him during the statehood controversy alienated him completely. The conduct of William Loughton Smith, Theodore Sedgwick, and others in attempting to delay the admission of Tennessee in 1796 of course destroyed for the Federalists the small amount of support they had in the West.

For forty years of statehood Tennessee was a one-party state. Political contests during that period were therefore based not upon partisanship but upon personal and sectional differences. But even personal and sectional differences remained submerged until the administration of Archibald Roane (1801–1803), so that Sevier's first three terms were years of political harmony. Sevier worked carefully to maintain the confidence of Middle Tennessee's leading politician, Andrew Jackson, who eventually became his bitter enemy. It was largely through the governor's support that Jackson won handily in his race for Congress in 1796. A few years later when Sevier as governor was informed that Jackson wished to become a member of the superior court of the state, he told Jackson that he could consider himself "already appointed."

While Tennesseans were enjoying at least superficial harmony, Europeans were again at war. A struggle that had begun as a class conflict in France soon engulfed most of Great Britain and the Continent. Of considerable concern to Tennesseans and people of the West was the rumor that Spain would be forced to surrender to France the territory west of the Mississippi that France had given her in 1763, along with Spanish Florida to the south. Western settlers had agonized for years over the question of navigation of the Mississippi River and had only begun to prosper after Thomas Pinckney's treaty with Spain in 1795 had secured for Americans free

Tennessee's first governor was John Sevier, 1796–1801, 1803–1809. *Above right:* Archibald Roane, governor, 1801–1803; *below left:* Willie Blount, 1809–1815; *below right:* Joseph McMinn, 1815–1821.

navigation of the river together with the right to sell goods at New Orleans. A much more satisfying rumor was that England was also interested in that territory and might attempt to seize it before France did. To the western people, English occupation of Florida, New Orleans, and the Louisiana Territory was much more desirable, because in 1783 England had promised to guarantee to the Americans free navigation of the Mississippi River. Land prices in the West became depressed as prospective purchasers contemplated French seizure and the possible closing of navigation of the Mississippi. Senator Blount, still the holder of thousands of acres of western lands, determined to do all he could to prevent the land from falling into the hands of the French. He became a ready co-conspirator in a plan to secure the territory for England, a move that cost him his Senate seat and returned him to his home in Tennessee—in disgrace, said his enemies from the East.

The originator of the plan in which Blount became involved was Captain John Chisholm, a Knoxville tavern keeper and renegade soldier of fortune but a British subject. Chisholm apparently unfolded his scheme for the first time in November of 1796 when he discussed the matter with the British minister to America, Robert Liston. Chisholm asked that the British, who were at war with the French and the Spanish, finance expeditions of Americans and Indians against Florida and Louisiana in an effort to take possession of them on behalf of Great Britain. As compensation, the British would grant land to members of the expeditions, appoint Chisholm superintendent of Indian affairs, make Pensacola and New Orleans free ports, and guarantee free navigation of the Mississippi to all Americans. Liston was diplomatically cautious but finally agreed to send Chisholm to London to deal directly with the British authorities; the British, however, flatly rejected the plan.

Meanwhile, Blount had assumed the leadership of the conspiracy and promoted it under the misconception that the British government would be certain to cooperate. Blount's motives were economic. He and his brothers and their associates had greatly overexpanded their land speculations and faced financial bankruptcy because land values were seriously depressed by rumors that the French would soon occupy New Orleans. Success of the Blount scheme would restore land values in the West and thereby provide opportunities for immense profits. Since western interests would be promoted, Blount would also be a hero, with infinite possibilities for political advancement. Blount conferred in New York with a fellow speculator, Dr. Nicholas Romayne, who then went to England to talk with the British, while Blount returned to the Southwest to take preliminary steps for putting the plan in operation.

Blount's activities were interrupted, however, by the calling of a special session of Congress, and the senator was then forced to resort to the dangerous expedient of writing letters. One letter, dated April 21, 1797, was addressed to James Carey, an interpreter in the employ of the federal government and a friend of the senator. Blount confided in the communication that Chisholm's plan would probably be implemented in the fall of that year and that Blount would probably be at "the head of the business on the part of the British." Blount warned Carey against permitting Benjamin Hawkins, acting superintendent of Indian affairs, or any other federal employee to see the letter or to learn of the proposed venture. Finally, Blount cautioned Carey to "read this letter over three times, then burn it."

Nevertheless, Carey permitted a federal employee at Tellico Blockhouse to read the communication. Soon it fell in the hands of Blount's personal enemies in Knoxville, who forwarded it to President John Adams in Philadelphia. Adams referred it to the Senate. Although Blount was evasive about his authorship, several senators—including William Cocke of Tennessee—testified that the document was in Blount's handwriting, and Blount himself admitted it in correspondence with friends in Tennessee.

Blount was expelled immediately from the Senate, and the House of Representatives adopted impeachment charges. He thereupon returned to Tennessee, where he found Jackson, James White, and many other Tennesseans rallying strongly to his defense. The Adams administration was very unpopular in the state, and Blount was described in all sections as merely a victim of partisan prejudice. Legislators offered to return him to the Senate, but he refused, and in 1799 he became speaker of the state senate when James White of Knoxville resigned to become Indian commissioner.

In the meantime, in December 1798, the United States Senate proceeded with the impeachment of Blount, although they had expelled him from the Senate and he was holding another office at the time. Blount did not attend, of course, but he was represented by counsel. His defense was on the question of jurisdiction rather than his guilt or innocence of the charges that he had conspired to violate American neutrality, reduce the influence of American representatives with the Indians, seduce Carey from his duty and trust, and diminish the confidence of the Cherokee Indians in the United States. His lawyers contended that senators were not civil officers in the meaning of the impeachment clause of the Constitution and were therefore not subject to impeachment; and even if they were, Blount had been expelled and was no longer a senator. The Senate decided on January 11, 1799 that it had no jurisdiction in the case and dismissed the impeachment.

There is no doubt that Blount was guilty of the charges, but his provocation was great. Not only was his personal fortune in jeopardy, but the interests of the West were also involved. The Spaniards used the conspiracy as a pretext for their delay in evacuating Natchez, north of the treaty line of 1795, but it seems that the fears aroused by Blount's activities actually led them to evacuate sooner than they might have done otherwise. Also, the United States government was led to pay more attention to the needs of the West than had been the custom—a trend that culminated in the Louisiana Purchase, which placed the Mississippi River entirely in American territory and brought other benefits.

At the time of Blount's impeachment trial in Philadelphia, Blount as senate speaker presided in Knoxville over the impeachment trial of David Campbell, a state judge who had angered both Blount and Sevier with repeated criticism. Blount had been responsible for the Treaty of Holston which, upon being surveyed in 1797, placed many settlers, including the home of Judge Campbell, on the Indian side and thus beyond the bounds of legitimate settlement. When federal troops forcibly removed the judge and others from the Indian lands, Campbell was furious. He castigated Blount for the treaty and Sevier for his cooperation with federal officials in the forced removal. A short time later, when Blount sued another critic for slander, Campbell as judge dismissed the suit before it even came to trial. When Blount presented these facts to Sevier and claimed that Campbell had exhibited "either extreme ignorance of the law" or "corruption in office," Sevier urged house leaders to bring impeachment charges.

The house of representatives prepared impeachment charges and the trial opened on December 24, 1798 before the senate, which sat as a court and with Blount as not only the presiding officer but also the chief prosecutor. Campbell, charged with "contempt of the authority . . . and the high trust in him reposed," heard various witnesses testify both for and against him on three successive days, including Christmas. When the final vote came, only six senators voted "guilty"; seven votes—a two-thirds majority—were needed to convict.

Although Blount was disappointed at the outcome of the Campbell case, he nevertheless continued to rebuild his political strength. At one point he prepared to assume the governorship, as talk developed that Sevier, recently appointed brigadier general by President Adams, might be pressed into military service when relations between the United States and France became strained in 1798–1800.

Blount died suddenly on March 21,1800, however, and Jackson sought to become the new leader of Blount's political faction. Jackson had been elected to Congress in 1796, and in the following year he was elected to the United States Senate. Unhappy in Philadelphia, he resigned and was appointed to the state superior court. Daniel Smith from near Gallatin was chosen to serve in the Senate as Jackson's replacement until the next meeting of the legislature, at which time Joseph Anderson was chosen to fill out the term and William Cocke was elected to a six-year term. Soon Jackson's ambitions to control the state brought him into a head-on clash with Sevier. The East Tennessean emerged the victor. Jackson's political stature declined after 1803, and only his spectacular victory at New Orleans in 1815 returned him to power. Sevier died in Alabama in the same year.

After serving three terms, Sevier retired as governor in 1801 and was replaced by Archibald Roane. In his valedictory, Sevier spoke of the tremendous progress made in the state during the past six years. Roane, an East Tennessean who had helped write the constitution in 1796, was a scholar of mild temperament easily dominated by Jackson. He was a member of the first superior court of the state, and as a member of that body he had come to know Jackson, whose support helped to sweep him to an almost unanimous victory. He received 8,438 votes, while his opponent, Sheriff John Boyd of Nashville, polled fewer than a dozen votes. The governor was one of many Tennesseans who, born in Pennsylvania, had moved down the valley of Virginia and into Tennessee. He settled first in Jonesboro and then moved to Jefferson County, where he practiced law and served as attorney general.

With Sevier's political future uncertain, Jackson now moved to

make his political domination of the state complete by openly court-
ing East Tennesseans of prominence and exerting his influence over
Roane. Soon after Roane was inaugurated, General George Conway
died, and Jackson, desiring the prestige and influence of high military
rank, moved to gain the highest military position in the state. He was
encouraged by his friends and especially by Judge Campbell, who
had made enemies of both Sevier and Blount and now looked to
Jackson as a political mentor.

Sevier had for years considered himself the leading military man in
Tennessee by virtue of his successes against both the British and the
Indians, and he refused to permit Jackson to assume the position of
major general unchallenged. As the field officers of the state prepared to select Conway's successor, they found that they must choose
among Sevier, Jackson, and James Winchester of Sumner County.[1]
When votes were cast, Jackson and Sevier had 17 each and Winchester had three. Sevier proposed another ballot, confident that he
could secure two of the three votes given Winchester, because all
three had come from Winchester's personal friends in East Tennessee. Jackson refused, however, and insisted that the governor cast
the deciding vote, as directed by law. This Roane did—for Jackson—and the Hero of the Hermitage was elected. While this action
placed Jackson in the state's highest military position, it also assured
Roane of an opponent in 1803, since Sevier now made plans to
return to the gubernatorial chair.

As the two prepared for the inevitable clash in 1803, Jackson
carefully considered strategy to help Roane secure reelection. In
1797, shortly after his election to the Senate, Jackson had secured
information that wholesale land frauds had been perpetrated at
several of the land offices of the state. To his amazement, Jackson's
information seemed to implicate prominent men who included
Sevier and—interestingly—Jackson's brother-in-law, Stockley Donelson. As Jackson allegedly observed, "When you set a bear trap, you
never can tell what particular bear is going to blunder into it." James
Glasgow, North Carolina's secretary of state, was intricately involved
and was forced to resign from office, while North Carolina
authorities tried on several occasions to bring Donelson to North

---

[1] Field officers—two majors and one colonel—were elected in each of three
military districts by the freemen between eighteen and fifty years of age who were
subject to military duty. The field officers in the three districts elected a brigadier
general, and together they selected a major general.

Carolina for trial; Jackson's kinsman was saved only by Roane's refusal to grant extradition.

Jackson published his charges alleging that Sevier had forged 165 warrants for 640 acres each and that the governor had bribed Glasgow to issue grants of land to him based on the warrants. The main charge against Sevier dealt with an arrangement he had made in 1795 with Glasgow to void a serious monetary loss that Sevier had suffered through no fault of his own. Sevier still had in his possession a great number of land warrants acquired under the Confiscation Act of 1779; he had purchased land confiscated from alleged Tories, but some of these Tories were able to retain the land by proving that they were unjustly charged. Although Sevier was then entitled to the same number of acres of substitute lands, there was almost no unappropriated land of value in Washington County. He therefore arranged with Glasgow to shift the warrants (changing the "consideration" from fifty shillings to $10) to the virgin country west of the Cumberland Plateau. For this favor Sevier gave Glasgow three of the warrants, saying in his letter that he hoped they would be sufficient to pay the fees to which Glasgow was entitled. Jackson, however, claimed that the three warrants, which he said were worth at least $960, constituted a bribe to Glasgow for performing an illegal act. Sevier and his friends insisted that Glasgow had committed no crime—that the payment was no more than a reasonable compensation for services rendered. Although there were some irregularities in Sevier's conduct, the people apparently condoned them and ignored the remainder of Jackson's charges. It was Andrew Jackson rather than John Sevier who suffered the greater loss of popularity as a result of the controversy. Sevier was elected by a comfortable vote of 6,780 to 4,923 for Roane.

Sevier was inaugurated on September 23, and scarcely a week had elapsed when the feud with Jackson was reopened. After a chance meeting on the streets of Knoxville during which each berated the other, Sevier wrote Jackson on October 2:

> Your ungentlemanly and Gasconading conduct of yesterday have unmasked yourself to me and to the world. The voice of the Assembly has made you a Judge, and this alone has made you worthy of . . . notice; to this office I have respect and this alone makes you worthy of my notice.

When Jackson proposed a duel near Knoxville, Sevier informed him that dueling in Tennessee was illegal and proposed that they meet outside the state. The governor wrote:

> I have some regard for the laws of the State over which I have the honor to preside, although you, a Judge, appear to have none. It is hoped that if by any strange and unexpected event you should ever be metamorphosed into an upright and virtuous Judge, you will feel the propriety of being Governed and Guided by the laws of the State you are sacredly bound to obey and regard. As to answering all your jargon of pretended bravery, I assure you it is perfectly beneath my character, having never heard of any you ever exhibited.

Jackson continued to lose in his encounters with Sevier, and his popularity and power declined. On October 11 Jackson did "pronounce, Publish, and declare to the world" that "his Excellency, John Sevier, Esq., Governor, Captain-general, and Commander-in-Chief of the land and naval forces of the State of Tennessee" was "a base coward and poltroon," but the two failed to meet in a duel. Jackson, in a fighting mood, a few days later exchanged blows with William Maclin, Tennessee's secretary of state, after he heard Maclin speak approvingly of Sevier. In the following year the governor's partisans in the legislature separated the state into two militia divisions, each commanded by a major general, so that Jackson lost command of the eastern division. In 1804 Jackson resigned his position on the superior court and vainly sought an appointment as governor of the Louisiana Territory, but the post went instead to W. C. C. Claiborne, a friend and former protégé of Sevier. Jackson retired to his plantation at the Hermitage with a deep sense of rejection, but emerged in 1806 to fight a duel with Charles Dickinson, an encounter which nearly cost him his life. His association, however brief, with Aaron Burr, who later was tried for treason, temporarily cost him just about all of his remaining stature before the people.

Sevier was reelected in 1805, this time defeating challenger Roane by a vote of 10,730 to 5,909. Two years later he was again elected when William Cocke offered only token opposition. He became the subject of a lengthy and flattering legislative resolution of appreciation upon his retirement from the gubernatorial chair in 1809. He was promptly elected to the state senate from Knox County and to Congress in 1811. He was still congressman when he died in 1815, on a federal mission to determine a Creek boundary in Alabama.

The gubernatorial contest of 1809 brought forth former United

States Senator William Cocke and Montgomery County farmer Willie Blount, who boasted widely of his blood relationship (half-brother) to the late territorial governor. Voting was largely along sectional lines. Middle Tennessee, now containing nearly two-thirds of the state's population, elected Blount, although Cocke carried East Tennessee by a substantial majority. Blount was reelected in 1811 and again in 1813.

Not long after Blount's election, Judge William Cocke was jailed, impeached, and convicted. Legislators during the first few decades of statehood carefully scrutinized the conduct of public officials, particularly judges. Judge David Campbell was impeached twice (in 1798 and 1803) but on each occasion was acquitted. Sevier and others were critical of Jackson while he was on the bench, and he ultimately resigned. But in 1812 Judge Cocke, who recently had been elected to preside over the first judicial circuit, became the first jurist to be impeached and convicted. Accused of using his office for private gain, he was jailed in Knoxville as noted above, and was subsequently tried, convicted, and removed from office by the state senate, of which his son, John Cocke, was speaker. Interestingly, Cocke was elected to the legislature the following year, and in 1814 President Madison named him agent to the Chickasaw Indians. He thereupon moved to Columbus, Mississippi, where he died in 1823.

A matter to which legislators turned their attention not long after Blount's inauguration was that of legislative reapportionment and the movement of the capital to Nashville. The constitution of 1796 had called for periodic reapportion of the legislature so that the lawmakers might be fairly distributed among the various counties according to the number of taxable inhabitants. The number of representatives was established at 26 until the population reached 40,000 taxable inhabitants, and the representatives could not exceed 40. The number of senators was to be not less than one-third or more than one-half the number of house members. In 1812 Blount called the legislature into special session to consider the matter of reapportionment. Ten years earlier, East Tennessee had had a clear majority in both houses—8 of the 13 senators and 15 of the 26 representatives. In the apportionment of 1812, however, the population of West Tennessee (as present-day Middle Tennessee was then called) had increased to such an extent that the section gained a majority in both the senate and the house of representatives. The westerners, exhilarated at the thought of controlling the legislature and consigning the eastern counties to a minority status, promptly voted to move the seat of government to Nashville. Consequently, when the legislature assembled in regular session in September 1812, they met in Nashville. The capital was returned to Knoxville for a two-year period (1817–1818) and then moved back west to stay.

Tennessee and the War of 1812 ஜ⊷ The second war with England, the War of 1812, overshadowed everything else in Blount's tenure as governor. For several decades after independence, the United States failed to gain the respect among the nations of the world that it deserved as a free and independent country. For thirteen years after the Revolution ended, Great Britain kept troops on American soil. For several years the British refused to negotiate a satisfactory treaty of commerce with the Americans. After the French Revolution broadened into a European struggle, both the French and the British stopped and searched American ships on the Atlantic and sometimes seized their cargoes as contraband of war. Because the British had the largest navy, they caused more damage to our trade than did the French.

The Americans had other complaints against the British. That nation practiced "impressment of American seamen"; that is, British vessels stopped American ships to search for British deserters and often seized sailors and "impressed" them into the British navy. While they were usually careful to seize only deserters, there was always the possibility of mistaken identity. When the captain of the British ship *Leopard* fired on the American *Chesapeake* in 1807 because its captain refused to permit a search for deserters, Americans were furious. Tennesseans across the state held mass meetings of protest, and legislators adopted a resolution asserting that "the latest encroachment" should be resisted. Early in 1809 they addressed a letter to President Madison, assuring him that the people of Tennessee would "make any sacrifices" necessary to preserve the honor and integrity of their country.

Like other westerners, Tennesseans were interested in expansion. Indeed, Congressman Felix Grundy expressed the sentiment of many when he exclaimed on the floor of the House of Representatives in 1811, "I therefore feel anxious not only to add the Floridas to the South, but Canada to the North of this empire." Canada belonged to Great Britain, and Florida was claimed by Spain. Tennes-

seans, however, had strongly supported Jefferson's claim that West
Florida (now southern Alabama and Mississippi) had been included
in the Louisiana Purchase of 1803. As prices paid for their cargoes
declined at New Orleans because of trade interruptions incident to
the European war, Tennesseans sought to use a shortcut to the Gulf
of Mobile, which was possible because of the proximity of the Coosa
and Tombigbee rivers to branches of the Tennessee. Mobile could be
seized even in a war with England, Americans claimed, if they could
establish its strategic need. In 1811 a new and vigorous group of
young Congressmen took office in Washington. All of them, including Tennesseans Grundy, John Rhea, and John Sevier, John C.
Calhoun of South Carolina, William Crawford of Georgia, and
Henry Clay of Kentucky, believed that the United States had ample
cause to declare war upon Great Britain immediately. Tennessee's
senators were not silent. Joseph Anderson, dean of the Tennessee
congressional delegation, talked of war and helped plan military
strategies against Canada when war came. George W. Campbell, a
Tennessee senator, informed both Governor Blount and Major
General Jackson in 1811 that war was inevitable. He believed that a
military victory would be required to lift the United States "from her
present degraded position in the eyes of the world."

Finally, the southern Indians, especially the Creeks, were a source
of constant trouble for Tennesseans. Jackson and other prominent
leaders had claimed for years that the British encouraged the Indians
to make raids on the southern settlements, and presented evidence
that they actually supplied the red men with guns and ammunition.
Congressman Rhea believed that only by taking Canada could we
pay England back for inciting "Indians to disturb and harass our
frontier" and "murder and scalp helpless women and children."

Although congressmen from the East opposed war, they could not
withstand the influence of the South and West. Consequently, on
June 18, 1812, war was declared, with Tennesseans and others of
those sections voting unanimously in favor of the declaration. The
news of war reached Tennessee in time to be a subject for Fourth of
July orations across the state. Governor Blount publicly stated that
"our cause is a good one," and legislators unanimously resolved that
the declaration was "an act of indispensable necessity for the sovereign welfare, happiness, and safety of the . . . people."

Major General Andrew Jackson hailed the war as a new day.
Already greatly encouraged by the election of Blount to the govern-

orship, Jackson saw in the opportunity to command on the field of battle a chance to recoup his political fortunes at home. He was not to be disappointed. In October, President Madison asked Governor Blount for 1,500 men to take Florida. Blount called upon Jackson, who hastily mustered 2,000 men into service and proceeded south. Unknown to the Tennesseans, a majority of Congress opposed a war of conquest against Spanish Florida. When Jackson arrived at Natchez, he was ordered to proceed no further and a few days later was dismissed without pay, supplies, or transportation because Congress had failed to sanction President Madison's plans. Jackson courageously escorted the men back to Nashville and won enroute the admiration of his troops and the sobriquet of "Old Hickory," which he proudly wore for the remainder of his life.

Meanwhile, two other groups of soldiers marched off to war. Colonel John Williams, Governor Blount's adjutant general, led several hundred men to join Georgia troops in a proposed conquest of Florida. Like Jackson's men, they were denied the opportunity of conquest in the Spanish territory and contented themselves with a few forays against hostile Indians before returning to their homes in East Tennessee. Other troops were sent north under General James Winchester of Sumner County, who had been commissioned a brigadier general to participate in what proved an unsuccessful attempt to invade Canada. Winchester's troops were surprised by a combination of British and Indian forces early in January 1813 at Frenchtown near the River Raisin, where the Tennesseans were forced to surrender.

A major part of Tennessee's military activity during the War of 1812 was against the Creek Indians, following the massacre of Americans in August 1813 at Fort Mims (in southern Alabama). The attack was the work of a faction of the Creeks called the "Red Sticks." Although the action was probably due more to a civil war among the Creeks—between the primitive Red Sticks and the more civilized mixed-breeds—than to incitement by British, the warlike faction became British allies, and thus the Creek War was a phase of the War of 1812.

Without waiting for federal authorization, the Tennessee legislature called for 3,500 volunteers, and in accord with the tradition that was to give Tennessee the name of "Volunteer State," recruitment was enthusiastic. Two armies were organized, one under the command of General Jackson in Middle Tennessee and the other under

General John Cocke in East Tennessee. Jackson had been seriously wounded in a brawl with Jesse and Thomas Hart Benton after he served as William Carroll's second in a duel with Jesse, but he left his bed of convalescence to assume command. After establishing a supply base called Fort Deposit at the "bend" of the Tennessee River, Jackson cut a road to the Coosa River. There he built Fort Strother, only thirteen miles from the Creek town of Tallushatchee, which he soon destroyed with a force led by General John Coffee. Jackson marched to the relief of the friendly Creek town of Talladega, which was beseiged by the Red Sticks. A quick end to the war was prevented, however, when a portion of Cocke's army attacked a Creek faction that was attempting to sue for peace.

Jackson also had trouble because of the disposition of his troops. Mutiny was caused first by the lack of supplies and later by disputes regarding terms of service. Although he dealt vigorously with the mutineers, on one occasion putting a gun across the back of a horse and promising to shoot the first soldier who took another step toward home, Jackson finally had to release his troops and wait for another army to be recruited. When that was accomplished, he was able to crush the Creeks at the Battle of Tohopeka, or Horseshoe Bend, on March 27, 1814. In this bloody engagement not only Jackson but other Tennesseans, including William Carroll, John Williams, and Sam Houston, achieved reputations that were to pave their roads to political success.

Jackson was soon appointed major general in the United States army and was given command of the Seventh Military District; Carroll succeeded him as major general of the Middle Tennessee militia. These generals and other Tennesseans soon engaged the British along the Gulf coast. After successfully defending Mobile and driving the British out of Pensacola, Jackson assumed command at New Orleans. His successful repulse on January 8, 1815 of the British effort to take New Orleans was the high water mark of his military career and a stepping-stone toward the presidency. Although the battle was fought after the treaty of peace had been signed with the British, the Battle of New Orleans contributed greatly to the rise of a spirit of nationalism in the United States and increased respect for the nation abroad. It has been argued that if the British had taken New Orleans, they would have refused to execute the treaty, still not ratified, and would have attempted to restore the Louisiana country to Spain.

Jackson's popularity was further increased in 1818 by his invasion of Spanish East Florida, a region long desired by the United States. Jackson was instructed to chase the marauding Seminole Indians back into Spanish territory, if necessary, but he also took possession of the forts at St. Marks and Pensacola and seized and executed two British subjects who had been aiding the Indians. Although Jackson claimed he had received authorization from President Monroe, his actions became the subject of a congressional investigation, which merely increased his stature as a national hero. After the United States acquired the territory in 1819 in a purchase agreement, Jackson served for a few months as the territorial governor. Thus Jackson, who ten years earlier had almost despaired of any opportunity for political success, was now hailed as a hero second only to Washington and fully qualified to become president of the country!

McMinn Elected Governor ॑३॓ With the end of the War of 1812 also came the end of Blount's six years as governor, and in the election of 1815 there was no dearth of candidates. Five men ran. They included Jesse Wharton, who had served in both houses of Congress; Robert Weakley, who had not only served in Congress but had also been speaker of the senate; Thomas Johnson, who had helped write the state constitution and later served in the legislature; Robert C. Foster, who had been speaker of the house of representatives; and Joseph McMinn who not only served in the constitutional convention but also was chosen three times as speaker of the senate. People of the Western District divided their votes among Wharton, Weakley, Johnson, and Foster, but East Tennesseans concentrated on Joseph McMinn of Hawkins County, who like many others in East Tennessee had been born in Pennsylvania and had entered Tennessee through the Valley of Virginia. Although its voters were now a minority, East Tennessee was chiefly responsible for McMinn's more than 15,600 votes, while his opponents split the remaining 22,000 votes. He was the last East Tennessean to serve as governor until 1853, when Andrew Johnson of Greeneville was chosen.

McMinn was reelected twice. His six years in the governor's chair began in widespread prosperity and ended in depression. He was a popular governor—at least until the advent of hard times in 1819— but he proposed little by way of innovation. He preferred instead to follow the patterns set by John Sevier and others with regard to Indian affairs and other matters.

The state grew considerably during McMinn's administration, as evidenced by the census of 1820, which showed a population almost twice that of ten years earlier. During his term the Jackson Purchase of 1818 cleared the vast and fertile area between the Tennessee and Mississippi rivers of the Chickasaw claims and brought vast agricultural growth to the state.

Closely associated with both the prosperity and the depression that followed was the development of banking throughout the state. Use of distant markets and the many commercial transactions made by Tennesseans caused credit facilities and bills of exchange to become necessary. The Bank of Nashville was the first bank in Tennessee. It was chartered in 1807, and in 1811 its charter was renewed for ten years. At the same time the Bank of the State of Tennessee at Knoxville was chartered for thirty years. Branches were approved for Nashville, Clarksville, Jonesboro, Columbia, and Franklin. Within the next few years banks were established at Fayetteville, Kingston, Maryville, Murfreesboro, Rogersville, Shelbyville, Winchester, and perhaps elsewhere. Many of these banks followed very poor banking practices from the very beginning by lending money without adequate collateral and by retaining little or no reserve.

The banks of that time differed somewhat from those of today in that they not only received deposits and made loans but also issued negotiable notes. When a person borrowed money, he received a printed note that circulated as money. The bank was supposed to redeem the notes in gold or silver (specie) upon demand, but few people made this demand, believing that the banks could redeem their notes.

The orgy of speculation encouraged by the banks led to the inevitable hard times of 1819. The price of cotton and other products fell, mortgages were foreclosed, trade lagged, and people suddenly became afraid that their paper notes would become worthless. They rushed to the banks to exchange them for specie only to find that all the banks had suspended specie payment except the Bank of the State of Tennessee at Knoxville, of which Hugh Lawson White was president.

The depression was most serious in the Cumberland area, where the boom had reached greater heights than in the eastern division. During the session of 1819, the Middle Tennessee legislators pushed through a "stay law" called the "Endorsement Act," which postponed the execution of judgments for two years unless the creditor agreed to accept depreciated paper money in payment. This enabled the merchants to hold off their eastern creditors at least temporarily. In 1820, at the insistence of Middle Tennesseans, McMinn called a special session of the legislature to deal with the problems. Felix Grundy promptly offered a bill that provided additional relief for debtors. As mentioned earlier, Grundy had been a War Hawk in 1811 but had resigned his seat in Congress in 1814 and had resumed the practice of law in Nashville. In 1819, however, he became a member of the state legislature and soon championed the cause of the debtors by proposing the creation of a new "Bank of the State of Tennessee" (generally called "the new state bank" to avoid confusion with "the old state bank" of Knoxville), which would be entirely state owned. Through its loan offices in Nashville and agencies in all the counties, the new bank was authorized to lend at 6 percent interest a minimum of $1 million to the hard-pressed citizens. The paper money issued for this purpose was to be backed by the proceeds of the sale of the state's public lands. The new bank, although helpful, did not solve all the problems. Depression continued for several years. The bank itself met with many problems. Officials of the other banks, having been opposed to the establishment of the new bank in the first place, refused to cooperate with it. Books were kept in a deplorable manner, and some funds were apparently embezzled. When McMinn's term ended in 1821 the people were still plagued with hard times. It was during the administration of the next governor, William Carroll, also of Pennsylvania, that prosperity returned to the Volunteer State.

SUGGESTED READINGS

Books
Thomas P. Abernethy, *The Burr Conspiracy* (New York, 1954); Abernethy, *The South in the New Nation* (Baton Rouge, 1961); Claude A. Campbell, *The Development of Banking in Tennessee* (Nashville, 1932); Samuel Carter, *Blaze of Glory: The Fight for New Orleans, 1814–1815* (New York, 1971); William N. Chambers, *Old Bullion Benton: Senator from the New West* (New York, 1956); David Crockett, *Autobiography of David Crockett* (New York, 1923); Carl Driver, *John Sevier: Pioneer of the Old Southwest* (Chapel Hill, 1932); R. E. Folk, *Battle of New Orleans: Its Real Meaning* (Nashville, 1935); Reginald Horsman, *The Causes of the War of*

1812 (Philadelphia, 1962); Marquis James, *The Life of Andrew Jackson* (Indianapolis, 1938); James, *The Raven: A Biography of Sam Houston* (New York, 1929); Eric Russell Lacy, *Vanquished Volunteers: East Tennessee Sectionalism from Statehood to Secession* (Johnson City, Tenn., 1965); Joseph Parks, *Felix Grundy: Champion of Democracy* (Baton Rouge, 1949); Robert V. Remini, *Andrew Jackson and the Course of American Empire, 1767–1821* (New York, 1977); Ronald N. Satz, *American Indian Policy in the Jacksonian Era* (Lincoln, Neb., 1975); James A. Shackford, *David Crockett: The Man and the Legend,* ed. John B. Shackford (Chapel Hill, 1956); Arthur P. Whitaker, *The Mississippi Question, 1795–1803* (New York, 1934).

Articles
Thomas P. Abernethy, "The Early Development of Commerce and Banking in Tennessee," *MVHR* 14 (Dec. 1927), 311–25; William E. Beard, "Joseph McMinn, Tennessee's Fourth Governor," *THQ* 4 (June 1945), 154–66; Aaron Boom, "John Coffee, Citizen Soldier," *THQ* 22 (Sept. 1963), 223–37; William N. Chambers, "Thwarted Warrior: The Last Years of Thomas Hart Benton in Tennessee, 1812–1815," *ETHSP* 22 (1950), 19–44; Paul M. Fink, "Russell Bean, Tennessee's First Native Son," *ETHSP* 37 (1965), 31–48; Stanley J. Folmsbee and Anna Grace Catron, "The Early Career of David Crockett," *ETHSP* 28 (1956), 58–85; L. Paul Gresham, "Hugh Lawson White as a Tennessee Politician and Banker, 1807–1827," *ETHSP* 18 (1946), 25–46; David Edwin Harrell, "James Winchester," *THQ* 17 (Dec. 1958), 301–17; Joseph T. Hatfield, "William C. C. Claiborne, Congress, and Republicanism, 1797–1804," 11 *THQ* 24 (Summer 1965), 157–80; Leota D. Maiden, "Colonel John Williams," *ETHSP* 30 (1958), 7–46; Robert V. Remini, (ed.), "Andrew Jackson's Account of the Battle of New Orleans," *THQ* 26 (Spring 1967), 23–42; Norman Risjord, "The War Hawks and the War of 1812," *Indiana Magazine of History* 60 (1964), 155–58; C. G. Sellers, Jr., "Banking and Finance in Jackson's Tennessee," *NCHR* 41 (June 1954), 61–84; Joe Gray Taylor, "Andrew Jackson and the Aaron Burr Conspiracy," *WTHSP* I (1947), 81–90; W. A. Walker, Jr., "Martial Sons: Tennessee Enthusiasm for the War of 1812," *THQ* 20 (March 1961), 20–37.

9.

N O possession was so highly prized on the frontier as land, and speculators such as William Blount and John Sevier numbered their acres in the hundreds of thousands. The Indians owned the land by right of prior occupation, of course, and it was only with reluctance that they surrendered it to the hoards of whites who came in increasing numbers. But within four decades after Tennessee became a state, the natives had been expelled to lands west of the Mississippi River. The transfer of Indians and the acquisition of public lands vied with politics and war during the first quarter-century for prime attention in the minds of Tennesseans.

The Cherokee were numerous and well established in East Tennessee by the time of statehood. Their towns extended from western North Carolina into northern Georgia. The Chickasaw Indians claimed and hunted the land eastward from the Mississippi to the Tennessee River, although they lived primarily south of Tennessee in what is now the state of Mississippi. At the time of statehood in 1796, approximately three-fourths of Tennessee was still claimed by these two major tribes. Other Indians located both to the north and to the south included the Iroquois, Shawnee, and Creek, and they also hunted on the land during game season but always returned to their towns and settlements on less disputed and safer grounds. The tribes jealously guarded their lands against the encroachments of the whites but slowly gave way before the advancing European civilization until late in the 1830s, when they were forcibly removed.

Even before the Revolution began, British superintendents of Indian affairs, in cooperation with the colonial governors of North Carolina and Virginia, negotiated with the Cherokee for lands along the Holston and Watauga rivers. Some land rights were gained in 1768 and 1770 in the treaties of Hard Labor, Fort Stanwix, and Lochaber. A few years later Richard Henderson negotiated the Transylvania Purchase, by which Indians surrendered their claims to a substantial portion of Middle Tennessee. Negotiations continued after the Southwest Territory was created in 1790. As superintendent of Indian affairs, Governor Blount negotiated the Treaty of the Holston in 1791, by which the Cherokee surrendered title to all lands east of the Clinch River and north of a line from near Kingston to the North Carolina boundary. The Holston line, finally surveyed in 1797 by Benjamin Hawkins, showed that some of the settlers had established homes on Indian territory, and those who refused to move peacefully were forcibly ejected. The legislature protested the action of federal authorities, and Congress responded with the appointment of commissioners who induced the Indians to cede two additional tracts. One tract lay between the Hawkins line (east of Chilhowee Mountain) and the Tennessee and Little Tennessee rivers; the other lay between the Clinch River and the eastern edge of the Cumberland Plateau. This treaty, guaranteeing the Cherokee "the remainder of their country forever," was signed at Tellico Blockhouse on October 2, 1798 and later became known as the First Treaty of Tellico.

Tennesseans, disappointed by the smallness of the cession, urged federal authorities to seek more land. President Adams refused, however, and state officials awaited the results of the presidential election of 1800 with considerable interest. Thomas Jefferson was strongly supported by the west and was sympathetic to its problems, and when he became president in 1801, Tennesseans confidently reopened negotiations with Washington authorities. Soon after Jefferson's inauguration, the new president recommended the extinction of Cherokee claims north of the Duck River, but it was October 1805 before Indians ceded all their claims north of the Duck River in the Third Treaty of Tellico.[1] These negotiations, concluded by Indian Agent Return Jonathan Meigs and Daniel Smith, relinquished Indian claims to approximately the northern two-thirds of the section of the state that lay between the Tennessee River on the east and the west. Inasmuch as it included the entire width of the Cumberland Plateau, the Indian barrier between the eastern settlements and the

---

[1] The Second Treaty of Tellico did not include lands in Tennessee.

Cumberland was now removed, a change that facilitated civil jurisdiction over contiguous territory.

A few days later the commissioners, believing the Cherokee leaders to be "possessed of a spirit of conciliation," secured the valuable land occupied by the United States garrison at Southwest Point (Kingston). The acquisition included a road through the Cherokee Nation from Tellico to the Tombigbee River that would facilitate travel and mail delivery from Knoxville to New Orleans. The tribe was paid an additional $1,600 and was assured that Southwest Point was a "desirable place" to locate the capital of the state.[2]

In the following year authorities purchased the claims of the Cherokee and Creeks to the area between the Duck River and the southern boundary of the state. Meigs and Smith purchased Creek claims for $14,000. Secretary of War Henry Dearborn received a delegation of Cherokee in Washington shortly thereafter and purchased their claim to the area. The Cherokee were given $10,000, a gristmill, and a cotton gin; Chief Black Fox received an annuity of $100 for life.

As a result of these Indian cessions, shown in map 5, migration to Tennessee increased enormously. During the first decade of the nineteenth century the free white population increased 137 percent and the slave population grew by almost twice that amount—a development that made necessary the creation of many new counties. During the first eleven years of statehood the number of counties in East Tennessee increased from eight to seventeen and those in Middle Tennessee from three to about six times that number.

Meanwhile, Tennesseans became interested in President Jefferson's proposal to remove all the Indians living east of the Mississippi River to the recently acquired area known as the Louisiana Purchase. Indian Agent Meigs was instructed by Washington superiors to spread the idea of removal among the Cherokee, and he was at first so successful that he had to undo some of his work because Congress had not appropriated enough money to remove all who were willing to go. Of those who did move, the largest number seems to have been from the Tennessee part of the Cherokee country. Not having any specific lands assigned to them, the Indians became involved in

[2] The legislature cooperated by providing in 1805 that the "next meeting" of the General Assembly would be held at Southwest Point. It did meet there for one day—on September 21, 1807—but enacted no measures except to adopt a resolution moving the capital back to Knoxville.

difficulties with their new neighbors in the west. In 1817 these Indians sent a delegation to a conference of the eastern Cherokee and a federal commission headed by Andrew Jackson and Governor Joseph McMinn. As a result, the Upper Cherokee obtained an

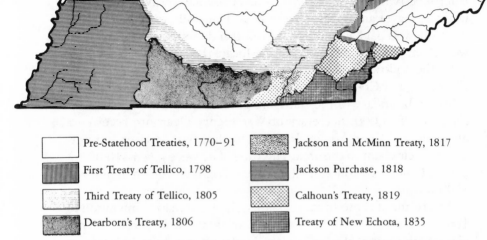

	Pre-Statehood Treaties, 1770–91		Jackson and McMinn Treaty, 1817
	First Treaty of Tellico, 1798		Jackson Purchase, 1818
	Third Treaty of Tellico, 1805		Calhoun's Treaty, 1819
	Dearborn's Treaty, 1806		Treaty of New Echota, 1835

Map 5. Indian Treaty Cessions. Conflicting Chickasaw claims with the Cherokee east of the Tennessee River had been removed by treaties of 1805 and 1816.

assignment of lands along the Arkansas and White rivers in exchange for a Cherokee cession of land in Georgia and the Sequatchie Valley in Tennessee. The United States promised to pay expenses for any Indians who wished to migrate to the west.

Governor McMinn was appointed as a federal agent to arrange for the general removal of the Cherokee, but that nation as a whole continued to reject all proposals, including an offer of $200,000 for all their lands in the East. Most opposed to removal were Cherokee of mixed blood and others who had adopted much of the white man's civilization. Some had accumulated considerable property and conveniences and of course did not wish to revert to primitive ways of living on the frontier. The Cherokee council sent a delegation to Washington to protest the pressure on the uncivilized Indians of the hill country, but Secretary of War John C. Calhoun countered with a demand that the tribe make another large cession of land to compensate for the additional territory necessary for Cherokee who had already moved west or were about to do so. The delegation finally agreed, and in Calhoun's Treaty of February 1819, the Cherokee ceded three tracts, including first the remainder of the Cherokee claim north of the Tennessee River and lying east and west of the Sequatchie Valley cession made in 1817 under the Jackson-McMinn Treaty. Also ceded was the Hiwassee District, which included a large tract between the Hiwassee and Little Tennessee and a smaller tract north of the Little Tennessee. Four new counties were soon created in these areas, and one county was enlarged.

The last claims of the Chickasaw Indians in Tennessee were extinguished. Leaders of that tribe had agreed in 1783 to a boundary running along the watershed between the Tennessee and Cumberland rivers, and in 1805 and 1816 the Chickasaw had relinquished the remainder of their conflicting claims to the Cherokee cessions in Middle Tennessee. But their claims to the area between the Tennessee and Mississippi rivers still remained unchallenged by any other tribe, and it was to that land that whites next gave their attention. In 1818 Andrew Jackson and former Kentucky Governor Isaac Shelby were appointed commissioners, with an assignment to negotiate with the Chickasaw for their claims of the Western District and western Kentucky. The land in those areas, they told the Indians, had been given by North Carolina and Virginia to Revolutionary War soldiers thirty-five years before, and the United States could no longer promise to keep settlers out of the region. Chickasaw leaders then agreed to sell the fertile and valuable soil for $300,000 to be paid in annual installments for twenty years. It was the most important single cession of Indian lands within the state of Tennessee.

Following the acquisition of West Tennessee (for many years called the "Western District" and the "Jackson Purchase"), thousands of people moved in from the east. The first county to be established was Hardin (1819), followed a few days later by Shelby, where fellow speculators Judge John Overton, General James Winchester, and General Jackson established the town of Memphis. By 1824, only six years after the area was cleared for settlement, sixteen county jurisdictions had been established.

The Removal of the Cherokee ஜ஭ As a result of the treaties consummated between 1791 and 1819, all of Tennessee had been cleared of Indian claims except the southeastern corner of the state, which remained under control of the Cherokee. Sixteen years were to pass before those Indians could be induced to surrender that territory and their extensive holdings in neighboring North Carolina, Alabama, and especially Georgia, where they had become largely concentrated by 1819. The people of Tennessee, who had previously been the chief advocates of removal, were content to let the Georgians complete the task.

The resolution with which the Cherokee resisted the federal removal policy may be explained largely by their progress in civilization, which was considerably greater than that of other southern tribes. Especially noteworthy was agricultural development in the growing of cotton, tobacco, corn, and other crops. There was also a considerable amount of domestic manufacturing. According to an official census published in 1828, the total Cherokee population was about 15,000. They owned about 1,000 slaves, 22,400 head of cattle, 7,600 horses, 1,800 spinning wheels, 700 looms, and had 12 sawmills, 55 blacksmith shops, and 6 cotton gins. The aggregate value of their property was estimated in that year at $2 million.

Almost all people of mixed blood could speak English, and many could read and write, as could a considerable number of the full-blooded Cherokee. After Sequoyah had invented his syllabary in the 1820s, making possible the writing and printing of the Cherokee language, a large number of the Indians learned to read and write in their native tongue. There was probably less illiteracy among the Cherokee than among the whites living in the same states. A printing press was obtained, and a newspaper, the *Cherokee Phoenix,* was published from 1828 to 1832 in the two languages, English and Cherokee. As early as 1817 the Cherokee had set up a republican form of government with an elected council. In 1827 they adopted a constitution modeled after that of the United States and hoped for admission into the Union as a state—a proposal that aroused indignation in the states where they resided.

There were two main causes of the rapid progress of the Cherokee in civilization: (1) the policy of the United States of supplying seeds, farm implements, and some training in agriculture, and (2) the work of Christian missionaries. The former seems to have originated in a provision of the Holston Treaty stating that the United States would supply the Cherokee with "useful instruments of husbandry." The federal agents to those Indians, particularly R. J. Meigs, worked earnestly in cooperation with missionaries to make the civilizing program effective.

Attempts to Christianize the Cherokee were made during the colonial period, but it was not until the early years of the nineteenth century that substantial success was achieved. Then the Moravians, Presbyterians, Methodists, Baptists, and the interdenominational American Board of Commissioners for Foreign Missions established mission schools in the Cherokee country. Several were located in East Tennessee, including two Presbyterian schools started by the Reverend Gideon Blackburn in 1804.

The most successful school in the Cherokee country was the Brainerd Mission, which was started in 1817 by the American Board, then under Congregational-Presbyterian control, on Chickamauga Creek near the site of Chattanooga. The mission had the advantage of outstanding leadership, first under its organizer, Cyrus Kingsbury, and later under the capable and highly educated Samuel Austin Worcester, who arrived when large numbers of the Cherokee were learning to read and write their own language. He was instrumental in starting their newspaper and translating the Bible and other types of religious literature into Cherokee. Several of the Brainerd pupils continued their studies at the more advanced school operated by the American Board at Cornwall, Connecticut. Two of them, Elias Boudinot and John Ridge, married white girls of the Cornwall area, and the ensuing furor resulted in the closing of the school.

Also contributing to the refusal of the Cherokee to move west was the encouragement given by most of the missionaries. Near the end of the controversy, however, some concluded that the combination of Jackson and Georgia was too strong to resist, and the missionaries advised yielding to the inevitable. Georgia's insistence on Indian removal was based on a number of factors, including a claim that the United States earlier had promised to clear the state of Indian title. Certainly not to be discounted was greed, which became accentuated by the discovery of gold in the Cherokee country and the sight of the fine farms and homes owned by the wealthier Indians.

Within a month after Jackson's election in November 1828, Georgia officials disregarded previous constitutional interpretations and extended jurisdiction of the state over the Indian country, effective in 1830. When a Cherokee delegation came to Washington to protest against the law, they were told that the federal government had no authority to interfere and that the Indians would have to submit to Georgia's jurisdiction or move west. Dissatisfied with the piecemeal removal policy, Jackson asked Congress for a general removal law that would give him more authority. Such a measure, which also appropriated $500,000 for removal purposes, was passed in May 1830, with Senator Hugh Lawson White of Knoxville and Congressman John Bell of Nashville acting as chief sponsors in the two houses. The only member of the Tennessee delegation to vote against the bill, David Crockett, was defeated for reelection. In 1832 the Supreme Court in *Worcester v. Georgia* declared the Georgia law unconstitutional on the grounds that the Constitution gave the United States exclusive jurisdiction in Indian affairs. Jackson refused to enforce the decision, however, and permitted Georgia to continue to exercise its unconstitutional authority. He seems to have believed that the Indians would be better off in the West and that under pressure from federal officials and Georgia combined they would be forced to accept the removal policy.

Georgia's oppressive jurisdiction was now applied with the utmost severity. The Cherokee lands were surveyed and disposed of by means of a lottery. New laws provided that no Indian could bring suit or testify in a Georgia court and prohibited Indian assemblies. Cherokee leaders found it necessary to move the Cherokee capital and the meetings of the council from New Echota across the state line to Red Clay, Tennessee. But Georgia refused to respect the boundary. Chief John Ross, the leader of the anti-removal faction, and his visitor, the celebrated author-composer John Howard Payne, were arrested at Red Clay and were taken back into Georgia. After being released, Payne wrote a bitter denunciation of Georgia's policy but failed to restrain that state.

Under pressure from Georgia officials, the Tennessee legislature, after three previous failures, finally passed on November 8, 1833 a law extending Tennessee jurisdiction over the Indian country. The Tennessee legislation, however, was more lenient than that of Georgia. The Tennessee law protected the property rights of the Indians and limited the criminal jurisdiction of the state courts in the Indian country to cases involving murder, rape, and larceny. An interesting case before the state supreme court resulted. In 1835 an Indian named James Foreman was brought to trial for murder but was acquitted on the grounds that the Tennessee law was unconstitutional in view of the decision in *Worcester v. Georgia*. The Foreman decision was reversed by the state supreme court. In delivering the court's opinion, Judge John Catron stated that the Indians were "mere wandering savages" and might even "deserve to be exterminated as savage and pernicious beasts"—a complete reversal of a position he had taken in a dissenting opinion several years earlier.[3]

The signing of the removal treaty was due to the growing conviction of Elias Boudinot, the editor of the *Cherokee Phoenix,* and of John Ridge (especially after Jackson had been reelected in 1832) that the only intelligent course for the Indians to follow meant negotiating the best possible terms with the government and moving west. The only alternative would be acceptance of the intolerable jurisdiction of Georgia and loss of independence as a nation. Boudinot and Ridge persuaded the elder chieftain, Major Ridge (John's father), and he became the leader of the faction. The beloved principal chief, John Ross, however, retained the support of the overwhelming majority for his anti-removal policy; he vainly hoped that Northern and Whig pressure would force the Jackson administration to abide by existing treaties and the Supreme Court's decision. The Ridges and Boudinot resorted to unethical tactics and by working hand in glove with the Georgia authorities attempted to reduce the influence of Ross and the other leaders of the anti-removal faction. In exchange, the Ridges and Boudinot were leniently treated by Georgia and were given large payments for their lands and other properties, but they were in violation of the Cherokee constitution and were therefore subject to the death penalty. When he signed the removal treaty, Major Ridge commented prophetically that he was signing his death warrant. After the removal of 1838, the Cherokee council, without the knowledge of John Ross, executed that death penalty on Major Ridge, his son, and Boudinot.

The Treaty of Removal was signed December 29, 1835 at an assembly of the Indians at New Echota called by the government agents William Carroll and John F. Schermerhorn. Of the 300 Indians who signed, only 79 were legal voters. The Ross faction had boycotted the assembly, and Ross, now realizing that removal was inevitable, had departed for Washington at the head of a delegation to negotiate a more satisfactory and legal treaty. Jackson ignored the Ross group, accepted instead the New Echota treaty, and submitted

[3] Catron's change of heart impressed Jackson, and two years later he appointed the Tennessee jurist to the United States Supreme Court.

it to the Senate. Although the treaty was repudiated by all but a small minority of the Cherokee, the Senate approved it on May 23, 1836.

By the treaty the Cherokee ceded all their lands east of the Mississippi for $5 million and agreed to move west within two years. But when that time expired in 1838, only a small number of the Cherokee had moved. The United States army evicted the remainder by force, and thousands of Indians died on their so-called Trail of Tears. Many Tennesseans were involved in the removal, and most of the camps in which Indians concentrated were in Tennessee. Some migrants were supervised by John Ross despite Jackson's protest and passed near the Nashville home of the retired president. Many of the Indians escaped removal by hiding out in the Great Smoky Mountains, however. They were later aided by a friendly North Carolinian, Will Thomas, in obtaining possession of the Qualla Reservation at Cherokee, North Carolina, where many descendants still live.

The Tennessee territory ceded by the Treaty of New Echota was the region south of the Hiwassee River and east of the Tennessee, together with a strip along the North Carolina border between the Hiwassee and the Little Tennessee rivers. Two new counties were created, and two others, one of them Hamilton, was greatly enlarged. In Hamilton County, Ross's Landing, soon to be renamed Chattanooga, already was an important shipping point in 1838.

The Public Lands ⧉ Closely associated with the Indian problem—and almost as vexatious—was the problem of the disposal of the public domain. After the Volunteer State was admitted in 1796, Tennesseans discovered that most of their best land was encumbered by North Carolina grants. Indeed, two years after the Revolution began, North Carolina had required all of her counties to open offices where claims might be made for lands that remained ungranted by either the British crown or the proprietors at the time independence was declared. As mentioned earlier, at about the same time North Carolina had recognized the settlements in the Watauga area and had created Washington County with approximately the same boundaries as those of the present state. Claims or "entries" began to be made immediately at an office created in the new county for that purpose, with John Carter as entry taker. After two years Sullivan County was created, and officials there followed the same pattern as did those in the Cumberland country a few years later

when the migration of 1779– 1780 resulted in the creation of Davidson County.

Near the end of the Revolution, North Carolina enacted several
measures designed to reward lavishly her soldiers of the "continental
line." In 1783 a law was passed setting aside for North Carolina
veterans of the Revolutionary War the northern half of the central
portion of present-day Tennessee—a tract 55 miles wide and more
than 100 miles in length, known as the "Military Reservation" (see
map 6). Preemption rights of pioneers on the Cumberland were to

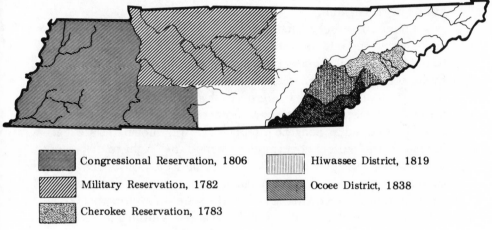

Congressional Reservation, 1806   Hiwassee District, 1819

Military Reservation, 1782   Ocoee District, 1838

Cherokee Reservation, 1783

Map 6. Public Lands of Tennessee

be respected, but veterans were given the remainder. Each private
soldier could receive at least 640 acres, but men of higher rank
received more—Major General Nathaniel Greene, for example, was
given an estate of 25,000 acres because of his rank and leadership. A
veteran's entitlement was in the form of a "warrant" issued to him
upon application and proof of service. It could be sold, given away,
traded, or inherited by his heirs. Thus, many veterans never saw the
land that became theirs—in most cases it fell into the hands of
speculators who purchased warrants from soldiers for a very small
price. As previously noted, William Blount and John Sevier were
among the landholders in Tennessee who numbered their acres in
the hundreds of thousands. Much of this land came from purchases
of warrants from North Carolina veterans. Although warrants
specified the number of acres, they did not designate any particular
plot of land. Thus, the veteran or his assigns were free to choose any

land not already occupied and within the provisions of the existing law. This system was especially beneficial to speculators, who could use warrants they purchased to put together huge tracts of land. A land office was opened at Hillsboro in May of 1783 with John Armstrong in charge of issuing warrants.

Not long after the Military Reservation Act was passed, North Carolina opened the Tennessee region south of the French Broad and east of the Tennessee River (except the Military Reservation) to the citizenry at large. Then, when the cession act of 1789 was passed, Congress claimed title to land that remained after North Carolina's claims were satisfied.

Tennesseans watched helplessly during the territorial period as lands within the territorial borders were distributed by the mother state. After statehood in 1796, Tennessee attempted to make a case for herself by asserting a "right to soil" that was allegedly inherent in the concept of statehood. Congress took a dim view of this assertion, however, and Governor Sevier and other leaders were not surprised when United States Senator Joseph Anderson informed state legislators that the federal government claimed the "right to dispose of the vacant and unappropriated soil" of Tennessee. Consequently, the state became involved in a triangular dispute with North Carolina and Congress over title to the land in the state—a dispute that waxed bitter during the decade after statehood and was ultimately settled in a compromise known as the "Compact of 1806."

According to the compact, Tennessee recognized the title of the United States to all ungranted lands in an area described as the "Congressional Reservation," which embraced all of West Tennessee and the southwestern corner of Middle Tennessee. In return, the United States surrendered to Tennessee all claims to land in the remainder of the state, subject to the following conditions: Tennessee should satisfy all future North Carolina grants in that area, outside the Cherokee Reservation; where existing claims permitted, Tennessee was to reserve 640 acres in each township of 36 square miles for the support of public schools; Tennessee was to appropriate two tracts of land, each 100,000 acres in size, in the Cherokee Reservation—one for the support of two colleges (to be located in East and Middle Tennessee) and the other for the support of an academy in each county in the state; and Tennessee was not to sell land for less than the national minimum land price (then two dollars per acre), except that occupants in the Cherokee Reservation should be permitted to purchase as much as 640 acres at a price of one dollar per acre. Governor Sevier hailed the measure as one that would make "additional burthens of taxation" unnecessary.

In the end, however, Tennessee received comparatively little revenue from the sale of the lands because claims from people in North Carolina continued to multiply and because legislators had sympathy for squatters on the Cumberland and in the Cherokee Reservation and not only gave them preemption rights to 200 acres each but also sold land to them at reduced prices. In 1818, when the Chickasaw Purchase opened West Tennessee to settlement, holders of North Carolina warrants flocked to that region and soon secured title to much of the best land. At about the same time, North Carolina published the muster rolls of her Revolutionary companies so that soldiers or their heirs who had not secured land could now do so by proving service. Eventually, military claims amounted to more than eight million acres outside of the Military Reservation.

One portion of Tennessee was not subject to claims made on the basis of warrants issued by North Carolina. That was the old Cherokee Reservation east of the Tennessee River and south of the French Broad River, which had been set aside when other Indian lands had been sequestered and was not available for the location of the North Carolina claims. Squatters occupied much of the Cherokee area, however, claimed preemption rights, and refused even to pay at the legal rate of one dollar per acre when assessed by law. The Hiwassee District, between the Little Tennessee and Hiwassee rivers and along the foothills of the Great Smokies, was acquired from the Cherokees in 1819 and was surveyed into townships and sections immediately. It was to be sold at the rate of two dollars per acre, but the Panic of 1819 kept the revenue smaller than expected. Soon the legislature dropped the price of the land, and some of it was sold for as little as 12½ cents per acre. The Ocoee District, between the Hiwassee and Tennessee rivers and the southern boundary of the state, plus the foothills region between the Hiwassee and the Little Tennessee rivers, became available for settlement when the Cherokee were forced to move across the Mississippi River in 1838. After this area was surveyed into townships and sections, it too was sold under a graduation system, with the prices ranging from $7.50 to a low of one cent an acre. Some of the revenue—about $150,000—was used during the 1830s for internal improvements, and the remainder became the major part of the common school fund of the state.

SUGGESTED READINGS

Books

Thomas P. Abernethy, *From Frontier to Plantation in Tennessee* (1932; rpt. University, Ala., 1967); Althea Bass, *Cherokee Messenger* (Norman, 1936); Robert S. Cotterill, *The Southern Indians* (Norman, 1954); Grant Foreman, *Advancing the Frontier, 1830–1860* (Norman, 1968); Foreman, *Indian Removal* (1932; rpt. Norman, 1972); Foreman, *Sequoyah* (Norman, 1938); Ralph H. Gabriel, *Elias Boudinot, Cherokee, and His America* (Norman, 1961); Gilbert E. Govan and James W. Livingood, *The Chattanooga Country* (1952; rpt. Knoxville, 1976); Reginald Horsman, *Expansion and American Indian Policy, 1789–1812* (East Lansing, Mich., 1967); Charles Hudson, *The Southeastern Indians* (Knoxville, 1976); Henry T. Malone, *Cherokees of the Old South: A People in Transition* (Athens, Ga. 1956); Theda Perdue, *Slavery and the Evolution of Cherokee Society, 1540–1866* (Knoxville, 1979); Francis P. Prucha, *American Indian Policy in the Formative Years, 1780–1834* (Cambridge, Mass., 1962); Ronald N. Satz, *American Indian Policy in the Jacksonian Era* (Lincoln, Neb., 1975); Jane F. Smith and Robert M. Kvasnicka, *Indian-White Relations: A Persistent Paradox* (Washington, D.C., 1976); Robert S. Walker, *Torchlights to the Cherokees: The Brainerd Mission* (New York, 1931); Robert H. White, *Messages of the Governors*, Vol. 1 (Nashville, 1952–1972).

Articles

Kenneth Penn Davis, "The Cherokee Removal, 1835–1838," *THQ* 32 (Winter 1973), 311–31; Edmund C. Gass, "The Constitutional Opinions of Justice John Catron," *ETHSP* 8 (1936), 54–73; Thomas B. Jones, "The Public Lands of Tennessee," *THQ* 27 (Spring 1968), 13–36; Henry T. Malone, "Return Jonathan Meigs: Indian Agent, Extraordinary," *ETHSP* 28 (1956), 3–22; Norvell Sevier Rose, "John Sevier and Marble Springs," *THQ* 29 (Fall 1970), 205–26; Charles G. Sellers, Jr., "James K. Polk's Political Apprenticeship," *ETHSP* 25 (1953), 37–53; St. George L. Sioussat, "Tennessee and the Removal of the Cherokee," *Sewanee Review*, 16 (July 1908), 337–44; Rennard Strickland, "From Clan to Court: Development of Cherokee Law," *THQ* 31 (Winter 1972), 316–27; Mary E. Young, "Indian Removal and Land Allotment: The Civilized Tribes and Jacksonian Justice," *AHR* 64 (1958–59), 31–45.

10.

ষ্ট Governor William Carroll: A Harbinger of Jacksonian Democracy

T HE Panic of 1819 and the relief measures enacted to combat it marked a turning point in the political structure of the state. Debtors facing financial ruin saw in the leadership of Felix Grundy, William Carroll, and others an opportunity to use political means to remain "even" with their creditors. The election of 1821 and the resulting democratic and humanitarian trends developed during the next dozen or more years supplied ample evidence that the extension of democracy was not to be denied. Interestingly, it was Governor Carroll, a spokesman for people who had had little or no voice in government, and not Andrew Jackson, who first brought "Jacksonian Democracy" to Tennessee. Because of the reforms accomplished or begun during his twelve years in office, Carroll has often been called the "Reform Governor."

Tennessee had come into the Union as a Jeffersonian Republican state over the vigorous protests of Eastern Federalists, who sought to delay the state's admission until after the presidential election of 1796. With the state safely in the Republican fold, people were satisfied to leave the affairs of government to the "natural leaders" for more than two decades, which meant that military heroes (such as Sevier) and the well-to-do and influential men (such as William Blount), who had something to gain from political control, ran the government. Blount, of course, had died at the turn of the century, and Sevier died fifteen years later. Although loose factional and sectional groupings among political leaders were apparent before, it was not until the Panic of 1819 and its aftermath that vigorous competition between factions became readily apparent.

Willie Blount considered himself heir to his half-brother's political domain, but the real leader for more than a decade was Andrew

Jackson's close friend, John Overton. Reputed to be the wealthiest man in the state, Overton was a lawyer, farmer, bank president, and land speculator with extensive holdings in Nashville and (after the Chickasaw claims were cleared in West Tennessee) in and around Memphis. Overton's brother-in-law, Hugh Lawson White, the powerful president of the Bank of Tennessee, and Pleasant M. Miller, a wealthy Knoxville businessman who had married one of Blount's daughters, led the Overton faction in East Tennessee. Jackson, United States Senator John Eaton, and Governor Joseph McMinn were also associated with the group. Although Jackson had served briefly in Congress and on the state superior court, he did not exercise much political power until after about 1823—his influence was curtailed by a variety of personal problems including his abrasive personality.

Enemies of Overton's conservative group became more aggressive during McMinn's administration. They, like the other faction, were held together by personal ties and friendships. Led by United States Senator John Williams of Knoxville and Congressman Newton Cannon and Andrew Erwin of Middle Tennessee, they also numbered among their members David Crockett of West Tennessee and State Senator Theoderick F. Bradford of Bedford County. In 1821 they found a new ally in William Carroll, who had ambitions to become governor. For a time they courted Felix Grundy, the champion of the debtor classes in the legislative debates of 1819, and at one point they even considered him a possible gubernatorial candidate, but his association with conservative banking interests of Nashville made them uncertain of his reliability.

Constitutional limitations prohibited McMinn from seeking another term in 1821, and a lively contest then developed between Carroll and Edward Ward, an aristocratic Davidson County planter and a neighbor and friend of Andrew Jackson. Carroll, a Nashville businessman and major general of the state militia, was a military hero whose Tennessee troops had withstood the heaviest shock of the British attack at New Orleans. Indeed, he had been considered second in command to Jackson, but the adulation that surrounded the Old Chief after 1815 all but totally obscured Carroll and others. Carroll had operated a general merchandise store in Nashville and for a while had owned an interest in a steamboat, but he had suffered near financial ruin in the Panic of 1819. He apparently recognized in the trauma of depression evidence of the rise of a new democratic

These four governors served during the eventful Jackson era. *Above left:* William Carroll, 1821–1827, 1829–1835; *above right:* Sam Houston, 1827–1829 (resigned after serving 1½ years of term); *below left:* William Hall, 1829 (served out Houston's term); *below right:* Newton Cannon, 1835–1839.

movement and was sympathetic to the debtor class; as a careful and judicious politician he neither condemned nor praised the work of Grundy and McMinn that had been designed to aid debtors. But Carroll did have harsh words for lending agencies and pleased all debtors by concluding that banks should be permitted to operate only under a "watchful eye." As a part of his social reform program, he advocated a revision of the penal code, construction of a "penitentiary house," state care for the insane, reorganization of the courts, internal improvements, and the establishment of a public school system. The common people received him gladly as he talked his way across the state.

Edward Ward, a wealthy, well-educated, and polished Virginia native who had been speaker of the state senate from 1815 to 1819, became the gubernatorial candidate of the Overton faction. He appeared as the friend of the creditors and the banks controlled by Overton, which continued to pay their stockholders sizable dividends made possible partly by severe policies on debtors. A candidate of "bank directors and the rich generally" and openly supported by Jackson, he called for an end to Grundy's state bank.

The results surprised no one. Carroll was elected by a vote of 31,290 to 7,294 and won a majority in every county but two. Although Ward had had the support of the then conservative Andrew Jackson, his "Virginia bearing," social position, wealth, and association with the rich and powerful brought him repudiation at the polls from which he never recovered. During the next fourteen years Carroll was politically invincible. With no opposition in 1823, 1825, and 1829, he had little difficulty in attaining reelection in 1831 and 1833.

Carroll turned his attention to reforms in his first appearance before the legislature. His efforts at an adjustment between debtor and creditor were helped greatly by the general improvement of the economic situation throughout the country during his first term as governor. At his insistence, legislators enacted a measure requiring banks to resume specie payment by April, 1824. Carroll's interest in a more humane attitude toward those convicted of crime did not meet with immediate attention, but legislators revised the criminal code and constructed a commodious prison in Nashville before he eventually left the gubernatorial chair.

Tennessee's criminal code had been taken from several sources, principally Pennsylvania and North Carolina. Both states had harsh codes, and local legislators adopted them with little modification. Horse thieves and murderers usually suffered death on the gallows; a perjurer might be sentenced to stand in the pillory for hours with his ears nailed, and afterwards both ears were severed from his body and left nailed on the pillory. In one case on record, a Stewart County man wounded another and was sentenced to be whipped publicly, cropped on both ears, and branded on the arms with hot wine. A Madison County man convicted of manslaughter was sentenced to be branded with the letter M. In Washington County, Elias Pybourn was convicted of horse stealing; he escaped the death penalty, but his sentence included confinement in the pillory for one hour, having both ears nailed to the pillory and severed at the end of the hour, thirty-nine lashes "well laid on," and branding with the letter H on the right cheek and the letter T on the other. An 1811 statute decreed that counterfeiters should receive

> 39 stripes on his, her, or their bare back, be imprisoned not less than six months, nor more than two years, shall sit in the pillory two hours on three different days, and shall be rendered infamous, and pay the costs of the prosecution, and shall also be branded on . . . the left thumb with the letter T.

In the meantime, reformers throughout the country talked of better treatment for those convicted of crime. Many believed that if the convict could be incarcerated for a time in a "penitentiary house" and accorded humane treatment, he would have the opportunity for the first time to contemplate the enormity of his crime and thereafter live an exemplary life. By the time Carroll became governor in 1821, several northern and eastern states had constructed modern penitentiaries.

Carroll wanted a prison where solitary confinement, coarse food, and hard labor might afford the criminal ample opportunity to repent. In 1825, at the suggestion of the General Assembly, Carroll procured information about the costs and operations of the prisons in Kentucky, Virginia, Ohio, New Jersey, New Hampshire, and Maryland. It was not until 1829, however, that legislators acted favorably upon his suggestions.

The law of 1829 made sweeping changes. It abolished the whipping post and the practices of cropping and confinement in the pillory and stocks. For some felonies formerly punishable by death, offenders would be confined in a new penitentiary where they would perform hard labor. Equally important was a provision for an elaborate penitentiary. Work was begun immediately, and the new prison was ready for use on January 1, 1831. A contemporary writer described it as a

> beautiful and substantial Prison. . . . It presents a front of three hundred and ten feet, and is three hundred and fifty in depth. The wings of the front building contain two hundred cells, and half of the center building is occupied by the Keeper, and the other half is used for a hospital, guard rooms, etc. The yard walls are four and a half feet thick at the bottom, and three at the top, and have an average height of twenty feet.

During the next three decades the penitentiary was enlarged, more land was bought, and the number of criminals housed at state expense increased. By 1860, the state prison had 352 cells—each measuring six and one-half feet in length, three feet in width, and seven feet in height—and housed more than 300 prisoners.

Contemporaneous with the movement for a revision of the criminal code was a growing demand for repeal of laws that provided for capital punishment and imprisonment of debtors. Continued agitation for the former failed to reap success, but in 1842 imprisonment for debt was abolished entirely.

One of the most important developments during Carroll's long tenure in the governor's office was the revision in 1834 of the state's fundamental law. For years legislators and interested citizens had expressed interest in a constitutional convention, and in 1819 the question was submitted to the qualified voters. Those wanting a convention argued that the time had come to dispossess the large landholders in the rich valleys of East Tennessee and the Cumberland Basin of the special tax privileges that makers of the constitution of 1796 had given them by declaring that all land should be taxed equally regardless of its value. Perhaps remembering the Philadelphia convention of 1787, however, opponents argued that it was dangerous to place such unlimited powers in the hands of a small group of convention delegates. At any rate, the proposal was defeated. A move for a convention was also defeated in 1821 and again a few years later. Considerably more interest was shown in 1831, when the question was again submitted to the people, but the efforts of the revisionists fell short by about 2,000 votes. Two years later when the question came up again, the people balloted for a convention by more than 8,000 votes. The outcome represented a culmination of efforts of years toward constitutional democracy. The pressure for reform had come principally from rural West and Middle Tennessee, while opposition came largely from the old established counties such as Carter, Davidson, Greene, Jefferson, Sullivan, and Washington.

The leaven of democracy, beginning with the Panic of 1819, had inspired the underprivileged to seek to wrest some of the powers and privileges from "the lords of the soil." As might have been expected, the common man wanted tax relief and more equitable representation. It was therefore only natural that these issues should become the principal ones at the convention.

Sixty delegates—18 from East Tennessee, 30 from the middle division, and 12 from the west—assembled on May 19, 1834 at Nashville. Few of them had claim to distinction, but former Governor Willie Blount, Newton Cannon, Adam Huntsman, John A. McKinney, Terry H. Cahal, William B. Carter, and Francis B. Fogg were exceptions. Blount acted as temporary chairman until Carter, of Carter County, was elected president.

The people as a whole apparently had confidence in the delegates, and it is highly doubtful whether at any time in 1833 or 1834 very many if any people seriously feared that a group of "radicals" would gain control and grossly upset the status quo. The editor of the Knoxville *Register,* one of the more conservative newspapers, voiced no profound fears, and the editor of a Nashville paper thought that the "sterling integrity and patriotism" of the delegates would insure Tennesseans of a revision devoid of extremes. The editor of another mid-state paper found "little to invite our censure," and "A Farmer," writing in the Nashville *Whig,* pointed to the growth of American democracy since 1796 and urged that confidence be placed in the delegates. Carter and Cahal were known as strong conservatives who had expressed fears of extremism, but Carter's election as president of the convention must have quieted the fears of both.

For many years the taxation clause—which provided for equal taxation of all land (except town lots, for which taxes might be as high as those for 200 acres of land)—had been a thorn in the flesh of small farmers who occupied land less valuable than that of others, especially in the valley and basin areas. When people asked why the constitution-makers of 1796 had restricted the taxing power of the legislature, the answer was that in 1796 there were few improvements on the land, that the restriction encouraged persons to invest in Tennessee lands, and that the founding fathers wanted to encourage landowners to improve their lands by guaranteeing that improvements would not increase taxes. Economic conditions had brought changes, said the delegates from the rural counties, and Adam Huntsman of Madison County and John A. McKinney of Hawkins County championed reform. They showed how "the poor man" might pay twenty-five times more tax money than "the rich man." They condemned a system according to which a town lot worth $10,000 and earning an annual rent of $600 was taxed for the same amount as one worth $20. By a vote of 43 to 13 the delegates adopted a provision stating that "all property should be taxed according to its value; that value to be ascertained in such manner as the Legislature shall direct. . . ."

Legislative representation was also debated extensively. Conservatives wanted to retain unamended the provisions that apportioned representation on the basis of free taxable inhabitants and limited the assembly to forty representatives and twenty senators. Especially objectionable to them was a movement led by Adam Huntsman, James Scott (representing Perry, Hardin, and McNairy counties), and others from other rural districts, to secure equal representation for all counties. Robert M. Burton of Lebanon believed that such a scheme would return Tennessee to the "rotten borough system of England," and asked, "Shall hills, mountains and rocks . . . be the basis of representation?" Cahal agreed. "Why [should] four hundred . . . voters in one county," he asked rhetorically, "possess as much political power . . . as four thousand in another . . . ?" After several days of debate delegates compromised by agreeing to apportion representation according to the number of qualified voters and to increase the number of representatives to a maximum of ninety-nine (seventy-five until the population reached $1\frac{1}{2}$ million) and to increase the number of senators to one-third the number of representatives.

Another change reflecting the democratic spirit of the times gave voters the right to elect county officials. Under the existing constitution, members of the county courts, who were chosen by the legislature for life, were empowered to elect sheriffs, trustees, coroners, and other officials. Such a practice had bred many abuses. West H. Humphreys of Fayette County believed that the popular election of all officials would "call forth the best talents" and improve the quality of officeholders. Delegates agreed and gave voters the right to select justices of the peace, sheriffs, trustees, registers, and other public officials for specified terms of office.

The slavery question had developed into a burning issue by 1834 and had been debated thoroughly in Virginia and other Southern states. Tennesseans, however, like Virginians, decided not to tamper with the troublesome question. By a close vote of 30 to 27 they wrote into the constitution a provision that the legislature could pass no laws for the emancipation of slaves without the consent of their owners. Free Negroes had voted under the old constitution, but under the new one they were denied that privilege.

Other changes were made. The legislature of 1834 was commanded to select a permanent location for the state's capital within the first week of its session. Duelists were disqualified from holding office, divorces could be granted only by the courts, and lotteries were prohibited. Judges could no longer hold office for life but were to be selected by the legislature for terms of twelve years.[1] Property qualifications were removed as a condition for officeholding.

A significant change involved the amending process. Under the constitution of 1796, two-thirds of the legislators were given authority to submit to voters the question of a convention. If a majority of citizens voting for representatives wanted a convention at which revision would be considered, then the next General Assembly was commanded to call one. Under the constitutional provision of 1834, an assembly might propose amendments by a simple majority. The next legislature, to meet two years later, was required to act on the proposed changes; if members accepted the amendments by a two-thirds vote, the matter was to be submitted to the people for acceptance or rejection, but a majority of the number of votes for representatives was required for approval. Amendments could not be considered more often than once in six years. Interestingly, the delegates retained a provision prohibiting ministers of the gospel from accepting seats in the legislature, but it defeated efforts of prohibitionists to exclude alcoholics.

Unlike the delegates to the convention of 1796, those of 1834 directed that their work be submitted to the voters for rejection or approval. Consequently, on the first Thursday of March 1835, the people went to the polls and accepted the revised constitution by a vote of 42,666 to 17,691. Only four counties—Davidson, Smith,

[1] An amendment providing for the popular election of judges and district attorneys was approved in 1853. Efforts in 1858 to call another constitutional convention to limit the size of the state debt failed. No additional efforts to amend were made until after the Civil War.

Williamson, and Robertson—showed majorities against ratification. On March 27, Governor Carroll proclaimed the revised document to be the fundamental law of the state.

As important as were Carroll's reforms and encouragement of democratic expansion, it was Andrew Jackson's amazing display of political strength in 1824 and his elevation to the presidency four years later that excited Tennesseans and rendered the new West a powerful contender for political control in Washington.

Presidential Elections of 1824 and 1828 ᠑᠍ Perhaps no more controversial figure than Andrew Jackson has ever performed on the American political stage. Contemporaries were seldom neutral where he was concerned; they either loved him or despised him. Some of the great state and national leaders of the times became his bitter enemies; yet to thousands of laborers and yeoman farmers, he was the "Old Hero"—the "Hero of the Common Man."[2]

Jackson emerged from the Battle of New Orleans in 1815 as a national hero, and his friends immediately attached political significance to his victory. William Carroll was among the first to approach him on the question of becoming a presidential candidate. On a recent visit with political leaders in nearby states, Carroll said, he had talked with many who expressed a distinct interest in seeing the Old Hero's name on the ballot in 1820. Jackson remained in relative seclusion, however, but John Overton, John Eaton, and other state leaders also urged him to run.

While Jackson said little, events in Florida three years after the Battle of New Orleans again brought him into the national limelight. A group of Seminole Indians, escaped slaves, freebooters, and smugglers, using the Spanish-owned peninsula as a base of operations, had robbed and terrified American settlements in Georgia, South Carolina, and Alabama for several years. In 1818, Secretary of War John C. Calhoun had dispatched Jackson to the Florida frontier with orders to "adopt the necessary measures" to end the border troubles. Jackson later claimed that Congressman John Rhea of

---

[2] Both contemporaries and historians of a later period have described Jackson as a complex figure. James Parton, writing little more than a decade after Jackson's death, despaired at the conflicting sources that his research uncovered and concluded that his subject was both a patriot and a traitor. James Parton, *Life of Andrew Jackson*, vol. 1 (New York, 1860), vii.

Above: Indian fighter and hero of the Battle of New Orleans, Jackson was active in state politics for three decades before becoming the nation's seventh president. *Below:* Jackson's home, The Hermitage, is a National Historic Landmark.

Blountville had also indicated to him that the administration would not object if he invaded the peninsula and, "without implicating the Government," took possession of it on behalf of the United States. Accordingly, when a band of renegades appeared in Georgia, Jackson chased them back into Florida. Not content with that, he crossed the Florida border, destroyed several Spanish posts, drove the governor and garrison out of Pensacola, executed two British subjects, and returned to United States territory. The episode caused President Monroe considerable embarrassment as he tried to explain the action to Spanish and British authorities, and the skillful diplomacy of Secretary of State John Quincy Adams was required to smooth over the international quarrel. To the Western frontiersmen, however, Jackson had done no wrong, and was an even greater hero than after New Orleans. Thousands of Tennesseans hailed him in Nashville when he arrived from Florida and unanimously agreed that his conduct was "marked with energy, valor, skill and patriotism, not surpassed in the annals of our country."

Although Jackson's raid interrupted negotiations with Spain for the purchase of Florida and the adjustment of the disputed boundaries of the Louisiana Purchase, in the long run it facilitated the completion of the Adams-Onís Treaty of 1819 by which those aims were achieved. After the treaty was ratified in 1821, Jackson was named governor of the Territory of Florida, but he resigned and returned to Nashville after serving for only a few months.

In the meantime, the Overton faction, aware of the rising tide of democracy in Tennessee after 1821 and smarting from the defeat of Edward Ward in that year, cast about for a strong and popular candidate whose election to high office might restore them to power. They considered running Jackson for the presidency in 1820 but became discouraged by the apparent popularity of President Monroe. Soon after the Virginian's second inauguration, however, they pushed Jackson forward as a presidential contender for 1824. They received considerable encouragement in July 1822, when members of the state legislature unanimously endorsed him. Describing Jackson as one who was "calm in deliberation, cautious in decision, and efficient in action," the legislators concluded that "the welfare of the country may be safely entrusted to the hands of him who has experienced every privation, and encountered every danger to promote its safety, its honor, and its glory." Jackson still was noncommittal on the question of state and national politics, but he encouraged his supporters a few months later by declining President Monroe's offer of an appointment as minister to Mexico.

Serious debate ensued within the Jackson ranks early in 1823. The three-pronged question among the leaders was whether to run Jackson for governor in 1823 against Carroll, have him oppose incumbent John Williams for the United States Senate, or let him appear untested in the presidential race in 1824. A vigorous minority feared that the Hero might suffer defeat in a contest against the popular Carroll, which would destroy his chances for the presidency; the minority therefore insisted that he not become involved at all until 1824. Pleasant M. Miller, however, entreated Jackson to run for governor. He contended that the General could purge the state administration of the Carroll-Erwin men, enhance his own prestige in time for the presidential contest of 1824 and, incidentally, help elect a legislature that would send Miller instead of Williams to the United States Senate. The majority, however, was convinced that Jackson could defeat Williams in the Senate race and that the victory would increase Jackson's prestige and make him a strong presidential candidate. On the day before the contest, leaders hastened to the Hermitage to urge the Old Hero to go to Murfreesboro and appear before the legislators. Jackson rode all night in order to arrive in time. His personal appearance was sufficient to win the undecided voters, and he was elected by a vote of 35 to 25. The General apparently had little ambition to go to the Senate, but his supporters attached great significance to the victory and openly boasted that it would elect him President in 1824.

People across the country viewed the approaching presidential election with great interest. In each of the earlier contests the party nominee had been selected by a congressional caucus, that is, by the party members serving in Congress. Because only the Republican party was active (the Federalists did not nominate a candidate after 1816), many people believed that nomination by caucus would be unfair. Opponents of "King Caucus" found vociferous support in the West, where seeds of democracy were germinating rapidly and where the settlers, deprived of much influence in the nation's capital, hoped to ride into power on the shoulders of Jackson or Henry Clay. When the caucus nominated William Crawford of Georgia (who had quarreled earlier with Jackson), western Republicans therefore vowed that they would not support the nominee. When western politicians could not agree on a single candidate, both Jackson and

Clay were pushed forward. John Quincy Adams, son of the second President, was selected by party stalwarts in the East. John C. Calhoun, whose supporters urged him to run, compromised by agreeing to accept the vice presidency.

The outcome of the election exceeded the dreams of even Jackson's most sanguine supporters, although Adams and not Jackson became President. Jackson carried eleven states and received 99 electoral votes to Adam's 84, Crawford's 41, and Clay's 37. Of the popular votes, he polled 152,901 to 114,023 for Adams. Because Jackson did not have a majority of electoral votes, it became the duty of the House of Representatives to choose the President from the top three candidates. Crawford had suffered a stroke of paralysis during the campaign and was not given serious consideration. Adams was elected thanks to the powerful influence of Clay, whose years of service in Washington enabled him to know personally most of the members of the lower house and persuade them to vote for Adams as the more experienced candidate.

The Old Hero accepted his defeat graciously until he heard that Adams had appointed Clay as secretary of state. The apparent "bargain and corruption" disturbed Jackson, and he vowed he would get even with the "conniving" Adams and the "Judas of the West" from Kentucky. Shortly after the inauguration he resigned his Senate seat and returned to Tennessee to develop plans for 1828. Hugh Lawson White was elected to the vacated Senate seat.

Jackson remained relatively quiet during the next three years, but he maintained a voluminous correspondence with political leaders. John Eaton and John Overton took the lead in strengthening Jackson's support and were especially pleased with the consummation of an alliance with some of the Calhoun men. They also urged old-line Jackson men such as John Coffee, William B. Lewis, and Sam Houston to work amicably with Martin Van Buren of New York, Thomas Hart Benton of Missouri, and others who controlled votes in other states.

The General opened the campaign of 1828 on the same note with which he had closed four years earlier—the charge of a "corrupt bargain" between Adams and Clay. The campaign had scarcely begun when it degenerated into mudslinging as supporters of each candidate sought to outdo one another in propagating malicious charges. The Adams men found plenty of ammunition. After Jackson and Rachel Donelson Robards had married in the mistaken belief that the Virginia legislature had granted her a divorce from her first husband, Jackson's enemies widely publicized this impropriety and represented Rachel as a woman unfit by refinement or talent to become the First Lady. Critics also condemned the Hero for executing six deserters in the Creek campaign; animadversions ran the gamut from slave peddling to dueling, from associating with Aaron Burr to misconduct in Florida. Adam's career did not offer so fertile a field for political propagandists, but some in Tennessee claimed that he was a Federalist masquerading in Republican garb. Legislators pronounced his administration "injurious to the interests and dangerous to the liberties of the country." The "surest remedy for these evils," they resolved, "is the election of Andrew Jackson to the Presidency of this Union."

Careful political observers conceded a Jackson victory several weeks before the election. Backwoodsmen of the West and factory workers of the East may not have comprehended Clay's American system and Adams's nationalism, but they had no trouble understanding the Old Hero's simple message of corruption and aristocracy in Washington. Jackson now embodied their conceptions of democracy, and they readily united behind him to expel the "aristocratic rascals" from the nation's capital. Jackson carried the West and South solidly and received all of the electoral votes of Pennsylvania and part of those of New York, Maryland, and even Maine; his margin was 178 to 83 for Adams. In Tennessee, where he received 44,193 votes to 2,240 for Adams, he appeared to have wooed and won most of his old enemies. Jackson, who in 1821 could not elect a governor in Tennessee and who two years earlier had been criticized for trying to bully legislators, had become the state's most powerful politician. Twice as many Tennesseans went to the polls in 1828 as had voted in 1824.

Sam Houston Elected Governor ខ្ Carroll's twelve years in the gubernatorial chair were interrupted in 1827 when the governor, having served three consecutive terms, was constitutionally barred from seeking reelection. He had hoped to replace United States Senator John Eaton, who had been in Washington since his appointment in 1818 to fill out the unexpired term of George W. Campbell, but Carroll lacked the support of Jackson. Eaton, who was widely known to be among Jackson's closest friends, was consequently elected to a second full senatorial term in November 1826. Carroll fretted but applied his talents to the gubernatorial campaign of Sam Houston, who also had the support of Jackson.

Houston won easily. He defeated Willie Blount, whose political star had apparently set, and Newton Cannon, a prominent Williamson County planter who was handicapped by the widespread knowledge that he was unfriendly to the ambitions and aspirations of Jackson. Houston was inaugurated on October 1, 1827.

The colorful and dramatic Houston was born in Virginia in 1793, but had moved at the age of fourteen with his widowed mother and eight brothers and sisters to Blount County. The "wild and impetuous" youth (as Houston later described himself) soon ran away from home and took up abode with the Cherokee Indians for three years; the Cherokee named him "The Raven." Enlisting in the United States Army in 1813, he served under Jackson in the Creek campaign and received a wound at Horseshoe Bend that was to plague him for the rest of his life. During the campaign he developed great admiration for Jackson, and the two became fast friends.

For a decade after the war Houston followed a varied career, including the study and practice of law at Lebanon and Nashville, election to the office of district attorney general, and service as major general of the Tennessee militia. In August 1822, he was elected to Congress with the support of Carroll and Jackson, and he remained in Washington until 1827. He was an active supporter of Old Hickory in 1824 and again in 1828.

Houston's term was but an interlude in the Carroll administrations. The Raven continued the sound fiscal policies and the reforms instituted by Carroll and was considered a protégé of his predecessor. Fortune for Houston began to turn soon after his inauguration. Charges were brought against him by the Masonic Lodge of Nashville for dueling, and in 1828 he was expelled from the order. At the same time, a noticeable coolness developed between him and Carroll, his erstwhile mentor. The former governor, chagrined that he had not been chosen for the United States Senate and somewhat miffed at Houston for openly accepting both his support and that of Jackson, made plans to return to the governor's chair in 1829. Houston denied that he had agreed to serve for only one term. He exhibited considerable independence and, no doubt with Jackson's encouragement, promptly announced that he would oppose Carroll's attempt to perpetuate his control of the state administration by seeking reelection.

A contest between the two was settled when Houston suddenly surprised everyone by resigning the gubernatorial office, withdrawing from the race for reelection, and taking up temporary residence again with a group of Cherokee Indians who had moved to the West. He became the first governor in the history of the state not to serve out the term for which he was elected.

Houston's strange conduct has generally been attributed to domestic troubles. The romantically inclined chieftain (his Indian friends referred to him as "Squaw's Man") had decided after his election as governor to "settle down." Consequently, on January 22, 1829, Houston, then thirty-five, married eighteen-year-old Eliza Allen, whose father, Colonel John Allen of Gallatin, was his close friend and admirer. The young bride remained with him for only a short while before she returned to her parents in Gallatin. Houston refused to issue a public statement about his marital affairs, but he wrote to Colonel Allen that Eliza had been "cold" to him and that he did not believe she loved him. After a brief sojourn with the Indians, Houston headed for Texas. He secured a divorce, was married again, and reared a family. His claim to greatness rests more with his accomplishments in the Lone Star State than in Tennessee.

Houston's resignation elevated William Hall, speaker of the senate, to the governorship. Born in North Carolina in 1775, Hall had moved with his parents to Castalian Springs in Sumner County when he was only ten years old. At the age of twenty-two he was elected to the house of representatives, and later served four terms in the senate. During the War of 1812 he fought under Jackson and rose to the rank of brigadier general. Hall's term of office as governor was only five and one-half months. No attempt was made to push him into the race in 1829, but he was elected to Congress two years after he retired from the gubernatorial chair. Carroll was therefore elected to a fourth term without opposition.

The fourteen years of Carroll's administration constituted a highly significant period for Tennessee. Andrew Jackson, the pride of Tennessee and the West, in 1824 became the state's first presidential candidate and was elected in 1828 and 1832. During the 1830s Tennesseans joined in the reaction against the Hero of the Hermitage. Jackson lived for almost a decade after he vacated the White

House in 1837, but at no time during that period did a Democratic presidential candidate win the electoral votes of Tennessee. This seeming anomaly in the conduct of voters in the Volunteer State is discussed in the next chapter.

SUGGESTED READINGS

Books

Thomas P. Abernethy, *From Frontier to Plantation in Tennessee* (1932; rpt. University, Ala., 1967); Claude G. Bowers, *The Party Battles of the Jackson Period* (Boston, 1929); William N. Chambers, *Old Bullion Benton: Senator from the New West* (New York, 1956); Clement Eaton, *Henry Clay and the Art of American Politics* (Boston, 1957); Llerena Friend, *Sam Houston, The Great Designer* (Austin, 1954); Robert V. Remini, *The Election of Andrew Jackson* (New York, 1963); Remini, *Andrew Jackson* (New York, 1966); Arthur M. Schlesinger, Jr., *The Age of Jackson* (Boston, 1945); Charles G. Sellers, Jr., *James K. Polk, Jacksonian, 1795–1843* (Princeton, 1957; Glyndon G. Van Deusen, *The Jacksonian Era, 1828–1848* (New York, 1959); John W. Ward, *Andrew Jackson, Symbol of an Age* (Oxford, 1955); Florence Weston, *The Presidential Election of 1828* (Washington, D.C., 1938).

Articles

Thomas P. Abernethy, "Andrew Jackson," *AHR* 33 (Oct. 1927), 64–77; Paul H. Bergeron, "The Nullification Controversy Revisited," *THQ* 35 (Fall 1976), 263–75; Bergeron, "Tennessee's Response to the Nullification Crisis, 1832–1833," *JSH* 39 (Feb. 1973), 23–44; Bergeron (ed.), "A Tennessean Blasts Calhoun and Nullification," *THQ* 26 (Winter 1967), 383–86; James C. Curtis, "Andrew Jackson and His Cabinet—Some New Evidence," *THQ* 27 (Summer 1968), 157–64; Reda C. Goff, "A Physical Profile of Andrew Jackson," *THQ* 28 (Fall 1969), 297–309; Perry M. Goldman, "Political Rhetoric in the Age of Jackson," *THQ* 29 (Winter 1970–71), 360–71; Louis R. Harlan, "Public Career of William Berkeley Lewis," *THQ* 7 (March, June 1948), 3–37, 118–51; Gerald S. Henig, "The Jacksonian Attitude toward Abolitionism in the 1830's," *THQ* 28 (Spring 1969), 42–56; Carlton Jackson, "—Another Time, Another Place—The Attempted Assassination of President Andrew Jackson," *THQ* 26 (Summer 1967), 184–90; Isabel Thompson Kelsay, "The Presidential Campaign of 1828," *ETHSP* 5 (1933), 69–80; Richard B. Latner, "A New Look at Jacksonian Politics," *JAH* 62 (March 1975), 943–69; Richard P. McCormick, "New Perspectives on Jacksonian Politics," *AHR* 65 (Jan. 1960), 288–301; John M. McFaul, "Expediency vs. Morality:

Jacksonian Politics and Slavery," *JAH* 62 (June 1975), 24–39; Chase C. Mooney, "The Question of Slavery and the Free Negro in the Tennessee Constitutional Convention of 1834," *JSH* 12 (Nov. 1946), 487–509; William G. Morgan, "John Quincy Adams versus Andrew Jackson: Their Biographers and the 'Corrupt Bargain' Charge," *THQ* 26 (Spring 1967), 43–58; Richard J. Moss, "Jackson Democracy: A Note on the Origins and Growth of the Term," *THQ* 34 (Summer 1975), 145–53; James Edward Murphy, "Jackson and the Tennessee Opposition," *THQ* 30 (Spring 1971), 50–69; R. Beeler Satterfield, "The Uncertain Trumpet of the Tennessee Jacksonians," *THQ* 26 (Spring 1967), 79–96; Charles Grier Sellers, Jr., "Jackson Men with Feet of Clay," *AHR* 62 (April 1957), 537–51; Culver H. Smith, "Propaganda Technique in the Jackson Campaign of 1828," *ETHSP* 6 (1934), 44–66; Major L. Wilson, "Andrew Jackson: The Great Compromiser," *THQ* 26 (Spring 1967), 64–78.

11.

ॐ *The Rise of the Whigs*

ALTHOUGH expediency scarcely accomplished a union, at least it provided the political factions in Tennessee with a working arrangement after Jackson's contests for the presidency began. Tennessee politicians who expected favors of any kind from Washington knew that they must at least give lip service to the Chief. But the bond that held them together—the political power of President Andrew Jackson—lasted only halfway through the Hero's second term.

While Jackson had held a half-dozen political offices from time to time, he had not occupied any of them long enough to establish a positive record. He had been ambitious to exert a controlling hand in Tennessee politics but had not been very successful, as, for example, when he misjudged the political temper of the rising democracy in 1821 and supported Edward Ward for governor. It was only after he demonstrated charismatic charm in 1824 that his political stock rose. His election to the presidency in 1828 caused his enemies to forget—at least temporarily—past animosities.

That a strong reaction against Jackson should become openly apparent by late 1834 and early 1835 no doubt surprised the casual observer. After all, Jackson had carried Tennessee solidly in 1824, 1828, and 1832. Too, in the nullification controversy of 1832 and early 1833, Tennesseans spoke strongly for the Union and rallied in support of Jackson's nationalistic position. A realignment of the politcal factions in 1832 seemed to point toward union behind Jackson. Finally, smoldering resentments, although admitted, were kept reasonably quiet.

Jackson carried Tennessee in November 1832 by a 20–1 majority. Yet, some of the enthusiasm for him had begun to waiver as evidenced by the fact that only about one-half the number voting in 1828 even bothered to go to the polls in 1832—49.8 percent of the eligible voters as compared with 28.8 percent. This drop may be attributed to several factors; it is certainly true that the "stay at home" vote bespoke some dissatisfaction with the Chief and indicated that perhaps his charismatic grip upon the imagination of the people might be loosening. The Jackson party did not win a presidential election again until 1856, by which time Jackson had been dead for a decade and new issues had arisen.

The nullification controversy of 1832 arose after Vice President John C. Calhoun had suggested that a state, as a means of protection against objectionable congressional legislation, might suspend the operation of such legislation within its borders by calling a convention and nullifying it. A law called into question in this manner by a sovereign state then would be scrutinized by the other states just as they would consider a proposed constitutional amendment. If three-fourths of the states "ratified" the statute, only then would the complaining state be forced to obey it. But even then, the brilliant South Carolina theorist and politician concluded, a state might avoid compliance by withdrawing from the Union. The controversy was a signal for unionists and states' righters to choose sides; the Webster-Hayne debates on the Senate floor in 1830 were only some of many occasions when Calhoun's proposals were thoroughly discussed.

As long as nullification was considered only a theory, many Tennesseans agreed that the concept had merit. But when in late 1832 South Carolina sought to apply it by nullifying the tariff acts of 1828 and 1832, Tennesseans immediately affirmed that such a policy could destroy the Union. When on December 10, 1832 Jackson issued his Nullification Proclamation, in which he threatened to send troops into South Carolina to enforce the tariff laws, Tennesseans rallied to Jackson. Even Governor Carroll, generally outside the Jackson fold, wrote to the President to offer 10,000 Tennesseans to march into South Carolina. Both men and weapons, the governor said, were at the chief's disposal. Similarly, State Senator Theoderick F. Bradford, whom most people regarded as a consistent anti-Jacksonian, commended the President on the floor of the Senate for upholding the laws of the country against a doctrine that could bring down upon the nation "the horrors of civil war." In the legislative halls, in the press, and on the streets Jackson was upheld and nullifi-cation vilified.

The nullification controversy was apparently the high water mark of Jackson's support in Tennessee. Events and developments were soon to indicate, however, that the commendations for Jackson as expressed during the controversy applied to the Union and not to Jackson personally. To conclude that Tennesseans condemned nul-lification because they were "passionately pro-Jackson" is to ignore the strong reaction against the Chief that became clearly apparent two years later, as well as the seeds of dissent that were sown during the preceding decades of frontier politics. It is also important to recognize that a strong passion for the Union had existed in Tennes-see from the early days of statehood and had unified even the divergent political factions.

Reference has been made earlier to the shifting pattern of factional politics. By the time of Jackson's second inauguration, John Overton still supplied leadership for the Jackson cause and was ably assisted by William B. Lewis, John Eaton, and others. Newspaper support came from Allen A. Hall's Nashville *Republican*. The anti-Jackson alliance continued to consist of William B. Carter and John Williams of East Tennessee, Andrew Erwin, Newton Cannon, and Bradford of Middle Tennessee, and David Crockett of the Western District; all were reasonably quiet about their distrust of the Chief because of Jackson's power and position. They decided against establishing a Henry Clay newspaper in Nashville only after very careful consider-ation. Soon after the election of 1828, mild dissension and jealousies developed within the Jackson camps, because some refused to con-cede that Overton and his inner circle should be the exclusive executor of Jackson's political will in Tennessee. Hugh Lawson White and Felix Grundy, both in the United States Senate, were joined by Congressmen James K. Polk of Columbia and Cave Johnson of Clarksville and were heard through Samuel H. Laughlin's Nashville *Banner*. These leaders resented Overton's power over Jackson—and probably his personal wealth and conservative politics—and even courted members of the Erwin faction. Governor Carroll, a consummate politician, was able to work within both the pro- and the anti-Jackson camps. He retained the support of the Erwin faction and gave to it a large share of the state's patronage, but he also sided early with the Overton group by supporting Martin Van Buren as Jackson's successor. Congressman John Bell, Theoderick

John Henry Eaton (1790–1856) was a strong supporter of Jackson and served as United States senator (1818–1829) and secretary of war (1829–1831).

Bradford, and others successfully worked in and out of the Jackson camps.

But the smoldering resentments were difficult to keep beneath the surface. The Hero had built enemies over a long period. Commercial classes were angered in 1832 when Jackson vetoed a bill to recharter the Second Bank of the United States. Hundreds gathered in Nashville in April 1833, for example, to defend western credit and denounce as "unfortunate," "unwise," and "most unjust" a report prepared by James K. Polk in defense of Jackson's position. Admirers of Calhoun among the cotton planters thought that Jackson had unfairly condemned the South Carolinian but said little in view of the Chief's strong defense of the Union.

Despite the rumblings of unrest both within and outside the Jackson ranks, the General's national popularity still would have enabled him to remain in control at home had he not been resolutely determined to designate Van Buren as his successor. The "Little Magician" was never popular in Tennessee. He had supported William H. Crawford in 1824 but had moved into the Jackson orbit only after Jackson's manifestation of strength. Four years later Van Buren delivered New York's electoral votes to the Chief. For this and other deeds, Jackson had appointed him secretary of state in 1829 and arranged his nomination for vice president in 1832. Tennesseans, however, believed that he had mesmerized Jackson, and they refused to consider him a suitable choice to carry the banner of Jacksonian Democracy. Most people of the Volunteer State hoped that Hugh Lawson White could succeed the Old Hero. Believing that the president's nod was tantamount to the party nomination, they turned the full impact of their wrath against Van Buren in an effort to dissuade the Chief. As events developed, John Bell and White became the leaders of the anti-Jackson group in Tennessee.

John Bell is often considered the "creator" of the Whig party in Tennessee, although the Nashville congressman had no intention of leaving the Democratic party when he broke with Jackson. He had had little reason to support Jackson—on many issues he silently disagreed with the Chief's policies and was displeased at Jackson's coolness toward him—but Bell avoided an open break because of the President's political power. On the nullification issue, for example, Bell had been sympathetic to Calhoun. To friends, Bell conceded his concern about Jackson's Force Bill, which Bell thought unwise and unconstitutional; yet, as chairman of the House Judiciary Committee, he felt that political expediency required his support of the bill. That Bell was sympathetic to the United States Bank was well known and was pleasing to many of his Nashville constituents, although in 1832 he voted with the administration forces against rechartering it.

A factor that greatly affected Bell's relations with Jackson was the rivalry between himself and Polk for speaker of the House of Representatives in 1834. Polk had served in the House since 1825, and Bell had been first elected the following year; both were able men and both sought Jackson's support. The Chief did not endorse either candidate, but all members of Congress knew that Jackson favored Polk. Bell emerged the victor[1] after 10 ballots, but his support came largely from those who had opposed Jackson on the bank and other issues. Both Jackson and Polk then proceeded to denounce Bell. Jackson hinted to friends that the new speaker was exhibiting too much independence and was "politically gone" unless he lent greater moral support to Jackson's anti-bank policy. Polk condemned him for alleged "treachery."

Although the breach between the president and the speaker widened daily, both hesitated to move in a manner that would bring an irreparable breach. In selecting committee chairmen, for example, Bell named Polk to head the Ways and Means Committee and placed other Jackson men in high posts. On other matters Bell tried to be equally circumspect. Not long after he became speaker, however, he let it become known that he would not support Van Buren for the Democratic nomination in 1836 and that he might support Richard M. Johnson of Kentucky or Hugh Lawson White.

The possibility of White's candidacy had become a topic for political gossip as early as the constitutional convention of 1834. In December of that year the Tennessee congressional delegation, with the exception of Grundy, Polk, and Cave Johnson, met informally at the Washington residence of Congressman Balie Peyton and endorsed White for the nomination. The meeting at Peyton's was widely discussed. The legislature of Alabama endorsed White two weeks later, and leaders in other states discussed him as a possible nominee. Democratic leaders close to Jackson worried little about White's candidacy in a Democratic convention, for they were confi-

---

[1] Late in the next year Polk again contested the speakership with Bell and, with Jackson's support, defeated him. Bell unsuccessfully challenged him in 1837, and Polk continued as speaker until his resignation in 1839 to become a candidate for governor.

dent that he would be overwhelmed by Jackson's choice. They did, of course, fear a split in party ranks should White emerge as an opposition candidate.

White at first discouraged the move to endorse him. He had entered the Senate in 1825 as a supporter of Old Hickory's candidacy for the presidency; after Jackson became chief executive, he supported the general in matters regarding the bank and Indian removal, and Jackson in turn spoke of him as an "upright and incorruptible patriot." White was determined, however, not to be intimidated by either Jackson or Jackson men. White's supporters were encouraged considerably, then, when he stated publicly, after being told that Jackson had threatened to ruin him politically if he ran for President, that "despotic power" had never controlled him and that he would not "be the slave of any man or set of men." Such a statement well described the character of the thin, narrow-faced banker and judge whose cold blue eyes bespoke a stubborn puritan spirit. Describing himself as "stubborn and unyielding in disposition," time and again he had refused to compromise his high principles for political or economic gain.

When Congress adjourned in spring 1835, the struggle for political possession of Tennessee reached major proportions. Bell returned to Nashville in May and was asked by friends to deliver a major address at the city's fashionable Vauxhall Gardens. There, in a stirring oration on May 23, Bell "lighted the torch of revolt against the Democratic party." He strongly defended White's record, declared that White was an able and deserving friend of Jacksonian Democracy, and claimed that the Knoxvillian had been far more consistent in his support of the Chief's policies than had Van Buren. When Bell finished the two-hour address, none could question his open declaration of war on Jackson's choice for the White House. Bell left no stone unturned in his efforts to further the cause of Hugh Lawson White.

Jackson realized now that the supporters of White were serious and determined to press for the Democratic nomination, regardless of what he might say about the matter. For Bell, he expressed words of scorn; it was he who had mesmerized the Knoxvillian, and in the process he had committed political suicide. For White, instead of indignation, Jackson expressed only sympathy. If the senator could be shaken free from his lethargy and the polluting grip of John Bell's "cunning and management," the Chief said, he could be induced to stop the revolt and thus save himself from political ruin. Especially disturbing to the President was the fact that many of the leading newspapers and local politicians in the state supported White and Bell, while the Jacksonians said little. "How is it," Jackson wrote Polk, "that there is no man in the . . . [Democratic] ranks to take the stump, and relieve Tennessee from her degraded attitude of abandoning principle to sustain men who have apostatised [*sic*] from the republican fold for the sake of office?" If he were free to do it, Jackson admonished Polk, he would set the state firmly upon its democratic legs and hurl "Mr. Bell, Davy Crockett and Company . . . from the confidence of the people." Their only object, Jackson believed, was to destroy him politically and to hand him "down to posterity as an old dotard, ruled by corrupt office holders. . . ."

In the meantime, Jackson had decided that the Democratic candidate should be chosen by a convention in which all the states were represented. (The caucus system had been discarded after the election of 1824.) Consequently, the Jacksonians proclaimed that in May 1835 a free and open convention would be held in Baltimore. Accordingly, three days before Bell's Vauxhall Gardens speech, Democrats assembled as scheduled and nominated Van Buren as Jackson had planned. White's supporters made no effort to nominate their man, so convinced were they that the Jackson faction completely controlled the convention, which they called a "packed jury," and would secure the nomination of Van Buren. Tennessee Democrats sent no delegation, but a spectator from Murfreesboro, Edmund Rucker, was picked from the crowd, seated as the Tennessee "delegation," and permitted to cast all of the state's votes. The White-Bell group back home made much fun of the "Ruckerized convention," and the Jackson-Van Buren faction was mortified.

Although national issues obscured local ones, the Jackson forces could not ignore the gubernatorial campaign of 1835, in which Newton Cannon of Williamson County had challenged Governor Carroll. Cannon for many years had been a personal and political enemy of the Old General. During the early 1820's Cannon favored Crawford for the presidency and in 1827 he had been an unsuccessful candidate for governor against Sam Houston, Jackson's choice. He also had flaunted the chief by championing the United States Bank, and when Jackson successfully led the Democrats out of the old Republican party, Cannon became not a Democrat but a National Republican. The Bell-White revolt was the culmination of his dreams, and his announcement for governor contained a strongly worded endorsement of White for president.

Governor Carroll meanwhile permitted word to circulate that he would be responsive to a movement for a seventh term. He received Jackson's endorsement and promptly became a forthright supporter of Van Buren. Because Carroll had been a successful governor, he probably would have been elected again had not a major constitutional issue been involved. The constitution clearly specified that no person should serve as governor for more than six years in any term of eight. Carroll argued, however, that a "new" constitution had been framed in 1834 and that he, therefore, should be able to serve for another three consecutive terms under the "new" fundamental law. Flimsy argument that it was, Carroll ran in the expectation of establishing this interpretation of the constitutional revision and capitalizing upon his general popularity.

Although he was admittedly a man of mediocre talents, Cannon campaigned well on several firm issues. The dubious constitutionality of a fourth term did not sit well with many people, and Cannon kept the issue before them. Also very important, of course, was the claim that Cannon had been among the first to push forward the presidential candidacy of Hugh Lawson White against that of the Little Magician from New York, whose cause Carroll espoused in order to win Jackson's support. Cannon also spoke out for internal improvements and public schools, and his stand favoring a national bank gained him status among the rising commercial classes in the cities.

The election results were not surprising. Cannon received 41,970 votes, Carroll polled 31,205, and a third candidate, Parry W. Humphreys, also a White supporter, received 8,054. Cannon's strength had come mainly from East Tennessee, where White was most popular, and from the urban areas, particularly Nashville, where the Whig party was soon to show its strength. The opposition victories did not end with Cannon. The White-Bell party captured the state legislature and elected to the house speakership an outspoken White supporter, Ephraim H. Foster. The Jackson-Van Buren men claimed that Carroll had been defeated on the constitutional question, but the White supporters insisted that the chief issue had been that of White against Van Buren.

The developments over the previous few months stung the Old Chief to the quick, and he returned to Washington after the gubernatorial contest determined to crush the White movement and to destroy politically those associated with it. Jackson's chief lieutenants in Tennessee—Polk, Grundy, and Cave Johnson—were urged to work night and day to stop the revolt and return the bolters to the fold.

In the meantime the Whig party was formed in other states. It consisted of a variety of dissatisfied groups, including the National Republicans, who followed John Quincy Adams and Henry Clay; the states' rights Democrats, who had broken with Jackson when he threatened to use force against the nullifiers; the Anti-Masons, who had united in a protest against all secret orders; and the pro-bank and pro-internal improvement Democrats. In brief, these groups had one thing in common: their dislike of Jackson. The Chief had acted in such a dictatorial manner, they said, that he resembled King George III of colonial days. Therefore, they called themselves "Whigs" to remind people of an earlier group of patriots who had resisted dictatorship. The coalescence of the group was no surprise to a seasoned politician like Jackson, but opposition to him in Tennessee caught him completely off guard. Each new development cut him to the quick, and he reacted sometimes in anger and sometimes in pain.

Highly distressing to the Old Chief was a resolution adopted in the United States Senate in March 1834, censuring him for assuming "power not conferred by the constitution and the laws" after he ordered the removal of deposits from the United States Bank. Jackson's friends sought immediately to have the resolution repealed, or, as they said, "expunged." In Tennessee, the Chief's friends introduced resolutions in the house and senate to "instruct" Tennessee's senators in Washington to vote for expunging the censure. The legislators hoped also to embarrass White, who as senator opposed expunging but was expected to obey the instruction or resign.

White said little during the debate in Nashville and hid behind empty rhetoric. He had not been in favor of censuring the President in the first place, he said, but now that it had been written into the records he did not want to expunge it. To expunge, he said, would be to "obliterate" and "mutilate" the record and thus take away from the right to vote of those senators who had ruled on the matter earlier. He would not object to "repealing," "rescinding," or "reversing" the resolution, but he would resign before he would vote to expunge.

Senator James L. Totten of West Tennessee and Representative Joseph C. Guild of Sumner County, both Jacksonians, sponsored resolutions instructing Tennessee's senators to vote to expunge the resolution. "To expunge from the journals" of the Senate, Guild said, was the only "rightful" and "adequate" remedy. Totten and Guild were ably answered by Representative Addison A. Anderson of Jefferson County. Tracing the word "expunge" to its Latin origin and its eventual adoption into the Anglo-Saxon language, Anderson said that it could mean only to "erase," "efface," and "obliterate." He opposed such action, and he praised Senator White for his stand to maintain the integrity of the congressional journals. The resolution to instruct was then tabled and all later efforts to remove it failed, despite the fact that on more than one occasion Jackson sent the legislators free issues of the Washington *Globe* containing speeches by Thomas Hart Benton favoring expunging. This action probably hurt Jackson's cause more than it helped, because he was promptly accused of trying to interfere with legislative proceedings.[2]

Even before a vote could be taken on the resolution to instruct, White's group had forced to the floor the question of the senator's reelection.[3] He was chosen without a dissenting vote. Soon thereafter the legislators endorsed the Knoxvillian for President by a house vote of 60 to 12 and 23 to 2 in the senate. They also had a word to say about Jackson. While expressing general approval of the policies of the "distinguished Chief Magistrate" who was "qualified by his principles, energy and great popularity," the lawmakers condemned the "tendency to a usurpation of the rights and powers of the people" in the Baltimore convention and made a plea for freedom of elections.

White accepted the legislative endorsement, and Jackson promptly read him out of the party. A vigorous campaign ensued. The President spent the summer at the Hermitage, but his stay became a political campaign for Van Buren rather than a vacation. At several places Jackson denounced White as a "red hot Federalist." Bell, Jackson said, was an "apostate." In Nashville, the President was feted at a barbecue given at the Hermitage, and hundreds of guests heard him again denounce the senator as a Federalist and a sympathizer with Whigs, nullifiers, and bank men.

[2] The censure was not expunged until 1837. With Thomas Hart Benton taking the lead, and Daniel Webster, Henry Clay, and John C. Calhoun vainly objecting, the Jacksonians had the satisfaction of seeing the secretary of the Senate draw lines around the resolution condemning the chief and write across it, "Expunged by order of the Senate, this 16th day of January, 1837."

[3] White had been elected in 1825 to fill out Jackson's unexpired term and was reelected in 1829.

The White forces were not idle. They made the chief issue White's opposition to Van Buren rather than to Jackson. They presented the senator, not Van Buren, as the true wearer of the mantle of Jacksonian Democracy. The White forces shunned any appearance of adhering to another party, although outside the state they were generally considered Whigs. White on several occasions emphasized that he was not "in the confidence of any party" and stoutly maintained that the only matter of disagreement between him and the President was Jackson's officious and inexcusable determination to choose Van Buren as his successor.

Whigs throughout the nation considered White one of their own. Realizing that they lacked strength against an established party such as the Democrats and against a hero such as Jackson, the Whigs believed that their best chance for success lay in nominating several candidates in the hope that the choice of a President would eventually have to be made in the House of Representatives. Consequently, Daniel Webster of Massachusetts and William Henry Harrison of Ohio also became candidates.

The Jacksonians in Tennessee argued that a Jackson-controlled Democrat such as Van Buren would be better than Harrison or Webster. The Nashville *Union,* which supported Van Buren, presented damaging statistics just before the election. White's name would appear on the ballot in only 11 of the 26 states; those 11 states had only 133 electoral votes, whereas 148 votes were necessary for election. Therefore, White's only hope was his selection by members of the House of Representatives, where Webster and Harrison men predominated.

Tennesseans voted for White despite the fact that his chances of being elected were slim indeed. The vote was 35,962 to 26,120. Even Old Hickory's Hermitage precinct voted 61 to 20 for White. It was a stunning blow to the Democratic party in Tennessee and to the Old Hero himself despite the fact that Van Buren won the presidency by a comfortable electoral majority.[4] White's strength came mainly from the eastern and western sections of the state. In the Jackson stronghold of Middle Tennessee, where Polk, Grundy, and Cave Johnson waged a hard battle, each candidate carried twelve counties.

The victory was more than a personal one for Bell and White. It

[4] White carried only one other state—Georgia—but did receive 40 percent or more of the votes in Mississippi, North Carolina, Virginia, and Missouri.

was the birth pangs of the Whig party in Tennessee, although White's men had carefully avoided that label. For the next twenty years Tennessee was to be a two-party state, and Jackson, who died nine years later, was not to see his state again in the Democratic fold in a presidential contest.

While Tennesseans in Washington and at home fought political battles, others in Texas sought to cast aside the Mexican yoke. Tennesseans had been among the first Anglo-Americans to migrate to Texas. The Panic of 1819 served as an impetus for westward movement. The establishment of Mexican independence in 1821 left Americans free to negotiate with the new government instead of the Spanish, and Stephen F. Austin therefore negotiated in that year a contract to establish a settlement of 300 families, among whom were some Tennesseans. Within the next three years many others from Tennessee joined the exodus to Texas.

Foremost among Tennesseans who migrated westward was Sam Houston. After his unfortunate marriage he had resigned the governorship of the state and had moved west. A few years later Houston became active in Texas affairs and served as chairman of a committee that wrote a Texas constitution. By November 1835, he was commander in chief of the Texas forces, and he soon became the first president of the Lone Star Republic.

Others from Tennessee also became prominent in Texas affairs. George Campbell Childress wrote the Texas declaration of independence. He had been editor of the *National Banner and Nashville Advertiser* before his departure for Texas early in 1836. Childress applied for a grant of land in a colony headed by another Tennessean, Sterling C. Robertson, and immediately became active in public affairs. Two brothers, William H. and John A. Wharton, migrated several years before Childress. In 1836 William H. Wharton and Stephen Austin visited many cities, including Nashville, New York, and Philadelphia, in search of aid for the new republic. John A. Wharton was editor of a Texas paper called the *Advocate of the People's Rights.* Several men from Davidson County, including Sterling Robertson, organized a company known as the "Texas Association," and expressed the intention of leading hundreds of Tennesseans to Texas.

Although Mexican officials at first welcomed the Americans, their enthusiasm soon cooled when they heard ambitious Yankees talk of annexing Texas and noted increasing trouble between the Americans and the natives. Finally, in 1830, Mexico forbade further immigration from the United States. Stephen Austin presented demands before Mexican officials, including one to repeal the ban on immigration, but he was arrested and imprisoned. Actual hostilities began in October 1835 at Gonzales, and Houston was named commander in chief of the army.

Tennesseans viewed these events with alarm. Soon after news of the outbreak was received, meetings were held across the state to arouse interest in helping the Texans. Hundreds of young men departed immediately by land and sea to shoulder arms in the cause of Texas liberty. General Richard G. Dunlap boasted that he would raise a force of more than two thousand men if the Texans would furnish transportation. Early in the following year, the ill-fated David Crockett arrived with a few friends to join, as he said, "the volunteers from the United States."

When armed bands left Tennessee and other states to fight in the cause for Texas independence, the Mexican *chargé d'affaires* in Washington complained bitterly. Finally, Mexican officials issued a circular in which they threatened to punish as pirates all armed foreigners entering Texas. Men from the Volunteer State were not intimidated, however, and continued to fight against Mexican oppression.

In the meantime, Texans were winning on the field of battle. On April 21, Houston defeated and captured Santa Anna at San Jacinto in the last major battle of the war. Interest in the welfare of Texans did not subside, however. Meetings were held throughout Tennessee to consider sending food, clothing, and other relief to the destitute. Tennesseans appointed themselves personal guardians of Texas liberty and independence, and stood ready to strike when the need arose. John A. Rogers of East Tennessee, for example, wrote Austin that in his opinion 30,000 or 40,000 men would volunteer to repel the invader should he attack again.

Many Tennesseans gave their lives in the cause for Texas independence, but none was better known that David Crockett. Drama and fiction have been kind to the memory of the "King of the Wild Frontier." He joined Colonel William B. Travis at the Alamo in February 1836 and was with him when the Mexicans slaughtered the small band of defenders on March 6. Stories differ about the last hours of Crockett and the other defenders of the Alamo, but if the Frontier King was not among the last five or six survivors, slaying scores of hapless Mexicans on all sides, it should not detract from his

David Crockett, frontiersman and hero of the Alamo, moved to Texas in 1835 after serving two terms in Congress from Tennessee.

glory. He was one of Tennessee's great fighting men—a person of indomitable bravery and intrepid courage, whose life was dedicated to the frontier ideals of liberty and freedom.

In Washington, President Jackson was reluctant to push the matter of annexation. Representative John Bell presented a memorial from a Nashville delegation requesting recognition of the new republic, and Hugh Lawson White presented the same memorial in the Senate. On the last day of his presidential term, Jackson appointed a *chargé d'affaires* to Texas and received a Texas minister. Texans had expressed their desire for annexation soon after the Battle of San Jacinto, but it was not until 1845 that the American Congress acted favorably.

Although the Texas Revolution and the revolt against Jackson overshadowed everything else during Cannon's first term, at least one important law, enacted in December 1835, should be mentioned. This measure established a new supreme court in accordance with the constitutional provision of 1835. Legislators were in agreement that the judicial body should be composed of three members and, in order that all sections of the state might be equally represented, that not more than one justice should reside in any one of the three grand divisions of the state. The salary was fixed at $1,800 per annum, and the term was set at twelve years. William B. Turley, William B. Reese, and Nathan Green were selected as justices.

The White-Bell forces had avoided the Whig label in 1836, but within a year it was evident that they had assumed the principles of the party. Not until 1839 did White reluctantly accept the Whig classification, although others by that time had embraced the new party both in name and in principle. From the beginning there had been no hesitancy on the part of Governor Cannon, who boldly announced for reelection in 1837 as a Whig. Democrats had difficulty finding a candidate to oppose Cannon, so pessimistic were they about their chances of victory. Finally, however, General Robert Armstrong, a successful military leader but poor political campaigner, agreed to run. Cannon's chief issue was the financial Panic of 1837, which he carefully blamed on Jackson and Van Buren. The governor won by a majority of more than 17,000, and his party also gained control of both houses of the legislature.

The Panic of 1837 caused economic issues to loom large during Cannon's second term. Farm prices were depressed, many merchants were bankrupt, and some of the principal banks were near financial ruin. Legislators, after considerable debate, decided upon sweeping "new deal" legislation that included establishing a state bank with broad powers and authorizing the issuance of internal improvement bonds to the amount of $4 million, largely in payment of state subscriptions of 50 percent of the stock of railroad and turnpike companies. The bank was to have a capital stock of $5 million, and was required to set aside from its profits annually $100,000 for common schools and $18,000 for academies. This legislation consolidated the commercial classes and for a time relieved pressures on debtors, but it was not until after Cannon had left the gubernatorial chair that prosperity returned.

In the meantime, ambitious and impetuous Whigs became embarrassed by the fact that both of the state's senators were Democrats. The Whigs therefore decided upon a bold course designed to replace Felix Grundy, whose term would expire in 1839, with a man of their own party. On December 15, 1837—some fifteen months before the term expired—the Whigs chose Ephraim H. Foster as Grundy's successor. Grundy, realizing that he could not defeat the Whig coalition, had refused to run, and William Carroll, backed by Democrats, was soundly defeated. Grundy, of course, had the right to remain in the Senate until March 1839, when his term expired, but Whigs—thinking that he would rather resign than comply—tried to remove him earlier by passing a resolution instructing him to vote against the Van Buren–sponsored subtreasury plan then before Congress. He surprised the Whigs by obeying the instruction, but within a few months resigned to become attorney general in Van Buren's cabinet. Governor Cannon then appointed Foster to fill out the remaining months of the unexpired term.

The period of 1834–1839 constituted a stormy half-decade in Tennessee politics. The Whig party was established, not originally as a segment of the national Whig group, but as a faction opposed to Jackson's arbitrary conduct in selecting his successor. The Tennessee group gained momentum with the gubernatorial election of 1835, enhanced its power and increased its membership with the presidential election of 1836, and by 1837 had gained strength equal to that of its rival. By that time the political map of the state had jelled, and party members remained loyal through the election of 1852. Of the 65 counties making returns in 1836, 53 continued to support the same party for the next 16 years. Of the 12 remaining, 6 supported

White in 1836 but voted for Democratic candidates thereafter, and the other 6 wavered from one party to the other.

Shortly after the election of 1836, a newspaper editor in West Tennessee described the campaign as having been a contest between the rural and the urban populations. The Whigs were said to have come largely from the wealthy city group, with some of the planter class scattered among the rural population; the Democrats were thought to be drawn mainly from the poor, agrarian group. Writers have tended to apply that interpretation to the parties during the twenty years of Whig-Democratic competition and have especially emphasized that Whigs were a class of aristocrats who distrusted "that scene of wild impulse, and . . . pure democracy." More recent studies, however, have modified this point of view and have shown that while large planter and commercial interests may have been exceedingly strong among Whigs, they did not dominate the party to the exclusion of all other people.

The two decades following the election of 1836 have been described as a period of "partisan fury" in Tennessee politics. Certainly never before or since has Tennessee had two political parties so nearly evenly matched.

SUGGESTED READINGS

Books

Thomas P. Abernethy, *From Frontier to Plantation in Tennessee* (1932; rpt. University, Ala., 1967); E. Malcolm Carroll, *Origins of the Whig Party* (Durham, 1925); Joseph H. Parks, *John Bell of Tennessee* (Baton Rouge, 1950); George R. Poage, *Henry Clay of the Whig Party* (New York, 1936); Charles Sellers, Jr., *James K. Polk, Jacksonian, 1795–1843* (Princeton, 1957); James A. Shackford, *David Crockett, the Man and the Legend*, ed. John B. Shackford (Chapel Hill, 1956); Glyndon G. Van Deusen, *The Life of Henry Clay* (Boston, 1937).

Articles

Thomas P. Abernethy, "The Origin of the Whig Party in Tennessee," *MVHR* 12 (March 1926), 504–22; Thomas B. Alexander, "Thomas A. R. Nelson as an Example of Whig Conservatism in Tennessee," *THQ* 15 (March 1956), 17–29; Robert Cassell, "Newton Cannon and State Politics, 1835–1839," *THQ* 15 (Dec. 1956), 305–21; Clement L. Grant, "The Public Career of Cave Johnson," *THQ* 10 (Sept. 1951), 195–223; L.

Paul Gresham, "Hugh Lawson White: Frontiersman, Lawyer, and Judge," *ETHSP* 19 (1947), 3–24; Gresham, "Hugh Lawson White as a Tennessee Politician and Banker," *ETHSP* 18 (1946), 25–46; Gresham, "The Public Career of Hugh Lawson White," *THQ* 3 (Dec. 1944), 291–318; Robert McBride, "David Crockett and His Memorials in Tennessee," *THQ* 26 (Fall 1967), 219–39; Chase C. Mooney, "The Political Career of Adam Huntsman," *THQ* 10 (June 1951), 99–126; Powell Moore, "The Political Background of the Revolt against Jackson in Tennessee," *JSH* 2 (Aug. 1936), 335–59; Norman L. Parks, "The Career of John Bell as Congressman from Tennessee," *THQ* 1 (Sept. 1942), 229–49; Ulrich B. Phillips, "The Southern Whigs, 1834–1854," in *Essays in American History Dedicated to Frederick Jackson Turner,* ed. Guy S. Ford (New York, 1910), 203–9; Charles Grier Sellers, Jr., "Who Were the Southern Whigs?" *AHR* 59 (Jan. 1954), 335–46; Glyndon G. Van Duesen, "Some Aspects of Whig Thought and Theory in the Jacksonian Period," *AHR* 63 (Jan. 1958), 305–22.

12.

~ *Transportation and Internal Improvements*

THE first settlers came to the frontier, as one contemporary observed, "anyway they could get thar." Whether
they walked, or came by horse, boat, or wagon, transportation was
always a major problem. The long hunters simply carried their furs
back east on their backs or, if the load was large, on the backs of pack
horses. Later, as established settlers produced crops for market,
boats and barges, trains of packhorses and wagons, and still later,
steamboats and locomotives, came into use.

Well-traveled turnpikes or railroad beds usually had their beginning as Indian trails (or traces) or as routes that wild animals had
followed for years. A half-dozen or more roads were in use by the
time of statehood. Perhaps the first and most traveled trail into
Tennessee was the Wilderness Road, which had been blazed by
Daniel Boone in 1775 from Long Island of the Holston through
Cumberland Gap into Kentucky territory. It was an extension of a
road down the Holston Valley through southwest Virginia and
served a vast number of people who sought their fortunes in the
trans-Allegheny West. Indeed, as it was widened later into a wagon
road, it became one of the most important and best-known routes in
western history. Three years later an important wagon road was
opened from Burke County, North Carolina to Jonesborough and
from there down the Tennessee valley. Ten years later in 1788, a road
was cut from Campbell's Station, a few miles west of Knoxville,
across the wilderness into the Cumberland settlements. This road,
known as the North Carolina Road or sometimes as "Avery's Road"
(after Peter Avery, who guided the expedition), greatly facilitated
travel between east and west. For years before, easterners moving

west had followed roughly the route James Robertson took in 1779—by the Wilderness Road through Cumberland Gap into Kentucky and southward through the Cumberland Valley into Nashville.

Other roads were built a few years after statehood. One connecting the east with the Cumberland settlements was the Walton Road from Southwest Point (Kingston) to Nashville. Its construction, coming as a result of a provision in the Holston Treaty for "free and unmolested use of a Road" between east and west, was ultimately paid for by a state appropriation and tolls collected from users after a lottery conducted in 1794 failed to raise the necessary revenue. Named for William Walton, one of the commissioners appointed to supervise its construction, the turnpike became the first toll road in the state. One of the best-known roads was the "Natchez Trace." Extending north from Natchez, it connected at Nashville with the Tennessee Path to Lexington, Kentucky. In 1804 the legislature appropriated $750 for a road from Southwest Point to the Cherokee Nation.

Roads, dusty in the summer and muddy in the winter, required constant work to keep them in a good state of repair. Legislators in 1804 authorized counties to lay out public roads and build bridges and also required all white males between the ages of 18 and 50 to work on the roads one day per month or pay 75 cents per day instead. Counties had already been authorized to place turnpikes (turnstiles) on the roads to collect tolls adequate for maintenance costs. Also, individuals and corporations were authorized to construct and open roads and to collect tolls for their use.

Much more important to the early settlers than roads was water transportation. Early settlements such as Nashville, Knoxville, and Clarksville were established on rivers, as were Memphis and Chattanooga later; flatboats and keelboats plied the waters from the days of the first settlements. Flatboats varied from primitive rafts to large flat-bottomed boats with cabins for passengers. Propelling flatboats upstream was almost impossible until the application of steam, so after owners reached their destination they usually destroyed or sold the boats and returned to Tennessee overland. The keelboat, lighter and narrower than flatboats, was framed around a long, stout piece of timber called a "keel" that made for easier steering. It could be navigated upstream by sails if the wind was adequate, or by poles in the hands of husky crewmen, who placed the ends of their poles on the bottom of the river and propelled the vessel upstream as they walked from prow to stern. Where the current was too deep or swift for poling, the crew tied ropes around nearby trees and pulled the boat upstream. Both methods, of course, involved back-breaking labor. In 1819, it required 67 days to propel a keelboat from New Orleans to Nashville.

Superior water transportation was one of several reasons why settlements in the Cumberland Valley grew more rapidly after 1800 than those of East Tennessee. Cumberland people had a reasonably direct access by river to the Gulf of Mexico at New Orleans, even though the Cumberland does follow a northward course for some distance before reaching the Ohio. But the much greater bend of the Tennessee into Alabama and its longer northward course across Tennessee and Kentucky to the Ohio, together with the serious obstructions at Muscle Shoals and elsewhere, meant that the inhabitants of the upper Tennessee Valley had a long and hazardous journey to reach the mouth of the Mississippi. Consequently, they were greatly interested in the possibility of a shortcut to the Gulf of Mobile, made feasible by the proximity of branches of the Mobile River to branches of the Tennessee. Residents of lower Middle Tennessee were interested in the proposal, made as early as 1807, that a road or canal be built to connect the Tombigbee, the western branch of the Mobile River, with Bear Creek, which flows into the Tennessee below the Muscle Shoals. East Tennesseans were more partial to a connection between the eastern tributaries of the Mobile—the Alabama and its branch, the Coosa—with the Hiwassee River, which would not only provide a shorter route to the gulf but would also bypass the obstructions at Muscle Shoals. A modification of this idea seems to have been used to some extent, beginning in 1821. The Cherokee Indians objected, however, and when a company was chartered by Tennessee in 1836 to build a Hiwassee-Coosa canal, the Indians absolutely refused to permit its construction. By the time the Indians were moved west, the railroad era had arrived, and the canal idea was considered obsolete.

Steamboats were on the Mississippi River by 1811, but nearly eight years had passed before one ventured on the Cumberland as far as Nashville. Arriving four years after Jackson's spectacular victory at New Orleans, the boat, named the *General Jackson*, attracted hundreds of people, who lined the banks. Within a short time others were in and out of Nashville, and the town, soon becoming a center for river traffic, exported tobacco, cotton, iron, and other products on a regular basis to New Orleans. Knoxville merchants joined those from other towns in purchasing goods from New Orleans that would be shipped to Nashville. Such goods were then transported overland to Knoxville.

The coming of the steamboat to Tennessee waters greatly stimulated interest in internal improvements, with major attention being given to the removal of obstructions to steamboat navigation in the principal rivers. Interest also was stimulated in the use of keelboats on the smaller streams and in turnpike building, so that outlying farmers might have more ready access to steamboat shipping points.

Busy legislators in 1830 enacted a comprehensive system of state aid for transportation and at the same time sought federal assistance in making internal improvements. On January 2, 1830, lawmakers appropriated $150,000; $60,000 each was earmarked for work in East and Middle Tennessee, and the remaining $30,000 was designated for the Western District. Although the funds were subsequently scattered among many local projects, an accomplishment of lasting value was the improvement of the Tennessee River between the Knoxville and Alabama line, which greatly facilitated navigation. Between 1832 and 1837, the federal government appropriated $135,000 for improvement of the Cumberland River below Nashville. Although President Andrew Jackson opposed federal aid for state transportation facilities in his veto of the Maysville Road Bill, he subsequently took the position that he would approve appropriations for river improvement up to the highest port of entry from the ocean, because such rivers were related to foreign commerce. Nashville was declared to be a port of entry, and under this interpretation the appropriation for improvement of the Cumberland was granted.

Interest in railroads began during the 1820s. East Tennesseans, conscious of a loss of both political and economic power to the west and central sections, embraced the railroad concept as the dawn of a new day. James G. M. Ramsey, a prominent Knoxville businessman and physician, expressed the belief of many that inasmuch as the logical market for East Tennessee was the Atlantic Seaboard, railroads would now make possible a very profitable connection with Charleston, Savannah, and other eastern ports. He was joined by other publicists, including the editor of the Rogersville *Rail-Road Advocate*, who in 1832 cautioned his fellow citizens that "Rail-roads are the only hope of East Tennessee." Charleston, wrote the editor, looked with "outstretched arms" to the West.

When a few years later the Louisville, Cincinnati, and Charleston Railroad was incorporated, 400 delegates met in Knoxville on July 4,1836 to help plan the difficult route over the mountains along the French Broad River to Knoxville and thence through the Cumberland Gap into Kentucky. Also in that year, the Hiwassee Railroad was chartered to build a road from Knoxville to Georgia, where it would connect with the projected extension of the South Carolina Railroad to the Tennessee River. Thus, Knoxville would be supplied with two separate rail connections with Charleston. Meanwhile, residents of Memphis became interested in the plans of railroad men in Charleston to expand westward. Major General Edmund Pendleton Gaines sought to tie Memphis not only with Charleston but also with Baltimore. Little was accomplished. Although one locomotive did run briefly from Memphis to LaGrange, railroad construction for the most part awaited the 1850s.

Partly to relieve conditions occasioned by the Panic of 1837, legislators in the following year enacted the Bank and Improvement Act, which provided for river improvement and turnpike and railroad construction. The law, like another state aid measure passed two years earlier, was not overly successful. The only tangible benefit was the construction of turnpikes, most of them in Middle Tennessee. State credit suffered because of the measures, and fewer than one-half of the bonds could be sold. Bonds issued to the railroad and turnpike companies in payment of the state subscriptions were sold by the companies at ruinous discounts; many were sold in the markets of the world for whatever they would bring—in some cases as little as 50 cents on the dollar. In 1840, the state aid laws were repealed by a large majority of both parties in the legislature. The railroad plans were the chief casualties of the depression.

The state aid system of 1836–1838 enabled 24 turnpike companies—19 in Middle Tennessee and 5 in West Tennessee—to qualify for state subscriptions, and they eventually received a total of $1,245,357 in state aid. A few of the companies failed, but the others managed to build more than 400 miles of turnpikes. The most important of the roads were those radiating from Nashville to neighboring towns, because the turnpikes greatly speeded the rise of the capital city, with its steamboat facilities, to a dominant economic

position and contributed to the prosperity of the whole Nashville
Basin. An unfortunate result was the accentuation of sectional an-
tagonisms, since East and West Tennessee had received little or no
benefit from the state subsidies. In 1841–1842, separate statehood
movements arose in both sections, and although other issues were
involved, the disparity of benefits in internal improvement contributed. David Fentress, a West Tennessee legislator, complained in
1842 of discrimination when he exclaimed on the floor of the house:

> Yes, it may now be said, with propriety, what was said of old Rome,
> "every road leads to Nashville." Yet the people of the most remote
> parts of the state have to pay their proportion of the taxes, raised to
> build these fine roads, though they may never have seen the beauti-
> ful city of Nashville. . . .

Fentress ventured a prophecy that if the selfish Middle Tennesseans
denied the "provinces" their paltry river funds, there would appear
in the Western District a "Peter the Hermit" and in East Tennessee
an "Attila the Hun" who would "preach a crusade" and lead an
avenging host that would "devastate and waste your Palestine."[1]
Legislators from Middle Tennessee might have been intimidated by
such a threat, for they promptly permitted the appropriation of
$200,000 for river improvement, the amount to be equally divided
between the eastern and western sections.

Tennesseans lost interest in railroads for almost a decade after the
Panic of 1837. It was not until sessions of the Southern and Western
Convention held in Memphis in July and November of 1845 that
interest was again aroused. The November meeting, presided over
by John C. Calhoun, attracted more than 600 delegates from sixteen
states and territories. Within the next few years the legislature had
chartered the Nashville & Chattanooga, the Memphis & Charleston,
and the East Tennessee & Georgia railroad companies, designed to
connect Nashville, Memphis, and Knoxville, respectively, with the
Georgia and South Carolina roads leading to the Atlantic Coast at
Charleston and Savannah. Despite this flurry of activity, the New
York-based *Railroad Gazette* published statistics on January 1, 1850,
indicating that while Georgia had completed 631 miles of railroad,
Alabama 111, Mississippi 98, and Kentucky 28, Tennessee had
finished none.

The first railroad completed in Tennessee was the Nashville and

[1] Folmsbee, *Sectionalism*, 219–20.

Chattanooga, finished in 1854. The incorporation of the company in December 1845 was the result of a vigorous campaign waged by Dr. James Overton and A. O. P. Nicholson of Nashville to overcome the indifference of a city apparently wedded to steamboat navigation. They were aided by the state geologist, Dr. Gerard Troost, who made a report concerning the feasibility of the road and the abundance of mineral resources, especially coal, along the route. The Memphis conventions of 1845 also created a fear that the establishment of a rail connection between Memphis and Charleston would take much of the trade of lower Middle Tennessee away from Nashville. From the organization of the company until long after the road's completion, Vernon K. Stevenson served as president. It was through his efforts and those of former Governor James C. Jones that funds to complete construction were obtained from stock sales in Charleston, Nashville, and other towns and counties along the route. To avoid much of the mountain barrier, Stevenson chose a route that dipped into Alabama and approached Chattanooga along the Tennessee River. The road was completed to the river at Bridgeport, Alabama by the beginning of 1853 and to Chattanooga in January, 1854. With the aid of booming business during the Civil War the company was able to pay off its bonds when they became due. Thus the Nashville and Chattanooga was not only the first Tennessee road completed but also the only one that the state aided without suffering any financial loss.

In 1850 the Western & Atlantic Railroad had completed tracks from Atlanta to Chattanooga. Officials had established December 1, 1849 as a target date for completion and when they learned that a tunnel at Dalton would not be ready until the following summer, they hauled a locomotive and cars around the tunnel so that they could chug into Chattanooga by December 1.

Other lines were soon completed (see map 7). Feeders to the Nashville & Chattanooga included the McMinnville & Manchester, which was completed in 1857, and a line operating to the Sewanee Mining Company near Tracy City, where coal was mined. Progress on the Nashville & Northwestern was being made when the Civil War broke out. Projected to run from Nashville to the Mississippi River at Hickman, Kentucky, the road had been built eastward from Hickman as far as McKenzie before the war began. But at the eastern end, the road had been built only a few miles from Nashville when the Union army assumed control and continued it as a war measure,

to the Tennessee River at New Johnsonville. In 1872, shortly after
the war, the Nashville & Northwestern was absorbed at the Nashville and Chattanooga, and the combination assumed the name of the
Nashville, Chattanooga, & St. Louis Railroad.

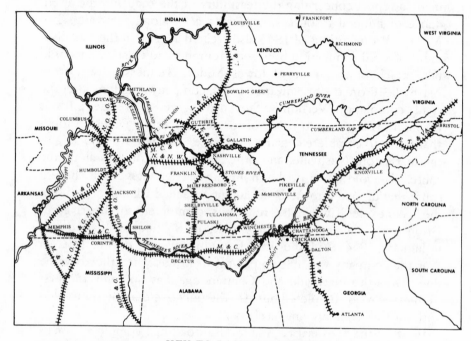

KEY TO RAILROAD NAMES

C. Br. Cleveland Branch, East
  Tennessee and Georgia
E.&K. Edgefield and Kentucky
E.T.&Ga. East Tennessee and Georgia
E.T.&Va. East Tennessee and Virginia
L.&N. Louisville and Nashville
M.&C. Memphis and Charleston
M.C.&L. Memphis, Clarksville,
  and Louisville

M.&O. Memphis and Ohio
M.&T. Mississippi and Tennessee
Mob.&O. Mobile and Ohio
N.&C. Nashville and Chattanooga
N.&N.W. Nashville and Northwestern
N.O.J.&G.N. New Orleans, Jackson,
  and Great Northern
N.O.&O. New Orleans and Ohio
N. & D. Nashville and Decatur
W.&A. Western and Atlantic

Map 7. Railroads in Tennessee at the Time of the Civil War

The Memphis & Charleston Railroad, chartered in 1846, made
little progress until the 1850s. Former Governor James C. Jones was
the first president of the company and was highly successful in selling
stock in widely separated locales. In New Orleans, for example, he

argued that the building of the road would greatly increase the amount of cotton that would be shipped down the Mississippi. In Charleston, however, he confidently predicted that a rail connection with the Atlantic Ocean would divert most of the Mississippi River trade to Charleston. When the Memphis and Charleston absorbed the old LaGrange and Memphis company, good use was made of the construction work done by the latter. The Memphis and Charleston also took over the railroad that had been built around Muscle Shoals. For some time Mississippi delayed the work by refusing to grant a charter unless the road was built through Holly Springs. Eventually this restriction was removed, and the original route was followed, cutting across merely the northeast corner of Mississippi by way of Corinth. The road was completed to Stevenson, Alabama in March 1857, and since arrangements had been made to use the tracks of the Nashville and Chattanooga for the remainder of the distance to Chattanooga, the rail connection between Memphis and the Atlantic seaboard was now complete.

Another part of the present Southern Railroad System built before the Civil War brought to reality East Tennesseans' early dream of seeing a railroad through their section that would connect at each end—through Georgia and Virginia—with lines leading to the Atlantic Seaboard. This aim was achieved by two companies, the East Tennessee and Georgia and the East Tennessee and Virginia, which were consolidated in 1869 under the name of East Tennessee, Virginia & Georgia.

The incorporation of the East Tennessee and Virginia Railroad on January 27, 1848 resulted from a dispute between railroad and river improvement interests during a convention at Greeneville in 1847. The legislature, however, failed to carry out the compromise recommendations of the convention—a state subscription to the railroad company and an appropriation of $250,000 for the improvement of the Holston and French Broad rivers. With great difficulty the supporters of the railroad succeeded in getting enough subscriptions to organize the company in 1849, and Dr. Samuel B. Cunningham of Jonesboro was elected president. To advance the project a group of Jonesboro citizens began the publication of the *Rail Road Journal* in 1850. Jonesboro and Greeneville became involved in a bitter controversy with Rogersville and other communities on the other side of Bay's Mountain over the location of the route. The eastern route won, and the Carter's Valley people had to be satisfied with a branch line, built by a separate company from Bull's Gap to Rogersville, which was not completed until after the war. When the East Tennessee and Virginia was opened in May 1858 throughout its entire length, from Knoxville to Bristol, it filled a gap in completed rail lines extending from such Eastern cities as Boston, New York, and Washington all the way to Atlanta, Charleston, Savannah, Montgomery, Nashville, New Orleans, and Mobile. East Tennessee's "isolated condition" at last had been ended.

Another railroad system of great importance in Tennessee is the Louisville & Nashville, familiarly known as the L.&N., which was financed largely by a subscription of a million dollars from the city of Louisville and by state aid under Tennessee's general laws. Its route in Tennessee was determined by the amounts subscribed by local governments along the alternative routes, and Gallatin and Sumner County won the contest. Completed on the eve of secession (October 1859), the road was viewed as a link binding the North and South. The legislatures of Tennessee and Kentucky met in Louisville and then joined in a Union-saving excursion to Columbus, Ohio. Eloquent Unionist speeches were made by political leaders of Tennessee who not long thereafter were to be identified with the Confederate States of America.

Other parts of the present L.&N. system were built by other companies, which were absorbed by the L.&N. after the Tennessee state-aid system collapsed during the Reconstruction period. Before the war, one line, generally known as the Nashville & Decatur Railroad and built by two companies, the Tennessee and Alabama and the Central Southern, connecting at Columbia, was completed from Nashville southward to the southern boundary of the state, where the line met an Alabama road from Decatur on the Memphis & Charleston Railroad. Another road later acquired by the L.&N. in which Middle Tennessee was greatly interested was the Edgefield and Kentucky. Early in 1860 it was completed, running from Edgefield (a suburb of Nashville) across the Cumberland River, northwestward to the Kentucky line at Guthrie.

Before the Civil War, West Tennesseans had also acquired rail connections with Mobile, New Orleans, and Columbus (Kentucky) as a result of the work of the Mobile & Ohio Railroad (now the Gulf, Mobile, & Ohio) and a group of companies now included in the Illinois Central system. Involved was a race between Mobile and

New Orleans in their efforts to achieve a connection by railroad with the mouth of the Ohio River. The aim of Mobile was to divert to its port much of the traffic going down the Mississippi River to New Orleans, but the citizens of the Crescent City were determined not only to counteract that effort but also to negate the influence of the Memphis & Charleston and other railroads in diverting traffic from "Old Man River." As it was finally built, the Mobile & Ohio entered Tennessee just north of Corinth, Mississippi, where it connected with the Memphis & Charleston Railroad, and proceeded north through Jackson and Trenton in the direction of Columbus, Kentucky, below the mouth of the Ohio. There the Mobile & Ohio made connection by ferry with Cairo, the terminus of the Illinois Central Railroad from Chicago. The section from Columbus to Jackson, Tennessee was completed by the end of 1858, but the longer portion between Jackson and Mobile was not finished until April 22, 1861, ten days after the Civil War had begun.

Meanwhile, the New Orleans, Jackson & Great Northern Railroad had been completed through Jackson, Mississippi to Canton; and the line was continued by Mississippi Central Railroad to Grand Junction, where the Memphis & Charleston crossed the Tennessee-Mississippi state line, and by the Mississippi Central & Tennessee Railroad to a connection with the Mobile & Ohio at Jackson, Tennessee. The line was finished in January 1860. By using the completed section of the Mobile & Ohio from Jackson to Columbus, New Orleans thus had the benefit of rail communication with the Northwest more than a year before its rival, Mobile. Also, the Mississippi & Tennessee Railroad built a line from Memphis to Grenada, Mississippi, on the Mississippi Central, which as it progressed southeastward gave the planters of northwestern Mississippi easier access to the river port of Memphis; when it was completed in July 1861, the line gave Memphis a direct rail connection with New Orleans. The Illinois Central, which came into possession of this whole system of roads after the war, in December 1873, completed the building of the "Cairo Extension," from Jackson, Tennessee to Cairo; that city and the Illinois Central were thus released from their dependence on the Mobile & Ohio.

Approximately 1,200 miles of railroads were built in Tennessee during the decade of the 1850s. They of course offered great potential for improvement and expansion of the state's economy when the

Civil War came. Rivers had been improved, and several thousands of miles of roads had also been built by that time. All played a significant role in the military strategy of the war.

SUGGESTED READINGS

Books
Gerald Capers, *The Biography of a River Town: Memphis, Its Heroic Age* (Chapel Hill, 1939); Thomas D. Clark, *The Beginning of the L&N* (Louisville, 1933); Jonathan Daniels, *The Devil's Backbone: Story of the Natchez Trace* (New York, 1961); Donald Davidson, *The Tennessee* (rpt. Knoxville, 1979), 1; Byrd Douglas, *Steamboatin' on the Cumberland* (Nashville, 1961); Stanley J. Folmsbee, *Sectionalism and Internal Improvements in Tennessee, 1796–1845* (Knoxville, 1939); Gilbert Govan and James W. Livingood, *Chattanooga Country* (rpt. Knoxville, 1976) Eric Russell Lacy, *Vanquished Volunteers* (Johnson City, 1965); Mary U. Rothrock (ed.), *The French Broad-Holston Country: A History of Knox County, Tennessee* (Knoxville, 1946).

Articles
Thomas E. Bailey, "Engine and Iron: A Story of Branchline Railroading in Middle Tennessee," *THQ* 28 (Fall 1969), 252–68; Jesse C. Burt, "The Nashville and Chattanooga Railroad, 1854–1872: The Era of Transition," *ETHSP* 23 (1951), 58–76; Thomas D. Clark, "The Building of the Memphis and Charleston Railroad," *ETHSP* 8 (1936), 9–25; Clark, "Development of the Nashville and Chattanooga Railroad," *THM*, Ser. 2, 3 (April 1935), 160–68; Stanley J. Folmsbee, "The Beginnings of the Railroad Movement in East Tennessee," *ETHSP* 5 (1933), 81–104, reprinted in White, *Tennessee: Old and New*, 2, 164–87; Folmsbee, "The Origins of the Nashville and Chattanooga Railroad," *ETHSP* 6 (1934), 81–95; Folmsbee, "The Turnpike Phase of Tennessee's Internal Improvement System of 1836–1838," *JSH* 3 (Nov. 1937), 453–77; James W. Holland, "The Building of the East Tennessee and Virginia Railroad," *ETHSP* 4 (1932), 83–101; "The East Tennessee and Georgia Railroad, 1836–1860," *ETHSP* 3 (1931), 89–107; Robert L. Kincaid, "The Wilderness Road in Tennessee," *ETHSP* 20 (1948), 37–48; James W. Livingood, "Chattanooga: A Rail Junction of the Old South," *THQ* 6 (Sept. 1947), 230–50; John C. Mehrling, "The Memphis and Charleston Railroad, *WTHSP* 19 (1965), 21–35.

13.

&✒ Slavery and the Free Negro

N EGRO slaves were some of the first people who came from North Carolina and Virginia to settle in Tennessee, several having accompanied John Sevier, James Robertson, and other whites who carved homes in the wilderness. Early records in Washington County indicate that blacks were before the courts in that county as early as 1778, and in the same year slaves helped Sevier cultivate his first corn crop on the Nolichucky. In 1779, one or more blacks accompanied James Robertson into the Cumberland Valley, and in the following year several came with Colonel John Donelson and party on their voyage from Fort Patrick Henry to the Cumberland bluffs.

When the Southwest Territory was organized in 1790, the 3,417 slaves constituted 10 percent of the total population, but by the time of statehood they had increased to 13.7 percent. Interestingly, four years after statehood the concentration was in the rich valleys of the Cumberland. About 20 percent of the total population of Middle Tennessee was slave, as contrasted with about 12 percent in the eastern counties at that time. Both the white and slave population increased at a considerable pace through the antebellum period, but the slave increase was proportionally larger, so that by 1860 there was about one black for every three whites in Tennessee. In 1800, the slave population was 13,584. By 1820 it had increased sixfold; the 80,107 blacks formed 18.9 percent of the total population. From 1820 to 1830 the black population nearly doubled, and from 1830 to 1860 it again increased about twofold.

The rapid increase in numbers can be explained in several ways. The rich lands of the Cumberland Valley were opened at about the time of the invention and widespread use of Eli Whitney's cotton gin. Too, Thomas Pinckney's treaty with Spain, which opened the Mississippi to trade and made production of cotton and tobacco a profitable occupation, was negotiated in 1795. Then, when the land between the Tennessee and Mississippi rivers was opened in 1818, that fertile area quickly lent itself to plantation-type cotton production. The close of the Creek War and the War of 1812 marked the beginning of an "era of good feeling" that brought about increased confidence in political stability and economic security and also inspired people to invest in land and slaves.

Of the three grand divisions of the state, East Tennessee had the smallest slave population. In some of the counties of that section, especially where farmers pursued subsistence agriculture, there were few if any slaves. But in the rich valleys of the Watauga, Holston, and French Broad from Bristol to Chattanooga, some farmers owned slaves, although none farmed large plantations as did planters of West Tennessee. Although the slave population in the 1790s in East Tennessee was about 12 percent of the total, it had decreased to 8 percent by 1860. On the other hand, the proportion in Middle Tennessee had increased substantially, so that in 1860 it was about 20 percent. Within the Middle Tennessee division, the slave population was concentrated in the fertile Central Basin—the cotton growers of Davidson, Maury, Rutherford, and Williamson held most of the blacks. In the Highland Rim, tobacco farmers also owned slaves but in fewer numbers than did those of the Basin counties. The Rim counties—Dickson, Hickman, Montgomery, and Stewart—also were iron producers, and iron manufacturers such as Montgomery Bell, James and Elias Napier, and others held slaves in large numbers. In West Tennessee, nearly 40 percent of the population in 1860 were slaves. Within that region the slaveholding people were heavily concentrated in the southwestern counties of Shelby, Fayette, and Haywood, where cotton was produced on plantations very similar to those of Mississippi and the deep South. In the northern counties of West Tennessee, where the growing season was too short for cotton, the black population was small.

Tennessee was a state of small landholdings and slaveholdings when compared with states of the deep South, and men such as Montgomery Bell, who held more than 300 slaves in 1850, G. A. Washington of Robertson County, who held 274 in 1860, and John W. Jones of Fayette County, who owned 235 in 1850, were indeed

Harry Primm, of near Charlotte, was about ninety-five years old when this picture was made in 1938. He was a slave in his early twenties when the Civil War ended.

rare. There were about 36,844 slaveholding families in 1860, in a white population of 826,722. Of those who held slaves, nearly 60 percent owned five or fewer; 21 percent held only one slave. Even in the cotton counties of the southwest, the average holding was about four slaves. The result was that the slaveholder in Tennessee had more personal contact with his Negroes than did the plantation owners of the deep South, and the Tennessee planter came to understand their problems and infirmities. Except in the cotton counties, few if any owners employed overseers. A typical small slaveowner was one who worked side by side with his slaves in fields of corn, cotton, and tobacco.

Farmers without skilled slaves frequently hired Negroes from neighborhood owners. Iron manufacturers also depended upon hired slaves from neighborhood masters to enable them to produce at maximum capacity during busy seasons. Hiring was beneficial to both parties, since the persons hiring would not have to maintain a full corps of slaves at all times, and owners could have their Negroes employed in remunerative work during slow periods. The price paid for hired blacks varied with the use made of the slave, the supply and demand for labor, and the price of goods that they produced. An unskilled worker would earn no more than $80 to $100 per year, in addition to the necessities of life provided by the employer. The ironmongers of Middle Tennessee occasionally paid as much as $200 per year for skilled workers, and a blacksmith belonging to Samuel P. Polk earned $487.76 for his master in 1852.

Federal census records prove inadequate in determining the number of slaves hired in any given year. It is apparent, however, that the hiring was done in industrial areas to a greater extent than in counties without industry, and that the practice began at a very early date and continued throughout the slaveholding period.

Tennessee's central location made it a slavetrading state, and from the early 1800s ample records appear of slave traffic. Of course, many planters bought and sold slaves, and administrators of estates, although not considered slavetraders, sold Negroes to settle estates. Although profits were substantial, a moral stigma was associated with slave dealing, which no doubt deterred some from engaging in the business. Nevertheless, John Overton, Isaac Bolton, Nathan Bedford Forrest, John Armfield, Isaac Franklin, and many others engaged in the trade. Overton bought and sold slaves before 1800 in Middle Tennessee, and Bolton and Forrest were two who made fortunes from the traffic in Memphis. Armfield joined Franklin in Sumner County in 1824, and they were highly successful on the Natchez Trace and throughout the South. Armfield and Franklin were described as men who had "a positive genius for speculating in slaves."

The prices of slaves depended upon many factors, including the age, quality, and skill of the Negroes. Over the state the average value of slaves in 1790 was from $150 to $200, but the price climbed substantially after that. The invention of the cotton gin in 1793 and the closing of the African slave trade in 1808 were material factors causing the increase. Except for a brief dip in prices during the late 1830s and the mid–1840s, the average price in the state as a whole rose steadily to 1860. Table 2 indicates the value for the two decades before the war.

Table 2.
PRICES OF SLAVES IN TENNESSEE, 1836–1859

Year	Average value	Year	Average value
1836	$584	1848	$467
1838	540	1850	507
1840	543	1852	547
1842	509	1854	606
1844	420	1856	689
1846	414	1859	855

Compiled from reports of the State Comptroller to the House of Representatives of the State of Tennessee, 1837–1860.

The highest valuation is found in the cotton country of West Tennessee. In 1838, for example, the average value in Haywood County was placed at $634, while that for Davidson and Rutherford (in Middle Tennessee) was $578 and $598 respectively, and for Johnson County (in East Tennessee) it was only $368.

Slaves were frequent subjects for legislative and judicial attention. The slave laws of North Carolina, established in an elaborate Slave Code in 1741, became the law for the Southwest Territory and the new state, thus insuring an orderly transfer of slavery from North Carolina to Tennessee. Under the North Carolina law, a slave was considered both a chattel and a person, and this concept was continued in Tennessee jurisprudence. As a chattel he was personal property subject to sale like any other property and legally under the control of his owner at all times. But as a person he was also entitled to expect from his master protection against the elements and against other people. He was "made after the image of the Creator," Justice Green wrote in 1846 in *Ford v. Ford,* with "mental capacities" and an "immortal principle in his nature" to make him "equal to his owner but for the accidental position in which fortune has placed him."

As representatives of the people, Tennessee legislators wrestled with their consciences with regard to the slave question, and frequently changed the state's position with regard to manumission. At the time of statehood, owners could free their slaves for "meritorious services," but the county court had the power of determining what and who was meritorious. In 1801 and for the next thirty years thereafter, the "meritorious service" provision was dropped, and an owner was allowed to emancipate whomever he wished. But in 1831, emancipation was made conditional upon the freedman's leaving the state. After 1854, manumission was possible only for blacks who would emigrate to Liberia.

Tennessee legislators, like those in other states, also gave attention to the problem of runaway slaves. North Carolina had developed a system of "patrols"; duties of patrol members included searching any slave not on his master's property to determine whether he carried a "pass" that gave him permission to be away. In 1806, the Tennessee legislature gave captains of the militia companies the responsibility of appointing members of the patrol and supervising their activities. Slaves determined to be runaways might be seized by members of the patrol and jailed until the owner could be located.

A series of developments in the early 1830s caused legislators to tighten control over slaves. These events—the wide circulation of abolition literature, the Nat Turner revolt in Virginia, rumors of threatened slave revolts in surrounding states, and the Amos Dresser[1] affair in Nashville—caused whites to reevaluate their position on slavery. Indicating a fear of insurrection, legislators in 1831 forbade all unlawful assemblages of slaves "in unusual numbers" or at "suspicious times and places." Blacks who assembled anyway and

[1] In July 1835, Dresser, a student at Lane Seminary in Cincinnati, was accused of distributing antislavery literature in Gallatin and Nashville. He was arrested in Nashville, given a semblance of a trial, stripped and flogged, and ordered out of the city.

refused to disperse upon orders from a sheriff or member of the patrol received twenty-five lashes. Powers and responsibilities of the patrol were expanded. Immigration of free Negroes was prohibited and, as mentioned, emancipation was forbidden unless the freedmen left the state. Courts were given discretionary powers to punish "conspiracy to rebel" as they saw fit. A law was passed in 1836, a year after the Dresser episode, that forbade distribution of abolition literature of any type. Offenders could be imprisoned for 5 to 10 years for the first offense and from 10 to 20 for the second.

Emancipation and colonization of slaves were subjects to which people outside the legislative halls addressed themselves from time to time. Thomas Embree and his sons, Elijah and Elihu—iron manufacturers of East Tennessee—were some of the earliest exponents of manumission. Thomas was outspoken. He called upon Tennessee legislators to make possible "a gradual abolition of slavery of every kind" and urged the people of Washington and Greene counties to form antislavery societies. Apparently unhappy in the environment of his slaveholding neighbors and meeting with little response to his agitations, he moved in 1800 with his wife and two daughters to Ohio. The iron business he left to his sons, who later reported to their father that their operations were successful.

Comparatively little antislavery sentiment developed before 1814. Shortly after the turn of the century Charles Osborn, a Quaker minister, preached against slavery in East Tennessee, but little is known of his activities. In December, 1814, eight Jefferson County citizens met at the home of Elihu Swain and formed the "Tennessee Society for Promoting the Manumission of Slaves." Two months later they met in the Lost Creek Meeting House of Friends and wrote a constitution that proclaimed, "freedom is the natural and unalienable right of all men. . . ." Neither immediate nor gradual emancipation was announced as a goal, but the fact that members were gradualists soon became apparent. The few who favored immediate abolition soon moved from the state, some of them settling in the Northwest Territory, where they became active in abolition work.

The vast majority of emancipationists who remained in the state actively propagated their doctrines for well over a decade. They organized local societies in Washington, Sullivan, Blount, Grainger, and Cocke counties, and established the "Manumission Society of Tennessee" in 1815. In the following year the first annual convention was held in Greene County, where leaders boasted of sixteen branches with 474 members. There they proclaimed the object of their organization to be:

> The gradual abolition of slavery . . . in our nation . . . by having laws passed declaring all those born after some fixed period, to be free at some reasonable age, and as a qualification for freedom that they be taught to read the Holy Scriptures and taught some occupation.

In 1822 and 1823 they restated their moderate position and proclaimed their desire to see "a gradual reform of our laws, so as to soften the bonds of slavery to those who now groan under the yoke" and "the gradual emancipation of slavery in our country." They proclaimed their gospel by petitions and speeches. In 1819, for example, thirty-five memorials with 1,975 signatures, each bearing a request for some kind of relief for the blacks, were submitted to the state legislature.

In 1819 Elihu Embree, one of the leaders in the Jefferson County and Greene County movements, began the publication of *The Manumission Intelligencer* at Jonesboro—the first paper established in the United States devoted wholly to antislavery agitation. The weekly suspended publication after one year, but in April 1820, Embree founded *The Emanicpator* as a monthly. His untimely death at the age of thirty-eight brought an end to the journal after only seven issues. It had met with phenomenal success, however, for after a few months it had a subscription list of approximately 2,000. Embree's achievements have been attributed to the fact that many people in East Tennessee shared his views on slavery, that they respected the high standing of the Embree family, and that in 1820 there were but two newspapers in that section of the state.

Shortly after Embree's death, Benjamin Lundy established at Mt. Pleasant, Ohio a paper called *The Genius of Universal Emancipation*. East Tennesseans persuaded him to come to Greeneville, where he continued publication from April 1822 to August 1824. Like Embree, Lundy was closely affiliated with the Manumission Society and represented it several times in annual meetings of the American Convention for Promoting the Abolition of Slavery. His departure in 1824 left the East Tennessee manumissionists without a paper.

Membership in the Manumission Society was confined primarily to people in East Tennessee, but in 1824 a group of Middle Tennesseans met at Columbia and formed the "Moral Religious Manumission Society." They denounced slavery as being "absolutely incompatible with the spirit of Christianity," deplored violence, and urged other manumission societies in the state to send preaching missionaries among the slaveholders.

The manumission societies in Tennessee were short-lived, and practically all had ceased to exist by the mid–1830s. Indeed, they had reached their zenith in the late 1820s, when twenty-five societies claimed a membership of 1,000. Few if any members had expressed radical sentiments, and all had favored a gradual and peaceful abolition of slavery and had advocated more humane treatment of blacks. At least two reasons may be assigned for the decline of interest. One, economic in nature, was the realization that the ever-increasing demand for cotton meant a higher value for the slave. The other was the violence factor associated with emancipation—the threat of radical abolitionists such as William Lloyd Garrison and Theodore Weld, who after 1831 advocated immediate and uncompensated emancipation by violent means if necessary to accomplish their objectives.

Colonization was too expensive to be popular among slaveholders, but the Tennessee Colonization Society was formed anyway in Nashville in 1829, with Philip Lindsley, head of the University of Nashville, as president. Well-meaning members of this "debating society" had no money, and during the first few years frequently complained that their "benevolent and important work" was being hindered because of a shortage of funds. After national colonization leaders appeared in the state on the society's behalf, state legislators in 1833 enacted a measure whereby $10 would be paid to the society for every Negro transported from Tennessee to Liberia, providing that not more than $500 was expended per year. This token amount was of course of no benefit to the owner of the slave, who had to assume most or all of the cost—estimated to be about $180 per black freed. Nor did the expense end there; the emancipator not only lost the value of the slave but assumed much of the expense of provisions sent to enable the freedmen to become established in their new environment.

Despite discouragement, Lindsley promptly called upon slave-owners from across the state to consider colonization. Several complied, and a total of about 700 blacks were sent to Liberia during the three decades prior to the Civil War. Among the larger cooperating slaveholders were General Logan Douglas of Williamson County, Montgomery Bell, who owned iron works throughout Middle Tennessee, and Christopher Strong, a large landowner in Dickson County. Douglas' slaves were placed in the hand of Samuel Henderson, who in December 1852 prepared two dozen or more slaves for departure. Strong's were placed in the hands of Robert McNeilly, a Charlotte attorney, who carried them to Liberia at about the same time. In 1853 Bell, old and infirm (he died two years later), offered to free any of his 300 slaves who would agree to go to Liberia. Eighty or more prepared to go, and were transported to Savannah, where on December 16, 1853 they boarded the *General Pierce* for Liberia.

The number freed and sent to Africa was only a small percentage of the number of free Negroes who remained in Tennessee. Although never large in number, free blacks were concentrated in East and Middle Tennessee and more particularly in the cities of Nashville, Memphis, and Knoxville. The heaviest concentration throughout the ante bellum period was in Davidson County, where 1,209 (about 17 percent) lived in 1860. Shelby, the only county west of the Tennessee River with an appreciable number of free blacks, ranked fifth in the state in 1860 with 276. During the first three decades of the nineteenth century the population increased from 309 to 4,555, but during the next thirty years the growth was not quite so rapid; the number was 7,300 in 1860.

Free blacks worked at a variety of occupations. Although most were common laborers, some were blacksmiths, domestic servants, hack and carriage drivers, bricklayers, tinners, janitors, seamstresses, and shoemakers. Most lived at a sub-standard level ecnomically, but, interestingly, many owned small lots of urban land which today would be worth millions. In 1850, for example, 4,380 of a population of 6,422 held real estate (about 85 percent), and in 1860, 5,874 owned real property valued in excess of $700,000. Several owned and operated barber shops or small businesses, and a few owned farms. Sherod Bryant of Davidson County, for example, in 1850 owned several hundred acres of land and 22 slaves.

Negroes became free as a result of emigration from other states, manumission, and self-purchase; some were free because their mothers were free or were white or Indian women. Of those who emigrated from other states, very few came from the lower South, but like the early white settlers, most came from Virginia and North Carolina. At mid-century, of the 1,500 born outside Tennessee and living in the state, nearly 1,100 were born in one of those two states. The most frequent reason owners gave for manumission was "meritorious service," and in their wills described at some length their affection for their slaves. Blacks who bought their own freedom were often skilled craftsmen or mechanics who were permitted to save money when they were hired out; these earnings were then applied to an agreed-upon purchase price.

Interestingly, there was an indeterminate number of blacks who occupied a position somewhere between that of freeman and slave. The courts recognized a class of nominal or *quasi* slaves—people who had been released from direction by a master but whose freedom had not been officially sanctioned by the county and state. But the courts also held that "a common reputation" of freedom in the community was sufficient evidence of a person's title to liberty. Also, there were examples where a legally recognized free black would assume for all practical purposes the status of a slave when working for a property owner.

Free Negroes, like the slaves, unfortunately left little or nothing to suggest how they viewed life. Newspapers and official records reflected the views of whites, who were sometimes strongly critical of this small and disadvantaged minority. Most whites took a negative view of the free black class in general, and some spoke of them as being shiftless, depraved, and dangerous to the maintenance of a satisfactory relationship between slave and master. Senator Spencer Jarnigan in 1833 believed that they were "corrupting the slave population," and Senator E. B. Littlefield thought they were "too lazy to work." They were kept under surveillance during most of the slaveholding period. As early as 1806, a statute was enacted providing for the registration and numbering of each free black or mulatto. His age, name, "color," "any apparent mark or scar," and an explanation of how and why he was free, were recorded, and the black was required, upon demand, to show "freedom papers." Other laws affecting free blacks were passed from time to time. In 1831 legislators forbade manumission by county courts without security that freedmen would be removed from the state; legislation also forbade migration into Tennessee from other states. Two years later, measures were enacted to encourage African colonization, and in 1834 the constitution was revised to prohibit freedmen from voting. In 1842 the law was modified to restore to county courts the right of emancipation and also to provide residence for freedmen who were Tennessee natives or who had lived in the state since 1836. In 1849, however, the act of 1831 was restored to the statute books, and in

1845 emancipation was permitted providing that those freed were removed to Africa. In 1858 free Negroes were permitted to enter slavery if they desired, and in the following year a measure was proposed that sought the removal to Africa of all of them or the forcible enslavement of all under forty-five years of age.

Some sources have described the free blacks as "a happy lot" who always had their "white folks" to "look out" for them. In the absence of historical data, this concept cannot be affirmed or refuted, but it of course expresses an attitude taken by the white establishment. The term "free black" was in any case a misnomer—"free blacks" were by no means "free" as the whites were. Like slavery, the condition was inherently demeaning—dehumanizing for the free blacks and confusing for all blacks and whites alike. Like slavery, it was a malignancy upon the social structure, and an assessment of "blame" in no way alleviated the problem.

The position of the churches on the slavery question is important, because the clergy, even more than newspaper editors, shaped the opinions of the people. Many of the early antislavery leaders, such as the Embrees, were Quakers, but this group was never strong in Tennessee. Methodists, Baptists, and Presbyterians took strong antislavery positions during the first three decades of the nineteenth century, but after 1830 they modified their stand, until by the 1850s many preachers in each of the three groups defended slavery. The shift was not so much the result of a change of conscience but rather a position of defense assumed by most Southerners after the abolition movement got under way in the 1830s. In Tennessee, where cotton and slavery were not as vital to the economy as in the lower South, ministers invariably compromised on issues. In the lower South, where the preponderance of Baptist slaveholders was exceeded only by Methodist slaveholders, slavery was defended with vigor and the opposition was assailed.

Members of the early Methodist movement in America took a strong antislavery position almost equivalent to that assumed by the Quakers. John Wesley had spoken against slavery, and Bishop Thomas Coke and Francis Asbury followed in Wesley's footsteps. According to one writer, "The Methodist Episcopal Church was virtually organized into a society for antislavery agitation. . . ." In 1808 the Western Conference met at Liberty Hill near Nashville and decreed that no member or preacher should buy or sell a slave "unjustly, inhumanely, or covetously." Presiding Elder James Axley and circuit rider Enoch Moore, prominent East Tennessee preachers, took strong antislavery positions and refused to permit a slaveholding member to lead in public prayer. At the annual Tennessee Conference held in Columbia in 1824, Methodists declared, "slavery is an evil to be deplored and . . . it should be counteracted by every judicious and religious exertion." The influence of the extremists wavered after 1825, however, and for the next two decades the Methodist church in Tennessee modified its stand on slavery. After the division of 1844–1845, leaders defended it. Peter Cartwright, a Methodist preacher who had moved to Illinois from Tennessee by the time of the division, condemned those "Methodist preachers, taken from comparative poverty, . . . who preached loudly against" slavery but who, after improving their financial status, "became popular among slaveholding families" and actually owned slaves themselves.

Baptists did not take such a strong position on slavery. In 1831 the Tennessee Association answered the query, "What ought to be done with a member that sells his colored brother to negro traders to be carried to a distant country against their [*sic*] will?" by advising simply that men should "act agreeable to the Gospel." In 1835 the editor of the Nashville *Baptist,* apparently disturbed by the abolition attack, wrote, "Southerners . . . will dispose of the [slavery] matter as they think properly, all the agitations of the Northerners to the contrary notwithstanding. . . ." After the organization of the Southern Baptist Convention in 1845, little antislavery sentiment was heard from the Tennessee Baptists.

The Presbyterians took similar positions on the slavery question. The Cumberland group had been founded in Tennessee in 1810 by the Reverend Finis Ewing, a slaveholder, and others. Ewing emancipated his slaves, took a bold stand against "the traffic in human souls," and announced that he was "determined not to hold, nor to give, nor to sell, nor to buy any slave for life." Three denominational organs, the Nashville *Revivalist,* the *Cumberland Presbyterian,* and the *Theological Medium,* strongly urged humane treatment and gradual emancipation. Members were exhorted to "Teach your slaves to read, and give them moral and religious instruction." In 1848 the General Assembly of the Cumberland Church met in Memphis and assumed a moderate stand on slavery. In response to a position taken by the Pennsylvania Synod in 1847 that slavery "is contrary to the principles of the Gospel . . . and ought to be abolished," members of the Memphis meeting decreed that "any attempt by jurisdictions of the church to agitate the exciting subject of slavery" was wrong and if persisted in would "gender [*sic*] strife, produce distraction in the church, and thereby hinder the progress of the Gospel."

In general, most ministers of the major religious groups accepted the evil as necessary. In East Tennessee, where antislavery sentiment was stronger than in the other two sections of the state, lived preachers who assumed the strongest antislavery positions. In areas where the parishioners did not hold slaves and were poor and backward the ministers invariably condemned the "rich" slaveowner. Some who despised slavery, including Cartwright, Samuel McAdow, and Barton W. Stone, moved to Illinois to escape the influence of what they believed to be the vilest of sins.

Frances Wright tried a different approach to the antislavery crusade in Shelby County in the 1820s. The radical Scot reformer visited the United States in 1818 and saw American slavery first-hand. On a later visit she saw its more repugnant aspects and determined to eradicate this "sin against humanity." She was a gradualist who believed that "to give liberty to a slave before he understands its value, is perhaps, rather to impose a penalty than to bestow a blessing." She believed that if blacks underwent a period of education and training, they could become prepared for freedom. She proposed to purchase Negroes and establish them in a colony where they might work and thus earn the costs of their purchase and transportation to some place outside the United States. Thomas Jefferson, James Madison, and James Monroe, all of whom had worked to rid the country of slavery, encouraged her.

In the autumn of 1825 Miss Wright purchased 1,940 acres on both sides of the Wolf River, about thirteen miles northeast of Memphis, named the vast estate "Nashoba" (a Chickasaw word for "wolf"), and sought a small contingent of blacks for her "noble" experiment. Negroes soon arrived from a variety of sources. Eight were purchased in Nashville, and six were donated by a South Carolina planter. Still others were bought in the vicinity of the colony. In the spring of 1826 land was cleared for corn and cotton, and an apple orchard was planted, but before the crops were harvested Miss Wright became ill. In the following spring she returned to Europe. The colony was left in charge of her sister, Camilla Wright, and a board of ten trustees, which included General LaFayette, Robert Dale Owen, and James Richardson.

The colony had little chance for success from the beginning; Miss Wright's departure coupled with her poor choice of associates— James Richardson and Richeson Whitby in particular—brought its downfall. Communications from Richardson to Benjamin Lundy indicated that at the time of her departure all was not well at the colony. As news of free love, loose morals, racial equality, and amalgamation came to be known, West Tennesseans threatened fire and destruction. The Nashoba group, always verbose, defended themselves eloquently, and Frances Wright returned to add her voice to their support. She determined to abandon the project, however, after she had observed the gross mismanagement that had taken place during her absence and resolved to take her Negroes to Haiti. Chartering her own ship, she accompanied them to the Haitian shores, where they were received by the governor and given land.

Frustration over the slavery question is evident in the constitutional convention of 1834. Despite the fact that antislavery sentiment had almost lost its force as an organized movement by 1834, some urged convention members to take action providing for the ultimate extinction of slavery. Many petitions were sent to Nashville, some seeking to free all children born to slave parents after 1835 and many seeking to establish a date—most said 1855 or 1856—after which slavery would be illegal. The debates on the issue illustrate the utter frustration experienced by many people throughout the South. No delegate pronounced slavery a "positive good," and many of the defenders admitted that it was an evil. Most confessed their inability to cope with race problems that would worsen with emancipation.

John A. McKinney, the Hawkins County delegate, was named chairman of a committee to respond to the antislavery petitions. Slavery, he said was an evil that even "the wisest heads and most benevolent hearts" had not found a way to eliminate. Like most people who face a seemingly insurmountable problem, McKinney resigned himself to his fate and attempted to rationalize and blame others. To establish a terminal date for slavery, he said would simply drive slaveholders into other states or cause them to sell their slaves outside the state in advance of the termination date. As "Unenviable as is the condition of the slave, unlovely as slavery is in all aspects, and as bitter as the draught that the slave is doomed to drink," McKinney wrote, still his condition was better than that of free Negroes. Finally, he sought to blame "misguided fanatics" of the North for Tennessee's problems. If such people "in those parts of the United States where

slavery does not now exist," he wrote, "will only refrain from inter-
meddling in a matter in which they have no concern and in which
their interference can do no possible good and may do much positive
evil, slavery, with all its ills, will be extinguished as certainly and as
speedily as the friends of humanity have any reason to expect."

Tennesseans reacted to these questions very much as the Virginians had two years earlier. The real problem, apparently—not
only in the convention but in the legislative halls—was not so much
slavery as the race problem. Tennesseans could have emancipated
their slaves, but they could not admit the blacks, free or slave, to a
position of equality.

Convention delegates ultimately wrote into the fundamental law
that "the General Assembly shall have no power to pass laws for the
emancipation of slaves without the consent of their owner or owners." The vote was 30 to 27. Of the 27 against, 14 delegates were
from East Tennessee, 10 from Middle Tennessee, and 3 from the
western division. At the same time the right to vote was taken from
free Negroes by the insertion of the word "white" between the
words "free" and "man." The vote on that question was 33 to 23.

The 1850s offered the embattled slaveholders and the suffering
slaves little relief, and widespread rumors of insurrections were
reported in 1856 in several of the Middle and West Tennessee
counties causing slaveowners to tighten their grip on slavery. For
example, a Fayette County slaveowner reported overhearing slaves
plotting insurrection and promptly had fifty-five of them thrown in
jail. Two kegs of powder were discovered in possession of slaves near
Columbia. Uprisings were reported also in Franklin and Perry counties. In Nashville the patrol was strengthened, Negro schools and
churches temporarily forbidden to operate, and all Negro assemblages after sundown prohibited. At Louisa Furnace in Montgomery County, a keg of powder was found under a church. Nearby,
a Negro preacher was heard haranguing a group of blacks—presum-
ably inciting them to insurrection—and upon his failure to obey an
overseer's order to desist, he was shot. According to a Nashville
newspaper, slaves planned to march on Clarksville on Christmas
Day, 1856, plunder its banks, and then flee to free territory in the
North. Ironmasters throughout the vicinity were notified by the
Clarksville city council on December 17 that no visiting slave would
be permitted to remain in the town for more than two hours unless
accompanied by a "responsible white person." Other uprisings were

reported from time to time. In 1859 two of Mrs. James Knox Polk's slaves were tried and condemned to execution for plotting insurrection.

By the 1850s Tennesseans were defending an institution that they had earlier tried to eradicate. While a few emancipationists such as Ezekiel Birdseye of Newport continued to work for peaceful abolition, such men were few in East Tennessee and could scarcely be found in the central and western divisions. Congressman John Savage spoke the sentiments of many people in 1850 when he exclaimed in the halls of Congress that he was "ready for war, subjugation, or extinction" before he would turn slaves "loose among us, to be our equals." It very obviously was the race question and no great affection for slavery itself that stood in the way of emancipation in Tennessee. But although slavery was dehumanizing for whites and blacks alike, a very long time passed before the American people were prepared to face the consequences of its elimination.

SUGGESTED READINGS

Books
Mary R. Campbell, *The Attitude of Tennesseans Toward the Union, 1847– 1861* (New York, 1961); Avery O. Craven, *The Coming of the Civil War* (Chicago, 1957); Arthur Y. Lloyd, *The Slavery Controversy, 1831–1860* (Chapel Hill, 1939); Chase C. Mooney, *Slavery in Tennessee* (Bloomington, 1957); Kenneth M. Stampp, *The Peculiar Institution: Slavery in the Ante-Bellum South* (New York, 1956).

Articles
Mary R. Campbell, "Tennessee and the Union, 1847–1861," *ETHSP* 10 (1938), 71–90; Robert E. Corlew, "Some Aspects of Slavery in Dickson County," *THQ* 10 (Sept., Dec. 1951), 224–48, 344–65; J. Treadwell Davis, "Nashoba (near Memphis, Tenn.): Frances Wright's Experiment in Self-Emancipation," *Southern Quarterly* (Oct. 1972), 63–90; Charles B. Dew, "Black Ironworkers and the Slave Insurrection Panic of 1856," *JSH* 41 (Aug. 1975), 321–38; O. B. Emerson, "Frances Wright and Her Nashoba Experiment," *THQ* 6 (Dec. 1947), 291–314; J. Merton England, "The Free Negro in Ante-Bellum Tennessee," *JSH* 9 (Feb. 1943), 37–58; Robert P. Hay, ". . . Andrew Jackson's Runaway Slave Ad . . .," *THQ* 36 (Winter 1977), 468–78; Isabel Howell, "John Armfield, Slave-trader," *THQ* 2 (March 1943), 3–29; Arthur F. Howington, " 'Not in the Condition of a Horse or an Ox.' *Ford v. Ford,* the Law of Testamentary Manumis-

sion and the Tennessee Courts' Recognition of Slave Humanity," *THQ* 34 (Fall 1975), 249–63; Asa E. Martin, "Anti-Slavery Societies of Tennessee," *THM* 1 (Dec. 1915), 261–81; Chase C. Mooney, "Some Institutional and Statistical Aspects of Slavery in Tennessee," *THQ* 1 (Sept. 1942), 195–228; J. W. Patton, "Progress of Emancipation in Tennessee," *JNH* 17 (Jan. 1932), 67–102; William Pease and Jane H. Pease, "A New View of Nashoba," *THQ* 19 (June 1960), 99–109; Bette B. Tilly, "The Spirit of Improvement: Reformism and Slavery in West Tennessee," *WTHSP* 28 (1974), 25–42.

14.

૨✥ *Economic, Social, and Cultural Development at Mid-Nineteenth Century*

TENNESSEANS at mid-century boasted of an increasing population, expanding agriculture, developing industry, and rapidly growing towns. Agrarian reforms resulted in a more efficient use of land and labor. Within the towns, infant industry brought a measure of wealth, which in turn was partly responsible for a growing awareness of cultural deprivation and a desire to share in the refinement that characterized larger urban areas. Reforms resulted in better treatment and better living conditions for unfortunate elements of society, and schools and churches grew along with the people.

The population had demonstrated phenomenal growth during those 70 years since James Robertson and John Donelson led people from Fort Patrick Henry to permanent settlements on the Cumberland River. The whites and "free coloreds" numbered 763,258 of a total of 1,002,717 people. The population had increased fourfold since 1800; it had more than doubled since 1820. There were at least two simple reasons for the growth. The fertile and inexpensive lands of the Basin and of the western district drew many people from the eastern states—Virginia and North and South Carolina, particularly. Second, each year the birth rate greatly exceeded the mortality rate. During the year ending June 1, 1850, for example, 23,093 free people were born, while fewer than 8,000 died. The population concentrated in the Basin counties of Davidson, Maury, Rutherford, Williamson, and Wilson and in the southwestern cotton-producing counties of Shelby and Fayette.

Most of the people at mid-century were farmers. Governor Sevier had spoken in 1799 of the great agricultural advantages enjoyed by

Tennesseans. "Providence," he asserted, "has blessed this State with a soil peculiarly calculated for the production of wheat, hemp, flax, cotton, tobacco, and indigo." During the next half-century, Tennesseans cultivated the soil intensively and produced in abundance all of the crops that the governor had enumerated except indigo. Corn was king, but much cotton was raised in the southwestern and south-central counties, and millions of pounds of tobacco were produced in the north-central counties. Wheat, oats, and a variety of other crops, including vegetables, were raised in great abundance. Agriculture was unquestionably the main economic pursuit and 120,000 house-holders in 1850 listed farming as their chief means of making a living.

East Tennessee was the first section to be settled, but at mid-century it was the poorest in agricultural production. Although the counties of the river valleys were fertile and productive, much of the other land was hilly, compelling farmers to pursue subsistence agriculture. East Tennesseans had a greater diversification of crops than did the farmers of the other two sections; they raised tobacco, wheat, cotton, flax, hemp and many fruits and vegetables.

Middle Tennessee consists of long mountain slopes, plateaus, and undulating lands, and includes the rich Central Basin and fertile bottoms of the Cumberland, Harpeth, and Tennessee rivers. A variety of crops, including cotton, corn, tobacco, and many vegeta-bles, was produced in the Basin and also on the peripheral Highland Rim. Tobacco was the principal money crop in the northern counties of Montgomery, Sumner, Robertson, Stewart, and Dickson, and in 1840 the state's yield was exceeded only by that of Kentucky and Virginia. Ten years later Maryland also had surpassed the Volunteer State in tobacco production, but by 1860, Tennessee had regained her spot just behind Kentucky and Virginia. Cotton was grown by John Donelson in Davidson County as early as 1780 but was not an important money crop in the central division until after the invention of the cotton gin.

West Tennessee was the last section to be settled, but the south-western counties soon surpassed the rest of the state in cotton production because of the fertile soil and long summers. At mid-century, this comparatively small area produced more than four-fifths of the state's cotton crop, and Colonel John Pope of Shelby County received a medal at the London Exposition in 1851 for "the best cotton known to the world." In 1810 (before West Tennessee was opened for settlement), the Volunteer State produced less than

3,000 bales, but by 1820, 50,000 bales were sold. At mid-century, the state's production of 194,532 bales was exceeded only by that of Alabama, Georgia, Mississippi, and South Carolina. On the eve of the Civil War, production had increased 50 percent over that of 1850.

Farmers in all sections of the state raised livestock and poultry. The earliest settlers had brought cattle into the wilderness, and James Robertson drove stock overland into the Cumberland area in 1780. In the raising of horses, mules, oxen, sheep, and swine, Tennessee compared favorably with the other Southern states, and in number of mules and swine Tennessee ranked at the top. Poultry—both turkeys and chickens—were raised not only for home consumption but also for the market. Middle Tennessee producers often drove flocks of 750 or more overland to Nashville, where they were placed on steamboats bound for New Orleans. Merino sheep, Berkshire hogs, and Shorthorn cattle were of special interest to Tennessee farmers. One of the most successful breeders was Mark Cockrill, who for several decades owned and farmed 5,000 acres of Davidson County land located on Charlotte Pike. He raised only choice cattle, horses and mules, Berkshire hogs, and sheep, and in 1851 he received at the World's Fair in London a premium for the finest wool in the world. Tennessee legislators presented him with a medal for his "devotion of a long life to the advancement . . . of agricultural resources," and a later assembly placed his bust in a position of honor in the capitol. Lucius Julius Polk and Ben Harlan of Maury County, Woods S. Miller of Gallatin, and L. C. Coleman of Nashville were well-known cattle and horse breeders. Animals produced by these men brought high prices, and Miller in 1840 wagered $500 that in any contest his would be judged superior to any in the state.

During a forty-year period before the Civil War, agricultural specialists were frequently critical of farm practices in the Volunteer State. Enlightened leaders such as Dr. Henry Brooks of Smith County, and Tolbert Fanning, editor of *The Agriculturist*, urged farmers to diversify and practice crop rotation, contour plowing, and terracing. Gideon J. Pillow, in speaking at a Middle Tennessee fair in Maury County in 1855, urged farmers to grow less cotton and raise more corn, oats, wheat, hay, and livestock.

Brooks was one of the many reformers who insisted that Tennessee cotton raisers and tobacco growers should turn to silk production. In 1829, Brooks told legislators of his own experiments with silkworms, of the small amount of labor necessary for their culture, and of expected benefits. He urged the assembly to appropriate public funds for silkworms eggs and mulberry seed to be distributed free of charge among interested farmers. Many editors of newspapers took up the cry, and soon a "Tennessee Silk Company and Agricultural School" was incorporated "to teach the art of the culture and manufacture of silk." A Nashvillian was convinced that silk could make Middle Tennessee "equal to the valley of the Piedmont or any region in the Chinese Empire." In 1840, silkmen sold nearly 1,100 pounds; more than 90 percent of this was produced in the eastern and middle divisions. By 1850, the output had doubled that of ten years earlier, and Tennessee then ranked first in production among the states. During the 1850s, however, the dream of an oriental empire of silk all but vanished, as farmer after farmer told of losing his cocoons. Production in 1860 amounted to only 71 pounds, and was limited almost entirely to the counties of Humphreys, Lincoln, and Sevier.

The interest in agricultural reform could not have been sustained without the State Agricultural Bureau, created in 1854. Its chief duties were to sponsor county agricultural organizations and to supervise county, division, and state fairs. To county organizations complying with certain regulations the bureau awarded a bounty of $200 that could be spent in any way beneficial to the agricultural interest of the county. The act of 1854 also provided $10,000 for fairs where farmers could exhibit their produce and compete with one another for premiums. Governor Johnson showed much interest, and in 1855, at his insistence, the legislature authorized the issuance of $30,000 in state bonds to purchase a permanent location for fairgrounds near Nashville and to construct the necessary buildings and fixtures.

Reformers continued their agitation until Southern economic life was paralyzed by the Civil War. Many of their ideas had been carried out, however, and much progress had been made. Values of land had increased considerably, and thousands of acres had been improved for cultivation.

Ante Bellum Industry. ‽ Comparatively little industrial development had taken place in Tennessee at mid-century. Social and economic prestige was associated with tillers of the soil and not with mechanics and laborers—this association no doubt made it difficult to lure Tennessee yeomen from the plow to the factory. Iron had been the principal industry; cotton, silk, and wool manufacture existed largely in the minds of a few who dreamed of industrial development in the Volunteer State.

Even before Tennessee became a state, iron forges and furnaces had been built by David Ross, James King, Moses Cavitt, Walter King, John Sevier, and Nicholas Perkins along the Holston, and by James Robertson in Middle Tennessee. Montgomery Bell purchased Robertson's interests in 1804, and soon became one of the state's greatest industrialists of the time. His advertisement in a Nashville paper in 1808 for 5,000 cords of wood which he would render into charcoal indicates the scale of his operations; at one time Bell owned or had an interest in more than a dozen furnaces and forges. Iron works were opened by other capitalists from time to time, especially in Washington, Unicoi, Greene, Hickman, Montgomery, Stewart, and Lewis counties. In 1850, the Chattanooga Foundry and Machine Shop was established; after the Civil War, the shop's business in iron and steel grew prodigiously. Also in Chattanooga, the Vulcan Iron Works was opened in 1860. By this time, Tennessee ranked third in bloomery output and was excelled only by Pennsylvania and New York. The Civil War brought renewed interest in the lead mines of East Tennessee, and in the 1860s much interest was shown in the Bumpass Cove area in Washington County, which had been productive earlier.

Copper and coal were also mined in East Tennessee at mid-century. Early settlers found copper, next to iron, to be the most useful metal. During the 1850s large quantities of copper were taken from mines in Polk County. The Hiwassee mine was opened in August 1850, and by 1854 at least fourteen mines produced several million pounds of copper annually; owners sold the copper in the markets of London, New York, and Boston. Charcoal was generally used instead of coal, but during the 1850s capitalists opened the Sewanee Mining Company and exploited rich coal veins in the southwestern part of the Cumberland Plateau.

Efforts to arouse interest in textiles met with little success. A joint committee appointed by the state legislators in 1845 was one of several groups that studied manufacturing possibilities from time to time. The committee told of successes in Alabama and elsewhere, pointed to Tennessee's natural resources, and contended that both slaves and free workers could be employed profitably in textile manufacture. Mark R. Cockrill believed that every county where cotton was grown in abundance could have one or two cotton mills. He proposed that fifteen planters in each county invest $4,000 each to get the project started; small blocks of stock could then be sold to interested citizens. This, Cockrill believed, would "render the South magnificently rich, and gloriously independent." Talk of industrial reform fell upon deaf ears, however. Although at mid-century factories had been established in Knoxville, Paris, Athens, Gallatin, Nashville, Murfressboro, and Franklin, the state's output was small. Less than $700,000 in manufactured goods was produced in 1860, while adjacent Georgia made goods valued at $2,371,207, and Massachusetts at more than $38,000,000. In the same year, only one wool factory was in operation in Tennessee, and the state's total output was worth only $8,100. Virginia's output of woolen goods, however, was valued at $717,827, Georgia's at $464,420, and North Carolina's at $291,000.

Probably the main reason for the sparsity of industrial development at mid-century was a lack of interest on the part of most of the people. Realizing that major political decisions were made by the farmers, politicians seldom talked about business interests. European immigrants from old-world industrial centers rarely came south; nativists such as William G. Brownlow had strongly urged them to settle in the North rather than in Tennessee. Landowners and men of capital turned their attention increasingly to cotton, which at mid-century continued to spiral upward in price.

Towns and Cities ⧸⧹ The large metropolitan centers of today did not exist in the mid–1800s; in fact, few cities in the entire country were as large as Memphis and Nashville are today. The state's capital, a sprawling town on the banks of the Cumberland River, was the largest and one of the oldest in the state and was primarily an agricultural and commercial center. Its 10,165 people pursued a variety of occupations, including flour-milling, sawmilling, and other small manufactures. By 1850, fifteen toll roads radiated from Nashville, making the capital the hub of the state. The Nashville and Chattanooga Railway was almost complete, and the first steam locomotive began operation in 1851.

Memphis, with a population of 8,841 at mid-century, was the state's second largest city. From its incorporation in 1826, the river town had grown rapidly; the census of 1830 indicated a population of only a few hundred, but ten years later nearly 2,000 people had settled there. Memphis became a major cotton center. At mid-century, factors handled 150,000 bales valued at $7,520,000 and by 1860 Memphis sold three times that amount. The river traffic, coupled with the promise of increased trade when railroad construction was completed, caused a New Orleans editor in 1850 to predict that Memphis would soon be "the most important town in the Southwest after New Orleans."

Knoxville had a population of 2,076 at mid-century and led the cultural and commercial life of East Tennessee. The Bank of the State of Tennessee was established there in 1811, and Knoxville continued as a town of strong financial interests. Steamboat transportation caused considerable growth during the 1830s, and the opening of rail facilities during the 1850s brought further expansion. As in Nashville, flour-milling and sawmilling were the chief industries.

Chattanooga was not incorporated until 1839, and at mid-century its population numbered only a few hundred families. Earlier, Chattanooga had been a stopping place for river traffic and was known as "Ross's Landing." In 1850, the Western and Atlantic Railroad began operation, reaching northward from Atlanta to Chattanooga and connecting with lines to Charleston and Savannah. A decade later, Chattanooga was a focal point of all the railroads in the Southeast. It was not until after the war that the town began a great period of growth and not until 1870 that Chattanooga became the seat of Hamilton County.

At mid-century, other towns in all sections of the state grew rapidly, and several had populations larger than those of Knoxville and Chattanooga. Columbia, established in the first decade of the nineteenth century and later the seat of Maury County, was the third largest town, with 2,977 people in 1850. Murfreesboro, the seat of Rutherford County, boasted 1,917, and nearby Lebanon, the seat of Wilson County, had 1,554. Pulaski, the Giles County seat, had 1,137 and Franklin, the seat of Williamson County, had 891. In West Tennessee, Jackson, with a population of 1,006, and Brownsville, with 971, ranked next behind Memphis. The migration from East Tennessee into the middle and western division—to say nothing of

Arkansas and Texas—kept towns in that section small. Greeneville, with 660, and Kingsport, with 320, ranked behind Knoxville and Chattanooga.

Ante Bellum Society ৯১ The picture of Southern society created by ante bellum writers and travelers from Europe and the Northeast became a stereotype widely accepted. This picture showed a threefold class society consisting of the lazy but well-to-do mint julip– drinking planters at the top and the equally lazy but more degenerate, shiftless, and hopeless poor whites—"that lawless and idle rabble"—near the bottom. Those at the top were arrogant; those at the bottom, surly. It was the worthy but exploited slave, however, who provided a foundation for the superstructure. Not until comparatively recently has a preponderance of evidence developed to suggest the existence of a strong middle class. The planter class, the poor whites, and the slaves were actually minorities; the vast majority of Tennesseans—and Southerners as a whole—were middle-class farmers who composed the backbone of the social and economic structure of the state and region.

European writers who traveled through Tennessee and the South supplied their readers with many interesting tales of frontier life. James Flint, for example, wrote that he had never seen such noisy and ill-mannered people as those west of the Unakas. On one occasion in 1818, shortly after Flint had seated himself in an East Tennessee tavern, a group of boisterous youths entered. The group engaged in "noisy gabbing, drinking, and swearing" the like of which Flint vowed he had never seen or heard before. Mrs. Frances Trollope, an English traveler who came several years later, found manners in West Tennessee to be even worse. She was amazed at the eating habits of people who dined in the Memphis hotels. On one occasion she watched horror-stricken as fifty diners rushed to the table and swallowed potatoes, meat, and bread with little or no mastication. Not a word was spoken; she heard only the sounds of smacking, chomping, and an "unceasing chorus of coughing." James E. Alexander, another English visitor, came to Nashville in the 1830s in hopes of finding people with better manners, but he could write only of his disappointment. At the sound of the dinner bell, Alexander watched scores of men rush into hotels and boardinghouses, spitting chewing tobacco in one direction and blowing their noses in the other, to devour chunks of roast beef and loaves of bread as though they were party sandwiches. He was horrified as men reached completely across the table, knives and forks in hand, to stab biscuits and steaks even before a blessing had been said. Hot coffee poured into saucers to cool, Alexander wrote, would be blown with such vigor as to send a spray across the room. Plates overflowing with food would be licked clean seconds later. Every person, he wrote, ate "as if it were [his] last meal. . . ."

The stories written by travelers were amusing and, if true, described exceptions rather than the rule. Many Tennesseans, especially in the towns and cities, had an appreciation of refinement and culture not unlike that of people in the East and Europe. Many artists who came to Nashville, Knoxville, and Memphis during the ante bellum period charmed audiences with their superb performances. Perhaps the most widely heralded artistic performances in ante bellum Tennessee came in the 1850s, when Jenny Lind was heard in Nashville and Memphis, Signor Luigi Arditi's Italian Opera Company performed in Nashville, Edwin Booth introduced Nashvillians to Shakespeare, and Christy's Minstrels thrilled audiences in Memphis. Nashville was described as being in "one wild uproar" on March 29, 1851, when Miss Lind arrived. From the presentation of her first selection, an aria from *Lucia di Lammermoor,* to her closing rendition of *Home, Sweet Home,* the Swedish Nightingale enthralled her audience and held it spellbound. Standing room at $3 was considered cheap in the newly constructed Adelphi Theater; in Memphis a capacity crowd paid $5 each to hear her, even though the performance was at eleven o'clock in the morning.

Nashville was the cultural center of the state, and a number of performers were seen and heard. In 1854, the Italian Opera Company was heard with Madame Rosa DeVries as prima donna. Miss Lind had introduced Nashvillians to Gaetano Donizetti, and Arditi opened with the Italian composer's tragic *Lucia de Lammermoor.* On succeeding evenings he presented Antonio Rossini's *Barber of Seville,* Vincenzo Bellini's *Norma* and *La Sonnambula,* and Giuseppe Verdi's *Ernani.* Although Miss DeVries could not reach the high notes sung by Jenny Lind, many believed her to be a greater artist. Her warm interpretation of *Norma* sent her audience into rapture; indeed, she was permitted to retire only "under a perfect deluge of bouquets." In March 1859, Edwin Booth appeared in Nashville and was billed as "the distinguished young tragedian." A man of melancholy and romantic countenance, graceful carriage, and poetic temperament, whom nature had cast as a nineteenth-century Hamlet, Booth for two weeks interpreted Shakespeare before capacity crowds. Although he was probably the most polished Hamlet Nashville audiences had seen, Booth played Macbeth equally well.

Memphis, a rapidly growing frontier town at mid-century, presented many cultural attractions. During the 1840s and 1850s many of those who performed in Nashville, including Miss Lind, Booth, and Ole Bull (a self-taught Norwegian violin virtuoso), also appeared in Memphis. Other stars included Boston-born soprana Signora Elisa Bascaccianti, a baritone named Signor Belletti, and Joseph Burke, a violinist. The 1850s were a decade of minstrelsy in Memphis, and a half-dozen groups—including Christy's—gave public performances.

Although Knoxville was not visited by Jenny Lind or Edwin Booth, Knoxvillians heard able artists of perhaps less renown. The faculties of East Tennessee University and East Tennessee Female Institute provided leadership for many musical and dramatic productions that drew on home talent. The Swiss Bell Ringers appeared before a capacity crowd in 1854; a few years later Anna Vail, accompanied by Theodore Schreiner, performed for Knoxvillians before returning to Europe. As in Memphis, minstrel groups were popular.

Education and Religion ⟨᠈᠈ Delegates to the constitutional convention of 1834 recognized that "knowledge, learning, and virtue" were "essential to the preservation of republican institutions" and commanded members of the General Assembly henceforth to "cherish science and literature." Legislators turned their attention to the matter very early in the state's history. The Compact of 1806 authorized support for schools from revenue received from the sale of public lands, but unfortunately, few funds were received from land sales. In 1830 the legislature made its first real attempt to establish a public school system, and money was distributed among counties in proportion to the free white population. This method proved unsatisfactory; the school money, wrote one school official, was "plundered by a thousand hands," and even the first state superintendent, Robert H. McEwen, was accused of mismanagement.

Governor Andrew Johnson turned his attention to the school situation in 1853, and at his insistence the legislature enacted what former state historian Robert H. White once called "the most important act for common schools . . . in Tennessee before the Civil War." The measure provided for a poll tax of 25 cents on free males and a property tax of 2½ cents on each $100 of taxable property. Efforts to revive the office of state superintendent were defeated (the state treasurer functioning in that capacity instead), but the tax, small as it was, almost doubled the amount of funds available for the public school program. Educators were encouraged and used their influence to expand facilities for public education across the state. Johnson, one to whom circumstance had denied the advantages of a formal education, was zealous to provide free public education for all. He told legislators that the school system fell "very far short" of the goal set at the constitutional convention of 1834 and no doubt observed with considerable dissatisfaction the census reports at mid-century, which indicated that from a total white population of 316, 409 persons more than twenty years of age, 77,522 of them could neither read nor write.

City systems were established in Nashville and Memphis during the 1850s. In 1852, Alfred Hume (later known as "the father of the Nashville public schools") examined urban educational facilities in the North and East. After visiting Cleveland, Boston, Providence, Philadelphia, and Baltimore, he presented to the city council a report that became the basis of Nashville's system. The city was to be zoned and at least one school located in each zone. Taxes levied to provide operating funds were to consist of a poll tax of $2.00 on free white males between the ages of twenty-one and fifty and a property tax of 20 cents on each $100 of taxable real estate. By 1860, the Nashville system boasted 35 teachers and a total enrollment of 1,892 pupils. The Memphis system was established in 1858 and was patterned after the one in Nashville.

Private schools and academies showed much greater vitality. Legislators authorized the establishment of academies in twenty-seven counties in 1806 and in most of the others by mid-century. Most had the usual financial problems but raised money from high tuition charges, gifts from affluent parents and other interested citizens, and the sale of lottery tickets. Most offered a variety of courses. In 1821 the faculty of Manhattan School in Maury County, for example, offered English grammar, trigonometry, navigation, logic, and natural philosophy. Students at Bolivar Male Academy studied astronomy, higher mathematics, Latin, Greek, French, and Hebrew.

Most of the academies admitted only men, but a few were established exclusively for women. One of the best-known schools for girls in the South was the Nashville Female Academy, a nonsectarian institution established in 1816. When President James Monroe visited Nashville in 1819, city officials proudly displayed the school and the President delivered an address before the 200 students and faculty members.

The Nashville academy reached its peak during the administration of the Reverend Collins D. Elliott, who served as its principal from 1844 to 1866. A strict disciplinarian and a strong believer in education for women, Elliott administered a sound program. As early as 1833, students of the French language were placed under the supervision of their professor, a native of France, who required them to converse on campus only in French. Able music instructors were also brought from Europe. A variety of subjects was taught, but the "Ornamental Department"—vocal music, instrumental music, painting, and fancy needlework—was the most popular. Elliot demanded long hours of study. He firmly announced to parents concerned about the conduct and welfare of their daughters that the "young ladies see no [male] company; never visit but with our approbation; read no novels [and] never leave the yard but in company with a teacher." The tuition in 1857 was $275, which defrayed all expenses. A Nashville newspaper at the time described the school as "the most extensive in the United States devoted to female education."

More than a dozen colleges flourished at mid-century. Davidson Academy had been reincorporated as Cumberland College in 1806. In 1826 the name was changed to the University of Nashville, two years after Dr. Philip Lindsley, an ordained Presbyterian minister, was appointed president. The school was closed temporarily in 1850 when Lindlsey resigned but was reopened in 1855 when Lindsley's son, John Berrien Lindsley, became chancellor. A person of remarkable talents, young Lindsley reorganized the university and merged with it the Western Military Institute, headed by Colonel Bushrod Johnson. On the eve of the Civil War the enrollment was 648. Several thousand students had been enrolled during the institution's fifty-year history, and hundreds had graduated with bachelor's and master's degrees. The medical school, operated in conjunction with the university, was considered to be one of the best in the country.

East Tennessee College (formerly Blount College) opened in

Philip Lindsley was the first president of the University of Nashville.

Knoxville in 1807 but closed two years later after the death of its president, Samuel Carrick. The school was reopened in 1820, and six years later, trustees, voting to change the location, purchased from Pleasant M. Miller the present site of the main campus of the University of Tennessee at Knoxville—a forty-acre hill located one mile west of the courthouse. A large building with a spire, clock, and ornaments was constructed. The physical plant and course offerings were expanded considerably after Joseph Estabrook was chosen as president in 1834, and the name was changed in 1840 to East Tennessee University in recognition of Estabrook's program of expansion.

Cumberland University, at Lebanon, was founded in 1842 under the auspices of the Cumberland Presbyterian Church. Its department of law, established in 1847, soon built a national reputation for the school. On the eve of the Civil War the institution had an enrollment of 500, nearly half of which were enrolled in the law department.

The forerunner of Southwestern at Memphis was Stewart College at Clarksville. In 1848 the Masonic Order acquired title to the property of Clarksville Academy but met with little success in its efforts to operate an institution of higher learning. In 1855 the property was purchased by the Presbyterian Synod of Nashville, and in the autumn of that year a school was opened under the name of "Stewart College." Emphasis was placed upon classical languages and literature.

Many other colleges, most of them small in enrollment, were established during the ante bellum period. Greeneville College, chartered in 1794 (a few days before Blount), had a precarious existence during its early years. After the Civil War, Greeneville was consolidated with Tusculum College, which in 1844 had been organized from Tusculum Academy. Samuel Doak, who established the first school in the Tennessee country, had received from North Carolina in 1783 a charter for Martin Academy, which became Washington College in 1795. Maryville College was begun in 1819 as Southern and Western Theological Seminary to train Presbyterian ministers. Among other colleges were: Jackson (Maury County, 1832), West Tennessee College (Jackson, 1844), Union University (Murfreesboro, 1845), Bethel College (McLemoresville, 1842, but later moved to McKenzie), Mossy Creek Baptist Seminary, a forerunner of Carson-Newman College (Jefferson County, 1851);

reconciliation with the mother church. By 1813, when efforts both to reunite with the Presbyterians and to join the Methodists had failed, the group considered that they had formed a separate Christian body and called themselves "Cumberland Presbyterians." Within five years new congregations had been formed in Alabama, Arkansas, Illinois, Kentucky, Mississippi, and Missouri.

The Disciples of Christ developed out of the teachings of Alexander Campbell and Barton W. Stone and emerged at about the same time as did the Cumberland Presbyterians. Both Campbell and Stone had been Presbyterian ministers, but like the leaders in the Cumberland group, they rejected the rigidity of Calvinism. Their cry for a return to the pristine purity of Christianity, their insistence that the Bible was the supreme authority in the church, and their persuasion that all men and not merely ministers of the gospel are commissioned to preach were reminiscent of Peter Waldo of the twelfth century and some of the Reformation leaders of the 1500s. Stone began his ministry in East Tennessee and Kentucky before 1800, but Campbell did not come to America from Scotland until 1809. By that time Stone had expressed the basic tenets of his faith: that the Bible was "the only sure guide to heaven," that ministers of the gospel should be treated like everyone else and not distinguished by a " 'Reverend' title,"—and that his presbytery—and all denominational bodies—should be dissolved and merged "into union with the Body of Christ."

Campbell was the embodiment of dissent. His great-grandfather had been a Roman Catholic, but his grandfather had rejected Romanism and united with the Church of England. Thomas, his father, had been an ordained minister in the Seceder Presbyterian Church, which had been formed from a schism in the Church of Scotland in 1733. After he determined that immersion was the only proper mode of baptism, he affiliated with the Baptist church for a while. He became known as a "reforming Baptist," and his followers generally were known as "Reformers" and "Disciples." He preached and debated leaders of other churches in all sections of Tennessee, but his principal following was in Nashville.

In 1832 the Stone and Campbell forces were united. They became variously known as Disciples, Churches of Christ, Christians, and Reformers. By 1842, the leaders were publishing *The Bible Advocate* in Paris, and a few years later the *Christian Review* in Nashville. At mid-century the Campbell and Stone forces, ranking fifth among the

and Lambuth, established by Presbyterians but taken over by Methodists (Jackson, 1842). One of the most promising institutions established before the Civil War was the University of the South, at Sewanee. The trustees received a charter in 1858 and proposed to offer an extensive program in arts and sciences. English, French, German, Spanish, Italian, and Oriental languages were to be taught, in addition to civil engineering, natural science, chemistry, and agriculture. Bishop Leonidas Polk laid the cornerstone in 1860 and dedicated the institution "for the cultivation of true religion, learning, and virtues." Because of the Civil War, the school did not function until 1865.

Disciplinary problems faced most of the college executives from time to time. In 1821 rules and regulations were prepared at East Tennessee College. Students could be expelled if they did not show "reverence and obedience" to the faculty or if they were guilty of blasphemy, fornication, robbery, dueling, or striking the president or one of the instructors. Among male students, fighting, wearing women's apparel, lying, defamation, and playing "at billiards, cards, dice or any other unlawful game" were punishable only by firm admonition. Similar rules were enforced at the other colleges. In 1844 a student at the University of Nashville was suspended for visiting "a house of dissipation." Another was dismissed two years earlier, not for moral turpitude but for poor scholarship.

Professional Education   Little progress was made during the ante bellum years toward developing professional schools. The licensing system was lax, and many people practiced a profession without the advantages of a formal education.

Perhaps the outstanding professional school of the period was the medical department of the University of Nashville, which opened in 1851 with twenty-eight-year-old John Berrien Lindsley as dean. The professorial staff of seven included, as mentioned, Paul Fitzsimmons Eve, a Georgia-born physician who had studied in the clinics of Paris and London and who had ministered to the wounded in Paris at the time of the July Revolution (1830) and in Warsaw in the Polish Revolution of 1831. Known as one of the ablest surgeons in America, Eve frequently performed difficult operations before medical students. He was one of the first to anesthetize patients, and he used both chloroform and sulfuric ether, although some of his colleagues were skeptical of both. Lindsley required of all candidates for graduation two full years' attendance at the professoral lectures, three years' service in the office of a practicing physician, composition of a thesis, and good moral character. At the time of the Civil War, the medical school had 456 students and ranked second among the schools of the nation in enrollment. Other medical schools of short duration were established in Memphis and Nashville before the Civil War.

All church-controlled colleges offered courses in theology. Perhaps the best-known department was at Cumberland University, which began operation in 1854. Richard Beard, professor of systematic theology, was probably the ablest of the instructors. Cumberland also opened a department of civil engineering in 1852. Surveying and construction were taught. Courses in surveying and civil engineering were suggested to the trustees at the University of Nashville in 1851, but apparently little attention was given to the proposal when the school reopened in 1855.

Young men who wished to enter the legal profession usually "read law" in the offices of a judge or an established practitioner, not infrequently performing clerical work in exchange for room and board. No particular period of study was required. But in 1847, Cumberland University opened the state's first significant law school and required a full year of study. Professor Abram Caruthers and other distinguished faculty members maintained high standards of scholarship. A law department opened at the University of Nashville a few years after the one at Cumberland, and in 1856 the West Tennessee Law School of the City of Memphis was chartered.

The English and scientific department at East Tennessee University had as one of its aims that of qualifying "young men to become teachers in the common schools and academies." Beginning in 1844, free tuition was provided for two men from each county in East Tennessee who would agree to devote three years to teaching after they completed a course of study. In 1855 a bill was introduced providing for the establishment of a normal school for training teachers, but the measure was defeated.

By 1860, nearly 3,000 short-term public schools were in operation, not including academies and private schools. Nearly 140,000 pupils attended public schools of the state and more than 15,000 were enrolled in the academies. More attended academies than in any other state in the South except Kentucky. The contrast in the

amount of financial support is significant. The funds available for the public schools totaled only $402,094; but for a much smaller number of pupils in the academies, nearly $600,000 was spent. Despite the progress of education in the state, Tennessee had one of the highest illiteracy rates in the Union. According to the census reports of 1860, more than 27,000 men and 43,000 women over twenty years of age could neither read nor write. Only North Carolina among the states of the South had more illiterate people than Tennessee.

At the time Tennessee became a state, the Presbyterian church was the strongest of the Protestant bodies on the frontier. These sturdy Calvinists cleared the forests, built schools and churches, and established a government, but by 1800 they were becoming a minority. Their insistence upon a well-educated clergy meant fewer Presbyterian preachers on the frontier, where rival Baptists and Methodists licensed people who felt the "call" to preach even if they did not meet rigid educational standards. In 1814, when Gideon Blackburn organized the First Church in Nashville, Presbyterians had 79 congregations in Tennessee. Despite dissension and spin-offs, Presbyterians at mid-century had established nearly 200 churches in the state and ranked fourth in the number of members—behind Methodists, Baptists, and Cumberland Presbyterians.

The Cumberland Presbyterian Church was organized in Tennessee and developed from a schism within the Presbyterian group. Many leaders of the Presbyterian church had been reluctant to participate in the Great Revival of 1800 because they questioned the sincerity of both the leaders and the converts. Ministers interested in the revival, however, soon secured control of the Cumberland Presbytery (which after 1802 embraced Middle Tennessee and part of Kentucky) and ordained or licensed for the ministry men whom Presbyterian authorities contended were unsound both educationally and doctrinally. The Cumberland group wished to reject the doctrines of predestination and foreordination, which to them meant "fatality." For several years both laymen and clergymen debated the subject. By 1810 only three ordained members of the revival group—Finis Ewing, Samuel King, and Samuel McAdow—remained; the others had returned to the Presbyterian fold without further argument. These determined men, however, met on February 3–4, 1810, in McAdow's home (now embraced within the Montgomery Bell State Park in Dickson County) and organized an independent presbytery but agreed to make sincere efforts to effect a

religious bodies in Tennessee, had 106 churches with a membership of more than 12,000 in the state. The congregations were concentrated chiefly in Middle and West Tennessee.

Frontier Baptist preachers were in East Tennessee almost as early as Presbyterians, and by 1800 they had gained a foothold in the Cumberland country. While the Baptists did not draw as many followers from the Great Revival of 1800 as did the Methodists and Cumberland Presbyterians, they did boast of more than 11,000 by 1812. By that time the Holston and Tennessee associations had been formed in East Tennessee and the Cumberland and Concord associations in the central division. Soon after Jackson purchased the area between the Tennessee and Mississippi rivers, the Western District Association and Forked Deer Association were formed.

Like the Presbyterians, the Tennessee Baptists suffered from controversies and schisms within the church. When Robert B. C. Howell came to Nashville from Virginia in 1835 to pastor the First Baptist Church, he found at least ten distinct Baptist sects whose members refused to take communion even with one another. Among the many discordant elements within the church was "Old Landmarkism," led by James R. Graves of Nashville. Graves had come to Nashville from Ohio in 1845, and at mid-century he was editor of the *Tennessee Baptist*; in this journal he condemned the regular Baptists and urged all to return to the "old landmarks" of New Testament Christianity. Like Campbell and Stone, Graves believed that emphasis upon human creeds had corrupted mankind, and he traced Baptists to the apostles. His influence was limited to Nashville and Middle Tennessee until after the Civil War, when he moved to Memphis to continue his struggle for a return to the original "landmarks."

Most of the Baptist churches in Tennessee became affiliated with the Southern Baptist Convention after its formation in 1845. By 1842, the slavery question had become an issue that involved ministers in both North and South, and Robert T. Daniel and others had preached throughout the state in favor of a Southern convention to meet the peculiar needs of the South and Southwest. When the Foreign Mission Board in 1844 refused to recommend a Georgia slaveholder for appointment as missinary to the Cherokee Indians, Baptists of the South formed a Southern Baptist Convention. In 1849 the First Church in Nashville became the meeting place for the annual convention.

Despite the various disruptive factors, Tennessee Baptists ranked second only to the Methodists during the ante bellum period. In 1860, the Baptists had nearly 700 churches and more than 35,000 members well distributed throughout the state; at least one church was located in every county. There were 21 congregations established in Sevier County, 19 in Wilson, and 18 in Carroll.

No religious body exerted more leadership in Tennessee church affairs during the ante bellum period than did the Methodists. In 1812, when the Tennessee Conference was formed, membership in the state was estimated at about 17,000. The Holston Conference was formed east of the mountains in 1824, and the Memphis Conference west of the mountains in 1840.

Tennessee Methodists were fortunate in that divisive forces did not impede their growth as in the Presbyterian and Baptist churches. Although Methodist Protestants had withdrawn in 1830 after a dispute over lay participation in church government and the powers of bishops, zealots had formed the Wesleyan Connection in 1843 over slavery, and the Free Methodists had coalesced a few years later over "holiness," none of these divisions affected the church in Tennessee. It was only in the sectional controversy of 1844–1845, when two distinct branches of Methodism—North and South—were formed, that Tennessee Methodists participated actively. Some Tennesseans, including Dr. Alexander L. P. Green and John B. McFerrin, joined other Southerners in signing a "Declaration of the Southern Delegates," which resolved that "the continued jurisdiction of the General Conference over the ministry in the slaveholding states would be inconsistent with success." Leaders from the Holston, Tennessee, and Memphis conferences met with other Southern leaders in Louisville in 1845 and formed the Methodist Episcopal Church, South.

By 1860, the Southern Methodist Church exceeded all other groups in membership in Tennessee. The Arminian doctrine of free grace, free will, and individual responsibility fitted well into the rising democratic spirit of the new West, and the courageous nature of the circuit-riding preacher enabled the gospel to be preached over a wide area. Bishop Asbury, for example, may have slept in "filthy houses and filthy beds" and have "taken the itch," but he also crossed the Appalachians sixty-two times and preached more than 15,000 sermons. Like the Baptists, the Methodists placed little emphasis upon a college-trained ministry. The sermons of the Methodist itinerants were simple but forceful and direct. Leaders at mid-century claimed nearly 1,000 churches in the area between Memphis and Bristol. At least one church was located in every county, and Madison had 33, Giles and Maury 26 each, and Davidson 20.

St. Paul's Church, organized in Franklin in 1827 by the Right Reverend James H. Otey, was probably the first Episcopal church to be formed in the state. Much of ante bellum Episcopal history centers around Otey. He came to Williamson County in 1825 to establish a school, but soon also sought to organize a congregation of worshipers. Shortly after St. Paul's was formed, Otey was called to Nashville, where he organized a congregation. In 1829 the Right Reverend John S. Ravenscroft, Bishop of North Carolina, visited the Nashville congregation and stirred "up the minds of the people by his bold and eloquent sermons." Construction work on Christ Church began soon thereafter, and services were held in the new building in 1831. By that time, St. John's had been built in Knoxville and St. Peter's in Columbia. Otey became the first bishop of the Protestant Episcopal Church in Tennessee in 1833, at which time communicants numbered 117.

By 1861, twenty-seven Episcopal clergymen and 1,500 communicants were in the state. Episcopalians concentrated in the larger towns such as Nashville and Memphis. Clergymen of note other than Otey included Leonidas Polk, Charles Tomes (who married Otey's daughter and became rector of a Nashville parish in 1848), and Thomas Wright of Memphis.

Few Catholics came into the state before the War of 1812, but in the early 1820s they came in large numbers, chiefly to perform construction work on Nashville's first bridge across the Cumberland River. In later years others came in to build railroads. In 1820 the Right Reverend Bishop David and Father Robert Abell offered the first mass in Nashville. Some years later the Right Reverend Richard Pius Miles became the first resident bishop of Tennessee, and established parishes, built churches, and founded seminaries. One of the churches was organized in north Nashville in 1853 to serve German families. John Anthony Vogel was ordained in 1858 by Miles, and was placed in charge of the church. Upon Miles's death in 1860, Bishop James Whelan succeeded him.

Not until some years later did Catholicism become established in Memphis. Father John R. Clary held services in the city at mid-century and shortly before the Civil War moved his congregation into the new St. Peter's Church. As in Nashville, railroad building aided in establishing a Catholic population in Memphis. In 1854 a large influx of Irishmen arrived from St. Louis for railroad work. By 1860 more than one-fifth of the 18,000 people in Memphis were Irish, most of whom were Catholics.

The German Lutherans, relatively few in number, centered largely in Sullivan County in East Tennessee, and some settled in nearby Greene and Cocke counties. Shortly after 1800, the Reverend William Jenkins organized the Shofner Church near Shelbvville in Middle Tennessee. Paul Henkel, a remarkably versatile author and preacher, was an early missionary in the state, and in 1820 two of his sons organized the Tennessee Synod as an independent body. Reminiscent of other frontier schisms, leaders sought fundamentals and believed that their congregation was based upon "the Holy Bible . . . and the Augsburg Confession of Faith as a pure emanation from the Bible." In 1855, J. C. Beyer organized a congregation in Memphis. It was not until 1859 that a church was organized in Nashville, and the Reverend Herman Eggers, a Pennsylvanian, became the first pastor. In 1860 the Holston Synod was formed from the Tennessee Synod and became much the stronger of the two, since most of the churches were in East Tennessee. When the Civil War began, Lutherans had only eighteen churches in the state, and fourteen of them were in the eastern division. It was not until twenty years after the war ended that the Tennessee and Holston synods agreed to join with the General Synod of the South, to form the United Synod in the South.

People of the Judaic faith lived mainly in the cities. A congregation was organized in 1851 in Nashville. Three years later, when Rabbi Alexander Iser, a Russian-Pole, arrived, the congregation was reorganized and chartered as "Khal Kodesh Mogen David," which meant a "Holy Congregation—Shield of David." A congregation was formed in Memphis in 1853, although by that time Jews had been in that city for at least a decade. By 1860 the Memphis synagogue had a membership of approximately seventy-five, and the Nashville group had about the same number. A smaller congregation, Beth El, House of God, was organized in Knoxville during the war.

Reforms: Care of the Unfortunates ஓ A movement for better care of the mentally ill did not begin as early as did the agitation for revision of the criminal code. (See Chapter 10). Although William Carroll had talked about the problem, and had urged legislative attention to it, it was not until after he had ceased to be governor and Dorothea Lynn Dix had awakened the public conscience that much was done. Earlier, Tennesseans for the most part had ignored the question completely or else had authorized county courts to appoint guardians for mentally defectives who owned property.

The first significant act came in 1832, when the legislature appropriated $10,000 for a hospital for the insane, to be located at Nashville. Funds were inadequate, however, and for fifteen years reformers were disappointed at the lack of progress. A legislative committee appointed in 1837 to investigate the hospital work, for example, found a half-built structure "in bad order" and "daily and hourly injuring" from exposure to rain and weather. Not until two years later was the hospital, consisting of sixty beds, ready for operation.

Reformers were far from satisfied with Tennessee's efforts to minister to the insane. Governor Polk in 1841 pointed to statistics showing that the state had approximately 800 people who were mentally defective, and he urged that hospital facilities be expanded. Governor Jones observed with regret what he characterized as public indifference to the "unfortunate class of our fellow-citizens." A legislative committee was appointed to study plans for enlarging facilities, but little had been done when Miss Dix arrived in Nashville in 1847. Dix, a Massachusetts-born reformer, had visited and studied almshouses and hospitals in many states as well as Europe, and reformers were not surprised when she told of Tennessee's inadequacies. She found the state hospital to be one of the worst in the country. The heating facilities, she said, were "a complete failure." There were no bathrooms; neither cisterns nor wells afforded an adequate water supply. She suggested to state officials the purchase of at least 100 acres of land readily accessible to all parts of the state and the building of a new hospital large enough to house at least 250 patients.

Legislators acted favorably upon her suggestions. The governor was authorized to appoint seven commissioners to purchase a tract of land and supervise the construction of a new hospital with the features Miss Dix had suggested. A site on the Murfreesboro Road, six miles from Nashville, was purchased, and construction was begun in the autumn of 1848. Work moved slowly, however, because of inadequate funds. Governor William Trousdale in his final legislative message (October 1851) observed that the hospital was at last ready for occupancy, and a few months later patients were transferred. Not until 1857, however, was the structure finished according to original specifications.

The humanitarian spirit also gave rise to a demand for public assistance for the blind and for deaf mutes. The first legislation on behalf of the blind came at the insistence of James Champlin, a blind son of an Overton County merchant, who in 1842 established a school for the blind in Nashville. Legislators appropriated little, but a few wealthy individuals contributed enough for building and operational costs. In the early 1850s legislators set aside $12,000 for a new school. Trustees purchased one and one-half acres on the Lebanon Road, where construction was begun immediately on a three-story building.

Similar attention focused upon help for deaf-mutes during the two decades before the Civil War. Tennessee became the seventh state to establish a school for the deaf in 1844, when the legislature appropriated money for a school at Knoxville. As in the case of education for the blind, interest in an institution for the deaf and dumb developed slowly. The school began operation with only six pupils, and by 1853 trustees reported that not more than twenty-five persons had availed themselves of the opportunities that the school afforded, although there were more than 500 deaf-mutes in the state, about one-fourth of school age.

Reforms: Efforts to Regulate Public Morals 〜 Throughout the colonial, Revolutionary, and early republic periods, drinking was quite common. Little thought was given to the moral issue. Nevertheless, a temperance movement developed soon after Tennessee became a state, and leaders boasted of their success during the first half of the nineteenth century. The first anti-liquor law affecting the state was enacted by North Carolina in 1779. The law restricted drinking to homes and establishments for travelers and made illegal the retailing of intoxicants in quantities of less than a quart, except in taverns and hotels. Legislators had of course intended to eliminate saloons whose sole business was the sale of liquor that could be consumed on the premises. Many "tippling houses" (as the saloons were called) existed in open violation of the law, however, and state legislators, apparently despairing of the enforcement of the enactment, legalized saloons in 1831. Proprietors were required to procure licenses from the clerks of the county courts and to give bond that they would keep peaceful and orderly houses and not permit gambling. It was called the general license system because any establishment, saloons as well as taverns, could be licensed to retail liquor.

In the meantime, prominent temperance leaders organized to combat demon rum. Some leaders formed temperance societies to dissuade people from the consumption of alcoholic beverages, others established temperance journals, and still others memorialized the legislature for stricter liquor laws. Two societies, probably the first in the state, were organized in 1829. One was at Kingsport, where members condemned intemperance and pledged themselves neither to vote for candidates who sought support with liquor nor to employ persons who drank while at work. The other society was at Nashville, where William Hume, Philip Lindsley, Robert Whyte, and other prominent citizens organized the "Nashville and Davidson County Temperance Society, Auxiliary to the American Temperance Society."

Legislators retained a close interest in the whiskey problem. When they assembled in 1837, many came to Nashville with specific instructions from their constituents to abolish tippling houses. Consequently, a measure was enacted early in the next year to repeal laws that licensed saloons and to prohibit the sale of intoxicants in quantities of less than a quart. The law was poorly enforced, and in 1846, eight years later, the Quart Law was repealed. Legislators returned to the licensing system, under which anyone might retail liquors who secured a license, provided he took an oath that he would not sell on Sunday, would not permit gambling, and would not sell to minors without written permission from their parents (or sell to slaves without permission from their masters). This law remained on the statute books until after the Civil War, except for two years (1856–1857) when the Quart Law of 1838 was resurrected.

Other efforts were made to regulate public morals during the ante bellum period. Newspapermen not infrequently editorialized upon the large amount of vice and misconduct, especially in the cities. Horseracing was frequently condemned; one correspondent described the track as a place of "noise and dust; hard drinking; profane cursing and swearing; quarrelling; fighting; bloody noses; black eyes;

fractured noses; [and] ragged citizens who can not give bread to their wives and children. . . ." Cardplaying was also condemned by some, and in 1815 legislators placed a heavy tax on vendors of cards. Two years later, Senator William C. Roadman, of East Tennessee, led a legislative battle to abolish billiard tables. The senator described the game as one that encouraged "the vice of gambling which will eventually be attended with pernicious consequences to society, by corrupting the morals of the youth of our country. . . ."

The continued agitation for reform reflected a growing awareness of social evil on the part of at least some of the people. Much crime and vice, nevertheless, continued, especially in the cities. The river town of Memphis teemed with robbers and gamblers, and Old Bell Tavern was a dive where confidence games were common and liquor could be had day and night. Sections of Nashville offered little by way of improvement. The river front, known as the "Jungle," was especially notorious for its cheap saloons, brothels, and hideouts for criminals.

Considerable economic and cultural progress had been made in Tennessee by the time the Civil War began. That disastrous struggle counteracted much of the good that had been wrought, but at the same time gains were made upon which future generations were to build.

SUGGESTED READINGS

Books
Peter Cartwright, *Autobiography of Peter Cartwright, the Backwoods Preacher* (Nashville, 1946); Blanche Henry Clark, *The Tennessee Yeoman* (Nashville, 1942); Catharine C. Cleveland, *The Great Revival in the West 1797–1805* (Chicago, 1916); Frank L. Owsley, *Plain Folk of the Old South* (Baton Rouge, 1949); Robert H. White, *Development of the Tennessee State Education Organization, 1796–1929* (Nashville, 1929).

Articles
Constantine G. Belissary, "Industry and Industrial Philosophy in Tennessee, 1850–1860," *ETHSP* 23 (1951), 46–57; Budd H. Bishop, "Art in Tennessee: The Early 19th Century," *THQ* 29 (Winter 1970–71), 379–89; Jesse C. Crowe, "The Origin and Development of Tennessee's Prison Problem, 1831–1871," *THQ* 15 (June 1956), 111–35; Robert E. Dalton,

"Montgomery Bell and the Narrows of Harpeth," *THQ* 35 (Spring 1976), 3–28; F. Garvin Davenport, "Culture Versus Frontier in Tennessee 1825–1850," *JSH* 5 (Feb. 1939), 18–33; Frank L. and Harriet C. Owsley, "Economic Basis of Society in the Late Antebellum South," *JSH* 6 (1940), 24–45; Owsley, "The Economic Structure of Rural Tennessee, 1850–1860," *JSH* (May 1942), 161–82; Tommy W. Rogers, "Migration from Tennessee During the Nineteenth Century: Origin and Destination of Tennessee Migrants, 1850–1860," *THQ* 27 (Summer 1968), 118–22; E. Bruce Thompson, "Reforms in the Care of the Insane in Tennessee, 1830–1850," *THQ* 3 (Dec. 1944), 319–34; Buford C. Utley, "The Early Academies of West Tennessee," *WTHSP* 8 (1954), 5–38; Charles P. White, "Early Experiments with Prison Labor in Tennessee," *ETHSP* 12 (1940), 45–69; Samuel Cole Williams, "Early Iron Works," *THQ* 6(March 1947), 39–46; Virginia Williams, "Tennessee's Public School Lands," *THQ* 3 (Dec. 1944), 335–48; John F. Woolverton, "Philip Lindsley and the Cause of Education in the Old Southwest," *THQ* 19 (March 1960), 3–22.

15.

Party Politics, 1839–1859

T HE political revolution of 1835 was like a knife thrust at the heart of the Democratic party in Tennessee, and the losses of 1836 and 1837 were like salt rubbed in raw wounds. So disorganized were its leaders that some seriously considered withdrawing from politics entirely. Cave Johnson, the Jackson stalwart from Clarksville, was so perturbed over the losses (which included his own congressional seat) that he considered moving to Mississippi. Jackson, in humiliation, retired to the Hermitage where he bitterly assailed the people's "damnable aspostacy," and Felix Grundy was at a loss to understand how people could so dishonor the Old Hero who had brought the highest civil and military honors to the state. Only Polk, the distinguished speaker of the House of Representatives, emerged unscathed. The Maury Countian now became the acknowledged head of the party and was viewed by Jackson and other Democrats as one who might rescue them from the clutches of the Whigs.

Polk Elected Governor ε≫ Shortly after the election of 1837, discouraged Democrats met in Nashville to reorganize and lay plans for regaining control. Speaker after speaker denounced the Whigs, and listeners shouted approval when Polk described them as Hamiltonian Federalists in disguise, censured them for shamefully deserting the standards of Jackson, and declared war on Henry Clay and Daniel Webster. Encouraged by the fighting spirit exhibited by Polk, Democrats vowed support when the congressman urged them all to cast off their lethargy and join him in thoroughly reorganizing the party down to the county and precinct levels.

Polk, who was 43, hoped eventually to become vice president, and many Democrats predicted he would be Van Buren's running mate in the next election. Many of his friends viewed the governor's office as a better stepping-stone to the White House than membership in Congress, and they moved to commit him to the gubernatorial race. Accordingly, supporters planned a rally in Murfreesboro on August 30, 1838, and invited Polk to deliver the principal address. On the appointed day some 2,000 Tennesseans gathered at the Rutherford county seat to consume hundreds of pounds of ham, barbecue, beef, and mutton—to say nothing of gallons of wine and whiskey—and to hear Polk denounce Whigs for their insistence upon a national bank and internal improvements at federal expense. The Whig plan of "building up a splendid and extravagant government," he said, would tax farmers and the poor in a discriminatory manner. After an hour of eating and drinking, the crowd returned to the speaker's stand to hear William Carroll praise Polk and disclaim any intention of seeking the gubernatorial chair himself. Jubilant Polk men then pushed the Maury Countian to the platform where he announced his candidacy for governor. Party leaders proclaimed Polk as their Moses and boldly predicted that he would lead them out of a Whig wilderness and into the folds of Democratic control.

James Knox Polk was descended from one of Middle Tennessee's prominent families. His elder cousin, Colonel William Polk, had been highly successful as a land speculator, and his father, Sam Polk, had grown wealthy as manager of Colonel Polk's holdings. Sam Polk had done well on his own as a land speculator, army contractor, merchant, and bank director. After graduating in 1818 from the University of North Carolina at the head of his class, young Polk studied law with Felix Grundy and became a practicing attorney at Columbia. Through Grundy's influence he obtained a clerkship in the state senate in 1819 and was elected to the lower house in 1823. There he voted for Jackson in the Chief's successful bid for the United States Senate seat held by John Williams, and two years later Polk followed the Old Hero to Washington and served in the House of Representatives until he was chosen governor in 1839.

Whigs nominated Cannon for a third term, and the candidates opened joint debates at Murfreesboro on April 11, 1839 and con-

The 1840s were years in which the Whig party seriously challenged the Jacksonian Democrats. Shown here are four governors who served during that decade. *Above left:* James K. Polk, 1839–1841 (Democrat); *above right:* James C. Jones, 1841–1845 (Whig); *below left:* Aaron V. Brown, 1845–1847 (Democrat); *below right:* Neill S. Brown, 1847–1849 (Whig).

ducted a campaign then unparalleled in the state's history. In the opening encounter, Polk spoke for two hours; then Cannon was heard. Polk's speech closely followed the platform that he had outlined in a twenty-eight page pamphlet circulated several weeks before. He contrasted the virtues of Jackson with the alleged iniquities of Henry Clay and John Quincy Adams and charged that Cannon and Tennessee Whigs were mere tools in the hands of the Kentuckian. Polk devoted little time to state issues but traced the genealogy of "Federal-Whiggery" to the Federalism of Adams and Hamilton and excoriated Cannon for jeopardizing the rights of the people by his insistence upon national and state banks. Governor Cannon then spoke for ninety minutes. He described the congressman as a "tool for Jackson," defended Henry Clay, blamed the Democrats for the depression of 1837, and spoke highly of a national and state banking system. A few days later they moved on to Lebanon, where Polk spoke for four hours, Cannon for nearly two, and John Bell for one hour. From Lebanon they went to Carthage, and from there to towns in the Cumberland Plateau. Large crowds attended the debates as they talked their way across the state, and from the beginning the people saw that Polk was master of the situation. Skillful in the use of sarcasm and abuse, the Maury Countian poked fun at the ponderous but self-confident Cannon and became a favorite with the people early in the series of debates.

Verbal fireworks did not provide the only attraction for the audiences. Bloody street fights broke out among belligerent Democrats and Whigs in several towns, and many people, including local candidates and speakers, carried weapons. After several joint meetings, Cannon, apparently sensing that he was no match for the skilled debater, pleaded that the press of state business required his attention more than did participation on the hustings. John Bell, Congressman William B. Campbell, Senator Ephraim Foster, and other Whigs were left to defend the governor as best they could. Interest was such that nearly 20,000 more people voted than had cast ballots in 1837.

Polk was elected, but the results were so close that for several days the outcome was in doubt. He lost the eastern and western sections, but his majority in Middle Tennessee was sufficient to win by about 2,500 votes. His party also captured control of both houses of the legislature and gained 3 additional congressional seats, giving Democrats a total of 6 out of 13. Party leaders across the state hailed the victory as a "great and glorious triumph"—a tremendous personal victory for Polk.

The Whigs, although disheartened, did not despair. Bell called a convention to meet in Nashville, where Whig leaders mapped strategy for recapturing control of the state. They blamed their defeat upon the unprecedented efforts of Polk, made plans to reorganize down to the precinct level, and predicted victory at the polls in 1840 and 1841.

The legislature assembled in October, and before the governor's message could be received, eager Democrats pushed through a resolution recommending Polk for vice president. After receiving Polk's message, legislators turned their attention to such matters as the Bank of Tennessee, internal improvements, public education, the construction of an asylum for the insane, and the election of United States senators. Perhaps it was the last named that created the greatest interest. Democrats found themselves in a position similar to that occupied by Whigs two years before. They controlled the gubernatorial chair and the legislature, but the United States senators, as well as a majority of the congressmen, were of the opposing party. Senator White's term would expire in 1841, and that of Ephraim Foster, who had replaced Felix Grundy in 1838, would expire in 1845. Victorious Democrats, unwilling to wait until the terms ended, unfolded a plan whereby the two senators would be forced to resign.

All United States senators at that time, having been elected by their respective state legislatures, were expected to carry out the instructions of their legislators or "graciously resign." Tennessee Democrats knew that White and Foster would quit before they would vote for key administrative measures then before the Congress. The Democratic-dominated legislature then passed resolutions instructing the two senators to "support in good faith the leading measures" proposed by President Van Buren. Foster resigned immediately (November 15, 1839), and Democrats promptly elected Grundy in his place. White resigned a few weeks later and returned immediately to Knoxville, where within a few months he died and became a martyr to his party's cause. Even though legislators selected a Knox County Democrat, Alexander Anderson, as White's replacement, they won few if any friends in the eastern section because of White's popularity with people of both political faiths.

The simple duties of the governor's office in Polk's day gave the

Maury Countian ample time to plan his political future. Legislative resolutions in Tennessee and elsewhere nominating him for vice president pleased him, and he wrote letters to acquaintances indicating his availability for the post. A delegation of Tennessee Democrats, including such stalwarts as Grundy, Carroll, Aaron Brown, Cave Johnson, and Samuel H. Laughlin, departed for the Baltimore convention in May 1840 with the intention of pushing Polk's candidacy.

Whigs in the meantime nominated William Henry Harrison, the clerk of an Ohio court who a quarter of a century earlier had defeated a coalition of Indians at Tippecanoe and had emerged as a hero. Party leaders in Tennessee had supported Henry Clay and General Winfield Scott and were amazed at Harrison's nomination. They nevertheless agreed to support the nominee and assembled in Nashville early in January to make plans for a statewide canvass.

Leaders of both parties had organized at the county and precinct levels, where they vied for grassroots support. Whigs surprised even themselves in the amount of noise and ballyhoo they engendered; brass bands, free barbecue and whiskey, pet raccoons, and log cabins—the last two items, especially, became symbolic of the party—were always on hand. Excitement ran high. Typical of the many Whig rallies was one held in Clarksville in late May, where more than 7,000 people assembled, made merry, partook of refreshments, and cheered for "Tippecanoe and Tyler, too." One politician, pleased with the enthusiasm, wrote that "there had never been anything to compare with it. . . . The very children are as deeply imbued with the party Spirit as the grown people."

The Democrats were not idle; even the ailing Hero of the Hermitage appeared at barbecues and rallies in Rutherford, Davidson, and Williamson counties before touring much of West Tennessee, and Polk left gubernatorial duties unattended while he excoriated Whig "clap-traps" who emphasized no issues other than "the log cabin, hard cider, and raccoon humbuggery." The combined efforts of Jackson, Polk, Grundy, Cave Johnson, and others were unavailing, however, and stunned Democrats witnessed the first presidential defeat in the history of their party. Harrison carried Tennessee by more than 12,000 votes and defeated Van Buren by an electoral majority of 234 to 60. Polk's failure to receive the vice presidential nomination had been one reason for Van Buren's loss of the Volunteer State, but the "Little Magician" had never been popular in

Tennessee, and the Whig barbecue and whiskey—not to mention thorough organization—cannot be discounted. In the minds of some Democrats the hopes engendered by Polk's victory in 1839 were shattered, and faith in the people's ability to distinguish sound issues and principles from "coonery and foolery" was destroyed.

James Chamberlain Jones Defeats Polk ჰ Democrats were yet to reach the depths of despair in the gubernatorial contests of 1841 and 1843. Polk had announced for reelection on July 4, 1840, even though the election was still more than a year away. He had used satire, ridicule, and effective debate against Cannon in 1839; still smarting from that defeat, Whigs sought a man who could beat him at his own game. After rejecting John Bell's brother-in-law, David W. Dickinson, they decided upon James C. (Lean Jimmy) Jones, whose political experience had been limited to one term in the legislature and brief service as a presidential elector in 1840.

Jones, Whigs believed, could match Polk with his stock of anecdotes and mimicry and could even add a bit of the folksy common touch that the distinguished and austere congressman lacked. Jones was an odd-looking man of only thirty-one years; he stood six feet or more and weighed only 125 pounds, and his solemn, almost grotesque countenance soon became a favorite among the people regardless of whether he told stories from the platform or walked among the crowds shaking hands and telling yarns without the least implication of condescension. The Whig press described him as able, efficient, and "a true Whig." Democrats were not at all worried and rejoiced that Bell or some other well-known person was not selected. Even Jackson wrote Polk that Jones's nomination was "well for the Democratic cause" and that Polk need have no fear.

The joint debates began at Murfreesboro on March 27, where a large crowd heard the candidates for nearly five hours. After that they talked their way across the state. Jones supported the national Whig policies, including a national bank, but his stock-in-trade was his anecdotes. Polk discussed state and national issues with dignity and sobriety, and his experience and broad understanding of government enabled him to deliver learned and convincing arguments in favor of the subtreasury system, of marketing unsold Tennessee bonds then in the hands of British brokers, and other issues. Jones's limited knowledge and experience handicapped him, but he refused to permit ignorance of the issues to embarrass him. His friendly and simple manner appealed to the rural populace, and he had only to appear before them stroking a raccoon fur to send them into gales of laughter.

The crowds gave Polk a respectful hearing, but they voted for Jones. The Whig candidate won by a majority of a little more than 3,000 votes. Whigs also gained control of the house of representatives but won only 12 of the 25 seats in the senate. The defeat was Polk's first before the people of Tennessee.

In his first message to the legislators, Governor Jones recommended that the school system be improved and that attention be given to internal improvements, sound currency, encouragement to manufacturing interests, and completion of the insane asylum. The immediate question before the legislature, however, was the election of two United States senators. Both seats were vacant. Alexander Anderson's term expired on March 3, 1841, and Grundy had died a few weeks after his appointment in November, 1840; A. O. P. Nicholson had been chosen in his place until the legislature could choose a successor. Although the Whigs controlled the house by a majority of three, Democrats held the senate by only one—a majority at first considered precarious because Senator Sam Turney, Democrat from the Cumberland Plateau district where Whigs were equally strong, could not be counted upon to hold steadfastly to the Democratic ranks.

Whigs were confident that they could elect both senators because the customary method of electing such officials was by a joint convention composed of the entire legislature. Democrats realized that they would be outvoted by the Whig majority in the house if they accepted the conventional method; they therefore concluded that each house should vote separately and hoped that the Whigs would compromise by naming one senator and permitting them to select the other. Whigs remained adamant, however, and those in the senate became known as the "Twelve Destructives." The Democratic majority, just as adamant, was called the "Immortal Thirteen." The result was that no agreement was reached, no senators were elected, and Tennessee was unrepresented in the upper house of Congress for the next two years. Blame was heaped generally upon the "Immortal Thirteen," but Jackson, watching carefully from the Hermitage, thought that Democrats had protected "the fundamental principles of our Republican system."

Successful in blocking the election of senators, the thirteen Democrats then resolved to obstruct other Whig legislation. They rejected the governor's nominations of bank directors on two occasions, and blocked an attempt to investigate the Bank of Tennessee, despite a Whig allegation that an investigation would bring forth "some awful disclosures." Jones disgustedly referred to the assembly as a "do-nothing" body.

For some time Democratic leaders assumed that Polk—now referred to by the Democratic press as the "Goliath of Modern Democracy"—would seek to avenge his defeat of 1841. Therefore, no other candidate was even suggested. Whigs, fearful that the magic of Jones's oratory might not again have its mesmerizing effect, were hesitant to renominate the incumbent. Ephraim H. Foster, however, assumed leadership of the party and dictated that Jones should run. Foster convinced party members and local leaders, who were organized even at the precinct level, that Tennessee was now truly a Whig state.

Polk, with an eye not only to the governorship but also to the vice presidency in 1844, announced the longest list of speaking engagements ever published by a gubernatorial aspirant and laid the groundwork for an extensive campaign. Jones promptly promised to meet the challenger wherever he went. Thus began the most thorough campaign the people had yet witnessed. Polk tried to ignore the work of the "Immortal Thirteen" and spent much of his time denouncing Henry Clay; it was generally assumed that Clay would be a presidential candidate in 1844. Jones, however, kept the Thirteen before the people. He chided Polk because of the obstructionist tactics of the Democratic legislators—and told jokes and tall tales. Polk's efforts to keep the campaign on a high plane of issues were ineffective, and Jones defeated the Maury Countian by nearly 4,000 votes. Whigs won both houses of the legislature and 5 of the 11 congressional seats. Polk's defeat was the darkest hour of his career; Whigs, however, hailed their victory as "one of the greatest triumphs" in the history of the party.

The two major issues before the Twenty-fifth General Assembly were the election of two United States senators and the selection of a permanent location for the state capital. With a majority of two in the senate and of five in the house, the Whigs had no difficulty in electing two senators from their own party. They promptly chose Ephraim H. Foster and Spencer Jarnigan—the men they had planned to elect two years before. They then proceeded to enact into law a method for electing senators so that the events of 1841 could not be repeated. Henceforth senators were to be chosen by the "two Houses assembled in Convention."

Deciding upon a permanent location of the capital was not so simple a matter. Members of the constitutional convention of 1834 had commanded the legislature of 1843 to select a permanent location within the first week of its session, the location not to be changed except by a two-thirds vote of both houses. During the state's brief history the capital had been located at four separate towns. Territorial Governor William Blount had established the seat of government in Knoxville. When Tennesseans drafted a constitution preparatory to becoming a state, they provided that the Knox County seat should continue as the capital until at least 1802. When the constitutional limit expired, legislators continued to meet in Knoxville for an indefinite period. In 1807 they met in Kingston for one day, in order to fulfill the terms of a treaty with the Cherokee Indians, but promptly returned to Knoxville. During the next decade the peripatetic legislature met in three different cities. Knoxville remained the seat of government until 1812, at which time the lawmakers moved to Nashville, but they returned to Knoxville in 1817. In the following year they moved to Murfreesboro. The capital remained there until 1826, at which time it was returned to Nashville.

Dozens of towns had been suggested both before and after the legislators convened. During the week-long debate, at least the following were considered: Nashville, Kingston, Lebanon, Hamilton (Sumner County), Sparta, Knoxville, Clarksville, McMinnville, Shelbyville, Chattanooga, Murfreesboro, Franklin, Harrison (Hamilton County), Woodbury, Columbia, Charlotte, Reynoldsburg (Humphreys County), Carrollsville (Wayne County), Carthage, Smithville, Jackson, Manchester, Monticello (Putnam County), and Taylorsville (Johnson County). Representative John W. Richardson of Rutherford County finally proposed that the capital be established "at the county town in the county of which the geographical center of the state may fall." A professor at the University of Nashville was employed to make a survey. His study revealed that the exact center was one and one-half miles east of Murfreesboro—Richardson's hometown. Those preferring Nashville prevailed, however, and seven days after sessions began Nashville had been chosen as the permanent seat of government. Plans were made immediately to construct a capitol on Campbell's Hill, near the center of town, which the city council of Nashville transferred to the state. A board of building commissioners was appointed, and William Strickland was engaged as architect.

James Knox Polk Elected President ⧉ An even more important development affecting Tennessee during Jones's second term was the nomination and election of James K. Polk as the eleventh president of the United States. After his second defeat for governor, he had returned to Columbia to practice law. His interest in politics continued unabated, however, and he kept up a wide correspondence with party leaders.

While plans were being made for the Democratic convention in May 1844, various people were mentioned for president, but Van Buren, with Jackson's support, had an advantage over the others. Polk was seldom mentioned in connection with the presidency, but he received prominent attention as a vice presidential possibility. In April, Van Buren weakened his chances considerably by opposing the annexation of Texas. Polk, who had been outspoken in favor of Texas, soon gained support, including an endorsement from Jackson. The able work of Gideon J. Pillow and others on the floor of the convention brought a strong movement for the Tennessean on the eighth ballot, and on the ninth vote Polk was chosen as the standard bearer for his party. Whigs, meanwhile, had nominated Henry Clay.

Polk made the principal issue that of expansion—"re-annexation of Texas and the re-occupation of Oregon." At the beginning of the campaign Clay spoke against annexation of Texas because it was against the wishes, he said, of "a considerable and respectable portion" of the people. Instead, he talked in favor of the regular Whig policies of a protective tariff, a national bank, and internal improvements.

In Tennessee the fact that voters were evenly divided between Whigs and Democrats made it evident that the contest would be close. Not only did pride in carrying Tennessee motivate Polk to action, but also the prospect of winning the state's thirteen electoral votes caused him to urge leaders to organize and campaign extensively on the local level. Oddly enough, the home state of Houston and Crockett voted against its son who promised annexation of Texas

Above: This was the Columbia boyhood home of James K. Polk. *Below:* Near Smyrna stands the birthplace of Sam Davis, the "Boy Hero of the Confederacy," who was hanged by the Federals in 1863 as a spy.

and opted in favor of a Kentuckian who hedged on the issue. Although Polk received 50.7 percent of the popular vote and won the presidency by an electoral vote of 170 to 105, he failed to carry Tennessee by 267 votes of about 120,000 cast.

Polk's failure to win his home state shocked Democrats and has confused historians. Certainly Tennesseans were expansionists and wanted Texas. But Clay had so modified his position on annexation that an expansionist could vote for him. Perhaps the best explanation is a simple one—Whig efficiency and organization and strong newspaper support brought people to the polls as in the past, while Democratic disharmony and inefficiency lost Polk a few votes across the state.

Polk's elation over his victory was offset by sadness when Andrew Jackson, his political mentor and friend of many years, died shortly after the inauguration. The Hero of the Hermitage had watched political events with unflagging interest after his retirement in 1837. During the campaign of 1844 he had published commendations of Polk and had been overjoyed when the Tennessean defeated Clay, whom Jackson earlier had called "that Judas of the West." Jackson had suffered from the effects of malaria and acute dysentery since the Indian wars, and at the time of Van Buren's inauguration in 1837 many feared that he would not reach the Hermitage alive. He had regained his health, but during the winter and spring of 1845 his condition steadily worsened. He died on June 8 and was buried beside his beloved Rachel at the Hermitage.

Flags were flown at half staff, and ceremonies in his honor were held throughout the state. Typical was a memorial service at Charlotte on July 18, where Jeremiah George Harris, editor of the Nashville *Union,* was the principal speaker. In a two-hour eulogy, Harris compared Jackson with Washington. He "was to the American people," Harris said,

> as the sun to the mariner. Like the father of his country, he descended to the grave loaded with all the civil and military honors of his countrymen. . . . The mother shall teach her infant to lisp their names [Washington's and Jackson's] in unison—the father shall teach him to emulate their sterling virtues.

Aaron V. Brown Elected Governor ೪ೞ While Jackson lay dying, Democrats perfected plans to regain the gubernatorial chair.

Aaron V. "Fat" Brown of Pulaski, a Democratic stalwart of long standing, had served ably in Congress and in both branches of the legislature, and he became his party's unanimous choice. Whigs discussed the names of Neill S. Brown, Gustavus A. Henry, and Ephraim Foster, and in the convention on March 20 they nominated Foster. The Whig nominee had served in the United States Senate and in both houses of the state legislature. Foster had been with Jackson during the Creek War and had supported the Chief for several years before joining the ranks of Bell and White. The two experienced men began their joint debates in Clarksville, and the speeches gave promise of another colorful campaign. Both were gifted orators and thrilled the crowds with their references to the Bible, motherhood, the Constitution, the flag, and classical literature.

Once again the election was close, and the decision was in doubt for several days. Foster won in East and West Tennessee, but Brown gained enough support in the central section to win. The final and official count gave Brown the victory by a majority of a little more than 1,600 votes. Democrats also gained control of the legislature, and jubilant leaders boasted that Tennessee had been "redeemed, regenerated, and disenthralled from the dominion of Whiggism."

The most important matter to come before the legislature during Brown's administration was the election of a United States senator to replace Foster, who had resigned to make the gubernatorial race. The Democratic caucus had expressed a preference for A. O. P. Nicholson, but W. C. Dunlap, Hopkins Turney, and General William Trousdale were also contenders. The Whigs, outnumbered in both house and senate, did not hope to elect a senator from their own party, but they sought to block the election of Nicholson. For two weeks legislators debated and voted but were unable to unite behind one candidate. Nicholson, who led on most of the early ballots, finally withdrew in exasperation, and his friends then supported Dunlap. At this point, the Whigs concentrated their strength on Turney, and elected him with the help of six Democrats. The disgusted Democratic majority termed Turney a traitor and turned him out of the party.

Two years later Whigs chose Neill S. "Lean" Brown, a Giles County native, to oppose "Fat" Brown. Again, national issues dominated the campaign, and the race between the two Browns was close. Whigs condemned Polk for his stand on the Oregon question and for his prosecution of the Mexican War. The people, weary of war, elected Neill Brown by a thousand votes and gave the Whigs a majority in both houses of the legislature. Once again the political pendulum had swung to the Whig side.

The legislature now faced the new election of a United States senator, and Whig leaders were determined not to reelect Spencer Jarnigan because he had supported the Democrat-sponsored Walker tariff (which reduced the levy on most items). Among Whigs considered were Governor Jones, Ephraim Foster, John Bell, Robertson Topp, John Netherland, and others, all of whom spent long hours wooing legislators in the legislative halls, in the lobby, and in the tavern taprooms. Bell, a member of the House of Representatives, was finally chosen on the 54th ballot after a month of debate. The competent Nashvillian served in the Senate until 1859 and became a candidate for President in the following year.

Texas, Oregon, and the Mexican War ঌ~ While Whigs and Democrats, almost equally divided, struggled for control of the state, national affairs also demanded attention. Texans sought annexation to the United States soon after they gained independence. Jackson had closed his political career by granting recognition to the republic, and William H. Wharton, a Tennessean who played an important role in the war for Texas independence, was named minister to the United States with instructions to "effect annexation."

In 1842 the legislatures of several states, including Tennessee, passed resolutions insisting upon annexation. Tennesseans urged representatives in Washington to "use every exertion in their power to procure the admission of Texas into the Union. . . ." In the following year, Aaron V. Brown, a member of the House of Representatives, wrote Jackson for advice. The Old Hero urged him to press for annexation at once.

Texas was annexed by joint resolution of Congress a few weeks before Polk's inauguration. By late December 1845, Texans had drafted a new constitution and accepted the American proposal, and the Lone Star State had become the 28th state of the Union.

The Oregon question was resolved with less difficulty. For more than three decades American and British interests in Oregon had been a subject for diplomatic negotiation. Joint occupation had been decided upon in 1818, and nine years later the two countries agreed to continue the arrangement indefinitely. In the early 1840s, as Americans swarmed westward, increased interest was manifested in Oregon, and a few expansionists insisted that the United States should assert its claim to all the territory; that is, to the line of 54°40'. The Oregon question became an issue in the campaign of 1844, and Polk declared in his inaugural address that Americans should take all of Oregon. A vociferous minority of Democrats even insisted that we should make war on Britain rather than surrender one inch of the claim.

In the quiet of White House conferences with party leaders, however, Polk questioned whether the country should risk war to acquire the disputed territory. Senators Thomas Hart Benton and John C. Calhoun refused to support the claims of the extremists and insisted upon compromise at the 49th parallel. Senator Hopkins Turney, also supporting compromise, wrote Polk that to insist upon all of Oregon would create an irreparable breach in the Democratic party. When British officials offered settlement at the 49th parallel, Polk submitted the matter to the Senate with his recommendation of acceptance. Consequently, the Senate voted 37 to 12 in favor of such a compromise. The final treaty was concluded on June 15, 1846.

California was not so easily acquired. On the contrary, only after war with Mexico could the Bear Flag State be added to the Union. Tennesseans had developed an intense dislike of Mexico after the Texas Revolution; the declaration of war, passed in May 1846, therefore met with general approval in the Volunteer State. The same enthusiasm that had inspired Americans to action in 1812 was renewed, and thousands of Tennesseans rushed forward to volunteer.

Nearly a week elapsed after the declaration of war before Governor Brown received orders from Washington to mobilize men for action. Tennesseans were mortified when they heard that the War Department wanted only one regiment of cavalry and two regiments of infantry from Tennessee—abut 2,800 men—and some went to other states to volunteer. Because more than ten times the number needed offered their services, the "privilege" of being taken into military service was determined by lottery. According to one Nashville newspaper, some disappointed volunteers offered to give as much as $250 for the right to fight in Mexico. Once organized, Tennessee troops were dispatched with haste across the border, where they fought bravely and played important roles in the battles of Cerro Gordo, Monterrey, and Chapultepec.

Tennesseans, like many others, were overconfident; they believed that the war would be brief and that the Mexicans would surrender after a few skirmishes. A Knoxville editor boldly declared that General Zachary Taylor was only awaiting the arrival of troops from Tennessee before he undertook what surely would be a hasty and triumphal march into Mexico City. As the war continued without victory and the stubborn resistance of the Mexican army brought loss of life to many who had marched proudly to war only a few months earlier, Tennessee Whigs became caustic in their denunciation of the administration's war policy. When dysentery, measles, and other illnesses took more lives than did Mexican bullets, Polk was described as a butcher who had brought on an "unwanted war," and General Gideon J. Pillow was denounced for the "terrible carnage."

On February 2, 1848, Nicholas P. Trist met Mexican officials at Guadalupe Hidalgo and signed a treaty of peace. When the treaty—which added the vast area known as the "Mexican Cession"—was presented to the Senate, both Bell and Turney voted with the majority to accept it. Although Bell had opposed acquisition of California and New Mexico, he felt justified in voting for the treaty because it would mean a cessation of hostilities.

Polk's term ended on March 4, 1849. Although many of his friends insisted that he become a candidate for a second term, Polk remained true to his pledge, made in 1844, that he would serve only four years. His administration had been successful, although not devoid of strife. He had led his country in the accomplishment of those goals most desired by his party, including the annexation of Texas, the reduction of the tariff, the reestablishment of the independent treasury plan, the settlement of the Oregon dispute, and the acquisition of California and New Mexico. After his term expired, Polk returned to Middle Tennessee and took up residence in the home formerly belonging to Felix Grundy. He died a few months later.

The Election of 1849, the Compromise of 1850, and the Nashville (Southern) Convention ᏋᏊ Shortly before treaty negotiations with Mexico began, Congressman David Wilmot of Pennsylvania attached to an appropriations measure a rider stipulating that slavery should be excluded from all territory acquired from Mexico. The proviso, successful in the House but not in the Senate, was the occasion for bitter controversy both in and out of Congress. Southerners had borne the brunt of the Mexican War, and Wilmot's attempt to exclude slaveholders from the newly gained lands raised a storm of protest. State senators in Tennessee agreed unanimously that they were "opposed to the 'Wilmot Proviso' in every shape and form. . . ." State Whigs and Democrats alike deplored it and shared President Polk's comment that it was a "mischievous and foolish amendment."

When Democrats assembled for a gubernatorial convention in the summer of 1849, passions were aroused. Delegates called for "a firm declaration of our purpose to resist the encroachments of northern fanaticism. . . ." In the event Congress enacted the proviso, Tennessee Democrats were ready "heart and soul, with a united front," to join with other Southern states, "through a southern convention or otherwise," to plan a course of action. Congress had no mandate, they said, to impair the rights of slaveholders or other property owners. Excoriation of the abolitionists and other "Northern fanatics" accomplished, Democrats turned their attention to the main purpose of the convention. They nominated William Trousdale, "the Warhorse of Sumner County," to oppose incumbent Governor Neill S. Brown.

The campaign was uneventful. The war, the Wilmot Proviso, and other national issues were debated. Although he was not as able on the hustings as Brown, Trousdale was known as a military hero who as a youth had quit school to enlist in the Creek War. He defeated the incumbent—who soon was appointed minister to Russia—by about 1,400 votes.

A Southern convention discussed by the Democrats in 1849 was already in the making. In December 1848, Senator Hopkins L. Turney and other Southern congressmen under the leadership of John C. Calhoun met in Washington to protest against the Wilmot Proviso and to formulate plans to avert dangers that threatened the South. They published an "Address to the People of the Southern States," in which they voiced hopes for a convention. In October 1849, a group of Mississippians called on people of the slave states to send delegates to Nashville in the following June to consider "the presentation of a united protest from the South against the attempt to exclude southern men with their slaves from the national territories" recently won from Mexico. Democrats in Tennessee welcomed the proposal, but Whigs, asserting that Tennessee should not be a "stamping ground" for seceders and nullifers, urged "the plotters to assemble elsewhere."

Before the delegates assembled in Nashville, Congress had begun consideration of measures that were to have an important bearing on North and South alike. In January 1850, Henry Clay—still an idol of Tennessee Whigs—introduced bills that eventually became the Compromise of 1850. Clay would settle many sectional issues by providing for the admission of California with its free-state constitution, creating a territorial government for the remainder of the Mexican Cession without restricting slavery, abolishing the slave trade but not slavery in the District of Columbia, and enacting a more effective fugitive slave law.

All of Tennessee's congressional delegation were heard on the compromise proposals. Bell agreed that California might be admitted as a free state, but he urged that a new slave state be carved from Texas to balance California and maintain the balance of power between South and North. Congressman Andrew Johnson urged Southerners to take a "stand against the encroachments of the North . . . upon southern institutions, and thereby save the Constitution from violation. . . . " In the final votes on the various measures Senator Bell favored all of them except the abolition of slave trade in the District of Columbia. Turney supported only the fugitive slave law. In the House, only one Tennessean voted for the District of Columbia bill, but the only other votes against the compromise measures were four votes (out of eleven) against the admission of California.

Meanwhile, delegates from most of the slaveholding states assembled in Nashville for a nine-day "Southern Convention." Langdon Cheves of South Carolina and other fire-eaters from the lower South were in charge. More than 100 Tennesseans attended after the Whig-dominated legislature defeated efforts of the Democrats to elect "official" delegates. Members denounced Northern abolitionists, declared the Wilmot proposal to be unconstitutional, demanded that a stringent fugitive slave law be enacted, suggested that the Mexican territory be divided along the Missouri Compromise line, and asserted that until some agreement was reached, all states had equal rights in the territories.

Following congressional passage of the compromise measures in September 1850, a second session of the Southern convention was held in November. Interest was shown only by extremists, because most Southerners accepted the Compromise of 1850 in good faith and believed that it would stem the rising tide of sectionalism. Gideon J. Pillow and Aaron V. Brown drafted "Tennessee resolutions" in which they urged that secession talk be ended and the compromise be accepted. Although Brown vilified Northern extremists who would "beggar" his children, "fire" his dwelling, and spread around him "all the horrors of a servile war," he still urged that "the past can be endured" and forgotten. Regardless of sectional feelings, he said, all Americans should strive to bind up the nation's wounds and preserve the Union and the Constitution. The Tennesseans were in the minority, however, and the states voted six to one to adopt stronger resolutions, including a recommendation that another convention be held soon to restore, if possible, "the constitutional rights of the South," and if not, "to provide for their safety and independence."

The Compromise of 1850 caused sectional bitterness to subside only for a short while. John Bell understood this well when he said to his constituents in the autumn of 1850:

> The crisis is not past; nor can perfect harmony be restored to the country until the North shall cease to vex the South upon the subject of slavery. . . . A spirit of conciliation and forbearance is demanded by patriotism and the exigencies of the times, as well on the part of the South, as on that of the North. . . .

Election of 1851 ᣟ᠍᠍᠍ With the ghost of sectional strife at least temporarily laid to rest, Tennesseans turned to the gubernatorial contest of 1851. Democrats nominated Trousdale, the incumbent, and Whigs chose Circuit Judge William B. Campbell, himself a hero of the Mexican War. The Compromise of 1850 was the main issue. Trousdale reluctantly accepted the measures but believed them to be oppressive and unjust to the South. He accused Campbell and the Whigs of being "too favorable to northern views. . . ." The Whig candidate, however, viewed the Compromise as "the work of wisdom" and urged Tennesseans to accept it in good faith. Campbell was elected by a majority of about 1,500 and became the last Whig to serve in the gubernatorial chair. Jubilant Whigs also captured control of both houses of the legislature.

Several matters of importance were disposed of by the General

Above left: William Trousdale, governor, 1849–1851; *above right:* William B. Campbell, 1851–1853; *below left:* Andrew Johnson, 1853–1857; *below right:* Isham G. Harris, 1857–1862. Harris was elected to serve until 1863 but fled upon the invasion by federal troops. Johnson was appointed "Military Governor" by President Lincoln and served 1862–1865.

Assembly while Campbell was governor. James C. Jones, a Memphis railroad executive and businessman after his retirement as governor, defeated former Governor Trousdale for United States senator. Because redistricting was necessary after the census of 1850, a committee of ten Whigs and five Democrats was appointed to recommend changes to the assembly and took pains to gerrymander counties to assure Whig majorities in Congress and in the legislature. In a general resolution that sought to define Tennessee's position on "federal relations," legislators resolved that the Constitution did not recognize the right of secession; that the state would aid the President in executing his constitutional powers; that the people of Tennessee recognized the right of revolution when "palpably, intolerably, and unconstitutionally oppressed"; and that in a spirit of "hope and kindness" Tennessee warned "her sister States of the North" that any modification of the fugitive slave law or failure to execute it would bring about "a train of deplorable consequences, from which a dissolution of the Union will be the most probable result."

Election of Andrew Johnson as Governor and the Decline of the Whigs ࠸ Dissension within the Whig party could be observed during the debates on the compromise; it was evident in the election of 1852, and continued until the party was destroyed. The nomination of Winfield Scott as the Whig presidential candidate in 1852 widened the breach between the Northern and Southern factions. Senators Bell and Jones supported the nominee, but Congressman William G. Brownlow and Meredith P. Gentry and others refused. Scott lost the election but carried the state by less than 2,000 votes. It was the last presidential election won by the Whigs in Tennessee. The victory did little to unify the unhappy party members. Even Bell admitted three months after the election that he saw "signs of a decisive breaking up" of the party.

When Whigs assembled in April 1853, to nominate a gubernatorial candidate, they tried to quiet dissension by talking of their achievements during the past two decades. They took pride in the fact that for six consecutive presidential elections they had carried Tennessee and in six of nine gubernatorial elections they had emerged victorious. The margin of victory in each case had been small, however, and leaders therefore stressed the need for unity.

Whigs chose Gustavus A. Henry, a Clarksville lawyer, and assured the rank-and-file Whigs that not only could he win but he also could restore party harmony.

Democrats nominated Andrew Johnson. The East Tennessee tailor had enjoyed a phenomenal rise in Tennessee politics. Born in 1808 in Raleigh, North Carolina, of a poor family, he was denied even the rudiments of a formal education. He was bound out to a local tailor at an early age but ran away from his master who promptly offered a $10 reward for his apprehension. In 1826 the 17-year-old youth and his widowed mother resolved to seek a new home across the mountains, and late in that year they arrived in Greeneville, where young Andrew established a tailor shop. Three years later he joined 26 others in a race for seven aldermanic positions and was successful by four votes. Shortly thereafter Johnson became mayor. He was elected to the legislature in 1835; defeated in his bid for reelection two years later, he was chosen again in 1839. In 1841 he began a term in the state senate. Two years later, pledging economy and reform in furthering the rights of the laboring classes, Johnson was elected to Congress, and he remained in Washington until his nomination for governor.

The doughty warriors conducted a vigorous joint campaign, beginning at Sparta on June 1. Johnson reaffirmed his pride in his plebeian origin and called upon all who earned a living by the sweat of their brows to support him. He took full credit for the Homestead Bill, then pending in Congress, and favored constitutional amendments by which the people might elect directly the President, vice President, United States senators, and justices of the Supreme Court. He frequently alluded to Henry's aristocratic origin, asserted that the Clarksvillian had voted when a member of the legislature against the best interests of the laboring classes, and accused him of refusing to honor Jackson and the heroes of New Orleans. Henry, the "Eagle Orator," had few peers as a polished speaker. He criticized Johnson for his participation in the work of the "Immortal Thirteen" during Jones's administration, charged him with being sympathetic to abolitionists, and asserted that his "White Basis Bill" (which Johnson had sponored in the legislature in 1842 and which provided for congressional apportionment in Tennessee without regard to the Negro population) was unconstitutional.

A record vote was cast, and for several days the outcome was in

Andrew Johnson, a state and national political leader for nearly fifty years, took pride in his profession as a tailor. His first tailor shop in Greeneville, pictured above, has been preserved as a national shrine.

doubt. The final count, however, revealed that Johnson had won by a majority of about 2,250 votes. Like most of the Democratic gubernatorial candidates before him, Johnson lost both the eastern and western sections of the state, but he received enough votes in Middle Tennessee to win. Whigs elected five of the ten congressmen, however, and won a substantial majority in the house of representatives. Their control of the legislature assured John Bell of reelection to the United States Senate, although two other Whigs, Henry and Thomas A. R. Nelson, received support.

The bitterness resulting from the Kansas-Nebraska Act in the following year destroyed the national unity of the Whigs. The measure, enacted in May, repealed the Missouri Compromise and provided for the organization of Kansas and Nebraska as territories without restriction as to slavery. Southern Democrats for many years had fought congressional intervention in the matter of slavery and interpreted the measure as a concession to the South. Harsh words were spoken, and Senator Jones excoriated Northern leaders. Congressman William Cullom, a Whig from Smith County, denounced the measure as the work of those who plotted "against the peace and quiet of the Union." His inflammatory words aroused Democratic Congressman William M. Churchwell of Knoxville, and a physical encounter between the two was stopped only when the sergeant-at-arms intervened. In the final vote, four of the six Tennessee Whigs in the House and one of the four Democrats voted against the pro-Southern measure. John Bell was the only Southern Whig in the Senate to vote against it.

The controversy over the Kansas-Nebraska Act produced ominous and sweeping changes in the nation's political structure. It sounded the death knell of the Whig party, and the addition of Jones and other Southern Whigs to the Democratic fold strengthened that party and increased the Southern influence within it. Unfortunately, the strong conservative influence that the Whig party had given to American politics was removed. Tennessee Democrats took control of the state and retained it, although they did lose the presidential election to Constitutional Unionist John Bell in 1860.

The Know-Nothing Movement 〜 The decline of the Whigs set the stage for the entrance of two new parties upon the

American political scene. The Republican party, organized in the North as a sectional, antislavery party, aroused little interest in Tennessee. The American or "Know-Nothing"[1] party, however, drew a considerable following from Whigs and discontented Democrats and for a short time replaced the Whigs as the "other" major party. The group had its origin in the Northeast, where the wave of immigration at mid-century had caused dissatisfaction among laborers. Many "native Americans" spoke of organizing a political party, the success of which they believed would give them an opportunity to limit the number of foreign laborers coming into the country. Because Irishmen were of the Catholic faith, the Catholic church became a target. The cardinal principle of the movement therefore became that of suppressing the influence of new immigrants and Catholics. A "Native American" convention called in Philadelphia in 1848 pledged support to Zachary Taylor for President.

In Tennessee, William G. Brownlow, a Methodist preacher and Whig newspaper editor and later Tennessee's Reconstruction governor, had attacked foreigners and Catholics as early as the 1830s, had prayed that the country might be "saved from the foreign influence and demagoguery of Democracy," and had warned his neighbors against all Catholics. He had criticized President Polk for appointing Catholic chaplains during the Mexican War and had condemned the President and his friends for contributing toward the building of a Catholic church in Washington. The new party was the answer to Brownlow's prayers. He believed that "Divine Providence" had "raised up" the new party "to purify the land and to perpetuate the . . . liberties of this country."

To many Whigs looking for new ideas and issues to cast before the electorate, the aura of irresistible attraction surrounding the novel party seemed to meet their needs. Party leaders did not hold a gubernatorial nominating convention in 1855, but when Meredith P. Gentry announced from his Bedford County home that "the overwhelming support" expressed in newspapers and private correspondence had convinced him that he should oppose Johnson's bid for reelection, the new party had a strong candidate. Gentry had

---

[1] The organization was formed as a secret oath-bound group, but members could recognize each other by signs. A member asked by an outsider what the organization stood for was instructed to answer, "I don't know." Hence, they came to be designated derisively as "Know-Nothings."

parted company with the national Whigs shortly after the nomination of Winfield Scott for president in 1852.

The campaign opened at Murfreesboro on May 1, where Johnson hacked at his protagonist as with a broadaxe. The Know-Nothing party, said the governor, was an ally "of the prince of darkness—the devil." When Johnson compared party members with the John A. Murrel gang,[2] local leaders shouted in unison, "It's a lie," and they drew weapons when the governor exclaimed, "Show me the dimension of a Know-Nothing, and I will show you a huge reptile, upon whose neck the foot of every honest man ought to be placed." Johnson paused only when he heard the cocking of pistols, but he was permitted to conclude his two-hour speech unharmed. After the opening at Murfreesboro, the two candidates talked their way across the state.

Although Gentry was an able orator and politician, he did not defend the Know-Nothing party and was a disappointment to his supporters. Johnson won by about 2,100 votes. As in 1853, Johnson failed to win the eastern and western sections but received sufficient majorities in the Middle Tennessee counties to bring him victory. He received 50.8 percent of the vote as compared to 50.9 percent two years earlier, as voting patterns established in past elections remained intact.

Although Know-Nothings lost the gubernatorial race, they elected six of the ten congressmen and gained control of the General Assembly. They elected Edward S. Cheatham as speaker of the senate and former Governor Neill S. Brown as speaker of the house of representatives.

Johnson's support of education, agriculture, better penitentiary conditions, and better working conditions for mechanics and laborers are discussed elsewhere. Other legislative accomplishments included appropriations to increase the number of volumes in the state library and to create the office of state librarian. The Hermitage property, consisting of Jackson's residence and 500 acres, was pur-

---

[2] Gentry R. McGee wrote in 1899, "John A. Murrel was a Tennessean of whom his countrymen have just cause to be ashamed. . . . He lived in Madison County, and organized all of the thieves, robbers, gamblers, cutthroats and ruffians he could . . . into one band of which he was the chief. They robbed boats on the rivers, stole horses and Negroes from farms, and killed people everywhere." McGee, *A History of Tennessee* (1899; rev. New York, 1930), 154–55.

chased for $48,000 and was promptly tendered to the federal government on the condition that a military academy similar to the one at West Point be established there. Although the offer was not accepted, when Johnson delivered his last message to the legislature in 1857 he reported that "the proposition . . . seemed to be favorably entertained by both houses of Congress."

Presidential Election of 1856 ⋙ Tennessee Democrats looked forward to the presidential election in 1856 with more assurance than they had mustered since Jackson swept to victory in 1828 and 1832. They had hoped to place either Andrew Johnson or Aaron V. Brown on the ticket as vice president, but they agreed readily to support the party nominees, James Buchanan and John C. Breckinridge. Andrew Jackson Donelson, Jackson's nephew and former personal secretary, led Tennessee Know-Nothings to the Philadelphia convention, where he won the vice presidential nomination under Millard Fillmore. Republicans had organized in the North in 1854 in opposition to the extension of slavery, and in 1856 they nominated John C. Frémont for President. Naturally, they received no significant support in Tennessee or in any other slave state.

The November election brought victory to the Democrats, both in the state and nation. For the first time since 1832 the party of Andrew Jackson won a presidential contest in the Volunteer State. For the first time since the Whig party was organized, West Tennesseans deserted their political alliance with voters in the eastern section and joined with those of the middle division to give the Democrats a majority of nearly 7,500. Brownlow, greatly discouraged, believed that his party was "utterly vanquished."

Gubernatorial Elections of 1857 and 1859 ⋙ The defeat in 1856 left the Know-Nothings with little enthusiasm for a gubernatorial contest in 1857. Nevertheless, they chose Robert Hatton of Wilson County—the "Demosthenes of the great American Whig–Know Nothing party"—to oppose Isham G. Harris of Shelby County, whom Democrats already had nominated. The campaign opened at Camden on May 25 and closed two months later when Harris and Hatton spoke in Nashville. Slavery and sectional equality in the territories were the principal issues. Much rancor characterized the campaign; fist fights developed in the crowds at several towns and on one occasion even between the two candidates. Harris's resounding majority of more than 11,000 votes brought an end to the Know-Nothing party in Tennessee. Democrats also had a clear majority in the house and senate.

Governor Harris, no newcomer to Tennessee politics, was to continue to exert tremendous influence in state and national affairs for another half-century. Born in Franklin County in 1818, he had studied law and was admitted to the bar in 1841. Six years later, at the age of twenty-nine, he was elected to the state senate and began a public career in which he was never to suffer a political defeat. In 1849 and again in 1851 he was elected to Congress but moved to Memphis in 1853, where he enjoyed a successful practice of law until his election as governor. After Reconstruction, he was elected to the United States Senate, where he served until his death in 1898.

The victorious Democrats outlined plans to take both United States Senate seats. Jones's term expired; as his replacement, legislators chose Governor Johnson over Neill S. Brown. Jubilant Democrats observed that Bell's term would expire in 1859, and they proceeded to elect A. O. P. Nicholson to replace him.

Two years later, remnants of Whigs, Know-Nothings, and antiadministration Democrats united to form what they called the "Opposition" party. They chose John Netherland of Hawkins County to oppose Harris. The impending national crisis overshadowed all state issues, and sixty-five debates centering around the impending strife were heard by crowds tense with excitement. Harris tried to link the new party with Republicans and abolitionists of the North, and told listeners that a vote for Netherland was a vote against the South. The Opposition candidate, however, disclaimed any connection with the radical elements of the North and pledged "unwavering firmness" in maintaining slavery under the Constitution. The rights and interests of the people of all sections, he said, should be carefully guarded.

Harris was again victorious, but his majority of 8,000 was considerably less than it had been two years earlier. Although the Opposition party failed to gain majorities in the legislature, its congressional candidates won seven of the seats. Bell and Brownlow took heart, and both predicted that their party would meet with success in 1861.

SUGGESTED READINGS

Books

Thomas B. Alexander, *Thomas A. R. Nelson of East Tennessee* (Nashville, 1956); William C. Binkley, *The Texas Revolution* (Baton Rouge, 1952); Mary R. Campbell, *Attitudes of Tennesseans Toward the Union, 1847–1861* (New York, 1961); James G. Sellers, *James K. Polk, Jacksonian, 1795–1843* (Princeton, 1957); Robert H. White, *Messages of the Governors of Tennessee*, vol. 3 (Nashville, 1952–).

Articles

Thomas B. Alexander, "The Presidential Campaign of 1840 in Tennessee," *THQ* 1 (March 1942), 21–43; Paul H. Bergeron, "The Election of 1843: A Whig Triumph in Tennessee," *THQ* 22 (June 1963), 123–36; Mary R. Campbell, "Tennessee and the Union," *ETHSP* 10 (1938), 71–90; Willie M. Caskey, "First Administration of Governor Andrew Johnson," *ETHSP* 1 (1929), 43–59; Caskey, "The Second Administration of Governor Andrew Johnson," *ETHSP* 2 (1930), 34–54; Turner J. Fakes, Jr., "Memphis and the Mexican War," *WTHSP* 2 (1948), 119–44; John Hope Franklin, "The Southern Expansionists of 1846," *JSH* 25 (Aug. 1959), 323–38; Billy H. Gilley, "Tennessee Opinion of the Mexican War as Reflected in the State Press," *ETHSP* 26 (1954), 7–26; Norman A. Graebner, "James K. Polk's Wartime Expansionist Policy," *ETHSP* 23 (1951), 32–45; Clement L. Grant, "Cave Johnson and the Presidential Campaign of 1844," *ETHSP* 25 (1953), 54–73; Robert Selph Henry, "Tennesseans and Territory," *THQ* 12 (Sept. 1953), 195–203; Thelma Jennings, "Tennessee and the Nashville Conventions of 1850," *THQ* 30 (Spring 1971), 70–82; Robert S. Lambert, "The Democratic National Convention of 1844," *THQ* 14 (March 1955), 3–23; Powell Moore, "*James K. Polk: Tennessee Politician,*" *JSH* 17 (Nov. 1951), 493–516; Moore, "James K. Polk and the 'Immortal Thirteen,' " *ETHSP* 11 (1939), 20–33; Moore, "James K. Polk and Tennessee Politics, 1839–1841," *ETHSP* 9 (1937), 31–52; Ray Gregg Osborne, "Political Career of James Chamberlain Jones," *THQ* 7 (Sept., Dec. 1948), 195–228, 322–34; Charles G. Sellers, "James K. Polk's Apprenticeship," *ETHSP* 25 (1953), 37–53; Clara B. Washburn, "Some Aspects of the Campaign of 1844 in Tennessee," *THQ* 4 (March 1945), 58–74.

16.

Dᴿ. James G. M. Ramsey, eminent East Tennessee physician, historian, businessman, and civic leader, frequently spoke out on political matters, but only after careful and considered thought. The friends to whom he wrote in 1858 no doubt were surprised when he expressed labored pessimism about the state of the Union he loved so dearly. But he could "conceal from no one," he wrote, his "deep conviction that the days of . . . [the] Union are numbered." The "antagonism" was "too strong, the estrangement . . . too deep" for the country ever to be reconciled. Tragically, Northern people had degenerated; in the place of the once "high toned New England spirit," only selfishness and corruption remained. On the other hand, in the South the "proud Cavalier spirit," the "virtue and integrity of the Huguenot," and the "probity and honor of the Presbyterian" had been intensified. "We are essentially two people," Ramsey wrote, as he concluded that a nation so different in refinement, tastes, passions, vices, and character could not stand.

The vast majority of Tennesseans, however, did not share Ramsey's pessimism. President Jackson had spoken the sentiment of most people when in 1832 he proposed to abort nullification by the use of force. State leaders had sought to discourage Southern nationalists in 1850 when fire-eaters met in Nashville for a Southern convention. Except for a few extremists, most people had accepted the Compromise of 1850 in good faith, and while few if any acquiesced in Daniel Webster's theory of an "indissoluble union," most saw no imminent need for secession. The majority believed that although the reins of government were temporarily in unfriendly hands, the ultimate victory lay with the "real" Union of constitutional democracy and equality among states. Disunion was not seriously considered, and Tennessee remained virtually free of secession talk until 1860.

But still the fear of abolitionism and "Black Republicanism" and their concomitant threats to the established social structure of the South were present before the sixties. Tennessee was a slave state whose slaveholders had millions of dollars invested in blacks. To most Tennesseans, the Republican party was synonymous with emancipation for slaves, and to describe another person as an "abolitionist" was an insult. Allen A. Hall, for example, editor of the Nashville *News,* in November 1859 shot and killed George G. Poindexter, editor of the *Union and American,* when Poindexter accused him of being an abolitionist. Another editor expressed his contempt for Republican leaders by describing all as political opportunists who would foment sectional strife, even to the point of destroying the republic, if it appeared expedient in their quest for power.

William H. Seward, a Republican leader in New York, seemed to Southern spokesmen to typify their conception of Republican abolitionists, and he became the target for abuse because of his scathing and persistent verbal attacks on slavery. In October 1858 he had asserted that war between the two sections was inevitable—an idea that became known as Seward's "irrepressible conflict doctrine" and was taken up by other Northern Republicans. To Tennesseans, the vast majority of whom believed that coexistence was possible and desirable, the statement was a "bomb-shell fired by a fanatic." It caused the few East Tennessee Republicans to repudiate the party and inspired Democrats to make slavery one of the major issues in the gubernatorial campaign of 1859. The Tennessee legislature branded Seward's comments "infamous" and called upon "national men of all parties throughout the Union" to do their duty by uniting to crush it.

Many people blamed Seward for John Brown's raid at Harper's Ferry in October 1859—an event described by a Nashville editor as "one of the most daring and reckless affairs which ever took place in this country." Andrew Johnson, then in the United States Senate, placed full blame for the incident upon Republican leaders. He ridiculed contentions by Republicans that Thomas Jefferson had considered Negroes and whites as equals; Johnson also pointed to inequalities of opportunity between the races in the North and urged Republicans to cease their agitation of the slavery question. The state legislature deplored the raid and placed the blame upon "the head of the Black Republican party, William H. Seward," whose "treasonable policy" might yet sound the death knell of the Union. A group of medical students from Tennessee enrolled at the University of Pennsylvania transferred to the University of Nashville when a professor remarked that the death penalty for Brown might be too severe. Beyond question, the defense of Brown by Northern abolitionists weakened the case of the strong Unionists in Tennessee and brought into the open extremists' talk of secession. Early in January 1860, Governor Harris told legislators that although he hoped "wise, temperate, and calm, firm counsel may avert the impending evils," he believed nevertheless in the right of revolution and feared that the right would have to be exercised "in case the reckless fanatics of the North should secure control of the government."

The Election of 1860 When Democrats met in Nashville in January to prepare for the national convention to be held in Charleston in April, their mood was not a conciliatory one. They condemned Seward's irrepressible conflict doctrine, indicted the Republican party for "its hostility to slavery . . . and its war upon the Constitution and upon the rights of the States," and warned that "if this war upon the Constitutional rights of the South is persisted in it must soon cease to be a war of words." They endorsed the Dred Scott decision and the administration of President Buchanan, and proposed Andrew Johnson as a favorite son nominee for the presidency.

The Opposition group met one month later, on Washington's birthday, and in the state's capital, "Know Nothing, American, Whig, and Opposition Friends" formed a "Grand National Union party." They did not draft a formal platform but pledged themselves to support the Constitution and the Union. The group deplored the agitation of the slavery controversy and, nominating John Bell, proclaimed that Bell's "superior qualifications . . . broad and expansive patriotism," and "unswerving devotion to the Union and the Constitution" rendered him the man best suited for the presidency. Neither Democrats nor Republicans could be entrusted to lead the country safely through the perilous days ahead, the group contended, and they urged people of conservative temperament throughout the nation to rally to the support of the Tennessee Unionist. Balie Peyton, Thomas A. R. Nelson, Horace Maynard, and others talked with politicians across the country in Bell's behalf, and newspapers in Philadelphia, Cincinnati, Baltimore, New Orleans, and other leading cities raised their standard for him. Three months later, conservatives met at Baltimore, formed the Constitutional Union party, and formally nominated Bell. Their simple platform called for support of "the Constitution of the Country, the Union of the States, and the enforcement of the laws." Bell, long-time Unionist and former United States senator and speaker of the House, pledged if elected not to "depart from the spirit and tenor of my past course" of maintaining "the Constitution and the Union."

In the meantime, Democrats assembled at Charleston. After considerable debate, Northern Democrats refused to write into the platform the demands of the Southern party members that slavery should be protected in the territories. After many delegates from the lower South had walked out in disgust, the convention adjourned, having nominated no one. A few weeks later, Northern Democrats met in Baltimore and selected Stephen A. Douglas of Illinois; Southern Democrats convened in Richmond and chose John C. Breckinridge. None of Tennessee's twenty-four delegates had bolted at Charleston, and they therefore reassembled with the "regulars" at Baltimore. When efforts at compromise proved unavailing and the Douglas men refused to make overtures to the Southerners, delegates from Virginia withdrew and those from Tennessee retired "for consultation." Only five Tennesseans decided to remain and participate in the nomination of Douglas. The other nineteen assembled at Richmond with the group that nominated Breckinridge; there Andrew Ewing "thanked God that he was now on a floor where he could speak without being hissed . . . or compelled to listen to nauseating speeches."

Republicans in the meantime confidently assembled in Chicago. Seward led on the first two ballots, but his supporters, apparently believing that he could not win in a national contest, cast him aside on the third ballot, and Abraham Lincoln was chosen. Republicans denied that Congress or a territorial legislature had the right to establish slavery in any of the territories and described secession as a "treasonous doctrine." No Tennessean took part in that party's deliberations, and no attempt was made to organize the party within the state. The party of John Bell rightly claimed to be the only one of national organization.

All candidates except Lincoln had organized support in Tennessee. Supporters of Douglas were limited largely to West Tennessee, where the Memphis *Appeal* kept his name before the public. His campaign in Tennessee was headed by William H. Polk, a brother of the former President, but made little headway despite the fact that Douglas himself visited the state in an effort to build strength. Weeks before the election the contest in Tennessee developed into a duel between Bell and Breckinridge. Supporters of the former included the old Whig hierarchy—Oliver P. Temple, William G. Brownlow, Neill S. Brown, Balie Peyton, Gustavus A. Henry, and Thomas A. R. Nelson—who disliked secession but also opposed any attempt by the federal government to coerce the states. Breckinridge supporters included old-line Democrats such as Andrew Johnson, Governor Harris, Landon C. Haynes, and Gideon J. Pillow, who called for congressional protection of slavery in the territories.

Although Lincoln received less than 40 percent of the popular vote, he carried the Northern states where the electoral vote was large and thus was elected President. In Tennessee, where Lincoln received no support, John Bell defeated Breckinridge by fewer than 5,000 votes. Table 3 shows how voters in the three divisions of the state balloted.

Table 3.

VOTES CAST IN TENNESSEE FOR PRESIDENTIAL CANDIDATES, 1860

	Candidate		
State division	*Bell*	*Breckinridge*	*Douglas*
East	22,320	18,904	1,659
Middle	29,006	34,452	2,187
West	18,384	11,697	7,548
Total	69,710	65,053	11,394

Note. These results are from the Nashville *Patriot,* November 26, 1860. Other newspapers gave only slightly different results; official returns cannot be located in the state archives.

Despite Douglas's initial popularity in West Tennessee, his support was negligible when compared with that of his two opponents. He carried only one county (Tipton) but lacked only 89 votes of defeating Bell in Shelby County. Bell's support was a straight Whig vote and differed in no important respect from the Whig votes of the preceding twenty years. Breckinridge carried the traditionally Democratic counties in Middle Tennessee and received a respectable vote in the cotton counties of West Tennessee.

Secession ⟨⟩ The election of Lincoln—by one section and by a minority vote—precipitated secession among the states of the deep South. Two days after the election the legislature of South Carolina called a convention, and on December 20 the delegates by unanimous vote adopted an ordinance of secession. Within a few weeks six other states—Georgia, Alabama, Florida, Mississippi, Louisiana, and Texas—joined the Palmetto State and set up a provisional government in Montgomery in early February.

Tennesseans, like other Southerners, were distressed at the success of a sectional candidate. Unlike the people of the cotton states, however, they were not ready to secede, and editors and spokesmen in the three sections deplored the hasty action of the deep South. The editor of the Memphis *Enquirer* denounced secession as a "madman's remedy," and the Memphis *Appeal* pointed to the profits made from the distribution of Northern-made goods, declared that the people of many of the Northern states were "as sound on the Negro question as the secessionists themselves," and advised that loyalty to the Union would pay dividends in the years to come. The editor of the Nashville *Union and American* condemned the deep South for leaving the border states "on a sinking ship." John Bell urged that Lincoln be supported. After all, Bell said, he had been elected constitutionally, and Northern extremists would be unable to get control of either house of Congress.

Governor Harris convened the legislature into extra session less than three weeks after South Carolina had seceded. Many Tennesseans believed that a "General Convention of the Slave States" should be held to discuss relations with the federal government. Prominent members of both the Democratic and the Constitutional Union parties had issued a joint statement to local politicians throughout the state, urging them to request the governor to call an extra session of the legislature that, once assembled, would be implored to aid in bringing about a convention of the Southern states. Members convened on January 7, 1861.

Legislators heard Governor Harris deliver a message strongly pro-Southern in tone. The slaveholding states had suffered many grievances, he said, that resulted from the "systematic, wanton, and long continued agitation of the slavery question." Now, Harris pointed out, the presidency was in the hands of a sectional party that had sworn undying enmity to slavery and the South. Although he had no doubt as to the necessity and propriety of calling a state convention to determine whether Tennessee should secede, he proposed that the lawmakers submit the question to the people. The legislators complied and set February 9, 1861 as the date for the referendum. The people were to vote for "convention" or for "no convention" and were also to select delegates so that a second poll would not be necessary if the convention were authorized.

In the meantime, leaders discussed compromises and ways of averting civil war. In the Senate, Andrew Johnson proposed a constitutional amendment calling for sectional alternation of the presidency and membership on the Supreme Court and a permanent division of the territories into free and slave sections. In Tennessee, Governor Harris suggested the establishment of a dividing line between free and slave territories and further proposed that authorities in any Northern state who refused to return fugitive slaves to their rightful owners should be required to pay double the value of the slave. Slaveowners should be guaranteed protection of their slave property while passing through or temporarily residing in any state, Harris claimed, and slavery should never be abolished in the District of Columbia or any other area in the slave states over which the United States had jurisdiction.

The only compromise proposal seriously considered by congressional leaders was Kentucky Senator John J. Crittenden's measure, which was similar in some respects to the suggestions made by Governor Harris. Although Tennesseans supported the Crittenden measure, little interest could be aroused among Republican leaders; therefore, all congressional attempts at compromise failed.

Tennessee sent delegates to the Washington Peace Conference held in the nation's capital on February 4, 1861. The meeting, called at the request of the Virginia legislature and presided over by former President John Tyler, was attended by delegates from twenty-one states. Eleven of Tennessee's twelve delegates stood staunchly for moderation, but their attempts at compromise, like the others, resulted in failure.

Preparatory to the February referendum in Tennessee, secessionists and Unionists strove to win victory at the polls. Union meetings were held throughout the state, and former Whigs such as Gustavus A. Henry, Brownlow, and others urged the people not to act precipitately, but to give the Republicans "a fair trial." The editor of the Nashville *Banner,* while admitting that "the sympathies of Tennesseans are decidedly Southern," believed also that Tennessee was decidedly "a Union State" if it could remain within the Union "upon terms of equality and justice." Prominent Democrats, however, including the editors of the Memphis *Avalanche* and the Nashville *Union and American,* urged the people to approve the holding of a convention, and to elect "states rights, anticoercion men."

On election day, the people rejected the convention by a vote of about 68,000 to 59,000. The total vote of the Union candidates was nearly four times that amassed by the disunion candidates. The people of West Tennessee voted for a convention, those of the eastern section opposed it, and people in Middle Tennessee were almost equally divided. The referendum did not end the controversy. The Unionists of East Tennessee hailed the vote as a great victory, and many believed that the state was destined to remain permanently within the Union.

Although the danger of precipitate action had been removed, secessionists did not despair. They excoriated Bell and other Unionists, claimed that the victory had given Lincoln new determination to "wage an irrepressible conflict," and resolved to continue their agitation. Extremists in Middle and West Tennessee urged friends to aid the cause of the seceded states, and hundreds in Franklin County, under the leadership of Peter Turney, signed petitions requesting that Franklin County be annexed to Alabama.

Tennesseans next turned their attention to Lincoln's inauguration, and John Bell and others hastened to Washington to be present for the ceremonies. In his inaugural address, the new President adopted a conciliatory tone but made clear that he considered secession illegal and would enforce the laws in all the states. People saw in the address whatever they wished to see, depending upon whether they were secessionists or Unionists. The editor of the Democratic *Union and American* called it "a declaration of war against the seceded states" and prophesied that "in less than thirty days . . . we shall have the clangor of resounding arms, with all its concomitants of death, carnage, and woe." The editor of the *Republican Banner,* however, considered the address "mild and conservative" and believed that Lincoln had dispelled the fear of "coercion." If war came, the editor wrote, it would not be the responsibility of the President.

A problem of immediate concern to Lincoln was what to do about federal forts in the South, particularly Fort Sumter, a fort and arsenal lying within the borders of South Carolina. A symbol of federal authority in the state, the fort lay at the mercy of the Confederates. President James Buchanan had tried in January to send provisions to the small force of eighty-four men, but when a ship bearing supplies entered the harbor a battery of South Carolina artillery fired upon it and drove it off. Confederates, now hoping to starve the small band into surrender, warned Lincoln that a similar attempt to reprovision the fort would result in war. The president, however, gave orders in April for an expedition to proceed. When Confederate authorities became aware of the move, they called upon the officer in charge of the fort, Major Robert Anderson, to surrender. His refusal brought fire from the Confederate batteries, and on April 13 Anderson surrendered. Two days later President Lincoln issued a call for 75,000 volunteers.

When Governor Harris received Lincoln's call for troops, he answered the message with characteristic vigor. "Tennessee will not furnish a single man for purposes of coercion," he telegraphed, "but 50,000 if necessary for the defense of our rights and those of our Southern brothers." Announcing that "in such an unholy crusade no gallant son of Tennessee will ever draw his sword," Harris issued a call for a second extra session of the legislature to convene in Nashville on April 25.

As legislators began to arrive for the extra session, they found sentiment in Middle Tennessee to be considerably different from what it had been only a few weeks earlier. In no other section of the state had people changed so rapidly from a Unionist to a secession position. Major Campbell Brown of Spring Hill, for example, who had just returned from a trip to England, was amazed at the transformation. Before his departure he had found "the union feeling . . . very strong" in Nashville; so strong, indeed, that he had "had a sufficiently disagreeable time in defending . . . [his] opinion." He was bitter because of "the villainous" way in which "the abolition journals and speakers of the North misrepresented . . . [the South] abroad." Immediately after the fall of Fort Sumter, however, he returned to Nashville from Spring Hill. To his "perfect surprise" he "found secession . . . at every corner." Confederate flags and secession parades were constantly in the streets and everybody was "ripe for joining the Confederacy." Enthusiastic anti-union rallies were reported in Clarksville, Fayetteville, Pulaski, Nashville, and elsewhere.

The legislators found Governor Harris in no mood for compromise. He blamed the President for having "wantonly inaugurated an internecine war upon the people of slave and nonslaveholding states," and he declared that the "real Union" (as "established by our fathers") no longer existed. Harris recommended the immediate enactment of a measure proclaiming that Tennessee had resumed her sovereignty and her independence from the United States. Accordingly, the lawmakers on May 6 drafted "A Declaration of Independence . . . Dissolving the Federal Relations between the State of Tennessee and the United States" and stipulated that it should be submitted to the people for ratification or rejection on June 8. The vote was 20 to 4 in the senate and 46 to 21 in the house. At the same session legislators proposed a "military league" with the Confederacy.

As the time for the referendum approached, prominent leaders of church, state, and press in Middle and West Tennessee urged ratification of the declaration of independence, while those of East Tennessee demanded that it be rejected. The Reverend James H. Otey and the Reverend Leonidas Polk, Episcopal bishops, declared themselves to be strongly in favor of secession, and Bishop Polk soon exchanged his clerical robe for a Confederate uniform. John Bell, Neill S. Brown, Cave Johnson, Return J. Meigs, E. H. Ewing, and Balie Peyton, all erstwhile prominent Unionists, issued a joint statement urging that coercion of the Southern states be resisted and commending the "wisdom, justice, and humanity" of Harris's refusal to furnish Lincoln with Tennessee troops. The editors of the five Nashville newspapers, who had often been bitter rivals and had advocated diverse policies, joined forces to urge that Tennessee be declared "independent forever of the United States Government." The editor of the Nashville *Republican Banner*, who had vehemently opposed secession earlier, now urged the people to vote for "the best interests of the state," and declared that "the rapidly developing policy [of the North] of . . . subjugation of the South . . . must serve to convince every patriotic and fair-minded man . . . that all hopes of a reconstruction of the Union" had been abandoned. One week later the editor, angered by what he saw in newspapers published in Northern cities, wrote: *"People of Tennessee!* If you could sit here in our offices and read all the journals of the North as we do, there would be little Northern sentiment left." On election day the editor had nothing but contempt for those who wanted a "union with a people . . . dead to all moral and constitutional obligations."

The Unionists, principally from East Tennessee, denounced the legislative action as unconstitutional and tried to rally support against separation. The two most effective leaders were Johnson and Thomas A. R. Nelson—men who had been bitter political enemies but who united efforts in a joint campaign to keep Tennessee in the union. Their work was in vain, however, as Tennesseans voted by a substantial majority in favor of "Separation" from the Union and "Representation" in the Confederacy. Only in East Tennessee, and in a few isolated areas elsewhere, did strong Unionist sentiment prevail. People in both the central and western divisions voted overwhelmingly for secession, indicating that there had been many defections from Unionist ranks within recent weeks. The vote is shown in table 4.

Table 4.
VOTES FOR AND AGAINST SEPARATION OF TENNESSEE FROM THE UNION

Voting population	Votes	
	For	Against
East Tennessee	14,780	32,923
Middle Tennessee	58,265	8,198
West Tennessee	29,127	6,117
Military camps	2,741	0
Total	104,913	47,238

Nashville *Union and American,* June 16, 1861.

A careful analysis of the returns shows that the people of the old Whig districts of East Tennessee, with Knoxville at the center, strongly opposed separation just as they had voted four months earlier against holding a convention. Democratic Sullivan and Meigs counties, which had voted for a convention, were for separation; they were joined by four other East Tennessee counties—Sequatchie,[1] Rhea, Polk, and Monroe. The Middle Tennessee counties of Bedford, Cannon, DeKalb, Rutherford, Smith, Jackson, Overton, White, Wilson, Williamson, and Van Buren, which had opposed a convention in February, now favored separation. The Middle and West Tennessee counties voted solidly for secession except for Fentress, Macon, Hardin,[2] and Wayne (in Middle Tennessee), and Carroll, Decatur, Henderson, and Weakley (in West Tennessee). Interestingly, the average wealth of East Tennessee families in 1860 was only $2,830, as compared with $5,530 for the state as a whole; for Middle Tennessee families it was $6,640, and $7,130 for those in West Tennessee. The eight middle and western counties opposed to separation were all below the state average and were in an economic class with East Tennessee.

Even before the referendum, Governor Harris made preparations to join the Confederacy. As authorized by the legislature, on May 7 he entered into a military league with the Confederate states, gave them permission to erect a battery at Memphis as a part of the Mississippi River fortifications, and encouraged volunteers to join the Southern forces. On May 24, Harris wrote Major General Gideon J. Pillow that he was "making every possible effort to organize and procure such military force as may be necessary to protect the state from invasion." On the following day, Harris ordered from a New Orleans firm "at any reasonable price" a "ten thousand stand of arms," with the "Endfield [sic] saber rifle bayonett [sic] or rifle musket" preferred.

Immediately after the referendum, United States Senator A. O. P. Nicholson resigned his seat in Washington and wrote Harris that he would "acquiesce cheerfully" in the result of the referendum. As Nicholson saw it, the people had declared their independence of the United States government, and he no longer had a right to a place in its Senate. He had not been a rabid secessionist—when South Carolina seceded he stated in Congress that he could not recognize the "de jure" secession of the state, although he did admit the "de facto" separation from the Union—but now he followed his state.

---

[1] Now a Middle Tennessee county, Sequatchie in 1861 was considered to be in East Tennessee. The towns of Knoxville and Chattanooga favored secession.

[2] Now a West Tennessee county, but then considered to be in Middle Tennessee.

Andrew Johnson, however, decided to retain his seat in the federal Senate.

John Bell, a Unionist until soon after Sumter, despaired of any concessions from the Lincoln administration and joined the ranks of the secessionists. A change of heart so pronounced by so able a leader deserves more than passing consideration. Soon after the Republican victory in November 1860, Bell openly expressed confidence in the President-elect and believed that Lincoln was sincere and courageous. Bell was confident that only one-third of the Republicans could be considered "dangerous" and that the rest had no desire to make war on Southern interests. Preparatory to the referendum of February 9, Bell made speeches in which he expressed confidence in the new administration, interpreted Lincoln's policy as one of conciliation, and criticized Harris for his strong stand on secession.

Bell had hurried to Washington for Lincoln's inauguration. As the recognized leader of the Tennessee Unionists and one who had been mentioned prominently for a seat in Lincoln's Cabinet, Bell was the logical person to dispense the patronage in the state. While in Washington, Bell had urged the new President to exercise care so that "no opportunity for a collision between the troops of the seceding States and those of the Government" might take place. Bell insisted that the bayonet could accomplish nothing of lasting value and suggested that if the seceding states rejected conciliation, "the wisest course would be to let them go in peace." The Tennessean left Washington confident that the policy of the new administration would be one of conciliation.

An important factor in Bell's change of heart was Lincoln's selection of Andrew Johnson—who had been in the Breckinridge camp in November 1860 and was a lifelong Democrat—as the chief patronage dispenser in the state instead of Bell or some other ex-Whig. Apparently Bell was in agreement with William G. Brownlow and was ready to carry to its logical conclusion the sentiment expressed by the Knoxville editor, who wrote that he had little desire to remain in the Union if Johnson was permitted "to monopolize the power and patronage of the Union party in Tennessee." Brownlow believed that such action on Lincoln's part merited "the scorn and condemnation of every honest man in the Union ranks." Bell and his Unionist friends in Tennessee had labored long and faithfully in their devotion to the letter and spirit of the Constitution; at last they became convinced that not only did Lincoln and the Republicans have little veneration for constitutional principles, but that they also connived with Johnson to build an allied political group in Tennessee from the elements that had proved in the past to be the least devoted to the defense of the fundamental law.

Historians have disputed the influence and responsibilities of Bell, and some have expressed the belief that if he had remained faithful to his earlier Unionist convictions Tennessee would not have seceded. Although Bell was influential, especially with the old-line Whig element, to suppose that he might have prevented Tennessee's secession is to attribute to him a degree of influence and power no one in the state possessed. The die was cast after Lincoln called for 75,000 volunteers, and no one could have persuaded Tennesseans to fight a war against the deep South. Bell remained in Nashville until the approach of the federal troops in 1862, then joined his children living in Rutherford County. Later he lived in Alabama and Georgia, but he returned to Tennessee after the war.

Tennesseans Prepare for War ॐ The second six months of 1861 was a period of hasty preparation for war. Harris appointed Gideon J. Pillow as commander of the Tennessee forces, with three subordinates in charge of each of the grand divisions of the state. On July 2, Governor Harris tendered to Confederate President Jefferson Davis 22 regiments of infantry, 2 regiments of cavalry, 10 companies of artillery, an engineering corps, and an ordinance bureau. The infantry, Harris wrote, was "fully armed and equipped ready for the field," and the cavalry was armed with sabers and double-barrelled shotguns. All cavalrymen were mounted. The tender was made with the hope that the Confederate states "at all times" would defend Tennessee from invasion. Davis of course accepted the troops, and on July 4 replaced Gideon J. Pillow with General Leonidas Polk.

Unionists of East Tennessee, in the meantime, posed a problem for the Harris government. People of that section had voted two to one against secession, and now viewed the actions of the Harris government with considerable· distaste. Antislavery and racial in their sentiments regarding Negroes and suspicious of the influence of slaveholders, they considered themselves to be "different" from the rest of the state. Some talked openly of joining Union forces in the event of war. Meetings were held in most of the counties, and finally a four-day session—June 17–20—was held in Greeneville in which all East Tennessee counties were represented except Rhea. There, leaders prepared and later presented, to the legislature a memorial asking that the counties of East Tennessee and "such counties of Middle Tennessee as desire to co-operate with them" be permitted to form a separate state which would remain loyal to the Union. "The hopeless and irreconcilable difference of opinion and purpose," they wrote, "leaves no alternative but the separation of the two sections of the state."

Governor Harris viewed the situation with alarm. Many East Tennesseans were "bent on rebellion," he wrote General Pillow on June 20, and feared an immediate "onslaught of Union men upon the southern rights men. . . ." Two weeks later, Landon C. Haynes, prominent Washington County Confederate sympathizer, told the governor that six regiments would be required to keep the eastern Unionists in line, since "moral power" could "no longer be relied on to crush the rebellion [against Tennessee]." While the Democratic-controlled legislature chose to ignore the Greeneville petition, Harris fumed about sending "a large force" into East Tennessee but for the moment gave attention to other pressing problems, including his bid for reelection.

Secessionists, now referring to themselves as the "Southern Rights Party" and supported by all the principal newspapers of the state except the Nashville *Republican Banner* and Brownlow's Knoxville *Whig,* assured the governor of a landslide victory. Brownlow had announced in March that he would carry the banner of the Unionists but withdrew several weeks later in favor of William H. Polk.

The gubernatorial contest was subordinated to the military developments. Polk accused Harris of trying to become a military dictator, blamed him for the state's secession, charged that he had exceeded his rights under the constitution, and predicted that Harris soon would go to the Confederate senate instead of serving out his term as governor even if he were reelected. Polk's supporters claimed that their candidate was acceptable to East Tennesseans and alleged that the election of Harris would drive all Unionists from the state. Supporters of Harris, however, pointed to the threat of invasion from the North and to Harris's determined efforts to defend the state against aggression. The editor of the Memphis *Appeal* wrote that all who even dared vote against Harris were committing treason.

Polk offered little appeal to voters, and Harris was elected by a 75,300 to 43,495 vote.

The secessionists secured large majorities also in both the house and senate. Legislators, convening in October 1861, redistricted the state into eleven Confederate congressional divisions. They chose Landon C. Haynes and Gustavus A. Henry as Confederate senators; Haynes was an East Tennessee Democrat and erstwhile Breckinridge supporter and Henry was a John Bell Whig from Clarksville. Although the two had been bitter enemies in days past, they now pledged "their whole souls, energies, and talents to the cause of Southern rights." On November 6, the people chose eleven representatives to the Confederate congress. Legislators met from October to December, before adjourning for Christmas, and enjoyed their last undisturbed session. When they resumed deliberations in January, the federal military command was making plans to take Forts Henry and Donelson, and the legislators soon fled to Memphis.

Loyalists in the four congressional districts of East Tennessee and northeastern Middle Tennessee had selected congressmen in an August election and sent them to Washington. Three—Horace Maynard, George W. Bridges, and Dr. A. J. Clements—were seated, but the other, Thomas A. R. Nelson, was arrested by Confederate authorities in Virginia. After a brief imprisonment, Nelson took the oath of allegiance to the Confederate government and was returned to his home.

Whether Tennesseans, in view of the circumstances, were justified in their declaration of separation from the federal Union will of course always remain an academic question. Had there been no invasion by federal troops—had Lincoln taken John Bell's advice about the use of force—Tennessee beyond any question would not have left the Union. Professor J. Milton Henry has ably contended that if the Tennessee conservatives, who were deeply devoted to the Union, had remained faithful to their original principles after the fall of Sumter, secession might have been prevented. As Professor Henry has shown, however, the conservatives had many reasons to lose confidence in Lincoln's administration. At length, they became convinced not only that Republicans had little veneration for constitutional principles but that party leaders were engaged in building an allied political group in Tennessee (with Andrew Johnson at the head) from people who were not devoted to the defense of the

Union. Once convinced that they had little to fear and perhaps more to gain from an alliance with the Confederates, they gave up their struggle for the Union. The determination of President-elect Lincoln to oppose all efforts at compromise, the precipitate secession of the deep Southern states without first calling a convention of slave states, and the strong Confederate proclivities of Governor Harris were decisive factors in the state's secession.

The vast majority of Tennesseans were Unionists until the fateful April days. The fall of Fort Sumter and Lincoln's call for troops convinced them that a search for a peaceful solution was futile. Living in a border state, they believed that they could not remain neutral but must join one side or the other. Perhaps many people, at least in Middle and West Tennessee, shared the sentiments of a West Tennessee farmer named B. W. Binkley, who wrote during the war: "I was for the Union so long as there was any hope of our remaining in it with peace and honor. When Lincoln issued his proclamation calling for 75,000 troops to whip . . . the Seceded States, I was satisfied that that day had passed, and now—though not what you'd term a regular Secessionist—I am the most uncompromising *rebel* you ever knew."

SUGGESTED READINGS

Books
Mary R. Campbell, *The Attitude of Tennesseans Toward the Union, 1847–1861* (New York, 1961); Dwight Dumond, *The Secession Movement, 1860–1861* (New York, 1931); James W. Patton, *Unionism and Reconstruction in Tennessee, 1860–1869* (Chapel Hill, 1934).

Articles
Mary R. Campbell, "The Significance of the Unionist Victory in the Election of February 9, 1861, in Tennessee," *ETHSP* 14 (1942), 11–30; Campbell, "Tennessee's Congressional Delegation in the Sectional Crisis of 1859–1860," *THQ* 19 (Dec. 1960), 348–71; LeRoy P. Graf, "Andrew Johnson and the Coming of the War," *THQ* 19 (Sept. 1960), 208–21; Howard Hall, "Franklin County in the Secession Crisis," *THQ*, 17 (March 1958), 37–44; Marguerite Bartlett Hamer, "The Presidential Campaign of 1860 in Tennessee," *ETHSP* 3 (1931), 3–22; J. Milton Henry, "The Revolution in Tennessee, February, 1861, to June, 1861," *THQ* 18 (June 1959), 99–119; Stanley F. Horn, "Isham G. Harris in the Pre-War Years," *THQ* 19 (Sept. 1960), 195–207; Eric Russell Lacy, "The Persistent State

of Franklin," *THQ* 23 (Dec. 1964), 321–32; John V. Mering, "The Slave-State Constitutional Unionists and the Politics of Consensus," *JSH* 43 (Aug. 1977), 395–410; Joseph H. Parks, "John Bell and Secession," *ETHSP* 16 (1944), 30–47; David L. Potter, "Attitude of the Tennessee Press Toward the Presidential Election of 1860," *THQ* 29 (Winter 1970–71), 390–95; Verton M. Queener, "East Tennessee Sentiment and the Secession Movement, November, 1860–June, 1861," *ETHSP* 20 (1948), 59–83; George C. Rable, "Anatomy of a Unionist: Andrew Johnson in the Secession Crisis," *THQ* 32 (Winter 1973), 332–54.

17.

The Civil War in Tennessee

THE Confederate states embarked upon a war for independence without adequately counting the costs. Limited resources placed them at a tremendous disadvantage. They were faced, for example, by an enemy whose white population outnumbered their own by nearly four to one and had nearly 90 percent of the country's industry, a standing army and navy, and a superior transportation system. By no means least among the disadvantages the South faced was that of defense, made difficult by the natural barriers that impeded effective communication. The Blue Ridge Mountains split the South into east and west, and the west was divided by the Mississippi River; the Tennessee and Cumberland rivers became highways into Tennessee and the Confederacy. On the other hand, the Confederates had some advantages. They had a superior fighting force commanded by competent officers, and they would wage war on home soil.

Tennesseans Prepare for War General Leonidas Polk was assigned command in the west on July 4, 1861, and he arrived in Memphis a few days later to take up his tasks with characteristic vigor. General Gideon J. Pillow already had begun the fortification of Memphis and Island Number 10 (in the Mississippi River below Columbus, Kentucky) and had begun fortifications 75 miles north of Memphis at a place later called Fort Pillow. Polk continued Pillow's work and also gave attention to pressing problems in East Tennessee. Upon Polk's recommendation, Felix Zollicoffer was commissioned with the rank of brigadier general and dispatched hastily to Knoxville

302

Above: Gustavus A. Henry was a Clarksville attorney, leading Whig, candidate for governor, and Confederate senator.

as the commander of a motley force of fewer than 4,000 recruits to attempt some kind of reconciliation with the dissidents of that area.

Polk clearly saw the strategic importance of the area assigned to him, and he urged President Jefferson Davis to combine all Confederate operations "west to east across the Mississippi Valley" under one commander. He suggested Albert Sidney Johnston as the man most likely to effect satisfactory coordination.

Johnston, Kentucky-born, had been a classmate of Jefferson Davis at Transylvania College in Lexington and a few years later was with him at West Point. He had fought briefly in the Black Hawk War and, with the outbreak of the war for Texas independence, journeyed to the Texas frontier, where he joined the Texas forces and rose to the rank of senior brigadier general. He acquired a plantation, became commander in chief of the Texas army, and then secretary of state of the new republic. Soon, however, he fell out with President Sam Houston and was wounded in a duel by a jealous subordinate. He returned briefly to Kentucky, where he became involved without much success in a variety of business enterprises and soon was back on his Texas plantation. At the outbreak of the Mexican War he reentered the military service and fought bravely at Monterrey. After the war he experienced financial difficulties resulting in bankruptcy at his plantation and again took up a military career. In 1855, he was placed in charge of the Second Cavalry and assigned to duties in the West. Two years later he was promoted to brigadier general and given command of the American military forces on the Pacific Coast. He had considered Texas his home, however, and the secession of that state brought him to Richmond, where President Davis commissioned him a general in the Confederate Army. On September 10, he was assigned to the command of Department Number Two, a vast area embracing Tennessee and Arkansas, a part of Mississippi, and sections of Kentucky, Missouri, Kansas, and the Indian territory where military operations were being carried on, and was given the title of "General Commanding the Western Department of the Confederate States of America." Tennesseans were jubilant about the appointment of the tall, muscular general of august appearance, and the Confederate press in Nashville and Memphis hailed him with enthusiasm.

Perhaps the most important task Johnston faced was that of devising an adequate defense for Tennessee. The general proceeded with haste, and soon established the "Line of the Cumberland," which he believed would be sufficient to protect the state and the western Confederacy. The thin line of troops extended from Columbus, Kentucky (on the Mississippi River), through Bowling Green, and to the Cumberland Gap on the east. Although seriously handicapped by lack of manpower, Johnston determined to fortify the strategic points of Henry and Donelson (forts on the Tennessee and Cumberland rivers, respectively, which Governor Isham G. Harris had begun to construct soon after the state had seceded) and the Cumberland Gap, where East Tennessee Unionists threatened revolt. His undermanned forces and precarious position soon were bolstered by regiments from Mississippi and Arkansas, and by Tennesseans recruited from the farms of West and Middle Tennessee.

To his amazement and consternation, Johnston found the people of Nashville and Middle Tennessee apathetic about defense. While workers at the Nashville Plow Company beat plowshares into swords at a fairly rapid rate, the more important Nashville Powder Mills in October could provide only 400 pounds of gunpowder per day, although officials of the company earlier had promised 10,000 pounds daily. Requests for slaves for use in construction work brought only scant response. The Nashville warehouses were laden with food, but transportation facilities were so poorly coordinated that General Zollicoffer's men in East Tennessee went hungry.

Johnston realized that time was precious and that defensive measures should be formulated with the manpower and supplies on hand. He recognized that the Tennessee and Cumberland rivers were veritable highways from the Ohio River into the heart of Tennessee, northern Mississippi, and Alabama, and Johnston ordered that work proceed without delay toward the completion of the strategic positions at Henry and Donelson. His apprehension was shared by Governor Harris, who on October 30 wrote President Davis that he believed invasion along "the northern border of this state" was imminent. Harris vainly requested that the President return the Tennessee troops then stationed in Virginia. If the Federals obtained control of Tennessee, he warned, then "the whole Confederacy" would face "incalculable mischief." On November 20, Harris sent terse messages to the governors of Alabama, Mississippi, and Louisiana, requesting aid. "Columbus and River definitely threatened by very large force," he telegraphed; "Have you an armed force that you can possibly send to our aid?"

Equally pressing were problems of inadequate weapons and

supplies. As early as August, Harris had ordered that constables in every county make "diligent inquiry" at each home in every civil district for weapons of all types. So poor was the response that in late November the legislature empowered militia captains to seize weapons wherever they could be found.

The first major activity on Johnston's front was on the right wing, when General Zollicoffer encountered a superior force led by General George H. Thomas on January 19, 1862 near Mill Springs, Kentucky. Zollicoffer had been ordered forward to the south bank of the Cumberland to observe Thomas, but the enthusiastic former newspaper editor had crossed the river, where he was killed and his troops routed. Tattered survivors retreated to Gainesboro and told of their defeat and the irreparable damage to Johnston's right flank.

Johnston in the meantime had inspected the works at Fort Henry and Fort Donelson and was appalled at the dilatory manner in which work proceeded. He had summarily ordered Brigadier General Lloyd Tilghman, a Kentuckian commanding at Hopkinsville, to assume charge of the two forts and to complete the work at once. "Sloth," he told Tilghman, would not "be tolerated." Brigadier General U. S. Grant, commanding Union forces at Cairo, and Captain Andrew H. Foote, commander of the Union flotilla on the western waters, proceeded in late January toward Henry and Donelson.

Fort Henry and Fort Donelson ੨✽ The forts had not been completed when Federals attacked in February 1862. On the morning of February 4, seven gunboats under the command of Captain Foote and 18,000 Federal soldiers under General Grant arrived in the vicinity of Fort Henry, which was held by fewer than 2,800 Confederates. A few shots were exchanged, and then on the following day Foote began heavy bombardment with his sixty-five naval guns. The twelve Confederate cannons were no match for Foote's guns, and after sustaining several hours of bombardment, Tilghman climbed to a parapet and raised a flag of surrender. Grant, having landed three miles downstream, had floundered in the slush and mud and had not reached the fort in time to participate in the fighting.

Strengthened by the addition of six new regiments of infantry that increased his command to 30,000 men, Grant moved rapidly toward Fort Donelson, where Confederates prepared diligently for defense. His strategy was the same as that planned for Fort Henry: Captain

Foote was to batter the garrison into submission with his naval guns while Grant blocked all escape routes and exacted terms of unconditional surrender.

Fort Donelson was commanded by General John B. Floyd, a political officer from Virginia who brought to Donelson an uneasy conscience and little military acumen. While secretary of war under President Buchanan, Floyd had allegedly misappropriated funds and unnecessarily transferred arms and ammunition to Southern forts. He therefore personally feared capture because he believed that he would be executed as a traitor should he fall into Federal hands. Floyd also apparently had little confidence in his staff, which consisted partly of Generals Gideon J. Pillow, Simon B. Buckner, and Bushrod Johnson, and Colonel Nathan Bedford Forrest—all men of some ability.

At dawn on February 13, Grant's men appeared about 700 yards from the outer defenses of the fort but were beaten off when they assaulted the Confederate center. Of far greater importance on the first day of the battle was the sudden change in the weather. A cold front changed the fair and mild afternoon into a cold, rainy evening and a near-zero night. When day dawned on the fourteenth, a two-inch snow blanketed many of the wounded and dying. Despite the cold weather, Confederates seemed to have victory within their grasp on February 14 and 15. On the fourteenth, the gunboats were driven off, and Foote was wounded twice. In mid-afternoon of the following day, Floyd, apparently having the enemy on the run, permitted General Pillow to withdraw his men completely from Wynn's Ferry Road, an escape route that led to Nashville. This gave Grant an opportunity to reorganize his assault and to surround the Confederates. On the night of the fifteenth, Floyd called his staff together to discuss surrender. Despite Forrest's assertion that he would get "out of this place . . . or bust hell wide open," Floyd, Pillow, and Buckner insisted that their men were demoralized, their supply of ammunition was exhausted, all avenues of retreat were blocked, and surrender was the only alternative. Floyd, Pillow, Johnson, and Forrest escaped; on the morning of the sixteenth, Buckner surrendered to Grant unconditionally.

The fall of Fort Donelson came as a distinct shock to the people of the South and was the worst loss the Confederates had suffered. Johnston's line now collapsed, and Nashville was abandoned. Federals under General Don Carlos Buell triumphantly marched into the

Nathan Bedford Forrest led his Confederate cavalry on campaigns still studied by military experts. *Below*: The remains of the earthworks and abandoned cannon from the Civil War can still be seen at Fort Donelson near Dover on the Cumberland River.

state's capital a few days later (February 24), and Tennessee and northern Mississippi were now at the mercy of the enemy. Tennesseans were dazed by the disastrous events that had taken place so suddenly, and Nashvillians were in panic. The heart of Tennessee— the Confederates' largest producer of iron and important storehouse of such vital items as powder, ammunition, weapons, staples, tents, clothing, and saddles—was lost to the enemy.

Despite suggestions by the press and pleas by Nashville Mayor Richard B. Cheatham and State Senator Washington Barrows that he defend the city, Johnston determined to evacuate all of Middle Tennessee. He stopped briefly at Murfreesboro and then trudged southward into Alabama and finally to Corinth, Mississippi.

In the meantime, Leonidas Polk, who commanded troops at Columbus, Kentucky, moved southward to defend Island Number 10 and went next to Corinth. Troops that remained at Island Number 10 were surrendered on April 8, a few hours after guns were silenced at Shiloh.

Shiloh ⟩⟨ "Shiloh," General Grant wrote years after the war ended, "was the severest battle fought at the West during the War. . . ." Certainly there had been nothing on the continent like it. Casualties numbered about 20,000—more than the combined totals of Donelson, Henry, and Bull Run (Virginia).

Johnston had suffered a tremendous loss of confidence and prestige after Donelson, and the Southern press joined politicians and even Johnston's own officers in heaping abuse upon him. The doughty general said little, but—at the instigation of Pierre Gustave Toutant Beauregard—moved to Corinth, where as ranking general he assumed command and proposed to make a stand.

Grant in the meantime unwittingly became embroiled in a controversy already brewing between General Henry W. Halleck, commander of the Department of Missouri with headquarters at St. Louis, and General Don Carlos Buell, commander of the Department of the Ohio headquartered at Louisville. Halleck actually had had Grant removed from his command for a short while; by the time he was restored, Confederates were gathering at Corinth. It was mid-March before Grant arrived at Savannah, and there he made plans to dislodge his enemy.

General Beauregard, a hero of Bull Run, was first to arrive at

Corinth and to realize the tremendous importance of making a stand there. Although outranked by Johnston, he assumed the major responsibility for concentrating nearly all of the available manpower in the Confederate West and for planning battle. By the first of April, Confederates were ready to strike at the Federal army encamped just north of the Mississippi-Tennessee border in the vicinity of a small Methodist Church called Shiloh.

The Confederate army that marched toward Shiloh was all that the West could offer, and Johnston soon commanded an army of 40,000 men. The First Corps, consisting of about 9,000 men, was commanded by fifty-six-year-old Leonidas Polk, a West Point graduate who had been an active Episcopal bishop before putting aside the clerical attire and casting his lot with the Confederate army. Braxton Bragg, forty-five-year-old West Point graduate and a hero of the Mexican War, commanded the Second Corps—the largest in the army and consisting of about 15,000 men. William J. Hardee's troups numbered about 4,500. "Old Reliable," as Hardee was called, was also a West Point graduate, a hero of the Mexican War, and an authority on infantry tactics. The Fourth Corps, consisting of three brigades totaling a little more than 6,000, was commanded by John C. Breckinridge. A Kentuckian who had served as vice president under Buchanan and the presidential candidate of the Southern Democrats in 1860, Breckinridge had replaced Major General Thomas L. Crittenden after Crittenden was arrested for habitual drunkenness.

Confederates arrived in the vicinity of Shiloh on April 4, but it was two days later before they were prepared for battle. Even so, they surprised the Federals in an early morning assault and found them dressing, cooking, and eating breakfast in the company streets. Grant, apparently not aware of the enemy's presence, was at his Savannah headquarters nine miles away, and Sherman, although on the field, at first discounted reports of his subordinates who said that advance enemy troops were near.

The first day of battle ended with the Confederates in control but at a fearful price. Federals had rallied quickly and had made a strong stand along an old sunken road and also at a spot Confederates called "the hornet's nest." Not only was the manpower loss tremendous on both sides, but it included General Johnston, who was struck in the thigh by a stray Minié ball that severed a major artery. Governor Isham G. Harris, riding near Johnston at the time, lowered the general from his horse but was unable to stop the profuse bleeding in time to save his life.

Confusion spread through the Confederate ranks as word of Johnston's death became known. Federals during the night were reinforced with nearly 30,000 fresh troops and early the next morning assaulted the Confederates with vigor. Beauregard, who assumed command when Johnston fell, decided by afternoon that the weary troops could hold no longer and by four o'clock began a retreat.

Beauregard received most of the criticism for the vital loss, particularly for not having pursued the advantage that was his late on the first day of battle. Recent scholarship, however, has ascribed the loss more to the Confederate failure to concentrate sufficient men on the right flank at the very beginning of the battle. This, together with the excessive expenditure of time and manpower at the Hornet's Nest, had of course occurred prior to the Creole's "lost opportunity"; these errors of judgment were the major factors in the defeat.[1]

The Confederates limped slowly back to Corinth, while the enemy remained in the battlefield area. Although more Federals than Confederates had actually been killed and wounded, the Union with its vast stores of reserve manpower could better afford to lose men and still win the battle. Confederates had now lost a chance to halt the enemy's determined drive into the West and to regain Tennessee. As the New Orleans writer George W. Cable later noted, "the South never smiled again after Shiloh."

Stone's River ?≈ After the Battle of Shiloh, the Army of Tennessee returned to Corinth, and General Bragg was placed in command. In the meantime, General Edmund Kirby Smith had taken charge of Confederate troops in East Tennessee, and he urged Bragg to join him in a campaign into Kentucky. The Blue Grass State, rich in food and supplies, might be won to the Confederacy, he thought, if a successful invasion were made. On August 16, General Smith marched from Knoxville into Kentucky and won a brilliant victory at Richmond. Two weeks later Bragg moved with nearly 30,000 men up the Sequatchie Valley, through Pikeville, Sparta, and Gainesville, and into Glasgow, Kentucky.

[1] For a discussion of debate about the "lost opportunity," see McDonough, *Shiloh—in Hell before Night* (Knoxville, 1977), 168ff.

The most vigorous fighting of the Kentucky campaign took place at Perryville on October 8, when Bragg met General Buell, who had pursued him from Corinth. Bragg, discouraged by the failure of Kentuckians to join his forces and fearing that Buell would crush him before he could escape, retreated in an orderly manner to Murfreesboro in November, where, joined by Generals Breckinridge and Forrest, he made plans to take Nashville.

General William S. Rosecrans, who in the meantime had assumed command of Federal troops at Nashville, made plans to dislodge Bragg and on December 26 began a movement toward Murfreesboro. He required four days to make the 30-mile trek, however, because General Joseph Wheeler, a young cavalry leader from Alabama, harassed him day and night and destroyed millions of dollars' worth of his supplies.

The battle began at daybreak on December 31 when a detachment of Bragg's men stumbled into a company of Federals a few miles west of Murfreesboro. The day went well for the Confederates, who by nightfall had pushed Rosecran's troops a distance of four miles or more. So convinced was Bragg of victory that he hastened into town early the next morning to notify President Davis. "The enemy has yielded his strong position and is falling back," he telegraphed; "God has granted us a happy New Year." Bragg was amazed upon his return at daylight to find Rosecrans still encamped in the area. Soldiers on both sides rested on New Year's Day while their commanding officers made plans for resuming the battle.

The tide of victory escaped the Confederates on January 2, when Rosecrans's men, reinforced by fresh troops, raked Breckinridge's charging infantry with artillery fire as the Confederate leader attempted to take a hill just west of Murfreesboro. On the following day, Bragg ordered a retreat, and the unhappy soldiers began a slow movement through Murfreesboro toward Chattanooga. Both officers and enlisted men complained about Bragg's ineptitude as a leader and urged that he be removed as commander of the Army of Tennessee. Victorious Federals now occupied Murfreesboro and Bragg went into winter quarters in Bedford and Coffee counties.

Forrest, restless and wishing to harass the enemy, meanwhile spent no time in winter quarters. He provided excitement and hope for Tennessee Confederates when, with fewer than 4,000 men, he attacked Federal outposts at Trenton, Humboldt, Union City, Lexington, and other points in West Tennessee. Forrest was rapidly becoming famous for his ability to take the enemy by complete surprise and destroy large stores of supplies.

Chickamauga and Chattanooga ᏋᏇ General Rosecrans, with 70,000 men, waited until June before moving toward the Confederates who, in anticipation of the advance, broke camp and retreated in an orderly fashion toward the southeast. By August, Bragg had arrived in Chattanooga, but he soon abandoned the town and retreated into northern Georgia. Rosecrans, believing that the Confederates would not stop until they reached Atlanta, pushed recklessly on and was amazed when on September 13 he found his enemy encamped and ready for battle approximately twenty miles south of Chattanooga, near Lafayette.

Early on the morning of September 19, the Army of Tennessee crossed the Chickamauga River to meet Rosecrans in what proved to be one of the bloodiest single days of the war. Generals James Longstreet and John B. Hood had arrived on the eighteenth with Confederate armies from the Virginia campaigns and by mid-afternoon on the nineteenth had ripped Rosecrans' army to shreds. Only the gallant stand of General George H. Thomas prevented a complete massacre of the Federal troops. Charles A. Dana, assistant secretary of war and an observer of the battle, wrote, "Bull Run had nothing more terrible than the rout and flight of these veteran soldiers."

The Federals then encamped at Chattanooga. Grant was sent to take command, and General William T. Sherman hastily moved his troops from Mississippi to join Grant. Bragg, who could have taken Chattanooga had he moved with haste after Chickamauga, quarreled with his subordinates, fatuously dispersed his troops, and vainly laid siege to Chattanooga in an effort to starve his enemy into surrender.

Grant in the meantime had been placed in charge of all operations east of the Mississippi and had moved hastily to Chattanooga to lift the siege. Because the Battle of Chattanooga began on November 23 in a dense fog at the base of Lookout Mountain, the fight has sometimes been called the "Battle above the Clouds." The Confederate positions on Missionary Ridge fell on the twenty-fifth before the charging bluecoats, who smashed the gray infantry back in a savage hand-to-hand encounter. The Confederates fled in panic and were regrouped at Dalton, Georgia, where they went into winter quarters. The Battle of Chattanooga was another serious blow to the reeling Confederates and marked the end of Bragg's career as a field commander. Joseph E. Johnston, who held the confidence of enlisted men and officers alike, was chosen to command the western army.

Federals Take East Tennessee &ep; In the meantime, General Ambrose E. Burnside had moved his Federal forces from Cincinnati to Knoxville. After Chickamauga, General Longstreet was sent to dislodge him, but on November 20 the Confederates were defeated at Fort Sanders. A few days later Sherman moved to aid Burnside, and Longstreet retreated into Virginia, leaving practically all of East Tennessee in undisputed control of the Unionists. A majority of the people had been Unionists all along and viewed Burnside's triumph with wild excitement.

General Sherman moved immediately into Georgia in pursuit of the retreating Confederates. During the next nine months his losses were more than twice those of the Confederates; still, by September 6 he had gained control of Atlanta. General Leonidas Polk was among the thousands of Tennesseans who had fallen in the defense of Georgia.

General John Bell Hood, one of Lee's ablest fighting generals, soon replaced General Bragg as the Confederate commander and planned bold strategy. After engaging the enemy in several skirmishes north of Atlanta, he decided to surprise Sherman by making a quick dash across Alabama and into Tennessee. If he could cut Sherman's supply lines, he might starve the Federals into submission. He dreamed of seizing vast stores of supplies at Nashville for his hungry and barefoot men, then moving to Louisville and Cincinnati, and finally joining Lee in Virginia for an assault on Washington. The fact that Hood had suffered the amputation of a leg in Virginia and no longer had the use of one arm did not deter him from moving forward upon a foolhardy venture.

Franklin and Nashville &ep; The first serious engagement of Hood's campaign in Tennessee occurred on November 30. General John M. Schofield, who had returned from an unsuccessful attempt to capture Forrest in West Tennessee, managed to slip past the Confederates during the night but was poorly prepared when

Hood encountered him in the afternoon at Franklin. He was driven from the field after five hours of fierce fighting and retreated during the night to the safety of the fortifications at Nashville, where Federal forces were commanded by General Thomas. Hood was left in possession of the field, but he had paid a fearful price. The Federals, fighting behind breastworks, had lost about 2,000 men; Hood's dead and wounded amounted to more than three times that number.

Although Grant feared that Hood might push immediately toward Louisville or even Chicago, the youthful Confederate commander determined to occupy the hills just south of Nashville and force Thomas to fight. Hood did not have long to wait. In a two-day encounter (December 15– 16), his forces were completely defeated. On the first day of battle, Hood retreated two miles to the foot of the Brentwood Hills. On the following afternoon, Schofield's infantry and cavalry completely broke the Confederate resistance and sent the reeling remnants in hasty retreat southward. Thomas, with about 70,000 men, listed his killed and wounded at slightly fewer than 4,000; Hood, with about 23,000 men, claimed that his losses did not exceed 1,500.

The Battle of Nashville was the last engagement of significance in the state. The retreating Confederates stopped at Brentwood long enough to form a semblance of organization and then proceeded southward. At Columbia they were joined by Forrest, who had retreated from Murfreesboro. Deaths at Franklin and Nashville, sickness, furloughs, and desertions had reduced the Army of Tennessee to an effective fighting force of only about 5,000 when the men finally joined the Confederate forces in North Carolina, where they eventually were surrendered to Sherman at Durham.

War Heroes ⧉ Many Tennesseans fought bravely; both the North and South had their share of men from the Volunteer State. A fair estimate is that about 100,000 wore the gray and approximately half that number wore the blue.

Many served with particular distinction in the Confederate army. Two officers—Alexander P. Stewart of Lebanon and Nathan Bedford Forrest of Memphis—rose to the rank of lieutenant general. Eight who attained the rank of major general were William B. Bate, John C. Brown, Benjamin F. Cheatham, Daniel S. Donelson, W. Y. C. Humes, Bushrod R. Johnson, John Porter McCown, and Cadmus M. Wilcox. More than thirty attained the rank of brigadier

Howard Pyle painted this view of the charge of Minnesota troops in the Battle of Nashville.

general, including Generals McComb, Pillow, and Zollicoffer. Commodore Matthew Fontaine Maury was the ablest Tennessean in the Confederate navy. Even before the war he was recognized as one of the world's greatest naval scientists.

Several Tennesseans became generals in the Federal army and served with equal valor. Included were James P. Brownlow, William B. Campbell, Samuel P. Carter, Joseph A. Cooper, Alvan C. Gillem, George Spalding, James G. Spears, and William J. Smith. One of the most competent of the Tennessee officers serving in the Federal navy was Admiral David G. Farragut, of Knoxville, who played an important role in the capture of New Orleans, Mobile, and other important points. During the war, Farragut rose to the rank of vice admiral and became the first full admiral in the history of the country in 1866.

Perhaps the real heroes were not the generals and admirals but the enlisted men who fought on the battle lines. All Tennesseans know the story of Sam Davis, the young Confederate who was hanged as a spy on November 27, 1863 near Pulaski. "I would die a thousand deaths before I would betray a friend," the youth exclaimed when Federals offered him his life if he would name the person who had given him detailed information about the movement of Federal troops. No less glory surrounds the memory of DeWitt S. Jobe, and his cousin, DeWitt Smith. Jobe (like Davis, a Coleman scout) carried valuable battle plans when he was seized by the enemy near Murfreesboro. Before the eyes of his captors Jobe tore the documents to shreds and hastily swallowed some of the pieces. The infuriated Federals beat him to death with rifle butts. When DeWitt Smith heard of his cousin's merciless slaughter, he left Bragg's army and returned to Middle Tennessee to wage his own private war of revenge. He killed more than fifty Yankees before being slain by cavalrymen near Nolensville.

Internal Affairs: Unrest in East Tennessee ैंश् While soldiers fought on the battlefields, the people at home faced many hardships. An immediate matter of major concern for Governor Harris was the strong Union movement in East Tennessee. The people of that section—most without slaves and without attachment to the "slavocracy" of Middle and West Tennessee, long conscious of themselves as a sectional minority within the state, confident of Federal assistance, and influenced by Union leaders such as Brownlow and Johnson—stood by the national government and thus destroyed the unanimity of the secession sentiment in the state.

Governor Harris determined upon a policy of conciliation with respect to East Tennessee and concurred with Polk in sending Felix Zollicoffer, a former Knoxvillian then living in Nashville, to command troops in the eastern section. Zollicoffer sought to carry out Harris's policies, and announced upon his arrival in Knoxville that his sole purpose was to "insure peace."

> All who desire peace can have peace [he stated], by quietly and harmlessly pursuing their lawful avocations [sic]. But Tennessee, having taken her stand with her sister States of the South, her honor and safety require that no aid shall be given within her borders to the arms of the tyrant Lincoln. . . .

Some East Tennessee Unionists were won to the Confederate side, but Brownlow, Johnson, Horace Maynard, and others steadfastly refused and aggressively championed the cause of the Union. Johnson and Maynard urged Lincoln to send a military force into East Tennessee, and Johnson pleaded with Washington legislators to send aid.

In November 1861, a small group of East Tennessee Unionists unfolded a daring plan. William Blount Carter, a Presbyterian minister living at Elizabethton, had journeyed to Washington in May to discuss problems with Lincoln, General George B. McClellan, and others. Carter, particularly wanting Federal troops to be sent into East Tennessee immediately, suggested that he and his friends would burn nine key bridges between Alabama and Virginia and that simultaneously Federal forces should move into Knoxville, where a general uprising would begin. He apparently thought that he had agreement from the President. On November 8, Carter performed his part of the bargain by destroying five of the bridges (and was paid $20,000 for his trouble), but Federal troops did not arrive. Unknown to Carter, General W. T. Sherman, who had been assigned the task of invading East Tennessee, had decided to hold his men in readiness to strike at Nashville instead of crossing the Cumberland Mountains. Consequently, the Union group was then without defense against the wrath of the Tennessee Confederates, whose spirit of conciliation was consumed in the fires of the railroad bridges.

Stern measures were demanded. A Nashville editor wrote that East Tennesseans obviously "could not appreciate magnanimity and leniency." General Zollicoffer imposed martial law, and Secretary of

War Judah P. Benjamin ordered that all bridge burners be hanged. Some of those implicated, including Carter, escaped the hangman's noose, but others suffered public execution.

For two years Confederate and Unionist neighbors waged a civil war of their own. By the use of martial law Unionists were silenced, but many went into hiding to await the day of deliverance, which belatedly came in the fall of 1863, when General Burnside arrived with his army and restored them to control. With Burnside came Brownlow who, by pen and tongue, kept the fires of hatred glowing. Trusted implicitly by Federal authorities, Brownlow became the section's journalistic lord and economic dictator. His influence spread from East Tennessee over the entire state when he was elected governor in March 1865.

Federal Occupation of Middle and West Tennessee ᏴᏙ While East Tennesseans waged their own civil war, Confederates in the rest of the state tried without much success to fight off the Yankee invader. After General Forrest carried to Nashville news of the fall of Fort Donelson, Governor Harris and other state officials fled to Memphis and eventually to the safety of the Confederate lines in Mississippi, and thus Middle and West Tennessee were in the hands of the Federals not long after Fort Donelson fell. Grant soon proclaimed martial law for much of West Tennessee.

Immediately after his military successes, President Lincoln determined upon a bold course. He established a "military governorship" for the state and chose as governor Andrew Johnson, who as a member of the United States Senate at the time had refused to follow his state into the Confederacy. Lincoln gave the East Tennessean broad powers, including that of suspending the writ of habeas corpus and the right to hold office at the pleasure of the President until "the loyal inhabitants" organized a civil government "in conformity with the Constitution of the United States." Both Lincoln and Johnson contended that none of the seceded states were out of the Union. They believed that the "disloyal" element, if given proper leadership, would follow the "loyal" group into full acceptance of Union control.

Objections to the appointment came from a wide area. The people of Middle and West Tennessee now looked upon Johnson as a traitor and viewed with disdain his appointment as military governor. They recalled that in his two gubernatorial contests in 1853 and 1855 he had failed to win East Tennessee; the central section had provided the small but necessary margin of victory both times. Johnson received hundreds of insulting and threatening letters. Every "dog has his day," one wrote, and "you will have yours. We are preparing a knise [nice] coat of feathers for that orcation [occasion]," the writer continued, "so when we have the chanse [chance] we will turn your black skin read [red]." Others informed Johnson of guerrilla bands that planned to intercept his train and seize him as he journeyed from Washington to Nashville. Assistant Secretary of War Thomas A. Scott, in Nashville at the time the appointment was being considered, telegraphed Washington authorities that Johnson would do more harm than good and urged instead the appointment of General William B. Campbell. General Buell advised General McClellan that such a provisional government with Johnson at the head would be "injudicious."

If Johnson had any misgivings about the situation, he did not show them. He assumed the position of governor with characteristic aggressiveness. A one-time slaveowner who supported the Southern Democratic ticket in 1860, Johnson horrified Tennesseans by denouncing secession leaders and suggesting that they should probably be executed. On March 18, six days after his arrival in Nashville, he issued "An Address to the People," in which he discussed reasons for his presence. The purpose of the military governorship, he said, was to aid in the prompt restoration of the state to its rightful place in the Union. He expressed only contempt for "intelligent and conscious treason in high places" but offered complete amnesty to "the erring and misguided" who would renounce their disloyalty and embrace the Union.

Johnson was disappointed and perhaps surprised when few people responded to his offers of pardon, and adamant public officials, newspaper editors, school teachers, and ministers of the gospel became objects of his vengeance. When Mayor Richard B. Cheatham and the city council refused to take an oath of allegiance, Johnson turned them out of office and arbitrarily appointed Union sympathizers in their places. Cheatham was imprisoned; former Governor Neill S. Brown, Judge Joseph Guild, and others were summarily arrested. The offices of several secessionist newspapers, including the *Daily Times,* the *Republican Banner,* the *Gazette,* and the *Patriot,* as well as the Baptist and Methodist publishing houses, were ordered closed for alleged disloyalty. Clergymen were jailed because of their "Confederate sermons," which Johnson believed were preached in every church in Nashville. His policies stirred the people to indignation and earned for him the sobriquet "Johnson the Tyrant," but he did not flinch from his avowed purposes. The failure of the native population to support his reconstruction program and the frequent threats to his authority by the Southern cavalry leaders Morgan and Forrest only made him more resolute. His frequent embroilment in quarrels with Generals Buell, Halleck, and Rosecrans, who earnestly sought his removal, added to his worries.

The threat to Johnson's reign as military governor was removed as an immediate possibility in January 1863, when Rosecrans drove Bragg from Murfreesboro, and was removed entirely in the autumn of that year when the Confederates withdrew southward from Chattanooga and General Burnside freed East Tennessee. After that, his rule, if contested at all, was disputed only by roving bands of guerrillas until Hood's invasion in 1864. The success of the Federal armies in Tennessee proved an invigorating tonic to the Union cause, and President Lincoln urged Johnson to prepare the state for reconstruction. "The whole struggle for Tennessee will have been profitless . . . if it so ends that Governor Johnson is put down and Governor Harris put up," the President wrote; "let the reconstruction be the work of such men only as can be trusted for the Union."

In December 1863, President Lincoln issued his "Proclamation of Amnesty and Reconstruction," designed to heal the nation's wounds as quickly and painlessly as possible. Amnesty and pardon, he said, would be accorded (with a few exceptions) to all who took an oath of allegiance to the federal government. When the number taking the oath equaled one-tenth of the voting population of 1860, loyalists should organize a government that would be recognized in Washington and accorded all the privileges and immunities the state had enjoyed before the war.

Lincoln's talk of leniency aroused little sympathy among Johnson and the Radicals. "The intelligent and influential leaders must suffer; the tall poppies must be struck down," Johnson told a group of followers. Lincoln's oath might absolve one from treason, but something more stringent—"a hard oath, a tight oath," Johnson said— must be used for those who wished to vote. Accordingly, when he issued a proclamation calling for an election of county officers on March 5, he prescribed an oath, referred to by many as Johnson's

"Damnesty oath," which all—Confederate sympathizers and ardent Unionists alike—must take. Prospective voters not only had to agree to support the Constitution and the government but also were required "ardently" to "desire the suppression of the present insurrection" and the extension to Tennessee of the Emancipation Proclamation. East Tennessee Unionists were humiliated at having to take an oath at all, and many conservative Unionists, in disgust, resolved not to take it. Johnson's prestige suffered, and the election proved, as one editor predicted, "a farce." Only Johnson's nomination for vice president at the Republican convention enabled him to regain respect among a large segment of Tennessee Unionists.

The presidential election created considerable interest in the state. The Lincoln-Johnson ticket was supported by the Johnson followers, of course, but it was opposed by both the secessionists and the Union Peace party, the latter being made up of loyal Unionists who favored a cessation of hostilities. The secessionists, though large in number, posed no problem because they were excluded by the test oath. Members of the Union Peace party presented more formidable opposition, and included prominent Unionists such as Emerson Etheridge, Thomas A. R. Nelson, and General William B. Campbell. They supported General George B. McClellan, commander in chief of the Federal armies in 1862, who had received the Democratic nomination on a platform declaring that "justice, humanity, liberty, and the public welfare demand that immediate efforts be made for a cessation of hostilities."

Violence and allegations of corrupt politics marred the campaign. Johnson pleased some by denouncing the "Tennessee aristocrats" and by advocating that the estates of the rich be seized and divided among free farmers, but he also angered many Unionists by his high-handed conduct. Violence flared not infrequently, and armed forces dispersed at least one group that had assembled for a McClellan rally. Only a small minority of Tennesseans voted and, as expected, they supported the Lincoln-Johnson ticket. Congress, however, rejected Tennessee's electoral votes on the grounds that the state was in rebellion and that no valid election had been held.

Unionists, encouraged by the reelection of Lincoln, immediately formed plans for reconstruction of Tennessee. Five hundred of them assembled in Nashville on January 9, 1865 to amend the constitution and provide for the restoration of civil government. They submitted to "the people" on February 22 a constitutional amendment abolishing slavery and a "schedule" accompanying the amendments that repudiated the ordinance of separation and the military league with the Confederacy and declared null and void all acts of the state government after May 6, 1861. Finally, they provided for an election of a governor and General Assembly on March 4 and nominated William G. Brownlow for governor. On the same day that Lincoln and Johnson were inaugurated, Brownlow, who in 1861 could not interest even East Tennesseans in his candidacy for governor, was elected chief executive. Only about 10 percent of the number of people voting in 1860 cast votes in 1865. Brownlow was inaugurated on April 5.

Johnson had been a controversial figure throughout his stay in the military governor's chair. That he was sincere and earnest few questioned, but his prejudices and personal dislikes,[2] never concealed, often were so violent and so biased that he drove otherwise loyal people into the camps of rebellion. His lack of broad sympathy and tact—qualities that characterized Lincoln—often caused him to be misunderstood. Johnson has been criticized for arbitrarily delaying reconstruction in the state, for employing methods that were "arbitrary, unconstitutional, and permanently injurious," and for excluding by his "Damnesty oath" many unquestionably loyal people from participation in reconstruction, thus destroying their interest in the work and losing their counsel, influence, and cooperation. Johnson unquestionably made mistakes, but he gave fearlessly and unsparingly for the Union cause in Tennessee. There were of course no precedents for him to follow; often without the cooperation and advice of the Federal military authorities, he had to make the rules as he went. He was loyal, self-sacrificing, and steadfastly devoted to a cause that he believed was just.

Conditions at Home ⁀ Destruction followed in the wake of the marching armies, and the deprivations suffered by the people only added to the anguish they experienced under Johnson. Diaries and letters described the hardships of war. Dr. James G. M. Ramsey told of the burning of his spacious home at the confluence of the Holston and French Broad rivers.

---

[2] "If Johnson were a snake," well-born Governor Isham G. Harris once observed, "he would lie in the grass to bite the heels of rich men's children." C. R. Hall, *Andrew Johnson, Military Governor of Tennessee* (Princeton, 1916), 22.

> I had the honor of a correspondence with the elite and distinguished [he wrote], . . . with A. Jackson, Calhoun, Polk, . . . [and] Democratic leaders and editors everywhere. . . . All my historical and antiquarian manuscripts—some of them containing the substance of my second volume of the History of Tennessee, . . . unpublished biographies of the leading master spirits of their day in Tennessee and elsewhere, . . . my library—medical, miscellaneous, . . . historical and literary, I had for many years been collecting from Europe and America, and which was, I believe, the best in the western states—were stolen, destroyed or burned.[3]

In Middle Tennessee, Mark Cockrill, who had won world renown during the 1850s as a cotton and wool producer, watched helplessly as Federal soldiers took from his Davidson County farm 20,000 bushels of corn, 26 horses, 60 head of cattle, 220 sheep, 200 tons of hay, 2,000 bushels of oats, and 2,000 pounds of cured bacon. At Murfreesboro, Mrs. Bettie Ridley Blackmore wrote of her people being "surrounded by a desperate, insolent, unscrupulous, but victorious foe" who burned her home and destroyed her father's property after General Bragg was driven out in January 1863. One writer compared some of West Tennessee to an Arkansas town where thousands of "old men, women, and children had been reduced to poverty."

Shortages of food and labor became acute throughout the state by 1863, as many farms went uncultivated for lack of adequate manpower. Vast stores of supplies had been taken to feed troops of both sides. Coffee, sugar, and salt, if available at all, sold at prices many times higher than those before the war. Both men and women smuggled food and medicines through the lines wherever possible. One Nashville woman, affecting great sorrow, carried a coffin packed with valuables through Federal lines at Nashville, and others concealed under their flowing skirts and spacious bustles coffee, quinine, sewing thread, and even boots and bolts of cloth. Most men were in uniform, and many slaves did not work. Although many Southern military authorities gave furloughs at planting and harvest time, still much land formerly cultivated went unworked.

Urban dwellers suffered more than their rural neighbors. Nashville, with Edgefield and other adjacent suburbs, had a population in

[3]William B. Hesseltine (ed.), *Dr. J. G. M. Ramsey, Autobiography and Letters* (Nashville, 1954), 55–56.

excess of 10,000 when the war broke out and was a rapidly growing, significant western city. In addition to being a manufacturing center, it had many wholesale business houses and was a major distribution center. Its docks on the Cumberland River serviced more than 100 steamboats, and its railroads connected with Louisville, Memphis, Chattanooga, and Decatur. A suspension bridge (destroyed as Federals approached) connected Nashville with Edgefield. Nashvillians strongly supported the Union until Fort Sumter; indeed, only a few weeks before Lincoln called for troops, the city council had warmly endorsed the Unionist sentiments expressed by Senator Andrew Johnson. Overnight, however, feelings changed, and Nashville quickly developed into a Confederate city. News of the fall of Fort Donelson threw Nashvillians into panic. Within an hour after the news was received, roads leading out of Nashville were crowded with people seeking residence elsewhere. Many others robbed and looted stores and shops. Prices soared. The editor of the *Daily Press* observed that by the spring of 1864 the city was "filled with thugs, highwaymen, robbers, and assassins." Still, they were able to get whiskey, and on August 4, 1864—a day President Lincoln had set aside for fasting and prayer—sixty persons went before the recorder's court on charges of public drunkenness. More whiskey was drunk in Nashville than in Boston, the *Daily Press* editor asserted.

Memphis was occupied by Federal troops soon after Nashville fell. This prosperous river town with a population of nearly 10,000 was one of the ten largest cities of the South. A major cotton center of the West, it was served by four railroads and regular steamboat service to all points north and south. Indeed, its reputation as a trading center caused it to be called the "Charleston of the West." Eight banks made it an important financial center.

The advent of Federal troops brought about an expected change in Memphis. Trade subsided, prices soared, hundreds of families moved elsewhere, and newcomers came in large numbers. By early 1863, the population was estimated at 11,000 original whites, 5,000 slaves, and 19,000 newcomers. As elsewhere, the propertied classes suffered along with the rest. Robertson Topp, for example, a politically powerful millionaire at the beginning of the war, saw his cotton seized or destroyed, his slaves freed, and, without adequate labor, he watched his Shelby County lands grow up in weeds and bushes, so that he was reduced to poverty by the end of the war.

Knoxville and Chattanooga were smaller than Nashville and

Memphis but were important and growing centers of trade and commerce at the beginning of the war. Knoxville in 1861 was a city divided on the Union issue; a majority of people supported the Confederacy, but they were surrounded by Union sympathizers. A commercial, manufacturing, and financial center of more than 5,000 people, it became a vital link between the upper and lower South because of the railroads. Confederate troops were headquartered in the town at the beginning of the war and remained there until 1863, when Federal troops marched in. As elsewhere, prices rose and supplies declined. Erstwhile Whig editor William G. Brownlow, on an extensive speaking tour of the North in 1863, told his audiences that Knoxville was a city of destitution; "not even a spool of thread," he told a Cincinnati audience, could be bought there. Throughout much of rural East Tennessee a wave of murders, whippings, and threats drove out a substantial portion of the population who wanted only peace.

Tennessee indeed had been a major battlefield of the Civil War. While the sufferings of the people are not to be compared with those of South Carolina or northern Virginia, they had been intense. The state also had been the subject of an experiment in government, headed by one whose temperament was not suited to the task. In East Tennessee, four years of bitterness left old wounds that required many years to heal, and the end of the war did not mean that the time of troubles had ended. The people were yet to suffer through four years of reconstruction under Governor Brownlow.

SUGGESTED READINGS

Books
Thomas B. Alexander, *Political Reconstruction in Tennessee* (Nashville, 1950); Thomas Lawrence Connelly, *Army of the Heartland: The Army of Tennessee, 1861–1862* (Baton Rouge, 1967); Connelly, *Autumn of Glory: The Army of Tennessee, 1862–1865* (Baton Rouge, 1971); Donald Davidson, *The Tennessee:* Vol. 2. *The New River, Civil War to TVA* (New York, 1948); John P. Dyer, *The Gallant Hood* (Indianapolis, 1950); Gilbert Govan and James W. Livingood, *Chattanooga Country* (1952; rpt. Knoxville, 1976); Robert S. Henry, *The Story of the Confederacy* (Indianapolis, 1931); Stanley Horn, *The Army of Tennessee: A Military History* (1953; rpt. Norman, 1968); Horn, *The Decisive Battle of Nashville* (rpt. Knoxville, 1968); James Lee McDonough, *Shiloh: In Hell Before Night* (Knoxville,

1977); Joseph H. Parks, *General Edmund Kirby Smith, CSA* (Baton Rouge, 1954); Parks, *General Leonidas Polk, CSA* (Baton Rouge, 1962); Digby Gordon Seymore, *Divided Loyalties: Fort Sanders and the Civil War in East Tennessee* (Knoxville, 1963).

Articles
Edwin C. Bearss, "Unconditional Surrender: The Fall of Fort Donelson," *THQ* 21 (March, June 1962), 47–65, 140–61; Jesse Burt, "East Tennessee, Lincoln, and Sherman," *ETHSP* 34, 35 (1962–1963), 3–25, 54–75; Sims Crownover, "The Battle of Franklin," *THQ* 14 (Dec. 1955), 291–322; Donald F. Dosch, "The Hornets' Nest at Shiloh," *THQ* 37 (Summer 1978), 175–89; Harold S. Fink, "The East Tennessee Campaign and the Battle of Knoxville in 1863," *ETHSP* 29 (1957), 79–117; Gilbert E. Govan and James W. Livingood, "Chattanooga under Military Occupation, 1863–1865," *JSH* 17 (Feb. 1951), 23–47; Ralph W. Haskins, "Andrew Johnson and the Preservation of the Union," *ETHSP* 33 (1961), 43–60; Stanley F. Horn, "Nashville During the Civil War," *THQ* 4 (March 1945), 3–22; Bobby L. Lovett, "The Negro's Civil War in Tennessee, 1861–1865," *JNH* 41 (Jan. 1976), 36–50; James L. McDonough, "Glory Can Not Atone: Shiloh—April 6–7, 1862," *THQ* 35 (Fall 1976), 279–95; James M. Merrill, "Capt. Andrew Hull Foote and the Civil War on Tennessee Waters," *THQ* 30 (Spring 1971), 83–93; Harriet C. Owsley, "Peace and the Presidential Election of 1864," *THQ* 18 (March 1959), 3–19; Joseph H. Parks, "Memphis Under Military Rule, 1862–1865," *ETHSP* 14 (1942), 31–58; Sarah Ridley Trimble (ed.), "Behind the Line in Middle Tennessee, 1863–1865, The Journal of Bettie Ridley Blackmore," *THQ* 12 (March 1953), 48–80; Peter F. Walker, "Building a Tennessee Army: Autumn, 1861," *THQ* 16 (June 1957), 99–116; Walker, "Holding the Tennessee Line," *THQ* 16 (Sept. 1957), 228–49; Walker, "Comand Failure: The Fall of Forts Henry and Donelson," *THQ* 16 (Dec. 1957), 335–60.

18.

Although Tennessee ceased to be a battlefield after Hood was defeated at Nashville in December 1864, Tennesseans experienced for another four years conditions that have been described as "neither peace nor war." The sufferings of people in the eastern section, so pronounced during hostilities, became more intense with the return of the blue and the gray, and street fights, rural feuds, and ambushes became common. In many parts of the state men returned to a land of waste and barrenness. Much of the state was "the womb of desolation," one newsman observed; "Government mules and horses are occupying the homes . . . in which . . . [Tennessee's] chivalric men so often slumbered." Another wrote with some degree of romantic imagination:

> Go from Memphis to Chattanooga, and it is like the march of Moscow in olden times. . . . Whether you go on the Salem, the Shelbyville, the Manchester, or any other pike [from Murfreesboro] for a distance of thirty miles either way, what do we behold? One wide wild, and dreary waste. . . . The fences are all burned down, the apple, the pear, and the plum trees burned in ashes long ago; the torch applied to . . . splendid mansions, the walls of which alone remain.

The death toll of Tennesseans in both armies was high. For others, survival was but a reprieve, because men weakened and diseased from years of military service prematurely filled graves. Amputation had been the only defense against gangrene and infections, and many men therefore hobbled back maimed or otherwise unfit for the heavy physical labor demanded by agricultural readjustment. The distress and destruction caused by the battling armies were augmented by

328

problems posed by freedmen who required time for orientation to their new status.

As noted earlier, William G. Brownlow was elevated to the governor's chair by a Unionist oligarchy in early 1865, and for four years he sought to suppress the ex-rebel majority and keep its leaders from positions of power. Historians have not been very kind to the memory of Brownlow. Most have followed the lead of his biographer, E. Merton Coulter, who viewed the Radical governor as a dangerous psychopath.[1] But in many respects he was probably not much different from many politicians of his own time or ours; he rewarded his friends and saw little reason for helping his enemies. Eloquent with tongue and pen, he probably suffered from a pronounced feeling of inferiority and, naturally given to verbosity, breathed fire and brimstone when he actually meant to produce little more than a smokescreen to conceal his own inadequacies. Along with his loquacity, his chief fault was his lack of balance and sound judgment on matters of grave importance.

Born in Wythe County, Virginia, Brownlow was orphaned at an early age and experienced an unhappy childhood. He grew up with few advantages and with very pronounced likes and dislikes. An uncle who reared him employed him on the farm and then bound him out to a carpenter who taught him the building trade. Although denied the advantages of a formal education, he learned to read and write and, like Abraham Lincoln and Andrew Johnson, read whatever books were at hand. He soon grew tired of the hammer and saw. Observing that in the Southern Appalachians the Christian ministry was a field which required "not much education, . . . but a large amount of religious fervor, excitability, and pugnacity," he became for ten years a circuit-riding Methodist minister. An eloquent speaker, he preached sermons that consisted largely of diatribes against Baptists and Presbyterians. In 1839 he began publication of the Elizabethton *Tennessee Whig* and thus embarked upon a journalistic career that thrust him into politics. A Whig, he entered actively into the social, economic, and political discussions of the day, assum-

[1] Coulter has written of Brownlow's elevation to the governorship: "It was a strange and dangerous act to set a person of Brownlow's record to rule over a million people. In peaceful times it would have been perilous; in the confusion incident to the closing of a civil war, it might seem preposterous. . . . For the promoting of the orderly progress of peace, it would have been impossible to make a worse choice." Coulter, *William G. Brownlow*, (1937; rpt. Knoxville, 1971), 262.

Above: William G. Brownlow was Tennessee's Reconstruction governor and served 1865–1869. He resigned February 25, 1869, to become United States senator. His term was completed by DeWitt Clinton Senter (*below*), who was elected to a full term in the following fall.

ing the character of a crusader in the causes he espoused. During the war he came to nurture special hatred for "rebels," and his two terms as governor afforded him an opportunity to demonstrate his hostility.

Brownlow assumed office on April 5, 1865, two days after the General Assembly convened, and as might be expected in the trauma of the war's aftermath, he urged legislators to deal out punitive legislation to the former Confederates. The criminal code, he said, should be strengthened to crush the guerrilla menace, and the state militia should be reorganized and strengthened. The franchise should be restricted to Union men only, freedmen must be protected from "those who fought to perpetuate slavery," and Confederate officers and bank directors should be held personally responsible for bank and railroad losses. He called for ratification of the Thirteenth Amendment and for prompt election of United States senators and representatives from the ranks of loyal people.

The legislature acting upon these recommendations consisted of Union men, chiefly former Whigs, most of whom were farmers and small merchants with little or no political experience. Soon after legislators began work they divided into two groups—those who completely accepted the governor's proposals and those who objected to some of his proscriptive recommendations. The former had a working majority, and Senate Speaker Samuel R. Rodgers defined the assembly's chief aim as being that of keeping loyal people from ever being "governed by rebels." They were known as "Radicals" and acquired their name by following the leadership of Washington Radicals, who advocated an extensive reconstruction program for the South. The others were called "Conservatives"; they followed the leadership of President Johnson and the Washington Conservatives who wished to put into effect the Lincoln-Johnson plan of reconstruction.

The Radicals enacted many new laws, most of which were designed to catch rebels in some act of wrongdoing. Horse stealing, housebreaking, burglary, and house or bridge burning were made capital offenses, and the gallows was prescribed for guerrillas and armed prowlers. They enacted laws to exclude former Confederates from the ballot box and permit only those of "unconditional Union sentiments" to vote. They also ratified the Thirteenth Amendment and offered a joint resolution authorizing the governor to "respond to the cries of the wounded and dying, the wail of the widow, [and] the weeping of the orphan" by proclaiming a reward of $5,000 for the arrest of former governor Isham G. Harris, whom they described as "responsible to a great extent for the war."

Tennesseans Restored to the Union in 1866 ᶝᵛ Various leaders presented plans for reconstructing the prostrate South. Both Lincoln and Johnson in 1865 contended that the Southern states had not been out of the Union but had existed in a state of suspended animation during their participation in the "rebellion." Now that the war was over, these states needed only to organize loyal governments, recognize federal authority, and elect representatives and senators to Congress. Radical leaders, however, asserted that the seceded states had committed treason by their acts and must therefore be reconstructed. Thaddeus Stevens, Radical leader in the House of Representatives, had suggested a "conquered province" theory, whereby Confederate states would become the property of Congress and be dealt with by that body as the members saw fit. Charles Sumner, equally powerful in the Senate, proposed a "state suicide" theory, in which he argued that the seceding states had lost their positions in the Union and were now territories subject to the exclusive jurisdiction of Congress. Governor Brownlow announced a plan to be used in case Southerners rose in a second civil war. Such a conflict was inevitable, he said, and—not missing a chance to castigate old enemies—predicted that Andrew Johnson would "in this second rebellion, take the place of Jeff Davis." After the "second rebellion" was put down and Johnson was executed, then the "loyal masses" should "make the entire Southern Confederacy as God found the earth when he commenced the work of creation, without form and void."

Johnson disagreed with the Radicals (and of course with Brownlow) and sought to have Tennessee restored immediately to its former relation with the federal government. He rejoiced at the state's acceptance of the Thirteenth Amendment and the election of United States senators and representatives. He received gladly a request from the legislature that

> the State of Tennessee be no longer considered in a state of insurrection, and that the loyal people of that state be granted all the rights and privileges that are granted . . . to the loyal citizens of any of the

sister states that are not considered in a state of rebellion against the Government of the United States.

The Radical Congress, however, much to the surprise and chagrin of Tennessee Radicals and to the dismay of Johnson, refused on December 4, 1865, to seat the Tennessee delegation. For several months the stalemate was debated both in and out of Congress. A joint committee on Reconstruction, consisting of nine members from the House and six from the Senate, was then established to study the situation in all of the Southern states. On April 30 the joint committee suggested to Congress that when a seceded state ratified the proposed Fourteenth Amendment, it should be given representation in Congress and thus, in effect, be readmitted to the Union.

Vigorous opposition to the Fourteenth Amendment already had developed in Tennessee and other Southern states. Some objected to one clause and some to another; to still others all four sections were equally obnoxious. The editor of the Nashville *Union and American* believed that the amendment was far more dangerous to American liberties than the Civil War itself, was "without parallel in American history," and was "aimed at a revolution of the social and political fabric. . . ."

Governor Brownlow called the General Assembly into special session on July 4, and the capitol became the scene of much excitement before the amendment was finally ratified. The senators promptly accepted the amendment, but Conservatives in the house determined to make a strong fight against it. Shortly before the session opened, when they discovered that they did not have sufficient strength to defeat the proposal, the Conservatives decided to accomplish their aims by absenting themselves and thus prevent the formation of a quorum, which consisted of two-thirds of those elected to the house. After convening and promptly adjourning for six days for lack of a quorum, the Radicals issued warrants of arrest for the absent members. On July 16, the sergeant-at-arms, with the assistance of Negro troops, arrested Representatives Pleasant Williams of Carter County and A. J. Martin of Jackson County and forcibly detained them in the capitol. Their applications for writs of habeas corpus were granted by Criminal Judge Thomas N. Frazier of Davidson County, but the legislature denied the court's jurisdiction. Only after the sheriff had formed a *posse comitatus* and stormed the capitol were the two prisoners set free. On July 18, the day before the

prisoners were released, however, the house ratified the amendment. Williams and Martin were recorded as being present but
having "failed and refused" to vote. Brownlow promptly telegraphed
Washington authorities that Tennessee Radicals had "fought the
battle and won it." On July 23 the President signed a congressional
resolution restoring Tennessee to its former relation with the Union,
and the state's congressional delegation was promptly seated in the
national assembly. Thus Tennessee escaped the military program of
reconstruction applied by the Radical Congress to the other ten
states of the Confederacy.

Negro Suffrage and the Election of 1867. ⧵❧ The Radical
oligarchy began in January 1867 to plan for the August election.
Throughout the month county conventions were held at which
Radical leaders urged the reelection of their chief. On Washington's
birthday, they assembled in Nashville, where they warmly praised
the governor and strongly condemned President Johnson.
Brownlow, the Radicals said, was a man of "firmness, courage, and
wisdom," whose "healthy mind . . . bears with like equanimity the
throes of pain and the perilous cares of State. . . ." They vowed that
they would not consider any other candidate for governor.

A bill that would give Negroes the privilege of voting was before
the legislature when the Radicals assembled, and they strongly recommended its passage. The measure had been written at the insistence of Brownlow, who had concluded for sometime that the votes
of loyal Negroes would probably be necessary to keep his regime in
power. Before the war the governor had been a staunch defender of
slavery, and more recently he had opposed Negro suffrage. Shortly
after the war he had suggested that blacks be colonized in Texas or
some other Western state. The goadings of the Northern press and
of Negro leaders, however, together with the realization that he
might lose the election in 1867, caused Brownlow to change his
views. Consequently, on February 26, he signed into law a measure
that enfranchised black men but excluded them from officeholding
and jury duty.

In the meantime, Conservatives held a nominating convention and
declared their support for an "immediate restoration of our disfranchised fellow-citizens to the rights, privileges, and immunities of

a full and complete citizenship." Also, they believed that "colored fellow-citizens" were entitled to all the rights and privileges of others. They praised Andrew Johnson, opposed martial law as enforced by "a standing army in our state," and nominated Emerson Etheridge of Dresden for governor. A man of unquestioned integrity, Etheridge had been both a legislator and a congressman before the war and had remained loyal to the Union during the conflict.

The incumbent governor was too ill to campaign extensively, but he had taken adequate measures to insure his victory even before Etheridge was nominated. During and after the debates on the Negro suffrage bill, the governor pushed through the legislature two measures that would give him more power. One, passed on February 20, provided for the raising of an armed force to be known as the Tennessee State Guard. Troops were necessary, he said, to stop "atrocious murders and numerous outrages" which had been committed by "violent and disloyal men." The second bill strengthened the franchise law by giving the governor authority to set aside registrations in any county. Brownlow, his dictatorial powers enhanced, was now ready for the gubernatorial campaign of 1867.

The governor's inability to campaign did not mean that he would not be represented on the hustings. Horace Maynard was popular especially among blacks and was joined by William B. Stokes (who became a gubernatorial candidate in 1869), Samuel M. Arnell, Columbia legislator and Radical leader, and others who carried Brownlow's candidacy to the people.

Etheridge was an able orator whose skill in the use of vituperative language matched that of Brownlow, but he must have realized early in the campaign that his chances of victory were indeed slim, especially after Radicals placed many obstacles in his way and even threatened his life. At Greeneville he was forced to defend himself against attackers, and at Elizabethton a Brownlow supporter threatened him with a gun. Disturbances occurred at Rogersville, Knoxville, Gallatin, Franklin, Fayetteville, Lewisburg, Pulaski, Columbia, and other towns.

On election day Radical whites and blacks delivered the majority that Brownlow expected and needed to win. The governor received 74,034 votes to 22,550 for Etheridge; all Radical candidates for Congress and all but three Radical candidates for the state legislature were elected.

The Impeachment of President Andrew Johnson ᖇᔓ Shortly after the election, Washington Radicals began seriously to consider impeaching President Johnson. Legislators in Tennessee were pleased with the movement and in October 1867 prepared a joint resolution requesting the state's delegation in Washington to vote for the impeachment articles. The Radical press, led by the Knoxville *Whig* and the Nashville *Daily Press and Times,* urged that no mercy be shown the chief executive. "Let Johnson be impeached, treason made odious, and the arch-traitor punished," wrote the editor of the Nashville paper.

Tennessee's House delegation did not need encouragement from the Radicals back home; their opinions had already been formed. With the exception of Congressman Isaac R. Hawkins, they voted for impeachment and denounced the President in the process. Congressman William B. Stokes charged Johnson with drunkenness while he served as military governor, described him as a man who had "no regard for truth," and denounced him for attempting to "put the rebels in power to again plant their heels upon our necks and crush the colored men into the dust." Congressman James Mullins of Bedford County believed that the President had ambitions to be "the sole legislator, the Nero of our day. The Czar of Russia had never assumed more despotic power and more absolute sway" than Johnson, Mullins fumed.

Tennessee's two senators who would sit as a court with their fellow solons in judgment of the charges brought against the President were David T. Patterson, a son-in-law of the chief executive, and Joseph S. Fowler. Radicals assumed that Patterson would vote for an acquittal, but Fowler, who had sided with them on many issues, kept both friend and foe in doubt until the final roll call. He received hundreds of visitors, as well as letters and telegrams urging him to vote for conviction. All of Tennessee's Radical delegation in the House of Representatives visited him and insisted that he should resign unless he could vote "what he well knows to be the sentiment of the loyal people of his state." Brownlow, Johnson's enemy of long standing, was alleged to have offered Fowler an appointment to the state supreme court if he would resign.

Upon final roll call both senators voted for acquittal. The Radicals failed by one vote to remove Johnson by impeachment. Senator Fowler was then excoriated by his erstwhile Radical cohorts, who characterized him as a "nineteenth century Judas."

The Ku Klux Klan 🙤 Brownlow's overwhelming victory in 1867 disturbed Conservative Unionists and former Confederates alike. Not only had ex-rebels suffered tremendous losses during the war, but they were kept out of influence in state government and were harassed by the Union League—a group that consisted of Northern Radicals dedicated to propagating the cause of the Republican party in the South. Lamenting their plight, the conservative group joined other Southerners in an illegal underground movement. In Tennessee the group took the name of Ku Klux Klan, and it spread to other Southern states.

The Klan was organized at Pulaski shortly after the war by a group of young men said to be seeking amusement and relief from boredom. By 1867, it had been transformed from a social club to a political organization designed to frighten blacks from the polls and Union Leagues from the South. The group grew rapidly, and leaders decided to hold a state meeting where a greater degree of centralization might be achieved.

Consequently, a secret convention was held at the new Maxwell House Hotel in Nashville in April 1867. So close-mouthed were leaders that they could assemble under the shadow of the capitol and in the presence of Federal troops and officers actually residing in the hotel. General Forrest was placed at the head of the organization, with the title of "Grand Wizard of the Empire." Each state constituted a Realm headed by a Grand Dragon, each congressional district a Dominion under a Grand Titan, and each county a Province governed by a Grand Giant. Local units were called Dens, headed by a Grand Cyclops. A constitution, or prescript, set forth the various duties of the officials. A revised prescript issued the following year stated that the purpose of the Klan were protection of "the weak, the innocent and the defenseless, from the indignities, wrongs, and outrages of the lawless, the violent, and the brutal;" aid to the suffering, especially "widows and orphans of Confederate soldiers;" protection and defense of the Constitution of the United States; and "aid in the execution of all constitutional laws."

For the next two years, activities of the Klan were reported widely. Disguised men staged numerous night parades in cities and towns throughout Middle and West Tennessee and in some counties of East Tennessee. Activity was reported in most of the counties, but especially in Maury, Lincoln, Giles, Marshall, and Humphreys (in Middle Tennessee), and in Obion, Hardeman, Fayette, Gibson, and Dyer (in

West Tennessee). Alleged depredations included murders, rapes, and whippings. Leaders in Negro affairs especially were abused and threatened. Even Brownlow reported having received threatening letters "accompanied with pictures of coffins, daggers, pistols, and the gallows," and Representative S. M. Arnell told of being forced to flee for his life when threatened in Columbia by Klansmen with "pistols and rope in hand." Troops, he told Brownlow, should be raised to "suppress all armed and masked parties. . . ."

To meet the new emergency Brownlow called lawmakers into extra session and requested legislation permitting widespread martial law. "These organized bands of assassins and robbers," he said of Klansmen, should "be declared outlaws by special legislation and punished with death wherever found."

At the same time, a group of former Confederate generals, including Benjamin F. Cheatham, W. B. Bate, Forrest, John C. Brown, Pillow, Bushrod R. Johnson and seven others assembled in Nashville to urge that peace and harmony should replace threats of war and violence. Denying that they were hostile to the state government or that they desired the overthrow of the federal government by illegal means, the generals regretted that "armed men" roved "through portions of the country," and believed that they would stop "as soon as the determination of the [state] leaders to have peace was made known."

Legislators, however, formed a committee to study Ku Klux Klan activity. Committee members took testimony of "a great many" witnesses and reported findings that "a perfect reign of terror" existed in many of the counties of West and Middle Tennessee. Armed and disguised men, they said, were

> going abroad . . . robbing poor Negroes . . taking them out of their houses at night, hanging, shooting and whipping them in a most cruel manner, and driving them from their houses. . . . Women and children . . . [were] subjected to the torture of the lash, and brutal assaults . . . committed upon them by these night prowlers. . . . In many instances the persons of females . . . [were] violated, and when the husband or father complained, he had been obliged to flee to save his own life.

Legislators then enacted two comprehensive measures. The first reestablished the state militia (the earlier act had expired) and gave the governor authority to declare martial law in any county where the law could not be enforced. The second, commonly called the Ku

Klux Klan Act, provided severe penalties for persons who "unite with, associate with, promote or encourage, any secret organization of persons that shall prowl through the country or towns . . . by day or night, disguised or otherwise, for the purpose of disturbing the peace." Violators were to be fined $500, imprisoned for not less than five years, and "rendered infamous." The same punishment was provided for persons who impeded the prosecution of the guilty. All citizens were authorized to arrest violators of the law.

When several months elapsed and no prominent ex-Confederate was charged with violating the Klan law, Brownlow employed Captain Seymour Barmore of Cincinnati to spy upon prominent citizens in an effort to obtain names for exemplary trials. The purpose of the ostentatious Barmore—who described himself as "the greatest detective in the world"—was soon discovered by Nashville Klansmen, who warned him to return to Cincinnati. He refused; instead he immediately caught a train to Pulaski, the center of Klan activity. There, dressed as a Klansman, he attended meetings of the Pulaski Klan and obtained the names of many of its members. The ruse was not discovered until Barmore had boarded a train for Nashville. At Columbia, however, Klansmen forcibly removed him. Six weeks later, on February 20, 1869, his body was recovered from the Duck River. A rope was about his neck, and a bullet had pierced his skull.

On the same day that Barmore's body was recovered from the murky waters, Brownlow declared martial law in the counties of Gibson, Giles, Haywood, Jackson, Lawrence, Madison, Marshall, Maury, and Overton, where he believed lawlessness abounded and where the Klan still operated unimpeded. A few weeks earlier the governor, after much difficulty, had raised the desired number of men to constitute the new state militia, and had placed General Joseph A. Cooper in command.

On February 25, 1869, Brownlow resigned in order to accept a seat in the United States Senate, and shortly thereafter General Forrest commanded that Klan masks and costumes be destroyed. Forrest believed that the Klan in large measure had accomplished its objectives, and he regretted that many acts of violence not committed by Klan members had been blamed upon the organization.

Freedmen's Bureau in Tennessee ᘒᘉ Many of the former slaves were understandably bewildered and unsettled in their new status. Many left the farms where they had worked and were soon destitute. Congress therefore formed the "Bureau of Refugees, Freedmen, and Abandoned Lands"—soon shortened to "Freedmen's Bureau"—to help Negroes. Bureau officials were given considerable power. They distributed food to the needy, supervised black contracts with white landowners, and established schools. Bureau officials also set aside for use of the freedmen tracts of land declared "abandoned" or land acquired by the government by sale or confiscation. Not more than forty acres could be leased to a freedman or refugee, which gave rise to the saying that blacks were to be given "forty acres and a mule."

General O. O. Howard, who had recently been in command of Federal troops in Tennessee, was named bureau commissioner, and General Clinton B. Fisk was named assistant commissioner in charge of a district embracing Kentucky and Tennessee. Subdistricts in Tennessee were formed, with headquarters at Nashville, Memphis, Chattanooga, Pulaski, and Knoxville. In order to dispel all hopes for a "free ride," Fisk told freedmen upon his arrival in Nashville that all would be expected to work. "Do not expect us to do all, nor half, but put your shoulders to the wheel and do for yourselves," he told a group of blacks in Nashville. Thousands of rations were issued to the destitute in the state, and at least four orphanages and two hospitals were established for them.

The Educational Division performed one of the most important functions of the bureau. Hundreds of teachers from the North, with a variety of motives, attitudes, and intentions, poured into the South. Most considered themselves the spiritual and intellectual successors to Grant and Sherman; the bluecoats had merely defeated armies, but the teachers had the more important task of conquering and enlightening the Southern mind. The "political rights of the blackest man" must be "put on a level with the whitest," they announced, and the South must be made safe for "the reddest Republican" or the "blackest Abolitionist." By September 1866, several thousand Negroes had been enrolled in forty-one schools. A few months later the legislature provided for the maintenance of Negro education, and soon many of the schools were being maintained entirely by the state.

Many native whites did not sympathize with the purposes or methods of the bureau; one scholar, Henry L. Swint, has written, "The Southern reaction to the presence of the Yankee teacher was definite, decided, and violent." Many white Southerners did not condemn Negro education; on the contrary, many had approved of it both before and after the war. They resented and feared the "typical Yankee teacher," however, who they believed would do more to foment racial unrest than to help.

Bureau officials received many reports of violence against schools and teachers. School buildings at Wartrace, Carthage, Decherd, Shelbyville, Brentwood, Athens, and other places were burned. Teachers at Carthage received advice to "go North where they belonged," and many elsewhere were threatened. M. M. Hiland, a Cheatham County white man who conducted a Negro school, reported in 1868 that he had received this note, signed "By order of the Grand Cyclops":

> M. M. Hiland, alias Nigro [*sic*] Hiland:—You are hereby notified to disband the school of which you are in charge at Jackson Chapel as it is contrary to the wishes of every respectable man in the vicinity and an insult to the refinement of the community. If this notice fails to effect its purpose, you may expect to find yourself suspended by a rope with your feet about six feet from terra firma. We hope you will give the same consideration; and in case of failure on your part, we intend to carry into execution the above mentioned plan.
> BEWARE! BEWARE!! BEWARE!!!

Despite threats and violence, officials continued to operate the schools. J. H. Barnum, assistant superintendent of the educational division of the bureau, toured Middle Tennessee in 1868 and found many people who "manifested a great interest in the subject of schools." Shortly thereafter, a reporter for the Nashville *Daily Press and Times* toured many of the counties and corroborated Barnum's report. The editor of the Nashville *Republican Banner* argued that the Southern whites should assume the task of educating the Negroes instead of waiting for the Northern people to do it.

While teachers taught Negroes reading, writing, and arithmetic, bureau officials taught them to vote the Republican ticket. In many of the Southern states, the bureau became little more than a political propaganda machine designed to perpetuate the Radicals in power, but in Tennessee the officials probably were less active than elsewhere.

The Radicals and the Railroads ✒ The Radicals found several ways to enrich themselves at the expense of the state treasury.

None, however, was more fantastic than that involving the railroads of the state. The decade of the 1850s had been an era of railroad expansion, and Tennessee, like other states, had loaned money to companies that would build railroads in or through the state. By 1861 a fairly satisfactory system of transportation had been built by companies that showed no danger of financial disaster at that time.

The wanton destruction of railroads and bridges during the war left the roads in disrepair and the companies in poor financial condition, although the federal government did build several hundred miles of lines and repaired others. After Appomattox, the Brownlow administration attempted to rebuild the entire system. By 1869 the legislature had appropriated nearly $14 million for the relief of the railroad companies.

Little of the money was spent on rolling stock, rails, and crossties, but instead found its way into the pockets of corrupt railroad officials and legislators. The Mineral Home Railway, for example, which existed entirely on paper—"not a shovel of dirt was ever dug, nor even a survey of the route attempted," an investigating committee later reported—received $100,000 in state bonds. Indeed, it remained for the legislature of 1879 to uncover all the sordid details of the flagrant misconduct of the railroad and government officials.

The Downfall of the Radicals Brownlow had been elected to succeed United States Senator David Patterson, whose term expired on March 4, 1869. Consequently, the governor resigned on February 25, 1869 and was succeeded by DeWitt C. Senter, speaker of the senate, whom Brownlow described as "a loyal man, capable, tried, and trusted, who is sound in his principles and who will steadily adhere to them upon the platform of the Union Republican party in Tennessee."

Brownlow based his description of the new governor upon the record. Senter, an East Tennessean, had served three terms in the legislature before the war and had voted against secession in 1861. He had been imprisoned by the Confederates, had been driven from his home by guerrillas, and had lived in Louisville during the war. In 1865 he returned and was elected to the state senate. There he voted for disfranchisement of the Confederates and otherwise supported Brownlow and the Radicals. As a member of the senate in 1867,

Senter had taken a leading role in the election of Brownlow to the United States Senate.

Senter proceeded cautiously during his first few weeks as governor and determined upon only slight modification of the Brownlow program. One of his first official acts was to declare the militia subordinate to civil government and to make clear that it did not supersede civil law. Shortly thereafter he mustered out the militia. With the removal of martial law, only disfranchisement kept the former Confederates from resuming positions of power, but in this respect Senter gave them little hope for immediate relief. Until the campaign for governor in 1869, Confederates had no reason to consider Senter anything but a "mild" Radical.

When Radicals held a gubernatorial convention in Nashville on May 20, 1869, the field of hopefuls had narrowed to Senter and General William B. Stokes, congressman from the third district, whom Brownlow had defeated previously in the election to the Senate. Each was supported by a faction determined to nominate its man, and soon the convention became—as one writer described it—"fit only for lunatics." A few days later, when the convention broke up in confusion, each faction held its own meeting and claimed its favorite to be the Radical nominee. Therefore, both Stokes and Senter became gubernatorial candidates.

Conservatives declined to nominate a candidate but vowed to support the Radical nominee who appeared most favorable to their cause. At first they leaned toward Stokes. He was a Middle Tennessean, while Senter, endorsed by the governor and considered the "administration candidate," was believed to favor continued disfranchisement. They soon shifted wholeheartedly to Senter, however, when it became apparent that enfranchisement of the Confederates would be the major issue.

On June 5 the campaign opened in Nashville. Stokes favored a gradual return of the ex-Confederates to the ballot box and suggested that this might be accomplished by a two-thirds vote of the legislators after each disfranchised person proved that he was peaceful and law abiding. Senter, however, proposed universal manhood suffrage and promised if elected to remove all restrictions. Brownlow, who always reserved the right to change his mind when he was not on a popular side, left Radicals dumbfounded by supporting Senter's stand. Brownlow was aware of the trends of the times, however; he also knew that the state supreme court six weeks earlier had rendered a unanimous decision declaring unconstitutional the legislative act that had conferred on the governor the power to set aside registrations of voters of a county where he detected fraud. The decision in effect reenfranchised about 30,000 ex-Confederates.

The campaign waxed bitter throughout the summer, and much strife was aroused wherever the candidates spoke. Although he knew that Stokes had the bulk of the Radical support, Governor Senter believed that he could be elected if enough ex-Confederates were given the right to vote before the election. Consequently, Senter began the wholesale removal of Radical registrars in counties across the state and replaced them with Conservatives. Thousands of former Rebels then registered, and were soon proudly announcing their intention of carrying the day for Senter. Toward the end of the campaign, Stokes, in Middle and West Tennessee, shifted to a position of universal suffrage. At Memphis he admitted, "suffrage is a dead letter—any man can get a certificate." At Huntingdon he promised to "enfranchise every man of God's green earth who will come up and ask for it."

Senter's election became a foregone conclusion. He received a majority of 65,297 out of 175,369 votes cast. Furthermore, the Conservatives ran their own candidates for the legislature and won control of both houses. The next General Assembly would have 20 Conservatives and 5 Radicals in the senate, and 66 Conservatives and 17 Radicals in the house. The election meant that Reconstruction was over in Tennessee and that the power of the Radical minority was broken.

The Conservative legislature began immediately to undo much of the Radical program. The State Guard Act and the "Act to Preserve the Peace" (Ku Klux Klan law) were repealed. Oaths for office-holders were removed. Most important of all, the legislature submitted to the people the question of electing delegates to a constitutional convention. By a five-to-one majority, the people voted in favor of the convention, which assembled in January 1870.

Radicals did not accept the revolution without a struggle. Stokes and others believed that the federal government would declare Senter's election illegal and urged Congress to place the state under military reconstruction. Their hopes were in vain, however, and their cause proved to be dead in Tennessee.

Thus, after four years of Radicalism, the government of Tennessee was again in the hands of the majority. Within recent years there has been a tendency among scholars to view the Reconstruction period in the South with greater objectivity. Certainly the Radicals were in power during a difficult time when the chief executive offered little by way of leadership. Admittedly, they tried to encourage industry, immigration, education, and civil rights for blacks during a time of the state's greatest need. Their major faults were those of ignoring the democratic principle of majority rule and accomplishing little toward restoring a spirit of comity so necessary for the continuation of an orderly society.

SUGGESTED READINGS

Books
E. Merton Coulter, *The South During Reconstruction, 1865–1877* (Baton Rouge, 1947); Coulter, *William G. Brownlow, Fighting Parson of the Southern Highlands* (Chapel Hill, 1937); James W. Patton, *Unionism and Reconstruction in Tennessee, 1860–1869* (Chapel Hill, 1934); Alrutheus A. Taylor, *The Negro in Tennessee, 1865–1880* (Washington, D.C., 1941); Lately Thomas, *The First President Johnson* (New York, 1968).

Articles
Thomas B. Alexander, "Kukluxism in Tennessee, 1865–1869," *THQ* 8 (Sept. 1949), 195–219; Alexander, "Whiggery and Reconstruction in Tennessee," *JSH* 16 (Aug.1950), 291–305; Peter H. Argersinger, "The Conservative as Radical: A Reconstruction Dilemma," *THQ* 34 (Summer 1975), 168–87; James B. Campbell, "East Tennessee During the Radical Regime, 1865–1869," *ETHSP* 20 (1948), 84–102; Weymouth T. Jordan, "The Freedmen's Bureau in Tennessee," *ETHSP* 11 (1939), 47–61; Gary L. Kornell, "Reconstruction in Nashville, 1867–1869," *THQ* 30 (Fall 1971), 277–87; William G. Miscamble, "Andrew Johnson and the Election of William G. ("Parson") Brownlow as Governor of Tennessee," *THQ* 37 (Fall 1978), 308–20; James C. Parker, "Tennessee Gubernatorial Election: 1869—The Victory of the Conservatives," *THQ* 33 (Spring 1974), 34–48; James W. Patton, "Tennessee's Attitude Toward the Impeachment and Trial of Andrew Johnson," *ETHSP* 9 (1937), 65–76; Paul David Phillips, "White Reaction to the Freedmen's Bureau in Tennessee," *THQ* 25 (Spring 1966), 50–62; Verton M. Queener, "Origin of the Republican Party in East Tennessee," *ETHSP* 13 (1941), 66–90; James Gilbert Ryan, "The Memphis Riots of 1866: Terror in a Black Community During Reconstruction," *JNH* 62 (July 1977), 243–57; J. A. Sharp, "The

Downfall of the Radicals in Tennessee," *ETHSP* 5 (1933), 105–24; J. Reuben Sheeler, "The Development of Unionism in East Tennessee, 1860–1866," *JNH* 29 (April 1944), 166–203; Frank B. Williams, "John Eaton, Jr., Editor, Politician, and School Administrator, 1865–1870," *THQ* 10 (Dec. 1951), 291–319.

19.

W ITH the Brownlow administration behind them, Tennesseans turned to other problems, most of which were legacies of the Civil War and Reconstruction. The people had called for a revision of the fundamental law soon after Governor Dewitt C. Senter's election, and early in January 1870 delegates convened for the first major constitutional convention in nearly four decades. After the convention adjourned, leaders focused attention upon the state debt, a Civil War-Reconstruction onus that increased at a disturbing rate and required settlement. Indeed, the state's entire economic system, with agricultural problems especially acute after the depression of 1873, needed rehabilitation. Some Southern leaders believed that an influx of industry and immigrants might be the answer to the South's sagging economy, and Tennessee had its share of protagonists of "New South" philosophy. Urban areas expanded during the postwar years, and Negroes became active in politics during the 1880s.

In the years after Reconstruction, Democrats became well entrenched and relegated Republicans to a minority status except in East Tennessee. The party constituency, which controlled West and Middle Tennessee, embodied several distinct elements. Those in control at this time have been referred to as "Redeemers," because they "redeemed" the state from the Radicals. Within Redeemer ranks were prewar Whigs, former Know-Nothings, and, of course, lifelong Democrats; the vast majority were former Confederates, although some had supported the Union before the Civil War but had rejected the Republican party rather than become associated with the extremes of Radicalism. The diverse group consisted of

347

both large and small farmers, businessmen and industrialists, and nostalgic proponents of the Old South, as well as those who looked with hope to a new era. Including men of such diverse antecedents as Andrew Johnson, Thomas A. R. Nelson, Isham G. Harris, A. O. P. Nicholson, and Nathan Bedford Forrest, the group was held together under one strong bond of union—the determination to prevent Radical extremists from ever again dominating the state as they had during the several years after Appomattox.

One scholar[1] of the quarter-century after Reconstruction has viewed the Democratic party as one in which voters' hopes for the future was the principal force in developing political alignments instead of economic differences or traditional party allegiances. Employing sophisticated quantitative techniques and a conceptual framework incorporating psychological and social models, he has viewed the "social elite" group—Redeemers, New South Democrats, and State Credit Democrats—as assuming an "optimistic" view respecting the future. Feeling socially and economically secure, they had little anxiety regarding their social and economic status and, putting the bitterness of 1861–1865 behind them, looked confidently to the future. An example was Robert L. (Bob) Taylor, earlier considered a leader of the agrarians, who in 1885 urged people to view the future with confidence and spoke grandiosely of a "grand structure of the New South" after "the debris and wreckage of the war's destruction" had been cleared away. The future, Taylor said, should be built upon the "enduring principles of free thought, free action, a free ballot, justice, law, order, the education of the masses, the autonomy of the states, constitutional government, one flag, and a reunited republic." On the other hand, Democratic dissidents— Bourbons,[2] unhappy farmers, and debt readjusters—saw a dim future because of their anxieties emerging from a feeling of guilt and inferiority associated with defeat and humiliation during the Civil War and Reconstruction. These feelings brought about anxieties concerning their future social, economic, and political status; they became defensive and developed a paranoid and reactionary political

---

[1] Hart, *Redeemers, Bourbons, and Populists: Tennessee, 1870–1896* (Baton Rouge, 1975), passim.

[2] The term "Bourbon" was used to denote prewar men of power, influence, and "ingrained conservatism" who considered themselves heir to the Jefferson-Jackson tradition and sought in the postwar days to reestablish and perpetuate their influence and control.

style in which they viewed all innovations as being "foreign" and "evil." These people who harbored such powerful irrational feelings were chiefly rural and small town whites who were suspicious of conspiratorial forces outside their geographic area that challenged their opportunities for upward mobility.

While Republican strength came chiefly from East Tennessee, the several counties along the Tennessee River in the west that had voted against secession were also counted within party ranks, as were West Tennessee counties such as Shelby, Fayette, and Haywood, which had a predominantly black population. Indeed, Negroes generally voted the Republican ticket wherever they lived, and they continued until the early 1890s (when black voting subsided) to help make the party competitive with Democrats. The powerful leaders, however, were the "Mountain Republicans" such as Leonidas C. Houk, who unseated the Horace Maynard machine and whose East Tennessee "ring" was the most successful Republican organization in the South between 1876 and 1900. Using federal patronage and employing organizational techniques not unlike those used in holding a military unit together, Houk organized mountain Republican neighbors into a tightly knit political machine able to challenge the aggressive and resourceful Democratic majority. Federal patronage under Grant and other Republican presidents, the bloody shirt, consciousness of a minority status, and economic issues held the party together. Of the congressional districts, the first and second were dominated by Republicans. Occasionally a Republican candidate would win in the third and also in the tenth, where the black population was large. Democrats controlled the others.

Delegates to the constitutional convention assembled according to plan on January 10, 1870. They were men of political talent and experience; many had been slaveholders and most were of conservative temperament. Neill Brown had been governor; others, including the chairman, were to hold that office later. A few had served in the United States or Confederate congresses, and more than one-half had been members of the state legislature. Most had fought in Federal or Southern armies, and four had been Confederate generals.

Radicals, both in Tennessee and Washington, watched the proceedings carefully. Those in Tennessee repeatedly urged Congress to place the state under military rule with other former Confederate states. Congressman Lewis Tillman of Shelbyville, for example, described the government as consisting only of Confederate leaders who were "trampling under foot" all semblance of law and order, and Secretary of State A. J. Fletcher saw Tennessee as a "seething volcano." The only solution to the problem, he wrote, was to reduce the state "to a territorial condition" so that the "loyal population" could be protected. Negro leaders convened in Nashville on January 2 and reported to Congress that "the Rebel party" in Tennessee was "un-Christian, inhuman, and beyond toleration"; blacks and other Unionists, they said, could find relief only through military reconstruction.

Delegates to the convention realized that their actions would be scrutinized carefully by Nashville and Washington Radicals. They wisely chose as chairman a prewar Whig, John C. Brown, who, although he had been a Confederate general, had repeatedly expressed his "heartfelt desire" to bind up the nation's wounds and lay the bitterness of civil war to rest. Delegates must raise their sights "above the passions of the hour," mark their deliberations with "wisdom, prudence, and moderation," "accept the situation" as it was, and "not seek to alter circumstances which have passed beyond . . . control," he told delegates. His strong hope, he said, was that Tennesseans could escape the federal military occupation that troubled citizens of some of the other Southern states.

Many issues were carefully discussed. The issue causing the most debate was that of suffrage. Should the law of 1867 that gave the freedmen the right to vote be written into the constitution? William Blount Carter believed it would bring about the destruction of "our republican system," but more rational heads prevailed, and delegates voted 56 to 18 to write black suffrage into the constitution. The question of making the payment of a poll tax a prerequisite for voting was discussed exhaustively. Five delegates prepared a statement in which they alleged that such a measure was "an unjust discrimination against the poor man"; others who had championed the cause of Negro suffrage said it would discourage freedmen from voting. Finally, however, the provision was included with the stipulation that money received from the tax would be used to support public education.

Few changes were made in the bill of rights except to prohibit slavery and provide for Negro suffrage. The delegates, learning a lesson from the Brownlow assemblies, prohibited future legislatures from lending the credit of the state in aid of "any person, association, company, corporation, or municipality," and limited the governor's control of the militia. They also provided that legislators could not be paid for more than 75 days of a regular session and 20 days of special session. To prevent hasty action on amendments to the federal Constitution, the delegates provided that no convention or General Assembly should act on any proposed amendments unless that convention or assembly had been elected after the submission of the proposed amendment. Partly to rid the state of Radical domination of the supreme court, the convention enlarged the judicial body to five members and provided that not more than two were to reside in any one grand division of the state. The exceedingly difficult process of amending the basic law as provided in the constitution of 1835 was retained, and long-delayed reforms changed the date of state elections to November of even numbered years and gave the governor veto power.

After a session of six weeks, the delegates adjourned on February 23 and submitted their work to the people for ratification. March 26 was the date set for the referendum. In the meantime, Radicals urged that the new constitution be rejected and hastened to Washington again to ask for military intervention in Tennessee. In fear of federal interference, House Speaker W. O. Perkins, and Senate Speaker D. B. Thomas issued a joint statement to Congress in which they refuted "false and mischievous" charges that the legislature and convention had been composed entirely of "rebels," and that the two bodies had enacted laws of discriminatory nature affecting Negroes and Union men. A careful examination of the constitution itself, they wrote, would indicate that delegates had secured "equal rights and liberties for all, and discriminations against none. . . ."

On the appointed day, voters ratified the "new" constitution by a vote of 98,128 to 33,972. Although the referendum apparently was a fair expression of the public sentiment, Radicals claiming discrimination carried their case to President Ulysses S. Grant and urged that he place the state under the Reconstruction laws of 1867. The chief executive, however, refused to send troops at their behest.

Perhaps the most significant observation that may be made about the constitution of 1870 is that, despite the trauma of four years of civil war, the basic fundamental law changed very little from that which the founding fathers had promulgated in 1796. And just as important, the constitution of 1870 has served the state in substantially the same form for more than one hundred years. All efforts to amend it since 1870 were unavailing until 1953, at which time delegates to a "limited" convention made several revisions. The fact that ratification came by a three-to-one majority was indicative of the confidence people placed in the delegates.

The first gubernatorial election under the new constitution came in November 1870 and resulted in a decisive Democratic victory. The work of John C. Brown in the convention had led to the Giles Countian's nomination; Republicans had selected William Wisener of Shelbyville, a prewar Whig and house speaker who had also served in the constitutional convention of 1870. On the hustings Brown told his listeners that although he had been a Whig, neither the "Democrat" nor the "Conservative" label offended him as long as he could be instrumental in defeating the Radicals. Not only was he elected by a two-to-one majority, but his party captured 20 of the 25 senatorial seats and 60 of the 75 places in the house. Democrats were chosen to fill all of the major offices of the state, and a few jubilant legislators announced plans to gerrymander districts so that Republicans would be excluded from all congressional and legislative seats. Impatiently, they awaited Brown's inauguration, which under the new constitution would not occur until October 1871.

Harmonious relations had not been a characteristic of the Democratic party, however, and soon overconfidence led to dissension. Thomas A. R. Nelson in 1872 talked with other former Unionists about forming a third party, and Andrew Johnson, whose indomitable ambition remained undimmed by the unjustified treatment given him by Washington Radicals, caused the defeat of the party's nominee for congressman-at-large by running as an independent. National lawmakers had assigned Tennessee yet another congressional seat, and because so little time remained before the election, the Tennessee legislature decided that the new seat should be filled by an election from the state at large. It was that race which threatened Democratic harmony and defeated the party's nominee. Benjamin F. Cheatham, former Confederate general, was the party's choice against Horace Maynard, the Republican nominee. Maynard, a prewar first district congressman, had been among those Radical leaders who opposed any form of leniency to former Confederates; thus he was especially objectionable to many Democrats. Andrew Johnson, although denounced from Memphis to Bristol as a party traitor—"a harsh, violent, oppressive, cruel and ambitious" man, said Frank G. Dunnington of Columbia—nevertheless ran as an inde-

These men served as governor during the twelve years after Reconstruction. *Above left:* John C. Brown, 1871–1875; *above right:* James D. Porter, 1875–1879; *below left:* Albert S. Marks, 1879–1881; *below right:* Alvin Hawkins, 1881–1883.

pendent Democrat and divided the party vote to such an extent that Maynard was elected. Governor Brown withstood a strong thrust to unseat him by Alfred A. Freeman of Haywood County. Although a substantial Democratic majority was elected to the legislature, party regulars were amazed to find that the Johnson independents and dissident Democrats such as Arthur S. Colyar could control the General Assembly through fusion with Republicans.

Republican hopes of gaining a larger measure of control received a serious setback in 1874 when Charles Sumner introduced and passed in Congress a civil rights bill. Although the measure was soon declared unconstitutional by the Supreme Court, it was sufficient—along with the scandals of the Grant era—to assure the election of a Democratic governor again in 1874. James D. Porter of Henry County defeated Congressman Maynard, the Republican nominee, by a two-to-one majority. A prewar Whig legislator, Porter had attained the rank of lieutenant colonel under General Cheatham during the war, had been a delegate to the constitutional convention of 1870, and, at the time of his election, was judge of the twelfth judicial circuit. He was renominated two years later and again won by a substantial vote.[3] In the same year Samuel J. Tilden, a Democratic nominee for president, carried Tennessee by a substantial vote but ultimately was "counted out" when a special committee formed by Congress awarded the disputed election to Republican Rutherford B. Hayes. Hayes promptly appointed United States Senator David M. Key of Chattanooga to his cabinet as postmaster general.

The legislature that assembled in 1875 elected Andrew Johnson to the United States Senate to replace Brownlow, whose term soon would expire and who was not a candidate for reelection. The former President had returned to Greeneville in March 1869 and had begun immediately to rebuild political fences. In April 1869, he told a Knoxville audience that he would devote the rest of his life to a vindication of his public career. When Johnson spoke to Negro groups, he not infrequently reminded them that it was he, not Lincoln, who had freed the slaves in Tennessee. Before farmer and debtor groups, he denounced the rich bondholders and implied that the legislators should repudiate the public debt. He had been nominated for the United States Senate soon after his return from Wash-

---

[3] Porter's vote in 1874 was 105,061 to 55,847 for Maynard. In 1876 he polled 123,740 votes to 73,695 for Dorsey B. Thomas and 10,436 for George Maney.

ington but had been defeated. In 1872 he was mentioned as a candidate for governor, but as already noted, he ran instead for congressman-at-large. Although defeated, he proved himself still to be a formidable campaigner, and in the autumn of 1874, he launched a statewide campaign in the interest of his senatorial candidacy. Legislators convening in January 1875 were presented with nearly a dozen names for consideration but soon narrowed their choices to Johnson, John C. Brown, and General William B. Bate—even though President Grant sent word that if Johnson were elected he would consider it a "personal insult." Despite Grant's influence (whether real or imagined), Johnson won on the 55th ballot after several days of voting. He considered the victory a great personal triumph because it would enable him to return to the body that had tried his impeachment. He took his seat on March 4, 1875 and promptly denounced President Grant as a charlatan, but suffered a stroke a few weeks later and died on July 31. David M. Key was appointed to fill the vacancy until an election could be held.

Legislators elected two United States senators in 1877. Four years remained in the term to which Johnson had been elected, and James E. Bailey, a prewar Whig from Clarksville, was chosen to that position. The term of Henry Cooper, elected in 1871, also expired. Isham G. Harris was selected and remained in the Senate until his death in 1898. After the war the secession governor had lived in Mexico and England until November 1867, when the legislature repealed a $5,000 reward offered for his capture. He promptly returned to Nashville and soon vigorously reentered state politics.

Governor Porter refused a third term in 1878, and Democrats nominated Albert S. Marks of Winchester, chancellor of the fourth district. A Confederate colonel during the Civil War, he had received a wound that required amputation of his right leg below the knee. Republicans chose E. M. Wight, a Chattanooga medical doctor, and the Greenback party, which had made a national appearance in 1876, nominated R. M. Edwards of Cleveland. The question of the state debt became the major issue in the contest, and solutions were offered in the platforms of each of the three parties.[4]

For more than a decade after Democratic restoration, the dominating issue in politics was that of the state debt. As observed earlier, Tennessee had pursued a very liberal policy in promoting the de-

---

[4] Marks polled 89,958 votes to 42,284 for Wight and 14,155 for Edwards.

velopment of banks and internal improvements during the four
decades before the election of Governor Brown. Although some of
the Southern states had established state-owned railroads, Tennessee had purchased stock in railroad and turnpike companies. Before
Brownlow's election, state funds had been invested generally in
sound banks and railroad companies, which were required to make
semiannual interest payments on the state bonds and to contribute to
a sinking fund for their retirement at maturity. Tennessee first issued
bonds in 1832 in order to purchase $500,00 of stock in the Union
Bank of Tennessee. More bond issues were authorized in 1836 and
1838 to aid internal improvements and to buy stock in the state-
owned Bank of Tennessee. None of the Bank of Tennessee bonds
had been retired by the time of the Civil War, but three-fourths of
the Union Bank bonds had been paid off. Other bonds also were
issued to complete the state capitol, to purchase the Hermitage
property, and to aid the agriculture bureau in erecting buildings at
the fairgrounds. The destruction occasioned by the Civil War
weakened the railroad companies to such an extent that after 1865
many of them no longer could make payments; the state, however,
was still liable for the debt and the accruing interest. The Brownlow
policy of free spending, which involved reckless and fraudulent loans
made even to hopelessly bankrupt lines, has been discussed in an
earlier chapter. At the time of Brownlow's election, the principal of
the "state debt proper"—which included obligations for the banks,
the internal improvement companies, the capitol, and the Hermitage
property—totaled $3,894,600; the principal on the railroad debt was
$16,213,000. By the time of Brown's election, the debt exceeded
$43 million, much of which was the "railroad debt."

Republicans agreed that the debt should be repaid; if the debt
were scaled down, however, it should be done only with the consent
of the creditors. Democrats were divided on the matter. Although all
Democrats blamed Republicans for the debt and accused them of
bad judgment and fraud, the "state credit" wing—which held the
reins of party control and monopolized the offices held by their
party—favored full payment and demanded that the state's credit be
maintained. Not only was such a position morally correct, they said,
but talk of default or scaling down the debt would frighten away
Northern and foreign capital, on which Tennesseans counted to help
diversify and expand the state's economy and end its overwhelming
dependence upon agriculture. The state credit group came princi-

pally but by no means exclusively from the ranks of former Whigs. Working in harmony with ex-Confederate leaders and conservative, business-minded Democrats, they dominated the party in the early years after Reconstruction and greatly influenced party policy for sometime thereafter.

Opinions of other elements in the party varied. Some people advocated outright repudiation; they said that the Brownlow administration, which issued many of the bonds, was a revolutionary government by usurpation and did not represent the whole people. John Savage of McMinnville, for example, believed northern bondholders should share heavily in the losses because of the destruction of Southern slave property—"the earnings of Southern people for two hundred years." Others recommended negotiation with bondholders to arrive at a fair but realistic figure consistent with the state's ability to pay. The latter group came to be known as "low tax" Democrats and ultimately played a major role in the final settlement. The low taxers did not find their leaders among the wealthy and business figures of the day; instead, their spokesmen were largely farmers and small town leaders from traditional Democratic rural counties. Tied closely to the soil, they supported low property taxes and were unlikely to embrace any part of the state credit position; only a substantial increase in prices of farm products could incline them in that direction.

The debt question did not become acute until after the Panic of 1873. Brown faced serious problems but he determined to uphold the integrity of the state by retiring matured bonds and paying interest due by the issuance of new bonds. In the campaign of 1872 he condemned those who upheld "the odious doctrine of repudiation," and shortly after his inauguration in 1873 he influenced the legislature to enact a funding act that authorized the issuance of more 6 percent bonds to fund the matured debt and the past-due interest owed by the state. The new bonds were recognized by the New York Stock Exchange Commission on Securities, and soon an active and confident market developed in Tennessee securities. The national depression that began late in 1873 affected Tennessee, however, and although the interest on the old bonds was met in 1874, it could not be met in the following year without raising taxes and borrowing money. Arthur S. Colyar, prominent lawyer, industrialist, publisher and chief supporter of Andrew Johnson's efforts at political rehabilitation, led a movement within the Democratic party to scale down the debt and reduce taxes and of course was joined in this effort by Johnson. When the former president was elected to the United States Senate early in 1875, the low tax group had won a major victory, even though Governor Porter had been elected a few months earlier on a platform that called for a continuation of Brown's repayment program. In mid-summer of 1875, the state defaulted in the payment of interest due. As the effects of the Panic of 1873 continued and the prices received by farmers for major crops continued to decline, it became apparent that the funding program had failed. By the time Porter's first term had ended in 1877, the state credit faction of the Democratic party acknowledged the reality of fast-growing sentiment favoring low taxes that was occasioned by hard times, and the group talked of an "honorable compromise" with creditors at less than par. When a committee of New York bankers met with legislators in March 1877 and proposed a settlement at 60 cents on the dollar in thirty-year bonds carrying 6 percent interest, the governor called the assembly into extra session to consider it. When this failed, bankers proposed a scaling of 50 cents on the dollar, but Tennessee legislators also rejected this plan in a second extra session. Thus when Porter's term ended, nothing by way of debt settlement had been accomplished.

Albert S. Marks, unlike his two predecessors, was not a prewar Whig but had supported the Southern Democratic candidate for President in 1860. As a judge he had not been associated with either the state credit group or the low taxers, but he was conceded to be the author of the 1878 platform, which had a strong agrarian flavor marked by an endorsement of scaling down the state debt. Therefore, legislators were not surprised when he told them soon after his inauguration that a compromise settlement fair and just to all should be developed. He soon formed a legislative committee to study the question and to make recommendations. The ensuing report showed that railroad officials during Brownlow's administration had conspired to defraud the state, had failed to comply with the terms of appropriation measures, and had given a generous present to the Brownlow family in order to insure protection. This evidence strengthened the demand that the "Brownlow debt" be repudiated and caused interest in favor of repudiating the entire "railroad" debt to mount. Finally, on the eve of adjournment in March 1879, legislators provided for funding the debt at the rate of 50 cents on the dollar with bonds bearing a 4 percent rate—subject to the will of the people expressed in a referendum. After the governor's commission determined that such a settlement was acceptable to the creditors, the question was submitted to the voters. Although those in the urban counties across the state supported the plan, rural voters from Memphis to Bristol rejected it, with opposition concentrated in Middle and West Tennessee. Indeed, only four counties west of the Tennessee River endorsed it, and only seven counties of the central sector supported it. Warren County, home of the influential low taxer John H. Savage, rejected it by an 8-to-1 margin. The proposal was defeated by a vote of 76,333 to 49,722.

The Redeemer coalition was not strong enough to withstand the dissension that developed over the debt, and division occurred within the party to such an extent that Republicans elected their candidate for governor in 1880. State credit men controlled the Democratic convention in that year and nominated former congressman and Confederate colonel John V. Wright of Maury County. Dissident low taxers, dissatisfied over state credit control—and especially because of a plank in the platform calling for settlement of the debt without a popular referendum—had already left the convention and nominated S. F. Wilson of Sumner County, a former Confederate soldier who had served in both the house and senate after Reconstruction. Republicans had already chosen a former Whig and Unionist, Alvin Hawkins of Huntingdon, and viewed the campaign with considerable confidence. On election day they won by a comfortable majority and immediately set out to solve the problem of the debt.[5]

Shortly after Hawkins' nomination, the New York–based "Committee of Tennessee Bondholders," representing nearly 300 American and foreign holders of the state's securities, had proposed that the debt be funded at par with a new series of bonds carrying 3 percent interest. When the measure was passed, having squeaked through the senate by one vote, low tax leaders determined to challenge the action in court. Early in 1882, however, supreme court members by a 3-to-2 vote declared the law unconstitutional. Hawkins immediately called the legislature into extra session to reconsider the matter but was still unable to effect a settlement.

Not only were Republicans unable to solve the debt question, but

[5] Hawkins polled 103,964 votes, Wright received 78,783, and Wilson got 57,080. Greenback candidate and former Union army officer R. M. Edwards garnered 3,459.

they also failed in a strong bid to elect Horace Maynard to the United States Senate. They did, however, play a role in the election of Howell E. Jackson when they shifted support to him instead of incumbent Democrat James E. Bailey after it became apparent that Maynard could not win. A prewar Whig but a newcomer to political office, Jackson received Republican support primarily because of his known support for high taxes.

It remained for Democrats to solve the debt problem. Despite division within the party—Duncan B. Cooper and James E. Bailey bolted the Democratic convention and carried about 10 percent of the delegates with them—Isham G. Harris and other Bourbons welded the party together sufficiently to elect former Confederate general and Sumner County native William B. Bate to the governor's chair. Bate had been outspoken on the debt issue and was viewed as a logical compromise candidate. Supported by Senator Harris, Memphis Negro leader Edward Shaw, and the bulk of the Democratic party, he won by a comfortable majority.[6]

Governor Bate's principal accomplishment was the settlement of the debt issue. His platform had called for payment in full of bonds held by "educational, literary, and charitable institutions," and by Sarach Childress Polk, widow of President Polk. The remainder would be paid on a "50 and 3" basis. In March 1883, the legislature enacted a measure calling substantially for a settlement of the entire indebtedness (amounting to nearly $29 million) as Bate had proposed. More than $26 million was funded at the rate of 50 cents on the dollar with bonds bearing 3 percent interest. The Polk and institutional bonds, funded at par, as mentioned, amounted to nearly $2.8 million.

The Bate settlement was aided by the improvement in the state's economy and helped win reelection for the Sumner Countian. In 1884, Republicans nominated Judge Frank T. Reid of Nashville, who denounced the debt settlement as one in which Tennessee had shirked its responsibilities. The candidates engaged in joint debate across the state. For a while the outcome appeared in doubt, but the final count showed Bate the winner by a vote of 132,201 to 125,246. In the following years, the governor announced that more than $8 million had been funded; three decades later the state had retired the

[6] Bate received 120,637 votes and Hawkins 93,168. Joseph H. Fussell, the state credit Democrat from Columbia who was supported by the bolters, received 4,814 votes, and John R. Beasley, Greenback candidate from Franklin County, got 9,660.

remaining bonds. Settlement of the debt question helped temporarily to restore harmony to the beleaguered Democrats.

Negroes in Politics ᶜᵂ Blacks became active in Tennessee politics soon after they gained the right to vote in 1867. They worked principally within the Republican party. Leaders entered local contests across the state; more than a dozen were elected to the legislature before 1900, and one, William Yardley, ran for governor. Among those who served in elective and appointive positions on the local level were Nashville banker, lawyer, and city councilman James C. Napier; Memphis lawyer Edward Shaw, who was in and out of both the Republican and Democratic parties; Knoxville lawyer and councilman, William Yardley; and Nashville reformer and congressional candidate of 1888, William H. Young.

Sampson W. Keeble, a Nashville barber, was elected to the house of representatives in 1872 and became the first black to serve as a state lawmaker. Twelve blacks were elected during the 1880s and for the most part were men of some influence and training. Four were lawyers, and at least four had been schoolteachers. At least half had attended college, and seven had held appointive or elective positions on the local level. One had served in the North Carolina legislature before moving to Tennessee. Their constituents were primarily black, and they reflected the political and economic interests of their race. Nine were from the five West Tennessee counties in which black outnumbered whites, one represented Davidson County, where blacks composed 40 percent of the population, and the other two were from Hamilton County, where the Negro population was about 30 percent of the total (see map 8).

The four elected in 1880 assumed a strong stand against discrimination in the use of public facilities. Thomas A. Sykes of Davidson County sought to repeal a state segregation law of 1875 that consigned blacks traveling on railroad lines to second-class accommodations and gave inkeepers and operators of places of amusement the right to exclude persons from their business establishments in the same manner that the owner of a private home might. He was ably supported by the other blacks—Thomas F. Cassels and Isaac F. Norris of Shelby County, and John W. Boyd of Tipton County—and most of the white Republicans, but he suffered defeat of the measure by the narrow margin of 31 to 29. The four blacks then issued a

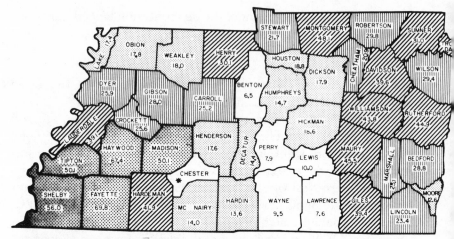

* Chester County, created in 1882, had 19.6% black
   population according to the census of 1890.

Map 8. Percentage of Blacks in Total Population of Tennessee by
Counties—1880. Source: Joseph H. Cartwright, *The Triumph of Jim Crow:
Tennessee Race Relations in the 1880s* (Knoxville: Univ. of Tennessee Press,
1976), 26–27.

protest in which they termed the act of 1875 a "violation of the spirit,
genius, and letter of our free government." "Four hundred thousand
black citizens are citizens *de jure,*" they wrote, "but are aliens *de facto*
and entitled to no rights which the railroads, hotels, and theaters are
bound to respect." Later in the session a "compromise" measure,
which the black legislators opposed, was enacted that specified separate but equal facilities on railroad cars for Negroes.

Others served later in the decade. In 1883, Boyd was joined by
Samuel A. McElwee of Haywood County, Leon Howard of Shelby
County, and David F. Rivers of Fayette County. William C. Hodge of
Hamilton County and Greene E. Evans and William A. Fields of
Shelby County were elected in 1885. Styles L. Hutchins of Hamilton
County and M. W. Gooden of Fayette County were elected in 1887,
along with McElwee, and they became the last blacks to serve until
1965, although J. M. H. Graham of Clarksville was elected in 1896
but was disqualified when house members discovered that he did not
meet the residence requirements. They sponsored anti-lynching
legislation, attempted to repeal the anti-miscegenation statute,
sought abolition of the prison lease system, argued for better schools
and educational opportunities for Negroes, and continued the work

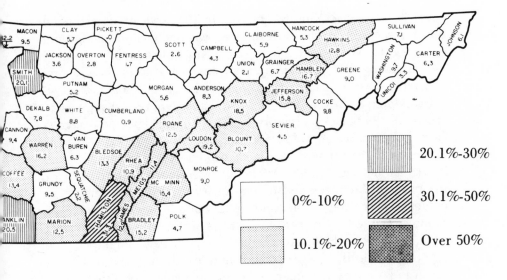

already begun for desegregation of public facilities and common carriers.

Despite the fact that black legislators were not very effective in attaining their goals, they did make their presence felt and did call to the attention of all that they were Americans entitled to the same rights as everyone else. There are probably many reasons why more blacks were not active in the legislative halls during the decades after Reconstruction. One certainly is that capable leaders were scarce. Not many possessed the charisma and native ability of McElwee, for example—a "magnetic speaker, forceful debater, and indefatigable worker" who earned degrees at Fisk University and Central Tennessee Law School in Nashville. Others, perhaps equally capable, lacked the political support, the material resources, or the political expertise necessary for a political campaign. A second reason is the absence of a substantial black population in the state, which during the two decades following Reconstruction was only about 25 perecent of the total. Still another reason is that most whites—Democrats and Republicans in the North as well as the South—simply did not want blacks to hold office. When legislators extended suffrage to Negroes in 1867, Tennessee became one of two states outside of New England to extend the franchise beyond the white male, and even in New England black officeholding was not encouraged.

A more significant matter for consideration is the change of attitude of whites toward black participation in politics between 1870 and 1890. When Keeble was elected in 1872, whites commended him for seeking office. Governor Brown invited him along with other legislators to a state dinner, and a Nashville newspaper quoted him as stating that at no time during his one term in the General Assembly was he discriminated against because of his race. Two decades later, however, white voters apparently agreed that they had seen enough of black legislators. Perhaps some had been too aggressive; at any rate the attitude among whites of "benign paternalism" as expressed in the early 1870s had changed to "overt hostility" by the late 1880s and early 1890s.[7] Whites apparently were unprepared for the push by McElwee and others for a proportionate amount of influence in the determination of policy and leadership; such bold action convinced them that the interests of the races fundamentally conflicted. Others believed that blacks in politics would impede the economy, radically change racial traditions, destroy the quality of urban and county government alike, and in general perpetuate more of the trauma that Tennesseans had experienced during the 1880s.

By the 1890s the poll tax, secret ballot, actions by partisan registrars, social and economic intimidation, violence, and corruption of the entire voting process had not only discouraged blacks from seeking office but prevented many from even voting. Tennesseans were indeed ready when the Supreme Court of the United States in 1896 affirmed segregation in *Plessy v. Ferguson.*

Industry and Agriculture ⧫ After the Civil War many pragmatic captains of industry came to regard the great struggle of 1861–1865 as simply a clash of economic systems and Appomattox as but a symbol of defeat for a decaying economic order. To them, the Old South of slavery and secession was dead, and upon its grave a New South of industry and commerce must be constructed. Weaving together the humanitarian and materialistic motives that characterized American imperialistic ventures in the Pacific at the end of the century, they sought to establish in the South an economic system comparable to that in the victorious North. They were joined by many articulate supporters of the "new South" philosophy in Tennessee and throughout the former Confederacy.

Scarcely had the noise of battle ceased in the Volunteer State when

---

[7] Cartwright, *The Triumph of Jim Crow* (Knoxville, 1976).

the urban press began a campaign for industry and "economic carpetbaggers." Arthur S. Colyar of Nashville, James E. Bailey of
Clarksville, Joseph B. Killebrew of Nashville, and others joined the
press by proclaiming the values of shifting from an economy dependent upon agriculture to one of industry. Yankees who only
recently had laid waste to the South were forgiven if they would
return with capital and industrial expertise. Indeed, editors throughout the state frequently admonished their readers against continuing
sectional animosities because such an attitude would frighten away
Northern businessmen and skilled laborers.

While capital did not flow into the state in the proportions that
some Tennesseans hoped for, fortune seekers from the North did
establish industries. Within two months after Appomattox, many
companies received charters. Among them were the Tennessee and
Kentucky Petroleum, Mining, and Manufacturing Company; the
East Tennessee Union Petroleum, Coal, Iron and Salt Company; the
Tennessee Mountain Petroleum and Mining Company; the New
York and Tennessee Petroleum and Mining Company; and the
Tennessee Mining and Manufacturing Company.

Although small towns became sites for some factories, the urban
areas—particularly Knoxville and Chattanooga—attracted most of
the industry. The Knoxville Industrial Association, organized soon
after the war, became a vigorous campaigner for industrial establishments. Although in 1868 members of the group complained
because Knoxville did not get its "fair share" of Yankee capital, by
the following year one-sixth of the business properties of Knoxville
were owned by Northern businessmen. By that date the Knoxville
Iron Company, which included a rolling mill, a foundry, a machine
shop, a nail mill, and a railroad spike machine, had been established
by a former federal military officer; other factories produced soap,
flour, paper, and a variety of products. According to a Richmond
newspaper in 1871, "no city of the South except Atlanta" had
"improved more rapidly since the war" than had Knoxville.

But Chattanooga grew even more rapidly. Although the main
street had been a "mudhole" as late as 1868, conditions soon improved. The twenty-two small industries that had employed 214
men in 1860 no longer represented a true picture of industrial
Chattanooga; by 1870 fifty-eight industrial establishments employed
nearly 2,000 workers. By that date J. T. Wilder, often described as
"the greatest of the carpetbaggers," and Colonel S. B. Lowe had

returned to Chattanooga. Wilder established the Roane Iron Company in Roane County and brought into the thriving business a defunct rolling mill in Chattanooga. In 1878 the Roane company made use of the first open hearth furnace south of the Ohio River. Colonel Lowe established the Vulcan Iron Works. Furniture factories, sawmills, gristmills, and many other types of factories had been established by 1883, but the iron works predominated. The editor of the Chattanooga *Daily Times* noted the progress with pride and wrote that

> the frozen fingers of the North have been laid in the warm palms of the South, and a healthful, invigorating temperature pervades them both as one body. They are moving in united thought—united action, placing wherever they tread some monument of their skill, industry, and patriotism, and garlanding the nation with their intelligence and virtue.

Memphians and Nashvillians of course joined in the search for industry. The Memphis Chamber of Commerce reorganized in 1865 to begin a vigorous campaign for industry. Soon such a "rush and roar of business" prompted a visitor from Kentucky to predict that the river town in a short time would surpass St. Louis as a manufacturing and commercial center. By 1870, Memphis had many business establishments and had become the largest processor of cottonseed in the Union, but then the yellow fever scourge struck and threatened to decimate half the population. The 1870s—not the 1860s—constituted the crucial decade of Memphis history; indeed, the financial structure became so depressed that the city surrendered its charter in 1879 and during the next few years had its affairs administered by the state government. By the early 1880s, however, the worst of the dread plague had past, and Memphis again moved forward commercially and industrially.

By 1869, Nashvillians could point to new liquor distilleries, sawmills, paper mills, gristmills, stove factories, and an oil refinery. A few years later the Nashville Woolen Mill Company was organized, and the cotton market in the capital was described by a Northern visitor as being "brisk." A Nashville editor in 1883 prophesied industrial greatness for the city, and urged the people to discover the "road to wealth" and happiness through "the workshop, the factory, the foundry, and the iron and coal beds."

Manufacturing plants of various sizes were constructed in other counties and towns. Immediately after the war, Julius Eckhardt Raht returned to his East Tennessee copper mines and opened offices in Cleveland. The Jackson Flouring Mills were built in Jackson in 1868, and the Jackson Woolen Manufacturing Company began operation a few years later. By 1880, one of the largest woolen mills in the state had been established at Tullahoma.

The industrial growth of the state had been comparatively rapid in the several years following Appomattox. By 1870 the value of manufactured goods for the state had increased nearly twofold over that of 1860; the number of plant units had increased from 2,500 to 5,300, and the number of industrial workers from 12,500 to 19,400. Development was arrested for a few years after the Panic of 1873 but by the end of the decade more people were employed than in 1870. Some plants had been consolidated and others had not reopened, so that only about 4,000 factories were in operation by that year; however, 22,445 people found employment in them. About one-fourth of the plants were grist and flour mills, but carriage and wagon shops flourished, as did tobacco and whiskey manufacturing establishments.

While the urban folk sought industry, the vast majority of Tennesseans quietly beat their swords into plowshares and returned to farming. It was indeed a simple life to which Tennessee farmers returned, but agriculture was to experience a revolution in the few years before the century ended. The typical farmer after the war returned to land grown up with weeds and bushes, with fences and outbuildings down or in a poor state of repair. His farming implements consisted of little more than a bull-tongue plow, a turning plow, and a shovel plow—all made by putting iron points on wooden stocks—a harrow, and the usual hand tools such as hoes, rakes, and shovels. The plows and harrows were pulled by mules or horses wearing collars woven of cornhusks and bridles and plow lines of cotton or leather fashioned at home. But during the thirty years following Reconstruction, a variety of new labor-saving implements came into use. A Bolivar newspaper reported in 1871 that cotton planters, with which one man could do the work of four, were coming into use on several of the larger West Tennessee farms. Primitive cotton pickers—hand-powered tools resembling vacuum cleaners—were being tried experimentally but had generally been found unsatisfactory. Reapers, already in use on large farms, were supplemented by binders and combines in the 1880s. Seed cleaners, corn shellers, new-fangled harrows (one was patented as the "Clod

Crusher"), and improved plows came into use on many Tennessee farms after Reconstruction.

Production increased rapidly, the number of farms multiplied, but farm prices fell, which meant that despite increased production, the value of farm products was actually less than in 1865 (see table 5). Tobacco doubled, from 21,456,452, pounds in 1870 to 49,175,550 in 1900. During the same time wheat production increased from 6 million bushels to nearly 12 million, and corn from 41 million bushels to more than 67 million. Cotton fluctuated. The number of bales in 1870, little more than 180 thousand, increased to more than 330 thousand in 1880, but dipped in 1900 to 235 thousand. But the value of all farm produce marketed declined to $55 million in 1890 from $86.5 million in 1870.

The Southern obsession with cotton, strongly criticized by New South exponents, reestablished itself quickly after the war, particularly in West Tennessee. Farmers in Shelby and Tipton counties, who collectively produced less than 35,000 bales in 1860, doubled production in 1880. Lauderdale also doubled production, and Dyer increased ninefold. Even in the northern counties, farmers successfully grew cotton. In twenty years Carroll County tripled production to more than 10,000 bales, and Henry's crop of 5,516 bales in 1880 was 25 times that produced in 1860.

State leaders gave attention to agriculture after Reconstruction and in 1871 formed the Bureau of Agriculture. Reorganizing the agency four years later into the Bureau of Agriculture, Statistics, and Mines, legislators empowered the employees to prepare soil maps and compile statistics on soil, climate, rural population, prices of land, and mineral resources. Joseph B. Killebrew, secretary of the agency, made an exhaustive study of agriculture in the early 1870s and found Tennessee farms and farmers to be in what he termed "fairly good condition." Memphis, he said, was a thriving cotton center and experienced in 1870 the greatest volume of sales in ten years. Although cotton sold for about twelve cents per pound—down from $1.90 in 1864—West Tennesseans, Killebrew wrote, were by no means discouraged. Middle Tennesseans produced a variety of crops, including cotton, corn, tobacco, potatoes, and peanuts, and East Tennesseans also produced grain and vegetable crops, fruits, and livestock.

In many conferences and addresses over the state, Killebrew urged farmers to adopt "the New South principles" of scientific

Table 5.
MARKET PRICES OF MAJOR CROPS GROWN IN TENNESSEE, 1870–1900

Crop	1870	1872	1874	1876	1878	1880	1882	1884	1886	1888	1890	1892	1894	1896	1898	1900
					Cents per pound											
Cotton	12.10	16.50	13.00	9.71	8.16	8.10	8.50	8.10	7.20	7.90	8.00	8.90	6.60	5.50	6.10	6.70
Tobacco	9.70	10.70	13.70	7.30	5.80	9.83	9.12	9.19	8.06	8.50	8.59	8.39	4.59	6.66	5.73	9.15
					Dollars per bushel											
Corn	.521	.383	.641	.361	.313	.340	.481	.349	.357	.331	.496	.393	.451	.214	.285	.350
Wheat	1.042	1.239	.948	1.036	.772	.952	.888	.645	.687	.927	.837	.624	.489	.721	.579	.621
Oats	.426	.322	.520	.349	.240	.349	.371	.272	.289	.270	.417	.315	.320	.183	.251	.253

Source: United States Bureau of the Census, *Historical Statistics of the United States, Colonial Times to 1957: A Statistical Abstract* (Washington: Government Printing Office, 1960), 297, 298, 302.

farming. This, the secretary said, should consist of at least the following: breakdown of larger farm units into smaller ones that the individual white farmer could work for himself; diversification of crops—more stock, hay, grains, fruits, and vegetables and less tobacco and cotton; enrichment of the soil through crop rotation, cover crops, and commercial fertilizers; and the attraction of immigrants who would purchase unoccupied lands. All of these principles worked to a certain degree. The number of farms had increased from 82,368 in 1860 to 172,412 in 1900. During the same time the size of the average farm had changed from 250 acres to 91 acres. Farmers by the end of the century were raising more different kinds of crops, but cotton and tobacco continued to be the chief money crops. Improved methods of soil fertilization were used, but as noted below, few immigrants came into Tennessee.

Immigration ?❧ In an effort to bring in immigrants from the North and from Europe, officials in 1867 commissioned Hermann Bokum, an East Tennessee Unionist, to compose a "handbook" advertising the economic potentialities of the state. European farmers and laborers, Bokum wrote, had constituted the backbone of the world's economic advancement, and he urged them to come to Tennessee—an area of virgin timber and minerals, cheap land and fertile soil, and peace-loving, hard-working people. Democrats who came into power in 1870 agreed with the Radicals on the immigration question and continued efforts to entice people from northern states and from Europe. Governor Porter, for example, in 1877 told an audience in Philadelphia that Tennessee had "mountains of iron and coal, with no one to work them." He urged the "dissatisifed sons of Pennsylvania" not to go West "but South."

Although people came from Prussia, France, England, Scotland, Ireland, and other European countries, their number was small. Equally few were the immigrants from Pennsylvania and other Northern states. Indeed the number of foreign-born in Tennessee in 1900 (17,746) was smaller than the number in 1860 (21,226) and thus was less than 2 per cent of the total population throughout the period.

By the mid–1880s Tennesseans had recovered from the trauma of war about as well as any state in the former Confederacy, and economic progress helped erase the heartaches and bitter memories.

The four urban areas were showing signs of becoming strong industrial centers.

SUGGESTED READINGS

Books

David Abshire, *The South Rejects a Prophet: The Life of Senator David M. Key, 1824–1900* (New York, 1967); Thomas B. Alexander, *Political Reconstruction in Tennessee* (Nashville, 1950) Joseph H. Cartwright, *The Triumph of Jim Crow: Tennessee Race Relations in the 1880s* (Knoxville, 1976); Roger L. Hart, *Redeemers, Bourbons, and Populists: Tennessee, 1870–1896* (Baton Rouge, 1975); Robert B. Jones, *Tennessee at the Crossroads: The State Debt Controversy, 1870–1883* (Knoxville, 1977); Mingo Scott, *The Negro in Tennessee Politics and Governmental Affairs, 1865–1965* (Nashville, 1964); James E. Thorogood, *A Financial History of Tennessee Since 1870 (Sewanee, 1949).*

Articles

Constantine G. Belissary, "Tennessee and Immigration, 1865–1880," *THQ* 7 (Sept. 1948), 229–48; Belissary, "The Rise of Industry and the Industrial Spirit in Tennessee, 1865–1885," *JSH* 19 (May 1953), 193–215; Joseph H. Cartwright, "Black Legislators in Tennessee in the 1880s: A Case Study in Black Political Leadership," *THQ* 32 (Fall 1973), 265–84; John H. Ellis, "Disease and the Destiny of a City: The 1878 Yellow Fever Epidemic in Memphis," *WTHSP* (1974), 75–89; Folmsbee, "The Origin of the First 'Jim Crow'Law," *JSH* 15 (May 1949), 235–47; William B. Hesseltine, "Tennessee's Invitation to Carpet-Baggers," *ETHSP* 4 (1932), 102–15; Sarah M. Howell, "The Editorials of Arthur S. Colyar, Nashville Prophet of the New South," *THQ* 27 (Fall 1968), 262–76; Timothy C. Jacobsen, "Joseph Buckner Killerbrew: Agrarianism in the New South," *THQ* 33 (Summer 1974), 157–74; Robert B. Jones, "Tennessee Gubernatorial Election: 1880—The Collapse of the Democratic Party," *THQ* 33 (Spring 1974), 49–61; J. Morgan Lousser, "Post-Reconstruction Suffrage Restrictions in Tennessee," *PSQ* 88 (Dec. 1973), 655–83; Gordon B. McKinney, "The Rise of the Houk Machine in East Tennessee," *ETHSP* 45 (1973), 61–77; Verton M. Queener, "A Decade of East Tennessee Republicanism, 1867–1876," *ETHSP* 14 (1942), 59–85; Queener, "The East Tennessee Republicans as a Minority Party, 1870–1896," *ETHSP* 15 (1943), 49–73; Samuel Boyd Smith, "Joseph Buckner Killebrew and the New South Movement in Tennessee," *ETHSP* 37 (1965), 5–22; Frank B. Williams, "The Poll Tax as a Suffrage Requirement in the South, 1870–1901," *JSH* 18 (Nov. 1952), 469–96.

20.

ఢ A Troubled Decade, 1886–1896

E VEN after the debt question was settled, factional politics continued unabated within the Democratic party. Several factions were evident, but as in the Jackson era, shifting realignments prevented polarization along lines proposed by any one of them. Motivation for alignment apparently was not only economic, social, and ideological, but also "status-anxiety" oriented, as described by Professor Roger L. Hart.[1] Bourbons, mentioned earlier, were conservative politicians of the "Old South" orientation who gained control in Tennessee largely through the influence of former governor Isham G. Harris, who was elected to the United States Senate in 1877. Although they lost control of the governor's office in 1886, they remained the strongest faction in the state for some time thereafter. In strong competition with the Bourbons was the New South group. Although relatively small in number, they exerted an influence disproportionate to their size because of the enormity of their resources, their enlightened leadership, and their success in bargaining with Republican leaders for mutually satisfactory legislation and patronage. During much of the time they looked for leadership to Colonel Arthur S. Colyar, a Nashville industrialist, lawyer, newspaper publisher, and politician who had organized a company that became the Tennessee Coal, Iron, and Railroad Company. A. J. Keller, Memphis newspaper editor, and Joseph Killebrew, Nashville agricultural and educational leader, were also prominent figures in the New South group. Not to be discounted was the small-farmer elements—sometimes called "wool-hat

[1] Hart *Redeemers, Bourbons and Populists: Tennessee, 1870–1896* (Baton Rouge, 1975).

boys"—who looked first to Andrew Johnson for leadership and later
to John P. Buchanan, who was elected governor in 1890.

The largest minority party was the Republican (see map 9) who,
thanks to the factionalism within the Democratic party, competed
with some degree of effectiveness during the period. Republicans
were also factionalized, largely with respect to a distribution of the
federal patronage, but they could usually patch up their differences
on election day. The enfranchisement of blacks increased the
number of Republican voters, and both blacks and whites usually
looked to Leonidas C. Houk of Knoxville and H. Clay Evans of
Chattanooga for leadership.

Other organized groups—Greenback, Prohibition, and Farmers'
Alliance—had influence in both Democratic and Republican ranks.
In 1890 the agricultural wing of the Democratic party, in league with
alliance men, elected the governor and controlled the legislature.
The entry of alliance men into the Republican party was far less
serious and at no time threatened to break that party's hold on the
eastern section of the state.

The "War of the Roses"—the Election of 1886 ॐ Lack of harmony
within the party, together with the rising threat from Republicans,
led Democrats urgently to seek a candidate in 1886 who could
inspire a degree of unity within the party. As the Bate administration
continued in power, the lack of harmony among followers of Harris
and Colyar became more pronounced, and the growing apathy of the
rural Democrats alarmed party leaders. "Our party needs reorganization," Robert Love Taylor from Happy Valley in Carter County
told Nashville Democrats early in January of 1886. "We have
been . . . discordant, belligerent, and . . . rent with feuds which
threatened to destroy the party," he said. To Taylor and other party
leaders, a factional truce appeared necessary if the political lifeblood
was to continue to flow in Democratic veins. Fortunately, state and
national issues were not of sufficient consequence to cause dissension within the party; if they became ominous, party leaders were
determined to compromise or postpone them in the interest of party
harmony. The selection of a candidate resulted in compromise.
Young men desired more recognition within the party, and rural
voters, perhaps inspired by the developing agrarian movements in
the South and West, could be awakened from their lethargy if a

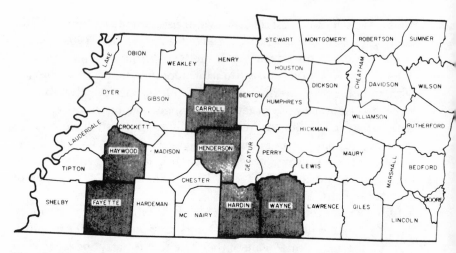

Map 9. Tennessee Counties (Shaded) with Republican Majorities in More Than 50 Percent of the Presidential and Gubernatorial Elections, 1880–1890. Source: Joseph H. Cartwright, *The Triumph of Jim Crow: Tennessee Race Relations in the 1880s* (Knoxville: Univ. of Tennessee Press, 1976), 64–65.

suitable candidate were nominated. The most satisfactory candidate, therefore, would be one who could satisfy the demands of the younger generation of Democrats, please the rural voters, appeal to Democrats in East Tennessee, and conciliate the industrial and Bourbon wings of the party.

Thirty-six-year-old Robert Love Taylor, an East Tennessean who captured the imagination of the young Democrats and the rural element, won the nomination on the 15th ballot. A man of conciliatory manners who could arouse the enthusiasm of the common people, Taylor understood well that his role as head of the state's majority party would be to unite the party factions. Even during the balloting, when the convention seemed deadlocked at one point, he had advised friends that he did "not want the nomination at the cost of [party] bitterness." His nomination presaged a decline of the influence of the Bourbons and launched the young East Tennessean upon a political career that would continue for nearly three decades.

Interestingly, the Republicans had nominated Taylor's brother, Alfred A. Taylor, seven weeks before the Democratic convention. A man of considerable ability but lacking his brother's personal magnetism, Alf was apparently selected to forestall the nomination of

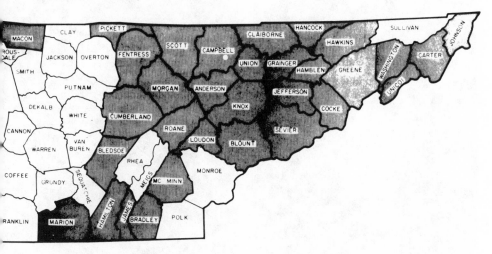

Bob, who Republicans feared might become the Democratic standard-bearer. Thus, the nomination of the brothers launched the "War of the Roses," a contest that attracted a greater degree of enthusiasm among voters than any other gubernatorial race until that time.

The Taylors were not newcomers to the political scene, and their forebears had been leaders in the civil and political affairs of East Tennessee for many years. Their father, Princeton-educated Nathaniel Greene Taylor, had served two terms in Congress, was an ordained Methodist minister, and considered himself "a farmer, minister, lawyer, politician, and civic leader." Their maternal uncle, Landon C. Haynes, was a prominent East Tennessee lawyer and politician for years and in 1861 was elected to the Confederate senate from Tennessee. Alf had served in the legislature and in 1878 was considered the popular choice for the Republican nomination for first district congressman, but a seasoned politician named Augustus Pettibone managed to win the nomination under conditions and by methods that many people believed questionable. The cry of fraud caused Alf's younger brother, Bob, to enter the race, and, although a Democrat, he managed to win the seat. The district was heavily Republican, and Bob soon lost his seat to Pettibone, who within two years had apparently managed to clear his name, but Bob's victory was sufficient to capture the attention of Democrats across the state. He soon established a newspaper in Johnson City, yet his heart lay in politics. In 1881 he sought without success James E. Bailey's seat in

The governors of the 1880s and 1890s—like those of the 1870s—were not outstanding, but they did play a role in helping the state to adjust to postwar conditions. *Above left:* William B. Bate, 1883–1887; *above right:* Robert Love Taylor, 1887–1891, 1897–1899; *below left:* John P. Buchanan, 1891–1893; *below right:* Peter Turney, 1893–1897.

the United States Senate and, in the following year, the Democratic nomination for governor. In 1884 he was chosen as Democratic presidential elector; his strong stand and hard work for Grover Cleveland won him an appointment as pension agent, and in 1885 he removed to Knoxville to assume the duties of that office.

Tennesseans have always been infatuated with a colorful political campaign; in 1886 they were not to be disappointed. The two brothers—already accustomed to the speakers' platform—arranged for forty-one joint debates across the state. Bob and Alf—both masters of the "fiddle" as well as satire and rural humor—stumped the state in a campaign that attracted nationwide attention. In the same spirit that Whigs and Democrats had chosen symbols in the campaign of 1844, Democrats and Republicans of 1886 chose the white rose of York and the red rose of Lancaster as their respective emblems. On many occasions the brothers traveled, slept, and ate together, but on the platform each defended his party with vigor. Both amused the crowds, but listeners generally agreed that Bob's "unpruned" rhetoric and droll anecdotes, his fiddle, and his charming manners outshone the attributes of Alf.

Enormous crowds of people thronged around the heroes on the hustings—3,000 met Bob at the outskirts of Murfreesboro and escorted him to his hotel, 8,000 listeners attended the hustings at Franklin, and 1,000 mounted men met the train on the outskirts of Columbia and escorted the two candidates into town.[2]

Issues were pushed into the background, and neither candidate advanced profound arguments and discussions on either national or state issues of the day. But the brothers did provide a "happy interlude" at a time when party and factional strife and racial and sectional bitterness still clouded the memories of many people. Bob Taylor's popularity with the rural masses enabled him to defeat his Republican brother by a majority of more than sixteen thousand votes. While the victory was by no means a landslide, the margin was more

---

[2] Many stories amused the audiences. On one occasion, Bob found Alf's speech (some people claimed that their father, Nathaniel, wrote the addresses for both sons) and committed it to memory. When the brothers met on the platform on the following day, Bob, speaking first, delivered Alf's speech. The embarrassed and chagrined Alf was left speechless.

Many stories centered around "fiddle" playing. Still told in Happy Valley is Bob's tale of a paroled convict who returned unexpectedly to his mountain home after a two-year stay in the penitentiary to find his wife tending her three-months-old baby. The parolee said nothing but merely took from beneath his coat a fiddle on which he played the mountain ballad, "Who's Been Here Since I've Been Gone?"

than twice that of Bate in 1884 and attested to Taylor's ability to win support.

Bob Taylor received the Democratic nomination again in 1888, but only on the fortieth ballot, after overcoming the determined opposition of the formidable Bourbon coalition. In the general election he defeated Republican contender Samuel W. Hawkins and Prohibition candidate J. C. Johnson.[3] Taylor's stand on the Blair bill, a measure that would provide federal aid to education, proved to be the major issue in the contest. Although Senator Howell E. Jackson and several members of the House from Tennessee supported the bill, most Tennesseans joined with other Southerners in the fear that federal aid would result in federally controlled schools. Therefore, when Taylor expressed approbation of the measure, a storm of protest arose. Students at Cumberland University burned him in effigy, and editors across the state decried his alleged apostasy to "Southern Democracy."

The work of Prohibition leaders reached its climax with a popular referendum shortly after Taylor's first inauguration. A variety of anti-liquor organizations had formed, including the Women's Christian Temperance Union, the Sons of Temperance, the Tennessee Order of Good Templars, and the Tennessee Temperance Alliance. These groups and their supporters were able to persuade legislators to submit the temperance question to the people.

On voting day communities across the state assumed a festive air, and "wets" and "drys" staged campaigns not unlike that of the Taylors a year earlier. The outcome of the referendum left no doubt as to how voters stood. The final count showed 135,197 against Prohibition and 117,504 for it. Although Prohibition leaders were able to keep the question from becoming a party issue, an examination of the vote county by county indicates that a preponderance of those counties that normally voted Republican supported and those normally Democratic were opposed. East Tennessee, where the movement was strongest, voted about 42,000 to 31,000 for it, but it was the Democratic voters of Middle and West Tennessee who defeated it. The vote in the central counties was about 71,000 to 41,000 against the amendment and about 43,000 to 35,000 against it in the western counties.

The defeat did not dampen the hopes of temperance leaders, and it

---

[3] The vote was 156,799 for Taylor, 139,041 for Hawkins, and 6,893 for Johnson.

FRANK LESLIE'S ILLUSTRATED NEWSPAPER

No. 1,619.—Vol. LXIII.] NEW YORK—FOR THE WEEK ENDING OCTOBER 2, 1886. [Price, 10 Cents.

ALFRED A. TAYLOR.   ROBERT L. TAYLOR.

NOVEL POLITICAL CAMPAIGN IN TENNESSEE—THE RIVAL CANDIDATES, "ALF" TAYLOR AND "BOB" TAYLOR, FIDDLING FOR VOTES.

FROM A SKETCH BY GEORGE SCHLEGEL.—SEE PAGE 105.

The "War of the Roses" in 1886 between Bob and Alf Taylor drew national attention to their "fiddle playing" and their oratory.

led to the formation of the Prohibition party. It also added impetus to
the feminist movement, as leaders sought to impress the temperance
people with the allegation that the measure would have passed
comfortably had women voted. Finally, it brought a flurry of bills
before the legislature that were designed to curb the flow of intoxicants and helped cause prohibition to become a major political issue
early in the twentieth century..

The administrations of Bob Taylor are remembered not for profound and far-reaching legislation but for the degree of stability that
Taylor gave to his party and for the several laws that modified rules of
suffrage. This legislation sought to preserve the purity of the ballot
box, promote honest elections, and raise revenue for schools. The
Dortch Law specified that in the more populous counties and cities
voters should mark printed ballots in secrecy unless they were blind
or otherwise physically disabled. A second measure, sometimes
referred to as the Myer's Registration Law, provided for registration
of voters in cities, towns, and civil districts having a voting population
of 500 or more. A third, the Lea Election Law, was designed to avoid
federal interference in state elections. It provided for separate ballot
boxes and for election officials in contests for state and federal
offices. A fourth law, enacted in a special session held early in 1890,
confirmed the payment of a poll tax as a prerequisite for voting, as
required by the constitution of 1870.

Taylor did not disappear from the political scene after the expira-
tion of his second term. A decade later—in 1896—he won another
term as governor and then served in the United States Senate.
Although he had defeated the Bourbon coalition and was able to win
office by his charismatic style, he was not strong enough to replace
the Bourbons with a faction of his own.

The Farmer's Movement ஜ~ After the Civil War, each year
brought rising agricultural costs and falling agricultural prices. Vigorous leaders soon organized the farmers and complained that
among businessmen there existed a conspiracy to discriminate
against tillers of the soil. Although Tennessee with its diversified
agriculture and relatively small Negro population differed somewhat
from the deep South and West, the effects of the agrarian movement
were felt strongly in the state.

The first farm organization of importance was formed soon after the war by Oliver Hudson Kelley of Washington, D.C. An employee of the Department of Agriculture, Kelley called the new organization the "Patrons of Husbandry," but soon it became known simply as the "Grange." "Its grand object is not only general improvement in husbandry," Kelley announced, "but to increase the general happiness, wealth, and prosperity of the country." Soon it spread to the South and West, so that by the early 1870s more than 1,000 chapters were located in Tennessee. Although in 1875 the nearly 20,000 members made Tennessee the third largest Grange state in the South, membership declined rapidly so that it became insignificant in the early 1880s.

Still, other organizations followed closely on the heels of the Grange, including the Greenback group, the Wheel, and the Farmers' Alliance. In contrast to the Grange, the Greenback movement was political in nature and advocated inflation of the currency through the issuance of paper money. Leaders nominated a candidate for each gubernatorial election from 1874 to 1884 (except in 1876) but did not muster sufficient strength to affect materially the outcome of the contests. The National Agricultural Wheel appeared in the state in 1884, and three years later the Farmers' Alliance was established. Both groups grew rapidly, especially in the central and western counties. In December 1888, the national organizations of the Wheel and Southern Alliance united under the name of "Farmers' and Laborers' Union of America." In July 1889, members of the two groups in Tennessee met in Nashville and united under the name of "Farmers' Alliance." The new organization consisted primarily of farmers but also included others closely associated with farmers, such as rural mechanics, teachers, physicians, ministers, and editors of agricultural papers. In 1890 Alliance leaders claimed a membership of more than 100,000 and openly sought to capture working control of the Democratic party; their voting strength, however, probably was less than one-half the number claimed.

In view of the organization's strength and purpose, it was only natural that the leaders should look with increasing interest to the election of 1890. John P. Buchanan of Rutherford County was the first president of the Tennessee Alliance, and in 1889 he became president of the combined Wheel and Alliance. The real power, however, lay with John H. McDowell of Obion County, who was a vice president of the southern branch of the Alliance and editor of a Nashville publication called *The Weekly Toiler*, the principal mouthpiece of the Alliance leaders. Before Democrats assembled in convention on July 15, 1890, McDowell had announced that he would not rest until Buchanan was nominated as the Democratic candidate for governor.

Three parties chose candidates. Among the Democrats, the Bourbon wing supported Josiah Patterson of Memphis, and the Colyar faction pushed forward Nashville businessman and railroad organizer Jere Baxter. When McDowell and rural groups mentioned Buchanan as a candidate, the urban press refused to take them seriously and made all manner of fun of Buchanan—his candidacy was "highly hilarious" to one of them. It was only after delegations from county after county lined up behind Buchanan that city editors conceded that he was not the buffoon they had earlier represented him to be. Finally, after six days of wrangling and twenty-six ballots, Democrats chose the Rutherford Countian as their standard-bearer. In his acceptance speech, he assured all that he would maintain the "great principles of Democracy as enunciated by Jackson, Polk, and Johnson." Republicans chose Lewis T. Baxter, a Nashville banker and businessman, and Prohibitionists nominated David Cato Kelley, a Methodist minister who had had a varied career.

Although he was not vigorously supported by the Bourbons, Buchanan won the election by a substantial majority. His rural supporters—the "hayseeds," as their urban opponents called them—would also control the legislature. In his inaugural address, Buchanan pointed to the spirit of Andrew Jackson, which "stalks abroad and lives in the hearts of the people," and promised his hearers that he, like the Old Hero, would champion the cause of the people against the "trusts" and all else.

The farmer-dominated General Assembly under Buchanan surprised critics by avoiding the extremes advocated by Western agrarians and generally illustrated the conservatism of the Tennessee Farmer's Alliance. Several significant laws were enacted. One provided for closer regulation of the sale of commercial fertilizers and another awarded pensions to totally disabled Confederate veterans. Other laws made more effective the poll tax requirement for voting passed during the Taylor administration, made trusts and other combinations in restraint of trade and production unlawful, restricted foreign corporations that did business in the state, classified Public Schools into Primary and Secondary, and enriched the curricula of both divisions by appropriating additional funds.

Buchanan, however, did not possess the personal magnetism of his predecessor and was unable to win nomination in 1892. While the Harris and Colyar factions found nothing to complain about in regard to the administration in general, they never fully accepted Buchanan, and they always regarded McDowell with suspicion. The governor's inability to settle the coal miners' insurrections in East Tennessee (which will be discussed later) and his use of state troops in an attempt to handle the situation angered many voters. Other people complained that Buchanan gave lucrative state jobs to Alliance men rather than to old-line Democrats. Especially galling was the fact that McDowell accepted a coveted state position but continued as editor of *The Toiler*. The formation of the new People's (or Populist) party, however, became the wedge that Democrats used to separate Buchanan from his party. National leaders of the new group sought to pull enough votes away from Democrats and Republicans to create a party of sufficient strength to capture the presidential nomination. The thought of leaving the party of the solid South was highly repugnant to old-line Democrats. Although Buchanan asserted that the formation of a third party of agrarians meant "the ruin of the South," none could deny that the movement had a strong appeal to many of the rural leaders, including McDowell. When the governor refused to break with McDowell, leading Democrats shifted their support to Peter Turney, chief justice of the supreme court. Turney's political star rose rapidly. Buchanan, realizing that he could not win the nomination, withdrew from the contest before the Democratic convention was held and left the field to Turney.

Three candidates in addition to Turney made the race. Governor Buchanan still had a respectable following among rural Democrats, and in August he was "drafted" by Alliance men, Populists, and "Buchanan Democrats," and ran as an independent. Republicans chose George W. Winstead of Dresden, and Prohibitionists named Edward H. East. The shadow of McDowell continued to fall across Buchanan's path. The governor was denounced as a tool of the agrarian leader, an advocate of racial integration, and a destroyer of the Democratic party. Even more damaging to his bid for reelection was the report of an alleged "deal" engineered by McDowell between Populists and Republicans. Buchanan's candidacy, according to the allegation, would take votes from Turney and insure a Republican victory; McDowell would receive $15,000 in cash and Republican support for the United States Senate. Buchanan's vehement denial did not convince the many who detested McDowell. Reports of the "deal," together with other rumors of Populist-Republican coalitions and the repercussions of the "Coal Miners' War" caused many erstwhile Buchanan supporters to break with the governor and hold to the party line. Consequently, Turney was elected although he received less than half of the votes cast, and the Bourbons were returned to power. The agrarian movement in Tennessee had reached its height during the Buchanan administration and showed that while the Alliance could win other Democratic factions when they were divided, it could not do so when the Democrats were united. Although Populist candidates entered 64 of the 99 house races, they won only 5. In the senate they gained only one seat, as jubilant Democrats took control of both legislative houses.

Peter Turney had enjoyed a distinguished career. The son of Senator Hopkins L. Turney, he had been prominent in politics before the war. In 1861 he had urged Tennesseans to secede and had formed a company of volunteers from his native county of Franklin. He served with distinction during the war and actively opposed Brownlow's reconstruction measures after his return to civilian life. Appointed to the supreme court in 1870, Turney became chief justice in 1886 and performed ably until he exchanged the bench for the governor's chair. He followed a conservative course that was in general satisfactory to party leaders and in 1894 was nominated for a second term because of that course and because of the threat of Republican and Populist fusion.

The Disputed Election of 1894 🍃 The gubernatorial contest of 1894 ended in a dispute and shook the Democratic party to its foundations. It got underway late in August after Republicans chose an able Chattanooga industrialist, H. Clay Evans, for the nomination. In addition to managing his extensive business interests in East Tennessee, the Pennsylvania-born industrialist had served four terms as alderman of Chattanooga, two terms as mayor, and one term as congressman. His support of the Lodge Federal Elections Bill ("Force Bill") while he was in Congress cost him reelection in 1890 and 1892 and weakened his appeal in the gubernatorial race of 1894, as the Democratic press taunted him with such epithets as "Force Bill Evans." Democratic leaders recognized him as one of the most formidable opponents Republicans could offer. Populists nominated

A. L. Mims, a Davidson County schoolteacher. Prohibitionists failed to choose a candidate, but they adopted a platform in harmony with that of the Populists.

Turney opened his campaign at Murfreesboro on September 13, despite a recurring illness. The sixty-seven-year-old governor spoke briefly before lunch and resumed his position on the platform after an hour of rest and refreshments. Within a few minutes he became exhausted, however, and was forced to call upon his brother to read the remainder of his speech. Democratic leaders now realized that Turney was too feeble to make the active and energetic campaign necessary for election; therefore, Edward Ward Carmack, vigorous editor of the Memphis *Commercial Appeal*, carried the governor's campaign from Memphis to Bristol. Turney's only other oratorical effort was an address in Chattanooga on Labor Day.

Evans, young and vigorous, opened his campaign at Huntington on September 5. From that time to his final address at Ashland City on November 5, the industrialist-politician eloquently talked his way across the state. He severely indicted President Cleveland for the manner in which he had handled the gold crisis and accused Turney of not knowing how to run the affairs of state "on business principles." The most serious charges Evans had to face were those alleging that he was a carpetbagger and that he had voted while a member of Congress for the "Force Bill," which would establish federal jurisdiction over congressional and presidential elections. In September, state Republican leaders announced that Governor William McKinley of Ohio, former Speaker of the House Thomas R. ("Czar") Reed of Maine, and other prominent party members would speak in Tennessee in the interest of Evans's candidacy. Only McKinley came; he delivered an address in Chattanooga on October 20. When the campaign closed at the Cheatham County seat on November 5, Republican chances for victory appeared the best in more than a decade.

Soon after the returns were tabulated but before they could be announced, Republicans and Democrats agreed that the election was very close. Turney had lost support in the urban-industrial areas of Nashville and Memphis; even in some rural counties he had not polled as many votes as Democrats had expected. Not until December 13, five weeks after the election, did the secretary of state make the returns public. The official count, which showed a small majority for Evans, gave the resurgent Republicans 105,104 votes, Turney

104,356, and Mims, 23,088. Republicans claimed the victory, but Democratic partisans contended that East Tennessee officials had permitted people to vote without poll tax receipts and that other examples of fraud could be proved in some of the counties where Evans had polled a majority. Two weeks later Turney issued notice that he would contest the election.

The legislature, dominated by Democrats, assembled on January 5 and promptly selected a "Committee on the Governor's Election" consisting of seven Democrats and five Republicans. After hearing allegations of fraud from both Turney's and Evans's attorneys, the committee in April filed both a majority and minority report. The former, signed by the seven Democrats, declared that many violations of the poll tax law had taken place in counties that Evans carried and declared that when the fraudulent votes were taken from the returns the official count should give Turney the victory by a majority of 2,000 votes. In the minority report the five Republicans questioned the authority of the committee, declared that the seven Democrats showed partiality from the beginning, and alleged that the majority did not seek to develop the whole truth. The contest, they believed, was as fair as any ever held in Tennessee, and they argued that the returns as originally reported should stand. On May 4, the members of the joint assembly voted 70 to 57 to accept the majority report. Consequently, Governor Turney took the oath of office for a second term on May 8.

Although Evans lost the governorship, he emerged as a hero and a martyr to Republican leaders. He enjoyed a movement to secure him the vice presidential nomination, and when convention leaders assembled his nomination seemed probable. Marcus Alonzo Hanna preferred another however; Evans therefore ran second to the choice of the Republican bosses. Evans nevertheless continued to be active in politics. He became commissioner of pensions under McKinley and consul general in London under Theodore Roosevelt.

Turney's victory—"counted in" as he was—was won at the expense of Democratic party harmony. The industrial wing had never warmed to the old neo-Confederate and had opposed the contest from the beginning, and Arthur S. Colyar had served as one of Evans's attorneys during the investigation. Among the 57 who opposed the acceptance of the majority report were 9 Democrats and 10 Populists. Many Democratic newspapers termed the action a "steal" second only to the Tilden-Hayes presidential election of 1876, and

Turney therefore began his second term without the support of a large segment of his party. His enemies soon had fresh ammunition for renewing their attacks. Increased state expenditures, the "Paste Pot" affair (in which Turney's enemies alleged that two of Turney's friends received $3,000 for pasting a few coupons on canceled bonds), failure to appropriate necessary funds for the Tennessee Centennial Exposition, expenses involved in calling the legislature into two extra sessions, and failure to assess railroad property at its true value brought increased dissension within the Democratic ranks and made evident to all that Turney's administration would pass unwept, unhonored, and unsung.

Convict Leasing and Prison Reform 〰 The system of convict leasing, so prevalent and profitable in the South after the Civil War, was abolished in Tennessee during the Turney administration. In comparison with other Southern states, Tennessee had made considerable improvement in penal reform during the ante bellum period, but the war disrupted economic progress and left the state with an enormous debt. The penitentiary, used during the war as a military prison, was in a dilapidated condition, and the enormous increase in prison population after the war added to the problems. Freed Negroes, hungry, confused, and ignorant of the white man's rules, and equally hungry and displaced whites, soon ran afoul of the law and were incarcerated. Negroes, who before the war seldom composed more than 5 percent of the prison population, made up more than half of the inmates by 1866.

State prison operations throughout the United States were still in their infancy and were emerging from an experimental stage. The prevailing belief among authorities was that the prisoners should defray their expenses by hard labor. Tennessee authorities before the war had used penitentiary inmates for a variety of tasks, such as work on the state capitol. Several states, including Kentucky, Missouri, Alabama, Indiana, and Illinois, had experimented with leasing and had discovered that from a businessman's point of view the system had many advantages. Felons were leased to individuals and companies who exploited them, and the state was thus relieved of the maintenance costs.

Because the economy had reached its nadir, Tennessee—and indeed the South in general—was ripe for a convict lease system. The treasury was empty, the prison population increased daily, and expenses involved in operating the penitentiary mounted. Moreover, businessmen from the Northeast who had settled in the state accentuated concepts of an independent capitalist society where labor was exploited and large gains were reaped by the investor. These ideas, combined with the concepts of a slave economy and mounting racial tensions caused by the war and reconstruction, made Tennessee a fertile field for the lease system. When several proposals to alleviate the prison conditions—including one to erect two additional penal institutions—failed because of the expense involved, legislators turned to leasing in the belief that it would pay prison costs and might even bring profits.

The first convicts were leased in July 1866 to a Nashville furniture concern. The firm built workshops on the penitentiary grounds and agreed to clothe and feed the prisoners and pay the state 43 cents per day per person. State officials rejoiced:

> Now every convict, old or young, skilled or unpracticed, clumsy, indolent, or vicious, is at once turned over, at forty-three cents per day; and it is the lessee's business to provide work profitable or otherwise, without regard to the character, condition or competency of the laborer. Possibly the convict may have been a good field hand, . . . but within the walls of the prison, no such employment is to be had and the laborer may be said to be both green and raw. Hence to instruct and to put mechanical tools into the hands of a novice, and pay forty cents per day, besides, is compensation greater than at first appears.

The prisoners, however, were not in sympathy with the arrangements. Some protested loudly and others refused to work. Finally, in June 1867, they burned the workshops. The contract was canceled in July 1869.

State officials promptly sought new lessees. Articulate industrialists such as Arthur S. Colyar had urged for several years that convicts could be used effectively in coal mines. Legislators were in agreement and accordingly established branch penitentiaries at the Tracy City and Battle Creek mines and leased the entire prison population to a Memphis firm having extensive mining interests in the eastern section of the state. In 1884, when the contract expired, a new agreement was made with the Tennessee Coal, Iron, and Railroad Company, which had mining interests in Tennessee and wanted to use the prisoners in the coal fields.

In the meantime, opposition to the lease system developed. Scores of miners, some of whom had been lured into Tennessee by promises of high wages, lost their jobs and protested vigorously against the use of convict labor in the mines. An organization known as the Mechanics and Manufacturers Association of Tennessee alleged that the leasing system was unfair to labor and that the living conditions of the "honest mechanics" were damaged by the "suicidal" system. Dr. John Berrien Lindsley and other humanitarians condemned the state for permitting the reformatory purposes of the penitentiary to become subservient to the desire for material gain, and leaders of the press charged that lessees mistreated prisoners, fed them inadequately, and created living conditions that were "hells on earth where men are made devils of. . . ." The warden and other prison officials, however, argued that conditions were no worse than those found in other states and pointed to the financial returns that the system brought to the state.

Officials of the Tennessee Coal, Iron, and Railroad Company signed a five-year lease in 1884 and agreed to pay the state $101,000 per year. The contract was renewed from time to time and ultimately expired on December 31,1895. Since the company had extensive coal and iron mines in East Tennessee, most of the convicts worked there. Others were subleased to other companies.

Criticisms of prison conditions brought legislative investigations. When the General Assembly convened in January 1885, the editor of the Chattanooga *Times* published a "shocking story" about prison conditions. A convict recently discharged had told of being forced to mine coal "in water a foot deep" and of being whipped with a lash of 13-ply sole leather braid. Prisoners who complained about the rough prison fare, much of which was unpalatable, received only kicks and the lash well laid on. Others confirmed the *Times* story. A legislative committee appointed to investigate the charges filed two reports. The majority found living conditions to be adequate and affirmed that the food was equal in quality to that "used by some of the best families of Nashville." The minority alleged that an objective investigation could not be conducted because prison officials, anticipating the visit of legislators, would not permit the committee to see conditions as they actually were. Additional investigations were made in 1887 and 1889. As before, the committees filed two reports. The minority in 1889 termed the whole system "a horror and shame upon the state," but the majority pointed to the profits that the system brought the state. Officials in the following year pointed to a net profit of $771,400, which was only $176,000 short of the entire cost of penal institutions since their beginning in 1829.

Despite the favorable majority reports from legislative committees, and regardless of the profits realized from the system, labor and manufacturing groups across the state joined a large segment of newspaper editors, ministers, lawyers, health officials, and public-spirited citizens to advocate elimination of leasing. They recommended the adoption of a central prison having manufacturing and agricultural facilities at which convicts might work. Agitation on the part of these groups, combined with a series of labor disturbances in East Tennessee, eventually led to the abolition of the lease system.

By 1891, free coal miners could maintain only a bare subsistence living, although the mining industry had grown to a respectable size in Tennessee and owners reaped sizable profits. Miners had objected to the use of convict labor for two decades; especially obnoxious to them was the use of felons as strikebreakers, but they could point to many other grievances. Some miners were paid in "scrip" (which required them to spend their wages at the company store or else have their scrip discounted in other stores), were forced to sign "iron-clad" contracts pledging confidence in company officials, and forbidden to engage in strikes. The inflamed miners for years had viewed the use of convict labor as a practice that would strip them of their small livelihood. Therefore, the East Tennessee mining communities were like tinderboxes; a spark might set off a conflagration.

Violence first ensued in July 1891 at Briceville (in Anderson County). Three hundred armed miners entered the stockade and forced convicts, officers, and guards to march to Coal Creek (now called Lake City) and there to entrain for Knoxville. A few days later Governor Buchanan, accompanied by a battalion of state militiamen, journeyed to Briceville. He heard the complaints of the miners, pleaded with them to observe the law, and then returned to Nashville, leaving the convicts and the militia at the mines. A few days later, 2,000 miners forced the convicts and soldiers to return to Knoxville. Governor Buchanan again journeyed eastward to hear complaints and ordered fourteen companies of militia to mobilize at Knoxville. After several days of negotiation, the governor and the miners agreed that the militia would be removed from the scene, that the convicts and guards would return to the mines, and that the miners would repose "confidence in the governor and general assembly."

The situation was far from settled. The governor called the legislature into special session shortly after his return to Nashville to consider a repeal of the lease law, but the measure was defeated in the house by a 2-to-1 margin. Miners then sought relief in the courts. Failing there, they again resorted to violence. On the night of October 31, 1891, several hundred miners surrounded the Briceville stockade, released the prisoners, burned the stockade and other buildings, and fled into the hills. Two nights later the miners liberated 200 convicts at Oliver Springs, in Roane County, and set fire to the buildings. Most of the convicts were apprehended and returned to the penitentiary in Nashville. In August 1892, outbreaks occurred at the Tracy City and Inman mines on the southern plateau. Buchanan pursued a vacillating course, but he did offer rewards for the apprehension and conviction of the leaders and sought to shift the blame to the legislature and the lessees. Some miners were arrested, but few were convicted.

The four gubernatorial candidates of 1892—Turney, Buchanan, Winstead, and East—pledged immediate abolition of the lease system. During the campaign, Colonel Colyar stated that the hiring of convicts as strikebreakers was no longer profitable, and Nathaniel Baxter, vice president of the Tennessee Coal, Iron, and Railroad Company, asserted that anti-leasing agitation and the Anderson, Roane, and Grundy trouble had "demoralized convicts" and rendered many of them no longer acceptable to industrialists.

Legislators of 1893 quickly found a substitute for the lease system. They provided for a new penitentiary to be "managed and conducted upon just, humane, and civilized principles" and to be large enough to house 1,500 convicts, and required the state to buy "not more than ten thousand . . . acres" of coal lands on which prisoners would work so that they would not compete with free miners. Consequently, state officials purchased 9,000 acres of coal lands in Morgan County, where they established the Brushy Mountain Prison, and for the penitentiary grounds they bought the Mark Cockrill farm, a 1,128-acre tract located approximately six miles west of Nashville on the south bank of the Cumberland River. Work on the prison—modern in every respect—began immediately. When completed in 1898, the prison had cost more than $800,000 and consisted of an administration building, two wings of 400 cells each, a hospital, and separate quarters for women. By the end of the century, the state had developed, through trial and error, a prison system comparable to some of the best in the country.

Humanitarians also severely criticized lack of separate facilities for juvenile offenders. The Reverend Collins D. Elliott, for example, in 1881 pointed with shame to more than 400 prisoners twenty-one years of age or under, and he urged legislators to establish a separate reformatory. Numerous religious and humanitarian groups petitioned the General Assembly to implement Elliott's suggestions, and Judge John C. Ferriss of Nashville canvassed the state in an effort to arouse public sentiment.

When it appeared that the state would do nothing, Colonel Edmund W. Cole provided money for the establishment of a reformatory for both youthful offenders and "abandoned children." The state accepted the gift and established the Tennessee Industrial School in 1887.

The period of 1886–1896 was a troubled decade in the state's development, but the "gold Democrats" of 1896 were to offer some hope to a troubled Democratic party. Although the state debt had been settled, difficulties still prevailed between the low taxers and the state credit group. Agrarian leaders were not to accept their demise lightly. Republicans were to take heart with the election of McKinley in 1896, and some erstwhile Democrats and also independents such as Nashville *Banner* publisher E. B. Stahlman were to give support to that party. The Taylor brothers' campaign of 1886 offered a "happy interlude" to troubled voters, and the abolition of the prison leasing system and the erection of a new penitentiary were solid achievements.

SUGGESTED READINGS

Books

Joseph Cartwright, *The Triumph of Jim Crow: Tennessee Race Relations in the 1880s* (Knoxville, 1976); Roger L. Hart, *Redeemers, Bourbons & Populists* (Baton Rouge, 1975); Paul E. Isaac, *Prohibition and Politics: Turbulent Decades in Tennessee, 1885–1920* (Knoxville, 1965); Daniel M. Robison, *Bob Taylor and the Agrarian Revolt in Tennessee* (Chapel Hill, 1935).

Articles

Lane L. Boutwell, "The Oratory of Robert Love Taylor," *THQ* 9 (March 1950), 10–45; Jesse C. Crowe, "Origin and Development of Tennessee's Prison Problem," *THQ* 15 (June 1956), 111–35; Pete Daniel, "The Tennessee Convict War," *THQ* 34 (Fall 1975), 273–92; Gerald H. Gaither, "The Negro Alliance Movement in Tennessee, 1888–1891," *WTHSP* 27 (1973), 50–62; Sarah M. Howell, "The Editorials of Arthur S. Colyar, Nashville Prophet of the South," *THQ* 27 (Fall 1968), 262–76; A. C. Hutson, Jr., "The Coal Miners' Insurrections of 1891 in Anderson County, Tennessee," *ETHSP* 7 (1935), 103–21; Hutson, "The Overthrow of the Convict Lease System in Tennessee," *ETHSP* 8 (1936), 82–103; J. Eugene Lewis, "The Tennessee Gubernatorial Campaign and Election of 1894," *THQ* 13 (June, Sept., Dec. 1954), 99–126, 224–43, 301–28; Gordon B. McKinney, "The Rise of the Houk Machine in East Tennessee," *ETHSP* 45 (1973), 61–77; McKinney, "Farewell to the Bloody Shirt: The Decline of the Houk Machine," *ETHSP* 46 (1974), 94–107; Verton M. Queener, "East Tennessee Republicans as a Minority Party, 1870–1896," *ETHSP* 15 (1943), 49–73; Queener, "The East Tennessee Republicans in State and Nation, 1870–1900," *THQ* 2 (June 1943), 99–128; Daniel M. Robison, "The Political Background of Tennessee's War of the Roses," *ETHSP* 5 (1933), 125–41; Robison, "Tennessee Politics and the Agrarian Revolt in Tennessee, 1886–1896," *MVHR* 20 (Dec. 1933), 365–80; J. A. Sharp, "The Entrance of the Farmers' Alliance into Tennessee Politics," *ETHSP* 9 (1937), 77–92; Sharp, "The Farmers' Alliance and the People's Party in Tennessee," *ETHSP* 10 (1938), 91–113; Robert L. Taylor, Jr., "Apprenticeship in the First District: Bob and Alf Taylor's Early Congressional Races," *THQ* 28 (Spring 1969), 24–41.

21.

A low ebb in tastes, refinement, and moral turpitude was reached in America in the several decades after the Civil War. The extremes of the Reconstruction era, the treatment accorded President Johnson by the Radical Congress, the graft and corruption of the Grant era, and the increased emphasis upon materialism generally left their marks upon American civilization. For better or worse, a new order of society was conceived, based upon liquid capital and centralization; conformity, not individualism, was the ultimate result. It was an era of millionaires. Captains of industry—some lacking in refinement and cultural background and having little regard for legal sanctions—plied their wares and reaped enormous profits; as these men conspicuously spent their wealth, millions of less fortunate Americans viewed their machinations with envy and disgust. The materialistic philosophy, admittedly more apparent in the lusty and confident North and East, also had its exponents and practitioners in Tennessee and the South.

The three decades following Reconstruction were years of reform movements—and Tennesseans had their share—perhaps because people were anxious to flee from guilty consciences or, on the other hand, perhaps because they sincerely desired to reap better things for themselves and their children. Although during the four decades after the war only one state registered less religious growth (as evidenced by church membership) than Tennessee did, still Tennesseans did enjoy increased emphasis upon education. For the first time in the history of the state a workable public school system was put into operation, and institutions of higher learning—financed largely by Northern industrialist-philanthropists—flourished. The century closed with the state's greatest display of fact and fancy—the Centennial Exposition of 1897.

Public Schools and Colleges ⧉ The Civil War disrupted the work of private schools, and soon after his election Governor Brownlow asked legislators to establish a public school system so that "thousands of children" would not "pass the school age hopelessly illiterate." Not until 1867, however, did the legislature comply. The law as finally enacted provided for centralized control; the new system would be headed by a state superintendent of the common schools, under whom county superintendents would work, and increased taxes would support the program. John Eaton, Jr., a New Hampshire–born minister of the gospel who had served as an army chaplain, a Freedman's Bureau official, and a newspaper editor in Memphis, was named state superintendent. A man of considerable energy, Eaton visited many counties of the state to determine school needs. In 1869 he prepared a comprehensive survey of educational needs and published it under the title, *The First Report of the Superintendent of Public Instruction of the State of Tennessee*. In the survey he called for increased appropriations to provide better school buildings, outhouses, and playgrounds, urged that normal schools for teachers be provided, and demanded that equal opportunities be given Negro pupils and teachers.

Within a few months after Eaton's report was published, the Radicals were swept from power. Iconoclastic Democrats, anxious to destroy the last vestige of Reconstruction and Brownlowism, tossed aside both the good and the evil including the educational program. They abolished the office of state superintendent and made the counties responsible for establishing schools. No provision was included for educating Negroes, but the Freedmen's Bureau schools remained in operation.

Public-spirited citizens continued, however, to espouse the need for a sound public school system, and soon the legislature was flooded with petitions requesting that changes be made. Both blacks and whites joined in the clamor. The State Convention of Colored Men, meeting in Nashville in 1871, petitioned Congress to establish a national system of schools. In the following year, Governor John C.

Brown called legislators into special session and recommended that they establish a constructive educational system, but his efforts were in vain. The lawmakers did, however, order several thousand copies printed of a comprehensive study of state educational needs, prepared by Joseph B. Killebrew, who in 1872 was assistant superintendent of public instruction. This report became the foundation for the educational law of 1873 and the present system of public education. Killebrew, like Eaton, emphasized pragmatic rather than cultural values of learning; he stressed the economic opportunities that stemmed from education. Men who had been trained to make a living would be less inclined to commit crime, he said, therefore, fewer prisoners would have to be maintained at state expense. Killebrew deplored the increasing illiteracy present in the state. Although during the 1860s the population had declined, illiteracy had increased 50 percent. A full-time state superintendent was mandatory, he said; adequate legislative appropriations were absolutely necessary. The failure of legislators to act in 1872 only brought additional petitions and condemnation upon state authorities.

When the General Assembly convened in 1873, Governor Brown told legislators that the high illiteracy rate caused Tennessee to rank "third in ignorance" among the states of the Union—a condition he described as "a disgrace to our people." Legislators then passed the school law of 1873, with broad provisions. A state superintendent of public instruction was to be appointed by the governor,[1] and county superintendents—"men of literary and scientific attainments"— were to be elected biennially by the county courts. Three school directors in each civil district would also be chosen by the county courts and would assist the county superintendent. A permanent school fund of $2,512,000[2] was reestablished, and 6 percent paid semiannually on the amount was to be used for the support of schools, in addition to the emoluments received from a poll tax and a property tax. County courts were authorized to levy additional taxes where local needs demanded them.

The decade following the enactment of the public school law was a difficult one for school officials. The state debt seemed to defy settlement, and the Panic of 1873 crippled the entire economy.

[1] Governor Brown appointed a young legislator from Knox County, John M. Fleming, who had edited the *Tennessee School Journal.*
[2] The school fund was a legal fiction—the amount existed on paper only, but the interest on it was paid regularly.

County superintendents outlined tales of woe. The state superintendent reported in 1875 that 60,000 fewer pupils were enrolled than in the previous year. By 1880 slow recovery was being made, but still the state superintendent wrote of "disaster and apprehensions of impoverishment. . . ."

Some of the financial handicaps were overcome by money provided by the Peabody Fund, established during the Reconstruction era by George Peabody, a Northern railroad executive and philanthropist. By 1870, Tennessee schools had received $17,000, and four years later they were receiving twice that amount annually. The Peabody Fund became one of the best administered and one of the most beneficial of all the philanthropic ventures by Northern businessmen after the war.

Several other school laws were enacted during the next two decades. A state board of education was established in 1875. In 1889 women became eligible for the office of county superintendent. Two years later the legislature made provision for secondary schools as well as primary schools; until that time secondary education had been largely a function of academies and private schools. In the same year the state superintendent was named an ex officio member of the state board of education, where his influence and knowledge could be used more effectively. In 1895 the board was authorized to specify standards and qualifications for county superintendents; to those who qualified, the board issued certificates that were to be filed with the chairman of the county courts. Two years later a more efficient accounting system was installed by requiring county trustees to make quarterly settlements with the county courts. In 1899 the "Uniform Textbook Law" established a state commission with responsibility for adopting a series of textbooks that could be used in all public schools.

"Teachers' institutes" did much to remedy the problem of poorly trained and incompetent teachers—a problem about which both county and state superintendents complained frequently. The institutes were begun in the 1870s but did not become popular until the following decade. They often continued from one to four weeks and were conducted by a college professor or a visiting school official. Not only did the participants discuss methodology, but they also studied spelling, grammar, geography, history, and other subjects. In 1884, State Superintendent Thomas H. Paine, confident that institutes would provide "marked improvement . . . in every grade throughout the state, planned at least one session for each senatorial district. In 1888 institutes were held in 90 counties and were attended by more than 4,000 teachers.

Perhaps as significant as the establishment of public schools were the formation and operation of more than a dozen new colleges and universities. The old University of Nashville, which had maintained outstanding schools of liberal arts and medicine before the war, took the lead in training teachers through the use of money provided by the Peabody Fund. "The Peabody State Normal School of the University of Nashville" was established in December 1875. University authorities, recognizing the need for teacher training in Tennessee and the South, soon closed the doors of the medical school and other departments and concentrated entirely upon preparing teachers. In 1878 the name was changed to "State Normal College" and a few years later to "Peabody Normal College." In 1881 the state legislature appropriated $10,000 per year for school maintenance and by 1895 had doubled its annual appropriation. Not until shortly after the turn of the century did school officials change the name to "George Peabody College for Teachers." The institution operated until 1979, at which time it was merged with Vanderbilt University.

Vanderbilt was chartered in 1873, and soon became one of the foremost institutions of the South. The financial generosity of Cornelius Vanderbilt and the untiring efforts of leaders in the Southern Methodist Episcopal Church, particularly Bishop Holland N. McTyeire and Landon C. Garland, were responsible for the institution. Garland became the first chancellor. In 1875 the university began full operation, with departments of law, medicine, religion, and arts and sciences. Despite some difficulties—including unfavorable publicity associated with the dismissal of Professor Alexander Winchell, whose ideas of evolution were diametrically opposed to those of the conservative Methodist board of trustees—the new university made solid progress. The selection in 1893 of Chancellor James Hampton Kirkland, a thirty-year-old professor of Latin, meant continued advancement and emphasis upon sound scholarship and able teaching. At the turn of the century, Nashvillians hailed the institution as "the pride of Nashville and of the whole South." Academic, theological, pharmaceutical, and engineering departments were maintained on the main campus; law, dental, and medical departments were operated in other parts of town.

The University of Tennessee may be traced to Blount College, founded in 1794, which became East Tennessee College and then East Tennessee University, receiving its present name in 1879. With the passage of the Morrill Act in 1862, Congress granted considerable land to the states, the proceeds from which were to be used for the development of agricultural and mechanical colleges. Tennessee, in the Confederacy at the time, could not avail itself of federal aid until 1869, two years after a special act had been passed. The legislature promptly established an agricultural and mechanical college as a part of the university and transferred to it the proceeds of the endowment resulting from the Morrill Act. By 1879, when the name was changed, four courses of study described as "agricultural, mechanical, classical, and scientific" were offered. Dr. Charles W. Dabney became president in 1887, and his sixteen years of service represented a period of solid growth for the university. In 1890 the school of law opened with a two-year curriculum, and three years later the university was opened to women.

The origin of the University of Tennessee at Chattanooga may be traced to Chattanooga University, a school organized by the Freedman's Aid Society of the Methodist Episcopal Church. After several years of acrimonious debate, the institution was consolidated with East Tennessee Wesleyan University at Athens under the name of U. S. Grant University. Dissatisfaction continued, and in the early 1890s a division was effected whereby the college of liberal arts was moved to Athens and the professional schools of medicine, law, and theology remained at Chattanooga. Not until after the turn of the century was the liberal arts school returned to Chattanooga, the name "University of Chattanooga" adopted, and control taken from the Methodist church and placed in the hands of a private board of trustees. In 1969 the university merged with the University of Tennessee.

The University of the South, at Sewanee, was established in 1857, but unable to begin operation until after the war, it soon emerged as one of the state's outstanding liberal arts colleges. The school was reopened in 1866 at Winchester but in the following year was moved back to the "Mountain," a few miles east of the Franklin County seat. It was reopened largely through the efforts of Bishop Charles T. Quintard and the philanthropy of his brothers, George and Edward. In 1868 only nine students were enrolled, but by 1870 the institution had 125. Enrollment fell slightly during the next two decades, but by 1890 it numbered several hundred, and three permanent buildings had been erected. The school also had one of the best libraries in the state.

Other colleges—Cumberland, Maryville, Southwestern, Lincoln Memorial, Tusculum, Bethel, Carson-Newman, Union, Lambuth, Nashville Bible School (David Lipscomb), and others too numerous to name—also made contributions within their own particular spheres of operation.

Several colleges for Negroes were established during the period. One of the best known, "Fisk School," was founded in Nashville in 1866 through the joint efforts of the American Missionary Association and the Western Freedmen's Aid Commission of Cincinnati. In 1867 the name was changed to Fisk University. George L. White soon organized the "Fisk Jubilee Singers," a group of students who toured the country and much of Europe and earned for the school more than $150,000. When members of the legislature heard the Negro chorus in 1879, they described the performance as "remarkable" and commended university officials for the progress in Negro education. By 1900 the buildings and grounds were valued at $350,000. Schools of arts and sciences, religion, and teacher training had graduated 433 students. Other institutions for Negroes established soon after the war included Nashville Normal and Theological Institute (later Roger Williams University), founded by Baptist leaders in 1866; Central Tennessee College, Nashville, chartered in 1866 by the Methodist Episcopal Church; Knoxville College, founded in 1875 by the United Presbyterian Church; Lane College, Jackson, established in 1882 by the Methodist Episcopal Church; and LeMoyne Normal and Commercial School, Memphis, founded in 1871 from funds supplied by F. Julius LeMoyne and the American Missionary Society of the Congregational Church.

By the turn of the century, Tennesseans could point to considerable educational progress since the basic law of 1873 was enacted. In the public schools the enrollment had more than doubled. The average length of terms now was nearly five months, as compared with a three-and-one-half month term in 1874. The number of schools had increased from 4,588 to 7,963, the number of institutes had increased sixfold, and the estimated value of school plant and equipment had increased threefold. Teachers, however, received a raise of only thirteen cents per month during the quarter-century; during the quadrennium of 1874–1878, the average monthly salary of teachers was $30.74, and twenty-five years later the figure was $30.87.

Religious Development ᨠ᜵ During the four decades that followed the Civil War, only one state registered a smaller increase in church membership than Tennessee. Northern bayonets ended the Southern bid for political independence and reunited the country politically, but they did not allay the sectional strife within the churches.

Methodists had divided sectionally in 1845 and were not reunited until 1939. Strife was bitter between the Northern and Southern wings of the church, especially in East Tennessee, during the several decades following Federal occupation of that section in 1863. "Parson" Brownlow followed the victorious Northern armies into the eastern section and urged members of the Southern church to join the "loyal" group. When many refused, the preacher-politician clandestinely urged returning Federal soldiers to attempt to intimidate ministers of the Southern church. The result was that some preachers were beaten, and many were not permitted to hold services. The Southern group retaliated. They charged that the Northern church was composed of radical politicians, abolitionists, and "grand thieves and rascals," all of whom sought "Negro equality." Members of the Ku Klux Klan took a hand and ordered all "carpet bag" preachers from the state. Despite the schism and bitterness, Methodist leaders added members and retained state leadership. Shortly after the turn of the century, nearly 200,000 persons were communicants of the Methodist Episcopal Church, South. The Northern Methodist Episcopal Church, the Methodist Protestant Church, the Wesleyan Methodist Connection, the Free Methodist Church, and the Methodist Episcopal Church of North America claimed another 50,000.

Baptists also made gains. Like the Methodists, they had divided sectionally before the war. About 1900, the Southern Baptist Convention claimed 160,000 members and was second only to the Methodists. Other groups, including the Primitive Baptists, the Free Will Baptists, the Northern Baptist Convention, the Regular Baptists, the General Baptists, the Duck River and Kindred Association of Baptists (sometimes called the Baptist Church of Christ), and the Two-Seed-in-the-Spirit Baptists claimed 22,000 members.

At the beginning of the war, the Presbyterian church divided into northern and southern branches, and the latter adopted the name "Presbyterian Church in the Confederate States of America." After the war, Southerners accepted the name "Presbyterian Church in the United States," as distinguished from the Northern group, which continued to employ the name "Presbyterian Church in the United States of America." The strongest of the Presbyterian bodies in Tennessee was the Cumberland Presbyterian Church, which had seceded from the main Presbyterian branch in 1810. By the turn of the century, Presbyterians of all kinds in the state numbered 75,000, including the United Presbyterian Church of North America and the Associated Reform Synod of the South in addition to the churches named above. The Cumberland group composed about one-half of that number.

The Church of Christ, the conservative wing of the Disciples of Christ, grew rapidly until by the end of the century it rivaled the dominant Methodist, Baptists, and Presbyterians. Before the Civil War, factions had developed among the Disciples; their main points of disagreement were the use of instrumental music in the churches, support of organized missions, and centralization. Nashville became a center of the Church of Christ movement. There, David Lipscomb, a gifted writer and spirited preacher, edited the *Gospel Advocate,* a conservative periodical with a wide circulation. Through this publication, Lipscomb and others of like persuasion drew the lines more closely. Various points of disagreement were developed but basically the quarrel narrowed down to instrumental music and "organizations" or "societies." Instrumental music and organized choirs were believed to discourage congregational participation; one writer referred to the organ as "an instrument of Satan." Missionary and Sunday school organizations were not scripturally approved; Christians should not make such a "departure from New Testament Christianity" by becoming affiliated with the movements. Efforts to bind the churches into into one centralized group met with Lipscomb's condemnation. "Decrees of Associations, Conferences, Synods, . . . and Romish councils" were unscriptural; therefore, any "meeting" that attempted to make recommendations to the churches for a centralized organization was "an improper assumption of power and authority" for which Lipscomb found "no authority in the Bible." At the turn of the century, the majority of the membership of the Church of Christ centered in Tennessee, with 41,411 members in the Volunteer State—more than three times that of Kentucky and Alabama. Of the eight adjacent states—Arkansas, Missouri, Virginia, North Carolina, Kentucky, Georgia, Alabama, and Mississippi—the total membership of all combined did not exceed that of Tennessee.

Many other groups of various sizes were also present in the state. Among them were the Protestant Episcopal, Lutheran, Catholic, Disciples or Christian, Church of God, and Church of the Nazarene. The last two were formed near the end of the nineteenth century.

Separate Negro churches were established soon after the Civil War. The vast majority of the freedmen became Methodists or Baptists. Before the war the Methodist Episcopal Church, South, claimed a black membership of more than 200,000. After the war the majority of them became members of the African Methodist Episcopal Church, which was founded before 1845, and which in 1906 had the largest Negro membership in the state. The Colored (later Christian), Methodist Episcopal Church, organized in Jackson in 1870, and the African Methodist Episcopal Zion Church also had sizable followings. Several Baptist congregations were formed even before the war. In Nashville the First Baptist Church, Colored, was established even before 1850. The Beale Street Baptist Church, Memphis, was one of the largest Negro groups formed after 1865. By the turn of the century several divisions in the Beale congregation had occurred, but the parent group still consisted of several thousand members. By 1906 the National Baptist Convention claimed 759 Negro congregations in Tennessee, and the Primitive Baptists and others claimed Negro churches and missions. Several other denominations, smaller in size, had Negro members. The Colored Cumberland Presbyterian Church was organized at Murfreesboro in 1869, and by 1906 seventy-nine Colored Cumberland Presbyterian congregations had been established in the state. Other denominations sponsoring Negro churches included: Presbyterian Church in the United States, United Presbyterian Church, Associated Reformed Synod of the South, Churches of Christ, Disciples of Christ, Church of the Living God, Seventh Day Adventist, Adventist Christian, and Roman Catholic.

Feminists, Prohibitionists, and Social Experimenters 🙚 Although American leaders of the women's suffrage movement did not attain rights at the ballot box until 1920, when the Tennessee legislature ratified the Nineteenth Amendment, many outstanding women had actively sought equal rights for over a century. During the first half of the nineteenth century, feminist activity was confined almost entirely to the Northern states. Not until after the Civil War was it introduced into the more conservative South.

The women's rights movement in Tennessee probably had its beginning in August 1876, when Mrs. Napoleon Cromwell of Mississippi addressed the Democratic gubernatorial convention in Nashville. "Woman is as free by nature as man," Mrs. Cromwell told the Tennesseans, who received her with both laughter and applause. Developing an issue with which she could reach every Democrat in the convention, she deplored the fact that Negro men could vote but that the mothers, sisters, wives, and daughters of the men assembled could not. She thus urged the unity of the white race by enfranchising women. Even the racial issue could not break the barrier, however, and her request that Democrats endorse woman suffrage met with only laughter and scorn from those present.

Mrs. Cromwell's appearance was apparently an isolated incident, and more than a decade elapsed before Tennesseans manifested much interest in women's rights. In 1885 Mrs. Elizabeth Lyle Saxon was appointed by leaders of the National Woman Suffrage Association as state president for Tennessee, but she moved from the state in 1886 before any steps were taken to organize a state chapter. Two years later Memphians organized a women's suffrage league with forty-five members. Mrs. Lide A. Meriwether, who for the next two decades was the state's leading suffragette, was elected president. Other groups were soon formed in Nashville, Maryville, and elsewhere, but leaders met with little encouragement. Although Mrs. Meriwether toured much of the state during the summer of 1895, she could claim in December of that year only five organizations with a total membership of 128. She had secured endorsements of her goals by 535 women, however, and had sponsored the appearances in Memphis of Susan B. Anthony and Carrie Chapman Catt, two of the country's leading feminists.

The century closed with a flurry of activity on the part of a few determined leaders. Mrs. Meriwether staged a state suffrage convention in Nashville in May 1897, where delegates heard leaders from Kentucky, Alabama, and elsewhere. During the convention, Mrs. Meriwether organized a group called the Tennessee Equal Rights

Association. Five months later the National Council of Women of the United States met in Nashville and heard Susan B. Anthony pledge that she "would not rest until a woman's name stood for as much as a man's name [and] until a woman's opinion was worth as much as a man's. . . ." In 1900, delegates of the Tennessee Equal Rights Association convened in Memphis. There they heard Carrie Chapman Catt denounce all who supported the concept of inequality of rights for men and women.

Customs of long standing are not easily overturned, and, as was to be expected, the feminists met with considerable opposition. Some of the most caustic critics were newspaper editors, women, and ministers. The editor of the Nashville *American,* for example, in 1887 described feminist agitation as a movement "which purposes . . . a radical and fundmental change in the theory and policy of government." Editors were quick to publish statements by women who contended that "woman's place was in the home." Ministers frequently urged women to remain in their "place" if they did not wish to violate the will of God. Mrs. Meriwether usually countered their arguments—especially those of "disloyal" women—with spirited replies. Mrs. Bettie M. Donelson of Nashville wrote in retrospect that "it required a woman of strong purpose and heart to be counted as a suffragist and brave the caricatures from the artists' pencils, and the malicious and undeserved reproach from the pens of editors and literary critics." Despite discouragement, feminists at the threshold of the twentieth century could point to some solid achievements during the preceding two decades and looked with confidence to the future.

For several decades before the Civil War, Tennesseans had joined temperance leaders in other states in seeking the passage of laws that would prohibit or curtail the manufacture, sale, and consumption of intoxicating beverages. The movement subsided during the war but was revived in the first decade after Reconstruction. A variety of temperance organizations, stage productions (the most popular of which was "Ten Nights in a Bar Room"), and editorial comment kept the issue before the public.

A significant piece of legislation known as the "Four Mile Law" was enacted in 1877 and, while modified from time to time, became the ultimate lever by which "King Alcohol" was removed from the state. The law simply forbade retail liquor sales within four miles of any chartered school outside an incorporated town. At first the law had only limited application, but later local community leaders who wanted to abolish their saloons simply surrendered their municipal status and obtained chartered schools. In 1887 the first of a series of amendments was added, this one applying the law to all schools whether incorporated or not.

Temperance forces, with leaders of the Protestant churches in the forefront, accelerated their agitation during the final decade of the twentieth century. Efforts to extend the Four Mile Law to the entire state failed in each biennium from 1889 through 1897, but in 1899, although local option was rejected, the provisions of the Four Mile Law were extended to towns of 2,000 or less provided they incorporated after the law was passed. Towns in this population category could, therefore, if they so desired, surrender their charters, reincorporate, and thereby become dry automatically. This, the beginning of the extension of the Four Mile Law that brought prohibition to all cities ten years later, was hailed by leaders as a great step forward toward their ultimate goal.

Although the Prohibition party was organized nationally soon after the Civil War, it was not established in Tennessee until 1883. Five years later, The Tennessee Temperance Alliance joined forces with the party. The Prohibitionists abandoned their earlier nonpartisan position, bitterly attacked Governor Bob Taylor and Senator Isham G. Harris as friends of the liquor interests, and nominated a candidate (J. C. Johnson) for governor in 1888. Although Johnson received only about 7,000 votes out of more than 300,000 cast, Prohibitionists felt encouraged and promptly made plans for 1890. The Reverend David Cato Kelley, pastor of a Methodist church in Gallatin, became the party's candidate in that year. Kelley entered vigorously into the race and received nearly twice as many votes as Johnson had in 1888, and under his leadership the Prohibition party attained the peak of its strength. During the remainder of the decade, the party nominated candidates for governor (except in 1894), but none received more than token support.

Although not attaining their ultimate goal during the nineteenth century, temperance advocates did lay solid groundwork for themselves and others who carried the fight into the twentieth century. The nineteenth-century leaders deserved considerable credit for the law of 1909, which was to add Tennessee to the rapidly expanding list of dry states.

Some reformers sought to revise the economy and social order by establishing communistic societies; still others came into Tennessee in small groups simply to establish homes but to live cooperatively. Indeed, there were so many such experiments that the Volunteer State of the nineteenth century has been referred to as a "social and economic laboratory."

For decades before the Civil War, promoters in Europe had tried to sell Tennessee lands. A brochure of 1842 published in London, for example, described "east Tennessee U.S.A." as a place of "fertile meadows, bold limpid streams, evergreen pastures . . . [affording] every requisite for comfort, convenience, and pleasure." The German-Swiss emigration after 1840 brought foreign-born to Tennessee, and they established such communities as Gruetli (Grundy County), Byrnyffynon (Scott County), Wartburg (Morgan County), and Hohenwald (Lewis County). The short-lived colony of Nashoba in Shelby County, established by Scotswoman Frances Wright in the 1820s as an experiment designed to prepare slaves for life in a free society, has been discussed in an earlier chapter.

Rugby, a settlement made in 1880 in northern Morgan County, has been a subject frequently exploited by journalists and historians alike. Thomas Hughes, a well-to-do English lawyer, writer (his best known work was *Tom Brown's School Days*), member of Parliament, liberal activist and social reformer, had considered for some time the establishment of a settlement where young sons of the English upper classes, "with good education and small capital," not finding profitable outlets for their talents in the anachronistic social structure of their time, could establish a "kingdom" in the virgin forests of America where they could enjoy high thinking and plain living. Even the humblest of members, Hughes said, living by "the labour of their own hands, . . . would be able to meet princes in the gate without embarrassment and self-assertion."

Hughes bought 75,000 acres from a group of Boston capitalists who had earlier considered the land for a settlement of working-class New Englanders idled by financial depression. He officially opened the colony in October 1880. Within less than a year, Rugby (named for an English School where Hughes had studied) had a population of 300 residents and more than a dozen buildings either completed or under construction, including the three-story Tabard Inn.

Many problems attended Hughes' venture into "enchanted solitude," and within little more than a decade his "new Jerusalem" had failed. It had, as John Egerton has written, "no sudden end, but a slow

and inexorable decline."[3] Cold winters and dry hot summers took
their toll, a contaminated water supply brought death by typhoid
fever, one in a series of fires destroyed the majestic Tabard Inn, and
mistakes in management were made. Some of the colonists returned
to England, but many others remained and established communities
in the area. Clarkrange (named for Cyrus Clark, who moved to the
area with six colonizing families in 1879), Burrville, Glades, Skene,
Deer Lodge, and Armathwaite were established by people who were
affiliated in one way or another with the colony.

Ruskin Colony originated in the minds of an Indianian named
Julius Augustus Wayland—a self-styled "grass roots Socialist" de-
scribed by one Marxist historian as "the greatest propagandist of
Socialism that has ever lived." Wayland already had a sizable following through the wide circulation of his newspaper, *The Coming
Nation*, when he established in Dickson County the "Ruskin
Cooperative Association" in July 1894. Impressed by the writings of
John Ruskin (for whom the colony was named), Edward Bellamy,
and Henry George, Wayland believed that he could establish an
agrarian paradise far from the noise and strife of the complex industrial society. Incorporated under the laws of the state, the group soon
had several hundred stockholders and colonists.

At first things went well at Ruskin. While the newspaper was the
chief source of income, settlers also acquired a herd of dairy cows and
began to market not only agricultural produce but a variety of
manufactured items including men's suspenders, chewing gum, and
patent medicine. Internal dissension developed to such an extent by
the summer of 1895 that Wayland decided to abandon the colony
and return to Kansas, where he soon established another newspaper.
Others remained for another four years.

Despite problems incident to Wayland's departure, the group
continued to exhibit vitality, and the year of 1897 was probably its
zenith. To the newspaper and other enterprises were added sawmills
and gristmills, a machine shop, a cannery, a diversified agricultural
operation, and a mail order business that served thousands.

Crippling dissension developed in 1898 and resulted in litigation
that closed the colony in 1899. The internal problems were such that
two dominant groups—the original charter group, consisting largely
of tempermentally gentle people who sincerely believed in the spirit

[3] Egerton, *Visions of Utopia* (Knoxville, 1977).

of cooperation but not in Marx's concept of a class struggle, and the "newcomers," who were a more radical and less educated group— could not work together and sought through the courts a dissolution of the colony and a division of the resources among the stockholders. Following a lengthy lawsuit in which the stockholders sustained considerable losses, the colony was dissolved. Some of the colonists continued to live in Tennessee, but others carried the remnants of the colony to Georgia, where they established a new Ruskin that lasted less than two years.

Bob Taylor Returns to the Gubernatorial Chair. :≥ Many observers thought that Democratic chances for success in 1896 had floundered on the rock of political controversy of 1894. National Democrats, torn between supporters of the gold and silver standards, ultimately patched up their differences sufficiently to rally behind William Jennings Bryan, who won the presidential nomination after a resounding oration denouncing the group favoring the gold standard. Gold and silver leaders in Tennessee at first refused to compromise; Congressman Josiah Patterson of Memphis championed the gold standard and veteran United States senator and Bourbon leader Isham G. Harris supported the silver. Finally, Robert Love Taylor, whose eloquent rhetoric and skillfully maneuvered bow had mesmerized voters in 1886, came forward to capture the nomination as a champion of free silver. On a financially successful lecture tour in the West at the time, Taylor hastily returned to chide party leaders for their "dissension and discord" and blamed them for departing "from the true policies of old-fashioned Democratic government." The Hero of Happy Valley promised all-out war on Republicans and Populists alike.

The thunder of Populism was little more than an echo now, but Republican leaders, hoping to capitalize upon Democratic dissension, revived cries of the "martyrdom" of H. Clay Evans and pledged themselves to defeat resurgent Democrats. Populists again nominated A. L. Mims of Nashville, and Republicans chose George N. Tillman, also of Nashville. An able orator, Tillman pointed to promises of "Republican prosperity" and to the depression under Cleveland, accused Taylor of running for governor as a steppingstone to the United States Senate, and denounced the Democratic party for its conduct in 1894.

In a close contest, Taylor won by polling about 7,000 more votes than Tillman.[4] Democrats gained a 4-to-1 majority in the legislature and maintained their usual majority in Congress. The overwhelming success of the party was attributable partly to the magnetism of Bob Taylor and to the return of many Populists to the Democratic fold. Tillman's allegations of fraud and eagerness to contest the election soon disappeared when the Democratic-controlled legislature discouraged him by enacting a law requiring contestants to post penal bonds of $25,000.

Trouble between the United States and Spain already was brewing when Taylor was elected. Many American capitalists by this time had made enormous profits from the development of Cuban sugar. Supported by the United States government, they were angered by Spain's mismanagement of the affairs of the island. In 1895, Cubans staged an insurrection, destroying much property belonging to American businessmen, and the Republican party in the following year elected McKinley on a platform that favored the independence of Cuba.

Conditions became worse after McKinley's inauguration. In January 1898, the United States sent the battleship *Maine* to Havana to protect American lives. A few weeks later when the vessel was blown up and several officers and 258 crewmen were killed, Americans blamed Spain and prepared for war. On April 28 the United States declared war to make Cuba safe from Spanish "treachery and inhumanity" and to join in an imperialistic race for colonies in the Pacific.

Four Tennessee regiments were mustered into service, and other Tennesseans served in additional regiments or in the navy or marines. The First Tennessee, originally commanded by Colonel William Crawford Smith, fought heroically at Manila. When Colonel Smith died of heat prostration, Lieutenant Colonel Gracey Childers assumed command and led the regiment for the remainder of the battle. The Second Tennessee Regiment was under the command of Colonel Kellar Anderson, the Third Tennessee was led by Colonel J. P. Fyffe, and the Fourth Tennessee Regiment was commanded by Colonel George Leroy Brown. All were sent to Cuba but saw little if any action. When the troops returned late in 1899, Benton McMillin had been elected governor (having defeated Republican James A. Fowler by a vote of 105,640 to 72,611 in 1898) and welcomed the

[4] Taylor received 156,333 votes, Tillman 149,374, and Mims about 12,000.

veterans home in a florid address before a large throng of Middle Tennesseans.

The Tennessee Centennial Exposition ?~ The greatest extravaganza during the Taylor administration—and perhaps the greatest that Tennesseans had witnessed to that date—was the Tennessee Centennial. Preparations were not complete on the 100th anniversary of Tennessee's statehood; on June 1, 1896, officials merely had opened and dedicated Centennial Park, announcing hopefully that the celebration would begin in the following spring. Less than a year later, their hopes were realized when at noon on May 1, 1897, President William McKinley pressed a button in Washington that officially opened the gates in Nashville to the Tennessee Centennial Exposition. For six months thereafter, people from all parts of the world viewed the exhibits.

The "centennial dream" had originated in the mind of a prominent Nashville businessman named Douglas Anderson. In 1892 Anderson had written letters to editors of various newspapers and suggested that preparations be made immediately for a celebration to be held in 1896. He proposed that six cities—Nashville, Knoxville, Chattanooga, Memphis, Columbia, and Jackson—compete for the privilege of staging it. For two years the idea "existed on oral wind and printers' puffs," Anderson later wrote, but in 1894 Nashvillians, who in 1880 had staged a successful celebration of the 100th anniversary of their city, began to prepare in earnest for the exposition. A Centennial Association was organized to arouse interest in Tennessee's history and make preliminary plans for an exposition.

Shortly before opening day, Professor R. L. C. White prepared a list of 100 questions on Tennessee history and called it his "Centennial Dream." He published the questions in newspapers and offered rewards for correct answers. The Association published the *Official Guide to the Tennessee Centennial and International Exposition and City of Nashville,* which described in detail the wonders visitors could see. Readers of the *Guide* had their attention called to a "six-day tour" that featured displays in the Mineral and Forestry buildings, the Parthenon, Little Egypt, Vanity Fair, and the like. Hotel rates for room and board were quoted at from 2 to 4 dollars per day, carfare was 5 cents, and individual meals cost 25 cents.

On opening day, thousands of visitors heard the usual bursts of oratory and cannon; they heard Governor Taylor, in a spirit of levity not uncommon to the Hero of Happy Valley, describe his vision of the world 100 years hence.

> Who can tell what another century will unfold? I think I see a vision of the future opening before me. I see triumphs in art, and achievements in science, undreamed of by the artisans and philosophers of the past. I see the sun darkened by clouds of men and women flying in the air. I see throngs of passengers entering electric tubes in New York and emerging in San Francisco two hours before they started. I see the gloved and umbrellaed leaders of the Populist party sitting in their horseless carriages and singing the harvest song, while the self-adjusting automatic reapers sweep unattended through the fields, cutting and binding and shocking the golden grain. I see swarms of foreign pauper dukes and counts kissing American millionaire girls across the ocean, through the kissophone. I see the women marching in bloomers to the ballot box and the men at home singing lullabies to the squalling babies. I see every Republican in America drawing a pension, every Democrat holding an office, and every "cullud pusson" riding on a free pass; and then I think the millennium will be near at hand.

With the speech-making over, visitors entered to view the great and the majestic, the weird and the fantastic. They walked along winding, graveled roads bordered by buildings, beautiful flowers, fountains, and lakes. Most of the buildings were of wood plastered to resemble pale gray stone. A replica of the Athenian Parthenon housed an extensive art exhibit. Nearby stood the Frectheum, another reproduction of a building on the Acropolis of Athens, which was devoted to historical relics. There, Robert T. Quarles and G. P. Thruston displayed a rare collection of state historical relics, maps, and artifacts. Other buildings exhibited what Gentry R. McGee[5] termed "a marvelous array of almost everything to be found in a civilized country." Laces and various other textiles, jewelry, firearms and ammunition, and the finest specimens of timber, iron, coal, stone, and other minerals were on display. Another building housed vehicles from wooden-wheeled oxcarts to "the most elegant and elaborate palace cars."

Vanity Fair, "so replete with strange people, strange sights, and strange noises," was an unusual attraction. Within this section of the exposition were reproductions of the streets of Cairo, a Chinese village, a "Colorado goldmine," and a display designed "to show the

[5] McGee, *History of Tennessee,* (New York, 1899) 259.

progress of the Negro race from the old plantation days to the present." Here and there were sideshow men who clamored for all to see "the greatest show on earth."

The musical presentations provided one of the highlights of the exposition. On many occasions the large pipe organ in the auditorium, a novelty to some visitors, could be heard. Vocalists and choruses, including the Fisk Jubilee Singers, entertained thousands. Many bands and orchestras attracted large audiences, but the Marine Band of Cincinnati, the "Legion Band," the "Prohibition Band," the Centennial Orchestra, and Victor Herbert and his Twenty-Second Regiment Band of New York were the most popular. The last named was wildly cheered; listeners claimed that they played Verdi and Stephen Foster with equal skill and feeling. When the band departed for New York, a group of Nashvillians followed them to the train as though they were reluctant to permit such talent to leave Tennessee.

Hundreds of thousands had viewed the exhibits when the exposition closed on November 1. As Gentry R. McGee[6] wrote two years later,

> When the first blasts of November winds were scattering the fallen leaves the grand exposition closed. It had been one of the most successful and creditable ever undertaken and carried out by a single state. Every department had shown the wonderful progress of the state since her pioneer days, and the creation and management of the great exhibit had shown the genius and energy of the men and women who had charge of its fortunes.

General Albert Sidney Johnston, who thirty-five years earlier had called vainly for a few Nashville-owned slaves to assist him in constructing Forts Donelson and Henry, would not have thought Nashvillians capable of such a display of energy, nor would General John B. Hood's barefoot men, who saw only gloom and despair when they trudged toward the capital only three decades earlier, ever have recognized the Davidson County seat. The Exposition was truly Tennessee's greatest contribution to the gilded age.

SUGGESTED READINGS

Books
John Egerton, *Visions of Utopia: Nashoba, Rugby, Ruskin, and the "New*

[6] *Ibid.,* 259–260.

Communities" in Tennessee's Past (Knoxville, 1977); Stanley J. Folmsbee, *Tennessee Establishes a State University* (Knoxville, 1961); David E. Harrell, Jr., *Quest for a Christian America* (Nashville, 1966); Paul Isaac, *Prohibition and Politics: Turbulent Decades in Tennessee, 1885–1920* (Knoxville, 1965); Henry McRaven, *Nashville, Athens of the South* (Chapel Hill, 1949); Edwin Mims, *History of Vanderbilt University* (Nashville, 1946); A. Elizabeth Taylor, *The Woman Suffrage Movement in Tennessee* (New York, 1957); Robert H. White, *Development of the Tennessee Educational Organization, 1796–1929* (Nashville, 1929).

Articles

Douglas Anderson, "The Centennial Idea and the Centennial 'Dream'," *THM,* Ser. 2, 3 (Jan. 1935), 107–10; W. H. G. Armytage, "New Light on the English Background of Thomas Hughes' Rugby Colony in Tennessee," *ETHSP* 21 (1949), 69–84; Francelia Butler, "The Ruskin Commonwealth: A Unique Experiment," *THQ* 23 (Dec. 1964), 33–42; Dick B. Clough, "Teacher Institutes in Tennessee, 1870–1900," *THQ* 31 (Spring 1972), 61–73; Marguerite Bartlett Hamer, "Thomas Hughes and His American Rugby," *NCHR* 5 (Oct. 1928), 391–413; David Edwin Harrell, Jr., "The Disciples of Christ and Social Force in Tennessee, 1865–1900," *ETHSP* 38 (1966), 30–47; Joseph C. Kiger, "Social Thought as Voiced in Rural Middle Tennessee Newspapers, 1878–1898," *THQ* 9 (June 1950), 131–54; Grace Leab, "Tennessee Temperance Activities, 1870–1899," *ETHSP* 21 (1949), 52–68; Grace Sloan, "Tennessee: Social and Economic Laboratory," *Sewanee Review* 46, (Jan.–March, April–June, July–Sept. 1939), 36–44, 158–66, 312–36; Brian L. Stagg, "Tennessee's Rugby Colony," *THQ* 37 (Fall 1968), 209–24.

22.

TENNESSEE politics during the twentieth century have been varied and dramatic. Republicans, destined to remain the minority party, have been surprisingly successful partly because of their ability to capitalize upon Democratic factionalism. Although Bob Taylor had brought some degree of unity among dissident Democrats, latent factionalism emerged again soon after the twentieth century began. The close of the first decade brought the election of a Republican governor—the second since Reconstruction.

Prohibition was the principal issue during the first decade of the century. The matter was by no means confined to capitol hill; it occupied pulpits, classrooms, and lecture halls, and permeated almost every avenue of society. When the decade ended, whiskey could not be legally marketed or manufactured anywhere in the state. The prohibition issue, along with a street gunfight which claimed the life of the prohibition spokesman and Democratic leader, Edward Ward Carmack, were the principal factors in destroying Democratic unity.

Democratic Control ဇ The twentieth century opened with a concerted effort by Republicans to win the Volunteer State for President William McKinley. "Tennessee ought to be Republican," wrote newspaper editor and Republican leader William Rule of Knoxville in the summer of 1900; "there are one hundred thousand white men in the state of Tennessee who would rejoice to have the Republican party triumphant. . . ." Alf Taylor, John C. Houk, and

Ben W. Hooper were among those who pointed to Republican industrialization and prosperity urging Tennesseans to reject the presidential candidacy of William Jennings Bryan. Democrats were in control of the election machinery, however, and the Democratic organization carried the day for Bryan. Indeed, the Nebraskan received 55.4 percent of the votes cast. Republicans, temporarily disheartened but not disillusioned, sought ways to disenchant groups within the majority party.

In the meantime, the Democrat-controlled legislature turned its attention to state and local matters. Benton McMillin became governor in 1899 and was reelected by a comfortable majority in the following year. During the campaigns of 1898 and 1900 he had manifested a distinct interest in the conditions of the public schools, and several educational measures of merit were enacted while he was governor. Included were laws that empowered school boards in each county to establish a high school, established uniformity in the use of textbooks throughout the state, increased appropriations for teachers' institutes, and designated one day of each school year as "Arbor Day." A sinking fund for the retirement of bonded indebtedness was established, and the state capitol was refurbished.

One central theme—prohibition—dominated Tennessee politics during the first ten years of the century. The issue was not new to the Volunteer State. It had appeared before McMillin assumed the governorship, and it continued until the liquor traffic was declared illegal ten years later. The basic prohibition measure was the Four Mile Law of 1877, which banned the retail sale of all intoxicating beverages within four miles of a chartered school outside an incorporated town. The law had been amended in 1887 to apply to any country school, whether chartered or not, and this had had the effect of prohibiting retail traffic in almost all of rural Tennessee. It was amended again in 1899 to forbid the sale of intoxicants within four miles of schools in towns of 2,000 or less, providing that they incorporated after the passage of the amendment. Already incorporated towns of this size could surrender their charters and reincorporate by a special act of the legislature. These basic prohibition measures had been enacted without the great public interest that was soon to be manifested during the first decade of the twentieth century.

With the turn of the century, several groups had formed with the purpose of arousing public interest. The Tennessee Anti-Saloon

William Jennings Bryan was well known in Tennessee for several decades before he aided with the prosecution in the Scopes trial (1925). Here he is, second from left, during one of his visits to the state. Governor Benton McMillin is on the extreme right.

League was organized in 1899, and members of the Women's Christian Temperance Union increased their activity considerably after 1900. Church leaders, especially from the dominant Baptist and Methodist groups, began to exert an increasing influence upon prohibition. The league, founded in Ohio in 1893 and established on a national basis two years later, became an important force in the legislature after 1901. The league's strategy was simple—to extend the provision of the Four Mile Law to the towns and cities.

Temperance forces in 1901 met liquor lobbyists head on in the state capital, and while proponents of temperance failed in their efforts to pass the Peeler bill, which would have extended the Four Mile Law to cities of 5,000, they were effective in getting several minor bills passed, such as one prohibiting the distribution of intoxicants in the capitol or on the capitol grounds. They were especially irritated at the defeat of the Peeler Bill and resolved to organize in greater forces when the legislature convened later. In the meantime they would influence the election of friendly candidates to the legislature in counties where temperance forces were sufficiently strong. New county organizations were formed, and in 1902 the *Anti-Saloon Journal* began publication in Bristol.

McMillin was not a candidate for a third term, and Democrats therefore nominated James B. Frazier, who had practiced law in Chattanooga for twenty years. Although he lacked political experience, Frazier was elected in 1902[1] and again in 1904[2] by comfortable majorities. Temperance advocates failed to persuade Democrats to include a plank on prohibition in 1902 but were successful in 1904. Frazier, not wishing to alienate the liquor interests in the cities, supported the Four Mile Law as amended but did not wish to apply it to the nine cities not affected by it. Jesse Littleton, his Republican opponent in 1904, favored local option across the state.

Temperance leaders, effective in securing the election of several friendly legislators, were influential in the passage of several measures in 1903. The Adams law extended provisions of the Four Mile Law to all towns of 5,000 that would reincorporate after the passage of the measure. A referendum held in interested towns of 2,000 to

---

[1] Frazier received 98,902 votes; Judge Henry T. Campbell, of Carter County, polled 59,007 as the Republican candidate; and R. S. Cheves, the Prohibitionist, received 2,198.

[2] Frazier received 131,503, and Jesse M. Littleton, Republican, received 103,409.

5,000 would address the question of rechartering and would be an expression of opinion on local option. Several dozen towns promptly held referendums, and in most the prohibitionists were successful; a notable exception, however, was Lynchburg, home of Jack Daniel whiskey, where the vote was 76 to 0 against rechartering. Efforts in 1905 to extend the Four Mile Law to towns larger than 5,000 were unsuccessful. Temperance leaders blamed their failures in 1905 upon the influence of Senate Speaker John I. Cox, powerful East Tennessee Democrat, whom they had worked unsuccessfully to defeat in his bid for a senate seat.

Another matter that commanded Governor Frazier's attention was the coal mines of East Tennessee, where many mine owners, in their desire for profits, operated unsafe mines. Consequently, at his insistence, an act was passed providing for "the regulation and inspection of mines," and "for the safety, welfare, and protection of persons employed therein. . . ." Rigid standards and penalties were established. Two years later, Frazier noted with pride that since enforcement of the law had begun, no lives had been lost in the mines and no damaging explosions had occurred. Other matters receiving legislative attention were education and the reduction of the bonded indebtedness.

Shortly after his second inauguration, Frazier resigned and was elected to the United States Senate to fill out the unexpired term of Senator William B. Bate, who had died on March 9. The haste with which the legislature acted in electing him shook the Democratic party and contributed to the ultimate success of the Republicans in the gubernatorial election of 1910. Scarcely was Bate buried before Frazier and two other leading Democrats and former governors, Robert Love Taylor and Benton McMillin, announced their candidacy. All had friends, but Frazier as incumbent governor had a very active supporter in John I. Cox who, as speaker of the senate, stood to succeed the governor. The two were able to secure the party nomination of Frazier six days after Bate died and his election six days after that. Taylor, on a lecture tour outside the state, was unable to make all of the contacts he considered necessary for his campaign and was irate at the haste with which Cox and Frazier had acted. Prohibitionists had never admired Cox, and they joined with Taylor's friends in condemnation of the new governor. Taylor, who had sought a Senate seat in 1898 when Thomas B. Turley was elected, had considered himself to be the front-runner for any vacancy that

The twelve-year period of 1899–1911 focused attention on prohibition and brought division within the dominant Democratic party. The governors during the period were: *above left:* Benton McMillin, 1899–1903; *above right:* James B. Frazier, 1903–1905; *below left:* John I. Cox, 1905–1907; *below right:* Malcolm R. Patterson, 1907–1911. Frazier resigned in March 1905, and Cox completed the term and was elected to a full term in the following fall.

might occur within the foreseeable future. He therefore grudgingly turned his attention to the other United States senator, Edward Ward Carmack, a close political ally of Frazier and Cox, whose term would expire in 1907.

Cox employed his time during most of the remainder of the term in preparing for the gubernatorial election of 1906. No major legislative innovations were suggested during his one and one-half years as governor, except that the General Assembly did provide for a state flag, designed by LeRoy Reeves, and approved the purchase of 11,000 acres in Bledsoe, White, and Van Buren counties (the "Herbert Domain") as a place for convict labor.

The political strife of 1905 brought significant, colorful, and powerful party leaders to the fore. As mentioned in an earlier chapter, Taylor had served three terms as governor during the 1880s and 1890s and remained a popular and powerful leader. Carmack, a Sumner County native, had begun a legal, political, and publishing career at Columbia. There he had served on the Maury County court and was elected to the state legislature in 1884. He joined the editorial staff of the Nashville *American* shortly after his house term ended and in 1888 founded the Nashville *Democrat,* which soon merged with the Nashville *American.* The *American* was controlled by Duncan Cooper, and Carmack became editor in chief. His capability as an editor soon won for him an editorial post with the powerful Memphis *Commercial* (later *Commercial-Appeal*), where he wrote editorials on imperialism, free silver, and policies generally supported by William Jennings Bryan. He held the editorial position for four years before resigning in 1896 in a quarrel over editorial policy. He then decided to run for Congress in the Memphis district against the incumbent, Josiah Patterson, a gold Democrat, whose support of a hard-money policy in Washington did not sit well with Memphis silver advocates. He won the seat only after a bitter contest, the outcome of which ultimately had to be settled in the House itself. He remained there until 1901, when he was elected to the Senate to fill a seat occupied since 1898 by Turley, who had finished out Isham G. Harris's term. In the Senate he soon established a reputation as an able orator and as a member of a Senate committee to investigate brutalities inflicted by American troops upon Filipino insurgents.

Another powerful Democrat to emerge at the time was Malcolm R. Patterson, a son of Josiah Patterson. Born in Alabama but reared in Memphis and educated at Vanderbilt University, Patterson was an experienced politician and had practiced law and served as an attorney general in Memphis. In 1896 he had been his father's campaign manager in the bitter congressional contest won by Carmack and then had been elected to Congress when Carmack went to the Senate. Patterson was reelected in 1902 and 1904, and in 1905 announced that he would seek the gubernatorial nomination in the following year.

Democrats selected nominees for both governor and United States senator in May 1906. The senatorial candidate was chosen in a primary election (the first primary in the state) after Carmack and Taylor had discussed issues across the state. Carmack recognized temperance as the major issue and immediately emerged as a champion of that cause. When he sought to brand Taylor as a tool of the liquor interests, Our Bob was quick to point out that as governor he had signed the Four Mile Law of 1887, had endorsed all temperance legislation, and had supported the prohibition amendment of 1887. Carmack, he said, had not championed any of the prohibition causes while a newspaper editor and had ridiculed candidates of the Prohibition party. The charm and charisma of Bob Taylor defeated the brilliant oratory of Carmack; Taylor received 74,000 votes to Carmack's 66,000 and won 75 of the 96 counties.

In the Democratic convention held in Nashville, Patterson vied with Cox for the gubernatorial nomination. Patterson attacked Cox for attempting to govern by "machine politics," favored "mild" prohibition, but expressed disfavor with any "legislation not based upon the will of the people." Cox, however, now professing sympathy for the temperance cause, promised to extend the Adams law to the larger cities. Neither candidate was endorsed by the Anti-Saloon League, however, but the Democratic platform approved league objectives by supporting the extension of the Adams act with the consent of the people affected. After a stormy convention, Patterson was nominated.

Republicans believed that because of Democratic factionalism they might elect a governor, and they therefore nominated the able and popular H. Clay Evans, who had been "counted out" of the office in 1894 by a Democratic legislature. Evans had come into Chattanooga as a Northern soldier but had remained to become a powerful industrialist and Republican politician. He was elected mayor of

Chattanooga for several terms, served in Congress, and held such appointive positions as assistant postmaster general and consul general of London. In league with industrialist Newell Sanders, he was able in 1906 to wrest control of the party from Walter P. Brownlow, a distant cousin of the late governor, and had become one of the most powerful Republicans in the southeast. Although he championed prohibition and increased state appropriations for Confederate pensions, Evans was defeated and Malcolm Patterson became governor.[3]

Patterson's first term was a relatively progressive one and fairly free of strife except for the whiskey question. Laws were passed forbidding gambling at horseracing, creating a tax equalization board, prohibiting the manufacture or sale of adulterated or improperly branded food or drugs (the "State Pure Food and Drug Act"), and purchasing a mansion for the governor. For the governor, a specially created commission bought a house on Seventh Avenue, one-half block from the capitol. Succeeding governors lived there until 1922, when the building was razed to make room for a war memorial building.

The prohibitionists in the 1907 legislative session principally sought to extend the concept of the Four Mile Law to the large cities. Subsequently, they passed the Pendleton Bill (named for its sponsor, Senator I. L. Pendleton of Davidson County), by which voters in the cities could abolish the liquor trade by voting to reincorporate. But only in Knoxville were they successful, and prohibitionists soon realized that voters in Nashville, Chattanooga, Memphis, and LaFollette would probably never accept prohibition unless forced to do so by state or federal law. Members of the Anti-Saloon League therefore announced plans in October of 1907 to seek the abolition of every saloon, distillery, and brewery in the state. They would also accelerate efforts to pass federal legislation banning the shipment of liquor from wet states into dry states, and they would exert pressure to defeat any candidate who did not endorse their program. Few were surprised when a few weeks later the Women's Christian Temperance Union (WCTU) met at the state capitol and unanimously endorsed the drive for statewide prohibition. After the state convention of women adjourned, 600 delegates to a national convention of

[3] Patterson received 111,856 votes to 92,804 for Evans.

the WCTU assembled in Nashville to hear Carrie Nation pledge to "carry on the war until the last saloon is gone." Church leaders from Memphis to Bristol joined the fray.

At about the same time the prohibitionists prepared for a statewide fight against the liquor traffic, Edward Ward Carmack announced that he would attempt to unseat Governor Patterson in 1908. After his defeat for reelection to the Senate in 1906, Carmack had continued to write and lecture and remain active in politics. He received hundreds of communications from people across the state urging him to seek another office. A group of "Nashville Ladies" begged him not to become discouraged but to "fill the high destiny we fully believe is yet in reserve for you—as President of the United States." A Lebanon lawyer wrote to express a belief that he could "get the nomination for governor for the asking," while a Knoxvillian informed him that the "good people" would elect him if he would denounce "this damnable whiskey influence that corrupts everything." Carmack was probably influenced by such popular pressure and made the decision to run for governor, although it countered the advice of some of his wiser friends, including Memphis lawyer (and later United States senator) Kenneth D. McKellar. Carmack had not declared a position on statewide prohibition at the time and apparently gave considerable thought to the subject during the fall and winter of 1907–1908. In 1906 he had said he had "never been among the extreme or fanatical elements of temperance," and as late as February 1908 he had expressed a preference for local option. But Carmack was a man of tremendous political talents looking for a cause—and an office. A few weeks later he announced a platform calling for statewide prohibition and was warmly endorsed by prohibition leaders across the state.

Not since the days of the Whigs and Democrats had a successful governor been so aggressively challenged after one term in office, and Patterson therefore determined to make a strong bid to remain in Nashville. Recognizing that with Carmack the principal issue would be the liquor traffic, Patterson at first sought to make peace with prohibitionists by pointing out that he had signed the Pendleton measure and that more than 400 saloons had been closed during his administration. But when he rejected statewide prohibition by declaring that local option was the only "safe, fair, and democratic procedure," he lost his final chance to win any measure of support from prohibitionists.

Carmack's determination to seek the Democratic nomination on a prohibitionist platform brought division within party ranks. Prominent leaders lined up on both sides; former Populists and independents backed Carmack, while a majority of the party regulars supported Patterson. Able campaign managers were secured for each candidate; George Armistead, a well-known newspaper publisher of Franklin, supported Carmack, and Austin Peay, a Clarksville lawyer who was later to serve as governor, managed the campaign for Patterson. Most of the urban press supported Patterson, with the exception of Luke Lea's Nashville *Tennessean*, while a majority of the rural press declared for Carmack.

In an effort to avoid as much divisiveness as possible, party leaders agreed upon a direct primary as the fairest means of determining the party's candidate. This decision itself was reached only after much discussion among Democrats, with the state Democratic executive committee proposing an indirect, county unit primary based upon the form prescribed in the federal Constitution for electing presidential candidates; the candidate who received a majority of the popular votes in a county would secure all of that county's votes in the state convention.

The direct primary was ultimately decided upon, and in April Carmack and Patterson began a canvass across the state. While prohibition was the principal issue, the candidates also debated such matters as big business and the railroads, the need for a direct primary law for all state offices, and party loyalty. It was on the latter issue that Patterson was most effective; he charged Carmack with sacrificing his Democratic principles to ride into office upon the wave of emotionalism created by the prohibitionists. On the liquor question, Patterson continued to refer to his record of moderation and to champion local option as the only fair way of solving the liquor problem. At rallies across the state tempers flared, bands played, choirs sang, and people marched and fought; not since the days of Bob and Alf Taylor had the people seen so much excitement in a political contest.

After a heated campaign Patterson won the nomination by about 7,000 votes. His support had come principally from the still wet counties of Davidson, Hamilton, and Shelby—a fact that made temperance forces more determined than ever to bring about statewide prohibition. Carmack's support came from East Tennessee and much of rural West Tennessee. The Patterson forces interpreted the primary results as a mandate for moderation and local option.

Meanwhile, Republicans had become just as inharmonious—if not more so—than the Democrats. There were able leaders among the Republicans who had quarreled bitterly for years over federal patronage, prohibition, and legislative apportionment. They included Walter P. Brownlow and Alf Taylor from the first district, Nathan W. Hale and John C. Houk from the second district, and H. Clay Evans and Newell Sanders of the third district. By 1908, the Republicans were divided into the Sanders Regulars and the "Home Rule Group" led by Houk. When they assembled in Nashville on March 25 for a convention, they became engaged, as the editor of the Knoxville *Journal* wrote, in a free-for-all that lasted "for an hour or more, in which heads were skinned, noses mashed, and clothing of delegates torn." Sanders was choked to the point of unconsciousness, locks and latches were hacked off the doors to the house chamber, and thousands of dollars' worth of furniture was destroyed. Nevertheless, a few weeks later Republican Regulars under Sanders and Evans reassembled and nominated George N. Tillman of Nashville for governor. Tillman had been defeated by Bob Taylor in a close gubernatorial race in 1896 and sought support in 1908 by declaring himself for statewide prohibition.

Both candidates campaigned across the state, and Tillman correctly assessed prohibition to be "the main issue before the people." Patterson, however, interrupted the campaign in October, when violence in the Reelfoot Lake region persuaded him to return to Nashville and mobilize the state guard to quell the disturbances.

For years natives had lived and fished along the lake banks in defiance of rights of owners. Difficulties finally arose when owners formed the West Tennessee Land Company and announced plans to drain the lake and develop real estate operations in the area. After threats and minor acts of violence, natives seized two prominent company lawyers, Quentin Rankin and Colonel Robert Z. Taylor, and determined to kill them. Rankin was hanged and shot, but Taylor miraculously escaped. Guardsmen and law enforcement officers soon rounded up and brought to trial some of the mob, and Patterson returned to the hustings as one who had upheld law and order.

In the general election, Patterson defeated Tillman by a vote of 133,166 to 113,233. Democrats considered their victory to be another endorsement of local option. The presidential contest of the same year had been all but overshadowed by the gubernatorial race.

William Jennings Bryan experienced little difficulty in winning Tennessee's electoral votes over William Howard Taft.

Soon after the primary election Carmack became editor of the Nashville *Tennessean*, a newspaper recently established by Luke Lea, a young Nashville lawyer and politician. Bitter over his defeat, Carmack considered contesting the results of the primary, but finally agreed to drop charges. Tersely announcing that "the fight against liquor must go on," he soon began to use the editorial columns of the newspaper to denounce many things and many people, and among the first of his enemies to receive scathing denunciation were Governor Patterson and Duncan B. Cooper. Cooper was an intimate friend and adviser to Governor Patterson and, as previously noted, a former employer of Carmack while Carmack was editor of Cooper's Nashville *American*.

Enmity between Carmack and Cooper, which ultimately resulted in the death of the fiery editor, probably began in 1896 when Cooper championed the cause of Malcoln Patterson's father, Josiah, during his close but unsuccessful race against Carmack for Congress. Later, in 1906, Cooper warmly supported Bob Taylor in his successful race against incumbent Carmack for the United States Senate and Patterson in his successful campaign for governor. The two victories made Cooper a powerful politician in Tennessee. Carmack in his race against Patterson in 1908 bitterly charged that "Baldheaded Dunc" (sometimes it was "a little bald-headed Angel named Dunc") was in unholy league with Governor Patterson against the people, and he urged voters to support him in turning both out of power.

While others ignored Carmack's barbs, Cooper, an elderly Confederate veteran who had retired from business interests but who continued to enjoy recognition and association with those in power, bitterly resented them. He apparently read the newspapers closely and was highly offended at the sight of derogatory remarks about himself. While members of his family tried to dissuade him, he procured a pistol, apparently for the purpose of being prepared should he encounter his antagonist. Late in the afternoon of November 9, 1908, Cooper and his son Robin, a young Nashville lawyer, met Carmack apparently by chance on the corner of Union Street and Seventh Avenue. The three were armed; guns were fired, and within minutes Carmack lay dead in the street and Robin Cooper had been painfully wounded.

The Coopers were jailed and indicted. Testimony at the trial indicated that Carmack had apparently fired first and had struck Robin Cooper in the throat and shoulder; Robin Cooper then fired three shots at Carmack, any one of which could have been fatal; two penetrated the heart and one severed the spinal cord. No shots were fired by the elder Cooper, who although armed did not even draw his weapon.

The shooting aroused people of the state as nothing else could. The sensationalist Nashville *Tennessean* described the shooting as "murder premeditated, deliberately planned, and executed in cold blooded style"; it was, indeed, a "dastardly crime without parallel in the annals of the state." For weeks thereafter the paper kept up a daily drumfire of extravagant propaganda. Carmack's widow received thousands of letters and telegrams of sympathy. A Memphis lawyer offered her his services "without charge" to "prosecute the assassin," and another telegraphed that "Cooper was always a dirty rascal, [while] Ned was a gentleman and never stooped to a small thing. . . ." J. E. Egerton, principal of Columbia Military Academy, wrote to extend a five-year scholarship to nine-year-old Edward Ward Carmack, Jr. Memorial services were held across the state for the fallen warrior; more than 7,000 gathered in the Ryman Auditorium in Nashville to revere the memory of Carmack and resolve to "drive the liquor power from the State."

Riding the crest of inflamed public emotion, prosecuting attorneys presented a strong case in circuit court against the Coopers. Both were found guilty and were sentenced to twenty years in prison for second-degree murder. The case then was appealed to the supreme court. There, in a three-to-two decision after ten weeks of deliberation the judgment of the circuit court was upheld with respect to Duncan Cooper, but the case against Robin was remanded for a new trial. Governor Patterson promptly pardoned Duncan Cooper. "It took the Supreme Court seventy-two days to decide this case and it decided it the wrong way," the governor asserted. "It took me seventy-two minutes and I decided it the right way." Few people were surprised at the pardon, but all were shocked at Patterson's haste and the attitude he took toward the deliberate judgment of the court.

Patterson had clearly signed his own political death warrant when he pardoned Duncan Cooper. The governor was already criticized for excessive use of the pardoning power, and Tennesseans from Mountain City to Memphis deplored his haste with respect to

Cooper. Equally important was the impetus that both the slaying and the pardon gave to the cause of prohibitionists; Carmack became a much more powerful political figure in death than he had been in life.

When legislators assembled on the first Monday in January 1909, they were overwhelmed by church and prohibition leaders on the one hand and liquor lobbyists on the other. Prohibitionists secured control of the legislature and elected as senate speaker William Kinney, a Haywood County lawyer; Hillsman Taylor, a son of Colonel Robert Z. Taylor and a son-in-law of former governor Bob Taylor, was chosen as house speaker. Senator O. K. Holladay, a prohibitionist Democrat from Putnam County, promptly introduced a bill to accomplish statewide prohibition. Patterson implored lawmakers to respect the concept of local option, but the ghost of Carmack and the pressure from thousands who had joined the prohibition cause prevailed. By a vote of 20 to 13 in the senate and 62 to 36 in the house, the Holladay bill was passed—thanks to a coalition of East Tennessee Republicans and prohibition Democrats. While the *Tennessean* proclaimed that "Tennessee has been redeemed," members of the WCTU held thanksgiving services on the spot where Carmack had died. Patterson's veto of the measure, in which he condemned "this new and strange spirit of radicalism" by which the "sacred principle" of self-government on the local level was ignored, resulted in more ridicule of the hapless governor; legislators overrode the veto by about the same majority that had passed the measure in the first place. Then, the Manufacturers' Bill, designed to halt the manufacture of intoxicants in the state, was enacted and then passed over the governor's veto. It was to become effective no later than January 1, 1910.

Among other laws passed were the General Education Law of 1909 (to be discussed in another chapter) and a general election law that struck at the roots of the governor's political control. The election law gave the General Assembly the power to select the state election board, to consist of two members from the majority party and one from the minority party. The board, then, would select bipartisan commissions in the counties. Traditionally, the board members had been appointed by the governor, who always chose members of his own party. Patterson and the regular Democrats vigorously opposed the law, but it was passed by a coalition of Republicans and prohibition Democrats. The coalition presaged the advent of fusion politics in the state.

In the meantime, as indicated, the Carmack Democrats had organized into the "Independent Democrats," with Luke Lea and E. B.
Stahlman as the chief spokesmen. The first test of their strength
came in the Democratic primary during the summer of 1910, when
five candidates for the supreme court ran as Independents against the
nominees of the Regular Democrats. Shortly before the court had
rendered a decision in the Carmack case, Governor Patterson was
accused of having attempted to influence the decision of Chief
Justice W. D. Beard, an old friend of his father, Josiah Patterson. A
report was then widely circulated among the Carmack group that
Patterson, at the head of the Regular Democratic machine, was
trying to control the courts. Beard charged that he would stand only
for a "free and untrammeled judiciary," repudiated Patterson, and
soon announced that he and other court members would not run as
party nominees in a primary as directed by the Democratic state
executive committee but would run as Independents. This stand by
Beard united Independent Democrats as nothing else had; leaders
immediately convened in Nashville and nominated three incumbent
justices—Beard, John K. Shields, and M. M. Neil—and Grafton
Green and David L. Lansdon. The Regulars nominated incumbents
W. K. McAlister and Bennett D. Bell, and R. E. Maiden, R. M.
Barton, and R. C. Cooke.

The Independents may have had an understanding with Republicans. At any rate, the Republican state committee—over the vigorous protest of Jesse M. Littleton, Republican candidate for governor
in 1904, who first advocated offering a Republican judicial slate and
then threw his support behind the Democratic Regulars—endorsed
the Independent ticket and studiously took action to prevent the
name of any Republican from being placed on the ballot. The entire
Independent slate was victorious in the August primary by more
than 40,000 votes. More than 25,000 were polled in East Tennessee,
indicating that Republicans had crossed party lines en masse to help
elect them. When Independents announced support of Republican
candidate Ben W. Hooper later that year, Democratic Regulars again
charged them with party disloyalty.

Ben W. Hooper Elected Governor ⧉ The Democratic Regulars nominated Patterson for another term. Republicans assembled
in Nashville a few days after the Democratic primary in one of the

largest conventions in the history of the party. After considering more than a dozen men, including an active prohibitionist from Newport named Ben W. Hooper, and Alfred Taylor who had continued to remain politically active after his defeat at the hands of Bob Taylor nearly 25 years earlier, leaders chose Hooper.

A thirty-nine-year-old lawyer, Hooper was not without political experience. He had served in the state legislature, had been an assistant United States attorney for the eastern district of the state, was a captain in the Spanish-American War, and had been a party leader for nearly two decades. His mild and genial manner was appealing, and the fact that he was a prohibitionist made him acceptable to the Independent Democrats. Within a few weeks Independents formally endorsed him, and Hooper carried the banner of the Fusionists.

In the meantime, Patterson faced the hopelessness of the contest. Championing local option when prohibition was gaining momentum, accused by some of having plotted Carmack's murder, charged with attempting to tamper with the judiciary, and faced with a division within his own party that could not be healed before the election, Patterson received a final blow when the only newspaper supporting him (the Nashville *American*) was purchased in early September by Luke Lea and merged with the anti-Patterson *Tennessean*. On September 10 the governor withdrew, pleading a desire "to harmonize the discordant elements in the Democratic party." Three weeks later the Regular Democrats announced from a "Harmony Convention" that they had nominated the old conciliator and spellbinder of earlier times, Bob Taylor, then a United States Senator.

The campaign between the two East Tennesseans waxed warm. Despite his sixty years and his desire to remain in the Senate (which he effectively concealed throughout the campaign), Taylor met Hooper in acrid debate across the state. Hooper, "an avowed friend of total abstinence," received the support of the Anti-Saloon League, the WCTU, and various church groups. He attacked with vigor the pardoning record of both Taylor and Patterson, blamed the Democratic Regulars for "maladministration," and charged that Taylor if elected would be simply a tool of the Patterson machine. Taylor denied that he was in any way attached to Patterson, and in oratorical tones reminiscent of days of old, championed the cause of public education, good government, good roads, and separation of church and state. This time, however, even the magnetism and charm of Bob Taylor could not heal the Democratic breach, and Hooper was elected by a vote of 133,074 to 121,694. The orator had not resigned his Senate seat, of course, and so he returned to Washington, where he served until his death in 1912. Talk by Regulars of contesting the election soon subsided, and on January 25, 1911 Hooper became the first Republican governor after Alvin Hawkins, who had been inaugurated thirty years before.

SUGGESTED READINGS

Books

Everett Robert Boyce (ed.), *The Unwanted Boy: The Autobiography of Governor Ben W. Hooper* (Knoxville, 1963); Paul E. Isaac, *Prohibition and Politics: Turbulent Decades in Tennessee, 1885–1920* (Knoxville, 1965); John Berry McFerrin, *Caldwell and Company: A Southern Financial Empire* (Chapel Hill, 1939); Kenneth D. McKellar, *Tennessee Senators As Seen by One of Their Successors* (Kingsport, 1942); William D. Miller, *Memphis During the Progressive Era* (Memphis, 1957); A Elizabeth Taylor, *Woman Suffrage Movement in Tennessee* (New York, 1957).

Articles

Paul E. Isaac, "The Problems of a Republican Governor in a Southern State: Ben Hooper in Tennessee," *THQ* 27 (Fall, 1968), 229–48; Eric Russell Lacy, "Tennessee Teetotalism: Social Forces and the Politics of Progressivism," *THQ* 24 (Fall 1965), 219–40; William D. Miller, "The Progressive Movement in Memphis," *THQ* 15 (March 1956), 3–16; J. Winfield Qualls, "Fusion Victory and the Tennessee Senatorship, 1910–1911," *WTHSP* 15 (1961), 79–92; Verton M. Queener, "The East Tennessee Republican Party, 1900–1914," *ETHSP* 22 (1950), 94–127; Leslie F. Roblyer, "The Fight for Local Prohibition in Knoxville, Tennessee, 1907," *ETHSP* 26 (1954) 27–37; Robert Saunders, "Southern Populists and the Negro, 1893–1905," *JNH* 54 (Jan. 1969), 240–61; J. M. Shahan, "The Rhetoric of Reform: The 1906 Gubernatorial Race in Tennessee," *THQ* 35 (Spring 1976), 65–82; Russell L. Stockard, "The Election and First Administration of Ben W. Hooper as Governor of Tennessee," *ETHSP* 26 (1954), 38–59.

23.

THE period 1911–1923 began and ended with a Republican in the governor's chair. The election of the first had been made possible by division within Democratic ranks over prohibition and the resulting fusion between Independent Democrats and Republicans. The election of the second came about with the Republican landslide of 1920 and the popularity of Alfred Taylor, who served from 1921 to 1923. Political strife was overshadowed briefly by World War I, and Tennesseans joined other Americans in 1917 in undertaking the first armed invasion of European soil in the history of the republic.

Conflict between the Fusionists, who had a tenuous majority in the house, and the Regular Democrats, who controlled the senate, developed soon after the legislative session opened. Thirty-seven Regulars first tried to nullify the Independent Democrat–Republican alignment by refusing to take their oaths as house members, and the Regulars were able to delay Hooper's inauguration until January 25. Finally, after they had given up hope of unseating Hooper and the Fusionists had dropped plans to contest several disputed legislative seats, the assembly turned its attention to legislative matters.

Of considerable concern to legislators was the election of a successor to United States Senator James B. Frazier, whose term would expire on March 4, 1911. Regulars concentrated upon Benton McMillin, but the Fusionists, with the support of Mayor Edward H. Crump of Memphis who permitted open saloons in defiance of the law, elected Luke Lea. Prohibitionists had not become endeared to Lea only because of his association with Carmack; his promise to support federal legislation preventing the shipment of intoxicants into dry states increased their enthusiasm for him.

Another matter of almost equal concern was the election law of 1909. When Regulars with a few Independent votes passed a bill modifying the measure in such a manner that Democrats would have complete control of the state's election machinery, thirty-four Fusionists (with money supplied by Industrialist Republican leader Newell Sanders) fled to Decatur, Alabama to prevent the formation of a quorum. Thus when Governor Hooper promptly vetoed the measure, no action could be taken on a move to override the veto. Finally, after an absence of two months, the legislators returned to pass a general appropriations bill following an agreement among Crump, Lea, Sanders, and Independent leader E. B. Stahlman of the Nashville *Banner.* Crump would permit the Shelby delegation to vote with the Fusionists on the election law and the Fusionists agreed to support measures beneficial to Memphis. The session ended with the election law of 1909 and the prohibition laws intact.

Hooper was a candidate to succeed himself in the gubernatorial contest of 1912, and McMillin was chosen by the Regular Democrats and a few Independents. With the strong support of Newell Sanders (recently appointed to the executive committee of the Republican National Committee), Hooper defended his record and charged that the election of McMillin would be a "return to lawlessness." McMillin defended the Democratic platform, which advocated repeal of statewide prohibition and a return to the Patterson position of local option in the cities. He decried the division within the Democratic ranks and promised to end the "temporary reign of Republicans." Prohibition and the election laws were the main issues.

McMillin's campaign was made difficult by several developments. His son died several days before the election, and he naturally withdrew from additional appearances on the hustings. Then, at the same election, Democrats staged a United States senatorial primary to select a candidate to succeed Newell Sanders, whom Hooper had appointed to the Senate when Bob Taylor died. Patterson was the only candidate, and his enemies identified him with McMillin—an association detrimental to McMillin's candidacy for governor. At any rate, most Independents joined Republicans in voting for Hooper, and the East Tennessee incumbent was reelected by a vote of 124,641 to 116,610.

The legislative session of 1913, like that of 1911, was one of

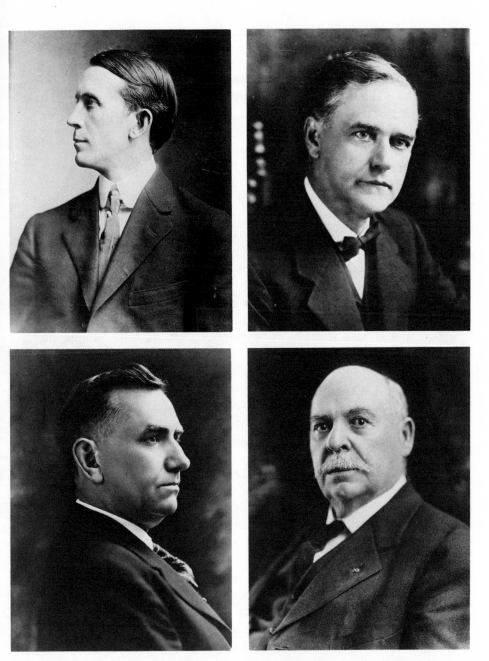

Ben W. Hooper and Alfred A. Taylor were two of the four Republican
governors of the twentieth century. Shown here are the governors from
1911 to 1923. *Above left:* Hooper, 1911–1915; *above right:* Tom C. Rye,
1915–1919; *below left:* A. H. Roberts, 1919–1921; *below right:* Taylor,
1921–1923.

considerable turbulence. Whether Fusionists or Regulars held control depended upon how Ed Crump wished the Shelby delegation to act. The result was that Crump worked with the Fusionists during the first part of the session but switched to the Regulars after Hooper called for enforcement legislation designed to close the Memphis saloons.

With the support of the Shelby delegation, Democratic Regulars revised the election law of 1909 to regain complete control of the state and county election commissions. Again, as in 1911, Fusionists prevented the majority from passing the measure over the governor's veto; they left the state and thus broke the quorum. Several months later they returned long enough to vote on a general appropriation measure but again departed so that those who remained ultimately adjourned in frustration.

Governor Hooper's proposed measures to enforce the prohibition laws had not been acted upon, and he therefore called the legislature into special session early in September. Among other things, he asked for laws to close saloons, to remove local officials who refused to enforce prohibition, and to regulate the shipment of liquor into the state. Although the measures passed the senate, the special session ended on September 27—before they could be brought to a vote by the tumultous members of the house.

Governor Hooper promptly called the legislature into a second extra session two weeks later and urged members to "restore the majesty of the law in the cities of Tennessee or face the rising tide of public indignation." This time he was more successful, as Democratic legislators realized that some enforcement was necessary. Despite opposition from Mayor Crump and other officials from the large cities, legislators—in an unusually brief session of five days—passed several laws; the most important were the Nuisance Law and two anti-shipment laws called the "Jug Bills." Under the Nuisance Law an attorney general, city or county attorney, or 10 citizens might secure the closing of saloons, "bawdy houses," and gambling establishments by court order if it could be clearly shown that police officials had refused to act. The anti-shipment laws prohibited the shipment of liquor from county to county within the state and forbade the transportation of intoxicants into the state from "wet" states; an important exception provided that individuals could carry or have delivered to their places of residence quantities of one gallon or less at a time. The laws were of course designed to close the saloons but not necessarily to prevent drinking at home.

Another important action taken by legislators in 1913 was the election of John K. Shields to a six-year term in the United States Senate after W. R. ("Sawney") Webb had been chosen to fill the remaining two months of the late Senator Bob Taylor's unexpired term.[1] Shields had been a member of the state supreme court for several years and had become chief justice in 1910 upon the death of W. D. Beard.

State Democrats Unite behind Wilson for President ⟩⟩⟩⟩ In the meantime, Democrats on the national level elected a president of the United States—the second Democrat since before the Civil War. The advent of Woodrow Wilson upon the political stage pleased Independent Democrats, and two years before Wilson's election they enthusiastically received rumors of his candidacy. Wilson captured the attention of astute political observers across the country in November 1910, when he was elected governor of normally Republican New Jersey. Immediately after the election the editor of the Chattanooga *Daily Times* hailed him as the hope of his party and boldly predicted that he would win the nomination in 1912. Luke Lea, owner of the newly merged *Tennessean and American,* joined the *Daily Times* in endorsing Wilson for the presidency. The Nashville *Banner,* on whose staff Wilson's brother, Joseph, was employed as city editor, saw him as one who could return the country "to the statesmanship of the old days." During the next two years, news about Wilson (whose father, Joseph R. Wilson, had taught at Southwestern Presbyterian Seminary at Clarksville from 1885 to 1892) dominated the front pages of the Democratic press of the state; his western tour in 1911—his first substantial bid for the nomination— was closely followed.

When Wilson visited Nashville in February 1912 to dedicate the new building of the Young Men's Christian Association, he found Independents solidly behind him, but the Regulars divided among

[1] When Taylor died (March 13, 1912), Governor Hooper appointed Newell Sanders to serve until the legislature met to choose a successor. Sanders' term thus expired when the legislature convened (January 24, 1913), and Webb was chosen to fill the remaining weeks of Taylor's term, which officially expired on March 3, 1913.

three other major contenders for the nomination. Senator Bob Taylor led the forces of House Speaker Champ Clark; Hilary E. Howse, the defiant anti-prohibitionist mayor of Nashville, championed the cause of Senator Oscar Underwood of Alabama; and the *Commercial Appeal* of Memphis and Nathaniel Baxter of Nashville upheld the interests of Judson Harmon of Ohio. The division of Democratic ranks continued through the state convention in May and the Baltimore convention a few weeks later.

Those who hoped that Democratic division would cause Wilson to lose the state were to be disappointed. President Taft had been nominated by the Republicans, of course, but Theodore Roosevelt's political ambitions had helped create a breach in the party, so that the Progressives nominated Roosevelt. The warm summer weather and the apparent hopelessness of the situation caused the rotund Taft to limit his speaking engagements considerably after early June, but Roosevelt, with the vigor that characterized his entire life, carried his campaign to Memphis, Jackson, Chattanooga, Knoxville, and points across the country. Because Tennesseans had elected a progressive Republican governor two years before, many observers believed that the state would vote Republican or Progressive. Democrats were able to close ranks sufficiently, however, to gain for Wilson a little more than half the popular vote and thus, of course, all the electoral votes. Taft and Roosevelt shared the remaining popular votes about equally.

Thomas C. Rye Elected Governor ࢰ Democrats had settled their quarrels enough in 1914 to regain the governor's chair. They nominated a relatively unknown attorney general of the thirteenth district, Thomas C. Rye of Henry County, a prohibitionist who had practiced law in Memphis and was generally acceptable to party leaders in all sections of the state. In an obvious effort to heal the breach, Democrats wrote a platform favoring prohibition.

Both Republicans and Independents nominated Hooper for a third term, but Independents were so weakened by defectors—and especially Luke Lea, who now turned the full strength of his powerful newspaper in favor of Rye—that they entertained little hope of success. Interestingly, former Governor Patterson, once the nemesis of the prohibitionists but now a teetotaler and under the employ of the American Anti-Saloon League, also declared strongly for Rye.

The result was a victory for Rye by a vote of 137,656 to 116,667. He won the Memphis vote by 12 to 1 majority, carried West Tennessee and Middle Tennessee without difficulty, and considerably reduced the majority that Hooper had won two years before. Hooper blamed his defeat upon the overconfidence of his supporters and ballot theft by the Democrats in Memphis and Nashville; the real reason, however, was that a large number of Independent Democrats had had enough of Fusion politics and had decided to vote with the Regulars. Democrats also secured control of the General Assembly.

The most controversial legislation passed during Rye's administration was the Ouster Law, enacted in January 1915. It provided for the removal of officials who neglected their duties, appeared intoxicated in public, engaged in gambling, or violated a penal statute involving moral turpitude. The generally expressed purpose of the measure was to remove officials who did not enforce the law, but more specifically it was aimed at Memphis Mayor Crump and other city officials who permitted saloons to operate in defiance of the law. Ouster suits could be filed by state, county, or city attorneys or upon petition by ten or more citizens.

Suit was filed against Crump under the provisions of the law in October 1915. The chancery court in which the suit was tried declared that Crump had not enforced prohibition laws and that he could no longer hold office. In the meantime, the Memphis mayor had been reelected to another term that would begin January 1, 1916. Nevertheless, the supreme court, to which the chancery decision was appealed, issued a stay order on January 1 that prevented him from taking office; six weeks later the court sustained the decision of the chancery court and stated that Crump had been properly ousted. Suits were also filed against Mayor Hilary E. Howse of Nashville and officials of other cities of the state. Howse admitted that he had not enforced the law in the capital because, he said, the people of the city were against prohibition.

Shortly after Crump's removal, Governor Rye called the legislature into special session to inquire "into the official conduct and fidelity of circuit and criminal court judges and district attorneys of the state," particularly Judge Jesse Edgington and Attorney General Z. Newton Estes of Memphis. The legislature convened on March 21 and brought impeachment proceedings against the two a few weeks later. Both were convicted and removed from office. Considerable interest was also shown in an attempt to remove Sheriff

J. A. Reichman of Shelby County, but testimony before the chancery court indicated that facts would not support the allegations.

Other legislation during Rye's two terms provided for the creation of a control board for charitable and penal institutions, a state highway commission, the registration of automobiles and trucks, a special highway tax to match federal funds, a general budget system, and a law prohibiting the sale at any soft drink stand of any beverage containing more than 0.5 percent alcohol. Of great significance was an act of 1917 requiring that party nominations for major offices be made by primary elections instead of by conventions. A proposal for a woman suffrage amendment was defeated at the polls in 1917.

The elections of 1916 created considerable interest. Wilson was nominated again for president and defeated Charles E. Hughes by a comfortable majority in the state, although his national margin was small indeed. In the gubernatorial election, Rye defeated John W. Overall of Liberty, who for some years had been a United States marshal for Middle Tennessee and a prominent Republican.[2] Principal interest centered in the senatorial race in which Congressman Kenneth D. McKellar defeated former Governor Ben W. Hooper.

McKellar was born in Alabama but moved to Memphis as a young man. He was graduated at the University of Alabama and became a successful lawyer in Memphis before his election in 1911 to Congress, where he served until his election to the Senate. The primary of 1915 saw McKellar's defeat of Luke Lea, the incumbent; former Governor Patterson and George L. Berry (later a member of the Senate) were also candidates in the bitter contest. During the vigorous campaign before the general election, tempers flared frequently. McKellar defeated Hooper by about the same majority that Rye polled in the governor's race.

In the meantime, Europeans had gone to war, and Tennesseans watched developments with increasing interest as hostilities progressed. Pro-ally press accounts in the four major cities kept the people informed. When President Wilson asked for a declaration of war against the Central Powers on April 6, 1917, the Tennessee congressional delegation supported him with a unanimous vote.

Nearly 80,000 Tennesseans were mustered into service, and most of them became a part of the Thirtieth ("Old Hickory") Infantry Division. The more experienced men had served in Mexico in 1916,

[2] The vote was 146,758 to 117,817.

when General John J. Pershing unsuccessfully attempted to capture the Mexican rebel Francisco Villa, but most received very little training until they reached France. The First Tennessee Ambulance Company left Memphis on June 7, 1917 and became the first group from Tennessee to go on active duty.

Park Field near Millington trained pilots for air defense. Although no regular training camps for infantry were located within the state, the University of Tennessee, University of the South, and other institutions of higher learning participated in the training of officers through the establishment of Reserve Officer Training Corps programs.

Tennessee troops were sent to France soon after they were mustered into service. After a period of intensive training, the Thirtieth Division relieved British troops on August 17, 1918, and the Fifty-ninth Brigade, commanded by General Lawrence D. Tyson of Knoxville, was involved in almost continuous action until the armistice was signed on November 11. General Tyson was awarded the Distinguished Service Cross, and Colonel Cary F. Spence was cited for heroic service. The Fifty-fifth Brigade, which also included many Tennessee units, was equally distinguished. More than 1,800 Tennesseans lost their lives during the war. Six received the Congressional Medal of Honor for outstanding service.

While troops marched off to war, civilians played necessary and important roles at home. Rutledge Smith of Cookeville became chairman of the Tennessee Council of Defense, which was to coordinate all war-related activities and to prepare the people for emergencies that might arise. W. E. Myer of Smith County became state chairman of the Fuel Administration; Harcourt A. Morgan, dean of the College of Agriculture of the University of Tennessee, headed the Food Administration in the state; Lee Brock of Nashville became chairman of the Fair Price Committee; and Percy Maddin of Nashville became chairman of the Legal Advisory Board. Thousands went to work in industrial plants and munitions factories; indeed, more than 20,000 promptly found work at the DuPont powder factory built at a cost of $80 million on the Cumberland River near Nashville at a settlement soon to be called "Old Hickory." Thousands of others, perhaps of less renown, raised victory gardens, bought war bonds, and encouraged the war effort generally.

The Volunteer State had its usual quota of heroes during the war. Admiral Albert Gleaves was in charge of transporting United States troops to Europe. The fact that almost two million men were sent overseas offers adequate testimony to the efficiency of this officer. Admiral William B. Caperton of Spring Hill became Tennessee's first full admiral since David Farragut. The Marine Corps, the Aviation Corps, and many other units of the armed forces inducted large numbers of Tennesseans. Lieutenant Edward Buford of Nashville was probably Tennessee's most noted ace; the Tennessee aviators who lost their lives included Lieutenants Claude O. Lowe and Charles McGhee Tyson, the son of General Tyson, who was honored by the naming of the McGhee Tyson Airport near Knoxville. Luke Lea, already well known for his activities on the political and publishing circuits of Tennessee, rose to the rank of colonel and even led a group of men into Holland in an effort to capture Kaiser Wilhelm II from the Netherlands, where he had taken refuge after Germany fell.

No Tennessee hero gained greater publicity than did Alvin C. York, a farm boy from the Cumberland Mountain area. During the Battle of Argonne Forest, York found his detachment decimated and, becoming separated from his remaining comrades, staged a one-man offensive against the German army. He is reported to have killed twenty German soldiers, captured a German major, and prevailed upon his prisoner to persuade 131 other Germans to surrender. The young Tennessee corporal created a sensation when he proudly marched his prisoners to the American lines. York was promoted to sergeant and was awarded the Distinguished Service Cross and the Congressional Medal of Honor. Congress voted him a resolution of appreciation; the people of Tennessee deeded a farm to him in his home county of Fentress and named an agricultural institute in his honor. In 1968, a bronze statue was erected in his honor at the state capitol.

Administration of Governor Albert H. Roberts ఄ The entrance of the United States into World War I in April 1917 did not dampen the interest of Tennesseans in state and national politics. Voters were not surprised when Governor Rye announced that he would seek election to the United States Senate instead of reelection to a third term as governor. The principal candidates for the Democratic gubernatorial nomination in 1918 were Chancellor Albert H. Roberts of Overton County and Austin Peay of Clarksville. The two men vigorously stumped the state before Democratic voters. Roberts won by about 12,000 votes and then defeated the Republican nominee, Judge H. B. Lindsay of Campbell County, by nearly 40,000 votes in the general election.

Senator Shields, the incumbent, defeated Rye in the senatorial primary by a small majority and won over H. Clay Evans in the general election by more than 30,000 votes. Shields had been elected to the Senate in 1913, the last time a General Assembly elected a United States senator. (The Seventeenth Amendment, which gives the people the right to elect United States senators, went into effect later in that year.) He found Rye a formidable foe in the primary. Rye had the open support of former governor Patterson and the tacit support of President Wilson, and Shields was forced to cancel plans to remain in Washington and returned instead to campaign. His warm support from Ed Crump and Senator McKellar was sufficient to net him a victory, although he failed to win Middle Tennessee.

The first item of business under the Roberts administration was the ratification of the Eighteenth Amendment, which prohibited the manufacture, sale and consumption of alcholic beverages. Inasmuch as Tennessee had been legally "dry" since 1909, ratification was considered a perfunctory matter. By a vote of 28 to 2 in the senate and 82 to 2 in the house, Tennessee became the 23rd state to vote favorably on the proposed amendment. Other states were quick to ratify it, and it became effective on January 16, 1920.

Of greater significance were laws revising the tax structure of the state. For a decade the expenses of operating the government had exceeded the revenue to such an extent that the deficit amounted to several million dollars. Roberts made economy in government and tax reform his chief issues. Inadequate laws, poor collections, and incompetent and corrupt officials, he told legislators, were moving the state toward bankruptcy. He therefore discharged unnecessary state employees and urged tax revision upon the legislature. The result was a "sliding scale" assessment law and legislation that gave the State Railroad Commission power to assess taxes on public utilities, including telephone and telegraph, electric power, gas, and water companies, in addition to the railroads.

Other significant laws were passed. One million dollars were appropriated, to be matched jointly by Davidson County and the City of Nashville, for the construction of a war memorial building.

Land was purchased and work was begun at once. Two measures were but a prelude to the bitter struggle for ratification of the Women's Suffrage Amendment. One granted women limited suffrage by giving them the right to vote in municipal and presidential elections, and the other, the Married Women's Emancipation Act, gave married women the same rights with respect to property as those held by unmarried women. Other laws repealed an act of 1915 abolishing capital punishment, levied a special tax for school support, and established a state textbook commission.

Tennessee Ratifies the Nineteenth Amendment ๛ The question of woman suffrage was not new to Tennesseans. As early as 1883 a bill had been introduced in the senate to permit women to vote in matters pertaining to schools, and a few years later a woman suffrage league was organized in Memphis. More than thirty-five years were to elapse, however, before suffrage leaders could claim even a partial victory.

In the meantime, faithful feminists sought to educate the people on the matter at hand. In 1906 they conducted the Southern Woman Suffrage Conference at Memphis and organized the Tennessee Equal Suffrage Association. Within the next decade many other organizations were formed on the local level in all of the major cities. Frequently liberal members of college faculties were at the head; the Vanderbilt Equal Suffrage League became a model for leaders at other colleges and universities throughout the state. Prominent individuals from other states, including officers of the National American Woman Suffrage Association, addressed and encouraged Tennessee leaders from time to time. In the forefront of state and local activity was Sue Shelton White of Henderson. She frequented legislative and congressional halls alike, called upon President Wilson on many occasions, demonstrated with other women in front of the White House, and was arrested and sentenced—for lighting a fire on the White House lawn—to the Old Work House in Washington, where she promptly went on a hunger strike until she was released.

Both Governor Hooper and Governor Rye favored enfranchisement during their administrations, but not until Governor Roberts was in office did women achieve their goal. In 1913 a proposed amendment that Hooper favored was defeated before the people. In 1917 feminists sponsored a bill with Rye's approval to give women the right to vote in presidential and municipal elections, but this bill was also defeated. When the measure passed two years later, leaders considered it only a token; they ignored it and concentrated the full measure of their force upon ratification of the proposed Nineteenth Amendment.

By the summer of 1920, some 35 states had ratified the Nineteenth Amendment and 8 had rejected it. (Approval of 36 or three-fourths of the states, was of course required for constitutional ratification). Of the remaining 5, Tennessee, Vermont, and Connecticut were the only ones that suffrage leaders believed might ratify it. Inasmuch as legislators in Vermont and Connecticut refused to vote on the question until after the November elections, Governor Roberts was urged to call a special session so that Tennesseans might express their desire through their elected representatives. Even President Wilson, believing perhaps that membership in the League of Nations might be accomplished by the senators elected in 1920, telegraphed Roberts to urge him to call a special session. Democratic presidential nominee James M. Cox of Ohio also urged Roberts to act, as did many prominent state leaders of both parties. One avid Democrat saw great significance in the matter for his party and wrote Roberts that if Tennessee did not ratify immediately, "some Republicans state will" and "[will] rob Tennessee of its chance for glory and the Democratic party of its . . . opportunity for success at the polls in November."

Roberts needed little persuasion. Once convinced of its legality, he called the special session to convene on August 9. Former governor Rye, as president of the "Men's Ratification Committee," and a variety of women's organizations began immediately to lobby for ratification. They were met by the Tennessee division of the Southern Women's League for the Rejection of the Susan B. Anthony Amendment and also by a variety of conservative politicians, preachers, and general citizens who argued that ratification would cause women to lose their femininity, violate the laws of God, elevate Negroes to high political offices, destroy democratic government, and even bring on a destructive war of the sexes. Those favoring ratification had the help of such prominent national figures as Carrie Chapman Catt, long associated with the movement for women's rights, and Senator McKellar. Those opposing ratification welcomed Congressman Finis J. Garrett and newspaper publisher E. B. Stahlman to capitol hill.

Observers noted from the beginning that the real struggle would
be in the house of representatives. Two days after convening, members of the senate voted 25 to 4 for ratification. After several days of
debate, House Speaker Seth Walker, who had earlier favored ratification but who had changed his mind when the special session was
called, moved that the resolution be tabled. This attempt to defeat
woman suffrage failed by a vote of 48 to 48. Ratificationists then
moved the adoption of the amendment. Harry T. Burn of McMinn
County had voted to table, but now he voted with the 48
ratificationists; this vote accomplished the adoption of the amendment by 49 to 47. So that he might have the right to move recon-
sideration of the action and perhaps still defeat ratification after
tempers had cooled and interest had abated, Speaker Walker then
changed his vote also.

A few disgruntled legislators then secured a restraining order from
a circuit judge enjoining Governor Roberts from certifying the vote
and reporting the results to the secretary of state in Washington. At
least thirty anti-suffrage house members, thinking the question now
would be reopened for debate and seeking to prevent the formation
of a quorum, entrained for Decatur, Alabama. The chief justice of
the state supreme court, however, granted a petition to dissolve the
injunction, and Governor Roberts thereupon certified the vote of
ratification to the secretary of state in Washington. Any additional
efforts to undo the work of the suffrage advocates were to no avail,
and thus Tennessee became the pivotal state in the nation's acceptance of the Nineteenth Amendment.

A Republican Victory ୧ ➤ Scarcely had the smoke cleared
from the ratification struggle when the November elections were
held. Despite growing dissatisfaction over Roberts' handling of
taxes, labor problems, and other matters of concern, Democrats had
chosen the incumbent in a summer primary over a real estate executive named William R. Crabtree, who had been mayor of Chattanooga and also a senator from Hamilton County. Roberts' small
margin of victory in the primary over the little-known Chattanooga
contender caused Republicans to take heart. Republican State
Chairman Hal H. Clements, pointing to the widespread dissatisfaction with Roberts' tax program, predicted that a Republican would
be elected "no matter whom . . . [we] nominate for governor." The

Above: Tennessee's unique position as the 36th state to vote on ratification of the Susan B. Anthony amendment caused the state's legislators to be wooed by both those who championed and opposed the amendment. *Below:* Tennessee, the 36th state to ratify the Nineteenth Amendment, was depicted by cartoonists as being the pivotal state in bringing suffrage to women. Carrie C. Catt Papers, Tennessee State Library and Archives, Nashville.

race soon narrowed to former Agriculture Commissioner Jesse Littleton of Chattanooga and Alfred A. Taylor, who was well remembered for his race with his brother Bob Taylor in 1886. By a 3 to 1 majority Taylor trounced his opponent in the Republican primary and stood forth as a unifier of his party.

Large crowds of both Democrats and Republicans came to hear Taylor, who was often joined on the podium by his foxhound, "Old Limber," and a quartet composed of his three sons and a friend who sang mountain ballads and religious songs.

Taylor captured the hearts (and votes) of the people and won the governorship by a majority of 229,143 to 185,890. He polled more than 70 percent of the vote in his native East Tennessee and ran well in the rest of the state. A majority of women apparently voted for Taylor, especially in East Tennessee; Robert had alienated many Democratic regulars by his support of woman suffrage, and he failed to endear himself to feminist leaders because of the negative attitude toward suffrage exhibited by many of his party leaders. The widespread popularity of Taylor, the national movement toward the Republican party after the war, the divisiveness still found within the Democratic party, the unpopularity of Roberts' tax program, and Roberts' attitude toward organized labor were other reasons for his defeat.

In the meantime Ohio Senator Warren G. Harding and Ohio Governor James M. Cox had been nominated for President by their respective parties, and both sought to draw attention to themselves by urging Tennessee legislators to ratify the suffrage amendment. On election day Harding won Tennessee by more than 12,000 votes. Although Cox's margin over Roberts exceeded 20,000 votes, Cox could not overcome the large number of woman voters in East Tennessee, who followed the lead of their husbands and fathers. The Volunteer State thus became the first Southern state to break ranks from the solid South since Reconstruction.

Taylor's two years in the governor's chair were frustrating ones for the aging chief executive, and his administration was only a few months old when he began to look forward to the end of his term and the chance to pursue a more sedentary life. Not only did he face a legislature controlled by Democrats, but he also had to contend with factionalism within his own party, as the Littleton group led by Senator John C. Houk refused to cooperate with him. Taylor identified as most important the state's need for better rural schools and highways, economy in government, and a revision of the tax program, but he was unable to supply the leadership necessary to bring about much improvement because of the lack of cooperation of legislators. During his administration new laws created the office of state tax commissioner, expanded the power of the Railroad and Public Utilities Commission, provided money for the establishment of Andrew Johnson's tailor shop in Greeneville as a shrine, and formed the Tennessee Historical Committee to collect and preserve antiquities of the state. Governor Taylor was especially interested in the continuation and expansion of the nitrate manufacturing plant begun at Muscle Shoals during the war. He headed a delegation of Tennesseans to Washington in an effort to persuade Congress not to abandon the project. Sources close to the governor told of his effectiveness in helping to avoid serious labor difficulties between the expanding unions and Tennessee's growing industry.

Democrats Victorious in 1922 ⧢ Widespread discontent with Taylor's program foretold of the success of the Democrats in 1922, and a strongly contested primary soon developed between Austin Peay of Clarksville and the veteran campaigner and "old war horse of Tennessee Democracy," seventy-seven-year-old Benton McMillin. Peay had managed Patterson's successful campaign in 1908 but had withdrawn from politics for the next decade while he expanded his law practice and farming interests in Clarksville. McMillin had served two terms as governor, had more recently been ambassador to Peru, had twice been a candidate for the United States Senate and, despite his advanced years, maintained an active interest in public affairs. Both men favored strict economy and a revision of the tax program. Ed Crump of Memphis and Stahlman, publisher of the Nashville *Banner,* supported McMillin; Lea, publisher of the *Tennessean,* and Clarence Saunders, a wealthy Memphian who had founded the Piggly Wiggly grocery chain, supported Peay. McMillin carried East Tennessee, and both candidates ran well in the central counties, but Peay won West Tennessee because of a tremendous majority in Shelby County. Although Peay was a tobacco farmer, he lost the rural vote to McMillin; Peay's urban vote brought him victory.

Republicans nominated Taylor for a second term, and soon the doughty incumbent and Peay were on the hustings proposing in many respects the same platform but offering a marked contrast in style. Both advocated economy in government, reorganization of the highway and tax departments, repeal of the law expanding the interest rate (from 6 percent to 8 percent) that lending agencies could charge, improved educational facilities, and a lightening of the tax burdens on landowners. Once again Taylor played his fiddle, told stories of "Old Limber," and beamed as a quartet of his three sons and a friend sang the old-time melodies. Peay, on the other hand, wore a Prince Albert coat and high stiff collar and formally lectured the people on lower taxes, better education and highways, and the need to curb the rising cost of living. Both men had powerful supporters. Lea of the *Tennessean* battled Stahlman of the *Banner* with political journalism of a quality very much in the Nashville tradition.[3] To *Banner* reporter Ralph McGill, Peay was a "czar," an "autocrat," and an "egotist"; the seventy-two-year-old Taylor was an "iron man" who was given a "generous welcome" wherever he appeared and reaped "enthusiastic applause." Crump played only a small role, but Clarence Saunders, his strong rival in Memphis, actively threw support and organizational ability behind Peay. The result was a victory for the Clarksvillian by a vote of 141,002 to 102,586. Peay gained the rural vote and won Middle Tennessee by more than a 2-to-1 majority, including Davidson County by about the same count. Although he lost East Tennessee by 15,000 votes, his margin in the western counties was 18,000.

At the same time, Senator McKellar defeated Newell Sanders by a substantial vote and continued a distinguished career that did not end until 1952. The legislature was also Democratic, insuring party control of the state.

The election of 1922 produced innovations in campaign techniques. For the first time radio was used, and Saunders' techniques in "selling" the candidacy of Peay just as he would sell merchandise anticipated more streamlined and better organized campaigns of the future. Among the journalists, Luke Lea was a clear winner and he continued to exert a tremendous influence upon Tennessee politics until his financial and political downfall in the early 1930s.

The period 1911–1923 was a reform decade in Tennessee de-

---

[3] During the war Lea allegedly tried to have the German-born Stahlman declared an "enemy alien" and deported.

velopment. The martyr image of the deceased Edward Ward Carmack carried over into the decade which followed his death and was a factor in the reform movement that followed. Ancillary to the prohibition enforcement statutes were laws against gambling on racehorses and cockfighting and attempts to provide for workman's compensation and to abolish capital punishment. The Seventeenth Amendment called for the popular election of United States senators, the Eighteenth for prohibition, and the Nineteenth for woman suffrage. All were readily accepted by Tennesseans, although the Nineteenth did have difficulty in the house of representatives. The election of Austin Peay foretold continued reform and better transportation and education facilities.

SUGGESTED READINGS

Books
Everett Robert Boyce (ed.), *The Unwanted Boy: The Autobiography of Governor Ben W. Hooper* (Knoxville, 1963); Paul E. Isaac, *Prohibition and Politics: Turbulent Decades in Tennessee, 1885–1920* (Knoxville, 1965); Kenneth D. McKellar, *Tennessee Senators As Seen by One of Their Successors* (Kingsport, 1942); William D. Miller, *Memphis During the Progressive Era, 1900–1917* (Memphis, 1957); Tom Skeyhall (ed.), *Sergeant York: His Own Story* (New York, 1928); A. Elizabeth Taylor, *The Woman Suffrage Movement in Tennessee* (New York, 1957); Rufus Terral, *Newell Sanders: A Biography* (Kingsport, 1935).

Articles
Arthur E. Buck, "Administrative Reorganization in Tennessee," *National Municipal Review* 12 (1923), 592–600; Philip A. Grant, Jr., Tennesseans in the 63rd Congress, 1913–15," *THQ* 29 (Fall 1970), 278–86; Paul E. Isaac, "The Problems of a Republican Governor in a Southern State: Ben Hooper in Tennessee," *THQ* 27 (Fall 1968), 229–48; Arthur S. Link, "Democratic Politics and the Presidential Campaign of 1912 in Tennessee," *ETHSP* 18 (1946), 107–30; James P. Louis, "Sue Shelton White and the Woman Suffrage Movement," *THQ* 22 (June 1963), 170–90; Joseph T. MacPherson, Jr., "Democratic Progressivism in Tennessee: The Administrations of Governor Austin Peay, 1923–1927," *ETHSP* 40 (1968), 50–61; William D. Miller, "The Progressive Movement in Memphis," *THQ* 15 (March 1956), 3–16; Gary W. Reichard, "The Aberration of 1920: An Analysis of Harding's Victory in

Tennessee," *JSH* 36 (Feb. 1970), 33–49; Reichard, "The Defeat of Governor Roberts," *THQ* 30 (Spring 1971), 94–109; Russell L. Stockard, "The Election and Second Administration of Governor Ben W. Hooper of Tennessee as Reflected in the State Press," *ETHSP* 32 (1960), 51–71; Margaret Ripley Wolfe, "Lucius Polk Brown: Tennessee Pure Food and Drug Inspector, 1908–1915," *THQ* 29 (Spring 1970), 62–78.

24.

Prosperity, Depression, and TVA, 1923–1937

THE decades of the twenties and thirties were years of reckless prosperity and excruciating depression. On the national scene, one of the most inept men ever to reside in the White House served as president at the beginning of the period, and one of the ablest came at the end. Scandals pervaded the administration of President Harding. Calvin Coolidge and Herbert Hoover cast about for solutions to very difficult problems; finally the confident and able Franklin D. Roosevelt led the American people into an experiment designed to end the ravages of panic and depression.

In Tennessee, the election in 1922 of Austin Peay brought to the capitol one of Tennessee's ablest governors. Peay died before he had completed his third term; he was followed by the mediocre administrations of Henry Horton and Hill McAlister. While Peay's election by no means ended political strife in Tennessee, it did bring years of constructive government during which Republicans and Democrats cooperated—at least on some matters—for the betterment of the state. Administrative reorganization, highway construction, and educational advancement marked the governor's accomplishments.

Horton's administration began in prosperity and ended in depression. His efforts to continue the constructive policies of Peay met with little success. When the Bank of Tennessee and other financial institutions failed, some of which had millions of state dollars on deposit, Horton was accused of poor judgment and fraud. McAlister served through the first New Deal and then was succeeded by Gordon Browning in 1937.

Peay as Governor ¿❧ Immediately after the November 1922 elections, Peay determined to make administrative reorganization one of his major goals. Most people agreed that it was long overdue. The constitution of 1870 had created four state administrative offices—governor, secretary of state, treasurer, and comptroller—but during the half-century that followed, governmental agencies, boards, commissions, and bureaus had increased at such a rate that duplication of effort, confusion, and gross extravagance seemed the order of the day. Acting independently of the state superintendent of education, for example, were the library commission, state librarian, free library committee, textbook commission, historical committee, and various examining boards. More than 1,000 employees worked in 64 departments, boards, commissions, and agencies at salaries totaling more than $1 million. Agency heads sought approval of their programs and appropriations for operation—in competition with each other—directly from the General Assembly. Legislators, the majority of whom served for only one term, were usually unfamiliar with the operation of state government; indeed many had sought election to the legislature not because they were dedicated lawmakers but primarily because they sought recognition in their respecve hometowns in order to develop a law practice or business. In many respects the governor was a figurehead instead of a strong executive who gave leadership to an efficient state program. Many observers believed that the number of state workers could be halved, costs of governmental operation cut considerably, and greater efficiency achieved.

In his inaugural address on January 16 the new governor therefore included reorganization among the goals he wished to accomplish. To the 3,000 well-wishers who assembled in the Ryman Auditorium to witness the ceremony, Peay spoke words of confidence and reform. He cautioned legislators against dissipating their energies in "legislation of a distracting character" and urged them to seek instead a businesslike administration of public affairs by a program of fiscal responsibility and tax relief. On the following day he sent to the legislature his recommended program, which emphasized economy, efficiency, and reform.

Within a few days, legislators, conceding the popular mandate, enacted a bill entitled "An act to reorganize the administration of the state in order to secure better service and thorough coordination and consolidation, and to promote economy and efficiency in the work of

Roads and schools were the major issues during the progressive administration of Austin Peay (*above*). Elected in 1923, he was the first governor
since Harris to be chosen for three consecutive terms. His death on
October 2, 1927, brought to the state house Henry H. Horton (*below*), a
Marshall County farmer who finished out Peay's term and then was elected
to two full terms.

the government. . . ." Eight departments, including those of finance
and taxation, agriculture, highways and public works, education,
institutions, health, insurance and banking, and labor were established. Each was headed by a commissioner appointed by the governor and answerable only to him. Some of the existing agencies
were abolished, but most were consolidated for more effective operation under these departments. The law become one of Peay's major
accomplishments, and his supporters claimed that it saved the state
millions of dollars. Very important to the chief executive personally,
it clearly shifted control of the state government from the hands of
the General Assembly to those of the governor. Indeed, for the first
time in the 127-year history of the state, the governor now held the
"supreme executive power" that had nominally been granted him by
the constitution.

With the reorganization going into effect on February 1, Peay now
turned to other matters. Economy in all aspects of state government
became his watchword—he even complained bitterly that a
Springfield judge caused the state an unnecessary expense of $90.
"When a dollar is wasted," he wrote the judge, "I suffer real grief."
Inequities in the tax structure worried him, and he secured passage of
a 3 percent tax on net profits of corporations. The tax not only
brought in much needed revenue but strengthened his support in
rural areas where farmers bore a heavy incidence of taxation.

Road building, public education, and conservation were the other
reforms that received high priority in Peay's program. At the time of
his election a majority of Tennesseans traveled in horse-drawn
vehicles over narrow, dusty or muddy roads. But the ubiquitous
Model T Ford, not to mention new power-driven vehicles produced
by other manufacturers, brought the staggering realization that the
state's roads must be reconstructed and expanded. Highway expenditures had ranked fourth (behind education, Confederate pensions,
and charitable institutions) in 1920 but took the lead during Peay's
first year in office and for the remainder of the decade required
greater expenditures than all other services combined. Financing the
program proved difficult. Urging a massive bond issue were cement
companies, which stood to profit from large state contracts, and
bankers, who would receive commissions on bond sales. But Peay
was committed to a pay-as-you-go plan. Ultimately he prevailed and
the program was funded from automobile registration fees, federal
aid, and a gasoline tax. By lifting the incidence of the tax from the

backs of the landowners and placing it in the laps of those who used the roads, Peay again endeared himself to the rural people of the state, who also profited tremendously from the new system. Good roads enhanced land values and brought growth to towns and cities.

Improvements in transportation also benefited education, as consolidation became practical and doomed the antiquated one-room schoolhouse. Educational development, discussed elsewhere, was one of Peay's greatest accomplishments, attributable in no small measure to the capabilities of his commissioner of education, Perry L. Harned of Clarksville. State expenditures for education doubled during Peay's incumbency, from $4.3 million in 1923–1924 to more than $8 million in 1927–1928, and the school term increased from 127 days to 155 days.

Although much had been accomplished elsewhere in the conservation of natural resources by the 1920s, it was not until the Peay administration that significant action was taken. But by the end of the governor's third term, Reelfoot Lake State Park was in operation and land had been acquired for the Great Smoky Mountains National Park along the boundary of Tennessee and North Carolina. Reelfoot Lake was created in 1811–1812 after devastating earthquakes opened giant fissures in the earth, permitting waters from the Mississippi River to engulf more than 25,000 acres in the northwestern corner of Tennessee and southwestern Kentucky. Soon thereafter squatters established homesteads in the surrounding swampy area and lived by hunting and fishing. Near the end of the century, however, enterprising businessmen began to show an interest in developing the area, and for several years landowners, squatters, and government officials quarrelled and sometimes fought over the use of the lake and the surrounding shorelines. The state designated the lake a common fishery and game preserve in 1909, but efforts to improve the terrain brought complaints from landowners both north and south of the waters. Finally, in 1925, Governor Peay proposed the establishment of a state park in the area. Consequently, the legislature authorized the purchase of a wide band of property around the lake, formed a commission to serve as a regulatory agency, and prepared the way for "Reelfoot Lake Park and Fish Game Preserve."

Establishment of the Great Smoky Mountains National Park took more time. After considerable negotiation among officials of Tennessee, North Carolina, and the United States government, Peay in

1927 sought a bond issue of $1.5 million as Tennessee's part toward the purchase of land for the national park. The Tennessee Great Smoky Mountains Park Commission, consisting of seven members, was created with power to acquire the land and assume control over the administration of it. More than 425,000 acres was eventually acquired, and titles to the tracts began to be transferred to the National Park Service in February 1930. Peay was dead by that time, but the honor and credit were his.

Although Peay was the first governor since before the Civil War to be elected to three consecutive terms, he met with determined opposition each time he sought reelection. As mentioned earlier, he had not sought the support of Memphis boss Ed Crump in 1922. But by 1924, Clarence Saunders' financial problems meant that he could help Peay very little in Memphis, and the governor decided to deal with Crump. Peay promised the Memphis boss that he could name a member of the election commission and also the location in Memphis of the University of Tennessee Medical units in return for his support.

The Memphis arrangement convinced Peay's enemies that the governor was unbeatable in 1924, but they made a thorough search for a strong candidate before they abandoned hope. Stahlman and Jesse Beasley of Murfreesboro (McMillin's campaign manager in 1920) even tried to persuade eighty-year-old Benton McMillin to run after former governor Albert H. Roberts refused to do so, but to no avail. They finally chose John R. Neal, a brilliant but quixotic political figure and former University of Tennessee law professor. In his lengthy political career, Neal ultimately was to lose 28 statewide elections, 9 of them for governor. The epitome of the absent-minded professor, he was said to have slept in his clothes, refused to take baths, and seldom graded students' papers while pursuing a teaching career. Peay's enemies, despairing of success in the primary, resolved to concentrate their efforts upon the general election. Captain Thomas F. Peck of Monroe County, who had served earlier as commissioner of agriculture, had been nominated by Republicans. During the campaign, both Peck and E. B. Stahlman, publisher of the Nashville *Banner,* kept up a daily assault upon the governor's program, and Peck sought to portray himself as the only friend of the farmer.

On election day the Republican turnout for President Calvin Coolidge gave Peck a lead in East Tennessee that Peay could not overcome, and Peck claimed that section by more than 20,000 votes. The incumbent governor swept the other two sections, however, taking West Tennessee by 74 percent of the vote. Peay won by a vote of 152,000 to 121,238.

Considerable interest also centered in 1924 upon the election of a United States senator. Incumbent John K. Shields was challenged in the primary by General Lawrence D. Tyson, a Knoxville war hero, who had commanded one of the two brigades of the Thirtieth ("Old Hickory") Division—in fact, he had commanded all of the Tennessee National Guard when the troops were first mustered into service. He had received the Distinguished Service Cross and won other honors for his actions in the Meuse-Argonne sector. Shields had served competently in the Senate but had lost popularity after he voted against President Wilson's peace treaty, which would have placed the United States in the League of Nations; indeed, a highlight of the campaign was a letter written by Wilson criticizing the incumbent for not supporting his policies. In the primary Tyson defeated the incumbent by 20,000 votes and won in the general election by a margin nearly twice that figure. In the presidential race, Democrat John W. Davis carried Tennessee comfortably, although he lost to President Coolidge by a substantial vote.

Peay fought successfully for adoption of most of his program in 1925, but he incurred the animosity of an increasing minority of legislators who chafed under the centralization of government in the governor's office. His veto of a bill to give each lawmaker a bonus of $450 for "postage, stenographic hire, and other necessary expenses" incurred additional unrest. And while he had developed friends who admired his courage and dedication, he had also made powerful enemies across the state, particularly among the bosses in Nashville and Memphis. He therefore took under careful consideration the question of a third campaign in 1926; only after he received hundreds of letters from Mountain City to Memphis during January and February of that year did he formally announce for another term. Suffering ill health at the time, he ran against the advice of his friends—principally, he said, because he believed that there was no one else to carry on his program. Nevertheless, astute observers knew that he would challenge Senator McKellar in 1928 if his health improved.

A number of gubernatorial hopefuls—legislators and others— attempted to develop support for themselves as early as 1925, but the opposition ultimately crystallized behind Hill McAlister, a Nashville lawyer then serving his fourth term as state treasurer. Although his personality invited comparison with Coolidge, McAlister hoped to develop support largely from the political bosses of Nashville and Memphis but also from other people across the state who for one reason or another had become disenchanted with Peay.

McAlister had reason to hope. Nashville was the base of operations for at least three political leaders of considerable power. *Banner* publisher E. B. Stahlman and Mayor Hillary B. Howse agreed upon their contempt for Peay, but *Tennessean* publisher and businessman Luke Lea again was Peay's strong supporter. Stahlman and Howse could control the Davidson County vote because of Howse's position and the concentration of the *Banner* circulation in Nashville; Lea's support was not concentrated at the municipal level but scattered across the state. In Memphis, Peay had lost the support of both Saunders and Crump.

Although Saunders vigorously opposed a third term for Peay, his effectiveness diminished considerably when he continued to encounter serious financial and legal difficulties in his grocery chain. Crump, however, had become a powerful figure by 1926 because of his growing control in Shelby County. He believed that Peay was taxing Shelby to support the rest of the state; after all, he argued, from 1923 to 1926 Peay had collected more than $1.9 million in automobile license fees from Shelby yet had spent less than $25,000 on roads there. The incidence of the gasoline and tobacco tax also weighed heavily upon Memphis and Shelby, while the tax revenues were used to support Peay's programs throughout the state. Crump not only feared Peay's threat to his own power base in Memphis but also believed that another Peay victory at the governor's level would bring the executive into a successful contest against Senator McKellar in 1928. Crump had become so able a defender of the interests of Memphis and Shelby County that by 1926 he could deliver the vast majority of the county's votes to anyone he chose.

On election day Democrats chose Peay by a narrow margin of 8,000 votes. Shelby County, which before had vigorously supported the incumbent, this time delivered a 13,000 majority for McAlister. Although the urban areas gave McAlister a 7,000 vote majority, 60 percent of the rural vote was for Peay. Thanks to the Shelby turnout, West Tennessee gave McAlister a substantial majority, and in Middle Tennessee the vote was about evenly divided; in the eastern section, however, nearly 70 percent of the ballots went to Peay, and without East Tennessee's support Peay would not have been reelected. This election contrasted with that of 1922, when Peay received only 26 percent of the votes in the eastern section. But the incumbent governor had assiduously courted the mountain vote for at least two years; he had given that Republican section good roads, good schools, and the Great Smoky Mountains National Park. He had played fair with the eastern people and had tried, as he said, to be governor of the whole state, not just Democratic Middle and West Tennessee.

Peay had little difficulty in the general election. Many Republicans revolted against continued control by National Committeeman J. Will Taylor and refused to vote for his candidate, Walter White, an undistinguished superintendent of public school from Rhea County. Peay defeated the Republican by a vote of 85,000 to 46,000.

Despite his substantial victory, Peay continued to face major difficulties. His health did not improve, and he continued to encounter problems with the legislature. Two factions, the urban and the rural, were readily discernible in the Democratic party by 1927, and without the help of Republican legislators from East Tennessee, Peay would have accomplished little in 1927. With a marginal coalition—Republicans and rural Democrats—he was able to pass several significant laws. He quickly secured a renewal of the tobacco tax and moved the educational and road building program forward. But in mid-February 1927, he contracted a serious respiratory ailment while in Washington on state business. Legislators recessed for six weeks while he recuperated, but differences between them and the chief executive continued. They became especially hostile after the governor, unable by veto to halt their plans for a $750 bonus for each and every senator and representative, ultimately blocked execution of their pork barrel legislation by taking them to court. Peay was widely hailed for his courageous stand for responsible government, and some began to talk of him as a vice presidential candidate in 1928, but on October 2, 1927, he died of a massive heart attack.

Peay's death brought to the governor's chair Henry H. Horton, a sixty-one-year-old Marshall County farmer who had not been active on the state level until his election to the senate in 1926. Without a political base and devoid of much talent for public administration, Horton had the misfortune to succeed a strong and experienced executive at a time when boss fought boss for a controlling hand in state government and financial depression brought many of the wealthy to ruin.

Luke Lea now became much more intimately associated with Horton than he had been with Peay, and in his quest for power he soon made a mockery of some of the reforms Peay had accomplished. But Horton in his weakness found strength in Lea. The Nashville publisher reached the height of his stormy career while Horton was governor and for a few years became the most powerful political figure in the state. Lea brought with him to the political stage Rogers Caldwell, a successful businessman with whom he had become associated in a variety of activities. Caldwell, with his brothers, Dandridge, Meredith, and C. W., had formed in 1917 an investment bank interested mainly in municipal bonds of the Southern states, which they called Caldwell and Company. Within a decade the Caldwells' industry and imagination had made the concern a financial empire with holdings in several states ranging from banks to baseball. In 1926, Lea and Caldwell made the first of several joint ventures— the purchase of a controlling interest in the Holston National Bank of Knoxville—and by 1927 had entered into a half-dozen or more additional transactions, including the purchase of the newspapers mentioned earlier. Horton's close association and involvement with the two was to lead to a groundswell of opposition and a move toward impeachment of the governor.

A few months after Horton took the oath of office, he announced his candidacy for a full term in the August 1928 primary. He was opposed by State Treasurer Hill McAlister, who had decided to run again, this time with the strong support of Stahlman, Mayor Howse, and Ed Crump. In one of the bitterest campaigns in state political history, McAlister made Horton's association with Lea and Caldwell the chief campaign issue.

McAlister insisted with some truth that Lea, not Horton, was the "real" governor. Even before Peay's death, Lea had sought to force C. Neil Bass, the commissioner of highways, to specify without competitive bids the use of "Kyrock"—a product of the Caldwell-owned Kentucky Rock Asphalt Company—in building certain Tennessee highways. After Peay's death Bass had no one to defend him, and continued pressure led to his resignation in February 1928. McAlister cited Bass's dismissal as an example of Lea's high-handed operation. The leader in the assault upon Lea and Horton was Stahlman's *Banner,* which daily pictured Lea as "Governor in Fact" and Horton as "Governor in Name." In a series of cartoons, Caldwell—the "Kyrock Kid"—was shown holding huge moneybags, Lea "the dictator" was dubbed "Musso-LEA-ni," and Horton—the "Governor-in-Name"—was usually mired in Kyrock. In Memphis, Crump worked more quietly behind the scenes than did Stahlman in Nashville, but the Memphis boss did hold rallies in support of McAlister. Crump also bought advertising space in which to criticize Saunders (who supported Horton) and, through the Memphis *Press-Scimitar,* which supported McAlister, denounced the "three Rock-Asphalteers, Lea, Caldwell, and Horton," as little more than "promoters and political hijackers."

Lea extolled Horton through his chain of newspapers. His Knoxville *Journal* urged Republicans to vote in the Democratic primary, and his *Tennessean* praised Rogers Caldwell as one of America's great businessmen. Through the Memphis *Commercial Appeal* he wooed West Tennessee voters who did not wish to follow Crump's lead. In all his newspapers Lea depicted McAlister as a weak and defeated politician who was only a tool in the hands of Ed Crump and the machine politicians of the big cities.

Also in the race was Lewis Pope of Pikeville, who had served as commissioner of institutions under Peay. A man of character and integrity, he, like Bass, had lasted only a short time under Horton and Lea. His dismissal, he claimed, had come at the hands of Lea because he had refused to "play politics." He won the endorsement of Austin Peay's widow and, like McAlister, pictured Horton as a mere tool in the hands of Lea.

Horton won the nomination by a majority of fewer than 6,000 votes in one of the closest races of the twentieth century. Crump delivered Shelby County to McAlister by a vote of 24,069 to 3,693; the Davidson vote was more than two to one against the governor, but the huge rural support for Horton brought him the victory. Thanks to the Crump influence in Shelby, West Tennessee delivered 53 percent of its vote to McAlister, but Horton ran strong in East Tennessee, where Peay had polled heavily two years earlier. The final vote was 97,000 for Horton, 92,000 for McAlister, and 27,000 for Pope.

In November, Tennesseans again voted Republican in the presidential election but chose Horton governor by a substantial majority. Prohibition continued to be an issue in the national contest, and Al Smith—never popular in the hinterlands anyway—was described as a

Catholic who would repeal the Eighteenth Amendment. This vote for Hoover was the last time Tennesseans voted Republican until the Eisenhower era of the 1950s.

Earlier, Horton had promised to continue Governor Peay's policies of road construction and educational development. When efforts failed to secure the necessary funds through a revision of the tax structure, Horton turned to bonds. Accordingly, the legislature provided in 1929 for the floating of bonds worth $28,796,000, most of which would be used for roads and bridges. Several months later, on December 2, 1929, Governor Horton called the assembly into special session to issue additional bonds for highway construction.

By a state statute of 1913 that was revised in 1929, money received from the sale of bonds could be deposited in approved state banks until it was needed to pay for the projects for which the bonds had been issued. This meant, of course, that favored banks sometimes had the use of state money for several months or even a year or longer if road construction or other projects moved slowly. The result was that large amounts of state funds found their way into the Bank of Tennessee and other banks controlled by Caldwell. The Bank of Tennessee, established in 1919 largely as a depository for Caldwell and Company, showed in June 1929 a state's balance of $40,000; two years later the balance was $2,269,000. Other Caldwell-Lea banks showed a total state balance in excess of $10 million. The collapse of the stock market in October 1929 and the onset of the Great Depression resulted in numerous bank failures across the country. Those owned and controlled by the Caldwells were among them, and a sizable loss for the state of Tennessee resulted.

Before the financial storm struck, another gubernatorial election had been held, and Horton was chosen for another term. It was a calm campaign indeed compared with that of 1928. Horton faced only a nominal challenger, a Shelby County attorney and farmer named L. E. Gwinn, who was an enemy of Crump but had the support of Hill McAlister and former governors Roberts and McMillin. To the amazement of political sages, Lea's *Commercial Appeal* warmly endorsed Crump for Congress, and the Boss of Shelby, announcing that he and Mayor Watkins Overton had appreciated Horton's efforts to build good roads into Memphis and to enlarge the mental hospital at Bolivar, supported the incumbent governor. Twenty-odd thousand Memphians changed their minds about Horton at Crump's behest, and Gwinn was swamped by the governor's majority of nearly 45,000 votes.[1]

In the same primary, circumstances necessitated the holding of two elections for the same United States senatorial seat. Senator Tyson had died in August 1929, and William E. Brock of Chattanooga had been appointed to serve until an election could be held. Therefore, the two contests developed as mentioned—one for the short term to fill out Tyson's term, which would expire in 1931, and the other for the long term, or the full six years beginning in 1931. Brock won the short term easily over John R. Neal, and Congressman Cordell Hull of the fourth district defeated former House of Representatives Speaker Andrew L. Todd of Murfreesboro and won the long term. Hull had served continuously in the House since 1907 except for two years (1921–1923) and had emerged as an authority on tax and tariff reform. The normally mild-mannered congressman had campaigned against Luke Lea in 1916 and had labeled him a "professional mudslinger," "chronic troublemaker," "political gorilla," and a person "seized with that spirit which caused the herd of swine to run into the river and drown." Lea had not forgotten these diatribes and tried to persuade Congressman Joseph Byrns (who later became speaker of the House) to enter the race against Hull, but to no avail. Neither Lea nor Crump played any role in the race.

In the general elections the Democratic candidates won handily despite efforts of the Republican gubernatorial candidate C. Arthur Bruce to make the large amount of state funds deposited in the Caldwell-Lea banks a major issue. The reaction against President Hoover brought even the defeat of veteran congressman B. Carroll Reese of the first district.

Four days after the election, on November 8, the newspapers of the state carried accounts of the closing of the Bank of Tennessee (owned by Caldwell and Lea); the State of Tennessee had a balance of $3,418,000 on deposit at the time. For several months prior to that time rumors circulated in financial circles that Caldwell and Company was in serious financial straits, but company officials had warmly denied them. The failure of the Bank of Tennessee, however, brought panic to thousands of Tennesseans from Memphis to Bris-

[1] The vote was 144,995 to 101,285. Horton won all three sections of the state, and received nearly 70 percent of the vote in West Tennessee.

tol. The Caldwell-controlled Holston-Union Bank of Knoxville suffered a run on November 10, when three-quarters of a million dollars were withdrawn, and it failed two days later. Other Caldwell-controlled banks either closed or merged with other solvent banks, and by November 14 Caldwell and Company had been placed in the hands of a receiver.

The State of Tennessee had had on deposit a total of $6,659,000 in the closed Lea-Caldwell banks at the time. When this fact became generally known, a storm of resentment arose against Horton, Lea, and Caldwell, and when the legislature convened in January 1931, demands were widely made for Horton's impeachment. Ed Crump, who had supported Horton in the August primary and as late as November 1930 was considered in the Horton-Lea camp, now denounced the governor and moved into the forefront of those seeking impeachment. Soon after the legislature convened it became readily apparent that Crump's forces would oppose those of Lea and Horton in the fight for impeachment. Both Horton and Crump issued statements through the press that were highly condemnatory of each other. Crump believed Horton's usefulness to the state had ended and that Lea and Caldwell would "go to [the penitentiary in] Atlanta."

A legislative committee was formed to draft articles of impeachment. They charged Horton with conspiring with Lea and Caldwell to defraud the state, having extravagantly spent money on furnishings for the governor's mansion, issuing false statements with regard to the state's money in the Caldwell banks, improperly using his pardoning power, and in general not being "fit and capable longer to hold the office of Governor." At first, sentiment was strong in the house, but after several long delays the movement failed. An analysis of the vote reflects the antagonism between the urban and rural factions and the still virulent power of Luke Lea. Many legislators chosen in the 1930 primary, when Lea was at the height of his power, preferred the discredited administration to the Memphis boss.

Constructive legislation that tightened the rules having to do with the depositing of the state's funds in state banks was enacted, but little else was done during the session. Horton had not been a candidate to succeed himself in 1932, and his departure from the governor's mansion early in the following year was not lamented. With him went Luke Lea, the principal political power in the state. Ed Crump, wrote the editor of the Chattanooga *Times,* "climbed in the saddle and became boss of Tennessee politics, succeeding Col. Luke Lea."

McAlister as Governor ᢒᢌ By the August 1932 primary, the nation was so deeply in the grip of the depression that bank and business failures were common across the country. In the governor's race, two-time loser McAlister ran with the endorsement of Ed Crump. Lewis Pope also ran again, this time on the slogan "Lewis S. Pope, the taxpayer's hope;" he promised revision of the tax structure, aid to education, and complete independence from the bosses. Malcolm R. Patterson, long in retirement in Memphis, ran as the administration candidate—with whatever support the wounded Horton-Lea group might give him. Crump delivered a majority of more than 25,000 votes in Shelby County to McAlister, who won the nomination by fewer than 10,000.[2]

The closeness of the race and Crump's methods of conducting elections in Memphis aroused a storm of protest and charges of fraud. Pope's campaign manager, Sam Carmack (a cousin of the slain Edward Ward Carmack), announced that the Pikeville attorney would contest the election because many of the Shelby precincts were "trained with this revolting fraud." Crump had used "cossack methods," charged the editor of the *Commercial Appeal*, and had "rounded up voters by the truckload" and taken them "like so many dumb, driven cattle" to the polls to vote for McAlister. Crump, however, bought advertising space to deny that he had conducted anything but a fair election. He denounced "the Liars, Blackguards, and thieves"who criticized him, and described McAlister as a "clean, honest, courageous and efficient" man who would "run the rascals out of the state house in Nashville." Although Pope filed charges of fraud, his claims were not sustained by the Democratic state committee. He then announced that he would run as an independent in the November election.

Pope's race in the general election disappointed his supporters; he finished third behind McAlister and John McCall of Memphis, the Republican candidate. On the national scene Franklin Delano Roosevelt swept the nation with promises of a "new deal" that would

[2] McAlister received 117,400, Pope 108,400, and Patterson 60,520. Pope went into West Tennessee with a 9,000 vote lead but lost that section by 20,000 votes. He received 45 percent of the rural vote, while McAlister won the urban support.

restore the country to prosperity. Tennesseans, who had voted for Herbert Hoover in 1928, now overwhelmingly repudiated the incumbent president in favor of the winsome chief executive of New York. The Lea-controlled *Tennessean* ignored McAlister's election but concentrated instead upon the promised reforms of President-elect Roosevelt.

Like the rest of the country, Tennessee was in the depths of depression when McAlister became governor and Roosevelt became President. In 1928, President Hoover and millions of other naïvely confident Americans had seen a vision of America without poverty. The euphoria had vanished by the time McAlister took office, and many people were in need. Indeed, by 1931, many people in Nashville, Memphis, Knoxville, and Chattanooga were without adequate food, clothing, and shelter. The Red Cross, Salvation Army, and similar organizations had spent the bulk of their resources, and many people looked to the federal government for aid. In April 1930, Tennessee was granted more than one million dollars of federal funds, which was soon spent in highway construction. Sometime later, funds under the Reconstruction Finance Corporation became available, and late in 1932 work projects under the Emergency Relief and Construction Act were begun in Knox and other counties. Even so, destitution was widespread. The Fisher Body Company of Memphis closed early in 1933, putting 1,200 men out of work; by the end of the year more than one-third of the major industrial establishments of the state had closed.

As mentioned earlier, financial institutions in Tennessee were in dire straits by the time of McAlister's inauguration. Following the example of more than a dozen other chief executives across the nation, the governor proclaimed a six-day banking holiday on March 1. By March 4, when President Roosevelt was inaugurated, scarcely a bank in the country engaged in normal operations. The President called Congress into extra session immediately and recommended legislation designed to restore popular confidence in the lending agencies.

After a quick thorough examination of all banks, treasury officials decided that sound ones would open during the week of March 12. On Sunday evening President Roosevelt assured the people in a "fireside chat" that their money was safer "in a reopened bank than under the mattress." Accordingly, stable banks located in the four

Above left: Kenneth D. McKellar (1869–1957) was an ally of Ed Crump, staunch supporter of the New Deal, and, with Senator George Norris, led the fight for TVA. *Above right:* Cordell Hull (1871–1955) was a state legislator and circuit judge before serving for nearly three decades in the United States House and Senate. He became secretary of state under Franklin D. Roosevelt and was mentioned as a presidential candidate in 1940. *Below:* TVA's Norris Dam created the first of the man-made "Great Lakes of the South."

major cities resumed operation on March 14, and others reopened later in the week. The Federal Deposit Insurance Corporation was soon established to insure deposits to the extent of $5,000 for each depositor. By summer, bank officals across the state told of the restoration of confidence in their institutions and proudly reported that more money was being placed in checking accounts than was being withdrawn.

Several relief agencies were created within the first few weeks after President Roosevelt's inauguration. The Civilian Conservation Corps (CCC), designed to provide relief and vocational training for a vast number of unemployed young men and boys, was established by Congress two weeks after the banks reopened. Camps were constructed across the country where needy young men were put to work planting trees, building roads, and performing a variety of other chores. By the end of the year, thirty-three camps had been set up in Tennessee. When McAlister's second term expired in 1937, more than 7,000 Tennesseans had been enrolled in the CCC. They had planted millions of pine seedlings, developed parks, erected fire observation towers, and accomplished many other worthwhile tasks.

Other agencies of relief established in 1933 included the Public Works Administration (PWA) and the Civil Works Administration (CWA). The former, created in May as a part of the National Industrial Recovery Act, provided work for thousands of unemployed. More than 500 projects were undertaken in Tennessee, including the construction of bridges, public housing projects, and municipal water systems, and the paving of streets and roads. Although the CWA received criticism throughout the nation, it employed hundreds of Tennesseans who cleaned county courthouses (of dirt), refurbished jails and schools, landscaped roadsides, raked leaves, and performed other chores.

The most important problem facing the Roosevelt administration—at least as far as Tennesseans were concerned—was that of restoring agriculture to a healthy and prosperous condition. Farm prices were declining daily, but the farmer's fixed costs—such as taxes and interest on borrowed money—remained constant. The situation in Tennessee, and indeed throughout the South, was critical when the Agriculture Adjustment Act was passed in May 1933. Under the act, payments were to be made to farmers who agreed under contract to curtail production of crops designed for market.

Cotton, the first crop to come under the provision of the act, was grown in 36 counties of southern Middle and West Tennessee and had declined in price from a high of 35 cents per pound in 1919 to 6 cents in 1932. A referendum indicated that nearly 90 percent of the cotton growers of the state wished to come under the program. Within a few weeks, 46,504 farmers signed contracts to remove 264,287 acres from production; for this they were paid $4,665,404.

Wheat, corn, tobacco, and other commodities also came within the program. Before the act was declared unconstitutional in 1936, Tennessee farmers had received payments in excess of $20 million for limiting production. Replacement legislation (including the Soil Conservation and Domestic Allotment Act) was soon enacted.

Tennessee Farmers also benefited from other New Deal legislation. The Emergency Farm Mortgage Act, the Farm Credit Administration, and the expansion of the Federal Land Banks enabled Tennesseans to borrow millions of dollars for agricultural purposes.

One of the soundest and most far-reaching of the New Deal agencies was the Works Progress Administration (WPA), established in 1935 with Harry Hopkins as director. It was the chief work relief agency until World War II made it no longer necessary. Colonel Harry S. Berry, who had served briefly as commissioner of highways under Governor Horton, was named administrator for Tennessee. In September, Berry announced that plans had been completed for farm-to-market roads costing $22 million and employing 5,000 men—a program from which "every county" would benefit. Its other projects included the construction of a variety of public buildings such as schools and courthouses, establishment of more than 100 parks, and provisions for many playgrounds and playing fields. By 1939 employment had been provided for more than 25,000 persons in the state.

Under the WPA people who could be employed were separated from those who were unable to work, and the latter received surplus commodities in the form of food and clothing. In order to supplement provisions supplied by the federal government, Tennessee in 1935 established the State Welfare Commission, with operating funds provided from bonds, to administer assistance to the needy. Thousands were soon placed on the rolls.

The National Youth Administration was created as a part of the WPA and became effective in Tennessee in September 1935 in time for the school year. This program provided constructive training for unemployed youths not in school and also gave aid to those who required it to remain in school. Students performed clerical tasks for school administrators, swept buildings, prepared food in cafeterias, fired furnaces, and performed many other jobs for which the government paid them a few cents per hour to enable them to attend high school or college.

Although Tennesseans participated in almost all of the New Deal agencies, certainly the most significant for the people of the Volunteer State was the Tennessee Valley Authority. Before the coming of TVA, the valley of the Tennessee River was an underdeveloped area with a relatively low level of agricultural and industrial development. Many of the people subsisted on a cash income of less than $100 per year. Although Secretary of Labor Frances Perkins may have exaggerated in 1933 when she said that few of the residents wore shoes, many people were on relief because of the depression. The difficulties of navigating the river, the widespread poverty in the area, and soil erosion caused by uncontrolled rivers and streams provided important impetus for the creation of TVA. In addition, the architects of the New Deal sought to produce electric power from water power, and TVA would offer a "yardstick" for determining the costs of producing electricity in this manner.

The Tennessee River had been troublesome to navigators long before the coming of Franklin D. Roosevelt. The Muscle Shoals area had been an obstruction to navigation from the time of John Donelson, and it was not until about the turn of the nineteenth century that canals were constructed around the shoals. Hales Bar Dam, built 33 miles below Chattanooga in 1913 by the Tennessee Electric Power Company, also greatly aided navigation upstream.

Washington, Detroit, and other cities watched construction at Muscle Shoals for several reasons. The federal government began building Wilson Dam in 1916 to produce nitrate for defense purposes, and in 1921 Henry Ford offered to lease the dam and other power facilities to produce nitrogenous fertilizer. Senator Kenneth D. McKellar enthusiastically supported Ford's bid, envisioning the great benefits that would result from such manufacture.

In the meantime, however, Nebraska Senator George W. Norris—"the Father of TVA"—opposed Ford's plan and urged the federal government to develop the area itself. Fearing monopolies in the field of electric power, Norris preferred to see the federal government operate hydroelectric plants because, he said, rates charged by the government could serve as a measuring rod for ascertaining the fairness of rates charged by privately operated power companies. McKellar soon joined the Norris camp, especially after 1928, when the Nebraskan agreed to include fertilizer production in his plans and agreed with McKellar that states should be compensated for tax losses resulting from a dam-building program. Norris was able to secure congressional approval for his plans twice before 1933, but they were vetoed by Presidents Coolidge and Hoover.

The law that established the Tennessee Valley Authority was passed a few weeks after President Roosevelt's inauguration. Broad in scope, it provided not only for power production but also for flood control, navigation improvement, reforestation, retirement of poor farmland, and "the development of the natural resources of the Tennessee River drainage basin and its adjoining territory for the general social and economic welfare of the Nation." A government corporation was created to carry out the intentions of the act; the first members of the TVA Governing Board were Arthur E. Morgan, Harcourt A. Morgan, and David E. Lilienthal.

Dams were soon under construction, and within a comparatively short time the Tennessee River was described as "the world's most modern waterway." The tonnage carried on the river increased annually, and Knoxville, Chattanooga, and other Tennessee cities benefited immensely from the increased trade and commerce.

Electric power production, however, became the chief function of TVA. Power could be produced so cheaply that almost everyone could afford it. With the development of the Rural Electric Administration, TVA electric power was made available even to Tennesseans in remote areas of the state. In 1933 the people in the area served by TVA consumed only 1.5 billion kilowatt-hours of electricity, but by 1945 consumption had increased to 11.5 billion, and 15 years later it had reached 57.2 billion. Inexpensive power became a magnet for industry, and industrial employment in the region served by TVA increased nearly 100 percent in two decades. The location of the Oak Ridge plant for the production of atomic bombs was selected in 1942 partly because of the availability of TVA power; for the same reason Tullahoma was chosen in 1949 as the site of the Arnold Engineering Development Center.

In addition to power production and improved navigation, TVA contributed importantly to flood control, soil conservation, and reforestation. It encouraged better farming methods through research and farm demonstrations. Research led to development of the proper types of fertilizer for the various soils and made the new products available to the farmer at a reasonable price. As a result of this improvement in fertilizers, the phosphate deposits in Tennessee have become more valuable, with a greatly expanded and steady market. Through the programs of TVA, the Department of Agriculture, and other public agencies, farmers in the valley have greatly increased their use of fertilizers, shifted a million acres from row crops to close-growing crops, terraced a million acres, and established nearly a million acres of improved pastures. Research by TVA has also led to the invention of new equipment for better farming and had aided in the shift to soil-building agriculture. Further, the chief forester of TVA has worked with the forestry services of the states to develop plans for erosion control, reforestation, and forest improvement.

The great lakes formed by the dams have resulted in many areas ideal for fish and wildlife and for swimming and boating. In combination with the Great Smoky Mountains National Park, opened in 1930, the TVA lakes and the Museum of Atomic Energy at Oak Ridge have made eastern Tennessee one of the most attractive regions for tourists in the nation. More people travel to the Great Smokies than to any other national park in the United States. Another tourist haven is the "Land-between-the-Lakes" development between TVA's Kentucky Lake on the Tennessee River and Barkley Lake on the Cumberland River. Stimulated by the authority's recreation program, Tennessee has greatly expanded the development of its state parks, the marking of historic sites, and the restoration of historic buildings. As a result, the tourist business has become an increasingly important source of revenue.

The depression brought suffering and Washington brought relief, and Tennesseans continued their avid interest in state politics. By the mid-thirties, few people disputed that Ed Crump was the principal political boss in Tennessee. Austin Peay was dead, the Caldwells had experienced the collapse of their fortune and power, the powerful Nashville *Tennessean* was in the hands of receivers, and Luke Lea and his son Luke Lea, Jr. had been incarcerated in the North Carolina State Prison at Raleigh.[3]

---

[3] After a series of legal maneuvers in several states, the Leas were convicted of conspiracy to defraud the Central Bank and Trust Company of North Carolina and were incarcerated in May 1934. Luke Lea, Jr. was paroled within a few months, but his father served for about two years. Both received full pardons in 1937.

No one felt the domination of Crump more than McAlister, even though he won reelection in 1934 by a comfortable majority. He was again opposed by Lewis Pope in what veteran *Tennessean* political commentator Joe Hatcher called "one of the bitterest and most stubborn fights ever staged in the state." Few issues emerged. Pope referred to McAlister seldom by name but simply as "Crump's puppet"; McAlister derisively spoke of Pope as the Bolter"—to show that he had deserted the Democratic party. Throughout the state the incumbent governor urged loyalists to vote Democratic, but Pope cautioned his supporters to "take your shotguns to the polls" to prevent Crump from stealing the election. At the same time, Congressman Gordon Browning unsuccessfully challenged United States Senator Nathan Bachman, who, Browning said, was "not the choice of the people" but had been appointed to the Senate by "his relative," Governor McAlister.[4] Senator McKellar, seeking reelection, had only nominal opposition from perennial candidate John R. Neal. McAlister won in the primary by about 50,000 votes and Bachman by about 40,000. Although Pope gained a majority in the Third, Fourth, and Eighth Congressional districts, he lost Shelby County by a vote of 39,218 to 3,574.

In the general election, veteran Republican political leader and former governor Ben W. Hooper developed a fusion ticket of Republicans and disgruntled Democrats. He persuaded Republican John McCall not to run for governor; instead Republicans and dissatisfied Democrats united behind Pope for governor and Hooper for United States senator. McAlister, Bachman, and McKeller toured the state together; the name of Franklin D. Roosevelt and the Democratic party was sufficient to win for them a victory over the Fusionists by more than 75,000.

Although McAlister had won both the primary and general election without the Shelby votes, he continued to feel the dominating hand of Ed Crump. When on one occasion he acted on his own, proposing a sales tax to reduce the state debt and to provide assistance for the public schools, he incurred the lasting enmity of the Red Snapper from Memphis. The powerful Shelby delegation, at Crump's behest, vigorously opposed the sales tax and launched a

[4] Bachman, who was acceptable to Crump, had been appointed to Cordell Hull's seat when Roosevelt named the Carthage senator secretary of state. Bachman was to serve until the next election (1934), at which time he ran for the two remaining years in the term.

Above: Edward H. Crump (1874–1954) was a powerful political leader for forty years. *Below:* Hill McAlister was governor from 1933 to 1937–thanks to Crump's support.

successful fight that was destined to bring about new alignments. After a bitter fight, the legislature failed to enact a new revenue bill, and the governor was forced to call the lawmakers into an extra session just to enact an appropriation measure that did not include the governor's recommendations for increased taxes and expenditures. Crump and McAlister also disagreed about the liquor question. The Eighteenth Amendment had been repealed, but the governor refused to give in to Crump's demands that Memphis and other large cities be permitted to sell alcohol.

McAlister did not seek reelection; Crump had termed him "our sorriest governor"—one who had kept the sales tax "hidden in his stony heart" and "tried in a sneaking way" to put it over on the people. He retired to his home in Nashville but later took the office of referee in bankruptcy.

The gubernatorial campaign of 1936 brought out two formidable opponents—Burgin E. Dossett of Campbell County and Congressman Gordon Browning of Huntingdon. Dossett, a superintendent of county schools, former state commander of the American Legion, and manager of McAlister's campaign in 1934, announced his candidacy early in the spring and had the support of the governor and Senator McKellar. Browning announced a few weeks later. The congressman, already known across the state from his race in 1934 against Bachman, had commanded a battery of artillery in a regiment commanded by Luke Lea during the First World War and had served in the House of Representatives with distinction for twelve years.

The candidates took to the stump early in June, and Browning soon emerged as the favorite. He promised to "clean up" the "corrupt" state government, institute reforms in state finances, encourage and support TVA, and maintain prohibition. Dossett would repeal the state's "bone dry" prohibition to bring in badly needed revenue. He claimed that Browning was not sincere in his claims of support for TVA.

Crump, interested in supporting a winner, was at first indifferent to the candidates and began a series of conferences with Senator McKellar and others on July 12. One week later he announced his support for Browning. Politicians were amazed that the Memphis boss would support an old friend of Luke Lea. But despite some misgivings about Browning, Crump did not care for McAlister's inner circle, and he had good reason to believe that Browning would win even without Shelby support. On election day Browning won by a 2-to-1 margin. Shelby voted almost 60,000 to 825 for Browning, and the governor-elect was so impressed that he promptly telegraphed the Memphis boss that there were "60,000 reasons" why he loved Shelby County. He faced only token opposition in November and prepared for his January inauguration and an administration of reform.

In the presidential contest, Tennesseans gave Roosevelt an overwhelming endorsement, as did voters throughout the country. It was a year for Democrats. Even veteran Republican Congressman J. Will Taylor of the second District retained his seat by only a 1,500 vote margin. The Democrats were back to stay—at least for awhile.

SUGGESTED READINGS

Books

T. H. Alexander, *Austin Peay, Governor of Tennessee* (Kingsport, 1929); Donald Davidson, *The Tennessee: The New River, Civil War to TVA*, Vol. 2 (New York, 1948); Wilmon Henry Droze, *High Dams and Slack Water: TVA Rebuilds a River* (Baton Rouge, 1965); Preston J. Hubbard, *The Origins of TVA* (Nashville, 1961); David E. Lilienthal, *TVA: Democracy on the March* (1944; paper rpt. Chicago, 1966); John Berry McFerrin, *Caldwell and Company: A Southern Financial Empire* (1939, rpt. Nashville, 1969); William D. Miller, *Mr. Crump of Memphis* (Baton Rouge, 1964); Jennings Perry, *Democracy Begins at Home: The Tennessee Fight on the Poll Tax* (New York, 1944).

Articles

James A. Burran, "The WPA in Nashville, 1935–1943," *THQ* 34 (Fall 1975), 293–306; Thomas H. Coode, "Tennessee Congressmen and the New Deal, 1933–1938," *WTHSP* 31 (1977), 32–58; Edward Felsenthal, "Kenneth Douglas McKellar: The 'Rich Uncle' of the TVA," *WTHSP* 20 (1966), 108–22; Jewell M. Galloway, "Speaker Joseph W. Byrns: Party Leader in the New Deal," *THQ* 25 (Spring 1966), 63–76; David D. Lee, "The Attempt to Impeach Governor Horton," *THQ* 34 (Summer 1975), 188–201; Lee, "The Triumph of Boss Crump: The Tennessee Gubernatorial Election of 1932," *THQ* 35 (Winter 1976), 393–413; Joseph T. MacPherson, "Democratic Progressivism in Tennessee: The Administration of Governor Austin Peay, 1923–1927," *ETHSP* 40 (1968), 50–61; William R. Majors, "Gordon Browning and Tennessee Politics, 1937–39," *THQ* 28 (Fall 1969), 166–81; William D. Miller, "The Browning-Crump Battle: The Crump Side," *ETHSP* 37 (1965),

77–88; J. Winfield Qualls, "The 1928 Presidential Election in West Tennessee: Was Race a Chief Factor?" *WTHSP* 27 (1973), 99–107; Franklin O. Rouse, "The Historical Background of Tennessee's Administrative Reorganizational Act of 1923," *ETHSP* 8 (1936), 104–20; Edward S. Shapiro, "Donald Davidson and the Tennessee Valley Authority: The Response of a Southern Conservative," *THQ* 33 (Winter 1974), 436–51; Judith M. Stanley, "Cordell Hull and the Democratic Party Unity," *THQ* 32 (Summer 1973), 169–87.

25.

T HE liaison of Boss Ed Crump and Governor Gordon W. Browning ended soon after Browning moved into the govenor's mansion. "I told him he could ride but that he could not drive," Browning said later of Crump. In 1939, the Memphis boss rode (or drove) back into power with Prentice Cooper of Shelbyville and consigned Browning to what many observers saw as political oblivion. Cooper, a conservative member of a prominent and wealthy Middle Tennessee family, became a respectable governor and had no difficulty in winning three consecutive terms. He thus became the first governor since the days of William Carroll to exercise undisputed executive power for six consecutive years. The Second World War claimed the attention of most people during Cooper's administration, and many young men (and some women) were in uniform in 1944 when Jim Nance McCord of Lewisburg succeeded Cooper and served two terms. With the elections of Cooper and McCord, Crump unquestionably controlled Tennessee politics. The voices of Luke Lea and others who had opposed Crump were stilled, and only Silliman Evans, a New Dealer from Texas who purchased the *Tennessean* in 1937 after it had become bankrupt, raised a strong voice against him.

The war gave Browning an opportunity to make a political comeback. The governor had been a popular field artillery officer in World War I, resumed his rank of captain in 1942, and was soon in Europe with the rest of the fighting forces. Rising to the rank of colonel, he was assigned to the task of establishing occupation measures in the conquered territories and ultimately became military governor of Bavaria. He returned to Tennessee a military hero and, in 1948, with

United States senatorial candidate Estes Kefauver, defeated Crump's candidates and broke the back of the Crump machine. Kefauver served in the Senate until his death in 1963. Browning, however, was unsuccessful in his attempt to win a fourth term and was defeated in 1952 in a four-man Democratic primary by thirty-two-year-old Frank Goad Clement of Dickson.

Although the Browning-Cooper-McCord era saw war and turbulent politics, it was a constructive period. Increased state income from taxes enabled leaders to bring about considerable improvements in education, transportation, and other public services.

Gordon W. Browning was inaugurated on January 15, 1937 in colorful pageantry on Memorial Square and assumed the office of governor with characteristic vigor. He first turned his attention to administrative reorganization. No comprehensive reorganization had taken place since Austin Peay, although many new boards, bureaus, and departments—incident chiefly to the New Deal and growing federal bureaucracy—had been created since Peay had died. The General Assembly immediately enacted the governor's recommended legislation, which provided—among other things—for the Department of Administration with a commissioner who would supervise the formulation of a budget, eliminate overlapping functions within departments, and study ways to promote greater economy and efficiency. Browning appointed to the post Wallace Edwards, former secretary to Governor Horton, and looked upon the new cabinet member as an executive assistant with considerable delegated authority and responsibility. The Department of Conservation was also created, with authority to supervise and regulate forestry, state parks, and fish and game management; in addition, the new commissioner was responsible for advertising to attract tourists to the Volunteer State. The New Deal program necessitated the creation of the Department of Institutions and Public Welfare, which was formed by a merger of the Welfare Commission and the Department of Institutions. Browning also implemented provisions for Tennessee to participate in the benefits of the federal social security program.

Perhaps the most pressing need facing the new governor was that of public education. Browning approved and adopted into his administration an "Eight Point Program" established by the Tennessee Educational Association and aimed at raising the state's minimum educational standards and teachers' pay. The bill, passed in March, appropriated more than $4 million, to establish a minimum term of eight months for elementary schools and a term of nine months for secondary schools, in addition to raising the salaries of most teachers.

Other legislation established a civil service system for state employees, provided for statewide automobile driver's license registration, set up a stricter hunting and fishing code and, as important as any other measure enacted, established a new debt-reorganization plan. Austin Peay had inaugurated a "pay-as-you-go" plan to finance new roads but, when that proved inadequate, raised revenue by issuing bonds. This policy was continued under Horton and MacAlister, so that between the years of Peay and Browning the debt rose from little more than $16 million to nearly $129 million. The governor sought counsel from financial experts in New York and soon presented to the legislature a plan to retire the indebtedness systematically during a period of years. Although the measure was enacted only after considerable opposition by the Shelby County delegation, it was hailed by creditors and the financial world as significant legislation.

Soon the legislature adjourned, and Browning was faced with another major decision when United States Senator Nathan Bachman died of a heart attack. The governor was flooded with advice from people of all political complexions, including President Roosevelt, who wanted to be sure that Browning did not appoint Cordell Hull, whom the president prized as his secretary of state. Browning had of course sought the Bachman seat in 1934 and nourished a latent ambition to serve in the Senate. He apparently considered resigning as governor so that the lieutenant governor could appoint him to the seat, but he was dissuaded by friends. Ultimately he appointed Major George L. Berry, a strong New Dealer and labor leader who in a rags-to-riches career had become wealthy as a printer and was now president of the Printers' Union with strong labor support. Although President Roosevelt hailed the appointment, Berry did not exercise the leadership as Roosevelt and Browning had hoped.

In the meantime, Edward Crump, who had delivered 60,000 votes to Browning in 1936, became disillusioned with his choice as governor. Soon the two were at dagger's point, and the controversy became the major factor in Browning's ultimate defeat in 1938. Crump had not only a latent fear of and dislike for Luke Lea, now in political disrepute, but also for anyone who had been associated with

Gordon W. Browning was a prominent political figure for thirty years. Six times a gubernatorial candidate, he was elected three times after serving in Congress for more than a decade. He was governor from 1937 to 1939 and from 1949 to 1953.

him. He had cautioned Browning about the "Lea crowd" before the governor's inauguration. He was therefore incensed when shortly after his inauguration Browning named Lewis Pope, an old Lea stalwart, to investigate corruption in the previous state administration and to collect back taxes. He was equally unhappy a little later with the appointment as comptroller of Marshall Priest, a strong man in the Horton administration, and of Wallace Edwards, who was to head the new Department of Administration. Later, Crump also claimed that Browning had not strongly supported TVA and that his associations with the private power trusts had been "overly friendly." Finally, on the prohibition question, Browning was "dry," while Crump supported local option in accordance with the wishes of leaders in Memphis and other cities. Basic to the dispute were the personalities of the two men: both wanted to control. By October 1937 Browning had become convinced that Crump was making preparations to oppose him for reelection in 1938 and that the 60,000 reasons why Browning had loved Shelby County in 1936 would work against him in 1938.

The governor was probably popular enough to weather the Crump and Shelby storm had he not called the legislature into special session to enact a county unit system, apparently a desperate attempt to break the back of the Shelby machine once and for all. Undemocratic on its face, the plan would nullify the great Shelby majorities. "Only a crazy man" would attempt a thing like that, Crump wrote. "Huey Long in his desperation didn't dare try" such a thing.

But Browning had the legislature under his control, despite strong opposition developing in Shelby, and he explained to legislators in special session the need for a revision of the primary voting law. Recounting the accomplishments of the session just recently adjourned, he alleged that the entire work of the assembly was threatened "because the Governor of the State could not pacify the resentment of an individual (Crump)." The Crump machine, which voted most Memphians as a bloc, had already registered 117,000 names as voters, Browning charged, but seldom in the past had more than one-half that number voted. "There is of course no one among you who believes that 117,000 voters have registered in any county in this state," he charged. He must choose, he said, between sitting supinely while Crump indulged in "such a sabotage" of his program and attempting to curtail the "invidious" power of the Memphis dictator. He therefore recommended the passage of a complicated unit plan such that "a definite influence in determining the results of a primary would be assigned and guaranteed to each county, in proportion to the vote cast for party nominees in the preceding election," limited only "by the comparative population of that county to others."

The unit bill, obviously, was designed to weaken the influence of Shelby County and to give more strength to the small rural counties. On October 15 the senate enacted the governor's bill by a vote of 20 to 13, despite the fact that scores of Crump's lieutenants roamed the legislative halls to defeat the measure. When the bill came before the house, United States Senator McKellar addressed legislators and denounced it as a violation of the principles of democracy. Despite the influence of Crump and McKellar, the unit bill squeaked by the house by a seven-vote majority. Crump's forces promptly announced plans to file suit, and early in the next year the state supreme court declared the measure unconstitutional. Voters would be discriminated against under the act, the court held, and a state could not confer the right of franchise upon one class and deprive another; a large vote concentrated in one area or one county could not within itself be regarded as prima facie evil unless violation of the law was involved.

The decision strengthened Crump's position and was a stiff blow to Browning, who was now depicted by an increasingly hostile press as one who would violate the laws of the state to establish a dictatorship. There were other means of counteracting Crump's power, however, and the governor immediately called the legislature into a second session at which they enacted a measure giving him control of the State Board of Elections. Encouraged by this, Browning ordered a purge of the Shelby County registration lists and soon reported the removal of more than 13,000 names of people improperly registered. When he opened his campaign for reelection in June of 1938, he denounced Crump and promised to destroy the Memphis machine.

The anti-Browning forces began to coalesce with the enactment of the unit bill, and in late winter Tenth District Congressman Walter Chandler of Memphis and State Senator Prentice Cooper of Shelbyville announced as gubernatorial candidates. Chandler soon withdrew, and the forty-three-year-old Cooper received the full support of the Crump machine.

Cooper was well qualified by background, education, and experience. His father had been speaker of the house of representatives and had practiced law for nearly a half century. Cooper had graduated from Princeton and Harvard (where he studied law), had served in both houses of the legislature, and had been attorney general in his district. He could not match Browning on the platform and therefore made relatively few speeches, but quietly went about his campaign discussing the issues of economy, education, roadbuilding, and taxation, often in the company of United States senatorial candidate A. T. (Tom) Stewart and William D. (Pete) Hudson, candidate for membership on the Public Utilities Commission. He welcomed Crump's support and treated the Memphis boss with respect but was apparently not submissive as McAlister had been. When Crump wrote a platform for him and asked that he sign and return it, Cooper apparently ignored the request. He also ignored Browning when the governor referred to him as "Little Lord Fauntleroy" who, as a puppet, responded only when Crump pulled the strings.

Crump entered the campaign with vigor and bought thousands of dollars of advertising space to portray Cooper as a competent man of dignity and refinement; Browning, however, he depicted as a bigoted boor. Indeed, Crump wrote, Browning was the type of person "who would milk his neighbor's cow through a hole in the fence." He was insincere; indeed, in his lifetime "his heart had beaten over two billion times without a single sincere beat." He was traitorous; "in the art galleries of Paris," Crump wrote, "there are twenty-seven pictures of Judas Iscariot—none look alike but all resemble Gordon Browning."

Browning, sensitive by nature, was wounded and made his campaign largely a contest against Crump. The "dictatorship" in Memphis had brought "corruption" to the ballot box, he told the crowds, where no one could receive fair treatment unless he bowed to Crump. Crump controlled even the federal bench in Memphis, the governor said, after United States District Judge John Martin answered "the swashbuckling governor" by enjoining him from sending the national guard to Memphis on election day to insure an honest election.

Toward the end of the campaign many people lost confidence in Browning; a hostile press now made him appear the very epitome of the dictator he purported to destroy in Memphis. The governor was also portrayed as a man who, with sufficient power, would run roughshod over the state and federal courts and the people themselves. The result was a resounding defeat for the Carroll Countian in an election that was about as one-sided as the one of 1936. Cooper won the primary by a vote of 231,852 to 158,854 and handily triumphed in the general election over negligible opposition. In the primary, he carried Shelby County by a vote of 57,225 to 9,315, took all of the congressional districts except the seventh and eighth, and won majorities in 62 of the 95 counties. Tom Stewart, also with Crump support, defeated incumbent Browning-appointee George L. Berry for the United States Senate by a substantial majority. In the congressional races, Albert Gore of Carthage defeated John J. Jewell of Murfreesboro by a small majority and continued to hold the House seat until his election to the Senate in 1952. For Browning the Democratic primary of 1938 was a humiliation and defeat; the governor soon after the election returned to Huntingdon to plan a comeback, while Crump increased his own power.

Cooper became a very satisfactory, although unspectacular, governor and numbered among his accomplishments several solid achievements. He was as conservative with the state's money as he was with his own. He granted few pardons, was tough on crime, and effectively used the highway patrol in breaking up roadside dives that promoted gambling and illegal liquor. He vigorously prosecuted violators of the small loan act and freed one-half of Tennessee's sixteen toll bridges. He received only nominal opposition in 1940 from George Dempster of Knoxville and won the general election without serious opposition in November.

Tennesseans had championed the candidacy of Cordell Hull for the presidency at the Democratic convention of 1940 but then for the third time gave FDR an overwhelming majority in his unprecedented bid for a third term. In the congressional races, Percy Priest as an independent defeated Joseph W. Byrns, Jr. in the general election after young Byrns incurred the wrath of Nashvillians by appearing soft on military defense and making uncomplimentary remarks about the king and queen of England at a time when the English people were fighting for their lives against Germany.

Cooper's austere and lackluster personality and his tight spending policy gained him strong opposition in 1942 when former fourth district congressman J. Ridley Mitchell challenged him. Mitchell entered the campaign with vigor and chose to make Boss Ed Crump and the poll tax the chief issues. At McKenzie, where Gordon Browning introduced him and described Crump as a dictator and his candidates as trained seals, Mitchell depicted the Memphis boss as a Hitler whose "political outfit will not repeal the poll tax" and "Charlie McCarthy" Cooper as "a stooge for Crump."

Crump had repeatedly refused to cooperate in the movement by the Tennessee Press Association and others to repeal the poll tax. The Shelby delegation in the legislature had beaten an attempt to repeal it in 1941, and in 1943, after the legislature repealed the tax, the supreme court in a 3-to-2 decision ruled the act unconstitutional. It was at this time that Silliman Evans, publisher of the Nashville *Tennessean,* increased his crusade against the poll tax and blamed Crump for the court action. The paper saw the Memphian's influence not only in the executive and legislative branches but now even in the supreme court. The *Tennessean* soon broke completely with Cooper over the issue, although the governor did call the legislature into extra session in 1944 to exempt servicemen from payment of the tax.

Crump was irate at the position taken by Evans and the *Tennessean,* but he was beside himself with rage when *Tennessean* editor Jennings Perry published in 1944 a hastily written book entitled *Democracy Begins at Home, The Tennessee Fight on the Poll Tax.* In a communication that he circulated among legislators and the press, and ultimately had placed in the *Congressional Record,* Crump refused to see the poll tax as a deterrent to democracy but regarded it instead as a means of insuring honest elections. As for Evans, Perry, and political writer Joe Hatcher, Crump viewed them as a "trio of mangy bubonic rats" who, as "conscientious liars," sought to malign him to gain standing for themselves before the people. Evans had a "foul mind and wicked heart," while Hatcher, filled with "ululation," was afflicted with "a diseased mind." But Perry—"an insipid ass"—had the "brains of a quagga" and wrote "just as one would expect of a wanderoo." Evans dismissed the attack as the frantic cry of a wounded old man who saw his power finally eroding—and the publisher was not far from wrong.

The election results were close enough to frighten the Memphis boss. Cooper's vote was 171,259 to 124,037 for Mitchell—a majority of 47,000, with nearly 45,000 coming from Shelby County. In the Senate race Edward Ward (Ned) Carmack, Jr. challenged Crump-supported incumbent A. T. (Tom) Stewart, and the results were even closer. Carmack went into Shelby County with a lead of nearly 20,000, but Stewart's 35,000 majority in Shelby kept a second Crump man in the Senate for at least another six-year term. Both Cooper and Stewart won handily in the general election that fall.

Prentice Cooper and Jim McCord were the governors during the 1940s.
Cooper (*above*) served from 1939 to 1945. McCord (*below*) was governor
from 1945 to 1949.

War and rumors of wars dominated the Cooper years, but they were years of solid achievement. The state debt was reduced from $123,598,000 to $83,517,000—the largest amount of debt reduction ever accomplished in a single administration. Aid to schools increased by 66 percent, appropriations for old age assistance doubled, and free textbooks were provided for children in the lower grades. A statewide system of tuberculosis hospitals was set up, and forest and park lands increased to 341,000 acres. The governor remained in Crump's good graces throughout his six years as chief executive, and only rarely did he not enjoy complete harmony with the legislature, although in 1939 a county option liquor bill was passed over his veto. In 1944 he was nominated for vice president in the Democratic convention but received only favorite son support.

Gordon Browning and most of the other able-bodied men not too old to fight had been mustered into service by 1944 and were engaged in combat in Europe, Africa, and the Pacific. Cooper, having served the constitutional limit of six years, was not a candidate for reelection and soon was named ambassador to Peru. The Democratic nomination fell to one of the party's most respected members of the House delegation, Fifth District Congressman Jim Nance McCord of Lewisburg. "Not since 1924 has the Tennessee Democracy staged a primary that was so unique," wrote veteran Nashville political reporter Ralph Perry, because "there was one candidate so far outstanding that the opposition was negligible." McCord defeated Rex Manning of Nashville and John R. Neal of Knoxville by more than a 10-to-1 majority in the primary and then won over John Wesley Kilgo of Greeneville in the November election by almost as large a margin. The "self-made man" from a poor family of eleven children had been billed as a "pure and wholesome plain country Democrat." For a quarter of a century he had served as mayor of Lewisburg and as a member of the Marshall County Court, had worked as a traveling salesman and auctioneer, and had published a newspaper. He had served as president of the Tennessee Press Association, had been a delegate to the Democratic National Convention in 1940, and was elected to Congress without opposition in 1942. McCord made no sweeping promises of reform but promised only to give the people honest government and to preside with a firm and even hand.

In 1946 the incumbent governor defeated Gordon Browning who, unlike most servicemen, had not been discharged from the military but still remained on army duty in occupied Germany.

Browning of course took no part in the campaign; Judge T. L. Coleman of Lebanon coordinated the labors of a host of servicemen and others who worked for the former governor's candidacy. McCord's victory of 187,119 to 120,535 for Browning was decisive but by no means overwhelming. Senator McKellar, whom Crump supported despite President Roosevelt's urging that he choose someone else, defeated Ned Carmack by an even larger majority—a victory that proved to be the last for the veteran senator and a defeat that ended the political aspirations of the son of a former senator and martyred prohibition leader.

McCord's major accomplishment—the sales tax—became the cause of his defeat in his bid for a third term. Astounded by conditions in the public schools, the need for capital outlay funds, and the lack of an equitable pay scale for teachers, McCord won a reluctant Crump to the support of a sales tax and then passed the measure in 1947 over opposition from Carmack, Silliman Evans, and others. The 2 per cent tax enabled school officials to establish a minimum wage scale for teachers, provide teachers with a retirement system, and fund expanding physical facilities in counties across the state.

In the meantime, Browning had returned to Tennessee, where he enjoyed a hero's welcome and soon entered vigorously into the gubernatorial race of 1948. He was joined by Third District Congressman Estes Kefauver, who challenged Stewart for the Senate seat. Crump continued to support McCord but, having become disillusioned with Stewart's poor showing in the election of 1942, threw his support to Judge John A. Mitchell of Cookeville. Stewart ran anyway—a fact that enabled Kefauver to win. Denouncing Crump as little more than the German dictator they had defeated in Europe, returning servicemen rallied behind Browning. The result was a solid victory for Browning and Kefauver and a defeat for the Crump machine from which it never fully recovered. Browning carried the Republican-dominated first and second districts, where Crump had been influential for years, and also won the other districts except for the tenth, where Crump still prevailed. Browning went into Shelby County with a majority of 85,000 votes, and even there he polled 20,000 of the 68,000 cast. The final vote was 240,676 to 183,938. Kefauver received 42 percent of the senatorial vote; his election, as mentioned, was made possible by a split of the opposition vote between Stewart and Mitchell.

Republicans were encouraged by the division in Democratic ranks

Chattanooga Congressman Estes Kefauver successfully challenged the Crump machine in 1948 and defeated two opponents for the United States Senate. He was the Democratic vice presidential nominee in 1956.

that gave rise to the Dixiecrat party, and they nominated for U.S. senator B. Carroll Reese, the long-time first district congressman. For governor they chose Roy Acuff, better known for his leadership of the Smoky Mountain Boys and his domination of the country music scene and the Grand Ole Opry from which stage he had become famous for his renditions of such old Tennessee favorites as "The Wabash Cannon Ball," "Great Speckled Bird," and "Night Train to Memphis." Although the crowds came to hear Acuff's music, they voted Democratic, and Browning and Kefauver won without serious trouble. In the presidential contest, Harry Truman won a plurality over the Republican, Dixiecrat, and other candidates.

Browning was inaugurated on January 17, 1949 and became the state's only governor to return to the office after a hiatus of twelve years. The old warhorse assumed his duties with characteristic vigor; indeed, as William R. Majors has written, he "took up where he had left off in 1937." Admitting on one occasion that he was "fortunate" as long as he could "keep Ed Crump a live issue in politics," he sought reform of the election laws to eliminate "election frauds, vote buying, and machine control by the Crump organization." Consequently the legislature enacted several election laws, including a significant measure that established a permanent registration system for voters in the urban counties. Other laws prohibited officials and candidates from serving as election officials, provided for the use of metal ballot boxes where voting machines were not used, and required orderly handling of absentee ballots. A "sunshine" provision required all election board meetings to be open to the public and all records and minutes of such meetings open for public inspection. Browning also turned his attention to schools and roads. He supported a four-point educational program that included higher salaries for teachers, money for capital outlay, and expanded benefits in the retirement system. His request for $148 million for the construction, improvement, and maintenance of farm-to-market roads passed the legislature in less than two weeks. He effectively defeated a bill for which the trucking industry had lobbied that would have increased the weight limits for large trucks. His proposals to bring together a constitutional convention to repeal the poll tax, classify property for tax assessment, extend the governor's term to four years, and simplify the means of amending the constitution were defeated and awaited the administration of Frank Goad Clement, his successor on capitol hill, for consideration and implementation.

Browning failed to develop a strong statewide coalition throughout the state, and this became a major cause of his defeat in 1952. He
looked for advice to his brother (former school executive F. L.
Browning) and a few others—Nashville attorneys John J. Hooker
and Jack Norman, Nashville Mayor Tom Cummings, and *Tennessean* publisher Silliman Evans—as a kind of "Kitchen Cabinet." But
in the final analysis he seldom trusted anyone's judgment except his
own—a characteristic that caused some people to describe him as
"stubborn" and "bull-headed." The result was a sizable vote in 1950
for a political unknown—Clifford Allen of Nashville—who had
served one term in the legislature. Browning had at first chosen to
ignore Allen and did not become active on the hustings until late in
the campaign when Allen became especially abusive. Only in the last
few days of the campaign did he even mention his opponent's name,
and then only to characterize him as being "the cheapest charlatan
that ever disgraced politics in Tennessee." Although Browning won
by a majority of 267,855 to 208,634, the size of Allen's vote scattered over the state indicated that Browning's charisma was wearing
thin. A strong candidate, observers noted, might unseat him if trends
against him continued.

A candidate for 1952 was not long in forthcoming. Frank Goad
Clement, a young Dickson lawyer associated with his father, Robert
S. Clement, announced on September 13, 1950. The reason for his
early announcement, he explained in a 900-word press release, was
that as a member of the Army Reserve he had been ordered into the
service as of September 15. He was assigned to the staff at nearby
Camp Gordon, Georgia, which was under the command of Brigadier
General Hatton Weems. Weems was connected with the Clement
family through marriage ties and maintained a lively correspondence
with Clement during his military service. Clement's duties were such
that he found time on weekends to return to Tennessee for speeches
before various civic, church, and fraternal groups. He was discharged
from service fifteen months later and began immediately to prepare
for the campaign.

Clement was a handsome man and a polished orator by years of
training, but he had no legislative and little administrative experience. He had graduated from law school at Vanderbilt University,
worked for a short time as an agent for the Federal Bureau of
Investigation, and then entered military service in 1943 for two years
before his ultimate discharge as a first lieutenant. Immediately after

"Far Hills," a Georgian home on a ten-acre site on Curtiswood Lane in Nashville, became the Governor's Mansion in 1949. Gordon Browning was the first governor to reside there.

the war he became general counsel for the Tennessee Railroad and Public Utilities Commission. He became known immediately as a church and civic leader, was elected state commander of the American Legion, organized the Young Democrats of Tennessee, and made speeches from Memphis to Bristol. His facility for quoting Scripture and his ability to captivate his audiences caused his political rallies to take on the flavor of old-time revivals that appealed to many people.

The Democratic primary of 1952 soon became the liveliest since the days of Bob and Alf Taylor. Although both Clifford Allen of Nashville and Clifford Pierce of Memphis also ran, the contest soon became a bitter man-to-man duel between Clement and Browning. Although Fourth District Congressman Albert Gore quietly challenged aging Senator Kenneth D. McKellar, the attention of the people was focused upon the contest between the 32-year-old challenger and the 63-year-old incumbent.

Clement opened his campaign on May 31 in Gallatin with a burst of oratory that captured the attention of people throughout the state. In a ringing tenpoint indictment of the Browning administration charging the governor with "corruption, graft, and favoritism," young Clement offered the people a new and untainted administration that would restore to the state "honesty, decency, and morality." The most important issue of the campaign soon became Clement's theme of "morality" versus "corruption."

Browning, a thirty-year veteran of the political and military wars, had never faced a challenger like Clement and he was stung by charges that he might be dishonest, indecent, and immoral. He first chose to ignore the Dickson lawyer, but he soon found that his antagonist must be answered. As the charges were expanded and Clement's confidence increased, Browning—as he was wont to do when frustrated or angered—not infrequently responded in an intemperate manner, which did nothing to help his cause but only gained sympathy for Clement. Accustomed to speaking to predominantly male audiences on public squares, Browning appeared ill at ease when on television. To many women and young voters, seeing the governor at close range for the first time, he appeared as little more than an out-of-date machine-type politician telling off-color jokes to the "boys."

Even so, Browning would probably have won the election had he not become involved in two matters that became grist for Clement's campaign mill. The first was the lease-purchase for office space of the Memorial Apartments on Seventh Avenue, a block southwest from the capitol. The other was his actions at the Democratic National Convention in Chicago in July.

The rapidly mushrooming bureaucracy of both the state and federal governments necessitated vastly increased office space even before Browning became governor. The legislature of 1951, at Browning's insistence, had authorized bonds for the construction near the capitol of a commodious office building to be named in honor of Cordell Hull. He also persuaded the legislature to authorize the outright purchase of the twelve-story Cotton States Building, one block south of the capitol. For these actions he generally was commended. But his method of purchasing the Memorial Apartments for office space raised questions in the minds of some observers and in the editorial columns of the Nashville *Banner*. These, when exploited by Clement, appeared that Browning's "cronies" were reaping huge profits at the expense of the taxpayers of the state.

According to Browning's lease-purchase plan, the state would buy the Memorial Apartments Building and, in turn, lease it to the federal government's Employment Security Division. Badly in need of office space, the federal agency would pay the state a rental of $115,000 per year. The state, in turn, would purchase the building by paying the rent collected for fifteen years to the owners and would then gain title to it. The total payment would amount to $1,725,000 over the fifteen-year period, but the governor's critics soon discovered that the building was worth less than one-half of that amount. When Clement and James G. Stahlman, publisher of the Nashville *Banner* and Clement's chief supporter, discovered that the people who recently had acquired the building and negotiated the sale to the state were close friends and political cronies of the governor, they had a major campaign issue. Stung by the charges of corruption, Browning answered by denying any wrongdoing. Instead, he said, it was the best business deal the state had ever made, because Tennessee would acquire title in 15 years to a million-dollar building for which it would have paid nothing.

Although Browning lost support as a result of the Memorial affair, he probably would have been reelected by a fair majority had it not been for his actions at the Democratic convention. Estes Kefauver was a contender for the presidential nomination, and Browning had campaigned for him in the Florida, Kansas, and Nebraska primaries. When a favorite son boom developed to nominate Browning for vice president, the governor quickly squelched it by urging all Tennesseans to work in harmony for Kefauver.

The real problem developed when Kefauver endorsed the movement sponsored by northern Democratic leaders to deny seats to any state delegation that refused to sign a loyalty pledge guaranteeing support to the presidential nominee, whoever he might be. This measure was of course designed to prevent the defections that had developed four years earlier and had resulted in the Dixiecrat movement. All delegations agreed except Virginia's, and Kefauver urged the Tennessee delegation to vote against seating them. Browning as chairman of the Tennessee group cast the state's vote against the Democrats from the Old Dominion, and Tennessee became the only Southern state to vote in this manner. Kefauver made little headway in his bid for the presidential nomination, and thousands of Tennesseans watching on television thought that their delegation had brought considerable discredit to the Volunteer State by "selling out the South."

Browning not only lost more than a week from the hustings; he also lost support. His enemies now described him as a "Yankee sympathizer," a "stooge for the left wing," a "scalawag," and one who had "sold out the South." The chagrined governor admitted to friends that he never should have gone to Chicago but was now forced to justify his actions before fickle voters. Clement, on the other hand, was described as one who "loved the South," who was "cradled in her bosom," and who would never betray her. When he spoke at Huntingdon, for example, banners above him read, "Frank Clement loves the South! We love Frank Clement."

The final four weeks of the campaign were days of increased activity by the Clement organization while the 63-year-old governor, exhausted by national as well as state responsibilities, tried unsuccessfully to keep pace. The result was a decisive, although not overwhelming, victory for Clement, who polled 302,491 votes to 245,166 for Browning. Allen trailed with 75,269, and Pierce received 24,191. Browning's efforts to inject Crump's endorsement of Clement into the campaign was of no avail, and Clement received a majority of nearly 40,000 outside Shelby County.

In the meantime, as mentioned, Gore had carried out a quiet but effective campaign against eighty-three-year old K. D. McKellar, who was seeking his seventh term as a United States senator. Unlike contenders in the gubernatorial campaign, neither candidate abused the other in any way; Gore's only issue was that the aging senator should be replaced by a younger man whose views were more in tune with the times. Gore won by a majority of 334,957 to 245,054. Both Clement and Gore won in the general elections without difficulty. The Democratic nominees for president and vice president, Governor Adlai Stevenson of Illinois and Senator John Sparkman of Alabama, failed to win the electoral vote in Tennessee. Thus the Volunteer State for the second time in a quarter-century voted Republican in a presidential contest.

SUGGESTED READINGS

Books
Cordell Hull, *The Memoirs of Cordell Hull,* 2 vols. (New York, 1948); Thomas A. Krueger, *And Promises to Keep: The Southern Conference for Human Welfare, 1938–1948* (Nashville, 1967); William D. Miller, *Mr. Crump of Memphis* (Baton Rouge, 1964); Jennings Perry, *Democracy Begins at Home: The Tennessee Fight on the Poll Tax* (New York, 1944).

Articles
James A. Burran, "The WPA in Nashville, 1935–1943," *THQ* 34 (Fall 1975), 293–306; William L. Davis, "Frank Clement: The First Campaign," *THQ* 35 (Spring 1976), 83–91; J. Bruce Gorman, "The Early Career of Estes Kefauver," *ETHSP* 42 (1970), 57–84; Allen H. Kitchens, "Political Upheaval in Tennessee: Boss Crump and the Senatorial Election of 1948," *WTHSP* 16 (1962), 104–26; William R. Majors, "Gordon Browning and Tennessee Politics, 1937–39," *THQ* 28 (Spring 1969), 57–69; Majors, "Gordon Browning and Tennessee Politics, 1949–1953," *THQ* 28 (Fall 1969), 166–81; William D. Miller, "The Browning-Crump Battle: The Crump Side," *ETHSP* 37 (1965), 77–88; Dean Pope, "The Senator from Tennessee," *WTHSP* 22 (1968), 102–22.

26.

৯৯ *Twentieth-Century Agriculture and Industry*

T HE state's economy has changed phenomenally during
the present century. Although much industrial progress
was made in the three decades after Reconstruction, Tennessee still
remained predominantly an agricultural state in 1900. During the
two decades after World War II, however, the Volunteer State
rapidly shifted from an agricultural to an industrial economy. By
1979, more than one-third of the people earned their living from
industrial jobs, while less than 6 percent received their major income
from farming. The standard of living of Tennesseans compared
favorably with that of people in the other states of the Southeast. The
per capita personal income of $5,432 exceeded that of the eight
contiguous states except for Georgia, Virginia, and North Carolina,
and had more than doubled during the decade.

Agriculture ৯৯ Agricultural development in the twentieth century has been marked by enormous advances in technology
and science. The greatest mechanical advance has been the invention
of the internal combustion engine tractor, which soon after World
War II replaced the horse and mule as the major source of work
power. At the turn of the century, electricity was unknown on the
farms, but with the advent of the Tennessee Valley Authority in
1933, that source of power came into use on most farms by the end of
that decade. By the 1970s the dairy farmer, as well as the row crop
and beef cattle farmer, was dependent upon electricity almost as
much as he was upon the soil.

Almost as important as the technological improvements was the revolution in the application of science to agriculture. County agents from Memphis to Bristol introduced farmers to a variety of new methods; farmers' cooperatives and other farm stores marketed commercial fertilizers that tripled and quadrupled production; and many new fungicides and weed killers were designed to decrease the amount of back-breaking toil once necessary to cultivation. By 1960 corn and cotton farmers used "pre-emergence" and "post-emergence" sprays that made necessary little or no cultivation of the crops between planting and harvesting.

Other major changes are evident, including a decline in farms and farm acreage (see map 10) but a decided increase in production. The number of farms multiplied steadily after the Civil War and until the 1920s; indeed, the number in 1860 (82,368) had tripled by 1910 (246,012) and reached a high of 252,774 by 1920. By 1930, however, the number had declined to 245,657, and by 1978 it had dropped to a little more than 100,000. There also had been a decline in the number of acres under cultivation and the size of individual farms. Farm acreage was at its height in 1900, when 20,342,058 acres were under cultivation with an average of 90.6 acres per farm. By 1930, however, 18,033,241 acres were under cultivation with an average of 73 per farm. In 1960, 16,081,285 acres were in farms, but by 1978 less than 13 million acres were cultivated.

Although farms and farm acreage have decreased steadily, production has increased enormously. The yield per acre of corn, cotton, wheat, tobacco, and all other crops has swelled because of improved farm practices and the use of modern fertilizers. The number of acres planted in corn, for example, was more than 2 million in 1950, while less than one-third that number was planted in 1979. But commercial fertilizers and improved hybrid varieties of seed corn have enabled farmers to triple production—the average yield per acre at mid-century was 32.5 bushels, while by the late 1970s many farmers produced 90 or more bushels per acre. The record yield by that year exceeded 6 billion bushels, and the average price that farmers received in 1978 was $1.96 per bushel. With the expanding livestock industry and the increase in swine production, the prospect for an increase in corn production is bright.

Agricultural development in Tennessee in the twentieth century may be divided for convenience into four broad periods. The first would include the first two decades of the century, when farmers enjoyed relative prosperity in comparison to the difficult decades

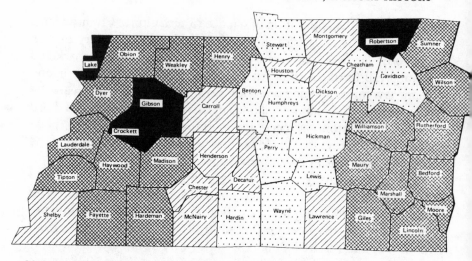

Map 10. Percentage of Land Area in Farms, Tennessee Counties, 1974.
Source: *Tennessee Statistical Abstract, 1977* (Knoxville: Center for Business
and Economic Research, Univ. of Tennessee, 1977).

following the Civil War; these years between the conclusion of the
Spanish-American War and World War I have been called the
"golden era of American agriculture." A second period would include the one and one-half decades from the end of World War I to
the New Deal; this period of course encompasses the depression of
1920, the subsequent efforts at relief by the federal government
under the Republican administrations of Harding, Coolidge, and
Hoover, and the first few years of the depression of 1929 and the
1930s. A third period would embrace the revolution occasioned by
the New Deal and World War II, and the fourth would be the three
decades of mechanization, coming after World War II, that drove the
horse and mule from the farm as a source of power in almost all but
the very hilly agricultural areas.

As the nineteenth century closed, the farmers' revolt ceased, and
farmers entered into an era of prosperity. As noted above, the
number of farms had more than doubled and the amount of cleared
land had increased considerably. Corn continued to be the major
crop and was grown in all sections of the state; in 1900 the crop was
valued at $28 million. Cotton was second in value, followed by
wheat, hay, and other crops. Cotton continued to be the major farm
product of southern West Tennessee, however; the five counties of

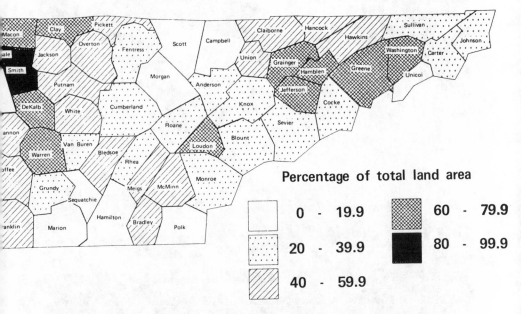

Percentage of total land area

0 - 19.9	60 - 79.9
20 - 39.9	80 - 99.9
40 - 59.9	

Shelby, Fayette, Haywood, Lauderdale, and Tipton produced more than one-half of the state's crop in 1900.

Concentration upon the production of animals for slaughter was also a major change by the turn of the century. Only a few years earlier most farmers had given little attention to selective breeding and had turned cattle and hogs loose during the year to roam in the forests and forage for themselves. Beef and dairying became important soon after the advent of the twentieth century, and by 1920 farmers throughout the state were producing good grades of cattle. Meat products in 1900 were valued at more than $19 million, greater than the value of any other agricultural product except corn. Indeed, Tennessee in that year ranked third among Southern states in meat production, just behind Texas and Kentucky. Dairy products were valued at more than $8 million. Poultry and eggs brought farmers almost as much.

Tennessee farmers at the dawn of the new century raised a variety of crops in addition to those mentioned. Tobacco remained important in the north-central counties, and farmers grew about 53.5 million pounds in 1900. Fruits and vegetables, long important, continued to bring profits. Among fruits, the apple orchards were far more numerous than all others. In 1900 the apple crop was valued at

Above: Memphis serves mid-America as the trade center of a seven-state region. *Below:* Chattanooga, historic Civil War battleground, is a thriving industrial city.

The wind tunnel at the Space Center at Tullahoma provides essential
information for the exploration of outer space.

more than $7 million; the total value of the peach, apricot, cherry, pear, and plum crop was a little less than $4 million. Others valued at one-half million or more included oats, Irish potatoes, sweet potatoes, peas, fruits, and sorghum.

"The farmers of our state are more prosperous," wrote Agriculture Commissioner John Thompson in 1908, "than at any time for 30 or 40 years past." The commissioner pointed to the increase in acreage under cultivation, the increase in production, and the growing farm income. The value of farm property and farm products doubled during the first decade of the new century. The enormous growth of urban areas had increased the domestic market enormously, and a profitable foreign market was also developing; thus the demand began to grow faster than the supply and brought welcome price increases.

Commissioner Thompson pointed to the state and county fairs and to the "Farmers' Institutes" as being extremely important in keeping farmers informed about new methods and markets. The first such institute, held in Jackson in 1899, proved to be very popular, and by 1908 the commissioner reported that 149 institutes had been conducted in 94 counties, in addition to regional institutes in each of the grand divisions of the state. The State Fair Association was organized in 1906 and offered prizes totaling $18,000. In a few years the amount of prize money was tripled. Tennesseans had won two grand prizes—in tobacco and forest products—at the Louisiana Purchase Exposition in St. Louis in 1904.

The prosperity of the years before World War I was stimulated considerably by the European demands for farm products after the war began. Cotton, for which Tennessee farmers received less than 12 cents per pound in 1912, brought 19.6 cents in 1916, nearly 28 cents at the close of the war, and an all-time high of 35.6 cents in 1919. Corn and tobacco also grew phenomenally in value. Corn, selling at 70 cents per bushel in 1914, had more than doubled in price four years later and brought $1.51 per bushel in 1919. Tobacco jumped from 9.7 cents per pound in 1914 to 27.9 cents when the war closed and then to a high of 31.2 cents in 1919. As prices rose, production grew. Animal products also increased during the war, although Texas fever, which invaded the state's beef industry early in the twentieth century, was a major cause of loss of beef as late as 1914.

The second period (1920–1933) opened and closed in agricultural depression, but between those years Tennessee farm prices held up reasonably well; prices did not approach the highs of 1919, however. The price of cotton dropped from 35.6 cents in that year to 13.9 cents in 1920; for the same years corn dropped from $1.51 to 62 cents per bushel, and tobacco from 31.2 cents to 17.3 cents per pound. In 1921, prices for cattle, sheep, and hogs had declined to about 50 per cent of their 1919 levels. During the 1920s industry and most of the rest of the country prospered, but not agriculture, because the productive capacity of the American farmer was obviously out of balance with foreign and domestic demands. The war years had been a time of heavy European demands; the postwar years had brought an inflationary spiral. Production from foreign countries in the 1920s—particularly South America, Australia, and Canada, in addition to Europe—greatly curtailed foreign markets, and improvements in technology at home caused overproduction. Although Tennessee congressmen were generally sympathetic to Washington's efforts to aid farmers, little of a constructive and lasting nature was accomplished there.

Officials of the State Department of Agriculture attempted to stimulate the economy during that time by encouraging immigrants to come to Tennessee and buy land. In 1922, the department issued a new edition of *Facts About Tennessee*, a pamphlet edited by Commissioner T. F. Peck and designed especially to inform potential immigrants of the advantages of living in Tennessee. Peck mentioned land available at low prices, salubrious climate, and productive soil. "There is a certainty of profitable returns," Peck wrote, "from whatever is put into the soil." He emphasized the growth of the cities and the resulting good prices for the produce of truck farmers. "Happiness, comfort, and health," he stressed, "await homeseekers in Tennessee, whose citizens gladly welcome newcomers to a region of schools, churches, social advantages, and good neighbors." Several groups of immigrants came into Lawrence, Franklin, and other counties but not in large enough numbers to have the desired effect upon the economy.

Although by 1922 Tennessee farmers had experienced relief from the depression, Peck's optimism was not warranted in the remainder of the decade. In that year, prices of cotton, corn, and tobacco climbed to 23.8 cents, 74.5 cents, and 22.8 cents, respectively, but

Above: Knoxville, where lakes and mountains meet, was the state's first capital. *Below:* Tennessee's capitol and nearby state buildings form the focal point for this view of Nashville.

they made no appreciable gains for the remainder of the decade. In 1930 the prices of the three products had sagged to 9.5 cents, and 12.8 cents.

The 1920s marked high hopes among tobacco growers for increased profits. The introduction of burley tobacco, which unlike the dark fired type did not require "firing," was a cause for optimism. At the close of World War I, burley was grown in only two or three counties of East Tennessee, but in 1921, after a concerted drive by the East Tennessee Tobacco Association and the Agriculture Extension Service to encourage its growth, 4,550,000 pounds were produced, with an average yield of 760 pounds per acre. Two years later production quadrupled, and a lucrative market was opened at Knoxville. Greene County became the leading burley producer in the state, and Greenville developed into one of the largest markets in the country. Although burley was confined largely to East Tennessee, farmers in the counties of Sumner, Bedford, Maury, and Giles also produced millions of pounds during the decade. Even though burley at times brought as much as 40 cents per pound, like other products, it experienced a decided decline in price at the end of the decade.

By 1933, drought and depressed prices had taken their toll among Tennessee farmers. Cotton had dropped to a new low—5.7 cents per pound—corn brought 31.9 cents per bushel, and tobacco fell to 10.5 cents per pound. A scorching drought in 1930 cut production to such an extent that experts in Nashville estimated the loss to farmers at one hundred million dollars. Along with prices, production had fallen considerably by 1933. The total value of farm products of the state declined from $314 million in 1929 to $132 million in 1932; the value of products sold by Tennessee farmers for the same period dropped from $161 million to $62 million. The registration of new passenger cars and trucks indicated the growing poverty. While 41,488 had been registered in 1928 and 55,211 in 1929, only 11,696 new vehicles were registered in the state in 1932.

Shortly after his inauguration in 1933, President Roosevelt told Congress of the dire conditions in Southern agriculture. The South was the nation's number one economic problem, he said; therefore, "an unprecedented condition calls for the trial of new means to rescue agriculture." Representative Joseph W. Byrns of Nashville, a member of the House for twenty-two years and later its Speaker, was among those who helped draft the Agricultural Adjustment Act (AAA), which President Roosevelt signed into law on May 12, 1933.

Manufacturers of chemical and allied products, such as the W. R. Grace Company of Memphis (*above*), represent one of Tennessee's leading industries. *Below:* Tennessee is a leading dairy state of the South.

This measure, which was to have a profound effect upon agriculture in Tennessee, was enacted mainly to raise farm prices to "parity"—a term defined as reestablishing "prices to farmers at a level that will give agricultural commodities a purchasing power with respect to articles farmers buy, equivalent to the purchasing power of articles in the base period . . . August, 1909–July, 1914." The measure authorized production controls through voluntary contracts with farmers to restrict their production of certain basic commodities such as cotton, wheat, corn, tobacco, and hogs—all important farm products in Tennessee. Producers were to be paid for their reductions in output by rental payments derived from a tax to be collected from the processors. State Commissioner of Agriculture O. E. Van Cleve hailed the act, praised the Tennessee delegation in Washington for supporting it, and estimated that in the Volunteer State the income of farmers would be more than doubled on the three essential crops of corn, cotton, and wheat.

Most crops had already been planted when the law was passed, and it was therefore clearly necessary to explain the act to farmers. At meetings held in every county during June it was carefully explained that some crops would have to be plowed under in order that farmers might benefit from the program. Other aspects of the law were discussed.

Cotton was the first crop to come under the AAA program. Governor McAlister, proclaiming July 12 as "Cotton Day," urged farmers to familiarize themselves with the program and to sign up to become eligible for payments. When the campaign ended, more than 46,500 farmers had signed contracts to remove a total of 264,287 acres from production. They were paid a total of $4,665,404 for an average of nearly $18 per acre during the first year. The law was changed in the following year, and nearly 90 per cent of the cotton farmers of the state signed contracts. Tennessee farmers participated in various aspects of the act until it was declared unconstitutional in January 1936. Producers of corn, tobacco, wheat, and hogs also benefited. Tennessee agriculture was being lifted "by its bootstraps," wrote the editor of the Clarksville *Leaf Chronicle* in July 1935, "out of the morass of depression."

Tennessee farmers participated in all the New Deal farm programs applicable to the state and received many benefits. They borrowed millions of dollars under the Commodity Credit Corporation program, enjoyed the benefits of electricity made available by TVA and

Above: Cotton is a principal money crop in the south central and south-western counties. *Below:* The soils of Tennessee, constituting the state's most important natural resource, provide fertile fields for tobacco cultivation.

the Rural Electrification Administration of 1935, and placed land in the soil bank under the revised Agricultural Adjustment Act of 1938. By 1936 the prices of cotton, corn, and tobacco had exhibited remarkable increases, and although prices declined during the brief recession in the following year, they regained their position by 1939 and continued to climb in the next decade.

During World War II there was considerable demand for agricultural products. Although the farm population decreased from 1,275,582 in 1940 to 981,501 in 1945 and the number of farms from 247,617 to 234,431, production increased considerably. The gain was due largely to improved mechanization. The Tennessee Home Food Supply Program was begun in 1940, under which each participating farmer agreed to grow a minimum of 75 percent of his family's food. Certificates of Recognition signed by Governor Prentice Cooper were given to those who participated. Governor Cooper was named chairman of the National Victory Garden Committee, and more than 200,000 families in the state cultivated gardens.

Many changes in agriculture have taken place since World War II, the fourth broad period in twentieth-century agricultural development. As mentioned earlier mules and horses, once the chief source of power on farms, began rapidly to disappear after the war and were replaced by tractors. In 1940 the number of tractors on farms was only 11,814, but five years later the number had doubled. By 1955 there were 84,869 tractors on farms, and by 1960 nearly 100,000. In 1960, nearly 12,000 farm operators reported the use of two or more tractors, and 718 stated that they operated farms on which five or more were used. The trend toward mechanization, improved methods of farming, superior seeds, selective breeding, and improved fertilizers and animal feeds have made greater production possible with less manpower and man-hours. Between 1910 and 1960, for example, the man-hours necessary to produce 100 bushels of wheat declined from 106 to 11.

At mid-century, 1,016,204 people lived on 231,631 farms; their land, buildings, livestock, and equipment were valued at two and one-third billion dollars. Many farmers were putting their land into permanent pasture for the grazing of dairy and beef cattle, and livestock became the state's largest single source of farm income. The gross value of dairy products was $105,148,000, and Tennessee ranked fifth in the nation in the production of cheese. Beef, pork, and mutton together were valued at $185 million and poultry at $40

The Tennessee River system of locks and navigable channels has been
called the "world's most modern waterway."

million. Cotton still was king, and the crop sold in 1951 brought $118 million. Corn was second at $106 million; tobacco came third at $67 million. Farmers cleared their forest lands to take advantage of high lumber prices brought about by the postwar boom. At mid-century Tennessee was the world's largest producer of hardwood flooring and also supplied millions of board feet for furniture manufacture and other construction.

By the 1960s cotton had declined in importance and had been replaced by tobacco, soybeans, and corn as important money crops. The cotton crop of 1967, curtailed by unseasonable weather and decreasing acreage, was the smallest in more than 100 years, and the yield of 336 pounds per acre was the lowest since 1951. In 1977, farmers produced 408 pounds per acre; the total crop value, lint and seed combined, was $66 million, which was $13 million lower than that of 1976. The number of acres planted in cotton—3,000,000—was 19 percent less than that of the previous year.

Tobacco became the principal money crop in 1966 but yielded first place in 1972 to soybeans, which have held the top spot since that time. It was in the mid-1960s that farmers began to produce soybeans in abundance. From a production of less than 4 million bushels at mid-century, farmers by the 1980s were producing twelve times that amount. Ten counties—Dyer, Gibson, Lauderdale, Obion, Tipton, Fayette, Shelby, Haywood, Lake, and Weakley, all in "West Tennessee"—early emerged as the chief producers, as traditional cotton farmers turned to the new crop.

Tobacco and corn continued to rank high as money crops, although hay comes second to soybeans in acres harvested. The value of the tobacco crop, $174 in 1977, was more than three times that of 1950, although the number of acres devoted to it remained virtually unchanged. Greeneville has continued to be the leading burley market, while Johnson City, Mountain City, and New Tazewell are not far behind. In Middle Tennessee, where several strains are grown— including burley, dark air-cured, and eastern dark-fired—Franklin, Sparta, Columbia, Hartsville, and Clarksville are the largest markets. Tennessee traditionally has ranked fifth among the sixteen major tobacco-producing states in crop value.

A variety of other farm produce brought income to Tennessee farmers, in addition to soybeans, tobacco, corn, wheat, and cotton. Indeed, 53 percent of the total farm income received by farmers came from livestock products. Meat animals—cattle, hogs, sheep, and lambs—account for about 33 percent. Poultry and eggs brought almost 6 percent. The dairying industry has declined and the number of cows milked in the 1980s was only about one-third the number milked in 1950. The sheep and wool industry also has declined.

Of major concern to agriculture in the last quarter of the twentieth century is the steady decline of farms, a poignant indication that the small farmer is the modern "vanishing American" in Tennessee as well as in the nation as a whole. But much of the land is becoming too valuable to cultivate, as urban areas encroach increasingly upon the farms.

Industry ⧫ The industrial development of the last three decades of the nineteenth century continued at even a greater rate after the beginning of the twentieth century. The capitalization of industry had reached a new high of $71,182,966 in 1899, and the value of manufactured products exceeded $92,500,000. Industrial workers numbered 45,963 and were paid a total of $14,727,506 in wages.

At the beginning of the century the leading industry was grist and flour milling, which accounted for more than 20 percent of the total products of the state's industries. Nashville was the chief center for flour milling, with Knoxville the leading center in the eastern part of the state and Memphis most important in the west. Because of the abundance of corn, wheat and water, most small towns had a grist or flour mill. The timber and lumber industry ranked second. Every county had an abundant supply of virgin timber and, consequently, many sawmills. Memphis was the largest inland hardwood lumber market in the world at the turn of the century; Nashville led in flooring and other hardwood products. Third place among the industries was held by iron and steel. Sixteen establishments employed nearly 2,000 wage earners, and their products were valued at $5,000,000. Ore was mined in both East and Middle Tennessee. Other important industries at the turn of the century included textiles (with an employment of 4,251), cottonseed products, and tobacco processing; the last-named industry experienced a gain of 252.7 percent within the decade.

During the first three decades of the twentieth century, industrial growth continued. The number of manufacturing establishments increased approximately 45 percent from 1904 to 1909, and five years later, when the war began, factory growth showed considerable development that continued throughout World War I. Many of the industries originating during the war were of a temporary nature, however, and immediately after the war some plants were closed. After the recession of 1920–1921, industry again developed strongly in the state until the depression began in 1929. The average number of wage earners in manufacturing increased 179 percent during the thirty-year period from 1899 to 1929. In the first decade alone of this period, the increase was 60 percent. Again, from 1914 to 1919 the number of wage earners increased 28 percent—largely because of the war prosperity and the demands of the Allies for war goods.

Considerable diversification took place in the first three decades of the century, and several new industries ranked foremost among manufactured goods of the state. Knit goods, as measured by the value of the annual output, ranked first in 1930, with an output value of $48,406,388. Lumber and timber products came second at $32,604,611. Grist and flour mill operations, which had ranked first in 1900, placed third in 1930, with products valued at $28,600,288. Rayon, shortenings and other vegetable cooking oils, animal and poultry feeds, and motor vehicles and parts were scarcely heard of in 1900 but were valued in the millions in 1930.

Although some plants constructed during the war had closed by 1919, others were able to convert to products for civilian consumer use. Among these was the DuPont Powder Plant at Old Hickory, which was manufacturing rayon and cellophane goods very shortly after arms were stacked. The plant was constructed in a record time of three months and was producing powder by July 1918. By summer of the following year, the town of Old Hickory consisted of 30,000 people and nearly 4,000 buildings, including homes, schools,

Above: Now a National Historic Landmark, the graphite reactor at Oak Ridge once served as a pilot plant for production of plutonium. *Below:* Built in two and one-half years, Oak Ridge became Tennessee's fifth largest city and had the world's first gaseous diffusion plant.

hotels, and city government buildings. A steel suspension bridge 540 feet long, with 1,260 feet of trestled approaches, spanned the Cumberland River, which separated the town from Nashville. Thousands of Tennesseans were soon employed in the manufacture of rayon and cellophane. Although operations were curtailed during and after the depression of 1929, the plant failed to close completely during that time.

The decade of the 1920s opened and closed in depression, but in an intervening seven-year period considerable industrial growth occurred. The number of commercial establishments increased 36 percent in the two-year period from 1927 to 1929 but declined 45 percent during the next four-year period. When the depression began, the number of wage earners in manufacturing had increased 179 percent during the first thirty years of the twentieth century. The population increased during the same period by only 39.7 percent; farmers obviously were exchanging the soil for factory jobs.

The increase in industrial development was largely responsible for the urban growth during the first three decades of the century. In 1929, Memphis, with a population of 162,351, produced manufactured products valued at nearly $200 million; Nashville, with a population of 118,342, produced goods valued at nearly $150 million; and Chattanooga ranked third with products worth well over $100 million. Memphis, the largest inland cotton market of the world, became the world's largest producer of cottonseed products. By the early 1920s the E. L. Bruce Company of Memphis had become the world's largest hardwood flooring manufacturer. Chattanooga, with a population of 57,895, was the leading knit goods center of the state and was second in the entire nation in the construction of steam boilers and in the manufacture of hosiery. Knoxville, with a population of 77,818, manufactured hundreds of different items—textiles, iron and steel products, marble and other stone products, knit goods, and lumber. Moreover, many of the small urban areas were in the process of developing large industrial establishments. The Kingsport Press of Kingsport was reputed to be the largest plant in the country devoted exclusively to the manufacture of books. Johnson City, the fifth largest urban area, had large hosiery mills, textile mills, and other factories. Jackson, almost as large as Johnson City, was a railroad center and was outstanding for its production of cottonseed products.

Although the depression of the 1930s caused many manufacturing establishments to close, considerable recovery was apparent by 1937. In that year 2,083 industrial plants in Tennessee paid total wages of $109,247,514 and produced goods valued at $707,986,784. Two years later, when World War II began in Europe, the number of plants had expanded to 2,289, which paid wages in the amount of $109,661,769 and produced goods valued at $728,087,825. By that year rayon and allied products had become one of the most valuable industries in the state, producing goods valued at $59,724,728. Meat packing ranked second and chemical products third among the top industrial establishments of Tennessee. The need for materials of war brought new industries to Tennessee, and many of these, including the Oak Ridge Atomic Energy Center and the Arnold Air Engineering Center at Tullahoma, remained operative after the war was over.

Immediately after World War II, state officials expanded efforts to bring industry into the state. Before that time, the State Planning Commission had conducted only limited research studies to determine which industries would develop best and which would be interested in coming to Tennessee. A comprehensive industrial survey was undertaken in the early 1940s, and in 1943 the commission published the first directory of manufacturers. In the following year, the commission began to maintain an inventory of available facilities for industries, and in 1945 it published *Industrial Resources of Tennessee*. In 1953, the Tennessee Industrial and Agricultural Development Commission was established primarily to develop new industry and to encourage the expansion of industries already operating in the state. The commission announced its plans to explain to all possible investors the advantages that the state held for industrial location. Advertising in the New York *Times* and other newspapers of wide circulation was begun before the year had passed, and in 1954, a traveling representative made frequent trips into northern cities to explain the attractions of Tennessee to potential investors. Not infrequently, state officials and prominent businessmen went as teams into New York, Chicago, Detroit, and other northern and eastern cities in search of investment capital. In 1945–1946 the state had expended only $17,889 for industrial development; in the biennium of 1958–1959 it spent $233,803. Further, the staff of the Industrial Commission expanded from four in 1948 to twenty in 1959.

By 1947—two years after the war ended—the manufacture of

chemical and allied products was the leading industry of the state. Food and kindred products and textile manufacturing ranked second and third, respectively. Industrial establishments had increased more than 50 percent since World War II began in 1939, and the total value added by manufacturing had more than tripled. In 1947 six major counties accounted for 50 percent of the total value added, 49 percent of the employees, and 39 percent of the establishments. Shelby (Memphis) rose to first place in value added, followed by Davidson (Nashville), Hamilton (Chattanooga), Sullivan (Kingsport and Bristol), and Knox (Knoxville).

Considerable growth continued in the 1950s. Of the states with 250,000 or more industrial jobs in 1955, Tennessee made the greatest industrial gains during the decade 1955–1965. Tennessee's 28 percent gain in manufacturing jobs compared with 25 percent in Florida, North Carolina, and South Carolina, and 21 percent in Texas.

In a publication released in 1961, the Division of Industrial Research hailed the year of 1960 as one that "will go down in the record books as one of the most dynamic in the history of the State"— during the record-breaking period of 1959–1960 nearly 40,000 jobs were created as new plants moved in and plants already established expanded. In 1960 the number of new industries selecting locations in Tennessee was 162, as compared to 99 in 1954; the number of expansions during the same period was 224 as compared to 136 in 1954. Chattanooga led with 26 new plants and 29 expansions. East Tennessee had 152 new and expanded plants—only 28 fewer than the total in Middle and West Tennessee combined.

By the 1970s, Tennessee had increased its relative position among the states in the three major categories of manufacturing income, manufacturing employment, and total value added by manufacturing. Manufacturing wages and salary disbursements during the twenty years since the early 1950s have more than doubled. Manufacture of apparel and related products continue to employ more people than any other single industry, with chemical and allied products not far behind. Each had increased about 40 percent over the preceding decade. Food products and electrical machinery also gave employment to a number of people.

As the fourth quarter of the twentieth century began, Tennessee continued to show a remarkable and healthy industrial diversity. Japanese industrialists soon gave Tennesseans precisely what Arthur Colyar and others who talked of a "New South" just after the Civil War longed for: a lesson in how to make money from industry. In October of 1980, Nissan Motors of Tokyo announced plans to build a $300 million truck assembly plant at Smyrna—this became the largest single capital investment by a private industry in the state. Soon, the company employed 2,000 people, added the Sentra automobile to truck assembly, and by 1989 employed well over 3,000 people. Late in the decade, Nissan began plans for a $490 million expansion which, when completed, would add another 2,000 employees. By 1990, Japanese companies had investments of more than $1 billion in the state and employed more than 8,000 Tennesseans.

An announcement by General Motors in the mid-eighties of an intention to develop a multi-billion Saturn plant in Williamson and Maury counties was, by 1990, adding to the economy and demographic growth of the state.

The significance of industry and commerce in the lives of Tennesseans is apparent by the decline in population in the predominantly rural counties and the increase in the urban counties. Especially in the rural areas of the Cumberland Plateau and west of the Tennessee River the population decline is apparent. But in counties having large federal agencies (such as Coffee and Montgomery) and counties having large cities, the population increase has been phenomenal. In 1960, for the first time, the state's urban population exceeded the rural population. By 1970, the figure had increased from 52.3 percent (1960) to 58.8 percent. The Memphis Delta region was 87.1 percent urban, mid-Cumberland 73.2 percent, Chattanooga area 60.6 percent, and the Knoxville area 47.5 percent. The black population, 15.8 percent of the state's total, generally concentrated more in the Memphis Delta and the southwestern part of the state than elsewhere except in the cities. The Upper Cumberland region, which had the smallest urban population, also had the smallest black population—less than 2 percent. Of the total black population of the state, more than 80 percent lived in urban areas.

On the eve of the twenty-first decennial census, the state's population was estimated at nearly 5 million and was predicted to rise to near 6 million by the year 2000.

More tourists travel to the Great Smokies than to any other national park.

SUGGESTED READINGS

Books

Betty V. Vickers, Ed., *Tennessee Statistical Abstract,* 1988 (Knoxville, 1988).

Articles

Charles B. Garrison, "Industrial Growth in The Tennessee Valley Region, 1959–1968," *American Journal of Agricultural Economics* (Feb. 1974), 50–60; Rayburn W. Johnson, "Population Trends in Tennessee from 1940 to 1950," THQ 11 (Sept. 1952), 254–62; Walter M. Kollmorgen, "Observations on Cultural Islands in Terms of Tennessee Agriculture," ETHSP 16 (1944), 65–78; John Rust, "The Origin and Development of the Cotton Picker," WTHSP 7 (1953), 38–56.

27.

ॐ *Education and Religion*

V ERY little was done to establish public schools of quality during the three decades following Reconstruction, in spite of the elaborate provisions of the Public School Law of 1873. Less than one-half of the children of school age attended schools of any type at the turn of the century; those who did went to five-month schools conducted by teachers of modest training who in some counties were paid as little as $18.50 per month. The first decade of the new century marked the decline of the academies—institutions that had been the "high schools" of the nineteenth century and had played a major role in the education of a large class of citizens—but witnessed a renaissance in the development of public education. The academies had been supported from a variety of sources, including lotteries, public subscriptions, small state appropriations, and tuition fees, but public-spirited citizens of the early twentieth century sought a school system financed entirely from public funds.

The tremendous progress made toward a satisfactory public school program early in the twentieth century was possible because of the efforts of scores of leaders from Memphis to Bristol who perceived a need for educational advancement and were determined to convince their fellow citizens of that need. Indeed, by the end of the first decade a variety of organizations such as the Cooperative Education Association (consisting of business, civic, and professional leaders), the State Teachers Association, and others had secured the passage of the General Education Law of 1909, which provided the core of the present-day education system in the state.

This law called for an annual appropriation of 25 percent of the gross revenue of the state for public education. Two-thirds of the amount was to go to the counties in proportion to their scholastic population. Thirteen percent was to establish and maintain four normal schools for the training of teachers, and the remainder was for the building and maintaining of high schools and libraries, and for the expansion and maintenance of the University of Tennessee.

The location of the four normal schools resulted in excitement and competition among cities in all sections of the state. The law required that an institution be located in each grand division of the state and that one be specified for Negroes. They were to be accessible and "centrally located" in locales where practice schools would be available and where "donations of land and buildings" might be available. Nearly two dozen towns and cities, generally supported by their county courts, ultimately submitted propositions for the location of the schools. From East Tennessee came proposals from Johnson City, Sweetwater, Cleveland, Dayton, and Athens. Cities of Middle Tennessee that made bids included Clarksville, Columbia, Cookeville, Fayetteville, Monterey, Murfreesboro, Shelbyville, Tullahoma, and Winchester. In West Tennessee, competition developed among Memphis, Covington, Humboldt, Huntingdon, Jackson, McKenzie, Milan, and Trenton.

State Board members, charged with the responsibility of choosing locations, visited each locale after carefully studying the respective proposals and in December of 1909 decided upon Johnson City, Murfreesboro, and Memphis as locations for the white schools, and Nashville for the school for Negroes. Governor Patterson informed legislators that more than $1 million had been pledged from the four cities and counties which, "with the amounts the state will pay," would "offer a full complement of trained teachers for our public schools" and establish for the state an educational system "second to none in the country." Middle Tennessee State Normal and East Tennessee State Normal opened in fall 1911, and West Tennessee State Normal and the Agricultural and Industrial State Normal for Negroes opened one year later.[1]

The next decade brought more accomplishments in education. During the Hooper administration (1911–1915) the general

[1] The names of these institutions were changed from time to time until now they are called East Tennessee State University, Middle Tennessee State University, Tennessee State University, and Memphis State University.

school fund was increased from 25 percent to more than 33 percent of the gross revenue, and legislation was enacted providing for uniform examinations and certification of teachers, compulsory school attendance, and transportation of pupils at state expense. In 1915, Tennessee Polytechnic Institute (now Tennessee Technological University) was established at Cookeville, and two years later a million-dollar bond issue was authorized to expand facilities at the University of Tennessee.

During the next two decades continued progress was made, although education at all levels was curtailed by the financial depression of the 1930s. Not only did Austin Peay appear friendly to the efforts of educational leaders, but his able commissioner of education, Perry L. Harned of Clarksville, effectively carried the needs to the people and obtained desired results. Legislation provided for an eight-month school term in 1925 and established a state salary schedule for teachers. The normal schools were changed to four-year colleges and money was appropriated for their expansion. A two-year normal was authorized for Clarksville in 1927 and was named for Austin Peay. The school opened in the fall of 1929 on the grounds and in the buildings formerly occupied by Southwestern Presbyterian University, which had recently moved to Memphis. Austin Peay was soon headed by Tennessee native Philander P. Claxton, who in the early 1900s had been one of the state's ablest campaigners for public education and had later served in many capacities, including that of commissioner of education of the United States. In the same year a branch of the University of Tennessee was authorized for Martin.[2] All state functions suffered from the depression, and educational funding was cut substantially. During one session legislators debated closing the colleges but finally compromised by slashing appropriations by two-thirds.

In the meantime the teachers had organized under the name of Tennessee Education Association, and with the support of the sectional associations the organization rapidly became the leader of the educational forces in the state. Leaders employed a full-time secretary in 1933 and provided for the creation of a "representative assembly" to serve as a legislative body and an administrative council to implement policies. Association leaders played impor-

[2] The institution at Clarksville today is called Austin Peay State University; the one at Martin is University of Tennessee at Martin.

Above: Shown here, looking west at the Knoxville campus, is the University of Tennessee. One of seven state universities in Tennessee, it also has principal campuses at Memphis, Martin, and Chattanooga. *Below:* Engineering building at Tennessee Technological University, the state university at Cookeville.

tant roles in influencing the legislature to enact the Eight Point Program during the late 1930s and 1940s. Additional operational funds were appropriated, free textbooks were provided for the first three grades, and a minimum salary was established for teachers.

Funds for education were increased sharply in 1947 when a 2 percent sales tax was levied. Although vigorously opposed by the Nashville *Tennessean* and others, the tax, increased from time to time by legislators, placed education of higher quality within the grasp of more Tennesseans. The 1947 legislature also established a teacher retirement system, which ten years later was combined with the federal social security system. Inadequate funding at all educational levels continues to perplex Tennesseans, and even today Tennessee spends less on pupils and teachers than do most of the other states of the Southeast. In 1976 Governor Blanton talked seriously of an income tax to help state government meet the increasing demands, but his proposals received little support from legislators and the populace in general.

Before the *Brown v. Topeka* case of 1954, only token efforts had been made in Tennessee toward integration of the schools—and that was in the area of higher education. The law school of the University of Tennessee had admitted blacks in 1952, for example, and some of the private institutions of higher learning had done so earlier. A group of black parents in Clinton had filed a suit as early as 1951 in the federal district court of Judge Robert L. Taylor in Knoxville seeking integration of the neighborhood schools in Clinton. The practice had been for the Clinton blacks of high school age to ride a bus eighteen miles into Knoxville to attend a school maintained there for Negroes. Taylor denied the plea, but three years later the United States Circuit Court of Appeals remanded the case to him and ordered him to rule in accordance with the *Brown* case. Early in 1956, Judge Taylor directed Clinton authorities to desegregate the schools "no later than" the fall school term.

In the meantime various white groups were organized to attempt to prevent or at least delay the integration of the schools. The Tennessee Federation for Constitutional Government was formed in July of 1955, and soon was joined in spirit by such other groups as "We the People," "Pro-Southern," and "Citizens Councils." Most of the groups—the Federation in particular—eschewed violence and attempted by persuasion (they brought in such speakers as Senators Strom Thurman and James Eastland, for example) and litigation to accomplish their ends. But it was an "outside agitator"—Frederick John Kasper of New Jersey—who was successful in fomenting unrest and generating a violent frame of mind among many people. Before he was jailed in Knoxville, Kasper developed such an explosive environment in Clinton that Governor Frank G. Clement was forced to send in troops to maintain order. State Adjutant General Joe W. Henry commanded a contingent of 600 battle-equipped national guardsmen with seven tanks, and moved them into Clinton a few days after schools opened when violence was threatened. Guardsmen remained only nine days, after which the school principal reported that his institution was operating on a normal basis. After that, few problems arose, and in May 1957, seventeen-year-old Bobby Cain became the first Negro ever to be graduated from an integrated public school in Tennessee.

Nashville schools were desegregated in the following fall. An attempt had been made in September of 1955, when a black Nashville barber named A. Z. Kelly tried to enroll his son in East High School and was refused. Three weeks later, Nashville lawyer and civil rights leader Z. Alexander Looby and his colleague, Avon Williams, filed suit on behalf of Kelly and twenty other plaintiffs seeking an end to segregation. The Supreme Court, however, in its May 1955 implementation order, had given local officials the right to develop their own desegregation plans. Consequently, both the city and the county government (the united Metropolitan government was not established until 1963) voted to delay integration indefinitely until a "study" could be undertaken. At that time the two governments maintained 25 black schools and officials alleged that blacks preferred their own segregated schools. But two years later, Nashville schools integrated the first grade only—a step not accomplished without trauma.

As early as June 1957, John Kasper who, as mentioned, had been arrested in Clinton for fomenting unrest, was in Nashville distributing anti-black literature and otherwise organizing white resistance movements. By August 27, when thirteen black children were registered at five formerly all-white schools, extremists had been worked up to a fever pitch. Demonstrations were staged, some pushing and shoving resulted, and the county-wide enrollment was more than 40 percent below normal. Shortly after midnight, on

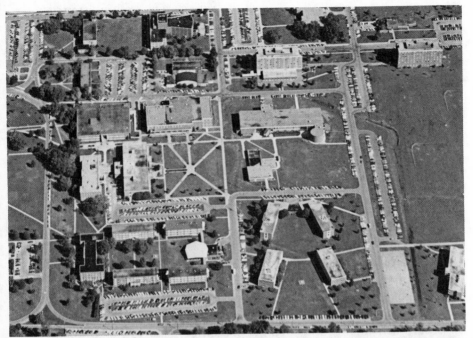

Above: Aerial view of Middle Tennessee State University, Murfreesboro.
Below: Portion of campus of Austin Peay State University, Clarksville.

September 9, the Hattie Cotton School, where 390 whites and one black had been enrolled, was dynamited and partly destroyed. The United States District Court for Middle Tennessee, presided over by Judge William E. Miller, had accepted the integration of the first grade with the understanding that the Nashville Board of Education would present an acceptable plan for the remaining grades by the end of the year. Among the remedies the board presented was a "three-school plan," widely heralded by segregationists. The plan simply called for three types of schools: (a) black schools for blacks who wanted their own; (b) white schools for whites who wanted their own; and (c) mixed schools for people who wanted integrated schools. Judge Miller, as expected, refused to accept it. Ultimately, the so-called stair-step, or grade-a-year, plan was accepted by Judge Miller. When in 1959 the concept was accepted by the United States Supreme Court, it became a model for other school systems throughout the South.

In Memphis, where the black population was proportionally larger than in the other Tennessee cities, leaders made no immediate efforts to desegregate grades one through twelve; indeed, it was 1961 before the public schools there were integrated. Leaders instead concentrated upon gaining admission for eligible students to Memphis State College (now Memphis State University). Consequently, the state board of education developed a plan whereby blacks would be admitted in the fall of 1955 at the graduate level and, working downward yearly, would ultimately be admitted to all classes by 1959. A few months later, District Judge Marion S. Boyd of Memphis approved the gradual plan, but in 1957 the United States Supreme Court found it unacceptable. The state board of education then opened all schools under its jurisdiction to blacks but permitted each institution to determine its own entrance requirements. The early 1960s came before all state institutions (shown in Map 11) accepted blacks below the graduate level. By 1966, Tennessee State University—traditionally all-black—had enrolled twenty-five or more whites.

During the twentieth century the University of Tennessee changed from a localized institution in East Tennessee to a statewide university. Soon after the turn of the century it began to meet the state's needs through farmers' institutes and programs of its agricultural experiment station, by working with secondary schools for the improvement of educational facilities, and by urging its alumni throughout the state to become more active in civic affairs. The immense recognition attained by the Summer School of the South, opened on the campus in 1902 by Dr. Philander P. Claxton with the aid of funds from the Southern Education Board, brought the institution a national reputation.

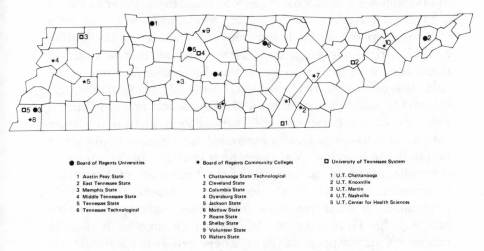

● Board of Regents Universities	✱ Board of Regents Community Colleges	☐ University of Tennessee System
1 Austin Peay State	1 Chattanooga State Technological	1 U.T. Chattanooga
2 East Tennessee State	2 Cleveland State	2 U.T. Knoxville
3 Memphis State	3 Columbia State	3 U.T. Martin
4 Middle Tennessee State	4 Dyersburg State	4 U.T. Nashville
5 Tennessee State	5 Jackson State	5 U.T. Center for Health Sciences
6 Tennessee Technological	6 Motlow State	
	7 Roane State	
	8 Shelby State	
	9 Volunteer State	
	10 Walters State	

Map 11. Public Higher Educational Institutions in Tennessee, 1976. Source: *Tennessee Statistical Abstract, 1977* (Knoxville: Center for Business and Economic Research, Univ. of Tennessee, 1977).

The most essential reform, achieved in 1909, was the broadening of the board of trustees to make the University representative of the whole state, thus removing the institution from the control of East Tennessee and Knoxville leaders. In 1911 the medical units were moved to Memphis, and in 1927 a branch of the University was established at Martin, as mentioned. The School of Social Work at Nashville became a part of the University in 1951, and in 1969 the University of Chattanooga was merged with the University of Tennessee to become the University of Tennessee at Chattanooga. The University's reputation as a school for graduate studies and scientific experimentation, including such new fields as atomic energy and outer space, has rapidly increased in recent years. In 1968, the institution was reorganized as a university system, with an administration for each campus headed by a chancellor.

University expansion into the Nashville area was halted in the spring of 1967 when blacks, hoping to see the state spend more money on an expansion of traditionally black Tennessee State University, claimed that the maintenance of the University of Tennessee Center in Nashville helped to perpetuate segregation. For some years the University had operated an extension night school in Nashville, but in 1967 officials announced plans to build a multi-million-dollar extension center—plans that apparently meant a full-scale university that (according to plaintiffs) would insure a continued existence of a dual system of higher education. United States District Court Judge Frank Gray, Jr. agreed that the state had maintained a racially segregated and discriminatory system and ruled that officials had an "affirmative duty" to "dismantle the dual system of public higher education which presently exists in Tennessee." He kept the matter under surveillance, and for ten years various cooperative programs were tried, including an out-of-court proposal for merging Tennessee State and the night school in Nashville under the governance of the University of Tennessee trustees but with the Tennessee State president, Frederick S. Humphries, as chief executive. The matter came up for review before Judge Gray again in 1977, at which time he found the various efforts and proposals to have been generally unsatisfactory. He therefore ruled that the two institutions "shall be merged under the governance of the State Board of Regents." "Merger," he wrote, was "a drastic remedy, but the State's actions have been egregious examples of constitutional violation." At the same time he ruled that state officials must devise and implement a comprehensive program of desegregation in all its colleges and universities. State officials then formed a twelve-member monitoring committee to oversee the process. University of Tennessee officials appealed the merger order to the United States Court of Appeals for the Sixth District where, in April 1979, the Court upheld Gray's ruling by a split decision. Although the University of Tennessee Board of Trustees announced plans to appeal the decision to the Supreme Court, Regents officials proceeded with plans to effect the merger.

Judges have come and gone, but the question of desegregation continues before the courts. In the mid-1980s, Federal Judge Thomas A. Wiseman, Jr., in Geier v. Alexander, tackled "Tennessee's dual system of higher education," and sought to eliminate it by "the maximization of educational opportunities for black citizens . . . and the improvement of [their] educational opportunities. . . ." In a stipulation of settlement to which both parties agreed, the Court established a "Desegregation Monitoring Committee" which would report periodically upon "the desegregation of all institutions." The enrollment at predominantly black Tennessee State University of Nashville was directed to consist of 50 percent whites and at least 50 percent white "upper level administrators" by 1993, while the predominantly white institutions were to increase substantially their black representation among both students and faculty. Tennessee State's mission was to become "the" regional urban university for Middle Tennessee and the Board of Regents and THEC were ordered to develop a plan for the "enhancement" of the university. As the 1980s ended, school authorities were making substantial progress toward meeting the court's directive.

Private institutions of higher learning that had been established soon after the Civil War continued to provide quality education in the twentieth century, although by the beginning of the fourth quarter of the century some were experiencing financial difficulties that threatened their continued existence. The George Peabody College for Teachers (Nashville) announced plans early in 1979 not to reopen in the fall. Regents officials urged a merger between Peabody and Tennessee State University, but after weeks of negotiations Peabody was merged with Vanderbilt University. In the fall 1979 term, the 100-year-old school was opened as the George Peabody College for Teachers of Vanderbilt University. Cumberland University, earlier experiencing difficulties, merged shortly after mid-century with Samford University of Birmingham, although a new two-year school called Cumberland College soon was established on the university grounds at Lebanon. Map 12 shows private institutions of higher learning in the state in 1976.

During the 1960s and 1970s state officials determined to make institutions of higher learning accessible to all citizens by establishing a system of community colleges across the state. Three were authorized in 1965, to be located in each grand division of the state. Cleveland, Columbia, and Jackson were chosen as sites, and community colleges were opened in those cities in the following year. Schools at Dyersburg and near Tullahoma (Motlow State) were opened in 1969, and at Morristown in the following year. Volunteer State at Gallatin, Shelby State at Memphis, and Roane State near Harriman, were opened in the early 1970s as a result of legislation enacted in 1969. Chattanooga State

Technical Institute, established in 1963, became Chattanooga State Technical Community College in 1973 when the legislature transferred governance to the Board of Regents.

Governance of the entire state system was changed in the 1960s and 1970s. The Tennessee Higher Education Commission was formed in 1967 with duties including those of studying use of public funds for higher education and analyzing programs and needs in the field of higher education. The nine members appointed by the governor are charged with developing a master plan for future development, among other duties. A few years later, in 1972, two governing boards replaced the State Board of Education, which had had the responsibility of governance at all levels. A board of regents was formed to supervise budgets and otherwise control institutions of higher learning (with the exception of the University of Tennessee system, which had its own governing board). Another board of education was formed to control public institutions below the college and university levels.

While educators in 1979 noted tremendous progress during the first eight decades of the century in making educational opportunities available to all people, they also were aware of the need to do more to develop an educational program of high quality. Educational leaders and the public at large expressed surprise in 1977 when a state board report revealed that nearly one-fourth of the high school graduates were awarded diplomas each year without having become proficient in the basic skills of mathematics and English. They expressed alarm in the following year, however, when more than one-half of the 71,764 eighth graders failed proficiency tests in language, mathematics, spelling, and reading. The "television generation" was found to be especially deficient in spelling and reading; nearly 55 percent failed in spelling and nearly 60 percent could not read at a satisfactory level. Urban dwellers were found to have scored lower than people living in the rural areas. Tennesseans in the 1980s became increasingly aware of a high illiteracy rate when studies showed that a large portion of the people could not read above the fourth grade level. Governor McWherter pledged more funds for adult education.

Religious Groups 🍃 The Roman Catholic, Judaic, and major Protestant denominations had become well established in Tennessee by the twentieth century. The largest and most influential continued to be the Methodist, Baptist, Presbyterian, and Church of Christ. By mid-twentieth century both union and division had occurred in some groups, and as the fourth quarter of the century got underway, some Protestant leaders talked of a union of the principal denominations.

The last detailed religious census taken by the federal government was compiled in 1936 (midway in the period considered here) and indicated that more than 900,000 Tennesseans of a population of about 2,750,000 were affiliated with a religious body. The Southern Baptist Church was in the forefront with 226,896 members and the Methodist Episcopal Church, South, second with 160,951. Three Presbyterian bodies (Southern, Northern, and Cumberland) had a combined membership of more than 140,000, and Roman Catholics counted almost 32,000.

Southern Baptists and Methodists were well distributed across the state. Twenty-one thousand Baptists were concentrated in Knox County, 16,000 in Shelby, and about 14,000 each in Davidson and Hamilton counties. Of the Methodists, Davidson had nearly 20,000 Shelby 18,600, Hamilton almost 9,000 and Knox about 7,000. Eight thousand Presbyterians were in Shelby and Davidson each, and about 6,000 each were in Knox and Hamilton counties. The Church of Christ, which was formed late in the nineteenth century from the conservative wing of the Disciples of Christ, was listed for the first time in the census records of 1906, with nearly 10,000 members in Davidson County and with more than 2,000 each in Knox and Rutherford. All of the religious groups have experienced considerable growth, of course, since the federal census of 1936.

Union among the various denominations was discussed by leaders of all faiths. Among the successful unions was one among Northern Methodists, Southern Methodists, and Methodist Protestants, in 1939. A somewhat unsuccessful union was attempted between the Northern Presbyterians and the Cumberland Presbyterians three decades earlier. The principal Methodist bodies (the Methodist Episcopal Church and the Methodist Episcopal Church, South) had divided and formed over the political sectional controversy more than a decade before the Civil War, as mentioned earlier. The Methodist Protestant Church had been organized as a protest against the formality of the Anglicans. Most of the Tennessee churches were affiliated with the Southern branch, although the Holston Conference of the Northern branch was maintained in East Tennessee. Although the union in 1939 was opposed by some of the churches in the Deep South, Tennesseans as a whole supported the movement. The Southern church brought to the union more than fifty colleges and universities, three of which were located in Tennessee (Scarritt College for Christian Workers in Nashville, Lambuth College at Jackson, and Martin College in Pulaski). In 1968 the Methodists joined with the Evangelical United Brethren to form the United Methodist Church, which probably made it the largest Protestant Christian body in the world.

A union among Presbyterian bodies had been considered for many years. Not long after the Cumberland group was formed in Tennessee in 1810, a few leaders discussed reunion with the mother church. After the Civil War brought division, a union between the Northern Presbyterians (Presbyterians in the United States of America) and the Cumberland Presbyterians, located primarily in the South and West, seemed mutually advantageous. Negotiations began in earnest soon after the beginning of the twentieth century, and a revision of church doctrine was made in 1903 by the Northern church to meet some of the demands of the Cumberlands. Although union was effected by majority vote of the latter group, a vigorous minority has continued the Cumberland church to the present time. More successful was the merging of the Northern and the United Presbyterians in 1958.

Another group strengthened by union in the twentieth century was the Pentecostal Church of the Nazarene. Several groups grew out of a Wesleyan revival of the late nineteenth century that professed the necessity of a return to the spiritual simplicity of John Wesley. The Pentecostal Mission had been organized in Nashville at the turn of the century, and in 1915 that group united with the Pentecostal Church of the Nazarene at Nashville. The former was concerned largely with foreign missions and the latter with home missions; thus the union greatly strengthened both bodies. Trevecca College is maintained in Nashville by the Nazarenes. According to the census of 1936, the membership of the church of Tennessee (5,416) was exceeded only by its membership in California, Oklahoma, and Kansas.

The claims of fundamentalism and those of "modernism" or religious liberalism aroused much concern among religious leaders during the first three decades of the twentieth century, and paved the way for the enactment of an anti-evolution law in 1925. The School of Religion of Vanderbilt University became the center of Biblical criticism after the university gained complete independence in 1914 from Methodist jurisdiction following litigation over a period of years. The chancellor, Dr. J. H. Kirkland, had been a leader in the movement to separate entirely from Methodist supervision, and he encouraged Dr. O. E. Brown, dean of the School of Religion, and other faculty members in their freedom of thought. The "Round Table," a literary club in Nashville whose membership included most of the faculty, thoroughly discussed liberal questions, including that of evolution. In 1926 the university published three lectures—by Brown, Kirkland, and Dr. Edwin Mims (a professor of English who took a strong position opposing an anti-evolution law)—in which the three argued for freedom of thought in matters of religion. Mims championed the cause of higher criticism of the Bible and urged all people to consider the great truths of the Bible as a whole and not out of context and insisted that they "rally . . . to this new standard of Jesus, emancipated from traditional interpretation" of the Scripture. Brown suggested that major areas of disagreement between fundamentalists and modernists concerned the Virgin Birth, the alleged inerrancy of the Bible, and evolution. He and Kirkland countered further allegations of the fundamentalists, principally that those who believe in evolution are essentially materialists who have abandoned faith in God for modern science, and that higher criticism denied or ignored the sacredness of the holy scriptures. Seeking to accommodate science and religion, Kirkland extolled the power of the mind and equated it with God. "In the beginning was force, and this force was mind," the chancellor wrote, "and this mind was God, and this God has been ever indwelling in the universe He has made, for without Him was not anything made that was made." The studies and assertions of Kirkland, Brown, and others soon resulted in charges that Vanderbilt was "a hotbed of Modernism" whose professors sought to undermine the faith of our fathers.

The talk of modernism reinforced the interest of many in old-time evangelistic revivals. T. DeWitt Talmadge, Billy Sunday, N. B. Hardeman, and others urged Tennesseans to depart from the paths of sin. In the long run, they paved the way for Billy Graham, who preached with tremendous success to thousands in Nashville and Memphis in 1951, 1954, and 1979. But it also aroused rural Tennesseans to such an extent that they prevailed in their insistence that an anti-evolution law be written into the statutes of the state.

The Anti-Evolution Controversy ᨏ As the twentieth century began, fundamentalists, steeped in a narrow interpretation of the faith, believed that Christianity was being assailed on all sides. Especially objectionable to them were higher criticism of the Bible, as mentioned, and suggestions that there may have been other "creations" besides that described in Genesis. Alexander Winchell, a noted naturalist, had been dismissed from the faculty at Methodist-supported Vanderbilt University in 1878 after he published *Pre-Adamites,* a work in which he suggested the existence of civilizations antedating the account of man as found in Genesis. But most objectionable of all to fundamentalists was Charles Darwin's theory of evolution, which seemed not only to contravene the Old Testament but to undermine the stature and dignity of man, who according to the Scriptures had been created a little lower than the angels and in the image of God.

Although some religious leaders were able to accommodate Darwinism to their faith, many others believed that the concepts expressed in the *Origin of the Species* conflicted directly with the story of creation as told in the Bible. Articles, books, and lectures by William Graham Sumner, Lester Frank Ward, and others in and out of the large universities fed the debate as stories of "such apostascy" circulated among fundamentalists. In 1900–1912, fundamentalist leaders reaffirmed their faith in the inerrancy of the Bible and the story of creation in twelve pamphlets entitled *The Fundamentals: A Testimony,* which received wide circulation in Tennessee, especially among the predominant Baptist and Methodist leaders. A variety of organizations such as the Anti-Evolution League and the Bible Crusaders of America, also enlisted a strong following in the Volunteer State, and speakers under the auspices of these groups were warmly received in all sections of the state.

Bryan, who had carried the state by large majorities in each of his three unsuccessful attempts to win the presidency, was well known in Tennessee, and people had read addresses he had made on the hustings in behalf of political candidates and in churches in support of fundamentalism. Some had noted with considerable interest a debate conducted in the columns of the New York *Times* in 1922 between the Great Commoner (as Bryan generally was called) and Harry Emerson Fosdick, the young "modernist" minister and writer in New York. After Bryan spoke in Nashville in 1924 on the subject "Is the Bible True?" and flayed Darwinism before a cheering crowd of several thousand, Protestant leaders in Middle Tennessee printed thousands of copies of the address and circulated the speech among legislators and others from Memphis to Bristol. Bills to outlaw the teaching of evolution were considered in Arkansas, Georgia, Kentucky, Minnesota, Mississippi, Missouri, New Hampshire, North Carolina, Oklahoma, West Virginia, and perhaps other states, and it is therefore not surprising that legislators in Tennessee gave the matter attention.

A few weeks after the General Assembly convened in January 1925, George Washington Butler, representative from Macon County, introduced House Bill 185, which would forbid the teaching in public schools of "any theory that denies the story of the Divine Creation of man as taught in the Bible, and to teach instead that man has descended from a lower order of animals." Those convicted were to pay a fine of $100 to $500. The bill was received by the public with mixed emotions, and newspaper editors, clergymen, educators, and public officials were found to be on both sides of the issue. The Nashville Baptist Pastors Council, for example, claimed its endorsement of the bill to speak for "ten thousand laymen of twenty local churches." The most serious indictment came from educators at the universities. Mims, as mentioned, was in the forefront at Vanderbilt University, and after the measure was passed, Chancellor James H. Kirkland wrote that the best "remedy for a narrow sectarianism and a belligerent fundamentalism" was "the building of new laboratories. . . ." Harcourt A. Morgan, president of the University of Tennessee, was unable to take a strong position because his operational budget depended upon appropriations from the state legislature, although many educators urged him to emulate the president of the University of Kentucky, who had waged a successful fight in 1922 against the anti-evolution movement in the legislature of his state. Morgan did write to Governor Peay, however, to describe how the measure would hinder further study and development of "the whole realm of plant and animal improvement"—an area in which he was vitally interested. R. Bruce Payne, president of George Peabody College for Teachers, continued his fight by urging a gubernatorial veto even after the legislation became law.

After considerable debate, legislators passed the measure and transmitted it to Peay. The governor, after "due deliberation," and after examining "tens of thousands of letters" and hearing appeals from many delegations, signed the bill nine days after its passage. Certainly no advocate of the measure, Peay apparently feared that a veto of the bill would defeat his highway and educational program. He viewed his signing of the bill as a way of winning rural support to his important measures and privately voiced a doubt that the law would ever be enforced.

The new law became a subject for considerable discussion in newspapers both within and without the state. Conservative papers and religious journals praised it but liberals deplored it. The Vanderbilt Agrarians believed it to be a step backward in civilization and Knoxville-born Joseph Wood Krutch, editor of *The Nation,* condemned it and blamed its passage upon "ignorant fundamentalists." Walter Lippmann, Henry L. Mencken, and other Eastern journalists joined in the ridicule.

The governor's signature was hardly dry when the press heralded the news that John Thomas Scopes, a young teacher of biology at Dayton, had been indicted by the Rhea County grand jury for violation of the statute. On May 26, 1925—one day after the indictment was reported—Dayton was a dateline for almost every major newspaper in the country. Interest spread abroad when Bryan announced that he would defend the fundamentalistic faith by assisting Attorney General A. Tom Stewart in the prosecution, and Dudley Field Malone, Arthur Garfield Hayes, and Clarence Darrow appeared to aid counsel for the defense.

The trial began on July 13, and for eight days Dayton indulged in a festive atmosphere. The details of the affair have been told in both truthful and exaggerated fashion by journalists, playwrights, novelists, and historians both in America and abroad. Scopes, found guilty, was fined $100, and Tennessee, now termed the "Monkey State" by Eastern punsters, was subjected to ridicule. In

Campus of Memphis State University, Memphis.

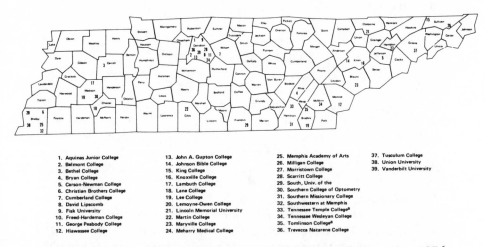

1. Aquinas Junior College	13. John A. Gupton College
2. Belmont College	14. Johnson Bible College
3. Bethel College	15. King College
4. Bryan College	16. Knoxville College
5. Carson-Newman College	17. Lambuth College
6. Christian Brothers College	18. Lane College
7. Cumberland College	19. Lee College
8. David Lipscomb	20. Lemoyne-Owen College
9. Fisk University	21. Lincoln Memorial University
10. Freed-Hardeman College	22. Martin College
11. George Peabody College	23. Maryville College
12. Hiawassee College	24. Meharry Medical College

25. Memphis Academy of Arts	37. Tusculum College
26. Milligan College	38. Union University
27. Morristown College	39. Vanderbilt University
28. Scarritt College	
29. South, Univ. of the	
30. Southern College of Optometry	
31. Southern Missionary College	
32. Southwestern at Memphis	
33. Tennessee Temple College[a]	
34. Tennessee Wesleyan College	
35. Tomlinson College[a]	
36. Trevecca Nazarene College	

Map 12. Private Higher Educational Institutions in Tennessee, 1976.
Source: *Tennessee Statistical Abstract, 1977* (Knoxville: Center for Business and Economic Research, Univ. of Tennessee, 1977).

Tennessee, however, fundamentalist religious groups experienced considerable growth, while more liberal ones declined in membership.

The law remained on the statute books until 1967. Various attempts at repeal during the four decades of the law's existence met with derision and opposition by conservatives. As late as 1959, some members of the Tennessee Academy of Science and various chapters of the American Association of University Professors, were summarily rebuffed when they petitioned the legislature for repeal. One high state official, for example, suggested that a college biology professor who had drafted a petition urging repeal should seek employment elsewhere if he did not wish to teach according to the laws of the state. At the same time the Rutherford County Court, hearing that the Middle Tennessee State University chapter of the American Association of University Professors had petitioned the legislature for repeal, unanimously condemned the "free-thinking" educators and asserted that members of the court—all "God-fearing men"—deplored such attempts to repeal the anti-evolution statute.

The repeal in 1967 came with relatively little effort and fanfare. Although last-ditch stands in defense of the original measure were made by a few conservatives, the law was repealed forty-two years after its passage.

SUGGESTED READINGS

Books
Ben W. Barrus, Milton L. Baughn, Thomas H. Campbell, *A People Called Cumberland Presbyterians* (Memphis, 1972); Cullen T. Carter, *History of the Methodist Church and Institutions in Middle Tennessee* (Nashville, 1956); Hugh D. Graham, *Crisis in Print: Desegregation and the Press in Tennessee* (Nashville, 1967); Andrew D. Holt, *The Struggle for a State System of Public Schools in Tennessee, 1903–1936* (New York, 1938); Laurence McMillan, *The Schoolmaker: Sawney Webb and the Bell Buckle Story* (Chapel Hill, 1971); Edwin Mims, *History of Vanderbilt University* (Nashville, 1946); James R. Montgomery, *The Volunteer State Forges Its University . . . 1887–1919* (Knoxville, 1966); Herman Norton, *Tennessee Christians: A History of the Christian Church in Tennessee* (Nashville, 1971); Rufus B. Spain, *At Ease in Zion: A Social History of Southern Baptists* (Nashville, 1967); Robert H. White, *Tennessee Educational Organization* Nashville, 1929).

28.

Intellectual and Social Life

T HE twentieth century opened in the liberalism of the Progressive Era and was followed by World War I and the conservatism of the 1920s. The second quarter of the century brought depression and the progressive New Deal. Perhaps the third quarter brought the most profound social and cultural changes to Tennessee and indeed to the nation. Women began to play more prominent roles in public affairs, and the aftermath of the Brown case of 1954 brought changes in the lives of blacks, including the integration of schools and other public facilities. Literature and universities flourished, and country music made Nashville a major center for music. The population doubled during the first 75 years of the century, and with the population increase came a shift from a rural to an urban society and culture. The four largest cities—Memphis, Nashville, Knoxville, and Chattanooga— continued to experience considerable growth. By the end of the 1970s the population of Memphis exceeded 700,000 and Nashville had well passed the half-million mark.

The first eight censuses of the twentieth century tell of the marked urban trend. The urban counties and those immediately surrounding them became larger, while many of the more remote counties actually lost population. For example, although the total population increased more than 12 percent during the 1940s, 43 of the 95 counties decreased in size. During the 1950s, the population increased nearly 8 percent, but 54 counties numbered fewer residents in 1960 than in 1950. Counties showing the largest gains during the period 1940–1960 were Anderson (which, containing Oak Ridge, showed a gain of 123.6 percent in 1950), Coffee,

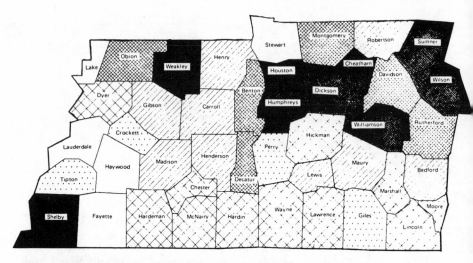

Map 13. Percentage Change in Total Population, Tennessee Counties, 1960– 1970. Source: *Tennessee Statistical Abstract, 1977* (Knoxville: Center for Business and Economic Research, Univ. of Tennessee, 1977).

Davidson, Hamblen, Hamilton, Knox, Roane, Rutherford, Sullivan, and Shelby. As mentioned, the 1960 census indicated for the first time that Tennessee had more urban dwellers than rural. Those living in towns and cities at that time, 52.3 percent, had increased to 58.8 percent in 1970. Map 13 shows population changes county by county for 1960– 1970. Estimates indicate that the figure may be as high as 75 percent in the 1990 census.

Three geographic belts in which population grew during the period 1940– 1960 are readily discernible. The first begins with Sullivan County on the Virginia line and extends southwest through Washington, Hamblen, Greene, Anderson, Knox, Roane, McMinn, and Bradley counties. A second belt begins at Bradley and Hamilton and runs northwest through Sequatchie, Warren, Coffee, Rutherford, Davidson, and Montgomery counties; the two belts together thus compose a "V" with the two branches moving northwest and northeast from the beginning point on the Georgia line. A third belt is Shelby County, which gained almost 30 percent during the 1950s; state statisticians estimate that this county will in 1980 experience a population increase of 112 percent over the population of 1950. Tables 6 and 7 show population change in Tennessee

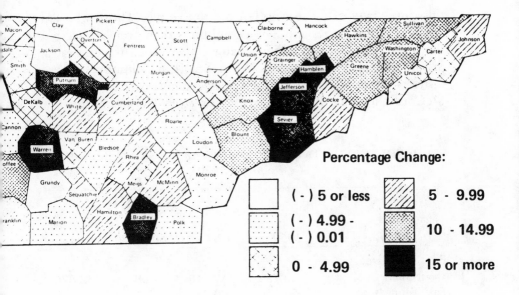

Percentage Change:

☐	(-) 5 or less
▨	5 - 9.99
▨	(-) 4.99 - (-) 0.01
▨	10 - 14.99
▨	0 - 4.99
■	15 or more

for 1960–1970 and compare the state's population with that in other parts of the country.

People of the 1970s were living longer than their grandparents of the early 1900s. Better health services were largely responsible. The state boasted 157 licensed hospitals with more than 32,000 beds by the 1970s. Costs of health care had also increased; in 1954 a day in a hospital cost $17.22, but by 1975 the figure had jumped to $121.99. As the number of births leveled off, so did the number of deaths. Senior citizens were more numerous than ever before; females in Tennessee could expect to live to age seventy-four and males to sixty-six.

Significant is the proportional decline of the black population in the state. The black population of 480,243 in 1900 was 23.8 percent of the total, but in 1980 blacks composed only 16 percent. High wages and good working conditions in Northern factories during and after World War II were particularly responsible for the exodus. Although World War I and the industrial prosperity of the 1920s lured many Tennessee Negroes to Northern cities, the depression of the 1930s caused many to return to the cotton fields of West Tennessee. Once again war brought mobility, and this time many of those who left did not return. Those who did enjoyed better wages and living conditions than ever before, but the white attitude toward them changed very little. In fact, a racial disturbance just at the end of World War II in Columbia's Negro district ("Mink Slide") lasted for a week and necessitated Governor McCord's sending the home guard to restore law and order.

Table 6.

CHANGES IN POPULATION IN TENNESSEE PLANNING REGIONS,
1960 AND 1970

Region	1960	1970	Percentage change 1960–1970	Population change
First Tennessee-Virginia	326,784	359,410	10.0	32,626
East Tennessee	654,236	700,985	7.1	46,749
Upper Cumberland	183,190	193,745	5.8	10,555
Southeast	389,348	419,656	7.8	30,308
Mid-Cumberland	681,580	793,618	16.4	112,038
South central	248,893	261,783	5.2	12,890
Northwest	205,999	220,975	7.3	14,976
Southwest	175,055	181,014	3.4	5,959
Memphis delta	702,004	792,978	13.0	90,974
Total	3,567,089	3,924,164	10.0	357.075

Source: U.S. Bureau of the Census, *U.S. Census of Population,* 1960 and 1970.

Indeed, at mid-century, most Tennessee whites clung to the attitude that their fathers had taken towards blacks in 1900. Respect for Negro rights had not characterized the American people at the turn of the century, and Tennesseans were no exception. The "separate but equal" decree of the Supreme Court (1896) had become the accepted dogma in Tennessee and throughout the country. Most newspaper editors referred disrespectfully to blacks, and politicians and civic leaders generally referred to them, if at all, with equal condescension; whites who associated with them were considered to be lowering the dignity of the Caucasian race. Politicians and editors alike roundly excoriated President Theodore Roosevelt in 1901 when he invited Booker T. Washington to lunch in the White House. Democratic leader Edward Ward Carmack, for example,

Table 7.
Population Comparisons, 1950, 1960, and 1970

Area	Population (thousands)			Percent change		Percentage of U.S. population	
	1950	1960	1970	1950–1970	1960–1970	1960	1970
Tennessee	3,291.7	3,567.1	3,923.7	19.2	10.0	2.0	1.9
Adjacent states							
Alabama	3,061.7	3,266.7	3,444.2	12.5	5.4	1.8	1.7
Arkansas	1,909.5	1,786.3	1,923.3	0.7	7.7	1.0	0.9
Georgia	3,444.6	3,943.1	4,589.6	33.2	16.4	2.2	2.3
Kentucky	2,944.8	3,038.2	3,218.7	9.3	5.9	1.7	1.6
Mississippi	2,178.9	2,178.1	2,216.9	1.7	1.8	1.2	1.1
Missouri	3,954.7	4,319.8	4,676.5	18.3	8.3	2.4	2.3
North Carolina	4,061.9	4,556.2	5,082.1	25.1	11.5	2.5	2.5
Virginia	3,318.7	3,966.9	4,648.5	40.1	17.2	2.2	2.3
Total	24,874.8	27,055.3	29,799.8	19.8	10.1	15.1	14.7
United States	151,325.8	179,323.2	203,211.9	34.3	13.3	100.0	100.0

Source: United States Bureau of the Census, U.S. Census of Population, 1970.

denounced the President for attempting to turn the White House into a "nigger restaurant," and the editor of the Memphis *Commercial Appeal* was mortified weeks later when he discovered that Roosevelt had issued no information that the executive mansion had "been disinfected or even the chair, knife, fork, plate and napkin deodorized." As late as 1917, after nearly two decades of "progressivism," aroused Shelby Countians could lynch a Negro accused of rape and murder and in the same week listen to a prominent Memphis lawyer and civic leader urge them to support the war effort to prevent Germany from turning back "the hands of Civilization . . . a hundred years."

The Supreme Court decision of 1954 (*Brown v. the Board of Education of Topeka*) ordered integration with all deliberate speed but found many people unready for such enormous social change. The decision was received with mixed emotions by Tennessee's political and civic leaders and newspaper editors. Except for Senators Gore and Kefauver and Representative J. Percy Priest, the Tennessee delegation in Washington expressed their disapproval by signing the Southern Manifesto, in which ninety-seven Southern congressmen pledged to continue the fight against integration. Although the majority of the major newspapers neither endorsed nor denounced the decision, most of those that did take a stand approved it. The small weekly Lexington *Progress* expressed the sentiments of many people when the editor wrote that the decision came as no surprise to Tennesseans because "by any and all standards we live by—those of our Constitution, . . . Christianity, and even those leading to the settlement of our country— Segregation was doomed."

Yet many people sought to block or at least delay the implementation of the Court decision. When blacks under the leadership of the National Association for the Advancement of Colored People (NAACP) filed implementation suits, segregationists sought to accomplish delays. As mentioned earlier, although Nashville schools began integration in 1957 despite protests and one case of dynamiting, by the fall of 1959 only four of the state's school districts had been integrated, and only 169 of Tennessee's 146,700 black children of school age attended integrated schools.

For many blacks, especially those of high school and college age, the wheels of justice ground much too slowly. Restive over discrimination in buses, restaurants, downtown stores, and theaters,

Above: Hollis F. Price, president of LeMoyne (now LeMoyne-Owen) College from 1943 to 1970, argued for moderation in Memphis during the civil rights struggle of the 1950s and 1960s. *Below:* Benjamin F. Hooks of Memphis became executive secretary of the NAACP in 1977.

Negroes began in 1960 a new tactic—the sit-in. Beginning in Nashville in February, where several hundred students from Fisk and Tennessee State University converged on lunch counters, the sit-ins spread to Chattanooga, Knoxville, and Memphis and brought poignantly to the public mind and conscience the second-class citizenship to which blacks were being subjected. When arrests, fines, and verbal and physical abuse did not deter the young blacks, several merchants in each of the cities agreed voluntarily to desegregate lunch counters. When in 1961, "freedom riders" began excursions into Southern cities to test segregation on buses and interstate carriers, blacks from Nashville and other Tennessee cities joined in.

Memphis had the largest black population among the cities, and authorities there faced the problem realistically by appointing a group composed of both blacks and whites—called the "Committee on Community Relations"—to prepare recommendations with respect to housing, recreational facilities, libraries, public transportation, and the like. After sit-ins and other demonstrations by blacks, libraries were desegregated in 1961, and other public facilities were integrated by the mid–1960s.

Desegregation without adequate economic opportunities, however, proved to be an empty victory for Memphis blacks, and leaders demanded better job opportunities. Such demands precipitated the Memphis garbage strike of 1968. "Toting the Man's garbage" offered little in money or status and paid less in wages than one-half the wages earned by New York City sanitation workers. When city officials refused to meet demands for better pay and working conditions, 1,300 workers walked off the job in February 1968. Soon the strike developed into a civil rights movement, and such men as Roy Wilkins and Martin Luther King were on the scene to offer leadership and encouragement. When in March 1968 more than 5,000 people joined in a demonstration march, they were confronted by the city police. Property was destroyed, one youth was killed, and sixty people were injured. King was in Memphis making preparation for a second march when he was killed (April 4, 1968)—the victim of a sniper's bullet fired from near the hotel balcony where he stood.

King's death not only removed an able leader and proponent of nonviolence but became a signal for violence and racial disturbances throughout the country. Preliminary estimates of damage in

Civil rights marchers in Memphis, 1968.

New York and Washington amounted to $15 million or more, and buildings in Nashville, Knoxville, Chattanooga, Memphis, and elsewhere in the state were looted and burned. Damages resulting from riots and looting in Tennessee were estimated at $700,000. Night curfews were ordered in a dozen towns and cities across the state.

The 1960s and 1970s were decades of marked progress for blacks in attaining equality in the white establishment. A. W. Willis, Jr., Memphis attorney and counsel for the NAACP, was elected to the legislature in 1964—the first Negro to be elected to the General Assembly in the twentieth century. Two years later, six others were elected, including Dr. Dorothy Brown, who became the first black woman in the history of the state to serve as a legislator. In 1968, Attorney Avon N. Williams was elected to the senate and has served continuously since that time. Frequently mentioned for a judicial position, Williams ably and effectively has been involved in hundreds of civil rights suits. Harold Ford, of Memphis, was elected to two terms in the legislature before being sent in 1974 to the federal House of Representatives. He thus became the first black Tennessean to serve his state in Congress. During the 1970s and 1980s, Alex Haley's widely-heralded *Roots* became a source of pride among blacks and whites alike. As the 1990s dawned, the talented writer turned his attention to a history of the state which is expected to circulate by the bicentennial celebration of 1996.

Literature ⧢ Tennessee has produced many talented authors who have contributed richly to the American literary heritage. The state's heroes, public figures, and picturesque environment have frequently been subjects fascinating authors and readers alike.

Among the public figures of the state, Andrew Jackson has been studied more than any other, and hundreds of books and articles have been written about him. The Old Chief was a complex figure indeed, and careful researchers have differed in their interpretation of his character and contributions. James Parton, a contemporary who published before the Civil War a three-volume account of his life and times, despaired at the conflicting sources uncovered by his

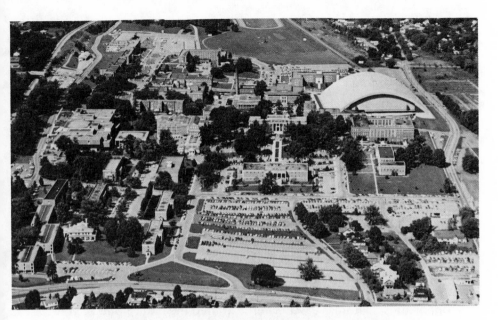

Above: A partial view of East Tennessee State University campus, Johnson City. *Below:* In 1966 Dorothy Brown, a Nashville physician, was elected to the state senate and became the first black woman to serve in the legislature.

research and concluded that Jackson was an enigma. He was "one of the greatest of generals," Parton wrote, but was "wholly ignorant of the art of war." He was a "most law-defying, law obeying citizen," a "democratic autocrat," an "urbane savage," and an "atrocious saint." Tennesseans John Eaton and Arthur S. Colyar prepared highly laudatory biographies about the hero during the nineteenth century.

Within the twentieth century, Jacksonian historiography has multiplied. Robert V. Remini is the foremost Jackson scholar today. He has portrayed the chief less as a symbol of the age than as a shrewd and able politician and leader. Other scholars headquartered at the Hermitage are currently editing Jackson's voluminous papers and correspondence, and their work promises to be definitive. Historians continue to quarrel about Jackson's true character and especially differ as to whether he was a sincere democrat or an opportunist. Thomas P. Abernethy argued the latter point of view, but Arthur Schlesinger, John Spencer Bassett, Marquis James and others have disagreed. Charles Grier Sellers, Jr. has discussed the controversy in some detail in his article "Andrew Jackson versus the Historians." Novelists have also drawn on Jackson lore. Two of the most successful works of fiction have been Irving Stone's *The President's Lady* and Noel B. Gerson's *Old Hickory.*

James K. Polk, Tennessee's other elected President, was a strong Jackson supporter aptly called "Young Hickory" and has also been a subject for biographers and novelists. For many years Polk was neglected by historians, but the publication of his diary not long after the beginning of the twentieth century brought about a reevaluation; modern historians now list him among the ten most successful Presidents (a group that also includes Jackson). The most widely recognized Polk scholar, Charles Grier Sellers, Jr., has published a dozen articles on Polk in addition to *James Knox Polk, Jacksonian* and *James Knox Polk, Continentalist,* the definitive works on the Maury Countian. The Polk papers are now being edited at Vanderbilt University, and four volumes have been published to date. Of the novels based on Polk's life, Noel B. Gerson's *The Slender Reed* has been one of the most successful.

The career of Tennessee's third President, Andrew Johnson, who succeeded to the office after Lincoln was assassinated, has been examined thoroughly. Shortly after the turn of the century, James S. Jones prepared a *Life of Andrew Johnson,* and in 1916 Clifton Hall published *Andrew Johnson, Military Governor of Tennessee*—an account highly critical of the East Tennessean's stay in Nashville as an appointee of President Lincoln during the war years. In the 1920s, four scholars prepared works on Johnson. Robert V. Winston wrote *Andrew Johnson, Plebian and Patriot;* Lloyd Paul Stryker, *Andrew Johnson, A Study in Courage;* Howard K. Beale, *The Critical Year: A Study of Andrew Johnson and Reconstruction;* and W. M. Caskey, two articles on Johnson's gubernatorial administrations. LeRoy P. Graf and Ralph W. Haskins, editors of the Johnson papers, published the first volume in the series in 1967 and continue their work at the University of Tennessee. Of the several historical novels based on the life of Johnson, the most successful was Gerson's *Yankee from Tennessee.*

John Sevier has become almost a legendary figure among writers of Tennessee biography. The Hero of King's Mountain—also called "Nolichucky Jack" and the "Warrior of the Watauga"—was successful, according to the inscription on his monument, in all thirty-five of his battles with the Redskins and the Redcoats. Sevier plays an important role in Lyman C. Draper's *King's Mountain and Its Heroes* (1887), Theodore Roosevelt's *Winning of the West* (1895), Samuel Cole Williams's *History of the Lost State of Franklin* (1924), Donald Davidson's *The Tennessee, I,* (1946), Wilma Dykeman's *The French Broad* (1955), and North Callahan's *Smoky Mountain Country* (1952). Full-length biographies of Sevier include F. M. Turner's *General John Sevier* (1910) and Carl Driver's *John Sevier, Pioneer of the Old Southwest* (1932). Among the novels centering around Sevier are Gerson's *The Cumberland Rifles* (1952), Florette Henri's *King's Mountain* (1950), and Helen T. Miller's *The Sound of Chariots* (1947). "Chucky Jack" has been the hero in a plethora of children's books and plays.

The careers of scores of other public figures have been scrutinized by historians and novelists. Among the historians, Joseph H. Parks, the most prolific biographer of Tennesseans, has penned studies of Felix Grundy (1940), John Bell (1950), General Edmund Kirby Smith (1954), and General Leonidas Polk (1962). Ably written biographies of others, including William Blount, David Crockett, Daniel Boone, Nathan Bedford Forrest, Sam Houston, Bob Taylor, and Edward Crump have circulated widely.

The many general histories of Tennessee have included multi-volume works by Philip Hamer, John Trotwood Moore, Dixon

Merritt, and the team of Folmsbee, Corlew, and Mitchell. A half-dozen authors have written one-volume works for use as texts in elementary schools. In 1899, Gentry R. McGee published a simple but comprehensive book called *A History of Tennessee* which, as revised later by C. B. Ijams of Jackson, was used as a textbook for more than a quarter of a century. William R. Garrett and Albert V. Goodpasture issued their *History of Tennessee* in 1905. Then, in 1925, S. E. Scates's *A School History of Tennessee* and in 1936 Robert H. White's *Tennessee, Its Growth and Progress* were issued. School histories currently in use include Joseph H. Parks and Stanley J. Folmsbee's *The Story of Tennessee,* Mary U. Rothrock's *This is Tennessee,* her *Discovering Tennessee,* and Jesse Burt's *Tennessee Story.*

With the exception of George W. Harris and Mary Noailles Murfree (who wrote under the pseudonym of Charles Egbert Craddock), Tennessee writers of fiction and poetry produced little work of quality until near the end of the first quarter of the twentieth century. Harris (1814–1869) lived most of his life in Knoxville and published a number of short comic works depicting characters of the East Tennessee mountains. His most famous character was "Sut Lovingood," a particularly incorrigible mountaineer rascal who could not stay out of trouble. Murfree was born in Murfreesboro; before she was thirty, she had placed short stories in the *Atlantic Monthly* and other journals. A collection of her short stories, *In the Tennessee Mountains* (1884), created a sensation and established her reputation. In the years that followed, she wrote more than a dozen novels and scores of short stories, focusing particularly on Appalachian Tennessee. Her talent for graphic detail and her ability to captivate the reader with her charm as a master storyteller accounted for her popularity.

Careful scholars of literature have maintained that, with the exception of Harris's and Murfree's works, Tennessee literature did not "truly come of age" until the appearance of a group of sixteen poets called "Fugitives"[1] at Vanderbilt University in 1922. Developing a little later was a group of twelve writers—mostly Vanderbilt instructors and students—known as "Agrarians."[2] Dur-

[1] John Crowe Ransom, Donald Davidson, Allen Tate, Robert Penn Warren, Merrill Moore, Laura Riding, Jesse Wills, Alec B. Stevenson, Walter Clyde Curry, Stanley Johnson, Sidney M. Hirsch, James Frank, William Yandell Elliott, William Frierson, Ridley Wills, and Alfred Starr.

[2] John Crowe Ransom, Donald Davidson, Allen Tate, Robert Penn Warren,

ing the period 1922–1925, the Fugitives published nineteen issues of a journal they called *The Fugitive,* which was devoted almost exclusively to verse. Sometimes called "the inaugurators of the Southern renaissance," the Fugitives were in close contact with the Agrarians, and several were within the ranks of both groups. The Agrarians, who published a variety of essays, articles, and books, were perhaps best known for their anthology published in 1930, entitled *I'll Take My Stand: The South and the Agrarian Tradition.* The work of both Fugitives and Agrarians was praised and condemned but scarcely ignored.

Creativity and individuality were the watchwords of the Fugitives. Indeed, as Donald Davidson has pointed out, they sought "to flee from the extremes of conventionalism" and to accept and use the best qualities of modern poetry "without . . . casting aside as unworthy all that is established as good in the past"; in this way, they hoped to capture and express the spirit of the "true Southern values." In the early issues of their journal, the Fugitives were not particularly interested in exploiting their identity as Southerners. They rebelled, they said, against "the high-caste Brahmins of the Old South." But as the disillusionment following World War I became magnified and the crass materialism of the mid–1920s became more apparent, they became convinced that industrial and commercial preoccupations were stripping the American people—and Southerners in particular—of their traditional and cultural birthright. They saw in their Southern heritage a society in which traditional and spiritual impulses were predominant and should be preserved. In this way the Fugitives were the precursors of the Agrarians.

Four Fugitive poets—Davidson, Ransom, Tate, and Warren—formed the nucleus of the Agrarians, who undertook to publish a criticism of American society and philosophy during the 1920s and 1930s. In some respects they were in the tradition of novelist Sinclair Lewis and editor H. L. Mencken, who saw in the emphasis upon materialism a departure from sound values. They were not debunkers and pessimists like Mencken, however; they were reformers who sought to turn society away from the monotony of conformity and the loss of identity in a lonely crowd. The true

---

Andrew Lytle, Stark Young, John G. Fletcher, Frank L. Owsley, Lyle Lanier, Herman C. Nixon, John D. Wade, and Henry B. Kline.

South they described as conservative, rural, and spiritually motivated—qualities that had become traditional largely through an agrarian economy. These qualities were worth keeping but would necessitate the repudiation of machinery and its materialistic philosophy, which threatened to strip man of his individuality. Learning from Sinclair Lewis and others of the standardization that industrialism had imposed upon other regions, the Agrarians rejoiced that it had been slow in developing in the South and questioned its worth in view of the problems in other regions where it had developed. Drawing upon the Bible, Thomas Jefferson, and John C. Calhoun, the Agrarians asserted that an economy of subsistence agriculture where men retained their self-respect and commanded the respect of their neighbors was superior to a surrender to "Progress"—which some were calling the "American way of life" but which would reduce man to the monotony of the assembly line and strip him of his individuality. In returning to a conservative past, the Agrarians shared the disillusionment of many people after World War I and believed that they could escape the problems that accompanied increasing population, urbanization, and racial turmoil.

Eastern critics dismissed the Agrarians as harmless literary diehards who could not forget the Confederacy. Such eminent historians as William B. Hesseltine, Henry Steele Commager, and Dixon Wecter dismissed them as provincial visionaries who advocated return to a "Golden Age" that never existed. Still others pictured them as scholars who had considerable literary ability but who wished perpetually to shed tears over the Lost Cause, to blame the North for America's problems, and to perpetuate a feudalistic society. It was said that the Agrarians completely ignored the many faults of the old system while extolling the virtues of courtesy, honor, and courage that they ascribed to the Old South. Writers of the 1960s have been kinder to the Agrarians. Indeed, C. Vann Woodward, Thomas Lawrence Connelly, and Louis D. Rubin are among the scholars who view them as serious, well-intentioned reformers within the American tradition. In his perceptive *The Burden of Southern History,* Woodward has indicated a belief that critics have not fully understood the intent and purpose of the Agrarians. Connelly has described *I'll Take My Stand* as only an "experimental beginning of a thirty-year reappraisal of American society" and an "attempt to define a Southern tradition that was worth defending and to criticize American society in general."

Regardless of the initial comments about their anthology, the Agrarians continued to be heard. Perhaps Davidson's best-known contribution is a two-volume work entitled *The Tennessee River,* published in 1946 and 1948 as a part of the Rivers of America series. Davidson, a native of Campbellsville, was a member of the English department at Vanderbilt University for more than thirty years. Lytle, born in Murfreesboro, wrote more than a half-dozen novels and for many years was editor of the *Sewanee Review.* Nixon taught for many years at Vanderbilt and is remembered for his interpretation of the rural South in *Forty Acres and Steel Mules* and his plea for social planning in *Possum Trot.* Warren, a Rhodes scholar, has written, with Cleanth Brooks, Jr., two widely used textbooks on poetry and fiction. His *Night Rider* (1939), a poignant story of the "Black Patch War," fought among tobacco farmers along the Tennessee-Kentucky border at the turn of the century, captivated the attention of readers, as did his later works including *Flood: A Romance of Our Time, All the King's Men,* and *A Place to Come To.* The last-named has a Tennessee setting. Owsley, a gifted teacher at Vanderbilt for many years, wrote *King Cotton Diplomacy, States Rights in the Confederacy,* and *Plain Folk of the Old South;* research for the last-named work came primarily from Tennessee materials, as Owsley sought to show the prevalence of a strong middle class in the states of the old Confederacy. Ransom, born in Pulaski, is best remembered for his work on the *Kenyon Review,* which he founded and edited until 1959.

T. S. Stribling's works contrasted with the more refined and gentle approach of the Fugitives. A son of a country merchant at Clifton, Stribling saw little value in writing of the Old South that Fugitives and Agrarians depicted as being so worthy of emulation. His first major work with a Tennessee setting was *Teeftallow* (1926), a story of poor whites surrounded by bigotry. *Bright Metal* (1928) tells of a cultured "foreigner" who married into a difficult Tennessee environment and sought to repudiate the myth that the Southern hill folk were gentle and hospitable. Indeed, the white people in most of his works are vulgar villains who operate only in terms of force, violence, and brutality.

The people and the picturesque countryside of the state have frequently been subjects for writers outside the state, particularly William Faulkner of Mississippi. Memphis was the "big city" nearest Faulkner's hometown of Oxford, and as a boy he knew it better than any other city. Few who have read *The Reivers, A*

Reminiscence (1962), a novel published shortly before his death, will forget the fictionalized account of the muddy roads leading into Memphis from Mississippi, the experiences of Boon Hogganbeck and Lucius Priest—the carefree Mississipians, and Everbe Corinthia, the Memphis prostitute with a warm heart.

Peter Taylor, a grandson of Governor Bob Taylor and a professor of literature at the University of Virginia, has written short stories with Southern scenes. Jesse Hill Ford has written predominantly of West Tennessee. His *Mountains of Gilead* is concerned with the Indian mounds around Humboldt, and *The Liberation of Lord Byron Jones* was concerned with race relations in West Tennessee.

James Agee was a Tennessee native whose impressions of Knoxville and the Cumberland Mountain country were lasting ones, even though he matriculated at Harvard after attending St. Andrews at Sewanee and lived predominantly in the East. His *Letters of James Agee to Father Flye* (1962) made occasional reference to Tennessee and demonstrated the literary talents of the youth in addition to the richness of his heart and soul. His Pulitzer prize-winning novel, *A Death in the Family,* which was later cast into a Broadway drama and a motion picture, opened with a scene in Knoxville of Agee as a child happily enjoying the companionship of his father. After his father died, he moved with his mother to Sewanee for a short time; it was there that Agee met the instructor who became his close friend and confidante, Father James Harold Flye.

David J. Harkness, an authority on literature by and about Tennesseans and about the South, has discovered certain characteristics that set Tennessee fiction apart in American literature. In contending that writers about Tennessee show "a preoccupation with kinship" and have a sense of the family as a shaper of society, he has cited Wilma Dykeman's *The Far Family* and Agee's *A Death in the Family* as examples. The preoccupation with historic image also appeals to writers about Tennessee, according to Harkness, and Andrew Lytle's *The Long Night* and *The Velvet Horn* and Alfred L. Crabb's *Dinner at Belmont, Home to Tennessee,* and *Journey to Nashville* are examples. Too, Tennessee writers are concerned with regional development, perhaps because of the distinct political and physical regions of the state. Here, Harkness points to Dykeman's *The Tall Woman,* Ed Bell's *Fish on the Steeple,* and Mildred Haun's *The Hawk's Done Gone* as typical. The variety of cultures in the state—those of the rich and poor, the landed gentry, and the barely subsisting mountain folk—are depicted by Wilma Dykeman, Andrew Lytle, Edd Winfield Parks, Anne Goodwin Winslow, T. S. Stribling, Robert Penn Warren, and others.

The most successful book ever penned by a Tennessean was Alex Haley's *Roots*. First published in the *Readers' Digest* in 1974, it ultimately was translated into twelve languages and telecast in 28 countries. Haley, a Henning native and retired sailor, spent twelve years in the preparation of the work. His story of Kunta Kinte's faith in his African heritage and the struggle for survival of his descendants inspired faith and hope in blacks and whites alike. Most whites, whose literary and entertainment pablum had consisted mainly of stories of Uncle Remus and Amos 'n Andy, gained new respect for blacks as they read of people of Africa's golden age and of peaceful and gentle Africans from whom the American blacks traced their ancestry.

Music and Drama ⧉ Tennesseans have been active in cultural fields other than literature. The Federal Theater Project of the 1930s, attempting to salvage a profession rendered bankrupt by the depression, provided federally financed dramatic productions for people in the major urban areas of the state—as indeed throughout the nation. By mid-century, many cities had their own "Little Theaters" and "Barn Theaters."

Tennesseans have been motion picture enthusiasts since the first "silents" began to be shown around the time of World War I, and by the late twenties and early thirties few towns did not boast one or more "picture shows." Many motion pictures have been made in Tennessee and with Tennessee performers. *All the Way Home,* a play based on James Agee's novel *A Death in the Family,* was filmed in Knoxville. Both the Agee novel and the drama had won Pulitzer prizes—the first time the award had been won by both an original novel and its dramatization. *The Liberation of Lord Byron Jones,* based on the novel by Jesse Hill Ford, was filmed in the Humboldt-Trenton areas. *Walking Tall,* the story of the heroism of Sheriff Buford Pusser, was filmed in the Savannah area. Claude Jarman, Pat Boone, and Dinah Shore of Nashville, Elvis Presley of Memphis, Elizabeth Patterson of Savannah, Patricia Neal, Polly Bergen, and Jerome Courtland of Knoxville, and Peggy Dow of Athens are among the many Tennesseans featured in major productions. Jarman was acclaimed for his role in *The Yearling,* and Miss Patterson for hers in *Intruder in the Dust, Welcome Stranger,* and *Miss Tatlock's Millions.* Patricia Neal won an Oscar for her performance in *Hud.*

Neal's remarkable career captured the attention and admiration of millions. Sustaining three massive strokes that left her temporarily paralyzed and unable to speak, she was restored to health and the stage largely through her own determination. "The neurosurgeon thought I would conk out," she was quoted as saying, "but Tennessee hillbillies don't conk that easy." In the fall of 1977 she participated in the dedication of the Patricia Neal Rehabilitation Center established in Knoxville as a part of the Fort Sanders Presbyterian Hospital.

The Volunteer State and particularly its capital have been described as the "music center of the world." Grace Moore, Mary Costa, James Melton, and Frances Geer are among many who have had outstanding operatic careers. A concert at the Kennedy Center in August 1977 featured the voices of three of Tennessee's outstanding Memphis opera stars—Ruth Welting, Nancy Tatum, and Mignon Dunn.

Memphis, which produced Elvis Presley, has been a center for the production of musical talent and, of course, the blues. Black singer Bessie Smith during the 1920s was the "Empress of the Blues" and was a contemporary of W. C. Handy, who became known as the "Father of the Blues" after he composed "The Memphis Blues" and "St. Louis Blues."

But it is Nashville that has truly been a "music capital of the world." Older Tennesseans will recall Beth Slater Whitson's "Meet Me Tonight in Dreamland" and "Let Me Call You Sweetheart," Francis Craig's "Near You," and Beasley Smith's "Night Train to Memphis" and "Sunday Down South," but to the modern generation the "Nashville Sound" means something else—country and western music and, of course, the Grand Ole Opry. "It isn't so much a sound as it is a way of doing things," recording artist Owen Bradley once said of "the sound." "It's a bunch of good musicians getting together and doing what comes naturally." Country music, first called "hillbilly," began as an expression of the rural South. Charles Wolfe has interpreted it as a form of art that "spoke to the people" of the region, "helping them to come to grips with the traumatic changes of the modern age; to meet the challenges to traditional values posed by industrialized and 'progress.'"[3]

[3] Charles K. Wolfe, *Tennessee Strings: The Story of Country Music in Tennessee* (Knoxville, 1977), vii.

Above: Internationally known as "Music City, U.S.A.," Nashville has its own Country Music Hall of Fame and Museum. *Below:* Shown here are eight of the Grand Ole Opry's best-known performers in 1931. They are: Sam McGee and Uncle Dave Macon, seated; and, from left, Kirk McGee, Dr. Humphrey Bate, Dorris Macon, Buster Bate, Alcyone Bate, and Lou Hesson. Courtesy of Charles K. Wolfe.

Although centers of country music have had their day, Tennessee and Nashville have been most consistently identified with it for more than a half-century.

The real impetus to country music was the establishment in 1925 of radio station WSM ("We Shield Millions") by the National Life and Accident Insurance Company. Operating with 1,000 watts, the station's signals reached not only Nashvillians but also thousands of rural people living within a radius of 100 miles or more. Announcer George Hay (The "Solemn Old Judge") who had had experience with country shows before joining the WSM staff, quickly perceived that of the thousands of people who heard the station's programs, a vast majority liked the old-time country music. Within a few months, Hay had made the "Saturday Night Barn Dance" the most popular segment of WSM's programming. Dr. Humphrey Bate, a Vanderbilt University Medical School graduate practicing at Castalian Springs, was among the first to broadcast country music from Nashville. Taking on a rustic air and appearance, Bate brought along a four-piece band called the "Possum Hunters," which included his thirteen-year-old daughter, Alcyone, who played the piano. But he was soon joined by the Crook Brothers band, harmonica artist Deford Bailey, the Clodhoppers, the Fruit Jar Drinkers, Uncle Dave Macon, and many others.

Uncle Dave became one of the Opry's favorites and truly symbolized the spirit of country music. Macon, often called the "Dixie Dewdrop" and "King of the Hillbillies," had been a vaudeville performer and banjo player. Before the Opry began, he made a living touring the South and performing in schoolhouses, at tobacco auctions, and on vaudeville stages. His "Keep My Skillet Good and Greasy" and "You Can't Do Wrong and Get By" occasionally annoyed city residents with more delicate tastes, but they thrilled the rural populace who crowded in to hear him. Uncle Dave and his Moonshiners soon became the most popular performers on the Opry, and he continued until his death in 1952.

The term "hillbilly music" offended some people who really enjoyed the music, and soon after World War II the terms "country" and "western" replaced "hillbilly." Interest mushroomed, and at mid-century Nashville was well on its way toward becoming the "recording center of the world" as well as the capital of country music. During the 1950s, "Music Row" along Sixteenth Avenue was a place where thousands of records were being cut by emerging new stars such as Johnny Cash, Marty Robbins, Chet Atkins, Owen Bradley, and hundreds o others. Bradley's Quonset Hut and Bradley's Barn became favorite re cording studios, and Bradley is often credited with being one who did more than any other to make the Nashville Sound heard around the world. Roy Acuff was already a nationally known figure, and Lester Flatt, Earl Scruggs, Ernest Tubb, and others cut hundreds of records.

By the late 1970s, Nashville had more than 250 recording studios, including Acuff-Rose, which was established in 1942 as the first Nashville-based publisher. It was Sun Records, however, that discovered Memphian Elvis Presley, who mixed country with the blues and introduced the American people to a different style that captured the hearts of teenagers and others around the world.

Tennessee Becomes Conscious of Its Past ⟩⟩⟩ During the second quarter of the twentieth century, Tennesseans became increasingly conscious of their past. Both the *American Historical Magazine* and the *Tennessee Historical Magazine* had been discontinued, but the Tennessee Historical Society, which actually traced its beginnings to the Tennessee Society for the Diffusion of Knowledge, formed in 1835, and the Tennessee Antiquarian Society, formed in 1820, was revitalized and began once again to meet periodically and to collect source materials.

The Tennessee Historical Committee was created in 1919 with its principal purpose the collection and preservation of materials about Tennesseans in World War I. In 1941 the name was changed to the Tennessee Historical Commission, and its areas of interest were expanded to incorporate general historical materials, the marking of historic sites, publication of historical works, and the broad function of diffusing historical knowledge about the state. The commission is composed of twenty-seven members, including the governor and commissioner of education who serve ex officio.

The commission has accomplished much in all of these areas of interest. One of its first significant acts was to encourage the writing of county histories and to subsidize one-half of the printing costs. Its publications have included the monumental *Messages of the Governors*, edited by State Historian Robert H. White, who before his death in 1971 had edited eight volumes extending to the end of the nineteenth century. The commission is also cooperating with the National Historical Publications Commissions in the editing and publishing of the papers of James K. Polk and Andrew Johnson. It has donated copies of its publications to schools and public libraries of the state and has erected more than a thousand historic markers.

The lakes formed by TVA's dams make the Tennessee region a popular center for recreation.

Further, the commission assumed a major role in the preservation of historic sites such as the Carter House in Franklin, Oaklands in Murfreesboro, Belle Meade Mansion in Nashville, and the Blount Mansion in Knoxville.

Largely through the commission's efforts, a new state library and archives building supplanted the crowded one-room facilities maintained for many years in the state capitol. Established in 1854 with an appropriation of $5,000 at the insistence of Governor Andrew Johnson, the State Library developed quite slowly over the years. The State Archives Department, created about fifty years later, had preserved their important documents in the basement of the War Memorial Building until the construction of the new building.

Today, the library and archives are under the direction of the state librarian and archivist, who supervises four divisions—the State Library Division, Public Libraries Division, Division of Administrative Services, and Archives Division. Until 1969 the state librarian served as chairman of the Tennessee Historical Commission.

There are three major historical societies in the state, in addition to societies in many counties. Appropriately, they are called the East Tennessee Historical Society, the West Tennessee Historical Society, and the Tennessee Historical Society. Each publishes a journal—the Tennessee Historical Society does so quarterly and the other two annually—subsidized by funds from the commission. Under the terms of a recent agreement, the Tennessee Historical Society also houses an extensive collection of historical materials in the State Library. The societies, through their journals and many activities, play important roles in stimulating interest in Tennessee history.

The celebration of the state sesquicentennial in 1946 did much to quicken interest in the state's history. The official ceremonies were held in Nashville from May 30 to June 3 under the direction of the sesquicentennial committee of the historical commission, of which Stanley F. Horn was chairman. Busts of Admiral David G. Farragut and Commander Matthew Fontaine Maury were unveiled in the house of representatives, a pageant entitled "Tennessee Through the Years" was staged at Dudley Stadium, and Dr. Walter R. Courtenay, pastor of the First Presbyterian Church of Nashville, preached a sesquicentennial sermon.

Ceremonies also were held in other Tennessee cities and in the

Library of Congress in Washington, D.C., under the auspices of members of the Tennessee State Society of Washington. Within the state, in addition to the ceremonies held in Nashville, the occasion was marked in Knoxville, Memphis, Chattanooga, Johnson City, Murfreesboro, Franklin, Monteagle, and elsewhere. In Knoxville, a monument to the memory of Sarah Hawkins Sevier, first wife of John Sevier, was unveiled on the courthouse lawn.

Even more elaborate plans began in 1971 for the state's participation in the nation's bicentennial celebration. The Tennessee American Revolution Bicentennial Commission of twenty-five members was formed in that year, with William L. (Dick) Barry of Lexington as chairman. Within a very short time 143 local bicentennial commissions were formed—one in each county and also in many of the cities and towns—seeking to commemorate the past, celebrate the richness of the present, and help build for a better future. Under the executive leadership of first David W. Bowen and later James C. Kelly, the commission spent over a million dollars from Memphis to Bristol on projects as varied as the tastes of the people. When the celebration ultimately ended, national authorities released figures indicating that Tennessee ranked fourth among the states of the nation in the number of outstanding events held in commemoration of the nation's beginning. The optimism that prevailed in the state after the event emphasized poignantly that most Tennesseans did not view their country with pessimism but looked toward the twenty-first century with considerable optimism.

SUGGESTED READINGS

Books

Oswald E. Brown, James H. Kirkland, and Edwin Mims, *God and the New Knowledge* (Nashville, 1926); Louise Cowan, *The Fugitive Group: A Literary History* (Baton Rouge, 1959); Ray Ginger, *Six Days or Forever: Tennessee v. John Thomas Scopes* (New York, 1958); Hugh Davis Graham, *Crisis in Print: Desegregation and the Press in Tennessee* (Nashville, 1968); David Harkness, *Tennessee in Recent Books, Music and Drama* (Knoxville, 1950); Thomas Krueger, *And Promises to Keep: The Southern Conference for Human Welfare, 1938–1948* (Nashville, 1967); Lester C. Lamon, *Black Tennesseans, 1900–1930* (Knoxville, 1976); Robert M. Miller, *American Protestantism and Social Issues, 1919–1939* (Chapel Hill, 1958); Twelve Southerners, *I'll Take my Stand* (New York, 1930); James W. Warren and

Adrian W. McClaren, *Tennessee Belles-Lettres: A Guide to Tennessee Literature* (Morristown, Tenn., 1977).

Articles
Kenneth K. Bailey, "The Enactment of Tennessee's Anti-Evolution Law," *JSH* 16 (Nov. 1950), 472–90; Thomas Lawrence Connelly, "The Vanderbilt Agrarians: Time and Place in Southern Tradition," *THQ* 22 (March 1963), 22–37; John H. DeWitt, Jr., "Early Radio Broadcasting in Middle Tennessee," *THQ* 31 (Spring 1972), 80–94; Jerry Henderson, "Nashville's Ryman Auditorium," *THQ* 27 (Winter 1968), 305–28; Elmo Howell, "William Faulkner and Tennessee," *THQ* 21 (Sept. 1962), 251–62; Rayburn W. Johnson, "Population Trends in Tennessee from 1940 to 1950," *THQ* 11 (Sept. 1952), 254–62; Lester C. Lamon, "The Black Community in Nashville and the Fisk University Student Strike of 1924–1925," *JSH* 33 (May 1974), 225–44; Lamon, "The Tennessee Agricultural and Industrial Normal School: Public Education for Black Tennesseans," *THQ* 32 (Spring 1973), 42–58; Dennis Loyd, "Tennessee's Mystery Woman Novelist," *THQ* 29 (Fall 1970), 272–77; James R. Montgomery and Gerald Gaither, "Evolution and Education in Tennessee: Decisions and Dilemmas," *THQ* 28 (Summer 1969), 141–55; Henry Lee Swint, "The Historical Activities of the State of Tennessee," *THQ* 17 (Dec. 1958), 291–300; Ferenc M. Szasz, "The Scopes Trial in Perspective," *THQ* 30 (Fall 1971), 288–98.

29.

&~ *The Clement-Ellington Years, 1953–1971*

T HE election of 1952 ended the political career of Gordon Browning and placed Frank Goad Clement in a position of power in state politics for nearly two decades. Indeed, at the time of his sudden death in 1969 he was said to have been considering still another race for governor. He served ten years as chief executive, delivered the keynote address at the Democratic convention in 1956, and twice ran for United States senator. During the eight years of this period when Clement was not governor, the mansion was occupied by his friend and commissioner of agriculture, Buford Ellington. Browning, who challenged the incumbent unsuccessfully in 1954, outlived both Ellington and Clement.

The period 1953–1971 was one of substantial progress for the Volunteer State. The sales tax was increased, and Tennessee's improved financial condition enabled state officials to increase services and improve educational facilities and teachers' pay. Three Tennesseans—Clement, Gore, and Kefauver—vied for national office, and Kefauver was the Democratic candidate for vice president in 1956.

Clement's inauguration in 1953 was the signal in many respects for a new era in Tennessee politics. "Constitutional reform," "reapportionment," and "racial integration"—words scarcely in the vocabulary of most Tennesseans in 1953—became household terms while the Dickson native was governor. Much reform legislation was enacted. The thirty-two-year-old governor—the youngest since James C. Jones was elected in 1841—maintained great hope for himself and the people he served. Promising "honesty, decency, and morality" in government, he told of his trust in God for guidance and his intention to keep the people informed of state operations as no other chief executive had done. "This office belongs to the people," a sign on the governor's office door proclaimed, and Clement told widely of his interest to operate the state's business "in a political goldfish bowl."

"The people of Tennessee have a right to expect certain qualifications in their leaders," the governor said. Public officials must have "character," "ability," and "diplomacy," he told his supporters, and he obviously implied that he brought this triumvirate of qualifications to the position. He told of a "lonely Figure"—a "foe of lies, dishonor, theft, and treachery"—who 2,000 years ago had championed the cause "of truth, honor, faith, and bravery" before being crucified and carried "into an airless tomb." It was his "fervent prayer," he said, that he could "so live as to be worthy of His sacrifice." He appointed an able, although inexperienced, cabinet. The first woman ever to serve on a Tennessee governor's staff—Christine Reynolds of Paris—was named to head the public welfare department. Jeanne S. Bodfish of Nashville was elected comptroller of the treasury with administration support.

To set the stage for "honesty, decency, and morality," Clement urged legislators to investigate Browning's administration to determine whether fraudulent and illegal operations had been carried on. While probe members in a 73-page report asserted that the highway department had bought more materials than were necessary and had abused the practice of competitive bidding for the purchase of heavy machinery, they found no evidence of illegal acts. But at Clement's insistence, new purchasing practices were instituted to insure that mistakes of the highway department would not be repeated. As a part of his "decency" program, Clement created a separate department of mental health to supervise and coordinate the work of all state mental health institutions and to seek "the growth and development" of mental health services throughout the state. By 1954, the governor told the Tennessee Press Association, the state had made "the greatest advance in all its history" in seeking mental health for all citizens.

Most of the Clement program was well received by the public, but one act—a measure to increase the weight limits for large trucks—brought criticism. For more than a decade the leaders of the trucking industry had complained that the weight limit allowed in Tennessee—42,000 pounds—was inadequate and much below that of the surrounding states. As a result, the industry had to circumvent the

Frank Goad Clement (*above*) was the first governor since William Carroll to serve in the state house for ten or more years. He was referred to as the "Humanitarian Governor" because of his emphasis upon mental health. He served from 1953 to 1959 and again from 1963 to 1967. Buford Ellington (*below*), Clement's close associate and cabinet member, served as governor from 1959 to 1963 and from 1967 to 1971.

state in interstate traffic, they said, or else maintain additional trucks in Tennessee upon which they would load and unload cargo at the borders in order to conform with the law. Those who argued that the state's highway system would not sustain the traffic of heavier loads were mistaken, trucking executives contended, and were probably on the payroll of the railroads. Robert M. Crichton and others in the industry had contributed heavily to the Clement campaign and career, and now they moved quickly to accomplish that which they had sought unsuccessfully in past administrations. When a measure was passed within one week raising the maximum weight to 55,980 pounds without even a public hearing, a storm of protest arose, and even Clement supporters Ed Crump and Nashville *Banner* publisher Jimmy Stahlman uttered outcries. So alarmed was Clement at the opposition expressed by Stahlman that the governor made immediate plans for a reconciliation with the publisher.

Gordon Browning had returned to his home in Huntingdon, where he observed the activities of the new administration with considerable interest. Unable fully to comprehend the magnitude of the juggernaut that had felled him in 1952, the veteran politician— hurt by the implications that he had been dishonest, immoral, and indecent—made plans in spite of the advice of friends to run again in 1954 in the belief that the voters of the state would not succumb a second time to the young governor's charismatic charms. Clement sought the advice of his close friends regarding strategy. "I am just a country politician," one cabinet official wrote him, "but I would avoid a knock-down, drag-out, mud-slinging campaign. . . ." Others also urged him to talk only of progress made during his two years as governor.

Careful observers knew from the beginning that Browning had scarcely a chance. "We [at the Nashville *Tennessean*], tried hard to persuade him not to run," veteran political observer Joe Hatcher said later. But the former governor bore unhealed wounds and hoped for a miracle. He tried to inject Clement's father—Dickson lawyer Robert S. Clement, "the power behind the throne"—into the campaign as a selfish influence peddler whose chief interest in government consisted in lining his own pockets at the expense of the taxpayers, and accused the incumbent of fraud, deception, and mismanagement. The former governor had successfully used Crump as an issue before, and he again injected the aged Memphian's name into the campaign. Clement was a puppet of the dictator, Browning said, who cared little for Tennessee but who wanted only to use the governor's office as a stepping-stone to Washington. Furthermore, the incumbent, Browning said, posed as a man of the people but drove only Cadillac automobiles given him by influence peddlers who were rewarded with legislative payoffs. Clement countered with the charges of 1952. Indeed, the only new issue was that of segregation, inasmuch as a decision in *Brown v. Topeka* had been handed down in May of that year. Browning flatly rejected the decision and boldly stated that he would "find a way" to keep the schools segregated while he was governor. While not endorsing the decision outright, Clement indicated that he would abide by the law of the land.

The sixty-five-year-old former governor was no match for the young incumbent and received the worst defeat of his long and distinguished career. Clement carried every county in the state except Carroll and won by a vote of 481,808 to 195,156. Raulston Schoolfield of Chattanooga, a strong segregationist, entered the contest a few weeks before the election and received fewer than 30,000 votes.

In the senatorial primary of that year, Sixth District Congressman Pat Sutton, a Southern Conservative from Lawrenceburg, was soundly defeated by incumbent Estes Kefauver, despite Sutton's use of a helicopter and a "round-the-clock talkathon" on television. The sixth district elected Ross Bass, Pulaski postmaster, to Sutton's place in Congress. Clement, Kefauver, and Bass had little difficulty winning in the general election in November. The work of the constitutional convention of 1953 had been ratified, changing the governor's term to four years, and in January 1955 Clement began the first four-year gubernatorial term in the state's history.

Clement emerged from the primary of 1954 the most powerful politician in the state. Young and handsome, he had confident bearing, an air of culture and refinement not universally found among Southern politicians, and he soon caught the eye of national leaders. By no means the least among his wide and developing circle of acquaintances was Billy Graham, whom Clement had invited to address the legislature in April 1953 and who for several years kept up an active correspondence with the governor. According to some reports, Clement and his adviser and secretary of state, Edward G. Friar, had developed a timetable that would project the young governor into the vice presidential nomination in 1956. After an inevitable loss to the popular Eisenhower and Nixon ticket through no fault of his own, he would then oppose Albert Gore in the senatorial race of 1958 and, from the Senate, would challenge all comers for the presidency in 1960.

A few weeks after the August primary, Clement was invited to a Democratic rally in Indianapolis, where he met Adlai Stevenson, National Democratic Chairman Stephen A. Mitchell, Speaker of the House Sam Rayburn, and other prominent Democrats. It was no mere coincidence that two years later he delivered the keynote address at the Democratic National Convention.

But several problems of varying magnitude began to appear that the governor had to solve if his success were to continue in the state and especially in the nation as a whole. One was a proper response to the *Brown* case mentioned earlier. While other leaders of states of the old Confederacy promised to "stand in the schoolhouse door" instead of submit to racial integration, Clement assumed a moderate position. He urged Tennesseans to seek a "Christian solution" and pleaded with blacks and whites alike to eschew violence; as the father of three young children, he said, "the benefits of all our children should be first in the minds" of everyone.

A second problem facing Clement early in his second year as governor was a serious rift in his own political organization. Three of his erstwhile advisers and close associates—Friar, Bodfish, and Crichton—became disillusioned with the governor, charged him with personal dishonesty, and alleged, among other things, that his father was "influence peddling" among legislators from Memphis to Bristol. But the magnetic charm of Clement prevailed. When, for example Friar purchased television time to tell his story of "Clement's perfidy," Clement bought time immediately after Friar's talk and devastatingly refuted each of his former adviser's charges. Friar was no match for Clement. He became a subject of ridicule to the vast throng of Clement supporters and eventually left the state; other defectors who chose to remain in Tennessee were cast into political oblivion. His credibility in no way shaken, the governor took on new laurels as one who had kept his own house in order.

A third issue to require serious consideration was reapportionment of the state legislature. The constitution of 1870 had provided for decennial reapportionment "according to the number of qualified voters," but the legislature had not obeyed the mandate since 1901. The state's urban areas, having experienced tremendous growth during the hundred years following the Civil War, were underrepresented, and the residents clamored for a division affording them their fair share. As early as 1953, leaders in Nashville and East Tennessee had talked of court action to bring relief, and in March 1955 they filed suit in chancery court in Davidson County. Although Chancellor Thomas Wardlaw Steele did not grant the relief sought, he did take a position that the issue was justiciable and not solely one for the legislature—the "courts represent the sovereign will of the people just as much as does the Legislature," he wrote. The chancellor focused attention on Governor Clement when he included in his ruling a belief that the governor would "exercise his constitutional duty" by convening a session of the legislature expressly for the purpose of enacting a valid apportionment act. Clement was besieged with communications from rural people who urged against reapportionment and from urban residents who argued that he should "do his constitutional duty." Clement took a moderate position and sided with neither faction. He did promise to bring the matter before the legislature in 1957—a ploy that apparently satisfied most people.

A fourth problem demanding Clement's attention was how to maintain his political independence without alienating anyone on the state and national levels. Tennessee at the time had "too much talent," Wilma Dykeman has written; it certainly is true that Estes Kefauver and Albert Gore vied with Clement for state and national attention, and each had his own following. Clement's supporters were in both camps, and Clement fought valiantly and successfully to retain them.

Early in 1956, as his stature increased in the state and the nation, Clement became a serious contender for the honor of delivering the keynote address before the Democratic National Convention. He soon drew the support of former president Harry Truman and others prominent in the party and ultimately was chosen from a list of nearly two dozen hopefuls, including Massachusetts Senator John F. Kennedy, Minnesota Senator Hubert Horatio Humphrey, Maine Governor Edmund Muskie, Oklahoma Senator Robert Kerr, and Washington Senator Henry M. Jackson. Seldom had there been so much national interest in a keynote address. Adlai Stevenson, who had described Clement as "one of those wonderful young men who is reinvigorating the Democratic party," was among those expressing satisfaction with the appointment. National newspaper columnists predicted a "spell-binding" oration.

Clement used the same format at Chicago that he had used in 1952 in his attacks upon the Browning administration. He projected himself as a prosecutor for "the people" and developed a ten-count indictment against the iniquities of the incumbent Eisenhower administration. He said that although Eisenhower had been an able battlefield general, he had exercised little leadership as a chief executive, while Nixon—that "Vice-Hatchetman slinging slander and spreading half-truths"—frightened the American people when they contemplated that he was only a heartbeat from the presidency. "How long, O how long America," Clement repeatedly intoned, would this leadership of mediocrity be tolerated by a responsible people. For forty minutes the Tennessee governor regaled Republicans and urged Democrats to move forward toward victory; he concluded by asking his listeners to look only "to God for guidance" and sing "in unison the inevitable victory hymn, 'Precious Lord, Take Our Hand, Lead Us On!'"

Although the speech won for Clement neither the presidential nor the vice presidential nomination, it did focus the country's attention upon the young governor. Estes Kefauver, in a close battle with John F. Kennedy, won the vice presidential nomination but was defeated along with presidential candidate Adlai Stevenson by the popular Eisenhower and Nixon. Even voters of Tennessee rejected its own son and supported the incumbent president.

Clement remained a powerful politician but was constitutionally ineligible to succeed himself in 1958. Still, he could point to considerable progress made during his six years as governor, and he strongly endorsed his first campaign manager and secretary of agriculture, Buford Ellington, as his successor.

The humdrum campaign of 1958 had none of the spectacular oratory and charges and counter-charges of the Browning-Clement years. Ellington had strong support from the rural populace but encountered serious opposition from the conservative Andrew ("Tip") Taylor of Jackson, Mayor Edmund Orgill of Memphis, and Clifford Allen of Nashville. Orgill and Allen ran with strong urban support. Thanks to support from the rural counties, the Marshall Countian won by a narrow margin. He received 213,415 votes; there were 204,629 for Taylor, 204,382 for Orgill, and 56,854 for Allen. Expressed as a percentage of total votes cast, Ellington received only 31 percent, while Taylor and Orgill each polled nearly 30 percent. Traditionally the victor had carried Shelby County, but in this election Ellington received only 18 percent of the Memphis vote, while Orgill and Taylor each received more than twice that much. In the same year Senator Gore resisted a strong challenge by Prentice Cooper and won a second term to the senate by a vote of 375,439 to 253,191 for Cooper. Gore carried all congressional districts except the third and eighth. Both Ellington and Gore were elected in the fall by large majorities.

While Clement was governor the sales tax had been increased from 2 percent to 3 percent (1955), but Ellington announced that the tax revenues were sufficient for his programs and that no new taxes would be necessary. He undertook a major reorganization of the administrative branch and abolished or consolidated many agencies and regulatory boards. Considerable landscaping on the capitol grounds and renovation of the capitol itself were accomplished while Ellington was governor.

In the year following Ellington's inauguration came the important presidential race in which Democrats returned to the White House, and the senatorial race in which incumbent Estes Kefauver was reelected. For the third time in succession, Tennesseans voted Republican in a presidential election, as Nixon and Lodge won by a small majority. In the senatorial race (primary), Kefauver was challenged by Circuit Judge Andrew ("Tip") Taylor, who had been defeated by Ellington two years earlier in the gubernatorial race. Although the Taylor forces billed their candidate as "our kind of folks" and represented Kefauver as one who numbered communists and northern liberals among his friends, the incumbent senator won by almost a 2-to-1 majority. While liberals saw in the Kefauver victory a chance for John Kennedy to win Tennessee's electoral votes in the fall, seasoned observers attributed the senator's reelection to his winsome personality and his intense campaign rather than to a liberal trend in the Volunteer State. Kefauver died two years after beginning his third term and was succeeded by Herbert S. Walters, who was appointed by the governor to fill the vacancy until the general election of 1964.

The gubernatorial elections of the 1960s were repeats of the 1950s, as Clement was elected for a third term in 1962, and Ellington returned for a second term in 1966. In the election of 1962, Clement was challenged by William W. Farris, a Memphis lawyer, and Rudy Olgiati, mayor of Chattanooga. Clement's 309,333 votes were a little more than 42 percent of the total cast, but they were sufficient to return him for a third and final term to the state capitol. Olgiati and Farris received 211,812 and 202,813 votes, respectively.

Two years later Clement announced for the United States Senate to fill out the unexpired term of Kefauver after Walters declined to run. He was challenged by Sixth District Congressman Ross Bass and M. M. Bullard of Newport. Bass had served in Congress since 1953 and had established a voting record that marked him as a liberal, while Clement was viewed more as a conservative. Bass carried 59 counties and won by a vote of 330,213 to 233,245 for Clement and 86,718 for Bullard. For the first time Clement lost Shelby County; Bass won majorities in the urban counties and polled more than 50,000 in Davidson County. In the general election, Bass was challenged by East Tennessee lawyer Howard H. Baker, Jr., whose father had served with distinction for more than a decade as second district congressman. In a surprisingly close race, Bass won by a vote of 568,905 to 517,330. In the other senatorial race, observers also were surprised at the strength shown by Memphis Republican Dan H. Kuykendall against incumbent Albert Gore. The vote in that election was 570,542 to 493,475. In the presidential election of that year, Tennessee reversed the trend toward voting for Republican presidential candidates and gave its eleven electoral votes to Lyndon B. Johnson and Hubert H. Humphrey.

Two years later, in 1966, it was Ellington's time to return to the governor's mansion; he was ably challenged in the Democratic primary by Nashville lawyer and businessman, John J. Hooker, Jr., a son of former Governor Browning's adviser and friend. With the support of Memphis blacks, Hooker carried Shelby County by a small margin but failed to win any of the other urban counties, including his home of Davidson. The rural areas also voted for Ellington, who won by a count of 413,950 to 360,105.

In the same year Clement, whose term as governor would expire in January, challenged Ross Bass, whose two years in the United States Senate had been a disappointment to liberals and conservatives alike. This time Clement polled solid majorities in Davidson, Shelby, and Hamilton counties, which enabled him to win with 51 percent of the vote. The final count was 384,322 to 366,078. But in the general election that fall, Clement was challenged by Howard Baker, Jr. Clement was no match for the handsome, straightforward Baker, who had gained in stature and public approval since his narrow defeat two years earlier; the vote was 483,063 to 383,843.

Clement carried Davidson County, but Baker swept the other urban centers and won handily in East Tennessee, where Clement had gained sizable majorities in past elections. In the same year, Ray Blanton, a McNairy County contractor, defeated the well-entrenched seventh district congressman, Tom Murray, by 400 votes. In a five-man race, Blanton polled only 29 percent of the total vote, but it was sufficient to launch a career that would ultimately carry him to the state house in Nashville.

As significant as any of the developments of the Clement-Ellington era were the matters of constitutional revision and legislative and congressional reapportionment. For more than a decade before Clement took office, reformers had talked of a need to revise the fundamental law. In 1952, they approved the calling of a convention, and that autumn they determined membership. Delegates consequently assembled in April 1953 for the first convention since 1870. Former Governor Prentice Cooper was elected chairman and former Governor Ben W. Hooper vice chairman. Delegates increased the governor's term from two to four years without the right of immediate succession, gave the governor the right to veto certain items in a bill without nullifying the entire bill, abolished the poll tax, increased the pay of legislators, and provided optional home rule for cities.

Since 1953, Tennesseans have held conventions at six-year intervals. In 1959, delegates considered extending the term of county officials and reducing the voting age to eighteen. Ultimately, they submitted to the people only the question of increasing the term of trustees from two to four years. In 1965, delegates considered matters of apportionment in the house and senate, authorized annual instead of biennial sessions of the legislature, allowed county courts to fill legislative vacancies, and placed legislators on a salary instead of paying them a per diem.

Reapportionment was a recurring theme. The constitution of 1796 had provided for senators and representatives to be apportioned among the counties and districts "according to the numbers of taxable inhabitants in each" as shown by a census to be taken every ten years. The constitution of 1834 had prescribed legislative reapportionment in 1841 and every ten years thereafter, and the constitution of 1870 likewise required decennial reapportionment.

But because no reapportionment had taken place since 1901 and the growth of cities had caused them to be grossly underrepresented, people in the urban areas undertook a vigorous campaign that ultimately resulted in the *Baker v. Carr* case begun in 1959 as a class-action suit. Plaintiffs in that suit alleged that although the population had increased from 2,021,000 in 1901 to 3,292,000 in 1950, with increased concentration in the cities, no effort had been made to reapportion the legislature. About 37 percent of the voting population elected 20 of the 33 senate members and 40 percent elected 63 of the 99 members of the house. A minority thus controlled the legislative body, with the result that collection of taxes and benefits from tax revenues were inequitable. Plaintiffs argued that they were denied equal protection of the laws as guaranteed by the Fourteenth Amendment of the federal Constitution. More specifically, they showed that a voter in Moore County, for example, had 17 times more representation than one in Davidson County, and that citizens of Moore and other small counties received many times the apportionment of benefits from the gasoline and other taxes.

A three-judge federal panel heard the case in 1959 and dismissed the complaint on the grounds that federal courts lacked jurisdiction in such matters, but complainants then appealed to the United States Supreme Court. Three years later (1962), the Court rendered the *Baker* decision. Along narrow grounds it reversed the ruling of the district court and held that federal courts did have jurisdiction and that "a justiciable cause of action" had been stated by the plaintiffs. The case then was remanded to the district court, with instructions to develop equitable reapportionment.

In view of the *Baker* decision, Governor Ellington called a special session of the legislature immediately. Members enacted a reapportionment measure in June, 1962, but it proved unsatisfactory to the district court, and legislators therefore tried again at the regular session in 1963. The house plan as adopted in that year was acceptable to the court, but the senate plan was not. The court ultimately established June 1, 1965 as the date when a plan proposed by the plaintiffs would become effective if the legislature could not develop something before that time. It soon became apparent that the federal courts wanted the districts evenly divided even if it meant cutting across county lines—a concept Tennesseans long respectful of county integrity and local government found highly distasteful. In the meantime Clement had been inaugurated and on May 28, seeking to bring the matter to a conclusion, signed into law an apportionment measure establishing new senatorial districts cutting across county lines. But the state supreme court ruled the act unconstitutional, and thus a convention was necessary to rewrite the constitution in a manner in which the question could be resolved.

At the same time, the governor signed into law a measure designed to correct population disparities among the congressional districts. This law, which divided Shelby County among the seventh, eighth, and ninth districts, was unsatisfactory to the three-judge district court. When the legislature failed in 1967 to meet the court's requirement for correcting disparities, the court imposed its own realignment, which was used for the first time in 1968.

A major accomplishment of Clement and Ellington was their able handling of the racial controversy that developed soon after the Supreme Court's decision of 1954. As mentioned earlier, Clement had been forced to send troops to keep order when blacks sought to integrate public schools in Clinton in August 1956. Although the segregationists criticised him, most people of the state understood the seriousness of the situation and viewed his actions approvingly. A dynamite blast at the school in the following year emphasized the continuing unrest there. Careful parliamentary maneuvering was necessary to sooth ruffled feelings on both sides as racial conflict widened on several fronts, but the two governors skillfully handled most of the problems in such a manner that major violence was avoided.

The Clement-Ellington years were a time of higher taxes and increased services to the people. Appropriations for highways and schools constituted the largest share of the expenditures. Clement on one occasion felt it necessary to defend increased taxes when he asserted, "we are spending more money than ever before in this business of State Government, yet we are saving money where money has never been saved before." The sales tax ultimately was increased (after Clement had left office) to a high of 6 percent, with the state receiving 4.5 percent and the counties and cities having the right to levy an additional 1.5 percent.

Despite the general acceptance of the Clement-Ellington program, the people of the Volunteer State turned increasingly toward the Republican party during the 1960s. Republican leaders, encouraged after Senator Howard H. Baker's defeat of Clement in 1966, turned their attention toward the presidential race of 1968 and the gubernatorial and senatorial contests of 1970. They were successful in all. Although Independent candidate George C. Wallace exhibited strong support in the presidential race, Republican Richard M. Nixon won Tennessee's electoral votes by a sound majority. Democrat Hubert H. Humphrey finished a poor third. In the same year, Republicans controlled the state house of representatives for the first time in modern history; they also increased their membership in the senate from eight to thirteen.

Both the gubernatorial and senatorial contests of 1970 brought forward candidates who were unknown outside their hometown areas but who proved to be strong vote-getters. In the Democratic primary, Hudley Crockett of Nashville challenged veteran Senator Albert Gore, who most observers believed would have little or no difficulty in winning nomination for a fourth term. Only near the end of the campaign did Gore realize the extent to which his support in the Volunteer State had deteriorated. He received a bare 51 percent of the popular vote—a fact indicating that he would have considerable difficulty in the fall elections, regardless of the Republican nominee. He lost the Sixth, Seventh, Eighth, and Ninth Congressional Districts; losses attributable more to his decreasing acceptance in the state than to strength on the part of Crockett. Third District Congressman William Brock, in the meantime, was having little difficulty in gaining the Republican nomination over entertainer Tex Ritter and other candidates; he received nearly 75 percent of the votes in the Republican primary.

In the gubernatorial primary, an array of candidates fought for the nomination. Robert L. Taylor of Memphis, grandson of the former governor and senator, resigned from the Court of Appeals to make the race, and Nashville schoolteacher and businesswoman Mary Anderson was heard across the state. The contest was between former Nashville Senator Stanley T. Snodgrass and Nashville businessman and lawyer John J. Hooker, however; and Hooker, of a prominent and powerful Nashville family, won handily. In the meantime, a politically unknown dentist from Memphis, Winfield Dunn, was successfully challenging several well-known Republicans— including Nashville businessman Maxey Jarman, William Jenkins of Knoxville, and Speaker of the House Claude Robertson, the last-named of whom had managed Senator Baker's successful campaign a few years earlier. Dunn's margin over Jarman was a bare 10,000 votes, but it was sufficient to win the right to challenge the Democratic nominee in the fall.

On the hustings during September and October, the handsome

and winsome Dunn spoke forcibly and effectively. He attacked Hooker's record as a businessman, and stressed the declining economy and increasing unemployment in Tennessee; Hooker told of Dunn's inexperience in public affairs. Occasionally speaking from the same platform, the two candidates discussed a multitude of issues, including governmental reorganization, consumer rights, health care, fiscal responsibility, highways, schools, law enforcement, environmental protection, and the state of the economy.

In as heated a general election as Tennesseans had witnessed in many years, Dunn won by a vote of 557,024 to 498,757 for Hooker. Douglas L. Heinsohn, running as an independent, polled nearly 25,000 votes. Dunn of course received solid majorities in the first three congressional districts and also carried the seventh and ninth districts. In the same general election, Congressman Brock had little difficulty in defeating Albert Gore. The Republican candidate effectively described Gore as one who had become so enamored with the liberal Eastern establishment that he had lost touch with the people of his home state. As expected, Brock carried the first three congressional districts, but surprised even himself in winning small majorities in the seventh and eighth districts. Like Dunn, he also carried the ninth district.

The Clement-Ellington era brought change and progress to Tennessee, and it also brought an end to the Democratic party's traditional stronghold in Tennessee politics. In three of the presidential elections Tennesseans voted Republican and, as the era ended, chose two Republican United States senators and a Republican governor. The obvious explanation was not so much a deterioration of Democratic leadership but a change in the Tennessee political mind from a position of blind loyalty to one of independence.

SUGGESTED READINGS

Books

Jack Anderson and Fred Blumenthal, *The Kefauver Story* (New York, 1956); Richard Cortner, *The Apportionment Cases* (Knoxville, 1971); Charles W. Crawford, *Yesterday's Memphis* (Miami, 1978); Albert Gore, *The Eye of the Storm: A People's Politics for the Seventies* (New York, 1970); Gore, *Let the Glory Out: My South and Its Politics* (New York, 1972); Joseph Bruce Gorman, *Kefauver: A Political Biography* (New York, 1971).

Articles
Robert E. Corlew III, "Frank Goad Clement and the Keynote Address of 1956," *THQ* 36 (Spring 1977), 95–107; William L. Davis, "Frank Clement: The First Campaign," *THQ* 35 (Spring 1976), 83–91; Richard M. Fried (ed.), "Fighting Words Never Delivered: Proposed Draft of Senator (Estes) Kefauver's (Democratic Presidential Nomination) Acceptance Speech," *THQ* 29 (Summer 1970), 176–83; Hugh Davis Graham, "Kefauver: A Political Biography," *THQ* 30 (Winter 1971), 413–18; Philip A. Grant, Jr., "Kefauver and the New Hampshire Presidential Primary," *THQ* 31 (Winter 1972), 372–80; William L. Majors, "Gordon Browning and Tennessee Politics, 1949–1953," *THQ* 28 (Fall 1969), 166–81; Neill R. McMillen, "Organized Resistance to School Desegregation in Tennessee," *THQ* 30 (Fall 1971), 315–28; Norman L. Parks, "Tennessee Politics Since Kefauver and Reece: A 'Generalist' View," *JOP* 28 (Feb. 1966), 144–66.

30.

እ Two Decades of Partisan Fury: Republicans and
Democrats Strive for Political Control,
1970–1990

During the 1970s and 1980s, Republicans and Democrats fought for political control of the state on an almost even basis. Republicans held the governor's office for twelve of the
twenty years and were successful in rebuilding their party to an extent
not witnessed in Tennessee for a hundred years. For six years they held
both U.S. Senate seats and exerted strong influence in both houses of
Congress. Their presidential candidates were appealing. In 1972,
voters balloted overwhelmingly for Richard Nixon; in most presidential races thereafter, through 1988, they cast the state's electoral
votes for the candidate of the GOP. Troubled Democrats received little
help from Governor Ray Blanton (1975–1979), but finally found a
winner in Ned Ray McWherter, a conservative West Tennessean,
whom they elected in 1986.

Democrats were plagued through the two decades by charges of
graft and corruption. Governor Blanton and several of his close associates went to prison, and, as the 1980s ended, federal charges and resulting indictments of high ranking party members not associated
with the governor's office scandalized Democrats and caused leaders to
seek a reorganization of the party.

The major problem state officials—regardless of party—faced was
the dichotomy of ever-increasing expenses in operating government
and the voters' mounting resistance to higher taxes. Repeatedly they
promised better schools, roads, and services should necessary operating
funds become available. Both Governors Dunn and Blanton suggested
a tax on incomes, but an ingrained fear residual in the minds of Tennesseans for decades prevented serious consideration of it. Alexander
and McWherter avoided the unpopular matter but did raise necessary
funds from other tax measures.

Administration of Winfield Dunn Winfield Dunn was the third Republican governor of the twentieth century but the first in nearly fifty years. As mentioned earlier, he had entered the Republican primary as a political unknown, but his platform charm and sincere manner won him the Republican nomination over formidable opponents and enabled him to defeat the Democratic nominee in the general election by a sound majority.

In his first message to the legislature, Dunn told of his goals. He wanted to establish a statewide kindergarten program, improve conditions in mental health institutions, improve the pay scale of certain underpaid state employees, and—at the same time—cut costs in government by a more efficient operation. He asked for $95 million in new taxes to finance his proposed programs.

The legislature then held one of the longest sessions in the state's history and ultimately trimmed $27 million from the governor's proposed budget. But lawmakers still provided for expenditures increased by $68 million, the highest single increase in the state's history. To raise these funds the sales tax was increased 0.5 percent. While Dunn's dreams of a statewide kindergarten program were curtailed by inadequate funds, many of his other goals were realized. In other action, legislators ratified the Twenty-sixth Amendment, which gave eighteen-year-olds the right to vote, approved a presidential preference primary for 1972, enacted a progressive drug law that provided leniency for first offenders, and adopted a modified Missouri Plan for public approval of incumbent judges. The census returns of 1970 had indicated that the state's congressional delegation would be cut from nine to eight, and reapportionment into eight districts became another matter for consideration.

Reapportionment remained for legislators who reassembled in February of 1972. Ultimately, the old eighth district was divided between the sixth and seventh; Shelby County was divided among those two and the new eighth district (See map 15). Expressing a belief that Democratic legislators were attempting to redraw the lines in a manner designed to eliminate Republican Ninth District Congressman Dan Kuykendall, Governor Dunn vetoed the redistricting measure, but legislators enacted it over his veto.

In the meantime, Tennesseans prepared for their first presidential preference primary, to be held on May 4, 1972. Democratic voters could not accept most of the candidates who sought their party's nomination—Shirley Chisholm, Eugene McCarthy, George McGovern, Edmund Muskie, and even Hubert Humphrey. Instead, they voted overwhelmingly for George Wallace; indeed, the Alabama governor's 335,858 votes were more than the combined total of all the other candidates. When Democrats in national convention turned to McGovern and (ultimately) Sargent Shriver, Tennessee Democrats and Republicans alike flocked to Richard Nixon and Spiro Agnew by more than a two-to-one majority. Seventh District Congressman Ray Blanton had challenged Senator Howard Baker; the incumbent won handily by a vote of 716,539 to 440,599. Both Nixon and Baker received a majority in all eight districts.

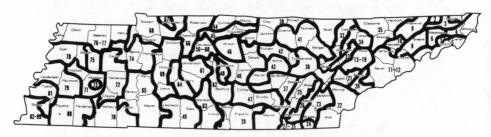

Map 14. Legislative Districts of Tennessee, 1976. Source: *Tennessee Statistical Abstract, 1977* (Knoxville: Center for Business and Economic Research, Univ. of Tennessee, 1977).

Legislators in 1974 approved a $2 billion operational budget—72 percent larger than that of Governor Dunn's during his first year in office. Turning to reforms, they enacted measures requiring candidates to make full disclosures of campaign financing, a "Sunshine Law" banning closed-door meetings of governmental agencies, and a provision for more committee time for full discussions of proposed legislation. Over the governor's veto they enacted a measure that would establish a medical school at East Tennessee State University at Johnson City.

The trauma of Watergate loosened Republican control in 1974, and the gubernatorial primaries of that year were viewed with considerable interest across the state. East Tennessee native, Lamar Alexander, who had served briefly as a Nixon aide, defeated Nat Winston in the Republican contest. A dozen Democrats sought their party's nomination, including such political veterans as Ross Bass, David Pack, and Stanley Snodgrass. Although newcomers Jake Butcher, Franklin Haney, and Hudley Crockett ran well, former Congressman Ray Blanton won the nomination with less than 25 per cent of the vote and with about

Map 15. United States Congressional Districts in Tennessee, 1989. Source: *Tennessee Statistical Abstract,* 1988 (Knoxville: Center for Business and Economic Research, University of Tennessee, 1988).

16,500 more votes than Butcher received. Blanton, a West Tennessee contractor and Hardin County native, had been elected to the legislature from McNairy and Chester counties in 1965 and in the following year had won a seat in Congress, where he remained until 1972, when he launched his unsuccessful race for the United States Senate.

In the general election party regularity prevailed, and Blanton won by more than 100,000 votes. (The final count gave Blanton 576,833 to 455,467 for Alexander.) Although Alexander carried the traditionally Republican First, Second, and Third Congressional districts, he lost the fourth by more than 50,000 votes and failed also to win a majority in any of the others. Blanton carried all of the Middle and West Tennessee counties except Henderson, Shelby, and Wayne, and won a majority in 72 of the 95 counties.

In other voting in 1974, Marilyn Lloyd, a Democrat, defeated incumbent Republican Congressman Lamar Baker in the third district; in the eighth, Democrat Harold E. Ford defeated Republican incum-

Winfield Dunn (*above*), a Memphis Republican, was governor from 1971 to 1975. He was succeeded by Democrat Ray Blanton (*below*) of McNairy County, who served until 1979.

bent Dan Kuykendall by fewer than a thousand votes and became the first black congressman in the state's history. Robert Clement, son of the late governor, won a seat on the Public Service Commission. Democrats, already in control of the legislature, gained twelve new seats in the house and one in the senate. Party campaign coordinator Tommy Burnett attributed the overwhelming Democratic victory to "able candidates" and "much effort," but Republican Tom Jensen of Knoxville blamed Watergate and a decline in the economy for his party's losses.

In the same election Tennesseans chose able members of the supreme court. Four of the justices chose not to run, and only incumbent William Fones of Memphis was chosen. Others elected included veteran political leader Joe Henry of Pulaski, Ray L. Brock and Robert Cooper of Chattanooga, and William J. Harbison of Columbia and Nashville. Cooper had been a judge of the Sixth Judicial Circuit and later of the Court of Appeals of the Eastern division; Harbison had taught at the Vanderbilt University School of Law and had served on the supreme court earlier as a special justice.

Legislators who assembled in 1975 were aware of a substantial economic slowdown that began early in 1974. Residential and commercial construction had declined considerably, and tax collections had fallen off substantially. Consequently, Governor Blanton proposed a "bare bones" budget of some $73 million less than that of 1974; conservative legislators, however, eventually cut nearly $50 million from that. Pay raises for teachers were cut, and salary increases for all state employees were limited to 2.5 percent.

The need for more money to finance state programs and the desire for the development of a more equitable tax plan caused Governor Blanton in 1977 to propose a state income tax. According to the governor's plan, the sales tax on June 1, 1977 would be decreased from 4.5 percent to 3 percent, and the income tax, varying from 1 percent to 3.5 percent on incomes, would become effective. People with an adjusted gross income of not more than $2,000 would pay 1 percent of it in taxes, while those with incomes of more than $10,000 would pay the higher rate. Although such a proposal would have benefited people in the poor to middle income groups, little or no support could be developed for the proposal. Legislators, aware of the long-standing opposition of Tennesseans to an income tax (despite the fact that nearly every other Southern state has such a tax), let the matter die without

Before being elected governor in 1986, Ned Ray McWherter (*above*) was a Dresden businessman and speaker of the house of representatives.

After a distinguished career as deputy commissioner of education of Tennessee, Dr. Otis Floyd (*below*) in 1987 became president of Tennessee State University.

action. Instead, they raised the sales tax to take care of rising costs of state government.

Legislators had first enacted a sales tax thirty years earlier when, in 1947, they established a 2 percent levy. Through the years it had been increased gradually, and now was raised to 4.5 percent. Local governments could levy up to 1.5 per cent, so that by April 1, 1976, most taxpayers across the state were paying 6 per cent on purchases. A $2.4 billion budget was proposed, which provided for a 9 percent increase for teachers and other state employees, aid for the Medicaid program, and money to continue the increasing operations of the state.

Later in the year, Governor Blanton and officials of Vanderbilt University cooperated to bring members of the United Nations to Nashville. It was the first time members of the UN had traveled as a group outside of New York City. One hundred and four delegates— lined up alphabetically from Albania to Zaire—arrived in Nashville via the airlines and rode in limousines to the university campus. UN Secretary General Kurt Waldheim was presented the Cordell Hull Peace Award, and delegates later feasted on Tennessee country ham, beef, and catfish in Centennial Park and heard the Nashville Sound at the new Opry House.

In the following year legislators gave attention to a variety of matters, including ethics legislation to improve the conduct and operation of the General Assembly and a new capital punishment law for perpetrators of major crimes.

The tremendous success of Alex Haley's *Roots,* mentioned earlier, brought recognition to the Henning native and to the state. On April 6, 1977, Haley addressed the legislature, the governor, and other officials, and subsequently was honored in Memphis and other cities across Tennessee. At the state museum in Nashville he was honored in ceremonies that included the unveiling of his portrait. A three-day celebration began on May 19 in Henning and ended with the dedication of his boyhood home as a historic site.

In Blanton's "State of the State" message of 1978, the governor told of progress during his four years as chief executive and described Tennessee's fiscal base as being the soundest in its history. Pledging to take his record "directly to the people," he told legislators that unemployment had been cut from 9.6 percent to 4.4 percent since he took office in 1975 and that more than 850 new plants and expansions were completed or planned, providing 46,000 new jobs for Tennesseans. He also told of improvements in the state's tourism program and in education. The state had moved from fiftieth in the nation to forty-fifth in expenditures per pupil, he said, and from thirty-ninth in salaries for teachers to thirty-sixth. He also told of improvements in correctional facilities, including the reopening of Brushy Mountain facilities that had been closed during the preceding administration.

Although the governor was eligible for a second term under the changes in the state constitution approved in March 1978, Blanton dramatically removed himself from the running in a meeting with 2,000 of his supporters at the governor's mansion on May 27. Again he told of the progress made during his administration, praised his cabinet members and other officials as people of high character and capability, and promised that his voice would continue to be heard in state and national matters even though he planned to retire to private life.

Constitutional Revision ॐ Constitutional revision was a matter to which Tennesseans continued to turn their attention during the 1970s. In the November 1968 elections, voters had approved a limited constitutional convention to be held in August 1971 to consider the classification of property for purposes of taxation. Voters had considered five proposals for revision, including lowering the voting age to eighteen and abolishing the limitation on the governor's right to succession, but only property classification—"Question Three"—was approved. Delegates who assembled according to the mandate elected William M. Leech, Jr., a Columbia attorney later to become state attorney general, as chairman. Then, in a relatively brief session, they divided property into three classifications—real property, intangible personal property, and tangible personal property—for taxation purposes. Real property was also divided into four subclassifications. Public utility property was to be assessed at 55 percent of its value, industrial and commercial property at 40 percent, and residential and farm property at 25 percent.

Of more significance was the convention of 1977, which assembled in Nashville in August to discuss a variety of matters including the executive, legislative, and judicial bodies. In close voting, J. D. Lee, a Madisonville attorney, defeated Leech for convention chairman. Delegates engaged in serious discussion from August to December and submitted their work to the voters on March 7, 1978.

Thirteen proposals ultimately went before the people, and twelve were accepted. Several were housekeeping measures—a rewriting of the constitution to conform to federal rulings. These included deletion of a provision prohibiting interracial marriages, a provision reducing the voting age to eighteen, and another deleting a requirement that schools be racially segregated. Several concerned the public at large only in a small way; one allowed the governor ten days to veto a bill instead of five, and others facilitated the signing of bills by the house and senate speakers, eliminated delay between organizational sessions and the regular sessions of the legislature, and improved means of filling vacancies in the General Assembly. Of interest to a much larger group of people was an increase in the homestead exemption from $1,000 to $5,000. Interest was also manifested in a provision that would place a limit upon state spending. According to the article, the rate of growth of appropriations from state tax revenues cannot exceed the estimated rate of growth of the state's economy—such rate to be determined by the legislature.

The proposal to lift the ceiling on interest rates perhaps received more attention than the others, although the governor's term, the structural changes in local government, and the judicial article—vigorously opposed by members of the supreme court and other judges and lawyers—were carefully discussed across the state. The constitution had specified that lending agencies could not charge more than 10 percent on loans. The price of money, however, had increased to such an extent that some lending agencies in the state had suspended operations and contended that they could not continue unless money, like other commodities, was placed in the open market. A study conducted at the University of Tennessee at Knoxville indicated that the state was losing more than $100 million annually in productivity, as well as thousands of jobs, because of tight credit. The *Wall Street Journal* reported that Nashville bankers had warned that retail sales of automobiles, furniture, and other commodities were curtailed because of the inability of Tennesseans to find adequate credit. The new constitutional proposal authorized the General Assembly to set maximum rates without any limit; in the event that the assembly failed to establish a rate, it would remain at 10 percent. Opponents of the proposal had argued that the legislature could not be relied upon to establish fair and equitable rates, but delegates claimed that the voters were responsible for the election of legislators who would be responsive to the people's needs. The proposal was opposed by the Nashville *Tennessean* and Governor Blanton, but was approved by more than 56 percent of voters going to the polls.

Delegates to the convention of 1953 had changed the governor's term from two years to four years but had denied an incumbent the right to succeed himself. The proposal adopted in 1978 lifted the one-term ceiling and gave the governor the right to serve two consecutive terms. It became effective immediately, and for nearly three months Governor Blanton considered a second term before ultimately deciding against it.

The proposal for local government established several distinct changes designed mainly to streamline county government. For many years county government had been in the hands of a county court composed of the justices of the peace who served six-year terms and presided over by a county judge or county chairman. The new article called for a "county legislative body" consisting of not more than twenty-five members elected for four-year terms from the districts of the county. An official called the "county executive" replaces the county judge, and he also serves four years. Indeed, all officials would serve four-year terms, with the right of succession, including the sheriff who traditionally has served two-year terms restricted to six consecutive years in office. The article makes counties eligible for home rule to the extent prescribed by the legislature and approved by a local referendum.

The judicial article called for sweeping changes and was defeated, as mentioned above. The present supreme court would have been retained, but a new court of appeals with at least eighteen judges to hear both civil and criminal cases would have been formed. A "court of discipline and removal" with power to censure, suspend, or remove any judge for misconduct was planned, and the position of attorney general was made appointive by the governor for a four-year term instead of being elective for an eight-year term by the supreme court. The constitution does not require judges to be lawyers, but the proposal would require all except general sessions judges to be members of the bar in good standing. Despite some very good sections, the article was believed by many to be too broad to be effective. Judges and lawyers believed that some degree of independence would be surrendered by the courts if the article were adopted. Especially objectionable was a clause that required courts to submit their rules to the legislature for approval. This clause appeared to be in conflict with the time-honored concept of separation of powers, and Chief Justice Joe Henry commented that it would produce a "devitalized, disorganized, demoralized, and subservient judiciary." The influence of Justice Henry and others was sufficient to defeat the proposal. More than 54 percent of those going to the polls voted against it.

Elections of 1976 and 1978 &❧ The elections of 1976 brought about additional Democratic gains, but two years later independent voters returned a Republican to the governor's mansion. Republicans held both United States Senate seats from 1971 to 1977. The elections of 1976, however, brought about the defeat of incumbent William Brock and the election of Democrat James Sasser. Jimmy Carter, Democratic nominee for President, ran stronger in Tennessee than leaders had predicted, and polled 56 percent of the vote to about 43 percent for incumbent Gerald Ford. Albert Gore, Jr., won the fourth congressional district seat vacated by Joe L. Evins, who had retired after thirty years in Washington. In the legislature, Democrats won 63 of the 99 house seats and 20 of the 33 senate seats.

Sasser, making his first race for public office, had soundly defeated John J. Hooker and others in the primaries, and received almost 44 percent of the popular vote to Hooker's 31 percent. Sasser had won a majority in every congressional district except the eighth, where Hooker received most of the black vote. Although Sasser had been chairman of the state Democratic organization, he had considerable difficulty forming a working organization in the early stages of his campaign. Lack of funds and name recognition constituted major problems. An endorsement by the Tennessee State Labor Council, however, brought both funds and votes. Hooker's failure to tour the state county by county had a detrimental effect when he decided to rely upon a "media campaign" instead.

After Sasser had won the primary, he was viewed by most Democrats as a sure winner in November. His vote of more than 750,000 was the largest ever polled in a political contest in Tennessee. Many voters had become disenchanted with national Republicans because of the Watergate scandal, and others had viewed Brock with little enthusiasm anyway throughout his six years in the Senate. Soon after his defeat, Brock was named national chairman of the Republican party.

Interest in the elections of 1978 centered primarily in the gubernatorial race, inasmuch as Democrats considered Howard Baker unbeatable. In the Democratic primary, a half-dozen candidates soon saw the contest develop into a two-man race between wealthy Knoxville banker Jake Butcher and Public Service Commissioner Robert Clement, a son of the former governor.

Neither Butcher nor Clement exhibited strong personalities or injected major issues. Butcher, a farm boy turned banker and millionaire, had run a close race in the primary of 1974 and had fallen short of Blanton's majority by only 16,000 votes. Spending a record $2 million on his campaign, Butcher outdistanced the former governor's son—who capitalized on name recognition—by a little more than 30,000 votes. Butcher carried the first, second, third, and eighth districts, and won Shelby County by nearly a two-to-one majority. Clement carried the fourth, sixth, and seventh districts but lost the fifth (Nashville) to Mayor Richard Fulton, who ran a poor third in the statewide race. Butcher received about 41 percent of the vote, Clement 37 percent, and Fulton 16 percent.

In the senatorial primary, where Democrats had difficulty finding someone to run, Nashvillian Jane Eskind handily defeated four men, including J. D. Lee of Madisonville, who had been chairman of the constitutional convention which had met earlier in the year.

In the Republican gubernatorial primary, 38-year-old Lamar Alexander easily defeated five opponents and won the party nomination. As mentioned, Alexander had managed Dunn's successful campaign in 1970, had been employed briefly with the federal government in Washington, and had lost to Ray Blanton in the general election of 1974. In the primary, he received 86 percent of all votes cast and even outpolled Howard Baker, who won the Republican nomination for the Senate without difficulty. In a walk across the state, Alexander was able to shed the "rich-boy" image that had plagued him in 1974 and to discuss in a down-to-earth manner some of the major issues of concern.

The general election in November fascinated Tennesseans and shook the majority Democratic party to its foundations. Despite the fact that wealthy Jake Butcher spent nearly $3 million on this campaign—mainly on billboards and the media—Alexander and Baker swept the state. They carried every congressional district except the eighth,

In 1966 Howard H. Baker, Jr. (*above*) became the first Republican to be elected to the Senate by popular vote. Jim Sasser (*below*) was elected to the Senate in 1976.

Lamar Alexander became the fourth Republican of the twentieth century to be elected governor. His election in 1978 came after an extensive campaign in which he walked across the state.

where Representative Harold Ford had united the black vote behind the Democrats, and carried blue-collar and silk-stocking districts alike by sizable majorities. Alexander polled 665,847 votes to 523,013 for Butcher and gained 56 percent of the vote. Baker received 645,771 votes to 464,756 for Eskind, or 55 percent of the total vote.

While Butcher explained the result by stating simply, "this just wasn't a Democratic year in Tennessee," and Jane Eskind explained her defeat as a result of having been identified with Jake Butcher, State Democratic Party Secretary Will T. Cheek was more realistic. He saw the results as indicative of a latent illness of party leadership. He called for a "calculated study" and believed that a total restructuring of the party might be in order. Senate Minority Leader Howard Baker and National Republican Party Chairman William Brock hailed the victories as the dawning of a new day in Tennessee politics, and Baker believed that "the Republican party is still a viable and effective entity" in Tennessee.

Alexander is Inaugurated ஐ While some Democrats blamed Governor Blanton for the party losses, the governor in the closing days of his administration had more serious problems before him. Never a favorite with the media, Blanton was criticized generally, but especially for his use of his pardoning power, particularly after his actions on the night of January 15—a few days before he was scheduled to leave office—when he granted executive clemency to 52 inmates of the state penitentiary, 20 of whom were convicted murderers. Included among the 52 was one Roger Humphreys, a son of one of the governor's strong supporters and patronage dispensers in East Tennessee. Two years earlier, Blanton had been criticized from Memphis to Bristol when he announced intentions to free Humphreys, who had been convicted earlier of slaying his former wife and her husband. A reason for the governor's precipitate action, apparently, was that Attorney General William M. Leech, Jr., had ruled a few days earlier that the incoming governor could be inaugurated at any time after midnight of January 15 and did not have to await the scheduled date of January 20. Blanton, however, denied that the ruling was a motivating factor in his actions and said that the pardoned convicts had been model prisoners and that crowded conditions at the penitentiary necessitated a curtailment of the prison population whenever it could be justified.

At any rate, two days later, in an unprecedented move, Alexander was inaugurated (January 18). He appointed an able cabinet, and in an eloquent message to the legislature assumed a position of a strong and responsible executive. When the legislature adjourned in May of 1979, both Lieutenant Governor Wilder and House Speaker McWherter spoke of "the spirit of cooperation that prevailed" between the Republican governor and the Democratic General Assembly.

Before adjourning to meet again in January of 1980, legislators enacted a number of constructive measures. Perhaps the most controversial—but one that ultimately passed with surprisingly little opposition—established a fluctuating interest ceiling on single-payment bank loans of more than $1,000 at a maximum of 5 percent above the Federal Reserve System's discount rate. At the time the measure was passed, the discount rate was 9.5 percent. Single payment loans of $1,000 or less were to be limited to 10 percent. But interest rates from the so-called small loan companies are permitted to average about twice the amount established by the banks. Other measures provided a budget of $3.5 billion to finance state government for the fiscal year, established a 7 percent raise for most state employees, raised the legal drinking age from 18 to 19, reorganized the State Board of Pardons and Paroles, and continued the 4.5 percent sales tax for another year.

Despite the increase in taxes along with a downturn in the economy, Alexander easily won a second term in 1982. Handily defeating Knoxville Mayor Randy Tyree, he became the first governor to win two consecutive four-year terms. Incumbent Senator Sasser turned back a bid by veteran Republican congressman Robin Beard. Among those running for congressional seats were Cissy Baker, 26-year-old daughter of Senator Howard Baker, and Jim Cooper and Robert Clement, both sons of former governors. Only Cooper was elected.

The mild-mannered Alexander became more aggressive in his second term, and pushed vigorously for reforms, especially in the field of education. The son of public school teachers, he took great interest in a "Better Schools Program," which would improve the lot of pupils and teachers alike. Sizable salary increases were provided for teachers who could qualify and more funds were provided for teaching supplies and equipment to enhance the pupils' computer skills as well as competencies in mathematics, science, and writing. To fund the extensive reforms, legislators raised the sales tax to an unprecedented 7.75 percent, which made Tennessee's tax the highest in the nation.

Alexander was not constitutionally eligible for a third term, and he soon became president of the University of Tennessee at Knoxville. Democrats nominated long-time Speaker of the House Ned Ray Mc-Wherter, who defeated former Governor Winfield Dunn in a contest which was not quite as close as it had been predicted to be. McWherter became only the second Democrat to be elected since Buford Ellington had been chosen in 1966.

McWherter as Governor 🐌 A West Tennessee conservative and businessman, McWherter recommended no increase in the sales tax and he soon became a favorite even among those whose support had been only lukewarm. Espousing the work ethic, he pledged to expend long hours on Capitol Hill in the interest of better government.

First to receive attention was the state's rapidly deteriorating road system, and the new governor called for a four cent increase in the gasoline tax designed to raise $100 million for pay-as-you-go road improvement and for connecting routes aimed at attracting industry. Other first term legislation made mandatory a seat-belt law, expanded Medicaid, and provided for salary increases for state employees. Second term legislation focused attention upon crowded prison conditions and called for building new places of incarceration, not to mention continued aid to education and mental health facilities.

Tennesseans during the 1970s and 1980s had far more than their share of white collar crime and corruption at the highest levels of government and business. Reference has been made earlier to the scandal-plagued administration of Ray Blanton, which resulted in the governor and several of his cronies going to prison. Jake Butcher, prominent Knoxville banker and twice candidate for governor, also served in prison on charges of bank fraud. Closely related was the indictment of Congressman Harold Ford, of Memphis, on charges which included trading political influence for Butcher bank loans. Governor McWherter and other prominent Democrats urged State Election Commission Chair Tommy Powell, of Memphis, to resign after he and others were indicted for setting up an illegal bingo hall in Memphis. One legislator committed suicide in 1989 rather than face charges of attempting to extort funds from the city of Knoxville, and a dozen legislators were accused of malfeasance in office in the same year. Some people predicted that the gubernatorial campaign of 1990, should a strong Republican candidate emerge, would be run with ethics in government a major issue.

As the final decade of the century dawned, Tennesseans realized that they lived in one of the most prosperous eras of the state's long history. Unemployment, at 5.3 percent, was at the lowest level in many years and well below the national average. Both foreign and domestic industry provided jobs for almost everyone who wished to work. The per capital income, at $12,880, was twice what it had been a decade earlier and the highest in history. Tennesseans faced their sesquicentennial with confidence.

Index

Abell, Father Robert, offers mass in Nashville, 247
Academies, established, 237–38
Acuff, Roy, runs for governor, 493; musician and entertainer, 567
Adams, John, President of United States, 101
Adams, John Quincy, President of United States, 170, 172, 193; castigated by Polk, 257
Adams Law, extends prohibition, 418
Adams-Onis Treaty of 1817, 170
Adventure, John Donelson's Flagship, 52
Agee, James, author, 563
Agrarian Movement; *see* Farmers' Movement
Agrarians, writers at Vanderbilt University, 559–60
Agriculture, on frontier, 117; main economic pursuit in 19th century, 228; during post-Civil War period, 367–70; decline in farm prices, 368, 369, 370; in 20th century, 500–16; expansion during 1920s, 507; effect of New Deal, 509–13; at mid-twentieth century, 513–14; recent growth and concerns, 515–16
Alabama, religion in, 244; mentioned, 183, 387
Alexander, Lamar, candidate for governor in 1974, 591; elected governor in 1978, 600, 603; pictured, 602; inauguration, 603–4; administration begins, 604–5
Allen, Clifford, candidate for governor in 1950, 494; candidate in 1952, 496, 499; runs again in 1958, 579

Anderson, Alexander, elected to U.S. Senate in 1841, 258; mentioned, 261
Anderson, Douglas, and Tennessee Centennial Exposition of 1897, 411
Anderson, Joseph, Territorial judge, 88; helps draft state constitution, 97; seeks governorship, 99; nominated for U.S. Senate, 99–100
Anderson, Col. Kellar, in Spanish-American War, 410
Anderson, Mary, candidate for governor in 1970, 585
Anderson, William and George, pioneers, 42
Anderson County, coal miners' war in, 390–91; vast growth during 1940s and 1950s, 545–46
Anthony, Susan B., in Memphis, 404–5
Anti-evolution controversy, 539, 541–42; background for, 540–41; tested in Scopes trial, 542; law repealed, 544
Anti-Saloon League, organized, 417–18
Appalachian Mountains, 7, 10
Armathwaite, established, 408
Armfield, John, slave trader, 212
Armistead, George, supports Carmack for governor, 425
Armstrong, John, land agent, 156
Armstrong, Gen. Robert, candidate for governor in 1837, 193
Arnell, Representative S.M., assaulted by KKK, 338
Arnold Air Engineering Center, 520
Arthur, Gabriel, first Englishman in Tennessee, 27

607